An Introduction to Corporate Compliance

Ruihua Chen

An Introduction to Corporate Compliance

Translated by Yong Gao

palgrave
macmillan

Ruihua Chen
Law School
Peking University
Beijing, China

Translated by
Yong Gao
Law Department
Beijing International Studies University
Beijing, China

ISBN 978-981-95-7256-4 ISBN 978-981-95-7257-1 (eBook)
https://doi.org/10.1007/978-981-95-7257-1

This Palgrave Macmillan imprint is published by the registered company Springer Nature Singapore Pte Ltd.
The registered company address is: 152 Beach Road, #21-01/04 Gateway East, Singapore 189721, Singapore

Preface

The present volume represents the current stage of my research on corporate compliance. *An Introduction to Corporate Compliance* distills the insights I have developed over six years of sustained inquiry and offers an initial theoretical framework for understanding corporate compliance management.

My engagement with this field began in 2019, prompted by close observation of corporate crime cases and renewed reflection on prevailing models of corporate governance. Even before that time, the legal profession had already developed compliance-related practice areas, and various regulatory authorities had issued guidance documents to support the establishment of corporate compliance programs. The "ZTE case" of 2018 further heightened public awareness of the challenges Chinese enterprises face when required to undertake compliance remediation under the scrutiny of foreign regulators or international organizations. As a result, a broader consensus gradually emerged: corporate compliance is not merely an internally driven component of corporate governance, but constitutes a significant evolution in regulatory philosophy and risk-management strategy. Fundamentally, corporate compliance should be understood as the effective control of compliance risk. The central task is to construct a systematic and functional compliance management framework capable of preventing, monitoring, and responding to such risks. This challenge is also inseparable from the larger strategic question of how to develop a model of corporate compliance suited to China's institutional conditions—what may be described as the "localization of corporate compliance."

Corporate compliance has emerged as a distinctly interdisciplinary field. Within legal scholarship, compliance—conceived as a mechanism for preventing and mitigating legal risk—intersects with core domains such as civil law, administrative law, criminal law, and criminal procedure, while also engaging numerous specialized areas of economic law, including antitrust, unfair competition, intellectual property, environmental and natural resources, financial, tax, and data protection law. Beyond the legal domain, corporate compliance encompasses corporate governance, risk management, and regulatory oversight, thereby drawing on insights from economics, management, and political science.

At present, theoretical research on corporate compliance remains at an early formative stage, both within legal scholarship and in related disciplines. Studies that integrate global developments with local realities are still relatively rare, and systematic theoretical frameworks for compliance are notably scarce. The field therefore urgently requires research that is both conceptually forward-looking and practically grounded. Being "conceptually forward-looking" entails engaging with leading international theories to extract insights of global relevance, while being "practically grounded" involves analyzing China's institutional realities to identify patterns and develop theories with genuine explanatory power. In advancing compliance scholarship, researchers must cultivate academic self-awareness and aim to contribute original theoretical insights. At the same time, they should avoid restricting their focus to technical discussions of "compliance skills," which risk reducing compliance to a rigid professional orthodoxy. Without the guidance of robust theoretical frameworks, compliance programs may become formalistic and fail to exercise meaningful control over compliance risk.

In response to these considerations, I have undertaken a systematic re-examination of corporate compliance. Building on a comprehensive review of existing scholarship, this book provides an analytical framework for understanding several core and contested issues in compliance theory. The study is organized around two central themes: the foundational theory of compliance and compliance incentives. The section on foundational theory establishes the conceptual underpinnings of corporate compliance management, clarifying its objectives, guiding principles, strategic orientations, and standards of effectiveness. The section on compliance incentives explores the external forces that shape compliance programs, detailing the regulatory pathways and incentive mechanisms through which enterprises are encouraged to design, implement, and sustain effective compliance management systems.

Building on existing scholarship, this book advances several key conceptual contributions. In defining compliance risk, it situates such risk alongside the four principal categories of strategic risk faced by enterprises—placing it on an equal footing with decision-making, operational, and financial risks. It further distinguishes between abstract compliance risk and concrete compliance risk, defining compliance risk as the likelihood of unlawful or non-compliant conduct and the potential adverse consequences, including sanctions, penalties, financial losses, or disqualification. Regarding compliance management models, the book examines their theoretical foundations and distinguishes two prevailing models in contemporary China: a management-oriented compliance model and a risk-oriented compliance model. It provides an analytical evaluation of the respective strengths and limitations of each approach. In the domain of effective compliance management, the book proposes two institutional models for assessing compliance effectiveness: a process-centered model and a results-centered model. It argues that effectiveness assessments must align with the overarching objectives of compliance programs and identifies three core elements: the effectiveness of program design, the effectiveness of program implementation, and the effectiveness of program outcomes. The book also offers a synthesized discussion of methodologies for evaluating compliance management effectiveness.

In examining the external mechanisms that drive corporate compliance, this book identifies three principal forces: administrative compliance, criminal compliance, and compliance promoted by international financial organizations. From these, it distills three fundamental modes of external compliance advancement: compliance guidance, compliance enforcement, and compliance incentives. The book traces the establishment and evolution of administrative compliance incentive mechanisms in China, analyzes the constructive role of international financial organizations in promoting compliance-oriented regulation, and provides a comparative study of criminal compliance incentive systems. It further explores the emergence of criminal compliance incentives in China and the institutional challenges they have faced.

Since 2020, the Supreme People's Procuratorate of China has launched a large-scale initiative—the Corporate Compliance Supervision and Inspection Reform Pilot. By applying compliance supervision and inspection measures to enterprises suspected of criminal offenses, the pilot integrated compliance incentives into the conditional non-prosecution framework. Enterprises that successfully met the compliance assessment criteria were granted non-prosecution decisions or other forms of lenient treatment. In 2024, due to a combination of institutional and practical factors, the pilot was brought to a close. Nevertheless, this book provides a detailed account of the reform's background, evolution, and controversies, offering future researchers a valuable resource for further study.

In studying corporate compliance, I have come to recognize that meaningful theoretical contribution requires not only sustained effort, adequate resources, and strong research capacity, but also a continuous infusion of intellectual nourishment drawn from both cutting-edge theory and institutional practice. Only through such engagement can researchers avoid confinement within academic dogma and generate original insights. In the context of corporate compliance, the true "sources of innovation" derive from both compliance theories and practices developed in Europe and the United States, as well as from China's own theoretical reflections and reform experiments. While maintaining a global perspective, scholars must also pursue a China-focused research agenda—grounded in local theory, attentive to domestic institutional realities, and engaged in rigorous dialogue on the major controversies shaping China's compliance landscape. By transforming practical experience into theoretical understanding, researchers can develop concepts capable of withstanding empirical scrutiny.

Like artificial intelligence, corporate compliance is a frontier topic of global significance. In this field, the Chinese academic community stands on essentially the same starting line as its counterparts in Europe and the United States, with no discernible disadvantage in resources, access to information, or research capacity. By employing rigorous methodologies and maintaining scholarly confidence, Chinese researchers are fully capable of making significant theoretical contributions to this emerging field.

Beijing, China
December 1, 2025

Ruihua Chen

Contents

About the Author

Ruihua Chen PhD in Law, is Professor of Law and Chair of the Academic Committee at Peking University Law School. His scholarly work focuses on criminal procedure, evidence law, theories of procedural justice and values, judicial institutions, and the normative foundations of corporate compliance.Professor Chen is the author of numerous influential monographs, including *The Jurisprudence of Criminal Procedure*, *Theories of Procedural Justice*, *Theories of Procedural Sanctions*, *An Introduction to Judicial System Reform*, *Visible Justice*, *Legal Research Methodology*, *The Legal Reasoning of Practitioners*, *The Philosophy of Criminal Defense*, *The Art of Criminal Defense*, *The Chinese Model of Criminal Procedure*, *Theoretical Issues in Criminal Evidence Law*, *Fundamentals of Corporate Compliance Theory*, and *China's Experience in Effective Corporate Compliance*, among others. His work has significantly shaped contemporary discourse on procedural law and corporate compliance in China.

About the Translator

Yong Gao is an associate professor at Beijing International Studies University, specializing in criminal justice, judicial systems, and comparative law. She obtained her PhD in Law from Peking University and was a visiting scholar at Duke University. Gao has authored and translated more than ten books and published over 30 academic articles.

CHAPTER 1

The Nature of Corporate Compliance

1.1 The Siemens AG Case as a Starting Point

Corporate compliance originated in the United States and has since evolved into a globally recognized model of corporate governance. However, its precise meaning remains contested, both within legal academia and among practitioners. This divergence reflects the fact that corporate compliance is not a unitary concept; rather, it encompasses multiple dimensions. Debates continue over the scope and substance of corporate compliance. For instance, some equate "compliance" solely with corporate compliance, while others emphasize its close connection to the legal liability of corporate executives. Similarly, some view compliance as synonymous with the prevention and avoidance of legal risks in general, whereas others argue that its core function lies specifically in managing the risks of administrative and criminal sanctions, rather than generic risk control. Moreover, there are contrasting views on the normative status of compliance. Some scholars contend that corporate compliance remains primarily a matter of corporate ethics and has not yet evolved into a fully coherent and enforceable legal regime. Others, however, argue that although corporate compliance initially emerged as an internal governance tool within the broader framework of corporate governance, it has gradually evolved—since the 1990s—into a significant legal institution, particularly with the formalization of regulatory and criminal compliance systems.

It is therefore necessary to provide a precise definition of corporate compliance and to clarify the divergent interpretations that surround the concept. By analyzing the example of Siemens AG and its establishment of a compliance mechanism, we can illuminate the multifaceted nature of corporate compliance. This analysis will then serve as the basis for a concise articulation of both its conceptual connotation and definitional scope.

In November 2006, Siemens AG came under investigation by the Munich Public Prosecutor's Office in Germany for its alleged involvement in overseas

R. Chen, *An Introduction to Corporate Compliance*,
https://doi.org/10.1007/978-981-95-7257-1_1

commercial bribery. In response, Siemens AG voluntarily disclosed its bribery practices in multiple countries to the U.S. Department of Justice (DOJ) and the Securities and Exchange Commission (SEC) and retained the U.S. law firm Debevoise & Plimpton to conduct an independent internal investigation, which lasted two years. Following the submission of the investigation report, Siemens AG entered into a Deferred Prosecution Agreement (DPA) with the DOJ. Under the terms of the agreement, the DOJ agreed to forgo criminal prosecution, provided that Siemens AG paid a fine of USD 448.5 million for violations of the accounting and internal controls provisions of the U.S. Foreign Corrupt Practices Act (FCPA). Concurrently, Siemens AG settled a civil enforcement action brought by the SEC. As part of the settlement, Siemens AG neither admitted nor denied the SEC's allegations regarding violations of the anti-bribery provisions, but agreed to disgorge USD 350 million in illicit gains. In addition, Siemens AG also reached a settlement with German prosecutors, agreeing to pay fines totaling approximately USD 800 million.

In the wake of the Siemens AG scandal, the company undertook a comprehensive overhaul of its management structure. Both the Chairman of the Supervisory Board and the Chief Executive Officer resigned, approximately 200 managers were dismissed, and over 100 senior executives were required to cooperate with the internal investigation. Siemens AG also reorganized its compliance division and appointed Dr. Theo Waigel, former German Minister of Finance, as an Independent Compliance Monitor. Beginning in 2009, Dr. Waigel was entrusted with supervising the company's ongoing compliance reforms. Siemens AG further engaged a number of external professional institutions—including independent accounting and law firms—to conduct what has been recognized as the most extensive internal corporate investigation in German history. The review encompassed over 5000 consulting agreements, 40 million bank account records, 100 million documents, and 127 million individual transactions. A large number of internal interviews were also conducted in the course of the investigation. The financial cost of this compliance reform effort was considerable. Siemens AG incurred several hundred million euros in expenses solely for the services provided by external professional firms.

Siemens AG has established an independent and authoritative compliance organizational structure. The function is led by a Chief Compliance Officer (CCO), who reports to the company's General Counsel and is also authorized to submit reports directly to both the Managing Board and the Supervisory Board of Siemens AG. The General Counsel, in turn, reports directly to the President and Chief Executive Officer. Originally centered on anti-corruption efforts, Siemens' compliance framework has since expanded significantly in scope. The company's current compliance program focuses on four principal areas: (1) anti-corruption, focused on preventing bribery and the abuse of public or corporate power for private gain; (2) antitrust compliance, which seeks to ensure adherence to the principles of fair competition; (3) data protection, with an emphasis on safeguarding personal and sensitive information; and (4) anti-money laundering, focused on preventing Siemens AG from being used as a vehicle for money laundering or the financing of terrorism.

Siemens' compliance system consists of two fundamental components: the *Code of Business Conduct* and a three-pillar institutional safeguard framework. The *Code of Business Conduct* sets forth the foundational principles of the company's compliance regime across eight key domains: (1) core standards of ethical conduct; (2) dealings with business partners and third parties; (3) prevention of conflicts of interest; (4) responsible use and protection of corporate assets; (5) management and protection of information; (6) environmental, health, and safety obligations; (7) procedures for submitting complaints and suggestions; and (8) implementation, monitoring, and enforcement of compliance mechanisms. Collectively, these provisions establish the normative basis for Siemens' internal compliance governance system.

The three-pillar institutional safeguard framework consists of three core functional elements: prevention, detection, and response. The prevention pillar encompasses six primary components: (1) compliance risk management; (2) the formulation of internal policies and procedures; (3) training and other forms of internal communication; (4) advisory and support mechanisms; (5) integration with human resources processes; and (6) collective initiatives, including integrity and anti-corruption programs. Among these, compliance risk management and training constitute the core components of the preventive mechanism. The detection pillar comprises four procedural mechanisms designed to uncover compliance risks or irregularities: (1) internal control systems; (2) auditing processes; (3) complaints and grievance handling; and (4) reporting obligations. The response pillar is oriented toward the prompt investigation and identification of compliance breaches, the imposition of disciplinary sanctions on responsible personnel, and the implementation of global case-tracking mechanisms. Following disciplinary actions, the relevant departments are obligated to implement the remedial recommendations proposed in the investigation reports and to rectify institutional deficiencies or procedural gaps in order to prevent the recurrence of similar violations.[1]

By analyzing the case of Siemens AG and its establishment of a comprehensive compliance system, several preliminary observations may be drawn. Siemens AG had engaged in overseas bribery, thereby violating anti-corruption laws in both the United States and Germany. Consequently, the company became the subject of a criminal investigation by German prosecutors, as well as parallel criminal and regulatory investigations initiated by the U.S. Department of Justice (DOJ) and the Securities and Exchange Commission (SEC). Had Siemens AG failed to cooperate with these investigations, make voluntary disclosures, and undertake a fundamental overhaul of its compliance program, it would have faced a high probability of criminal prosecution by the DOJ and conviction in U.S. federal court, in addition to enforcement actions and administrative sanctions by the SEC. Although corporate criminal liability is not

[1] Ruihua Chen, "Siemens' Compliance System," *China Lawyer*, no. 6 (2019).

formally recognized under German criminal law, Siemens AG remained subject to the imposition of significant administrative penalties. It may therefore be reasonably concluded that, in an effort to mitigate the risk of extensive administrative and criminal liability, Siemens AG chose to pursue a strategic course centered on the reconstruction and institutionalization of its compliance program.

Through the reconstruction of its compliance program, Siemens AG not only entered into settlement agreements with the U.S. Department of Justice (DOJ) and the Securities and Exchange Commission (SEC)—thereby securing lenient criminal and administrative treatment and avoiding substantial financial penalties, disqualification from public procurement markets, and reputational harm—but also, perhaps unexpectedly, seized the opportunity to reform its internal corporate governance structure. The company rebuilt its compliance function, promulgated a new code of business conduct, and implemented a compliance management system structured around the three foundational pillars of prevention, detection, and response. If the avoidance of severe criminal and administrative sanctions can be understood as an external incentive for corporations to develop compliance programs, corporate compliance may nonetheless be characterized as an internal mechanism of self-regulation—one that enables companies to pursue their own governance and risk management objectives. This insight, however, invites a more fundamental inquiry: in what essential respects does this compliance-driven model diverge from traditional approaches to corporate governance? Siemens' declared principle of "only doing compliant business" illustrates that corporate compliance entails the execution of all business activities in strict adherence to applicable laws and regulations. It requires not only the active prevention and rejection of unlawful conduct, but also the cultivation of a long-term organizational culture of legality—one that extends to employees, third parties, and all other commercial partners.

Given that academic research on this topic remains relatively underdeveloped, a systematic and rigorous examination of the nature of corporate compliance is both necessary and timely. This book draws upon Siemens' experience in reconstructing its compliance system to articulate the threefold conceptual meaning of corporate compliance, analyze its institutional and developmental evolution, and clarify several prevailing conceptual ambiguities, with the aim of distilling its fundamental attributes. Such a foundational inquiry not only ensures that theoretical research proceeds along a coherent and well-grounded trajectory, but also offers valuable guidance for regulatory authorities in gradually developing a practical and effective compliance regime—one that aligns with the internal logic and normative requirements of compliance corporate governance.

1.2 Defining the Concept of Corporate Compliance

Drawing upon Siemens' experience in reconstructing its compliance program, the concept of corporate compliance may be understood as comprising three fundamental dimensions. First, from a normative or foundational perspective, corporate compliance refers to the obligation of enterprises to conduct their business operations in accordance with applicable laws, regulations, and relevant rules. It also entails ensuring that employees, third parties, and other commercial partners engage in business practices that are lawful and compliant. Second, from the standpoint of corporate governance, compliance serves as an internal governance mechanism through which companies seek to prevent or mitigate the risk of legal sanctions, regulatory penalties, and other forms of liability arising from unlawful or non-compliant behavior. This dimension is oriented toward protecting the enterprise from significant financial losses, reputational harm, and disqualification from public or commercial participation. Third, from the perspective of external regulatory incentives, corporate compliance is promoted by regulatory authorities as a proactive strategy for preventing corporate misconduct. To this end, regulators encourage the establishment and implementation of robust compliance management systems and engage in various forms of compliance oversight.

1.2.1 The First Dimension of Compliance

At its most basic level, the term *corporate compliance* denotes the obligation to "follow rules" or "comply with legal provisions." Regardless of the specific structure or configuration of a compliance program or compliance management system, its fundamental purpose remains the same: to ensure that the enterprise conducts its business operations in accordance with applicable laws and regulations. This gives rise to a basic yet significant question: what specific legal norms and regulatory frameworks are corporations, in practice, required to observe?

In general, the legal and regulatory obligations that corporations must observe in business practice may be classified into four categories, according to the nature and source of the applicable rules. First, there are national laws and administrative regulations promulgated by legislatures and regulatory authorities, which constitute the core of the domestic legal framework. Second, there are commercial customs and ethical standards, including both formal codes of conduct issued by industry associations and informal, unwritten business practices and ethical norms. Third, corporations are subject to internally established rules and policies, such as corporate charters, codes of business conduct, and internal ethics guidelines. Fourth, companies may also be subject to relevant foreign laws, international treaties, and customary international practices, including the legal provisions of foreign jurisdictions in which they operate, international conventions to which their home country is a party, and regulatory frameworks established by international organizations.[2]

At its core, corporate compliance operates as an internal self-policing mechanism. The primary objective of a compliance management system is to ensure that employees, third parties, clients, and acquired entities comply with relevant laws and regulations in their business activities and that all such actors engage exclusively in lawful and compliant conduct. However, the expectation that a company should merely operate in accordance with the law represents a superficial understanding of compliance. From a corporate governance perspective, achieving legal compliance requires a proactive and systematic approach: enterprises must assess the specific legal and regulatory risks they encounter and establish internal mechanisms to prevent misconduct by employees, clients, third parties, and acquired companies. The essence of corporate compliance lies in its internal regulatory function—specifically, in the creation of systems designed to prevent, detect, and respond to potential violations within the organization. In this sense, corporate compliance is not merely a general obligation to "comply with the law," but a comprehensive, institutionalized self-policing system aimed at preventing, identifying, and responding to potential compliance risks.

1.2.2 The Second Dimension of Compliance

If our understanding of corporate compliance is confined to the previously discussed perspective, we risk reducing it to the relatively superficial notion of "operating in accordance with laws and regulations." However, from the standpoint of compliance management in actual corporate practice, compliance entails much more than the mere observance of legal norms or the fulfillment of regulatory obligations. At a more substantive level, corporate compliance refers to a governance system established by companies to proactively prevent unlawful or non-compliant conduct and to avoid or mitigate the various losses—legal, financial, reputational, or operational—that may result from such conduct. To fully understand this deeper dimension, it is necessary to conduct a concise analysis from four interrelated perspectives.

First and foremost, corporate compliance serves as a risk management mechanism aimed at mitigating compliance risk. This refers to the potential for a corporation to incur legal sanctions, regulatory penalties, financial losses, or reputational harm resulting from non-compliance with applicable laws, regulations, or ethical standards. The specific manifestations of compliance risk may vary considerably depending on the nature of an enterprise's business operations. For instance, banks commonly encounter compliance risks related to violations of anti-money laundering laws; healthcare companies are exposed to risks involving breaches of anti-bribery and anti-corruption legislation; big data

[2] Ruihua Chen, "Fundamental Issues of Corporate Compliance," *China Law Review*, no. 1 (2020).

firms are particularly vulnerable to infringements of data protection and information privacy laws; and enterprises engaged in cross-border trade may face significant risks under international export control regimes. To mitigate these risks and avoid the associated losses, companies must establish a robust compliance management system. Such a system should be viewed not merely as a legal compliance tool, but as a critical institutional pillar of modern corporate governance.

Second, corporate compliance operates as a governance framework aimed at addressing investigations, sanctions, and enforcement actions initiated by regulatory authorities. The core rationale for establishing a compliance system is not to insulate the company from all forms of legal risk, but to prevent regulatory enforcement and liability arising from unlawful or non-compliant conduct. In the course of their operations, enterprises inevitably encounter various risks and typically adopt broad-based risk management strategies. However, the objective of corporate compliance is not to manage ordinary business risks or to address legal risks in general or undefined terms. Instead, it is focused specifically on preventing risks associated with administrative penalties, regulatory sanctions, or legal accountability resulting from violations of applicable laws and regulations. The case of Siemens AG clearly illustrates this point: the company's core motivation for reconstructing its compliance program was to avert the imposition of severe administrative penalties and the threat of criminal prosecution.

Third, corporate compliance serves as a targeted mechanism for mitigating the risk of substantial financial loss, reputational damage, and disqualification from essential market participation. For enterprises suspected of unlawful or non-compliant conduct, the consequences of regulatory investigation or judicial conviction often extend significantly beyond administrative fines or criminal penalties. In many cases, such sanctions may result in the suspension or revocation of core business qualifications. For example, a company subject to regulatory sanctions or criminal conviction may: lose its eligibility for public listing; be barred from bidding for or contracting with government agencies; or have its franchise or operating licenses revoked. In China, the most severe administrative penalties imposed on non-compliant enterprises take the form of market disqualification measures—namely, the revocation of special business licenses and the cancellation of business registration. These penalties represent the most stringent forms of regulatory sanction under administrative law. As noted by the U.S. Department of Justice in reference to the far-reaching consequences of indictment, "to indict a corporation is tantamount to imposing the corporate death penalty." This striking formulation underscores the profound consequences of regulatory enforcement and criminal prosecution. Once convicted or sanctioned, a company may lose essential business qualifications, be barred from market participation, and suffer catastrophic financial and reputational damage. To avoid such outcomes, enterprises must establish robust compliance systems capable of identifying and preventing unlawful or non-compliant conduct by the company or its employees.

Ultimately, corporate compliance has developed into a distinctive and essential dimension of contemporary corporate governance. Traditional governance frameworks primarily focus on delineating the rights and responsibilities between shareholders and managerial authority. In this model, the board of directors—elected by shareholders—undertakes strategic decision-making and supervisory responsibilities, while senior executives—appointed by the board—are tasked with managing day-to-day operations. To strengthen financial oversight, companies may establish relatively independent internal audit departments or audit committees that report directly to the board. However, this conventional governance structure generally lacks an autonomous mechanism specifically designed to manage legal and regulatory risks. The integration of corporate compliance mechanisms addresses this structural deficiency by embedding a specialized risk management function within the governance framework. This is typically achieved through the formation of a compliance committee under the board, the appointment of a Chief Compliance Officer (CCO) at the executive level, the establishment of a dedicated compliance department at headquarters, and the deployment of compliance officers or units across business divisions and subsidiaries. Collectively, these arrangements constitute a top-down compliance management system that institutionalizes legal risk prevention within the broader corporate governance architecture.

By establishing a compliance management system, enterprises formulate codes of business conduct, set behavioral standards for employees, and put in place a compliance risk prevention system, a risk identification system, and a response system for misconduct. Through the timely monitoring and handling of business activities undertaken by the enterprise and its employees, enterprises achieve self-regulation, self-reporting, self-disclosure, and self-remediation. In this way, they can not only prevent and promptly detect violations of laws and regulations but also address and remedy institutional loopholes and deficiencies. To a certain extent, corporate compliance thus functions as a substitute for governmental regulation, helping to prevent unlawful conduct by enterprises and their employees.[3]

1.2.3 *The Third Dimension of Compliance*

Corporate compliance, as a mode of corporate governance, does not operate autonomously or possess inherent normative force. Its effectiveness hinges on the establishment of external incentive structures that motivate enterprises to actively adopt, maintain, and institutionalize compliance management practices. In the absence of such incentives, the compliance governance model tends to remain inert, lacking both immediacy and practical momentum. From a regulatory standpoint, public authorities have generally relied on three

[3] Ruihua Chen, "Three Dimensions of the Corporate Compliance System: A Comparative Law Perspective," *Journal of Comparative Law*, no. 3 (2019).

principal mechanisms to promote corporate compliance: compliance guidance, compliance mandates, and compliance incentives.

Compliance guidance constitutes a key mechanism through which regulatory authorities and judicial bodies promote corporate compliance. The term refers to administrative measures whereby public authorities issue compliance guidelines to assist enterprises in developing or strengthening their internal compliance management systems. By issuing compliance guidelines, regulators provide a foundational framework for effective compliance, setting forth the minimum standards that enterprises are expected to meet. In addition, these guidelines play a critical role in standardizing the methodologies and procedures used to evaluate the effectiveness of corporate compliance programs.

Compliance mandates represent another essential mechanism through which regulatory and judicial authorities foster the development of corporate compliance systems. The term refers to the imposition of a mandatory compliance regime, under which qualifying enterprises are legally obligated to implement compliance programs. Failure to fulfill this obligation may subject enterprises to administrative or legal liability. Because the law imposes a duty to establish a compliance system, non-compliance may be classified as a form of unlawful conduct, thereby exposing the enterprise to a range of potential sanctions, including administrative penalties, disqualification from market participation, or, in severe cases, revocation of the business license. As such, compliance mandates are widely regarded as an effective regulatory instrument for compelling companies to institutionalize compliance measures and integrate them into the broader framework of corporate governance.

Compliance incentives refer to regulatory or judicial mechanisms that offer lenient treatment to enterprises subject to enforcement or judicial proceedings, provided they have established effective compliance management systems. This approach represents a shift from traditional enforcement paradigms, which have historically relied on punitive measures to deter corporate misconduct. By introducing a compliance-based leniency mechanism, the legal system transitions from a solely punitive model to one that rewards corporate reform and proactive governance. Within this framework, enterprises that design and implement robust compliance programs—particularly those capable of preventing the recurrence of similar violations—may benefit from mitigated administrative or judicial sanctions. The underlying objective is to encourage companies under investigation to actively enhance their compliance infrastructure, thereby promoting the broader institutionalization of compliance practices across the corporate sector. By rewarding substantive and demonstrable improvements in compliance, regulatory authorities aim not only to incentivize legal conformity but also to reframe compliance as a strategic governance instrument—one voluntarily adopted by enterprises as part of their long-term risk management and corporate responsibility strategies.

From the standpoint of applicability, compliance incentives are generally classified into two types: *ex ante* compliance incentives and *ex post* compliance incentives. *Ex ante* compliance incentives are mechanisms by which regulatory or judicial authorities evaluate whether a company has already established an effective compliance management system before any unlawful or non-compliant conduct occurs. Depending on the assessed effectiveness of the pre-existing system, authorities may either exempt the enterprise from liability or impose reduced penalties. In contrast, *ex post* compliance incentives apply when, after a violation has taken place, a company proactively implements remedial measures by establishing or enhancing its compliance framework. These post-violation actions are designed to demonstrate the company's commitment to future legal conformity and may constitute the basis for regulatory or judicial leniency, resulting in mitigated sanctions.

The implementation of compliance incentive mechanisms facilitates the development of a model of negotiated corporate regulation within the legal system. Under this regulatory framework, enterprises that have committed legal or regulatory violations may be eligible for leniency contingent upon their commitment to, and implementation of, comprehensive compliance remediation measures. Such mechanisms enable corporations to avert the most severe sanctions, thereby strengthening their incentives to pursue institutional correction and institutionalize robust compliance systems. Once such proceedings are initiated, a failure to carry out compliance remediation permits regulatory or judicial authorities to exercise full discretion in imposing stringent sanctions. This conditional framework exerts substantial pressure on enterprises to engage in timely and substantive compliance remediation efforts. Conversely, enterprises that proactively engage in compliance remediation and successfully undergo regulatory review may receive significant benefits, such as the discontinuation of enforcement actions or the imposition of reduced penalties. Such outcome-based incentives reinforce corporate willingness to invest in sustained compliance efforts. Accordingly, compliance incentive mechanisms have been widely recognized across Europe, North America, and other jurisdictions as among the most effective regulatory instruments for promoting corporate compliance and fostering voluntary cooperation in enforcement contexts.

1.3 Categories of Compliance Risk

At present, two distinct theoretical models can be identified regarding the nature and function of corporate compliance: the management-oriented model and the risk-oriented model. The former is typically found in autonomous corporate compliance management and defines compliance as "corporate adherence to rules." It stresses a comprehensive review of compliance obligations and pursues the overarching goal of ensuring that all employees, business operations, and processes are conducted fully in accordance with laws and regulations. The latter, by contrast, is generally associated with the compliance remediation processes of enterprises subject to legal proceedings. It conceives of compliance as a "compliance risk control system," emphasizing the establishment of targeted compliance programs tailored to the specific risks faced by the enterprise, with the aim of achieving effective prevention, monitoring, and response to compliance risks.

Irrespective of the compliance model employed, there is broad consensus on the central importance of identifying and evaluating compliance risks, which are widely regarded as a cornerstone of effective compliance governance. This raises a critical conceptual question: what precisely constitutes a compliance risk? To date, definitions articulated in international compliance frameworks, domestic compliance guidelines, and academic analyses have converged on a common formulation: compliance risk denotes the likelihood of incurring adverse consequences—such as sanctions, penalties, financial loss, or reputational damage—stemming from violations of laws, regulations, or other applicable standards. From an analytical perspective, compliance risk is generally understood to comprise two fundamental components. The first is the "likelihood of non-compliance," which refers to the probability that an enterprise—or its agents—will breach legal, regulatory, or normative obligations. The second is the "likelihood of loss," which denotes the probability that such breaches will result in enforcement actions, sanctions, or other adverse outcomes. There is widespread scholarly agreement that these two dimensions—internal behavioral risk and external consequence risk—jointly constitute the structural foundation of compliance risk. However, ongoing debates concern how best to conceptualize the distinction between "internal risk" and "external risk," as well as how to define the scope and boundaries of each category.

For proponents of the management-oriented model, compliance risk is primarily conceptualized as the probability that a corporation will breach applicable norms. In this framework, "norms" are interpreted broadly to encompass both mandatory external obligations and voluntary internal undertakings. These include statutory laws, administrative regulations, and governmental directives, as well as internal corporate policies, procedural rules, codes of conduct, and ethical principles to which the corporation has explicitly or implicitly committed. Within this model, any failure to comply with external (legal and regulatory), internal (institutional), or ethical (moral) norms is considered to give rise to a compliance risk. Furthermore, this model posits that once a normative breach has occurred, the potential for any adverse consequence—termed "consequential risk"—is likewise encompassed within the broader structure of compliance risk. Such consequences include administrative sanctions, criminal prosecution, or international regulatory measures, as well as commercial opportunity loss, financial harm, or reputational damage. In summary, from the management-oriented perspective, any act of non-compliance—whether with legal, internal, or ethical standards—that entails the potential for adverse consequences is subsumed under the category of compliance risk.

This conceptualization of compliance risk has come under mounting academic and practical scrutiny, as it appears to diverge from core principles of compliance governance and has given rise to a host of adverse real-world implications. One of the most prevalent critiques is that norm violations vary widely in severity. Breaches of state-imposed mandatory legal norms are fundamentally distinct—in both nature and consequence—from failures to honor voluntary corporate undertakings. These divergent forms of non-compliance carry markedly different ramifications for national interests, public welfare, and the internal functioning and strategic priorities of the firm. A salient example is the contrast between a corporation that commits an environmental crime—such as severe pollution constituting a criminal offense—and one that merely breaches a contractual clause. The legal gravity, public condemnation, and reputational fallout of the former far surpass those of the latter. Critics further contend that the repercussions of non-compliance differ drastically depending on the normative regime in question. Criminal violations may lead to conviction and incarceration; breaches of administrative law may result in regulatory sanctions; civil infractions typically trigger lawsuits and compensatory liabilities, whereas breaches of ethical norms may only incur reputational censure or moral disapproval. In light of the significant divergence between internal behavioral risks and external consequence risks, it is increasingly debated whether enterprises ought to allocate compliance resources indiscriminately across all domains. Is a monolithic and undifferentiated compliance framework truly warranted?

Empirical observations indicate that risk control and management constitute the central concerns of corporate governance. In practice, the level of organizational commitment to risk mitigation varies significantly based on the inherent characteristics of the risk and the severity of its potential consequences. As a general principle, enterprises typically prioritize "strategic risks"—those with the potential to inflict substantial losses or catastrophic consequences—by dedicating considerable personnel, capital, and infrastructure and by instituting specialized risk management frameworks. Conversely, "general risks," which are expected to result in only limited harm, seldom warrant significant resource allocation or cost expenditure. In the area of compliance risk management, both international standards and domestic regulatory frameworks emphasize the "tone at the top" doctrine, which places ultimate responsibility for compliance on senior corporate leadership. This principle requires that compliance departments be institutionally independent, endowed with sufficient authority and resources, and tasked with developing, operating, and continually enhancing the compliance system. Executives are also expected to lead in shaping and disseminating a culture of compliance throughout the organization. However, if compliance risk is construed so expansively as to include the possibility of incurring any adverse consequence from any form of norm violation—be it legal, institutional, or ethical—then how can a firm reasonably justify the deployment of high-level governance resources to manage what amounts to an indeterminate and overgeneralized category of risk?

This suggests that the prevailing theoretical formulation of "compliance risk" may be conceptually unsound. The compliance risks confronting enterprises involved in legal or regulatory breaches should not be treated as ordinary; instead, they more appropriately fall within the category of "strategic risk." Strategic risks refer to high-impact threats that may result in substantial losses or precipitate catastrophic outcomes for the enterprise. Traditional corporate governance theory has consistently emphasized the centrality of managing strategic risks—particularly decision-making risk, operational risk, and financial risk—as the foundation for designing governance structures and internal control mechanisms. These risks are prioritized precisely because, if left unmanaged, they can result in profound disruptions to the firm's viability and long-term performance.

Decision-making risk denotes the possibility of fundamental misjudgments in a company's strategic orientation, core philosophy, or long-term business direction—miscalculations that may trigger severe, potentially catastrophic consequences. For instance, a critical error in strategic planning or a departure from a sustainable strategic path may result in serious organizational disruption, including the breakdown of key commercial relationships, loss of major clients, or collapse of financial liquidity chains. Operational risk—commonly referred to as business risk—originates from technical flaws or managerial inadequacies in the firm's routine operational activities. Such risks may manifest in the form of unprofitable capital allocations, market rejection of products or services, or sustained failure to achieve profitability. Severe financial losses can ensue when deficiencies in product innovation, business scaling, technological integration, or workforce management give rise to prolonged underperformance—or, in extreme cases, corporate insolvency and bankruptcy. Financial risk arises from serious misconduct, control failures, or managerial deficiencies in a company's financial operations. Such risks may stem from internal fraud, unauthorized or speculative investments, or systemic lapses in financial oversight. For example, a firm lacking a robust and transparent financial governance framework may be unable to prevent the misappropriation of funds or other acts that undermine financial integrity. These vulnerabilities can lead to significant financial losses and may ultimately jeopardize the company's fiscal sustainability. Because decision-making, operational, and financial risks constitute strategic-level threats rather than routine business problems, they are regarded as core priorities in corporate governance. Contemporary firms address these risks through comprehensive governance architectures, risk-specific internal control mechanisms, and institutionally embedded safeguards designed to ensure early detection and effective mitigation.

Like the three preceding categories of strategic risk, compliance risk should likewise be conceptualized as a form of strategic risk confronting modern enterprises. This is clearly evidenced by the responses of firms facing investigation for administrative or criminal wrongdoing. Why are such enterprises willing to submit to the requirements imposed by administrative regulators or judicial authorities, accept supervision and guidance from appointed compliance monitors, and undertake targeted compliance remediation measures? Empirical observations suggest that these firms are not responding to routine compliance matters or low-grade legal risks. Rather, they are confronting high-stakes legal exposures, including the threat of administrative penalties, criminal prosecution, and international regulatory sanctions. If left unaddressed, such risks may culminate in administrative or criminal penalties, enforcement actions by international financial institutions, or exclusion from both domestic and global markets. The potential consequences are severe: revocation of business licenses, disqualification from regulated industries, ineligibility for public procurement, restrictions on access to capital markets and credit institutions, and delisting from securities exchanges. Because these risks are existential in nature, firms under regulatory or prosecutorial scrutiny are often compelled to acknowledge misconduct, accept legal liability, and commit to compliance remediation—frequently involving the establishment or restructuring of a corporate compliance framework. From the perspective of rational choice theory, would any firm voluntarily submit to such intrusive, resource-intensive, and reputationally costly compliance supervision—absent the imminent threat of legal jeopardy or the imperative to safeguard vital operational interests? Would a rational enterprise undertake the restructuring of its governance architecture, the remediation of institutional deficiencies, or a wholesale transformation of its business model merely to avoid marginal reputational damage or limited financial loss?

The conceptualization of compliance risk as a form of strategic risk is reflected not only in the remediation efforts undertaken by companies under investigation, but also in the voluntary establishment of internal compliance systems by firms that are not subject to formal regulatory or prosecutorial scrutiny. A prominent example is Siemens AG, which, after completing compliance remediation under the supervision of the U.S. Department of Justice (DOJ) and the Securities and Exchange Commission (SEC), enhanced its anti-commercial bribery compliance framework. Building upon this foundation, the company autonomously established three additional specialized compliance management systems. A similar trajectory can be observed in the case of ZTE Corporation, which, under the oversight of both U.S. judicial and administrative authorities, initiated compliance remediation by establishing a robust export control compliance program. Based on subsequent internal compliance risk assessments, the company further expanded its compliance architecture to include dedicated programs focused on anti-commercial bribery compliance and data protection compliance. These two cases clearly demonstrate that, even in the absence of formal administrative enforcement or criminal proceedings, enterprises can proactively develop multiple specialized compliance management systems on the basis of identified and prioritized compliance risks.

Compliance risks identified through risk assessment and risk identification are conceptually distinct from both traditional legal risks and normative ethical risks. In the course of business operations, enterprises may incur losses arising from civil law violations or suffer reputational harm due to breaches of prevailing social or ethical norms. However, whether in the context of post-violation compliance remediation or voluntary compliance system development, such civil and ethical risks are generally not categorized as compliance risks. The rationale is straightforward: while such violations may result in limited or localized harm, they rarely produce broader societal consequences. Nor do they typically provoke administrative investigations, criminal proceedings, or enforcement actions by international financial institutions. They are unlikely to lead to administrative penalties, criminal liability, or international financial sanctions, nor do they result in restrictions on market access or operational disqualification within regulated sectors. Given these attributes, there is neither theoretical justification nor practical rationale for classifying civil or ethical risks as strategic in nature—let alone designing a dedicated compliance governance structure to address them. Accordingly, contemporary enterprises typically assign the management of civil and ethical risks to the legal affairs function, maintaining a clear institutional distinction between legal risk management and compliance governance.

As a category of strategic risk—comparable to decision-making, operational, and financial risks—compliance risk originates in legal risk but should not be equated with routine or general legal exposure. First, in terms of violation likelihood, compliance risk refers specifically to the possibility that an enterprise may contravene administrative regulations, engage in criminal conduct, or breach regulatory standards established by international financial institutions. Only such conduct—administrative infractions, criminal violations, and breaches of international financial compliance frameworks—falls within the legitimate scope of compliance risk governance. Second, regarding potential consequences, compliance risk primarily entails the possibility that a firm may face administrative sanctions, criminal prosecution, enforcement actions by international financial institutions, or the revocation or suspension of essential business qualifications. For example, breaches of administrative law may result in regulatory enforcement; criminal conduct can lead to indictment, conviction, and sentencing; and violations of international financial compliance standards may result in temporary or permanent exclusion from global financial markets. Moreover, these three categories of non-compliance often give rise to collateral consequences beyond the primary sanctions—such as the revocation or limitation of business licenses, franchise rights, or market access eligibility.

Given the potential for substantial losses arising from serious legal or regulatory violations, compliance risk can be broadly classified into three principal categories: administrative compliance risk, criminal compliance risk, and international financial compliance risk. Administrative compliance risk refers to the possibility that a company, in the course of its business activities, may contravene administrative laws or regulations, thereby incurring administrative sanctions and the potential revocation or suspension of operational licenses or regulatory qualifications. In response to such risks, administrative authorities may require the enterprise to implement a targeted administrative compliance management system tailored to the area of regulatory concern. Criminal compliance risk arises from violations of criminal law that may result in prosecution, conviction, sentencing, and the consequent disqualification from essential business qualifications or industry-specific certifications. In such cases, judicial authorities may require the enterprise to establish a specialized criminal compliance framework to address the underlying legal vulnerabilities. By contrast, international financial compliance risk refers to the possibility that a company, in the context of participating in procurement or lending programs administered by international financial institutions, may engage in prohibited conduct—such as corruption, fraud, or collusion—in violation of applicable integrity standards. In such cases, the institution may require the implementation of a dedicated integrity compliance system as a condition for continued participation or future eligibility.

1.4 The Evolution of Corporate Compliance

Corporate compliance first emerged in the United States. As early as the pre-1960s period, the concept of corporate compliance began to take shape within the broader context of commercial regulatory practice in the United States. In response to mounting public distrust of corporations, some companies adopted internal self-regulatory measures by codifying employee conduct and promoting adherence to legal and ethical norms. At the same time, several industry associations began formulating compliance guidelines intended to promote lawful and standardized business operations across the sector. Notably, the establishment of compliance frameworks—whether by corporations or industry associations—was not driven solely by the pursuit of legal adherence. Rather, it also served strategic purposes, including the delineation of market boundaries and the exercise of pricing control. This early phase of corporate compliance in the United States is best characterized as a "self-regulatory stage."[4]

Following the 1960s, a wave of corporate monopoly scandals fundamentally altered the trajectory of corporate compliance in the United States. More than a dozen major corporations—including General Electric and Westinghouse Electric—were found to have engaged in market allocation, price-fixing, and bid-rigging schemes to preserve their monopolistic dominance. These companies became the focus of large-scale criminal antitrust investigations conducted by the Antitrust Division of the U.S. Department of Justice. Ultimately, more than 30 corporations and over 40 individuals entered into plea agreements with federal prosecutors. In addition to multimillion-dollar fines imposed on the corporations, seven senior executives received custodial sentences. The criminal sanctions imposed on corporations and their executives sent shockwaves through American society and triggered a wave of corporate responses, with many firms initiating the establishment of antitrust compliance programs. During this period, regulatory authorities played a pivotal role in advancing the evolution of corporate compliance practices. Under emerging legal doctrines, corporations that had adopted compliance programs—and ensured their diligent oversight and good-faith implementation—could invoke the absence of corporate intent or culpability, thereby limiting or eliminating organizational

[4] Todd Haugh, "The Criminalization of Compliance," *Notre Dame Law Review* 92 (2017): 1215–1270.

liability for employee misconduct. As a result, beginning in the early 1970s, the institutionalization of compliance management systems began to gain traction across a number of highly regulated sectors. This era, which spanned nearly three decades, is commonly referred to as the "government-driven stage" of corporate compliance in the United States.[5]

During this period, corporate compliance assumed an increasingly prominent role in the enforcement of anti-bribery laws. In 1977, in response to mounting concerns over overseas bribery involving U.S. corporations, the United States enacted the Foreign Corrupt Practices Act (FCPA). The FCPA introduced stringent anti-bribery provisions and accounting requirements that imposed significant legal obligations not only on U.S. companies conducting business overseas, but also on foreign firms involved in corrupt activities within the United States and on foreign entities with U.S.-based subsidiaries or operations whose overseas conduct falls within the reach of U.S. jurisdiction. Enforcement of the FCPA is divided between the Department of Justice (DOJ), which exercises criminal jurisdiction over anti-bribery violations, and the Securities and Exchange Commission (SEC), which oversees civil enforcement.[6]

Since the early 1990s, the U.S. Department of Justice (DOJ) and the Securities and Exchange Commission (SEC) have significantly expanded the scope and intensity of their enforcement efforts against foreign bribery. Consequently, numerous multinational corporations have faced prosecution and conviction for engaging in various forms of commercial bribery. In addition to criminal penalties, such convictions often caused significant reputational harm, leading to the loss of business opportunities and exclusion from critical commercial engagements. To avoid such detrimental outcomes, many corporations began to prioritize internal legal risk management, with particular emphasis on building and strengthening compliance systems designed to prevent foreign bribery.[7]

From that point forward, the U.S. corporate compliance framework entered a new phase of institutional development. A defining feature of this phase was the transformation of compliance from a sector-specific regulatory tool into a broadly institutionalized model of corporate governance across the U.S. corporate landscape. At the same time, a compliance framework that had initially been shaped by criminal enforcement authorities was gradually adopted by a broad range of governmental agencies, resulting in the parallel integration of criminal compliance and administrative regulatory compliance into the overall compliance architecture.

[5] Feng Deng, "The Origins of Corporate Compliance and the Institutional Limitations in China," *Comparative Law Review*, no. 1 (2020).

[6] Ruihua Chen, "The U.S. Foreign Corrupt Practices Act and Issues of Corporate Compliance," *China Lawyer*, no. 2 (2019).

[7] Ruihua Chen, "Corporate Criminal Liability from the Perspective of Compliance," *Global Law Review*, no. 1 (2020).

In 1991, the United States Sentencing Commission issued the *Federal Sentencing Guidelines for Organizations* (FSGO), codified as Chapter Eight of the *Federal Sentencing Guidelines*, thereby establishing a structured framework for sentencing corporations and other organizations convicted of federal offenses. A core component of Chapter Eight is the articulation of general criteria for what constitutes an Effective Compliance Program, which may serve as a mitigating factor during sentencing. As revised, the standards in § 8B2.1 of the FSGO specify that an effective compliance program must, at a minimum, incorporate seven essential elements—commonly referred to as the "Seven Elements" of an effective compliance program. These include: (1) establishing standards and procedures to prevent and detect criminal conduct; (2) ensuring oversight by the organization's governing authority and high-level personnel, with specific individuals delegated operational responsibility and provided with adequate authority and resources; (3) using reasonable efforts to exclude individuals with a history of illegal or unethical conduct from positions of substantial authority; (4) communicating standards and procedures effectively through periodic training and other means; (5) implementing monitoring and auditing systems and establishing anonymous or confidential reporting mechanisms; (6) promoting and enforcing the program consistently through appropriate incentives and disciplinary measures; and (7) responding appropriately to detected misconduct and taking reasonable steps to prevent future offenses, including necessary program modifications.

The implementation of the *Federal Sentencing Guidelines for Organizations (FSGO)* served as a powerful catalyst for the development of corporate compliance across multiple dimensions. On the one hand, in order to deter corporate misconduct and criminal violations, enforcement authorities not only imposed monetary penalties but also introduced incentive mechanisms for companies that had implemented effective compliance programs. On the other hand, the Guidelines explicitly encouraged companies to cooperate with law enforcement investigations, voluntarily disclose unlawful conduct, promptly discipline culpable employees, and, in doing so, become eligible for reduced penalties in proportion to the degree of their cooperation. The emergence of this criminal compliance framework marked the first systematic use of affirmative incentives to promote the enhancement of internal compliance systems. As a result, corporations began to shift from passive observers of employee conduct to active advocates of lawful and rule-abiding business practices.

Indeed, the implementation of the *Federal Sentencing Guidelines for Organizations (FSGO)* marked a watershed moment in the evolution of the U.S. corporate compliance framework. Thereafter, corporations across the United States increasingly developed compliance programs based on the standards articulated in the Guidelines, which soon came to be viewed as a hallmark of sound corporate governance. At the same time, federal prosecutors came to play an increasingly pivotal role in promoting corporate compliance practices. Charging decisions began to depend heavily on the compliance-related standards set forth in the Guidelines, with prosecutors assessing whether companies had instituted adequate compliance measures prior to initiating criminal proceedings. Moreover, in negotiating Deferred Prosecution Agreements (DPAs) and Non-Prosecution Agreements (NPAs), prosecutors consistently evaluated whether the corporation had implemented—or had pledged to implement—compliance programs in line with the Guidelines. Following the conclusion of such agreements, these standards continued to serve as reference points for corporate compliance enhancement.[8]

The fourth phase in the evolution of corporate compliance in the United States is commonly referred to as "the stage of comprehensive regulatory oversight." In the early 2000s, the United States was shaken by a series of high-profile corporate fraud scandals involving companies such as Enron, WorldCom, and Lehman Brothers, all of which ultimately collapsed due to their involvement in systemic fraudulent activities. One of the most consequential developments during this period was the collapse of Arthur Andersen, then the world's largest accounting firm. The firm was criminally prosecuted for obstruction of justice after it was discovered to have destroyed key documents related to its audit of Enron. The indictment led to Arthur Andersen's rapid disintegration: it lost its license to conduct securities audits, forfeited nearly all of its clients, and experienced a mass departure of employees—many of whom either resigned or were laid off. The firm's downfall triggered widespread economic disruption.

In response to the crisis and in order to reinforce corporate internal controls, the United States enacted the Sarbanes–Oxley Act of 2002 (SOX)—the most far-reaching reform of federal securities regulation since the 1930s. The enactment of SOX marked a paradigm shift in the governance of publicly traded companies in the United States—from a disclosure-based model to one centered on substantive regulatory oversight. At the core of the Act was the requirement that companies establish comprehensive internal control systems and that senior management assume direct responsibility for their design, implementation, evaluation, and disclosure. Pursuant to SOX, the Public Company Accounting Oversight Board (PCAOB) issued foundational standards for internal control over financial reporting. These standards mandate that corporate management assess the effectiveness of internal controls and maintain thorough documentation and reporting of their evaluations. Specifically, management's responsibilities include: documenting the design of internal controls related to the recognition of all financial statement accounts and disclosures; testing the operational effectiveness of those controls across all components of the internal control framework; carrying out procedures sufficient to obtain persuasive evidence supporting the assessment, and retaining appropriate documentation; personally undertaking the evaluation—with assistance permitted from internal auditors, company personnel, or external consultants, but without delegation to external auditors or unrelated third parties; refraining from concluding that the internal controls are effective if one or

[8] Ruihua Chen, "Deferred Prosecution Agreements in the Context of Corporate Compliance," *Journal of Comparative Law*, no. 1 (2020).

more material weaknesses have been identified; and ensuring that all identified material weaknesses are disclosed in the internal control report.[9]

The *Dodd–Frank Wall Street Reform and Consumer Protection Act* of 2010, enacted in response to the 2008 global financial crisis, significantly contributed to the further institutionalization of corporate compliance in the United States. As observed by American legal scholars, the Act placed increased emphasis on internal whistleblower protections and corporate compliance procedures, encouraging companies to enhance and continuously refine their compliance programs in order to more effectively identify and prevent internal legal and regulatory violations.

Following the widespread implementation of corporate compliance systems in the United States, international organizations gradually embraced the concept of "corporate governance through compliance" and began to issue foundational standards to guide the establishment of compliance systems across relevant sectors. In April 2005, the Basel Committee on Banking Supervision issued *Compliance and the Compliance Function in Banks*, which established general principles for the creation of compliance departments within financial institutions. The document provided a clear definition of compliance risk, emphasized the role of senior management in driving compliance from the top, and laid out key principles of compliance governance. In March 2010, the Organisation for Economic Co-operation and Development (OECD) released its *Good Practice Guidance on Internal Controls, Ethics, and Compliance*, which established anti-bribery standards applicable to both member states and multinational enterprises, and introduced 12 core principles for effective compliance systems. In 2014, the International Organization for Standardization (ISO) published *Compliance management systems—Guidelines (ISO 19600:2014)*, which set forth globally recognized standards for effective compliance management in the form of an international normative framework. The issuance of this standard marked a key milestone in the institutionalization and maturation of effective compliance programs on a global scale.

Under the influence of the U.S. corporate compliance regime, other Western countries gradually adopted compliance-oriented models of corporate governance. Initially, the international diffusion of compliance practices was closely tied to global efforts to combat transnational commercial bribery. Over two decades after the enactment of the U.S. Foreign Corrupt Practices Act (FCPA), the United Kingdom passed the Bribery Act in 2011,[10] followed by France's enactment of the Sapin II Law in 2016.[11] In both jurisdictions, corporate compliance was institutionalized as a key incentive mechanism within their anti-corruption enforcement regimes, with minimum standards established for what constitutes an effective compliance program. Around the same time,

[9] Ruihua Chen, "Enron and Arthur Andersen Cases," *China Lawyer*, no. 4 (2020).

[10] Ruihua Chen, "The UK Bribery Act and Corporate Compliance," *China Lawyer*, no. 3 (2019).

[11] Ruihua Chen, "The Sapin II Law and Corporate Compliance in France," *China Lawyer*, no. 5 (2019).

countries such as Spain and Italy amended their criminal codes to formally incorporate compliance mechanisms—recognizing them both as statutory defenses to corporate criminal liability and as legally recognized mitigating circumstances during sentencing. These legislative developments form part of the international legal response to foreign bribery, and the associated compliance frameworks are generally categorized as "anti-corruption compliance"—or, more narrowly, as "narrow compliance" or "compliance in the narrow sense." Over time, compliance practices—initially focused on preventing corporate bribery—have been progressively extended to cover a wider array of regulatory domains, including anti-money laundering, antitrust, data protection, and export controls, thereby contributing to the normalization of compliance as a core component of corporate governance. What initially emerged as an incentive mechanism in criminal law has increasingly gained traction among administrative regulators, evolving into a key criterion for granting leniency in administrative enforcement proceedings across numerous jurisdictions. Through administrative settlement agreements, regulatory authorities not only encourage but increasingly mandate the establishment or improvement of internal compliance systems. This model of negotiated, compliance-based regulation has evolved into a standard enforcement tool across Western regulatory systems.[12]

While many international organizations have endorsed corporate compliance principles and issued standards for effective compliance programs, some have also come to act as de facto "international enforcement agents." In this role, they supervise compliance measures for companies participating in their procurement and tendering processes, thereby establishing compliance as an "incentive-based tool of transnational enforcement." A paradigmatic example of this development can be found in the World Bank Group, which exemplifies the broader category of international financial institutions. As such an institution, the World Bank is authorized to impose sanctions—such as cross-debarment and harmonized disciplinary measures—on firms found to have engaged in misconduct in connection with procurement activities, including corruption, fraud, collusion, coercion, and obstruction. However, where the misconduct is not considered egregious, companies are typically given an opportunity to remediate and seek sanction relief by implementing or restoring a robust and credible integrity compliance program.

The *World Bank Group Integrity Compliance Guidelines* represent a formal and authoritative benchmark for effective corporate compliance, promulgated by the World Bank. For sanctioned entities, the lifting of penalties is contingent upon their establishment or improvement of internal compliance systems in line with the requirements set forth in the Guidelines. To date, 44 Chinese companies have been sanctioned by the World Bank, most of which are state-owned enterprises (SOEs) penalized for fraudulent conduct. One notable

[12] Sean J. Griffith, "Corporate Governance in an Era of Compliance," *William & Mary Law Review* 57 (2016): 2075–2140.

example is Hunan Construction Engineering Group Corporation, which was subjected to a "conditional non-debarment" sanction due to misrepresentation of its performance history during the bidding process for a World Bank-financed project. During the three-year compliance monitoring period, the company—under the World Bank's supervision and guidance—implemented a comprehensive restructuring of its internal compliance system in accordance with the *Integrity Compliance Guidelines.* Upon demonstrating full adherence to the Bank's compliance standards, the company was officially removed from the list of sanctioned entities in 2017.[13]

1.5 Ex Ante and Ex Post Compliance Approaches

At its core, corporate compliance represents a governance model grounded in the prevention and control of legal and regulatory risks. However, without external pressure—whether from administrative regulators, judicial authorities, or international institutions—it is extremely difficult for enterprises to independently initiate and sustain the development of a robust compliance management system. Absent strong pressure and incentive mechanisms embedded in regulatory oversight, criminal enforcement, or international sanctions, companies are unlikely to develop the necessary motivation to undertake meaningful compliance reforms.

Since 2005, Chinese enterprises have developed their compliance frameworks through two principal pathways. The first is ex ante compliance, characterized by the development of institutionalized compliance systems under the guidance and oversight of administrative regulatory authorities, with an emphasis on proactively preventing compliance risks and embedding compliance into routine corporate governance. The second is ex post compliance, which emerges in response to enforcement pressure from domestic authorities or sanctions imposed by international institutions. In such cases, companies that have already engaged in regulatory misconduct undertake targeted compliance remediation efforts with the goal of reducing penalties or having sanctions lifted. Through these parallel developments, a dual-track compliance governance framework has gradually taken shape in China—comprising both proactive, risk-oriented ex ante compliance and reactive, corrective ex post compliance mechanisms.

Ex ante compliance—also referred to as routine compliance or autonomous compliance—describes a governance approach in which enterprises, absent any existing legal or regulatory violations, proactively construct compliance management systems based on ongoing assessments of compliance risk. The objective is to identify and mitigate potential risks before they materialize.[14] To date,

[13] Ruihua Chen, "Hunan Construction's Integrity Compliance Program," *China Lawyer*, no. 11 (2019).

[14] Yunxia Yin and Xiaoxia Li, "Motives and Implementation Paths of Corporate Compliance in China," *China Legal Review*, no. 3 (2020): 159.

a number of Chinese regulatory bodies have issued sector-specific compliance guidelines to facilitate the implementation of ex ante compliance. For example, financial regulators have introduced compliance frameworks for the financial industry; state-owned asset supervision authorities have released compliance rules for centrally managed state-owned enterprises; and the National Development and Reform Commission (NDRC), together with other agencies, has published the Guidelines on Compliance for Overseas Operations of Chinese Enterprises. Collectively, these documents offer authoritative benchmarks and regulatory references that guide enterprises in building sustainable, preventive compliance systems tailored to routine governance needs.

Nevertheless, in building routine compliance management systems, many enterprises lack a genuine awareness of compliance risk. Rather than developing risk-specific compliance frameworks grounded in the results of systematic risk assessments, they tend to equate compliance merely with the formal requirement of "operating in accordance with the law." They often attempt to guard against all conceivable risks indiscriminately, resulting in sweeping, all-encompassing compliance plans that purport to address a wide range—sometimes even dozens—of specialized compliance domains at once. Although such plans may appear exhaustive on paper, they often remain superficial in practice, lacking both specificity and functional utility. Without a risk-based and priority-driven design, these frameworks are unlikely to function as effective tools for the prevention and mitigation of compliance risks.[15]

Ex post compliance—also known as *post-crisis compliance remediation*, or simply *compliance remediation*—refers to a governance response in which enterprises, when confronted with administrative enforcement actions, criminal investigations, or international sanctions, undertake targeted institutional reforms to address systemic vulnerabilities and correct structural deficiencies in their business models, managerial practices, or decision-making procedures.[16] In China, regulatory agencies—most notably the State Administration for Market Regulation (SAMR)—have, in the context of antitrust enforcement actions, required certain enterprises to submit antitrust compliance remediation plans or to formally commit to undertaking compliance remediation measures. Likewise, under the supervision and guidance of the World Bank and other international financial institutions, enterprises sanctioned for violations of institutional rules may commit to undertaking compliance remediation in accordance with the World Bank's Integrity Compliance Guidelines. If they successfully implement the required compliance remediation measures and pass the compliance assessment, such enterprises may have their sanctions lifted and regain eligibility to participate in international procurement and bidding activities. These post-crisis compliance efforts—carried out under the

[15] Ruihua Chen, "Research on Deferred Prosecution Agreements for Corporate Compliance," *Chinese Journal of Criminal Law*, no. 1 (2021): 92.

[16] Yunxia Yin, Yanjun Zhuang, and Xiaoxia Li, "Corporate Agency and the 'Radiating Enforcement Effect' in Anti-Corruption," *SJTU Law Review*, no. 2 (2016).

supervision and direction of domestic regulatory bodies or international organizations—have played a pivotal role in prompting the establishment and institutionalization of compliance management systems within sanctioned enterprises.

Generally speaking, ex ante and ex post compliance represent two distinct compliance governance scenarios, each with its own scope of application and domain-specific utility. Both models may function independently and make meaningful contributions to the overall effectiveness of corporate compliance frameworks. However, both models also exhibit inherent limitations, and reliance on either approach in isolation is typically inadequate for constructing a truly robust and sustainable compliance management system. Among the two, ex ante compliance—characterized by its emphasis on preventive controls—offers distinct institutional advantages. Its greatest strength lies in its capacity for proactive risk management—enabling enterprises to detect, assess, and mitigate potential legal and regulatory risks before they crystallize. When effectively implemented, this model can significantly reduce, or even eliminate, the likelihood of non-compliance. Moreover, aside from the necessary investment of human, financial, and organizational resources, ex ante compliance generally spares enterprises from punitive measures. In particular, it helps them avoid the substantial consequences often associated with enforcement actions, such as monetary fines, disgorgement of unlawful gains, environmental remediation costs, or victim compensation liabilities. Equally important, ex ante compliance enables the selective and strategic allocation of compliance resources based on the specific risk landscape an enterprise faces. Through risk-based prioritization, companies can identify and concentrate on those compliance risks that are immediate, high-impact, or strategically significant. Such a targeted, risk-based approach enhances governance efficiency and strengthens the enterprise's ability to manage strategic compliance risks effectively.

Nevertheless, ex ante compliance is subject to certain inherent limitations. Given that the corporation is fundamentally a profit-oriented entity, it is unrealistic to expect corporations to invest substantial managerial or financial resources in compliance management in the absence of discernible or immediate returns. Ex ante compliance refers to routine compliance efforts undertaken under normal circumstances—specifically, when the enterprise does not face any imminent threat of sanction or regulatory enforcement. Such programs are premised on anticipating "possible violations" or "potential non-compliance" as hypothetical risks and typically have not been tested through enforcement scrutiny or legal challenge. Accordingly, their capacity to effectively prevent unlawful or non-compliant conduct remains largely untested and unproven. In the absence of strong external regulatory pressure and sufficiently robust incentive mechanisms, it is extremely difficult to expect a company to initiate self-driven reforms to its entrenched, dysfunctional business operations, commercial models, or organizational culture. Moreover, compliance—as a corporate self-regulation governance mechanism—requires not only significant financial and operational investment, but also clear commitment and strategic resolve from top management. In the absence of a triggering crisis, and without substantial coercive pressure from regulatory authorities, enforcement agencies, or international institutions—particularly in contexts where effective compliance incentives have yet to be institutionalized—the establishment of an internal compliance risk management system that extends across employees, management, subsidiaries, clients, third parties, and acquired entities through overlapping and multilayered protocols remains an exceptionally difficult undertaking.

By contrast, ex post compliance—undertaken in the aftermath of legal or regulatory violations and often triggered by significant organizational crises—possesses certain distinct advantages not inherent in ex ante compliance. First, ex post compliance is characterized by its crisis-response function and is not primarily aimed at establishing a comprehensive compliance management system, but rather at effectively responding to organizational crises arising from regulatory enforcement actions. Through effective compliance remediation, enterprises aim to obtain the most lenient resolution possible, thereby minimizing potential harm to corporate interests. Second, given the time-bound nature of compliance monitoring periods, ex post compliance typically pursues more realistic and readily achievable objectives. Rather than building an expansive, all-encompassing compliance risk control system, the focus is on establishing, improving, operationalizing, and enforcing targeted compliance programs directly tied to the specific violations at issue, with the aim of preventing the recurrence of the same or similar forms of misconduct. Third, compliance remediation entails a managerial process of "dismantling before reconstruction." This process begins with the diagnosis of the endogenous structural causes that contributed to the unlawful conduct, followed by targeted institutional correction, and then the structured reconstruction of the compliance system. The term "institutional correction," also known as "institutional remediation," refers to the effort by enterprises, through the compliance remediation process, to look beyond the surface manifestations of misconduct and identify systemic flaws and managerial vulnerabilities. It involves detecting "illicit factors" or "criminogenic elements" embedded within the company's business model or operational structure. Building upon this diagnostic foundation, companies are required to implement a structured set of corrective, remedial, and restorative measures aimed at closing regulatory loopholes and eliminating latent risks, thereby facilitating the decriminalization of the company's business model and operational practices. The subsequent phase of "systematic construction" refers to the process whereby the company, having completed institutional correction, proceeds to develop one or more targeted compliance programs that specifically address the nature of the prior violations, with the objective of preventing the recurrence of the same or similar types of misconduct.

Although ex post compliance carries the institutional advantages outlined above, it also presents certain non-negligible limitations. Across both Western jurisdictions and China, post-violation compliance initiatives aimed at managing corporate compliance risks effectively continue to encounter persistent structural obstacles. On the one hand, companies tend to exhibit varying degrees of instrumentalism in their compliance planning. Motivated by the prospect of securing leniency or exemption from liability, firms frequently adopt superficial remediation measures designed primarily to satisfy compliance assessment requirements, rather than pursuing substantive reforms to their internal governance structures or ingrained operational culture. On the other hand, in the absence of effective compliance remediation objectives and clearly defined assessment criteria, corporate remediation efforts often degenerate into a formalistic exercise in policy drafting and system design, emphasizing procedural construction over substantive implementation and enforcement. This approach tends to obscure the actual effectiveness of compliance in preventing, monitoring, and responding to unlawful conduct. As a result, oversight bodies tasked with conducting compliance assessments frequently engage in perfunctory evaluations, failing to rigorously determine whether the adopted compliance frameworks genuinely fulfill their deterrent and corrective functions.

1.6 Clarifying Core Concepts

1.6.1 Corporate Compliance Versus Executive Compliance

In Western jurisdictions, corporate compliance mechanisms have steadily developed over the past half-century and now constitute a central component of modern corporate governance. By contrast, in China, corporate compliance—introduced as a foreign regulatory model—has a relatively short history, having been adopted only within the last decade. It was not until 2018 that administrative regulators began to systematically promote the institutionalization of compliance management systems within the corporate sector. Given this relatively recent institutional development, there remains considerable debate regarding the conceptual boundaries and normative character of corporate compliance in the Chinese context. To achieve conceptual clarity and theoretical coherence, it is essential to further articulate the essential nature of corporate compliance and to clarify several of the core disagreements and interpretive ambiguities that continue to affect scholarly and regulatory discourse.

Some scholars argue that corporate compliance encompasses not only the legal obligations of the enterprise as an organizational entity but also the compliance duties incumbent upon senior corporate executives. Some even equate corporate compliance directly with "entrepreneurial risk control," viewing it primarily as a tool for managing the personal liability risks of business leaders. This perspective is particularly salient in the context of criminal law, where China's Criminal Law enshrines the doctrine of corporate criminal liability and enumerates nearly 200 offenses that may be imputed to corporate entities. Under this "dual punishment" regime, legal responsibility is imposed concurrently on both the corporate entity and the individuals directly accountable for the offense. Accordingly, some scholars argue that the establishment of a corporate compliance framework should fulfill a dual purpose: mitigating legal risks for the corporation and shielding senior executives from potential criminal liability.

The proposition that equates corporate compliance with entrepreneurial risk control is conceptually flawed and analytically unsound. This is because the essence of corporate compliance lies in constructing an institutional mechanism for the prevention, identification, and mitigation of unlawful or noncompliant conduct, thereby fostering a corporate culture grounded in legality and regulatory discipline. By implementing such a system, the enterprise delineates clear behavioral boundaries for senior management, ordinary employees, and third-party actors; assigns corresponding rights, obligations, and liabilities in accordance with applicable legal norms; and ensures that all parties are held to legal compliance, are deterred from engaging in misconduct, and are subject to accountability for any violations. Evidently, corporate compliance functions as a core instrument of internal governance—a framework of self-management, preventative oversight, and internal constraint applied by the enterprise to its senior leadership, employees, and external partners. The compliance framework is thus directed at managing institutional and operational risks faced by the corporation itself, rather than shielding entrepreneurs from personal liability or insulating executives from individual legal exposure. This marks the first and most fundamental conceptual distinction.

Secondly, the implementation of a corporate compliance framework enables the effective allocation and delimitation of liability between the enterprise and its executives, employees, third-party actors and even acquired or affiliated entities, thereby safeguarding the company's core legal and commercial interests. As enterprises expand, their internal governance structures tend to become increasingly intricate, with some corporations employing tens of thousands of staff or managing extensive networks of domestic and international subsidiaries. Such scale not only imposes considerable administrative burdens but also exposes enterprises to derivative legal liability arising from the conduct of executives, employees, or external partners. In business areas such as investment, mergers, and acquisitions, such risks are further exacerbated: unlawful conduct or regulatory breaches by target companies may inadvertently implicate the acquiring or parent enterprise, subjecting it to unintended legal exposure. The establishment of a compliance framework mitigates such risks by embedding institutional safeguards: providing regular compliance training to executives and employees, ensuring the ongoing transmission of compliance policies and procedures, distributing employee conduct manuals, and requiring written compliance undertakings. These measures function as critical evidentiary safeguards. In the event of misconduct by executives or employees, the enterprise may invoke its compliance infrastructure to demonstrate the exercise of due oversight and, accordingly, seek exemption from vicarious or derivative liability.

In doing so, the company achieves a substantive separation between institutional responsibility and individual culpability.[17]

Moreover, in cultivating relationships with third-party partners—such as suppliers, distributors, and agents—the adoption of a corporate compliance framework necessitates the implementation of proactive safeguards, including compliance risk assessments, due diligence investigations on prospective third parties, and targeted compliance oversight for entities identified as carrying heightened legal or regulatory risk. If such third parties subsequently engage in unlawful conduct, the enterprise's prior compliance measures may serve as key evidentiary support in asserting defenses against derivative or vicarious liability. Furthermore, in the context of investment, mergers, and acquisitions, the parent company may incur substantial legal exposure if the target enterprise is found to have committed prior regulatory or criminal violations. Under the principle of successor liability, such historical misconduct may be imputed to the acquiring entity. To mitigate such successor liability risks, acquiring companies should, prior to consummating the transaction, conduct comprehensive compliance risk assessments, perform detailed due diligence on the target entity, and implement pre-transaction compliance controls in accordance with institutional compliance standards. Accordingly, should post-acquisition violations emerge, the acquiring firm may invoke its pre-transaction compliance efforts as the foundation for legal defenses aimed at exemption from, or mitigation of, liability.

From the standpoint of compliance risk prevention, the essential function of corporate compliance lies in achieving a clear and enforceable delineation between corporate liability and the respective liabilities of senior management, employees, third-party partners, and acquired or affiliated entities. This legal demarcation is intended to shield the enterprise from being held vicariously or derivatively liable for unlawful or non-compliant acts committed by these actors, thereby serving as a mechanism for mitigating overall legal risk. Accordingly, corporate compliance must not be conflated with entrepreneurial risk management. On the contrary, it is designed precisely to differentiate corporate liability from the personal legal responsibilities of entrepreneurs, executives, or shareholders.

Thirdly, from the perspective of how enterprises manage compliance risks, corporate compliance inherently involves mechanisms of voluntary self-disclosure and internal investigation—procedures that often require the enterprise to impose disciplinary sanctions on senior executives and employees found to have engaged in unlawful or non-compliant behavior. Accordingly, the implementation of a corporate compliance framework does not function to shield entrepreneurs from liability. On the contrary, it may trigger the attribution of legal responsibility to corporate leaders themselves.

[17] Yunxia Yin and Xiaoxia Li, "Motives and Implementation Paths of Corporate Compliance in China," *China Legal Review*, no. 3 (2020): 159.

When a company becomes implicated in unlawful or non-compliant conduct, it may be subject to regulatory investigations and enforcement proceedings. To mitigate further loss, companies with established compliance mechanisms often undertake independent internal investigations in conjunction with cooperation efforts toward external regulators. Such inquiries typically seek to establish the underlying facts of the violation, diagnose structural deficiencies in the compliance framework, identify the individuals directly responsible for the misconduct, and impose internal disciplinary sanctions. Where warranted, senior executives found to bear legal responsibility may be referred to judicial authorities for potential prosecution. In certain cases, companies may proactively disclose violations previously unknown to regulators in order to obtain enhanced cooperation credit or leniency. However, such disclosures may implicate a broader group of employees and senior personnel, resulting in expanded disciplinary measures internally and increased legal exposure externally. Accordingly, the implementation of a corporate compliance mechanism does not serve to reduce the legal risks borne by entrepreneurs. On the contrary, it may result in disciplinary measures against accountable management and, in some instances, subject corporate leaders—including entrepreneurs—to direct legal liability.[18]

1.6.2 Compliance and Risk Control

Many enterprises maintain internal control or risk management departments that specialize in identifying, preventing, and mitigating operational and strategic risks. In the course of developing compliance systems—particularly within state-owned enterprises—it is not uncommon to observe corporate compliance being treated as functionally equivalent to risk management. In some cases, it has even been suggested that compliance departments be subordinated to existing risk control units. This raises a fundamental question: Is corporate compliance truly synonymous with risk control?

At its core, corporate compliance should be understood as a governance mechanism specifically designed to identify, prevent, and manage compliance risks. A rigorous inquiry into the nature of corporate compliance requires both a conceptual clarification of compliance risk itself and a systematic delineation of how such risks differ from other forms of corporate risk. Generally, the core function of corporate governance frameworks is to manage two principal relationships: first, between shareholders and corporate managers—that is, the traditional separation of ownership and control—and second, between controlling shareholders and minority shareholders. This latter relationship has long attracted extensive attention in both legal scholarship and economic theory. Notably, the "tunneling effect" hypothesis in economics describes how controlling shareholders may extract private benefits by diverting corporate assets

[18] Yunxia Yin, Yanjun Zhuang, and Xiaoxia Li, "Corporate Agency and the 'Radiating Enforcement Effect' in Anti-Corruption," *SJTU Law Review*, no. 2 (2016).

or opportunities, thereby infringing upon the interests of minority shareholders. The protection of minority shareholder rights remains one of the most enduring and complex challenges in modern corporate governance practice.[19]

At the corporate governance level, a foundational question arises: What categories of risk should enterprises prioritize in their risk prevention strategies? Among the many risks faced by modern firms, how should compliance risk be conceptualized and situated in relation to other core risk domains? In practice, many corporate decision-makers lack a nuanced understanding of the nature and classification of governance-related risks and, as a consequence, tend to underestimate the strategic significance of compliance risk. Some classify corporate governance risks into an expansive array of subcategories—such as investment risk, merger and acquisition risk, financing risk, sales and market risks, product quality concerns, technological vulnerabilities, intellectual property disputes, and labor-related risks—and regard compliance risk as just one among these operational or transactional categories. Such an approach clearly fails to capture the distinct nature of compliance risk. From a strategic perspective, enterprises are generally exposed to four principal categories of risk: decision-making risk, operational risk, financial risk, and compliance risk. The following section offers a concise analysis of the internal logic and interrelationships among these key dimensions of strategic risk.

The first type of strategic risk is decision-making risk. When a company makes major strategic decisions, determines its business direction, or sets long-term management objectives, any significant error in judgment or breakdown in oversight may result in organization-wide losses and catastrophic consequences—potentially threatening the company's continued existence. To mitigate such risks, contemporary corporations typically establish both a board of directors and a supervisory board to institutionalize rational and collective decision-making processes and to ensure the proper functioning of internal governance and oversight structures.

The second type of risk is operational risk, also known as business risk. Such risk arises in the course of business operations—including investment and mergers, market sales, and quality assurance—and refers to the possibility that investments may fail to generate returns, the enterprise may become unprofitable, or even face threats to its survival. Operational risk must be effectively prevented, identified, and addressed through business governance mechanisms embedded within the company's overall corporate governance structure. The Chief Executive Officer (CEO) holds primary responsibility for managing operational risk, while the executive team under their leadership serves as the core force driving the enterprise's business performance. However, operational risk falls fundamentally within the domain of economic analysis. To mitigate such risk, enterprises must examine the full cycle of investment and business

[19] Robert A.G. Monks and Nell Minow, *Corporate Governance*, 5th ed., trans. Li Weian et al. (Beijing: Renmin University Press, 2017), 81.

operations and formulate solutions aligned with market dynamics and economic laws.

The third type of risk is financial risk. It primarily refers to the risk of economic losses resulting from disorganized financial management, fraudulent practices, or corrupt behavior—threats that may prevent the enterprise from achieving profitability or may even push it to the brink of bankruptcy. A sound modern financial management system involves a wide array of interrelated and sophisticated components. In addition to appointing a Chief Financial Officer (CFO) and maintaining a specialized financial management department, companies must also institute auditing bodies to provide necessary oversight of financial affairs. Some companies go further by establishing a relatively independent audit committee under the board of directors to strengthen the authority and independence of financial oversight. Thus, financial management functions as an independent governance system, separate from the domain of operational management.

The fourth type of risk is compliance risk. Compliance risk, distinct from both operational and financial risk, refers to the possibility that a company may face administrative penalties or criminal prosecution due to unlawful, non-compliant, or even criminal conduct committed during the course of its business activities. As previously discussed, compliance risk may be categorized into three main types: regulatory enforcement risk, criminal liability risk, and the risk of sanctions imposed by international organizations. If left uncontrolled, compliance risk may result not only in legal liability, but also in the loss of special operating permits or the revocation of business licenses. These outcomes may inflict serious financial and reputational harm, potentially setting off a cascading effect that culminates in disastrous consequences for the enterprise.

It is therefore evident that the establishment of a corporate compliance mechanism is not intended to address "risk" in a general or abstract sense, but rather to prevent unlawful or non-compliant conduct and to contain the resulting consequences—such as regulatory sanctions, legal liability, economic losses, and the revocation of operational qualifications. In this respect, compliance risk is materially distinct not only from decision-making and operational risks, but also from financial risk. Accordingly, in companies that have established effective compliance programs, four major governance subsystems generally operate in parallel under the leadership of the board of directors: decision-making oversight, business operations, financial management, and compliance management. Each subsystem is tasked with managing a corresponding type of strategic risk—namely, decision-making risk, operational risk, financial risk, and compliance risk. These subsystems are structurally independent, mutually constraining, and endowed with significant authority in fulfilling their respective functions within the overall corporate governance framework. Therefore, corporate compliance should not be regarded as a generic form of risk control, but as a distinct governance mechanism specifically designed to identify, prevent, and respond to compliance risk.

1.6.3 *Compliance and Legal Risk Management*

In the process of establishing compliance management systems, many companies place their compliance units within the legal department, and it is not uncommon for the Chief Compliance Officer (CCO) to concurrently serve as the General Counsel or Chief Legal Officer. Based on this organizational structure, some argue that corporate compliance is essentially synonymous with legal risk management—that is, the compliance function is expected to prevent, identify, and respond to all legal risks encountered by the enterprise. Some further contend that, beyond administrative enforcement risk, criminal liability, and international sanctions, corporate compliance should also extend to the management of civil legal risks. This has led to the emergence of the so-called concept of "civil compliance." Others adopt an even broader perspective, arguing that legal risks arising from unlawful or criminal acts committed by third parties—which cause economic or other forms of harm to the enterprise—should likewise fall within the scope of compliance management. Accordingly, the implementation of corporate compliance mechanisms is sometimes expected to include measures to prevent victimization resulting from external criminal conduct.

If corporate compliance were truly synonymous with "legal risk management," then a company's legal department would suffice to fulfill that function, rendering the creation of an independent compliance department unnecessary. The case of Siemens AG serves as a particularly compelling counterexample. Although the company already had a legal department in place, it nonetheless undertook a comprehensive overhaul in the wake of its anti-bribery scandal to establish an independent and authoritative compliance organizational structure and to implement a specialized compliance management system. A similar institutional distinction can be observed in the case of ZTE Corporation. Despite having long maintained a legal department, ZTE only launched a full-scale reconstruction of its export control compliance system following investigations by the U.S. Department of Justice, the Department of Commerce, and the Department of the Treasury.

The experience of companies that have undertaken compliance program reconstruction clearly demonstrates that corporate compliance is not simply synonymous with general legal risk management. From the moment of its incorporation until its dissolution, bankruptcy, or revocation of business licenses, a company remains subject to a dense and evolving framework of legal norms and regulatory constraints and must contend with an unceasing stream of legal risks. If "legal risk" is defined as the possibility of being penalized or incurring losses due to violations of laws or regulations, then such risks are virtually omnipresent—embedded in every stage of a company's operations and decision-making processes. For example, if a company breaches civil contract law—whether through non-performance or fraudulent inducement—it may be subject to civil litigation and held liable for contractual damages. Similarly, if a company violates labor laws and infringes upon the lawful rights of its employees, it may be subject to judicial proceedings and civil liability. Moreover, companies may incur significant losses as a result of unlawful or criminal acts committed by third parties or colluding insiders—such as fraud, serious violations of rights, or corruption schemes involving both internal and external actors.[20]

This raises a fundamental question: Do the aforementioned legal risks fall within the scope of "compliance risk," and is corporate compliance intended to address all such legal exposures? The answer is clearly no. In reality, not all legal risks fall within the purview of compliance. Among the multitude of legal exposures that companies may face, those most closely associated with compliance are the ones that carry the gravest consequences—specifically, risks arising from violations of laws or regulations that subject the enterprise to regulatory sanctions, criminal prosecution, or other forms of state-imposed liability. For example, a company involved in commercial bribery may come under investigation by anti-unfair competition regulators or be subjected to criminal investigation by law enforcement agencies. A company that receives funds from corrupt officials or terrorist organizations in violation of anti-money laundering laws may be investigated by financial regulatory bodies or prosecuted by competent judicial authorities. Similarly, violations of cybersecurity or data protection laws—such as the unauthorized collection, misuse, or disclosure of personal information—may trigger regulatory investigations or lead to criminal proceedings before the courts. Violations of export control laws may result in administrative sanctions or even criminal charges. Likewise, the unlawful discharge of hazardous waste resulting in environmental damage may lead to administrative sanctions imposed by environmental regulators or criminal convictions.

Once an administrative enforcement proceeding is initiated by a regulatory authority, the enterprise may be subject to severe administrative sanctions. Likewise, the initiation of criminal proceedings by law enforcement authorities may result in a conviction and the imposition of criminal penalties. Furthermore, enterprises may be subject to sanctions imposed by international organizations such as the World Bank, which, once imposed, can result in substantial economic losses. Among the various consequences resulting from administrative penalties, criminal prosecutions, and international sanctions, the most severe is the disqualification of the enterprise from essential market participation. As previously analyzed, such disqualification may take several forms: the revocation of specific operating licenses, the denial of access to credit, the loss of bidding eligibility, or—most drastically—the cancellation of the enterprise's business license, which constitutes the legal death of the enterprise.

Precisely because regulatory sanctions, criminal prosecutions, and international organizational penalties can inflict such serious consequences on enterprises, the risks arising from these specific enforcement mechanisms are

[20] Yi Han, "Risk Control and Structural Pathways for Corporate Corporate Compliance," *Legal Studies Journal*, no. 9 (2019).

designated as a distinct form of compliance risk—one that must be clearly distinguished from general legal risk. It is precisely to manage such compliance risks that enterprises establish dedicated compliance infrastructures—including compliance committees, Chief Compliance Officers (CCOs), and compliance departments. Under the guidance of corporate codes of conduct and employee handbooks, these organizational structures facilitate the development of targeted systems for the prevention, detection, and response to compliance risk. This underscores that corporate compliance is not merely a subset of general legal risk management. Rather, it constitutes a dedicated governance architecture grounded in self-regulation, self-disclosure, self-prevention, and self-correction—expressly designed to address risks arising from administrative penalties, criminal liability, and international sanctions.

In both Chinese and Western corporations, it is common for the compliance function to remain organizationally integrated with the legal department. Often, the General Counsel or Chief Legal Officer concurrently serves as the Chief Compliance Officer (CCO), and the compliance department is situated within the legal division. However, this organizational overlap does not imply that the compliance function is merely responsible for general legal risk management. On the contrary, it highlights that the compliance department is primarily tasked with managing a specific subset of legal risk—namely, compliance risk—which, although part of the broader legal risk framework, is substantively distinct from ordinary legal risks. In enterprises where the compliance unit is embedded within the legal department, its principal function remains the prevention and mitigation of compliance risks. By contrast, conventional legal responsibilities—such as representing the enterprise as a plaintiff or defendant in civil proceedings, appearing before judicial or arbitral bodies, initiating administrative enforcement actions, or filing criminal complaints on behalf of the company as a harmed party—should be undertaken by legal professionals outside the compliance department.

1.6.4 *Compliance as Moral Responsibility or Legal Duty*

As a form of corporate governance, is corporate compliance best understood as a matter of ethics or as a matter of law? This question warrants serious attention, as scholarly opinion on the issue remains deeply divided. Some scholars contend that corporate compliance is fundamentally an ethical matter. It is, they argue, primarily concerned with internal self-regulation and corporate rule-making, and to date, few jurisdictions have formally incorporated compliance mechanisms into their foundational legal frameworks. They further argue that the effectiveness of compliance mechanisms ultimately hinges on cultivating a corporate culture grounded in legality and ethical norms—a transformation they view as moral in nature, rather than rooted in legal obligation. By contrast, other scholars maintain that corporate compliance is not merely an ethical aspiration but a legal institution. In both Western legal systems and China, administrative law has established compliance-based incentive mechanisms that grant leniency in enforcement, particularly through administrative settlement frameworks premised on effective compliance. Moreover, many Western jurisdictions have established criminal compliance mechanisms within their substantive criminal law frameworks, enabling companies to obtain lenient treatment in criminal proceedings in exchange for implementing effective compliance programs. At the same time, their criminal procedure laws provide for the use of Deferred Prosecution Agreements (DPAs) and Non-Prosecution Agreements (NPAs) for companies that demonstrate good-faith efforts to establish or enhance internal compliance systems. These legal developments make it evident that corporate compliance is no longer confined to the voluntary realm of corporate ethics, but has become an institutionalized component of national legal systems—firmly embedded within both administrative and criminal law structures.

Both perspectives contain elements of truth, yet each presents an incomplete and somewhat one-sided understanding of corporate compliance. Fundamentally, the debate reflects a lack of comprehensive understanding among scholars regarding the conceptual complexity of corporate compliance. As previously analyzed, corporate compliance constitutes a highly complex mode of corporate governance that encompasses multiple dimensions—both legal and ethical. From a positive standpoint, corporate compliance is often viewed as synonymous with lawful corporate conduct—implying that enterprises, like natural persons, are expected to conduct their business in accordance with applicable laws and regulations. In this sense, such compliance is closer to a normative expectation than a binding legal institution, as it emphasizes voluntary adherence rather than coercive legal enforceability. Conversely, from a risk-averse or defensive perspective, corporate compliance functions as a governance tool adopted to shield the enterprise from regulatory sanctions or criminal liability arising from unlawful or non-compliant conduct. To avert legal, financial, and reputational harm, enterprises have developed internal control systems aimed at preventing, detecting, and responding to compliance risks. Such mechanisms often reflect ethical imperatives rather than strictly legal obligations. Indeed, during the early stages of compliance system development, many Western corporations explicitly referred to their compliance units as "Ethics and Compliance Departments" and designated their heads as "Chief Ethics and Compliance Officers." Moreover, the implementation of compliance mechanisms is closely linked to the development of an internal corporate culture grounded in legality, discipline, and ethical conduct—commonly referred to as a "compliance culture."[21] These observations demonstrate that, although increasingly embedded in legal frameworks, corporate compliance retains a fundamentally ethical character.

However, corporate compliance cannot be classified solely as an ethical issue. If compliance were merely a matter of corporate morality, there would be

[21] Donald C. Langevoort, "Cultures of Compliance," *American Criminal Law Review* 54 (2017): 933–977.

little rationale for embedding compliance mechanisms within administrative and criminal law. Why, then, have administrative laws developed regulatory compliance systems and institutionalized administrative settlement mechanisms? And why should criminal law establish criminal compliance mechanisms? And why have criminal procedure laws adopted instruments such as deferred prosecution agreements (DPAs) and non-prosecution agreements (NPAs)? Even in China, as compliance mechanisms have been gradually incorporated into corporate governance practices, administrative law has begun to institutionalize compliance-based incentives. For instance, administrative settlement procedures now allow enterprises to rely on established compliance systems as a basis for resolving regulatory disputes. Likewise, the development of a compliance defense permits companies to invoke internal compliance programs as grounds for distinguishing corporate liability from that of individual employees. These developments demonstrate that compliance-based incentive structures have already been introduced into China's administrative legal framework, laying the foundation for an emerging regulatory compliance system. By contrast, China's criminal law and criminal procedure law have yet to incorporate compliance mechanisms into their formal incentive frameworks. Consequently, corporate compliance programs currently cannot serve as a legal basis for granting leniency in criminal enforcement actions against corporate entities. Nonetheless, drawing on the experiences of Western jurisdictions—where compliance mechanisms have been systematically incorporated into both substantive criminal law and criminal procedure—it is reasonable to expect that China will eventually integrate criminal compliance into its own criminal justice system.

Based on the regulatory and enforcement practices of Western jurisdictions, it is evident that authorities impose harsh sanctions and pursue legal liability against companies that either lack compliance programs or maintain systems deemed ineffective. By contrast, enterprises with effective compliance programs may be granted regulatory leniency. Administrative agencies may enter into settlement agreements, while criminal enforcement bodies may offer deferred prosecution agreements (DPAs) or non-prosecution agreements (NPAs)—often on the condition that the enterprise commits to revising or reinforcing its compliance framework. Even when administrative or criminal penalties are ultimately imposed, enforcement authorities often adopt a mitigated approach toward companies that have proactively implemented and sustained effective compliance systems. These enforcement practices clearly demonstrate that corporate compliance has been formally embedded within both administrative and criminal legal regimes, serving as a critical legal basis for determining the scope and degree of state-imposed sanctions on corporate misconduct. In Western legal systems, corporate compliance is no longer regarded as a purely voluntary or internal practice. Rather, it has been institutionalized as a legally recognized governance mechanism—jointly affirmed by administrative and criminal law—as a legitimate basis for regulatory forbearance and prosecutorial discretion.[22]

Furthermore, the evolution of corporate compliance illustrates a broader historical shift from ethics-based governance to law-based governance. From the 1960s through the 1990s, many Western corporations initiated the development of internal compliance management systems. During this period, corporate compliance mechanisms were largely limited to internal self-governance and organizational rule-making, with no binding legal obligations imposed by either administrative regulators or criminal enforcement bodies. Accordingly, compliance practices during this stage were generally regarded as falling outside the scope of formal legal regulation and were primarily grounded in corporate ethics and business morality.

This began to shift in the 1990s, as corporate misconduct and regulatory non-compliance became increasingly widespread and serious, prompting heightened concern across Western jurisdictions about the need for more robust corporate regulation and governance. The early 2000s marked a critical turning point: high-profile corporate scandals involving Enron, WorldCom, and Arthur Andersen generated widespread public alarm, particularly regarding the governance of publicly listed companies. In response, regulatory authorities placed renewed emphasis on internal control systems as a means to enforce lawful, transparent, and accountable corporate conduct. From that point forward, corporate compliance was no longer regarded as a matter of voluntary ethical commitment, but rather as a compulsory risk management strategy—adopted by companies to avert potentially catastrophic legal, financial, and reputational consequences.

To prevent the arbitrary exercise of discretion by regulatory and prosecutorial authorities, Western jurisdictions have incorporated standards of effective compliance into both administrative and criminal law. These standards delineate the conditions under which companies may enter into settlement agreements, and specify the criteria and extent of leniency that may be granted to enterprises demonstrating good-faith compliance efforts. The developmental trajectory of corporate compliance confirms this transformation: what originated as a voluntary ethics-based initiative has evolved into a legally institutionalized governance model, shaped by developments in both administrative and criminal law. Today, corporate compliance serves as a statutory basis for administrative regulators to externally compel internal supervision and reform, and for criminal enforcement bodies to require enterprises to establish mechanisms for preventing compliance risks, identifying violations, and responding to investigative proceedings.

Therefore, corporate compliance embodies both ethical and legal dimensions. On the one hand, it reflects an ethical commitment to lawful and

[22] Hong Li, "Compliance Programs and Corporate Criminal Liability," *Legal Studies Journal*, no. 9 (2019); Yanan Shi, "Implementation of Compliance Programs and Corporate Criminal Attribution," *Legal Studies Journal*, no. 9 (2019).

rule-abiding behavior, intended to prevent legal liability, economic loss, and reputational harm. On the other hand, it serves as a legal basis for administrative agencies to grant regulatory leniency and for criminal enforcement authorities to exercise prosecutorial discretion in favor of mitigation. Taken together, this dual nature demonstrates that corporate compliance, while rooted in ethical values, has become an integral part of modern legal and regulatory frameworks.

CHAPTER 2

The Fundamental Values of Corporate Compliance

2.1 Introduction

Corporate compliance refers to a governance framework oriented toward the prevention and control of compliance risks. As early as 2006, Chinese enterprises in the finance, securities, and futures sectors began embracing the concept of corporate compliance. In conducting overseas activities—such as investment, public listings, and cross-border mergers and acquisitions—these enterprises gradually adopted compliance management systems to meet host-country regulatory requirements and enhance their international competitiveness. In the years that followed, as foreign governments and international organizations imposed increasingly stringent compliance obligations on corporate operations, more Chinese enterprises involved in international trade and overseas business began establishing specialized compliance systems. With the deepening of China's reform and opening-up, numerous foreign enterprises conducting business, trade, and investment in China brought the concept of corporate compliance into the domestic corporate landscape. The compliance systems they implemented—anchored in risk prevention and control—have exerted a profound and lasting influence on Chinese enterprises. Corporate compliance is increasingly regarded as a form of strategic soft power—crucial for building corporate credibility, accessing market opportunities, and strengthening competitive advantage.[1]

No enterprise can establish an effective compliance management system solely through voluntary effort or spontaneous internal initiative.[2] Throughout the evolution of corporate compliance, administrative and judicial authorities have played a pivotal role. They have integrated compliance requirements into

[1] Ruihua Chen, "On the Sinicization of Corporate Compliance," *Legal Science* 3 (2020).

[2] Yunxia Yin, Yanjun Zhuang, and Xiaoxia Li, "Corporate Agency and the 'Radiating Enforcement Effect' in Anti-Corruption," *SJTU Law Review*, no. 2 (2016).

R. Chen, *An Introduction to Corporate Compliance*,
https://doi.org/10.1007/978-981-95-7257-1_2

regulatory and enforcement procedures and imposed mandatory obligations on enterprises. Moreover, when enterprises come under investigation for suspected legal or criminal violations, authorities often grant lenient treatment to those that have established compliance systems or formally committed to implementing compliance remediation. Such enforcement-based incentives represent the principal driving force behind the widespread adoption and institutionalization of compliance mechanisms.[3]

Since 2018, Chinese administrative authorities have progressively integrated the concept of corporate compliance into their regulatory framework. By issuing compliance management guidelines, implementing an administrative guidance system, promoting mandatory compliance regimes, and piloting administrative settlement procedures, regulators have actively encouraged enterprises to establish comprehensive compliance management systems. On the one hand, under the guidance and supervision of administrative authorities, virtually all centrally administered state-owned enterprises (central SOEs) and Chinese companies engaged in overseas operations have established systematic and institutionalized compliance management mechanisms. These typically include the issuance of compliance charters, internal compliance policies, and employee handbooks; the establishment of a structured compliance function; and the implementation of mechanisms for the prevention and identification of and response to compliance risks. Some enterprises, through dedicated risk assessments, have identified specific compliance risk areas and developed targeted compliance systems tailored to those risks. On the other hand, enterprises found to have engaged in illegal or non-compliant activities have, during regulatory investigations, either committed to improving their compliance systems or submitted targeted compliance remediation plans. In many cases, such initiatives have resulted in lenient treatment by administrative authorities, including exemption from administrative liability, reduction of penalties, or the conclusion of administrative settlement agreements.[4]

Broadly speaking, corporate compliance in China has developed along two primary trajectories: market-oriented compliance and crisis-responsive compliance.[5] The former refers to compliance management systems established by enterprises to gain access to business opportunities and enhance market competitiveness, with an emphasis on anticipating and controlling compliance risks. In the absence of imminent regulatory threats, companies adopting this model typically conduct compliance risk assessments and construct preventive, standardized, and systematized compliance frameworks aimed at mitigating potential violations. The latter, by contrast, refers to compliance remediation efforts undertaken in response to administrative investigations, where enterprises—

[3] Ruihua Chen, "On the Nature of Corporate Compliance," *Journal of Zhejiang Gongshang University*, no. 1 (2021).

[4] Ruihua Chen, "Three Dimensions of the Corporate Compliance System: A Comparative Law Perspective," *Journal of Comparative Law*, no. 3 (2019).

[5] Yunxia Yin and Xiaoxia Li, "Motives and Implementation Paths of Corporate Compliance in China," *China Legal Review*, no. 3 (2020): 159.

facing the imminent prospect of severe sanctions—seek to manage legal crises through targeted institutional reforms. Because misconduct has already been exposed, symbolic or hypothetical compliance frameworks are no longer viable. Instead, companies must address management deficiencies, institutional vulnerabilities, and the underlying causes of unlawful conduct in order to prevent recurrence and obtain more lenient treatment. The former may be described as a "routine compliance management system," whereas the latter may be characterized as a "crisis-responsive compliance remediation mechanism" or an "autonomous compliance management system."

Regardless of whether compliance is market-oriented or crisis-driven, any model designed to mitigate compliance risks necessitates the allocation of substantial human, financial, and material resources, along with comprehensive structural adjustments to the corporate governance framework. Some enterprises have established compliance management committees under their boards of directors, appointed Chief Compliance Officers (CCOs), created dedicated compliance departments, and assembled teams comprising hundreds of compliance personnel. In certain cases, annual compliance budgets have reached hundreds of millions of yuan. Why, then, are companies willing to commit such extensive resources to compliance system construction? Why do administrative regulators regard the development of compliance frameworks as a core regulatory tool—sometimes even granting leniency or making enforcement concessions to incentivize corporate participation? From a broader societal perspective, more profound normative concerns arise: when a company has already engaged in unlawful conduct and inflicted concrete harm on society, is it truly justifiable for regulatory authorities to grant leniency—or even absolve the enterprise of legal liability—merely on the basis that it has undertaken compliance remediation and, upon assessment, is deemed to have implemented effective preventive mechanisms? Can the retroactive establishment of a compliance program reasonably serve as a legitimate basis for favorable enforcement outcomes?

To answer these questions, it is necessary to analyze the legitimacy of corporate compliance. Western scholars have engaged in extensive debate on this issue, putting forward various theories to justify the intrinsic value of corporate compliance, such as the self-regulation theory, the business efficiency theory, the corporate social responsibility theory, and the ethical behavior theory. Other theories, such as the social utility theory and the theory of reducing the cost of illegality, have been proposed to explain the legitimacy of mechanisms designed to incentivize compliance.[6] In Chinese academic discourse, scholars tend to justify the significance of corporate compliance by highlighting its tangible benefits to enterprises. Frequently cited views include that compliance

[6]Ruihua Chen, *The Fundamentals of Corporate Compliance*, 2nd ed. (Beijing: Law Press, 2021), 109ff.

helps prevent legal risks, enhances corporate governance, fosters compliance culture, and even generates economic value.[7]

This chapter seeks to reassess the foundational value of corporate compliance in light of the practical evolution of China's compliance framework. It contends that corporate compliance possesses not only instrumental utility but also intrinsic moral value, as it promotes respect for ethical duties and the assumption of essential social responsibilities by enterprises. From the standpoint of corporate survival and development, compliance enables enterprises to mitigate losses, delimit liability, obtain leniency in administrative and criminal proceedings, and achieve long-term sustainable growth. From the regulatory perspective, corporate compliance helps overcome the structural limitations of external administrative oversight by introducing principles of negotiation, dialogue, compromise, and contractual governance. These mechanisms activate corporate self-regulatory capacity, enhance the effectiveness of external supervision, and provide a novel regulatory avenue for large enterprises to prevent unlawful or criminal conduct. From the perspective of the public interest, although the implementation of compliance mechanisms may appear to impose high management costs and confer additional benefits on implicated enterprises, it ultimately contributes to safeguarding the interests of numerous stakeholders and promoting the public good.

2.2 Compliance and Corporate Social Responsibility

Why should enterprises establish compliance management systems? Given that compliance does not directly create economic value and often demands the sacrifice of short-term profits, the allocation of considerable human, material, and financial resources, and a reduction in operational convenience and efficiency, a fundamental question emerges: Does corporate compliance reflect a value that goes beyond economic gain?

In addressing this question, scholars in the Western legal tradition have proposed two major theories to elucidate the normative foundations of corporate compliance: the corporate social responsibility theory and the ethical behavior theory. The former holds that as large corporations accumulate increasing power and societal influence, establishing compliance programs can promote the fulfillment of broader social responsibilities and enhance the publicness of corporate conduct. Such programs encourage enterprises to comply more fully with legal and regulatory standards concerning employee equality, consumer rights, environmental protection, and other areas of public interest. The latter theory emphasizes the role of compliance in shaping employee behavior. Once a compliance system is in place, employees tend to perceive a higher likelihood that misconduct will be detected—not by distant law enforcement agencies, but by internal personnel who are more attuned to their behavioral patterns.

[7] Zhile Wang, "Fundamental Issues in Corporate Compliance Programs," *Criminal Law Trends in Transition* (WeChat post), July 15, 2020.

This perception produces a preventive effect. Moreover, compliance programs help address marginal or ambiguous violations by leveraging employees' concerns for reputation, interpersonal relationships, and professional standing, thereby guiding them toward lawful and ethical conduct.[8]

While these theories are reasonably persuasive, they also raise a further question: By what concrete means do corporations ensure adherence to ethical obligations and the assumption of social responsibilities? To explore this issue in greater depth, we may briefly examine the experiences of Siemens AG in Germany and ZTE Corporation in China, both of which have developed robust compliance systems. Their respective approaches provide a more concrete and practical foundation for further analysis.

In 2008, after reaching a settlement agreement with the U.S. Department of Justice and the Securities and Exchange Commission, Siemens AG rebuilt its anti-commercial bribery compliance program during the monitoring period and, on that basis, established targeted compliance programs targeting antitrust, anti-money laundering, and data protection. Through this reconstruction, Siemens adopted a corporate philosophy of "only conducting compliant business" and "only earning clean money," thereby cultivating a compliance culture markedly different from the past. For Siemens—a company that once faced a life-or-death crisis—compliance became not only a "lifesaving remedy" but also a "preventive vaccine" for future development. The company has embraced "only conducting compliant business" as a core corporate value. As senior executives have explained: "We must uphold long-term values and not sacrifice sustainable development for short-term gain. It is true that we have lost some business by refusing to engage in non-compliant conduct, but in many more cases, our compliance efforts have helped us win contracts, because our partners see Siemens as a low-risk company—one that does not carry hidden compliance dangers."[9]

In 2018, following separate settlement agreements with the U.S. Department of Commerce and a U.S. federal court, ZTE Corporation launched a comprehensive overhaul of its export control compliance program. The company subsequently broadened its compliance governance framework to include additional areas such as anti-bribery and data protection. Through this reform process, ZTE developed a distinctive compliance culture. Senior management began issuing regular compliance reports to employees, shareholders, and business partners to communicate the company's progress in building its compliance systems. The compliance department was granted full veto authority over all business operations and commercial transactions, thereby institutionalizing the principle that compliance takes precedence over business interests and fundamentally transforming the company's compliance culture. While reconstructing its targeted compliance programs, ZTE prioritized the cultivation of

[8] Donald C. Langevoort, "Cultures of Compliance," *American Criminal Law Review* 54 (2017): 933–977.

[9] Ruihua Chen, "Siemens' Compliance System," *China Lawyer*, no. 6 (2019).

a strong compliance culture. In the area of export controls, the company underscored that "export compliance is everyone's responsibility," emphasizing that compliance not only creates value but also protects it. ZTE committed to conducting global business with integrity and in accordance with ethical standards, enshrining these principles in its Code of Business Conduct. The Code establishes integrity and ethical compliance as the company's core operational tenets, requiring all employees, customers, business partners, and investors to abide by applicable laws and regulations, and affirming that every employee bears the obligation to represent the company in an ethically responsible manner.[10]

These two cases demonstrate that the implementation of corporate compliance mechanisms, while requiring companies to forgo certain commercial interests and opportunities in the short term, has reshaped their business philosophy to varying degrees and fostered a steadily deepening culture of lawful and rules-based corporate governance. As companies pursue commercial objectives, they increasingly prioritize the assumption of social responsibility and the cultivation of a positive corporate image. This shift—through which enterprises are encouraged to adhere to ethical standards and fulfill their social obligations—reflects the intrinsic value that corporate compliance is ultimately designed to achieve.

In the early stages of compliance development, companies in several countries often associated the concept of "compliance" with "ethics," with some firms even naming their compliance departments "Ethics and Compliance Departments." Regulatory authorities in China have largely embraced this conceptual framework, regarding compliance not only as a managerial system and a mode of corporate governance but also as a normative culture to be actively cultivated. The notion of "compliance culture" refers to a system of values and ethical norms that reflect a company's commitment to both social and moral responsibility. As articulated in the official Guidelines for Compliance Management Systems issued by Chinese authorities, "compliance culture refers to the presence of values, ethical standards, and beliefs throughout an organization, which interact with the organization's structure and control systems to generate behavioral norms that lead to compliant outcomes."[11] The ethical and social responsibilities of corporations are primarily expressed through the establishment of robust compliance systems that promote lawful and rule-abiding conduct, institutionalize organization-wide adherence to compliance principles, and embed compliance considerations into all aspects of corporate decision-making, investment, operations, management, and supervision. Such systems also emphasize the prevention and identification of compliance risks and the appropriate handling of violations, thereby contributing to the

[10] Ruihua Chen, "ZTE's Targeted Compliance Program," *China Lawyer* 2 (2020).

[11] Standardization Theory & Strategy Institute. *ISO 37301:2021 Compliance Management Systems—Requirements and Guidance for Use: International Standard Interpretation*. "China Standardization" (WeChat post), April 14, 2021.

continuous improvement of the compliance framework. Through these efforts, companies not only ensure compliance in their business operations but also balance the pursuit of profit with the advancement of broader societal values—such as government integrity, environmental protection, labor rights, intellectual property rights, and the protection of personal privacy. At the same time, corporate compliance plays a vital role in fostering a fair and competitive marketplace, promoting the rule of law, and building a business environment defined by fairness, openness, and transparency.

During the initial stage of compliance development, enterprises are typically motivated by a desire to avoid harsh regulatory sanctions, criminal liability, and the risk of significant financial and reputational loss. This is particularly true for companies compelled to rebuild their compliance systems under the supervision of regulatory or enforcement authorities, where the primary objective is to protect commercial interests and ensure corporate survival. As compliance mechanisms mature, however, enterprises begin to institutionalize compliance through the issuance of codes of conduct and employee handbooks, the establishment and institutionalization of the compliance function, and the implementation of systems designed to prevent risks, identify violations, and respond to misconduct. Gradually, the ethos of compliance takes root across the organization, making law-abiding operations a standard practice among executives and employees. The commitment to "only doing compliant business" becomes a guiding operational principle, giving rise to a corporate culture shaped by legal and ethical discipline. Once this culture and value orientation are firmly embedded, enterprises not only adhere to legal and ethical standards internally, but also exercise effective compliance oversight over their leadership and workforce. In developing business relationships with third parties—such as suppliers, distributors, agents, or participants in mergers and acquisitions—they begin to extend compliance obligations externally. Through compliance risk assessments, due diligence, and ongoing monitoring, enterprises project their expectations of compliance onto their broader commercial ecosystem. In this way, a company with a well-functioning compliance program becomes a "disciplined" commercial entity—one that transmits its compliance culture to its business counterparts. This, in turn, creates a positive diffusion effect, whereby internalized compliance values propagate across commercial networks, fostering the broader institutionalization of lawful and ethical business practices.

In a broader sense, by developing targeted compliance programs, enterprises can uphold ethical standards in specific areas and assume corresponding social responsibilities. For example, anti-commercial bribery compliance programs help promote values such as integrity, transparency, and fair competition. Data protection compliance frameworks establish mechanisms for safeguarding customer information, thereby reinforcing the value of personal privacy. Similarly, anti-money laundering (AML) compliance systems enable enterprises to play an active role in preventing the misuse of financial institutions for money laundering and terrorist financing. Improvements in export control compliance help institutionalize adherence to import and export regulations and foster a business ethic grounded in lawful, rules-based international operations. Moreover, through the development of targeted compliance programs, companies can take on social responsibilities in areas such as environmental protection, intellectual property rights, and labor rights.

2.3 Compliance and Sustainable Corporate Development

Many enterprises that have established compliance management systems embrace the concept that "compliance creates value." At ZTE Corporation, for instance, compliance has become a core organizational value prioritized across all levels of the company. It is considered both a foundational principle and a non-negotiable baseline for operations—one of the firm's three strategic pillars and a necessary path toward sustainable development. First, ZTE regards compliance as a value-driven choice essential to long-term business viability. It supports the optimization of management costs and the maximization of operational efficiency. A robust compliance framework safeguards the company's sustainable growth while protecting the commercial interests of clients, partners, shareholders, employees, and other stakeholders—thereby generating lasting value. Second, ZTE is committed to building a world-class, highly efficient compliance management system characterized by organizational coherence and process integration. The company aims to fully embed compliance mechanisms into core business workflows, ensuring the seamless implementation of compliance standards. It aspires to become an industry benchmark for compliance excellence, transforming compliance into a competitive advantage, fulfilling increasingly rigorous client requirements, and ultimately achieving the goal of value creation through compliance.[12]

In advancing corporate compliance governance, Chinese regulatory authorities have incorporated the concept of "sustainable development" into the broader framework of corporate governance. The *Guidelines for Compliance Management Systems*—China's national standard for compliance—explicitly states that "compliance is the cornerstone of an organization's sustainable development" and serves as a critical safeguard for realizing the "principles of good governance." At first glance, the establishment and refinement of a compliance management system may appear to hinder a company's pursuit of high profits and rapid returns. Yet from a long-term perspective, law-abiding enterprises are far better positioned to avoid legal risks, regulatory sanctions, and the severe financial and reputational losses that may result from misconduct. In addition, the very act of building a sound compliance framework can generate direct economic benefits, enhance competitive advantage, and contribute to the development of a strong corporate image and brand identity. These outcomes collectively highlight the positive role that compliance plays in advancing corporate sustainability.

[12] Ruihua Chen, "ZTE's Export Control Compliance Program," *China Lawyer* 4 (2020).

2.3.1 *Preventing and Controlling Compliance Risks*

For a company that has neither engaged in unlawful conduct nor been subjected to regulatory investigation or criminal prosecution, what tangible benefits arise from establishing a compliance management system? The primary answer lies in its ability to effectively prevent and control compliance risks. As a core element of corporate governance, a compliance management system also functions as a key risk mitigation mechanism. In general, regardless of industry or business model, enterprises are exposed to four fundamental categories of risk: strategic risk, operational risk, financial risk, and legal risk. Strategic risk refers to major setbacks arising from flawed decisions regarding corporate direction or business model selection, often resulting in significant losses. Operational risk concerns threats to investment returns, sustainable profitability, or market position, potentially leading to an inability to recover investments. Financial risk stems from deficiencies in financial management—such as embezzlement, dereliction of duty, disorder, or inefficiency—that may cause substantial economic losses. Legal risk involves exposure to penalties, litigation, or impairment of lawful rights resulting from violations of laws or regulatory obligations. These four categories of risk represent the principal dimensions of modern enterprise risk governance. In this framework, the general meeting of shareholders and the board of directors are responsible for mitigating strategic risk through the formulation and oversight of corporate strategy. Senior management addresses operational risk through the execution of business operations. The finance department manages financial risk via effective oversight of financial activities. The legal affairs department is tasked with controlling legal risk by implementing a comprehensive legal risk prevention and management system.

So, what exactly constitutes compliance risk? Broadly defined, compliance risk originates from legal risk and forms an integral subset of it. Unlike general legal risks, compliance risk refers specifically to the potential consequences an enterprise may face due to violations of administrative regulations—such as regulatory penalties, criminal prosecution for unlawful conduct, disqualification from market participation, and other serious operational or reputational losses. Within the contemporary international economic legal framework, compliance risk also includes sanctions imposed by international financial institutions—such as restrictions or disqualifications from procurement and bidding opportunities—against companies found to have engaged in misconduct. These measures are widely regarded as a distinct form of compliance risk. From a corporate governance perspective, companies increasingly institutionalize compliance risk management by establishing board-level compliance committees, appointing Chief Compliance Officers (CCOs) with substantial authority, and creating relatively independent compliance departments. Many enterprises also designate compliance officers or teams at subsidiary or regional levels. In addition, companies typically adopt compliance charters, policies, and employee handbooks, and develop comprehensive systems for the prevention, identification, and management of compliance risks. The level of organizational attention devoted to compliance risk far exceeds that accorded to general legal risk.

The primary rationale for establishing a corporate compliance management system—and for ensuring its effective implementation—is to minimize the occurrence of compliance risks that could have catastrophic consequences for the enterprise. Once a company becomes exposed to such risks, it may face administrative sanctions, criminal liability, or international regulatory penalties. These outcomes can lead to disqualification from critical market access activities—such as franchising, public listing, and government procurement—or, in extreme cases, revocation of the company's business license, resulting in potentially existential threats. For this reason, most enterprises now regard compliance risk as a distinct and overriding category of legal risk, separate from general legal exposure. The fundamental purpose behind constructing a routine compliance management system is to prevent unlawful or criminal conduct that could endanger the survival of the business and trigger irreversible consequences.

Following its settlement agreements with the U.S. Department of Justice and the Securities and Exchange Commission, Siemens AG undertook sustained efforts over several years to establish a globally leading compliance management system. It achieved particularly notable progress in the development of its anti-commercial bribery compliance framework. Under the protection of this system, Siemens has not encountered any major, systemic overseas bribery incidents since 2006 and has avoided severe regulatory sanctions or legal liabilities related to such conduct. Similarly, after entering into two separate settlement agreements with the U.S. federal court and the Department of Commerce, China's ZTE Corporation developed three targeted compliance systems covering export control, anti-bribery, and data protection. To support the effective implementation of these systems, ZTE established two complementary departments: a compliance audit unit and a compliance management unit. Together, these entities have ensured the integration of compliance into all aspects of the company's operations, realizing enterprise-wide compliance and elevating compliance to one of the three strategic pillars of corporate governance. With this comprehensive framework in place, ZTE has successfully mitigated a broad range of compliance risks and has avoided renewed exposure to trade sanctions, administrative penalties, or potential criminal prosecution.

2.3.2 *Defining Corporate Liability Boundaries*

In addition to preventing potential compliance risks, the establishment of a compliance management system can generate further strategic benefits. Notably, enterprises with effective compliance programs are often able to implement mechanisms for risk transfer and liability separation between the company and its employees, clients, third-party business partners, and acquired entities. These mechanisms help insulate the enterprise from joint or vicarious liability arising from unlawful or criminal conduct committed by affiliated parties.

In 2017, China revised its Anti-Unfair Competition Law, introducing several new provisions regulating commercial bribery in the context of business operations. Notably, the amended law adopted a default liability regime, whereby acts of bribery committed by employees are presumptively attributed to the "business operator," thus imposing initial legal responsibility on the enterprise. However, the law also allows the enterprise to raise an affirmative defense: a business operator may be exempt from liability if it can provide evidence demonstrating that the employee's conduct was unrelated to securing a transaction opportunity or gaining a competitive advantage on behalf of the enterprise.[13]

According to authoritative interpretations, in order for an enterprise to establish that an employee's conduct was "unrelated to securing a business opportunity or competitive advantage" for the business operator, it must provide evidence that it had adopted lawful, compliant, and reasonable internal measures; exercised effective oversight; and did not acquiesce in or tolerate the employee's unlawful conduct. In other words, if the enterprise has established a compliance management system specifically aimed at preventing unfair competition—particularly commercial bribery—and has implemented prohibitive and disciplinary measures against such conduct, while also adopting preventive mechanisms such as compliance training and internal communication, it may be exempt from administrative liability for the employee's misconduct.

It is evident that the establishment of an effective compliance management system can function as both a "buffer zone" and a "firewall," enabling the enterprise to clearly delineate its own liability from that of its employees, clients, third-party business partners, and acquired entities. This functional separation may provide a legal basis for exempting the enterprise from administrative or criminal liability. The following section offers a brief analysis of this mechanism.

With respect to the relationship between corporate liability and employee liability, many jurisdictions have adopted strict liability regimes under which enterprises may be held vicariously liable solely on the basis of an employee's unlawful or criminal conduct, regardless of any fault or negligence on the part of the enterprise. A prominent example is the offense of "failure of commercial organizations to prevent bribery" under the United Kingdom's Bribery Act 2010, which imposes strict liability on companies for acts of bribery committed by their employees. Similarly, the offense of "failing to fulfill cybersecurity management obligations" under China's Criminal Law reflects a comparable approach, whereby enterprises may be held strictly liable for criminal acts committed by their employees. In such strict liability frameworks, the establishment of an effective compliance management system may serve as an affirmative

[13] Jiangping Xiao, "Main Progress in the New Anti-Unfair Competition Law," *China Market Regulation Studies* 12 (2017).

defense, allowing the enterprise to rebut the presumption of liability and avoid sanctions despite the occurrence of employee misconduct.

How, then, can an enterprise leverage elements of its compliance management system to effectively delineate its own liability from that of employees or associated individuals? First, enterprises typically adopt targeted compliance policies and codes of conduct tailored to address specific categories of compliance risks. These instruments delineate the permissible boundaries of employee conduct, impose clear prohibitions against unlawful or unethical behavior, and establish corresponding disciplinary mechanisms. Second, to mitigate compliance risks, enterprises are expected to conduct compliance training for employees and senior management. Such training includes both regular, periodic sessions and specialized programs targeting high-risk personnel. If the enterprise can present training records, signed employee acknowledgments, or compliance declarations, it may demonstrate that it has discharged its duty to inform, educate, and caution its personnel—thus negating any suggestion that it tolerated or was willfully blind to misconduct. Third, in the course of day-to-day operations, an enterprise that establishes real-time compliance monitoring measures, implements effective oversight mechanisms, and maintains bottom-up reporting systems—such as whistleblower hotlines for reporting employee misconduct—can be deemed to have in place an internal early-warning system capable of detecting and responding to unlawful or non-compliant behavior by its employees. Finally, when violations occur, if the enterprise initiates prompt internal investigations, conducts targeted anti-fraud inquiries where appropriate, imposes timely disciplinary sanctions, and undertakes institutional reforms to address weaknesses in the compliance framework, these actions may be viewed as concrete remedial measures.

With respect to the delineation of liability between enterprises and their clients, a well-functioning compliance management system can serve as a critical mechanism for liability separation. This is especially important in the financial sector, where the absence of a robust anti-money laundering (AML) compliance framework may expose financial institutions to legal liability for facilitating money laundering or for concealing or disguising criminal proceeds derived from corruption, terrorism, fraud, or other illicit activities perpetrated by clients. To mitigate these compliance risks, financial institutions must establish a client-oriented compliance risk assessment mechanism. At the core of this mechanism lies the implementation of customer due diligence (CDD) procedures, which involve comprehensive background checks on clients—including assessments of their identity, business operations, regulatory compliance status, and any history of legal or regulatory infractions. Building on this foundation, financial institutions are also expected to conduct real-time monitoring of high-value transactions and potentially suspicious activities. Such compliance controls serve not only to proactively prevent the emergence of client-induced compliance risks but also to significantly reduce the institution's legal exposure. Most importantly, they enable the enterprise to achieve a clear separation of liability in circumstances where clients are found to have engaged in unlawful conduct, thereby preventing the transfer of compliance risk from clients to the institution.

With respect to the allocation of liability between enterprises and their third-party business partners, many jurisdictions have adopted strict liability frameworks. Under such regimes, a company may be held vicariously or strictly liable for unlawful or criminal acts committed by third parties acting on its behalf or for its benefit, even in the absence of fault on the part of the company itself. However, where the enterprise has implemented adequate third-party compliance measures—including conducting compliance due diligence, maintaining ongoing risk monitoring, and establishing clear contractual exit mechanisms—it may be eligible for exemption from legal liability. These safeguards enable the enterprise to achieve an effective separation of responsibilities and to limit its legal exposure arising from misconduct by external partners.

In general, a company's third-party business partners can be grouped into three categories: upstream suppliers and vendors; midstream agents and consultants; and downstream distributors, resellers, and contractors. If any of these third parties engage in unlawful or criminal conduct, the enterprise may be exposed to joint or vicarious liability. To effectively insulate itself from such liability, the enterprise must establish a robust third-party compliance management framework. Specifically, to mitigate legal risks arising from third-party misconduct, enterprises should implement a comprehensive set of compliance controls across four key dimensions: first, by clearly communicating internal compliance policies to third parties and requiring adherence as a contractual condition; second, by conducting thorough third-party due diligence to identify and evaluate potential legal and compliance risks; third, by maintaining ongoing compliance monitoring and oversight throughout the duration of the business relationship; and fourth, by performing regular risk assessments and establishing clear exit mechanisms for third parties that fail to meet established compliance standards.

With respect to the relationship between corporate liability and the liability of acquired entities, many jurisdictions have established mechanisms for liability separation. By developing targeted compliance management systems, acquiring companies can prevent themselves from being implicated in the unlawful or criminal conduct of the entities they acquire and thereby achieve effective risk transfer. In certain national compliance frameworks, the doctrine of "successor liability" plays a significant role. This doctrine refers to the legal principle that, in the context of a merger or acquisition, the acquiring company may bear legal responsibility for violations or misconduct committed by the target company prior to the transaction. As a general rule of attribution under corporate law, successor liability requires the successor company to assume liability for the predecessor's unlawful acts, serving as an institutional safeguard against the evasion of legal responsibility through corporate restructuring. Under the U.S. Foreign Corrupt Practices Act (FCPA) of 1977, the principle of successor liability has become a critical basis for imposing both administrative and criminal liability. The U.S. Department of Justice and the Securities and Exchange Commission, the two primary enforcement agencies of the FCPA, have consistently relied on this doctrine to hold acquiring firms accountable for foreign bribery committed by their acquisition targets.[14]

In response to the principle of successor liability, many companies have established compliance management mechanisms specifically designed for mergers and acquisitions. Typically, these include conducting pre-acquisition due diligence and strengthening compliance programs and internal control systems after the acquisition is completed. This practice is motivated by four main considerations. First, due diligence allows the acquiring company to accurately evaluate the target entity. Contracts secured through bribery or transactions conducted via unlawful means are inherently unsustainable. Prior misconduct by the target company may not only expose the acquirer to legal liability but also jeopardize its reputation and long-term prospects. Investigating such issues in advance enables a more informed assessment of both legal exposure and the actual value of the target. Second, pre-acquisition due diligence reduces the risk of perpetuating corrupt practices. By identifying commercial and regional compliance risks, it lays the groundwork for the seamless integration of the target into the acquiring company's internal controls and compliance environment. Third, if potential violations are identified during due diligence, the acquiring company can proactively manage related legal risks by negotiating cost-sharing arrangements, liability allocations, and remediation measures. Fourth, a thorough due diligence process signals the acquiring company's commitment to transparency and its proactive approach to uncovering and preventing unlawful conduct.

2.3.3 *Incentive Effects of Leniency Policies*

For enterprises under regulatory investigation for unlawful or non-compliant conduct, what tangible benefits can be derived from establishing a compliance management system or committing to compliance remediation? In practice, when a company is suspected of violating administrative regulations, the creation of a compliance system—or a formal pledge to implement a corrective compliance plan—may serve as grounds for exemption from administrative penalties, reduction in sanctions, or eligibility to enter into administrative settlement agreements. By undertaking compliance remediation measures, the enterprise may secure lenient treatment and avoid the most severe enforcement outcomes. Moreover, even enterprises sanctioned by international financial institutions for misconduct such as corruption or fraud may be eligible for the lifting of those sanctions if they agree to undergo compliance supervision and succeed in rebuilding a credible, integrity-driven compliance program. This, in turn, can restore their eligibility to participate in international procurement and bidding activities.

[14] Yunxia Yin, Yanjun Zhuang, and Xiaoxia Li, "Corporate Agency and the 'Radiating Enforcement Effect' in Anti-Corruption," *SJTU Law Review*, no. 2 (2016).

In December 2020, China's State Administration for Market Regulation (SAMR) initiated an investigation into Alibaba Group for alleged abuse of its dominant position in the domestic online retail platform services market, in accordance with the Antitrust Law. In April 2021, SAMR issued an administrative penalty decision, ordering Alibaba to cease its illegal conduct and imposing a fine equivalent to 4% of its 2019 sales revenue in China—amounting to over RMB 18.2 billion. In addition, SAMR issued an administrative guidance document requiring Alibaba to undertake comprehensive compliance remediation, including the strict fulfillment of platform operator responsibilities, the enhancement of internal controls and compliance management, the maintenance of fair competition, and the protection of the lawful rights and interests of merchants and consumers. Alibaba was also required to submit annual compliance reports to SAMR for three consecutive years.[15]

In 2018, Harbin Electric Machinery Company Limited was subjected to a conditional suspension of eligibility by the Asian Development Bank (ADB) due to fraudulent conduct—specifically, the falsification of performance credentials—during its participation in an ADB-funded procurement project. Shortly thereafter, the company was placed under coordinated sanctions by multiple international financial institutions, including the World Bank. In response, Harbin Electric formally committed to undertaking compliance remediation. Under the oversight of the ADB, the company engaged a leading domestic compliance law firm to establish a comprehensive integrity-based compliance program. This entailed building a clearly structured compliance governance system, adopting a full suite of compliance management policies and effective operational workflows, and implementing all promised compliance remedial measures. Drawing on the integrity compliance guidelines of the World Bank and the ADB, as well as domestic compliance guidelines, the legal team developed four major compliance assessment modules, 18 specific evaluation criteria, and over 40 targeted improvement recommendations. They also refined 13 specialized compliance policies and developed 12 supporting implementation documents, including approval workflow forms, standardized compliance clauses, and compliance commitment letters, thereby ensuring alignment with both domestic and international regulatory requirements. On August 18, 2020, the Asian Development Bank officially confirmed the lifting of sanctions against Harbin Electric Machinery Company Limited, thereby restoring its eligibility to participate in international procurement and bidding activities.[16]

The two aforementioned cases demonstrate how enterprises—when subjected to administrative investigations or sanctions by international institutions

[15] "Alibaba Fined 18.2 Billion RMB, and Submitted Self-Inspection Compliance Reports to the State Administration for Market Regulation for Three Consecutive Years," *People's Daily*, April 10, 2021.

[16] Wei Wu et al., "KWM Assisted Harbin Electric Corporation in Lifting ADB Sanctions," *KWM Institute* (WeChat post), September 2, 2020.

due to unlawful or criminal conduct—may benefit from committing to comprehensive compliance remediation. Following the successful establishment of a compliance management system within the prescribed compliance monitoring period, and upon passing the requisite compliance assessments and inspections, the enterprises were ultimately granted lenient administrative penalties, non-prosecution decisions, or relief from international sanctions. Although the factual circumstances of these cases differ, they collectively illustrate that in regulatory environments where compliance incentive mechanisms are in place, companies under investigation that formally commit to developing a compliance framework may be granted the opportunity to undertake such reforms. If an enterprise completes its compliance remediation plan and establishes an effective compliance infrastructure during the compliance monitoring period, domestic authorities may impose mitigated administrative penalties, while international organizations may lift sanctions and reinstate the company's eligibility for public procurement and bidding activities. These developments underscore a critical insight: for enterprises facing legal or reputational crises, the establishment of a compliance management system can generate a concrete benefit—namely, eligibility for lenient enforcement treatment. Such treatment can help companies avoid more severe consequences, such as disqualification from strategic markets, and provides a viable path to legal rehabilitation and operational recovery.

2.3.4 *Compliance as a Source of Commercial Value*

The establishment of a compliance management system enables enterprises to prevent specific compliance risks; delineate corporate liability from that of employees, clients, third-party partners, and acquired entities; and obtain more lenient treatment during regulatory crises—thereby avoiding severe outcomes such as disqualification from critical market access. These constitute the negative or preventive benefits of compliance: the value of safeguarding against potential loss through the proactive construction of a compliance framework. In essence, such benefits are remedial in character. Beyond this, however, the effective implementation of a compliance management system can yield positive commercial returns. Enterprises with robust compliance infrastructures are better equipped to build reputational capital, strengthen competitive advantages, attract high-quality clients, cultivate reliable business partnerships, and secure valuable transactional opportunities. The widely used phrase "compliance creates value" refers precisely to this affirmative dimension

After years of rebuilding its compliance system, Siemens AG has grown into a multinational corporation with a compliance team of over one thousand professionals and has fostered a leading compliance culture within the industry. The sophistication and maturity of Siemens' compliance framework have earned the company a global reputation for excellence, enhancing its ability to attract a wide range of clients and business partners. Since 2018, China's ZTE Corporation has similarly undertaken a comprehensive compliance restructuring initiative, establishing a professional compliance management team with several hundred dedicated personnel. Advancing in parallel with its telecommunications technologies, ZTE's compliance infrastructure has supported sustained performance growth and drawn a large number of high-quality clients. This dual-track development has significantly strengthened the company's competitive position. What was once viewed as a non-revenue-generating function—compliance management—has thus become a strategic asset, instrumental in securing premium clients and unlocking market opportunities. Siemens' commitment to "only engaging in compliant business" and ZTE's philosophy that "compliance creates value" exemplify two expressions of a shared principle: that effective compliance governance can serve as a powerful driver of corporate commercial value.

First, an effective compliance program can enhance a company's organizational culture and public image, strengthen its business reputation, and attract more clients and investors. These outcomes contribute directly to greater competitive advantage and profitability. In turn, such gains incentivize sustained investment in the continuous improvement of the compliance framework, creating a virtuous cycle that steadily elevates the company's market value. Notably, in the context of mergers, acquisitions, or capital financing, an effective compliance program can significantly boost corporate valuation, thereby converting compliance governance into a source of demonstrable economic benefit. To a certain extent, a company's compliance infrastructure—much like the quality of its products—can produce a brand effect, significantly enhancing both its commercial reputation and public standing, and ultimately serving as a strategic asset in securing long-term commercial success.

Second, the broad adoption of compliance management mechanisms contributes to the establishment of a fair and orderly competitive environment. Within such a framework, enterprises that operate in accordance with laws and regulations are afforded the opportunity to compete on equal terms and pursue sustainable, long-term growth. In the short term, companies may seek to increase revenues through unlawful or unethical practices—such as bribing public officials, engaging in predatory competition, committing fraud, polluting the environment, or violating personal data privacy. While such misconduct may yield temporary economic gains, it fundamentally erodes the integrity of market competition, increases operational costs, and may result in greater losses over time, particularly if illicit practices become widespread across an industry. In contrast, from a long-term perspective, only enterprises that establish compliance management mechanisms and implement effective compliance programs can operate in accordance with laws and regulations, thereby securing a relatively fair and rules-based business environment—one that fosters predictability, drives sustainable commercial development, and ensures the continued protection of legitimate rights and interests. A company that develops through a culture of compliant operations will ultimately benefit from such integrity, gradually becoming a model enterprise within its industry. In doing so, it not only achieves its goals of sustainable development but also enhances its potential to evolve into a truly enduring institution—a "century-old enterprise" built on the foundation of lawful and responsible business conduct.

2.4 Compliance and Governmental Regulation

The evolution of corporate compliance systems reveals that early efforts—characterized by enterprises voluntarily establishing compliance programs—initially yielded certain positive outcomes in encouraging lawful and rule-abiding conduct. However, this spontaneous, self-regulatory approach ultimately proved inadequate and, in some instances, counterproductive. Notably, some companies came to regard compliance frameworks as mere "window dressing"—tools for masking legal risk or shielding themselves from liability—resulting in the proliferation of paper-based compliance plans that failed to deter or prevent unlawful activity. Since the 1990s, many jurisdictions across Europe and North America have incorporated compliance into both criminal and administrative legal frameworks. The establishment of a corporate compliance system has come to serve as a recognized basis for granting leniency to enterprises found in violation of the law, thereby institutionalizing compliance-based incentive mechanisms.[17] In the administrative context, the growing use of administrative settlement agreements marks a shift away from rigid punitive enforcement.[18] Regulatory authorities have increasingly embraced the mechanism of administrative contracts, allowing enterprises to obtain reduced sanctions in return for undertaking and implementing substantive compliance reforms. Building upon this foundation, regulatory authorities have strengthened the legal status of compliance by issuing authoritative compliance standards, implementing mandatory compliance regimes, and establishing liability exemption mechanisms for companies that demonstrate effective implementation. Collectively, these measures have made compliance a regulatory tool for supervising and promoting lawful, rule-based corporate conduct.

Why, then, has compliance become a widely favored regulatory instrument among administrative enforcement and regulatory agencies across jurisdictions? What specific advantages does it offer that have led to its broad adoption as a standard tool of administrative governance? In this regard, Western legal scholarship has put forward two principal theoretical explanations: the "social benefit theory" and the "violation cost-reduction theory." According to the former, corporate compliance programs enable governments to achieve ex ante prevention of unlawful conduct without increasing enforcement intensity or expanding budgetary allocations. By encouraging enterprises to establish internal compliance systems, regulators can shift from reactive enforcement to proactive risk mitigation, thereby alleviating the administrative burden. The implementation of compliance programs generates system-wide benefits for

[17] Todd Haugh, "The Criminalization of Compliance," *Notre Dame Law Review* 92 (2017): 1215–1270.

[18] Ruihua Chen, *Fundamentals of Corporate Compliance*, 2nd ed. (Beijing: Law Press, 2021), 187.

the judiciary by reducing investigative demands and lowering litigation costs. The latter theory emphasizes the functional utility of compliance in reducing the legal exposure of enterprises. Compliance programs not only facilitate the prevention of violations but also assist companies in identifying and assessing potential civil liabilities and criminal risks at an early stage, allowing for timely and strategic responses. Even in the aftermath of a violation, the existence of a compliance program may serve as grounds for affirmative defense, procedural leniency, or mitigation in sentencing. Moreover, it may obviate the need for overly intrusive regulatory interventions aimed at compelling corporate remediation.[19]

In the author's view, from the standpoint of governmental regulation, the introduction of compliance mechanisms—and their application as enforcement incentives—can effectively address the problem of external regulatory failure, significantly reduce the costs of administrative regulation, and function as a substitute for harsh punitive measures. More importantly, such mechanisms can stimulate enterprises to engage in proactive self-regulation, thereby enhancing the overall effectiveness of regulatory governance. This article advances a theoretical framework—the theory of effective regulation—to elucidate the distinctive value of corporate compliance in the context of public administration.

2.4.1 Limits of Traditional Enforcement

Regulatory authorities have traditionally embraced a punitive enforcement paradigm, viewing sanctions and penalties as primary instruments for addressing corporate violations. This model rests on the assumption that punishment serves a dual deterrent function: specific deterrence, by preventing the offending enterprise from committing further violations, and general deterrence, by dissuading other enterprises from engaging in similar misconduct. When confronted with suspected corporate non-compliance, administrative agencies often presume that imposing fines, revoking licenses, or applying other forms of punitive action will both curb repeat offenses and generate a broader deterrent effect within the industry.

However, this overly idealized enforcement philosophy often proves unrealistic when confronted with practical constraints. On the one hand, the legal framework governing corporate misconduct has grown increasingly stringent and complex, with an ever-expanding body of statutory provisions serving as the basis for determining violations. This proliferation of legal norms has placed mounting burdens on enforcement authorities, who now face high operational costs, an increasing number of technically complex cases, and persistently low levels of enforcement efficiency. On the other hand, selective enforcement has become a systemic phenomenon: while some enterprises are investigated and

[19] Sean J. Griffith, "Corporate Governance in an Era of Compliance," *William & Mary Law Review* 57 (2016): 2075–2140.

sanctioned, a significant number of similarly situated violators remain outside the reach of enforcement or even evade detection entirely. The result is a distorted enforcement landscape in which those subjected to investigation resign themselves to misfortune, while those who escape sanction cultivate a sense of complacent impunity—undermining respect for legal authority and eroding the deterrent effect of regulatory enforcement.

From the perspective of corporate regulation, China's enforcement and judicial practice has revealed a prevalent issue of "external regulatory failure"—the inability of government agencies to effectively detect, investigate, and prevent misconduct in large enterprises with complex governance structures when relying solely on traditional enforcement mechanisms. Such corporations often employ thousands of personnel, operate under multilayered governance systems (including shareholders' meetings, boards of directors, supervisory boards, and executive management), maintain numerous subsidiaries and branches across the country and abroad, engage hundreds of suppliers, agents, and distributors, and carry out frequent mergers and acquisitions, turning dozens of external entities into wholly or majority-owned affiliates each year. In comparison with the oversight of small enterprises that have limited personnel and simpler governance structures, the external regulation of large corporations proves significantly more costly, inefficient, and frequently ineffective. This regulatory challenge becomes particularly acute in specialized sectors such as tax administration, intellectual property protection, environmental regulation, anti-commercial bribery enforcement, and data protection—domains in which corporate misconduct is often highly concealed and strategically timed to evade regulatory detection. Large enterprises operating in these fields frequently possess advanced technical capabilities to resist investigative measures. Once a violation occurs, they can swiftly destroy, fabricate, or alter evidence and may even organize coordinated efforts among employees to mount a united front or provide false testimony, thereby obstructing regulatory investigations.

Moreover, even where a company does not itself organize, encourage, or acquiesce in unlawful or criminal conduct, a core challenge of corporate governance lies in establishing mechanisms capable of effectively preventing, detecting, and responding to violations committed by managers, employees, subsidiaries, clients, third-party business partners, or acquired entities. At stake is the design of a governance framework capable of systematically ensuring that all affiliated actors conduct business in accordance with applicable laws and regulations. This challenge is particularly pronounced in emerging high-tech industries, where early-stage business operations often evolve in regulatory gray zones. Driven by policy considerations that favor innovation and hindered by limited regulatory experience, government agencies may refrain from early intervention—allowing companies to grow unchecked during their formative years. By the time such enterprises reach substantial scale or when the industry structure begins to stabilize, regulators may belatedly recognize that the underlying business models or operational practices embody elements of illegality or criminality. In recent years, business formats such as peer-to-peer (P2P) lending, online financing platforms, and big data-driven commercial models have exhibited intrinsic legal vulnerabilities, giving rise to pervasive compliance risks across the sector. For regulators, however, this presents a persistent dilemma: continued tolerance may allow corporate illegality to proliferate and become entrenched, whereas the indiscriminate application of harsh punitive measures could push numerous enterprises to the brink of collapse—potentially inflicting severe damage on entire industries.

The foregoing analysis demonstrates that, as enterprises expand in scale and adopt increasingly complex governance structures—and as corporate misconduct grows more covert, specialized, and recurrent—administrative authorities are confronted with an escalating crisis of external regulatory failure. Against this backdrop, the integration of corporate compliance frameworks as a complement or an alternative to purely punitive regulatory approaches has emerged as not merely a policy option, but an inevitable requirement for effective governance. From a regulatory governance perspective, the adoption of compliance incentive mechanisms—under which enterprises that have established or committed to establishing effective compliance management systems are afforded lenient treatment—represents a viable institutional response to the limitations of external oversight identified above.

2.4.2 *Positive Effects of Compliance-Based Regulation*

In contrast to traditional regulatory approaches, compliance-oriented regulation represents a governance model in which enterprises, under external pressure and incentivized conditions established by regulatory authorities, are compelled to implement internal institutional reforms. Whereas conventional regulation may be described as a form of *external oversight*, compliance-based regulation more closely resembles *self-policing*. This regulatory model comprises two core components. First, regulators exert significant compliance pressure on enterprises, obligating them to establish formal compliance systems. For companies already embroiled in legal or regulatory crises, regulators may extend compelling incentives aimed at prompting compliance remediation measures and the reconstruction of internal compliance frameworks. Second, under such external pressure, enterprises are prompted to initiate internal investigations and propose compliance remediation plans aimed at rectifying institutional deficiencies and addressing latent managerial risks. Based on these measures, enterprises then proceed to establish or enhance their compliance management systems and reinforce internal control structures.

A paradigmatic example of how administrative authorities externally stimulate corporate initiatives to establish compliance systems is reflected in the administrative settlement cases concluded by the China Securities Regulatory Commission (CSRC) with enterprises suspected of administrative violations. In 2019, the CSRC reached a settlement agreement with Goldman Sachs (Asia) L.L.C. and eight additional applicants. In 2020, it entered into a similar agreement with Shanghai Sidu Company and four other applicants. These two cases remain among the most representative instances of administrative settlements concluded between the CSRC and corporate actors to date. In both cases, the applicants acknowledged the facts of their violations, paid substantial administrative settlement amounts, and undertook commitments to enhance their internal control and compliance management mechanisms. Upon completion of the agreed compliance reforms, they submitted written remediation reports to the CSRC. In exchange, the CSRC terminated its investigative proceedings concerning the alleged misconduct.[20]

What positive effects can be observed once corporate compliance is integrated into the regulatory and enforcement framework? First and foremost, when enforcement agencies signal the possibility of lenient treatment, implicated enterprises are more inclined to abandon adversarial postures in favor of comprehensive cooperation and compromise. This marks the infusion of a negotiated enforcement philosophy into the enforcement process. The development of a compliance program often serves as a key indicator of a company's willingness to cooperate with governmental investigations. Through settlement agreements with regulatory and criminal enforcement authorities, implicated enterprises typically commit to full cooperation—voluntarily acknowledging past misconduct and granting investigators extensive access to internal operations. Such cooperation frequently encompasses comprehensive internal audits, the restructuring of governance and management systems, and the removal of senior executives responsible for wrongdoing. In addition, whether initiated voluntarily or compelled by regulatory pressure, these enterprises may assume self-disclosure obligations, revealing not only further details of unlawful conduct but also the involvement of employees and senior management. This comprehensive cooperation functions as both an institutional acknowledgment of wrongdoing and an act of contrition while simultaneously facilitating the timely and effective prosecution of individual offenders. By doing so, the enterprise achieves a functional separation from culpable actors and establishes the foundation for a fundamental transformation of its governance framework.

Second, in pursuit of the most favorable case outcome, enterprises under investigation are often incentivized to undertake proactive remedial measures aimed at repairing the legal interests and social relationships harmed by their misconduct. These efforts help to establish a constructive foundation for subsequent compliance remediation. Typically, enterprises that commit to implementing a compliance program will voluntarily engage in restorative actions such as paying administrative fines, remitting back taxes, surrendering unlawful gains, and compensating affected victims. In certain instances, they may also

[20]Weiqiao Yang, "Behind the CSRC and Goldman Sachs Administrative Enforcement Settlement," *Board Magazine* (WeChat post), July 31, 2019; Xinyu Liu, "Settlement Exceeds 680 Million RMB! CSRC Reaches Administrative Settlement with Five Institutions Including Sidou," *Pengpai News* (WeChat post), January 20, 2020.

seek to remedy environmental harm or restore damaged community relations resulting from their unlawful acts. Under traditional regulatory frameworks, such remedial actions are generally imposed through mandatory administrative or judicial orders, and enterprises often respond with reluctance or minimal cooperation. In contrast, under a compliance-based regulatory approach, enterprises proactively undertake these restorative actions—repairing the legal interests and social relationships harmed by their misconduct—which in turn substantially mitigate the societal harm resulting from the underlying violations.

Third, in an effort to secure the most favorable resolution, companies under investigation often voluntarily assume internal regulatory responsibilities by reforming their management systems and governance structures, and by strengthening compliance oversight of risk-associated actors—including managers, subsidiaries, employees, clients, third-party business partners, and acquired entities. To some extent, the enterprise assumes quasi-regulatory functions, performing supervisory roles that would otherwise fall to enforcement authorities. Compared to externally imposed oversight, this form of internally driven compliance supervision often yields more effective results in preventing, identifying, and responding to corporate misconduct. For instance, through compliance risk assessments and due diligence on clients, third parties, and acquisition targets, enterprises can proactively identify high-risk areas and implement targeted compliance mechanisms. Compliance training and cultural initiatives help enhance employees' awareness of legal and ethical obligations, reducing the likelihood of violations. Mechanisms such as compliance reporting, whistleblower systems, and internal audits enable enterprises to monitor risks in real time—functioning as an internal "radar system." In the aftermath of violations, internal investigations allow companies to hold responsible individuals accountable, uncover systemic weaknesses, and devise improvement measures to strengthen their compliance frameworks. Under the supervision of administrative or judicial authorities, such enterprises can thus establish dynamic compliance systems that integrate ex ante prevention, ongoing monitoring, and ex post remediation—ultimately reducing the likelihood of future violations.

Finally, compared to traditional regulatory models, compliance-based regulation enables authorities to avoid constant direct intervention and reliance on severe punitive measures. Instead, regulators assume the roles of overseers, reviewers, and arbiters, guiding enterprises to rectify unlawful business practices by reforming their internal governance structures. This process encourages companies to gradually establish mechanisms for conducting business in accordance with laws and regulations, thereby fostering a compliance-oriented management framework and corporate culture. The establishment of corporate compliance mechanisms significantly reduces the resource burden on regulatory bodies by transforming external oversight into an incentive-based model of self-regulation. Enterprises are thus motivated to engage in proactive self-monitoring, self-reporting, and self-correction. Both administrative regulators and criminal enforcement agencies may reward companies that adopt compliance programs with leniency measures, including non-prosecution, reduced penalties, or even full exemptions from legal liability. In particular, authorities may enter into administrative settlement agreements or deferred prosecution agreements with such companies to supervise and facilitate the enhancement—or even complete reconstruction—of their compliance management systems.

In the process of improving or reconstructing compliance programs, regulatory and enforcement agencies function as facilitators, supervisors, and evaluators. With relatively limited investment of manpower and resources, they have achieved notable results in prompting enterprises to overhaul their compliance systems. Compared to the traditional model of "external regulation," this incentive-driven approach—whereby leniency is granted in exchange for genuine compliance reform—more effectively mobilizes corporate efforts to establish and enhance internal compliance structures. It also fosters stronger oversight of employees, subsidiaries, clients, third-party partners, and acquired entities, thereby preventing potential violations from within. In this light, the compliance-based regulatory model has significantly enhanced the efficiency of both administrative supervision and criminal enforcement. It has also encouraged enterprises to take initiative in internal governance and engage in proactive risk management. Administrative and judicial bodies have thus shifted from a reactive posture—merely responding to unlawful conduct—to a proactive role in driving corporate governance reforms, encouraging voluntary investigation and disclosure of violations, closing institutional loopholes, and continuously strengthening internal control systems. By relinquishing part of their punitive authority, these agencies have secured a more effective framework for achieving regulatory oversight and corporate governance. This, arguably, constitutes the most significant institutional benefit that the corporate compliance system confers upon administrative and judicial authorities.

2.5 Compliance and the Protection of Public Interests

In discussions on the normative value of corporate compliance, the so-called "ripple theory" has attracted significant attention. This theory holds that prosecuting a corporation is tantamount to imposing a corporate death penalty; sanctions imposed on a company often inflict harm on innocent third parties, including investors, employees, pension recipients, and customers. Accordingly, the logic of compliance should prioritize sparing the implicated corporation itself, while imposing strict and targeted accountability on the individuals directly responsible for the misconduct.[21]

Whether a corporation establishes a compliance management system on its own initiative or is compelled to implement compliance remediation under

[21] Liangfang Ye, "Development of the U.S. Deferred Prosecution Agreement System for Corporations," *Journal of Criminal Law in China*, no. 3 (2014).

government supervision, the improvement of such systems not only promotes the maximization of corporate interests and enhances the effectiveness of regulatory oversight, but also, as an objective consequence, contributes to the effective protection of social public interests. This dimension can be better understood by examining the value orientations of different compliance models.

First, the establishment of a routine compliance management system plays a crucial role in minimizing compliance risks, monitoring the legality of business operations, and promptly addressing identified management deficiencies and institutional vulnerabilities. As a mode of corporate governance, it protects the enterprise from internal misconduct; helps prevent administrative penalties, criminal prosecution, or governmental sanctions; and reduces potential losses related to corporate reputation, commercial opportunities, competitive advantage, and market access. In this sense, an effective compliance system functions as both a "protective umbrella" and a "defensive shield" for the enterprise.

Importantly, while primarily designed to avert corporate losses, such a system also contributes—objectively—to safeguarding the interests of various related parties. For instance, a sound compliance framework helps protect the rights and interests of investors, shareholders, and board members by insulating them from the economic harms caused by reputational damage, lost business opportunities, or diminished competitive positioning. At first glance, an effective compliance management system may appear to constrain the autonomy of employees, clients, subsidiaries, third-party business partners, and acquired entities and may even increase their responsibilities and potential exposure to liability. In substantive terms, however, such a system markedly reduces the risk of unlawful or criminal conduct by placing relevant actors within a stringent framework of internal discipline and self-regulation. Whether as employees, shareholders, investors, customers, or contractual partners, stakeholders generally prefer to engage with enterprises that uphold principles of honesty, integrity, and legal compliance. Such enterprises are better equipped to avoid legal, economic, and reputational risks and to achieve sustainable, long-term development—an outcome that serves the fundamental interests of all parties involved. By contrast, short-sighted and opportunistic business practices, including illegal or non-compliant conduct, may yield short-term profits or transactional gains that superficially benefit certain stakeholders. Yet once such conduct is exposed and sanctioned, the enterprise inevitably suffers varying degrees of financial loss, disqualification, and reputational harm—consequences that ultimately undermine the legitimate interests of all good-faith stakeholders.

Second, for stakeholders associated with an enterprise, a crisis-responsive compliance system can yield considerable long-term benefits. The Enron and Arthur Andersen scandals in the United States stand as cautionary lessons, demonstrating that the failure to establish effective internal controls and implement meaningful compliance programs can result in devastating consequences. When a corporation goes bankrupt or becomes subject to regulatory investigations and criminal proceedings, it not only is exposed to severe legal penalties and disqualification from market participation, but also inflicts varying degrees of economic and reputational harm on its employees, shareholders, investors, business partners, and clients. In the aftermath of the Arthur Andersen scandal, tens of thousands of employees were laid off or compelled to resign within a short span of time, countless individuals suffered significant financial losses, and the economy as a whole experienced marked instability. These painful lessons underscore that without a robust compliance infrastructure, the legitimate rights and interests of all corporate stakeholders remain fundamentally vulnerable.[22]

In contrast, when administrative investigations are launched by regulatory authorities or sanctions imposed by international organizations, an enterprise under scrutiny may, by cooperating with the investigation and undertaking meaningful remedial efforts, commit to a compliance remediation plan aimed at eliminating institutional deficiencies and managerial vulnerabilities. By adopting effective corrective measures to prevent future violations, the enterprise may become eligible to enter into an administrative settlement agreement with the regulatory body or be placed under a compliance supervision regime by the relevant international organization. Upon successful completion of the compliance remediation process and passage of the requisite compliance review, the enterprise may receive lenient treatment—such as a reduction or exemption of administrative penalties, or the lifting of sanctions. In any event, through targeted and responsive compliance remediation, an implicated enterprise can avert the most severe punitive outcomes—particularly the risk of disqualification from market participation—thereby alleviating its immediate existential crisis. A crisis-oriented compliance framework can prevent corporate insolvency or collapse; safeguard the economic interests of investors, shareholders, and directors; protect employees from the threat of mass unemployment; preserve customers' continued access to commercial opportunities; and shield business partners from the financial losses that would otherwise result from the enterprise's failure. Moreover, under sustained regulatory supervision, the enterprise can undertake a fundamental restructuring of its compliance management system, effecting a transformation into a law-abiding, rule-based commercial entity. Such structural reconstitution provides a durable and reliable safeguard for the interests of all stakeholders.

Furthermore, while safeguarding the interests of corporate stakeholders, corporate compliance also plays a vital role in protecting national interests and broader public welfare. On the one hand, when an enterprise conducts its operations in accordance with laws and regulations, mitigates compliance risks, avoids severe penalties, and prevents bankruptcy or collapse, it contributes to the maintenance of economic order, the prevention of financial instability and mass unemployment, and the preservation of key public interests, including fiscal revenue, investment, and employment. This is particularly significant in the case of large enterprises that serve as economic anchors within their

[22] Ruihua Chen, "Enron and Arthur Andersen Cases," *China Lawyer*, no. 4 (2020).

respective regions. Under the safeguards provided by a robust compliance management system, such enterprises can generate sustained value and make substantial contributions to society. Accordingly, when determining whether to impose sanctions or administrative penalties on a non-compliant enterprise, regulatory authorities typically conduct a necessary public interest assessment, treating the protection of public welfare as a central factor in their enforcement decisions.

On the other hand, once a corporate compliance system is effectively implemented, it can exert a powerful preventive function against unlawful and non-compliant conduct, thereby aligning more closely with national priorities and the broader public interest. Traditional administrative regulation has long relied on command-and-control mechanisms, while conventional enforcement has emphasized punitive deterrence through severe sanctions. However, with respect to corporate violations, these control- and punishment-centered approaches have often failed to address structural and systemic non-compliance within enterprises. In contrast, the institutionalization of corporate compliance represents a shift from traditional external regulation and governance to an incentive-based model that exchanges enforcement leniency for corporate self-correction and internal oversight. This transformation substantially strengthens enterprises' internal incentives to adopt compliance governance. As a preventive mechanism, corporate compliance offers clear advantages over traditional regulatory approaches: it enhances regulatory efficiency, lowers enforcement costs, reshapes corporate behavior and business models, and achieves a substantive "de-legalization" of unlawful practices. It enables enterprises to move beyond patterns of unchecked expansion and to embrace a governance paradigm committed exclusively to compliance-driven operations. This preventive capacity makes corporate compliance a particularly effective instrument for safeguarding national interests and promoting the broader public good.

2.6 Addressing Common Objections

In the preceding discussion, a preliminary case has been made for the intrinsic normative value of corporate compliance in fulfilling corporate social responsibility, along with its instrumental effectiveness in promoting sustainable development, ensuring regulatory efficiency, and safeguarding the public interest. These analyses indicate that compliance management operates not only as a form of moral obligation on the part of enterprises, but also as a utilitarian mechanism through which the interests of multiple stakeholders may be concurrently served. In particular, when contrasted with traditional models of corporate regulation and administrative enforcement, compliance-based regulatory approaches exhibit distinctive institutional advantages. Nevertheless, this line of analysis would remain incomplete without engaging with certain existing or anticipated objections to the legitimacy of corporate compliance. It is therefore necessary to address such critiques from a falsification-oriented perspective, in order to demonstrate that the normative and functional criticisms commonly leveled against compliance regimes fail to withstand critical scrutiny.

First, building a corporate compliance system typically entails significant investment in human, material, and financial resources and incurs substantial direct and opportunity costs. In some large enterprises, establishing a few targeted compliance programs may require assembling dedicated compliance teams comprising several hundred—or even over a thousand—staff members, with annual compliance budgets running into hundreds of millions or even billions of yuan. Moreover, to ensure the effective functioning of the compliance system, companies must commit considerable managerial resources—from the board of directors and senior executives to each department and subsidiary. In certain cases, compliance departments are even granted veto power over operational decisions, such that enterprises may be compelled to forgo transactions, projects, or business lines deemed to pose potential compliance risks. These realities underscore that compliance imposes real resource burdens and often fails to deliver immediate financial returns. On this basis, some critics challenge the legitimacy of compliance by arguing that the high costs involved may discourage companies from engaging in compliance efforts altogether—claiming that such efforts may prove disproportionate to the benefits, or even counterproductive.

The so-called high-cost compliance argument rests on factual premises but arrives at an untenable conclusion. It is indeed the case that building a compliance system entails substantial costs and resource commitments. However, such expenditures represent a price worth paying in the course of corporate development. In the early stages of compliance implementation, companies may not observe immediate returns on their investment. Yet as the system gradually proves effective in preventing, identifying, and responding to compliance risks, enterprises begin to cultivate a compliance culture—one that is firmly grounded in lawful and rule-based operations. Over time, compliance begins to generate both tangible and intangible benefits—such as enhanced corporate reputation, improved competitive positioning, expanded business opportunities, and the attraction of high-quality clients. Ultimately, compliance demonstrates its capacity to create value. Even more critically, the capacity of compliance systems to shield enterprises from severe regulatory sanctions, disqualification from market access, or bankruptcy reflects a form of latent commercial value—one that is difficult to quantify but of profound significance. The previously discussed cases of Siemens AG and ZTE Corporation, both of which undertook extensive compliance reforms, underscore the point that high compliance expenditures are not only justified but also essential. In the long run, it is the enterprise itself that stands to gain the most from a well-functioning compliance regime.

Admittedly, small and medium-sized enterprises (SMEs) may not have the capacity to establish comprehensive compliance programs on par with those implemented by large corporations. However, this does not constitute a legitimate reason to abandon compliance system development altogether. Compared with large enterprises, SMEs can adopt more streamlined and targeted compliance frameworks. For example, they may develop risk-specific compliance mechanisms, implement specialized institutional adjustments focused on key compliance vulnerabilities, appoint a limited number of highly qualified compliance officers, or delegate compliance management functions to external legal professionals who are authorized to exercise veto power over high-risk business activities. With regard to cost allocation, both large enterprises and SMEs can—and should—design compliance systems that vary in scale and complexity according to their respective capacities and risk profiles. There is no need to adopt a one-size-fits-all compliance model.

Second, one may argue that even the establishment of a compliance system cannot fully prevent or eliminate all instances of unlawful or non-compliant conduct. This concern is especially salient for large enterprises, which typically operate with expansive employee rosters, multilayered management structures, numerous subsidiaries, diverse client networks, and a wide array of third-party business partners. Even if the enterprise itself harbors no intent to engage in misconduct, it may nonetheless be unable to prevent violations committed by affiliated individuals or entities. Against this backdrop, a recurring objection arises: if corporate misconduct cannot be entirely eradicated, what is the substantive value of building a compliance management system in the first place?

To counter the so-called compliance is useless argument, it is essential to re-examine the practical value of corporate compliance. Like any other model of corporate governance, a compliance management system is designed to prevent specific risks and avert potential crises; it is no exception to this general rule. However, no matter how well-designed or rigorously implemented, no framework can eradicate all unlawful or non-compliant conduct—this is both an empirical fact and a matter of common sense. The key point, however, lies elsewhere: the fundamental purpose of establishing a compliance system is not to guarantee absolute legality, but to cultivate a governance model and compliance culture grounded in legality and regulatory responsibility. Its core objectives are to prevent compliance risks to the greatest extent possible, enable the timely and accurate detection of violations, and ensure proportionate and effective institutional responses to misconduct. In fulfilling these functions, compliance activates an internal mechanism of self-regulation, self-correction, and self-improvement. Under such a mechanism, systemic violations at the organizational level can be effectively curbed, and the likelihood of incurring vicarious or joint liability for misconduct by affiliated individuals can be substantially reduced. Even when violations occur, companies with sound compliance systems can conduct internal investigations, voluntarily disclose relevant facts, and initiate self-reporting—practices that markedly reduce the recurrence of similar misconduct. Moreover, through the gradual and sustained refinement of compliance systems, enterprises progressively close institutional loopholes and address latent risks, moving toward more mature and resilient governance structures. Over time, this institutional evolution tends to earn regulatory and judicial leniency—representing tangible, measurable benefits of compliance.

Finally, some may question whether regulatory authorities, in cases involving corporate misconduct, apply enforcement standards inconsistently—offering leniency to companies that pledge to establish compliance systems, while imposing harsher penalties on those that do not. Such differential treatment may be viewed as resulting in unequal enforcement or judicial outcomes and could be criticized as contravening the fundamental principle of equality before the law.

The so-called unfairness of compliance incentives argument fails to appreciate the distinctive normative value of corporate compliance. Enterprises that acknowledge their misconduct and undertake meaningful compliance commitments demonstrate a clear posture of remorse by cooperating with investigations and accepting legal responsibility. In doing so, they actively engage in remedial efforts to mitigate or reverse the harm caused by their violations, thereby restoring the legal interests that had been damaged. Through substantive compliance reforms, these companies rectify institutional deficiencies and managerial blind spots, significantly reducing the risk of repeated violations. Against this background, regulatory leniency—or even exemption from administrative penalties—granted to such enterprises is both legally justified and normatively sound. By contrast, enterprises that commit similar violations but refuse to acknowledge wrongdoing, fail to cooperate with enforcement authorities, neglect to implement any remedial measures, and take no steps toward structural reform remain at high risk of reoffending. Imposing more severe penalties on such non-compliant and uncooperative entities fully comports with the principle of proportionality in public law.

Overall, whether it is the "high-cost compliance" argument, the "compliance is useless" critique, or the claim that "compliance incentives are unfair," these objections each reflect only one dimension of a complex issue, while overlooking—or even dismissing—the essential value of corporate compliance. Compliance is not a flawless model of corporate governance, nor are compliance incentive mechanisms a fully matured regulatory paradigm. However, compared to traditional governance approaches, corporate compliance systems exhibit distinct and irreplaceable advantages. Likewise, relative to conventional modes of regulation, incentive-based compliance mechanisms can stimulate internal regulatory commitment and help remedy the persistent problem of external regulatory failure. Compliance may not constitute the optimal model of corporate governance, but it remains a governance approach that effectively mitigates compliance risks. Likewise, it may fall short of being the ideal regulatory framework, yet it functions as an incentive-based mechanism that produces fewer adverse effects and imposes lower overall costs.

CHAPTER 3

Principles of Corporate Compliance Management

3.1 Introduction

Corporate compliance is an internal control system oriented toward the prevention and mitigation of legal and regulatory risks. Through the establishment of a structured compliance management framework, enterprises can reduce or avoid unlawful and non-compliant behavior, develop long-term safeguards against compliance risks, and foster a corporate culture grounded in legality and regulatory adherence. Compliance initiatives may be categorized into two types based on the timing of their implementation: *routine compliance management system* and *crisis-responsive compliance remediation mechanism*. The former—also known as *ex ante compliance* or *autonomous compliance*—is undertaken in the absence of known violations, typically to enhance competitive advantage and expand access to business opportunities. The latter—referred to as *ex post compliance*—is undertaken following legal or regulatory violations and the commencement of regulatory investigations, functioning as a remedial mechanism aimed at securing leniency from enforcement authorities and avoiding severe legal, financial, or reputational consequences.

As a general rule, in the absence of external regulatory pressure, sanctions, or disciplinary incentives, compliance management systems established by enterprises often lack uniform evaluation criteria and are not subject to mandatory assessments or independent third-party verification. Consequently, such systems frequently fail to achieve effective control over compliance risks. By contrast, once enforcement proceedings are initiated by regulatory agencies or international financial institutions, the implicated enterprise not only faces potential administrative penalties, criminal liability, or financial sanctions, but must also undergo compliance inspections, evaluations, and certification procedures imposed by the competent authorities. In such circumstances, enterprises typically strive to meet the remediation requirements prescribed by the reviewing body and to align with its established compliance standards. In this

R. Chen, *An Introduction to Corporate Compliance*,
https://doi.org/10.1007/978-981-95-7257-1_3

sense, a ***routine compliance management system*** primarily addresses the challenge of building a compliance framework ***from nothing to something***, whereas a ***crisis-responsive compliance remediation mechanism*** is directed toward transforming that framework ***from ineffective to effective***.

The concept of "effective compliance management," also known as an "effective compliance program," refers to the set of compliance risk control objectives established by administrative authorities, judicial bodies, or international financial institutions for enterprises under investigation. In order to achieve the goal of effectively controlling compliance risks, such enterprises must put in place an internal control system that enables the proactive prevention of violations, continuous monitoring of business operations, and appropriate responses to unlawful or non-compliant conduct. To date, many countries have codified the key components of effective compliance management within their legal and regulatory frameworks. Likewise, a number of international compliance instruments have set forth the core features of an effective compliance program. However, these laws and instruments tend to focus on specific procedural or managerial elements, while failing to sufficiently articulate the overarching principles and normative foundations of effective compliance management.[1] Although the laws and regulations of certain jurisdictions purport to establish the "basic principles of effective compliance," these so-called principles often consist of specific institutional mechanisms and procedural requirements—such as due diligence, risk assessment, compliance communication and awareness-raising, and compliance auditing and monitoring—which are operational in nature and fall short of constituting fundamental normative guidelines for compliance governance.

For instance, U.K. anti-bribery legislation articulates the "Six Principles of Adequate Procedures" and recognizes them as a statutory defense available to implicated enterprises. However, several of these principles represent concrete managerial practices rather than overarching normative standards that inform the structural design and governance philosophy of compliance systems.[2] Similarly, although French law has defined key components of anti-corruption

[1] For example, the *Compliance Management Systems—Requirements with Guidance for Use* (ISO 37301), issued by the International Organization for Standardization (ISO) in 2021, states that an organization's compliance management system should reflect its "values, objectives, strategy, and compliance risks" and "take into account the organization's context." On this basis, such a system should adhere to fundamental principles, including "good governance," "proportionality," "integrity," "transparency," "accountability," and "sustainability." See Research Task Force on Corporate Compliance in Criminal Cases, *Case Handling Manual on Corporate Compliance in Criminal Proceedings* (Beijing: China Procuratorial Press), 399.

[2] The six principles of "adequate procedures" established in the *Bribery Act 2010 Guidance* issued by the U.K. Ministry of Justice in 2011 were reaffirmed in the *Criminal Finances Act 2017 Guidance*, and later adopted as general criteria for assessing compliance effectiveness in the *Corporate Compliance Evaluation Handbook* issued by the Serious Fraud Office (SFO) in 2020. These six principles include: proportionality, top-level commitment, risk assessment, due diligence, communication (including training), and monitoring and review. See Ruihua Chen, *The Chinese Experience of Effective Compliance* (Beijing: Peking University Press, 2023), 270–274.

compliance and subsequently introduced a core concept along with three institutional pillars, these provisions primarily enumerate concrete compliance mechanisms and fall short of articulating the underlying normative principles that guide effective compliance governance.[3] Likewise, the 1991 revision of the United States' *Federal Sentencing Guidelines* introduced seven elements of an effective compliance program, and since 2019, the U.S. Department of Justice has released the *Evaluation of Corporate Compliance Programs*, which sets forth principal criteria for evaluating program effectiveness. Nevertheless, neither the enumerated elements nor the articulated benchmarks can be regarded as fundamental normative principles in the strict sense underlying effective compliance management.[4]

Since the "ZTE incident" in 2018, Chinese regulatory authorities have progressively established a diversified compliance oversight regime in areas such as anti-monopoly enforcement, securities regulation, data governance, and anti-money laundering. This emerging regime integrates compliance guidance, mandatory compliance obligations, and incentive-based compliance mechanisms, aiming to promote the development of effective corporate compliance systems through a combination of administrative directives and regulatory pressure. Concurrently, under the guidance and supervision of State-owned Assets Supervision and Administration Commissions (SASACs) at various

[3] The *Sapin II Law*, enacted by the French Parliament in 2016, established seven core elements of corporate compliance programs: (1) a code of conduct; (2) an internal whistleblowing system; (3) risk assessments; (4) internal and external accounting controls; (5) a training program; (6) disciplinary procedures; and (7) internal monitoring and evaluation mechanisms. The *French Anti-Corruption Guidelines*, issued in 2020, aimed to provide companies with the necessary measures and procedures to raise awareness, prevent, detect, and sanction corruption-related offenses. The guidelines designate the principle of proportionality as a central tenet and outline three structural pillars of anti-corruption compliance: (1) top management commitment to anti-corruption; (2) risk identification; and (3) risk management. See Ruihua Chen, *The Chinese Experience of Effective Compliance* (Beijing: Peking University Press, 2023), 278–279.

[4] According to the 1991 revised U.S. Federal Sentencing Guidelines, an effective compliance program is not only an important basis for prosecutors to decide whether to prosecute a corporate defendant, but also a reference for judges when sentencing criminal corporations. The guidelines list the "general standards" for effective compliance: (1) establish compliance standards and procedures to reasonably prevent criminal conduct; (2) have corporate leaders and governing bodies (board of directors) monitor and manage the compliance program; (3) exclude individuals with prior illegal conduct or non-compliance with effective procedures from corporate compliance functions; (4) communicate corporate compliance policies and standards to employees through training and other means; (5) establish reasonable measures to ensure effective compliance, such as monitoring, auditing, and reporting systems to detect criminal conduct; (6) establish disciplinary mechanisms to strictly enforce compliance standards; and (7) continuously improve and update the compliance program. In April 2019, the U.S. Department of Justice, Criminal Division, issued the *Evaluation of Corporate Compliance Programs*, which, through multiple revisions, established three key elements of an effective compliance program: (1) the company has a well-designed written compliance program, considered a prerequisite for effectiveness; (2) the program is properly implemented and enforced within the organization; (3) mechanisms exist to effectively detect, correct, and report violations. See Ruihua Chen, *The Fundamentals of Corporate Compliance*, 3rd ed. (Beijing: Law Press, 2022), 102–109.

administrative levels, state-owned enterprises (SOEs) have actively pursued the construction of autonomous compliance frameworks. Central SOEs have taken the lead in building preliminary comprehensive compliance systems, and an increasing number of provincial-level SOEs have initiated their own compliance infrastructure programs.

With the active promotion of China's relevant regulatory authorities, the concept of effective compliance management has gradually taken root and has been incorporated into an expanding body of laws, regulations, and normative policy documents. Nevertheless, a critical question remains: In the course of compliance remediation, what fundamental principles should an implicated enterprise adhere to in order to achieve the objectives of effective compliance? Although certain documents enumerate guiding principles—such as proportionality and top-level commitment—they generally stop short of offering a systematic framework or comprehensive interpretation of these principles. The requirements for effective compliance remediation, as outlined in these materials, continue to center on operational aspects—namely, the construction of specific compliance mechanisms and procedural arrangements. Compliance guidelines and compliance management measures issued by regulatory agencies tend to focus primarily on enumerating institutional systems, organizational structures, and operational workflows, while offering little in the way of articulation or synthesis of the foundational principles underpinning effective compliance governance.[5] As a consequence, when regulators impose mandatory compliance obligations or evaluate the outcomes of a company's remediation efforts, there is often no clearly defined baseline against which the effectiveness of compliance can be measured. This results in excessive administrative discretion in the evaluation and acceptance of compliance remediation.

In light of the foregoing, this chapter undertakes a preliminary examination of the fundamental principles of effective compliance management. Drawing on a critical review of compliance legislation in selected jurisdictions, relevant international instruments, and practical experience from both autonomous compliance programs and crisis-driven compliance remediation, the author proposes six foundational principles of effective compliance governance. These principles are discussed in terms of their normative content, operational requirements, and practical application. Any effective compliance management

[5] In 2018, China's National Development and Reform Commission (NDRC), in collaboration with several other agencies, issued the *Guidelines for Compliance Management in Overseas Operations of Enterprises*, which established three fundamental principles for corporate compliance management: (1) independence, (2) practicality, and (3) comprehensiveness. In 2022, the State-owned Assets Supervision and Administration Commission of the State Council (SASAC) promulgated the *Administrative Measures for Compliance Management of Central State-Owned Enterprises*, which, while emphasizing the political orientation of compliance management, laid out key principles such as "comprehensive coverage," "clear division of responsibilities," and "pragmatic efficiency" for central SOEs. See Ruihua Chen, *Fundamentals of Corporate Compliance*, 2nd ed. (Beijing: Law Press, 2021), 467; see also *Administrative Measures for Compliance Management of Central State-Owned Enterprises* (SASAC, 2022), art. 5.

system should adhere to six minimum principles: the risk-based principle, the proportionality principle, the top-level commitment principle, the authority principle, the business process integration principle, and the sustainability principle. Only by meeting the requirements of these principles can an enterprise build an effective compliance management framework—or complete a substantive compliance remediation process—capable of ensuring that the system effectively prevents, detects, and mitigates compliance risks.

3.2 The Risk-Based Principle

Currently, under the guidance of administrative regulatory authorities, numerous state-owned enterprises (SOEs) in China have undertaken the development of compliance management systems. These initiatives are informed by the concept of *comprehensive compliance*, which prioritizes the establishment of a corporate governance model grounded in strict adherence to applicable laws and regulations. This model typically begins with a systematic review of a wide range of normative sources, including national legislation, administrative regulations, policy guidelines, international legal instruments, internal corporate rules, industry-specific standards, and professional codes of ethics. Based on this review, enterprises identify their compliance obligations. They then assess key areas of compliance risk in accordance with their business operations and industry context, and accordingly develop a compliance management system that covers all business processes, personnel, and operational activities.

This management-based model of compliance, while offering distinct advantages during the initial stages of system development, enables companies to mobilize institutional resources and rapidly establish top-down compliance frameworks to ensure implementation. However, from the standpoint of effective compliance management, this approach suffers from several structural shortcomings, including rigidity, mechanical execution, and operational inefficiency. It often fails to reflect the actual distribution of compliance risks across the enterprise or to accommodate the need for context-specific, scenario-based governance. As a result, it proves inadequate for the targeted prevention of unlawful or non-compliant conduct. In view of these limitations, a growing number of enterprises have adopted a risk-based approach to compliance.[6]

Unlike the management-based concept of compliance, the risk-based compliance principle originated in the course of compliance remediation undertaken by enterprises involved in legal proceedings and was later gradually adopted in the establishment of routine compliance management systems by many enterprises. As a general practice, when investigating enterprises suspected of violations of laws or regulations, both administrative regulatory authorities and international financial institutions often require the establishment of a targeted compliance program. Such compliance management follows

[6] ZTE Corporation, *Compliance Creates Value: ZTE's Compliance Practice* (Beijing: Law Press, 2023), 7–8.

the "risk-based" approach, which emphasizes, with the aim of effectively preventing the recurrence of identical or similar unlawful or criminal conduct, targeted institutional corrections based on an assessment of the compliance risks associated with the specific type of suspected misconduct, and subsequently the introduction of a targeted compliance management framework.

Numerous international compliance instruments and legal frameworks have entrenched the risk-based principle as a cornerstone of effective compliance management. A notable example is the International Organization for Standardization's *Compliance Management Systems—Requirements with Guidance for Use* (ISO 37301:2021), which explicitly requires organizations to "adopt a risk-based approach" and identifies compliance risk assessment as a foundational component of a compliance management system. The standard distinguishes between inherent compliance risk and residual compliance risk and mandates that organizations conduct compliance risk identification—including the identification of sources of compliance risk, the assignment of compliance risk levels, and the maintenance of both a compliance risk source register and a compliance risk level register. ISO 37301 further requires that compliance risk assessments be updated whenever significant changes occur, such as business model adjustments, organizational restructuring, major external developments, changes in compliance obligations, mergers and acquisitions, or the detection of non-compliance. Adopting a zero-tolerance stance toward non-compliance, the standard emphasizes the need to allocate limited resources and efforts to high-risk compliance matters as a priority, progressively extending management and oversight to the full spectrum of identified compliance risks.[7]

The United States was one of the earliest jurisdictions to develop formal standards for evaluating the effectiveness of corporate compliance programs. In its Evaluation of Corporate Compliance Programs, the U.S. Department of Justice regards the existence of a risk-assessment mechanism as a primary indicator of whether a compliance program is well-designed. Prosecutors begin by understanding the company's business, and then evaluate how the company has identified, assessed, and defined its risk profile, the extent of scrutiny applied, and the resources devoted to managing those risks. Regarding risk identification, prosecutors assess whether the company has analyzed and addressed risks derived from factors such as the location of its operations, industry sector, market competitiveness, regulatory environment, potential clients and business partners, use of third parties, gifts, travel and entertainment, and charitable and political contributions. As for the risk-assessment process, prosecutors evaluate the effectiveness of the company's risk assessment, how

[7] Research Task Force on Corporate Compliance in Criminal Cases under the Supreme People's Procuratorate of China, Case Handling Manual on Corporate Compliance in Criminal Proceedings (Beijing: China Procuratorial Press, 2022), 425–427.

the compliance program has been tailored based on that risk assessment, and whether the criteria are periodically updated.[8]

The United Kingdom's anti-bribery legislation sets out six "Principles of Adequate Procedures" as the foundation of effective compliance management. The third of these, the Risk Assessment Principle, requires companies to regularly evaluate the nature and severity of both internal and external bribery risks. This includes organization-wide risk assessments conducted at the senior management level, the allocation of adequate resources, the identification of relevant internal and external information sources, the performance of due diligence, and the accurate documentation of both the assessment process and its findings.[9]

France's 2016 anti-corruption legislation identified risk assessment as one of the seven essential components of effective compliance management. It requires companies to identify, analyze, and classify bribery risks based on their industry and geographic areas of operation, and to conduct periodic reassessments of these risks. The 2020 *French Anti-Corruption Guidelines* further refined this framework by designating risk identification and risk management as two core institutional pillars of effective compliance programs. *Risk identification* involves the use of diagnostic tools to detect, assess, and categorize corruption risks faced by the enterprise, followed by the implementation of graded risk control measures. *Risk management* refers to the adoption of appropriate procedures and controls to address identified risks, with the objective of preventing and detecting conduct that breaches the code of ethics or may constitute corruption, as well as enforcing appropriate sanctions where warranted.[10]

China's administrative regulatory authorities have increasingly emphasized compliance risk assessment, recognizing it as a foundational element of effective compliance management. For example, the *Administrative Measures for the Compliance Management of Central State-Owned Enterprises*, issued by the State-owned Assets Supervision and Administration Commission of the State Council (SASAC), defines compliance management as a governance activity aimed at the effective prevention and control of compliance risks. Under these Measures, enterprises are required to establish mechanisms for the identification, assessment, and early warning of compliance risks. This includes conducting systematic reviews of potential risks in business operations and management, establishing and regularly updating a compliance risk database, and analyzing the likelihood of occurrence, degree of impact, and potential consequences of such risks. Enterprises are further expected to issue timely warnings for risks that are particularly representative, widespread, or likely to result in serious consequences. In 2018, the National Development and Reform Commission

[8] Ruihua Chen, "Basic Standards for Effective Compliance Programs," *China Lawyer*, no. 9 (2019).

[9] Ruihua Chen, "The UK Bribery Act and Corporate Compliance," *China Lawyer*, no. 3 (2019).

[10] Ruihua Chen, "The Sapin II Law and Corporate Compliance in France," *China Lawyer*, no. 5 (2019); see also Ruihua Chen, "Standards of Effective Compliance in French Anti-Corruption Cases," *Qiaoqiao Legal Insight* (WeChat blog), June 29, 2022.

(NDRC), in coordination with other government agencies, issued the *Guidelines on Compliance Management for Enterprises Operating Overseas*, which likewise designate the identification, assessment, and management of compliance risks as key components of corporate compliance governance. According to the Guidelines, compliance risk identification refers to the process through which enterprises—focusing on key positions and core business functions—identify risks by means of internal compliance consultations, audits, performance evaluations, and internal investigations of misconduct, or by monitoring changes in external regulatory requirements. Based on the risks identified, enterprises are expected to conduct compliance risk assessments by analyzing the causes and sources of violations, the likelihood of occurrence, and the potential severity of consequences. They must also determine appropriate risk assessment criteria and prioritize risk management measures in light of their size, strategic objectives, market environment, and overall risk profile. For each category of identified and assessed risk, enterprises are required to establish and maintain sound risk response systems, including the implementation of appropriate control and remediation measures.[11]

While the aforementioned regulatory documents consistently emphasize the importance of compliance risk assessment and risk identification—recognizing them as key operational components of compliance management—they have thus far remained at the level of technical or procedural mechanisms, without being elevated to the status of foundational principles of effective compliance. From the perspective of building a genuinely effective compliance governance system, it is imperative to critically reflect on the dominant management-based model and, in its place, affirm the risk-based principle as a core normative standard that underpins compliance management.

Under the risk-based principle, corporate compliance should not be narrowly defined as mere rule adherence or lawful business conduct; rather, it should be understood as a form of corporate governance aimed at the effective prevention and control of compliance risks. In this framework, compliance risks are best conceptualized as strategic risks—on par with decision-making risk, operational risk, and financial risk. Such risks typically take the form of administrative penalties, criminal prosecution, or international financial sanctions, all of which share a common and particularly severe consequence: disqualification from market access. Disqualification consequences may include the suspension or revocation of business operations, special licenses, operating qualifications, or business permits; exclusion from public procurement or bidding processes; ineligibility for loans; delisting from stock exchanges; or the cancellation of business licenses. By contrast, general economic losses, reputational harm, or other minor adverse effects resulting from legal or regulatory violations should not, in themselves, be classified as compliance risks. It is

[11] Ruihua Chen, *Fundamentals of Corporate Compliance*, 2nd ed. (Beijing: Law Press, 2021), 471; *Administrative Measures for Compliance Management of Central State-Owned Enterprises* (SASAC, 2022), art. 20.

precisely the need to avoid these disqualification-related outcomes—arising from administrative, criminal, or cross-border enforcement actions—that elevates compliance risk to a matter of strategic significance. As such, compliance management becomes not merely a regulatory function but a form of strategic management, and emerges as a key issue in contemporary corporate governance.

In accordance with the risk-based principle, enterprises should avoid undertaking overly broad or unfocused inventories of compliance obligations. Instead, compliance risk assessment must be treated as the foundational task of compliance management. First, consistent with the concept of effective compliance management, enterprises should engage in scientifically grounded risk identification by distinguishing between abstract and concrete compliance risks. Through the evaluation of concrete risks, companies can identify real, imminent, and potentially consequential sources of systemic compliance risk—such as high-risk business operations, vulnerable personnel, and critical control points that may result in significant legal, financial, or reputational losses. Second, once these risk sources have been identified, enterprises should carry out a detailed analysis of their likelihood of occurrence, potential scope of impact, degree of severity, and the magnitude of their adverse consequences. Third, based on this analytical process, enterprises should assign a risk level to each identified risk, develop a risk ranking system, and adopt differentiated compliance management measures that correspond to the severity and probability of each risk.

Pursuant to the risk-based principle, enterprises should develop targeted compliance programs organized around discrete and clearly defined compliance risks. For such specialized compliance initiatives to be effectively implemented, two foundational components are required: (1) a general compliance management platform and (2) specialized compliance management elements. The general platform comprises the core structural features that support the regular operation of the overall compliance management system. These typically include a corporate compliance charter, a designated compliance leadership body, and a structured internal compliance organization, as well as three interrelated subsystems that support the effective operation of the compliance management framework: a risk prevention system, comprising compliance risk assessments, due diligence procedures, compliance training programs, declarations of compliance commitment, and internal communication and awareness initiatives; a risk monitoring system, incorporating compliance reporting mechanisms, whistleblower channels, compliance investigations, and audit procedures; and a risk response system, consisting of internal investigations, disciplinary measures, and institutional remediation mechanisms. By contrast, the specialized elements refer to risk-specific compliance measures tailored to address a particular category of compliance risk. These may include specialized codes of conduct, standards, and procedural protocols; dedicated employee handbooks; tailored compliance training programs and written statements of commitment; and risk-control mechanisms embedded within specific business processes.

Under the risk-based principle, both the regulatory assessment of compliance remediation undertaken by implicated enterprises and the proactive establishment of compliance management systems by non-implicated enterprises should adopt the effective prevention and control of compliance risks as the primary benchmark. For enterprises subject to regulatory investigations or enforcement actions, effective risk control refers to the demonstrable prevention of the recurrence of identical or similar misconduct. For enterprises not under investigation, it encompasses the ability to prevent the occurrence of unlawful or non-compliant conduct, to monitor the legality of business operations, and to respond to and remediate violations promptly and effectively. In the case of implicated enterprises, only where regulators determine that remediation efforts meet this standard may leniency or compliance-related incentives be granted. For non-implicated enterprises, only those that have achieved the stated objectives of compliance risk control will be considered to have satisfied relevant regulatory requirements and fulfilled their compliance management obligations.

3.3 The Principle of Proportionality

To build an effective compliance management system, enterprises should avoid the trap of a "one-size-fits-all" compliance program. Practical experience demonstrates that implementing an overly broad or rigidly standardized compliance framework—without taking into account factors such as organizational size, business model, industry-specific characteristics, and distinct compliance risk exposures—rarely achieves the objective of effective risk prevention and control. Such undifferentiated programs fail to distinguish between high-risk and low-risk areas, leading to the inefficient allocation of scarce compliance resources across all operations. As a result, enterprises are often unable to conduct risk-based due diligence proportionate to the scale and risk profile of specific transactions, and are ill-equipped to prevent unlawful or non-compliant conduct in high-risk sectors.

To achieve effective compliance management and avoid reducing compliance to a mere formality, enterprises must incorporate the principle of proportionality into the design and implementation of their compliance systems. According to this principle, companies should identify, assess, and manage compliance risks based on their specific characteristics—including organizational size, business operations, industry sector, governance structure, corporate culture, and risk exposure—and establish a compliance management framework that is proportionate to those risks. At the same time, regulatory authorities, judicial institutions, and international financial organizations overseeing the compliance remediation of implicated enterprises should also adhere to this principle. They should require companies to establish compliance structures that are aligned with the objectives of effective compliance, allocate compliance resources such as personnel and funding based on the principle of necessity, and design mechanisms for risk prevention, monitoring, and response in accordance with the principle of proportionality.

From the perspective of achieving effective compliance, the *principle of proportionality* comprises two specific dimensions: the *positive* and the *negative* proportionality principles. The positive aspect requires enterprises to invest adequate resources and establish necessary compliance management structures in the course of building their compliance systems. The goal is to meet the fundamental requirements of effective compliance remediation—namely, to prevent violations of laws and regulations and to cultivate a corporate culture of lawful and rule-based operations. By contrast, the negative proportionality principle emphasizes restraint: enterprises should limit their compliance-related investments and institutional arrangements to what is necessary for achieving effective outcomes. This means selecting management mechanisms that impose the least possible burden and cost on the enterprise, while still ensuring that the resources and systems deployed remain proportionate to the actual compliance risks they are intended to address.

On the one hand, a corporate compliance management system should observe the *principle of necessity*—meaning that, provided it can effectively prevent and control compliance risks, the enterprise should, wherever possible, adopt institutional arrangements that minimize harm, reduce burdens, or involve relatively lenient sanctions. On the other hand, under a narrow interpretation of the principle of proportionality, the configuration of a compliance program—including the establishment of compliance departments, allocation of compliance personnel, setting of evaluation timelines, designation of compliance monitors, and deployment of other compliance resources—should be commensurate with the enterprise's size, scope of operations, industry characteristics, the seriousness of the alleged misconduct, and the level of compliance risk involved. As a general rule, the larger the enterprise and the higher its risk profile, the more formalized, standardized, and sophisticated its compliance framework should be. Conversely, smaller enterprises with lower risk exposure should not be subjected to unduly stringent compliance requirements, as such demands may impose disproportionate compliance burdens. Excessive or unnecessary compliance obligations of this nature constitute "over-compliance" and run counter to the principle of proportionality.[12]

The principle of proportionality has been incorporated into the legal frameworks of numerous jurisdictions and is widely recognized as a foundational norm for effective compliance management. For example, under U.K. law, the *principle of proportionate procedures* is established as the primary element of the "adequate procedures" defense in anti-bribery compliance. This principle requires that the measures adopted by a commercial organization to prevent associated persons from engaging in bribery be *proportionate* to the level of bribery risk it faces, and to the nature, size, and complexity of the

[12] Ruihua Chen, "The Principle of Proportionality in Corporate Compliance Remediation," *Journal of Comparative Law*, no. 1 (2023).

organization's operations. These procedures must be clear, practical, accessible, and capable of being effectively implemented. More specifically, a compliance program aimed at preventing criminal misconduct should adopt a risk-based approach, under which the organization conducts a comprehensive internal risk assessment to ensure that its compliance measures are proportionate and tailored to the specific risks it faces. At the same time, recognizing that enterprises differ in the nature of their business activities, organizational scale, and operational complexity—and consequently in the types and degrees of compliance risks they encounter—each enterprise should develop a compliance management framework that corresponds to these defining characteristics.[13]

Similarly, the *French Anti-Corruption Guidelines* identify the *principle of proportionality* as a central pillar of corporate anti-corruption compliance.[14] Under this principle, enterprises are required to develop their anti-corruption compliance programs based on the specific risk profile they face. Such risks are shaped by a range of factors, including the nature of the company's operations; the types of products or services offered; its governance structure, organizational size, business divisions, geographic presence; and the categories of third-party business partners involved. To give effect to the proportionality principle, senior management is expected to allocate anti-corruption resources appropriately in line with the organization's risk exposure, in order to ensure the effective design, implementation, and oversight of the measures and procedures comprising the anti-corruption program. Moreover, in response to any conduct that violates the guidelines or qualifies as corrupt behavior, senior management must impose disciplinary measures that are both appropriate and proportionate to the misconduct in question.

Likewise, U.S. regulatory and enforcement authorities apply the *principle of proportionality* in guiding the compliance remediation efforts of corporate violators. Both the Department of Justice (DOJ) and the Securities and Exchange Commission (SEC) require companies to design compliance programs tailored to their specific needs, risk profiles, and operational challenges. An effective program must be grounded in a comprehensive risk assessment and should allocate compliance resources in a manner proportionate to the level and nature of the identified risks. In doing so, companies are expected to establish calibrated mechanisms for risk prevention, monitoring, and response, ensuring that compliance controls correspond appropriately to the scope and severity of the risks they are intended to mitigate.

In applying the principle of proportionality, U.S. prosecutors typically evaluate whether a company has allocated adequate compliance personnel and resources commensurate with its size, organizational structure, and risk exposure. When reviewing a company's risk assessment, prosecutors encourage the

[13] Yuanhuang Zhang et al., eds., *Global Survey on Corporate Compliance* (Beijing: Peking University Press, 2021), 95–96.

[14] Ruihua Chen, "Standards of Effective Compliance in French Anti-Corruption Cases," *Qiaoqiao Legal Insight* (WeChat blog), June 29, 2022.

targeted allocation of greater resources to higher-risk areas and expect timely adjustments to compliance procedures—such as due diligence processes and internal audits—as the company's risk landscape evolves. In determining whether to appoint an independent compliance monitor, prosecutors take into account whether the company has already implemented a compliance program or established internal control mechanisms. In cases where the company voluntarily discloses misconduct, cooperates with enforcement authorities, and commits to improving its internal controls, prosecutors may decline to impose a monitor. Instead, the company may be permitted to conduct self-monitoring, subject to periodic reporting on its compliance efforts.[15]

In the course of advancing compliance remediation, Chinese regulatory authorities have preliminarily recognized the principle of proportionality as a fundamental guideline for the development, evaluation, and review of corporate compliance programs. As a general rule, enterprises are expected to establish and progressively expand targeted compliance programs in response to changes in their organizational scale, business scope, and industry characteristics, thereby promoting the transition toward comprehensive compliance frameworks. In light of the specific nature of the alleged criminal misconduct, regulatory authorities should require enterprises to formulate targeted compliance programs designed to ensure that compliance remediation measures effectively prevent the recurrence of the same or similar unlawful conduct.

Furthermore, with respect to the allocation of compliance resources, implicated enterprises should establish compliance structures or designate compliance personnel in a manner proportionate to their organizational type, size, business scope, and industry characteristics. Based on the enterprise's specific circumstances—and provided that effective compliance remediation is ensured—such arrangements may include the establishment of a dedicated compliance department with full-time staff, the appointment of part-time compliance officers, or the engagement of external professionals to fulfill compliance responsibilities.

Moreover, compliance assessment authorities should, in line with the requirements for effective compliance evaluation and with reference to industry-specific assessment benchmarks, develop an *assessment index framework* tailored to the actual circumstances of the implicated enterprise. The weighting of individual indicators should be determined by factors such as the enterprise's type, size, scope of operations, industry characteristics, and the seriousness of the alleged misconduct. Particular emphasis should be placed on assigning greater weight to indicators covering critical compliance areas, structural vulnerabilities, and high-risk positions.

Finally, in view of the particular constraints faced by small and micro-sized enterprises—especially their limited capacity to allocate compliance resources—regulatory authorities should establish simplified compliance remediation

[15] Ruihua Chen, *The Chinese Experience of Effective Compliance* (Beijing: Peking University Press, 2023), 290–297.

requirements that are distinct from those applied to larger enterprises. For instance, regulators may conduct a direct review of the compliance plans and remediation reports submitted by such enterprises, without imposing additional procedural burdens. This review should primarily assess whether compliance commitments have been fulfilled, whether the compliance plan has been effectively implemented, and whether the compliance remediation measures taken have achieved substantive results.

3.4 The Principle of Top-Level Commitment

As an internal control framework designed to prevent and mitigate strategic risks, a corporate compliance management system is inherently vulnerable to being rendered ineffective or relegated to a purely nominal role. On the one hand, even a compliance program that appears comprehensive on paper will remain superficial unless it is supported by a genuine, organization-wide culture of compliance. If managers at various levels—driven by the imperative of maximizing economic returns—explicitly or implicitly encourage employees to engage in unlawful or non-compliant conduct, or tolerate such conduct by business units, subsidiaries, or third-party partners, the program will inevitably degenerate into a mere box-ticking exercise. On the other hand, if senior leadership fails to take the effective implementation of compliance measures seriously—whether by withholding adequate human and financial resources or by neglecting to lead by example in promoting a culture of integrity and compliance—the compliance function will risk being sidelined whenever operational departments question or resist its authority. In such circumstances, the compliance system will be incapable of fulfilling its essential purpose: to prevent, detect, and control compliance risks in a meaningful and sustainable manner.

To prevent the aforementioned problems, enterprises should incorporate the *principle of top-level commitment* into their compliance management systems and treat it as a foundational institutional safeguard for ensuring effective compliance governance. This principle emphasizes the leadership, oversight, and promotional role played by the board of directors and senior executives (collectively referred to as "top management") in the enterprise's compliance governance efforts. A key question, then, is: what are the specific responsibilities that top management assumes in the domain of compliance governance? The answer lies at the heart of understanding the scope and substance of the principle of top-level commitment. To accurately interpret this principle, it is essential to distinguish between *compliance governance* and *compliance management*. The former refers to the high-level responsibilities and commitments assumed by top management, while the latter concerns the day-to-day operational tasks carried out by dedicated compliance departments. The principle of top-level commitment does not require senior executives to micromanage compliance affairs or engage in every operational detail. Rather, it underscores the expectation that top management should treat compliance risks as strategic risks—equivalent in importance to decision-making risks, operational risks, and financial risks—and should integrate compliance governance into the company's overall strategic governance framework.

The principle of top-level commitment encompasses three interrelated dimensions. First, senior management bears the overarching responsibility for establishing and institutionalizing the corporate compliance management system. This entails spearheading the creation of an effective compliance governance structure, ensuring that the compliance framework is properly designed, implemented, and subject to continuous improvement. Second, top executives are charged with embedding a compliance culture across the organization. This involves making clear and demonstrable commitments to compliance governance, consistently communicating compliance values and expectations to employees, shareholders, subsidiaries, and external business partners, disseminating compliance knowledge, and providing regular and transparent reports on the performance and development of the compliance program. Third, senior leadership must safeguard the effective and sustainable functioning of the compliance system. This requires the allocation of adequate human, financial, and technological resources; sustained oversight to ensure that compliance controls are fully integrated into business operations; rigorous compliance review of proposed business activities; decisive rejection of projects or products that pose significant compliance risks; and the imposition of proportionate disciplinary measures against employees or managers who engage in unlawful, unethical, or non-compliant conduct.[16]

As a foundational principle for achieving effective compliance management, the principle of top-level commitment has been widely affirmed in international compliance frameworks and national legal systems. For instance, in April 2005, the Basel Committee on Banking Supervision released its document *Compliance and the Compliance Function in Banks*, which underscores that a compliance culture must originate at the highest levels of the organization. It affirms that compliance is most effective when the board of directors and senior management lead by example. Under the leadership and oversight of top executives, banks are expected to uphold elevated standards of compliance in all aspects of their operations, consistently seeking to align with both the letter and the spirit of the law.[17]

The *Compliance Management Systems—Requirements with Guidance for Use*, issued by the International Organization for Standardization (ISO), underscores that organizational compliance is achieved through top management's alignment of the organization's core values with recognized good governance principles, ethical requirements, and societal expectations. It places particular emphasis on three leadership responsibilities of top management: (1) demonstrating visible leadership and commitment to compliance; (2) establishing and maintaining a compliance policy that aligns with the standard's

[16] Ruihua Chen, "The Principle of Top-Level Commitment in Compliance Remediation," *Legal Science*, no. 3 (2023).

[17] Ruihua Chen, *Fundamentals of Corporate Compliance*, 2nd ed. (Beijing: Law Press, 2021), 450.

requirements; and (3) ensuring that compliance-related roles, responsibilities, and authorities are clearly defined, assigned, and effectively communicated across the organization.[18]

According to the *Evaluation of Corporate Compliance Programs* issued by the Criminal Division of the U.S. Department of Justice, an effective compliance program requires both senior and middle management to play an active role in creating and fostering a compliance culture. Prosecutors are directed to evaluate whether senior management has clearly and consistently articulated the company's ethical standards, communicated them accurately and without ambiguity, and exemplified those standards through their own conduct. They are likewise instructed to assess the extent to which middle management emphasizes compliance standards and encourages employees to adhere to them. In assessing the commitment of both senior and middle management, prosecutors should examine the leaders' actual conduct, their demonstrated commitment to compliance, and the effectiveness of their oversight in promoting and enforcing adherence to the company's compliance framework.[19]

Under U.K. law, the principle of top-level commitment is recognized as one of the six principles for establishing "adequate procedures" to prevent bribery, as set out in the *Bribery Act 2010 Guidance* issued by the U.K. Ministry of Justice. This principle requires senior management—including the board of directors, owners, and other equivalent bodies or individuals—to demonstrate a clear and genuine commitment to preventing bribery by persons associated with the organization. It further expects them to foster a compliance culture in which bribery is never acceptable.[20] Official guidance from U.K. authorities elaborates that, regardless of an organization's size, structure, or market position, top-level commitment is reflected in two main aspects: (1) senior management should communicate the organization's anti-bribery stance internally and externally; and (2) they should be actively and appropriately involved in developing, implementing, and overseeing anti-bribery procedures.[21]

Similar to the United Kingdom, France places strong emphasis on compliance oversight in the area of anti-corruption, recognizing senior management commitment, risk identification, and risk management as the three institutional pillars for the effective prevention of corruption.[22] In building an anti-corruption compliance framework, the commitment of senior executives to

[18] Research Task Force on Corporate Compliance in Criminal Cases under the Supreme People's Procuratorate of China, Case Handling Manual on Corporate Compliance in Criminal Proceedings (Beijing: China Procuratorial Press, 2022), 408–411.

[19] Ruihua Chen, "Basic Standards for Effective Compliance Programs: An Introduction to the U.S. DOJ's Evaluation of Corporate Compliance Programs," *China Lawyer*, no. 9 (2019).

[20] Yuanhuang Zhang et al., eds., *Global Survey on Corporate Compliance* (Beijing: Peking University Press, 2021), 95–96.

[21] Research Task Force on Corporate Compliance in Criminal Cases under the Supreme People's Procuratorate of China, Case Handling Manual on Corporate Compliance in Criminal Proceedings (Beijing: China Procuratorial Press, 2022), 449.

[22] Ruihua Chen, "Standards of Effective Compliance in French Anti-Corruption Cases," *Qiaoqiao Legal Insight* (WeChat blog), June 29, 2022.

anti-corruption—demonstrated through their execution of corporate responsibilities, leadership conduct, and day-to-day business practices—is regarded as the cornerstone of any effective anti-corruption program.

This commitment is demonstrated not only through senior management's determination to prevent and detect corruption within the organization, but also through the appropriate allocation of anti-corruption resources. Senior executives may either directly oversee the design, implementation, and monitoring of the anti-corruption program or delegate these responsibilities to qualified personnel, provided that such individuals report directly to top management. In doing so, senior leadership must ensure that delegated personnel possess the requisite knowledge—gained through prior experience or specialized training—are vested with sufficient authority, and are granted access to the information necessary to carry out their responsibilities. In addition, senior management is expected to review audit findings concerning the program's measures and procedures to ensure proper functioning. They should also take an active role in implementing key anti-corruption measures, communicate the company's anti-corruption program both internally and to external third-party partners, and affirm their unwavering commitment to ethical conduct and integrity. Finally, senior leadership must ensure that individuals who violate the code of conduct or engage in corrupt practices are subject to appropriate and proportionate disciplinary measures.[23]

Chinese regulatory authorities have increasingly recognized the importance of the principle of top-level commitment in promoting corporate compliance remediation and have gradually embedded this principle into the design of various institutional frameworks. In principle, senior corporate leadership is expected to play a central role in the compliance remediation process. First, companies are generally required to establish a compliance leadership team composed of the actual controller, principal executives, and directly responsible management personnel. Where appropriate, external professional institutions or experts may also be engaged to participate in or assist with the compliance process. Building on a comprehensive analysis and evaluation of the enterprise's compliance risks, the compliance leadership group shall formulate targeted compliance programs and establish corresponding internal policies and procedures. This institutional design, enshrined in authoritative regulatory instruments, formalizes the responsibility of senior leadership for establishing and guiding the organization's compliance governance structure. Second, the actual controller and principal executive of the enterprise must make an explicit compliance commitment within the targeted compliance programs, clearly affirming that compliance constitutes a core corporate value and that the enterprise adopts a zero-tolerance policy toward illegal and unethical conduct. They must ensure that compliance is embedded in the company's strategic objectives, development planning, and governance structures. This provision

[23] *The French Anti-Corruption Agency Guidelines*, https://www.agence-francaise-anticorruption.gouv.fr, accessed July 23, 2022.

establishes the responsibility of senior leadership for cultivating a compliance culture and designates the prevention of unlawful behavior as a foundational aim of the enterprise's compliance management framework. Third, enterprises are required to provide adequate human, financial, and material support to ensure the effective operation of the compliance management system. This includes staffing, training, internal communications, physical infrastructure, equipment, and funding. In addition, enterprises must establish a compliance performance appraisal mechanism that integrates compliance metrics into the evaluation of principal executives and other key personnel. These requirements establish a clear and normative basis for holding senior management accountable for the appropriate allocation of compliance-related resources.

3.5 The Principle of Authority

Traditionally, corporate legal departments have borne certain compliance responsibilities. However, these departments and their personnel often lack the institutional authority necessary to perform substantive compliance functions. In many cases, they are neither empowered to reject high-risk business activities nor authorized to investigate or discipline employees or managers who violate legal norms or internal compliance rules. This lack of enforcement capacity has weakened the influence of compliance management over both business operations and personnel matters, resulting in its progressive marginalization within the organization and undermining its effectiveness in identifying and mitigating compliance risks.

To avoid repeating the institutional shortcomings of traditional legal affairs departments and to ensure that the compliance function can genuinely fulfill its role in risk management, enterprises must ensure that the compliance department is endowed with real authority. This entails safeguarding its independence in performing its duties, granting it the power to oversee both business operations and personnel from a compliance perspective, and allocating resources proportionate to the scope and importance of its functions. This compliance governance concept may be concisely referred to as the *principle of authority*.

For example, according to the *Compliance Management Systems—Requirements with Guidance for Use (ISO 37301:2021)* issued by the International Organization for Standardization, effective performance of the compliance function requires the following safeguards: direct access of the compliance function to the governing body; independence of the compliance function, enabling it to operate autonomously (i.e., not being subject to interference from line management); appropriate authority of the compliance function to provide guidance, raise concerns, and promote compliance throughout the organization; adequate resources to establish, operate, maintain, and continually improve the compliance management system.[24]

The document *Compliance and the Compliance Function in Banks*, published by the Basel Committee on Banking Supervision, sets out ten key principles for managing compliance risk. Principles 5 and 6 underscore the independence of the compliance function and the need for adequate resources. Under these principles, the compliance function should have a formal and independent status within the bank and be headed by a compliance officer with authority to act independently and report to the board of directors—either directly or through a board committee. It should not be involved in the performance of activities it monitors, in order to avoid conflicts of interest. To fulfill its responsibilities, the compliance function should have the authority to access all records and information necessary for its work, to conduct investigations of possible breaches of compliance policy—either on its own or with external expert support—and to report its findings to senior management and, where necessary, directly to the board of directors. Furthermore, the bank should ensure that the compliance function is supported with adequate resources, including staff with the requisite qualifications and experience, and access to ongoing professional training and development.[25]

Chinese administrative regulatory authorities have also emphasized the importance of maintaining the independence of the compliance function, recognizing it as a fundamental principle of corporate compliance management. For instance, the *Guidelines on Compliance Management for Enterprises Engaged in Overseas Operations*, jointly issued by the National Development and Reform Commission (NDRC) and other relevant agencies, designate independence as one of the three core principles of compliance governance. In line with this principle, enterprises are required to ensure the structural independence of their compliance systems—particularly with respect to institutional design, organizational setup, personnel arrangements, and reporting lines—and to proactively prevent conflicts of interest to the greatest extent possible.[26]

From the perspective of achieving effective compliance management, the aforementioned documents and regulatory frameworks each highlight different aspects of compliance principles, but few have systematically defined the institutional authority of the compliance function in carrying out its responsibilities. In practice, for corporate compliance programs to function as effective mechanisms for preventing compliance risks, it is essential to implement the *principle of authority*. This principle consists of three core elements: *independence*, *prioritization*, and *adequate resourcing*.

[24] Research Task Force on Corporate Compliance in Criminal Cases under the Supreme People's Procuratorate of China, Case Handling Manual on Corporate Compliance in Criminal Proceedings (Beijing: China Procuratorial Press, 2022), 429.

[25] Ruihua Chen, *Fundamentals of Corporate Compliance*, 2nd ed. (Beijing: Law Press, 2021), 451–452.

[26] Ruihua Chen, *Fundamentals of Corporate Compliance*, 2nd ed. (Beijing: Law Press, 2021), 467.

First, *compliance independence* refers to the ability of the compliance function to operate autonomously—free from interference or restrictions by business units or other departments—while remaining under the overarching framework of top-level commitment. The head of compliance should occupy an independent position with the status of a senior executive. Whether serving as the chair of the compliance committee, the chief compliance officer (CCO), or the general counsel, the individual should not be assigned any decision-making, business, or financial management responsibilities that could compromise the compliance function. This separation of duties is essential to safeguarding the functional integrity and independence of the role. Enterprises should establish a relatively independent compliance department and a dedicated compliance team tasked exclusively with compliance management and not with business management activities that are inconsistent with the compliance function. In addition, a top-down compliance governance structure should be maintained to ensure clear lines of authority and accountability between the parent company and its subsidiaries, branches, departments, or field offices. This includes implementing a compliance oversight mechanism whereby the parent company's compliance department conducts inspections of subordinate compliance units, as well as an upward compliance reporting mechanism requiring lower-level compliance departments to report regularly to their superior compliance authority.

Second, the principle of *compliance priority* refers to the authoritative and determinative role that the compliance function must play in a company's decision-making processes, business activities, and management operations. Specifically, no major corporate decision should be made without undergoing a prior compliance review and receiving formal approval from the compliance department. In the operational domain, where business initiatives or product development plans present systemic compliance risks, the compliance department is authorized to raise objections and, if necessary, bypass business units to escalate the matter directly to top management. In such cases, the compliance department may recommend that the project be rejected or suspended pending senior-level review and authorization. Furthermore, where employees or senior executives are suspected of engaging in unlawful or non-compliant conduct, the compliance department has the authority to initiate an internal investigation. Upon verification of violations, the department may submit disciplinary recommendations to senior management for appropriate and proportionate sanctioning.

In particular, when addressing the disciplinary handling of individuals involved in unlawful or non-compliant conduct, enterprises must activate their internal compliance reporting and investigation mechanisms by establishing a comprehensive compliance inspection system. Designated compliance personnel should carry out prompt internal investigations and anti-fraud inquiries into suspected violations. These investigations serve two principal purposes: first, to ascertain the factual basis of the misconduct and to identify the internal structural factors that facilitated its occurrence; and second, to determine the specific employees and senior managers who bear direct responsibility. Based on the findings, appropriate accountability measures should be imposed, including reassignment, removal from office, or referral to judicial authorities for further legal action.

Finally, an effective compliance management system must ensure that the compliance function is supported by essential and sustainable resource guarantees. On the one hand, enterprises should ensure that compliance personnel are granted a level of authority and institutional standing commensurate with their responsibilities. For instance, the Chief Compliance Officer (CCO) should hold senior executive status and be entitled to attend top-level meetings, including those of the board of directors, supervisory board, and executive leadership team. Compliance officers at branch offices should occupy relatively senior positions, and part-time compliance representatives should be positioned at least at the deputy level within their respective departments or subsidiaries. On the other hand, enterprises must allocate adequate human, material, and financial resources to support compliance management, based on their organizational size, business scope, product profile, and risk exposure. In particular, companies should appoint full-time compliance personnel, including a sufficient number of specialized compliance officers, compliance coordinators, and compliance investigators, and ensure that an appropriate budget is earmarked to cover the operational needs of the compliance function.

3.6 The Principle of Business Process Integration

As a system for managing compliance risks, a compliance framework can fulfill its preventive, monitoring, and responsive functions only when it is deeply embedded within the enterprise's core business operations. However, many companies hastily adopt "comprehensive compliance" strategies by indiscriminately converting external legal and regulatory mandates into internal "compliance obligations" and then implementing a superficial form of "legal compliance management." Such practices often fail to conduct a rigorous and science-based identification and assessment of compliance risks specific to business activities, overlook the risk points inherent in operational processes, and neglect to develop targeted control measures tailored to those risks. Worse still, they often lack ongoing mechanisms for inspection, monitoring, and risk assessment, thereby failing to identify emerging regulatory gaps or managerial vulnerabilities and to drive the continuous enhancement of internal control measures. Ultimately, such an approach leads to a hollow model of "paper compliance."

To prevent the emergence of such deficiencies, enterprises must embed the principle of business process integration into the design and implementation of their compliance management systems. Under this principle, compliance functions should not remain external to core business operations, acting merely as observers, auditors, or veto authorities. Rather, compliance must be deeply integrated into every stage of the enterprise's operational workflow. This entails identifying specific compliance risk points within the business processes, establishing corresponding compliance control mechanisms, and implementing targeted, risk-based compliance measures that are aligned with the actual operational context and risk exposure of each business activity.

Although certain compliance guidelines issued by Chinese regulatory authorities call for the integration of compliance management into business operations, such requirements have yet to be formally recognized as a foundational principle of compliance governance. For instance, the *Administrative Measures for Compliance Management of Central State-Owned Enterprises* promulgated by the State-owned Assets Supervision and Administration Commission (SASAC) in 2020 explicitly adopt the principle of comprehensive coverage, requiring that compliance obligations be embedded across all domains and stages of corporate activity. These obligations must permeate the entire process of decision-making, execution, and oversight and be implemented at every level of the organization—including all departments, business units, and employees. This framework clearly embodies the core concept of business process integration. Moreover, the Measures stipulate that compliance review must be embedded as a mandatory procedural step within enterprise management processes. For major decision-making matters, the compliance opinion must be signed by the Chief Compliance Officer (CCO), who is responsible for issuing a clear determination on the legal and regulatory conformity of the proposed decision. Business units, functional departments, and compliance departments are further required to conduct periodic assessments of the implementation and effectiveness of such compliance reviews.[27]

Some enterprises, having been compelled to implement compliance remediation in response to major regulatory violations, have subsequently adopted more scientifically informed compliance management approaches. From the perspective of achieving substantive and effective compliance, these enterprises have initiated institutional reforms aimed at embedding compliance mechanisms into core business processes—and have, in some cases, achieved promising outcomes. A notable example is ZTE Corporation, which developed a structured risk control framework organized around the model of "Risk–Control–Process–Tool." Under this model, the company draws a clear distinction between abstract compliance risks and concrete compliance risks. The former are conceptualized as macro-level, generalized, and latent risks, while the latter are defined as micro-level, specific, and actual risks that arise in day-to-day business operations. Building upon the identification and analysis of concrete compliance risks, the company proceeded to designate Key Control Points (KCPs) within its various business processes. KCPs are defined as control mechanisms that serve to prevent, eliminate, or mitigate the impact of risks to an acceptable threshold. Such mechanisms may include, but are not limited to, inspections, verifications, evaluations, audits, reviews, decision-making

[27] *Administrative Measures for Compliance Management of Central State-Owned Enterprises* (SASAC, 2022), arts. 5 and 21.

procedures, performance appraisals, budgeting controls, early warning systems, risk assessments, authorization protocols, inventory verification, and the segregation of incompatible functions. In general, enterprises can determine whether a given risk control point qualifies as a Key Control Point (KCP) through a four-step evaluative process. First, does the process step involve any form of risk control mechanism? Second, are there dedicated controls specifically designed to eliminate risk factors or reduce them to an acceptable level? Third, would the potential impact of the identified risks exceed acceptable thresholds in the absence of such controls? Fourth, can any subsequent steps effectively mitigate or eliminate the consequences of those risks if they occur? By establishing a structured model to evaluate the attributes of control points, enterprises can classify the nature of each control point, determine whether it qualifies as a Key Control Point (KCP), and—drawing on risk assessment results and the specific characteristics of the business process—set KCPs accordingly. This enables the targeted and efficient allocation of compliance management resources and strengthens the organization's capacity to manage and mitigate compliance risks.[28]

ZTE Corporation's compliance management practices embody a fundamental approach to integrating compliance into core business processes—an approach that is fully aligned with the principle of business process integration. To facilitate the promotion and broader application of this experience, it is useful to provide a brief conceptual analysis of the underlying principle.

First, in the compliance risk assessment phase, enterprises should conduct a comprehensive and precise identification of concrete compliance risks inherent in their business processes. This requires pinpointing compliance risk sources—namely, those business areas, operational procedures, job functions, or personnel that carry a high probability of engaging in unlawful or non-compliant conduct. To accurately assess such risks, enterprises must disaggregate and tag these risk sources within each business process. Based on this mapping, they should analyze both the likelihood of risk occurrence and its potential impact, assign risk levels, and establish a clear prioritization framework for risk mitigation based on urgency and severity.

Second, during the compliance risk management phase, enterprises should adopt differentiated compliance control measures tailored to the specific risk sources identified within each segment of the business process, with the aim of eliminating potential vulnerabilities and addressing management blind spots. The concept of Key Control Points (KCPs), as developed by ZTE Corporation, provides a generally applicable reference model for enterprise-level compliance risk governance. Its central premise is that enterprises must design targeted risk control strategies aligned with the specific characteristics of each compliance risk, and formulate practical, enforceable implementation plans to embed those controls within day-to-day operations. By embedding compliance control

[28] ZTE Corporation, *Compliance Creates Value: ZTE's Compliance Practice* (Beijing: Law Press, 2023), 14–34.

requirements into operational workflows, enterprises can achieve the effective integration of compliance into business processes.

Third, with respect to the organization of compliance management, enterprises should promote the deep integration of compliance and business functions by assigning a sufficient number of part-time compliance officers, thereby positioning business operations as the first line of defense against compliance risks. To avoid the fragmentation commonly referred to as the "compliance-business divide," enterprises may appoint compliance liaisons or part-time compliance personnel within each business unit. These individuals are tasked with conveying applicable compliance rules, standards, and guidelines and with executing compliance-related responsibilities in accordance with the instructions of the central compliance team and the operational requirements of their respective departments. In cases where no liaison has been formally appointed, the general manager of the relevant unit or subsidiary may, by default, assume the role to ensure effective compliance implementation at the frontline level. At the same time, to incentivize greater participation of business departments in compliance governance, enterprises may adopt a "three lines of defense" framework for compliance risk control. Under this model, business units constitute the first line of defense and assume primary responsibility for embedding and executing compliance controls within daily operations. The compliance management department functions as the second line of defense, responsible for developing compliance policies, issuing standards and guidelines, and conducting ongoing monitoring to identify and mitigate compliance risks. The compliance audit or inspection department serves as the third line of defense, charged with receiving reports of non-compliance, conducting internal investigations, recommending disciplinary measures, and performing continuous compliance audits. These three lines are interdependent and operate in a coordinated manner, jointly establishing a comprehensive, layered compliance assurance system that enhances the organization's ability to prevent, detect, and respond to compliance risks effectively.

3.7 The Principle of Sustainability

In response to regulatory pressure, many enterprises have established compliance management systems within a short period of time. While such systems may initially prove effective in addressing previously exposed compliance risks—providing short-term benefits in terms of prevention, monitoring, and mitigation—they often lack the capacity for continuous adaptation and long-term effectiveness. As business operations expand and evolve, and as national laws and regulations are regularly revised, the nature and intensity of compliance risks also shift accordingly. If enterprises fail to conduct ongoing risk assessments, to systematically evaluate the effectiveness of their compliance frameworks, and to adjust them in line with regulatory and operational changes, their compliance systems risk becoming outdated and ineffective—unable to serve as reliable tools for risk governance in a dynamic legal environment.

To prevent such shortcomings, enterprises must embed the principle of sustainability into their compliance management systems. This principle entails the continuous adaptation and renewal of compliance frameworks in response to changes in external legal and regulatory requirements, as well as transformations in the nature and structure of internal compliance risks. Only through such ongoing responsiveness can the compliance system serve as a durable and effective mechanism for the prevention and control of compliance risks.

International compliance frameworks place explicit emphasis on the continuous improvement of compliance management systems. For example, *Compliance Management Systems—Requirements with Guidance for Use* (ISO 37301), issued by the International Organization for Standardization (ISO), identifies **sustainability** as one of the fundamental principles of compliance management. Under this standard, the effectiveness of a compliance management system depends on its ability to adapt to changes in the organization, its operating environment, applicable laws, regulations, and other compliance obligations and to be continually improved so as to enhance its suitability, adequacy, and effectiveness.

Given that an enterprise's context, business activities, customer base, and compliance obligations may evolve over time, it is essential to perform ongoing and periodic reassessments of compliance risks and to regularly review and update the compliance management system to ensure that it remains current and continues to support the achievement of compliance objectives. Where appropriate, the enterprise should also reassess and evaluate its compliance culture. In the event of non-compliance, the organization is expected to conduct a root cause analysis and update its compliance policies and procedures accordingly.[29]

Several national compliance guidelines likewise emphasize the need for continuous improvement in corporate compliance management systems. For example, *Principle 6—Monitoring and Review* of the *Six Principles of Adequate Procedures* set out in the U.K. Ministry of Justice's *Guidance to the UK Bribery Act 2010* requires commercial organizations to put in place procedures for monitoring and reviewing the effectiveness of their anti-bribery arrangements and for making improvements where necessary. In practice, this entails establishing internal and external monitoring mechanisms—such as employee surveys, internal controls, and other oversight measures—as well as implementing a regular compliance risk reporting process to ensure that senior management periodically reviews and assesses the ongoing adequacy and effectiveness of the compliance program.[30]

[29] Research Task Force on Corporate Compliance in Criminal Cases under the Supreme People's Procuratorate of China, Case Handling Manual on Corporate Compliance in Criminal Proceedings (Beijing: China Procuratorial Press, 2022), 441–442.

[30] Ruihua Chen, *The Chinese Experience of Effective Compliance* (Beijing: Peking University Press, 2023), 273.

Similarly, the *Resource Guide to the U.S. Foreign Corrupt Practices Act* (FCPA Resource Guide), jointly issued by the U.S. Department of Justice (DOJ) and the Securities and Exchange Commission (SEC), highlights the importance of continuous improvement, periodic testing, and review in corporate compliance programs. The Guide notes that as a company's business operations, risk environment, customer base, and applicable legal or policy frameworks evolve—and as weaknesses or deficiencies in existing compliance procedures are identified—companies should regularly review and update their compliance programs to ensure they remain effective and well-tailored to the company's specific risk profile. The Guide further states that enforcement authorities may give favorable consideration to companies that demonstrate a proactive commitment to revising and enhancing their compliance programs, including through mitigation of penalties, declinations, or other forms of leniency.[31]

At present, several compliance management guidelines issued by Chinese administrative authorities also emphasize the importance of continuously improving corporate compliance systems. For example, the *Administrative Measures for Compliance Management of Central State-Owned Enterprises*, issued by the State-owned Assets Supervision and Administration Commission (SASAC), require central SOEs to regularly review business processes, identify compliance risk points, embed compliance obligations and control measures into operational workflows, and strengthen compliance review at critical control points to enhance procedural oversight. Central SOEs are further required to establish real-time monitoring mechanisms for high-risk areas and key operational nodes to enable early warning and rapid response to emerging compliance risks. In parallel, they must develop a system for compliance risk identification, classification, and early warning, and maintain a regularly updated compliance risk database. In addition, enterprises are instructed to conduct periodic evaluations of the effectiveness of their compliance management systems, carry out targeted assessments of compliance performance in high-risk business segments, and ensure that the results of such evaluations are systematically applied to improve the overall adaptability and functionality of the compliance framework.[32]

However, given that compliance management systems have only recently been introduced into China's administrative regulatory framework and judicial incentive mechanisms, many enterprises remain in the early stages of developing and institutionalizing their compliance programs. Consequently, some regulatory authorities have not yet explicitly mandated the continuous updating of compliance systems, nor have they adopted it as a core criterion for assessing the effectiveness of compliance programs. Nevertheless, from the standpoint of effectively preventing and managing compliance risks, it is

[31] Ruihua Chen, *The Chinese Experience of Effective Compliance* (Beijing: Peking University Press, 2023), 295.

[32] *Administrative Measures for Compliance Management of Central State-Owned Enterprises* (SASAC, 2022), arts. 20 and 34.

imperative that enterprises embed the principle of sustainability into their compliance frameworks. This principle should serve as a foundational guideline for the design, refinement, and performance evaluation of compliance systems.

First, enterprises should proactively identify new sources of compliance risk in response to evolving internal and external conditions—such as changes in business operations, client structures, product portfolios, and relationships with commercial partners—and make corresponding adjustments to their compliance management systems. Specifically, companies should conduct regular compliance risk assessments to identify newly emerging risk-prone processes, operational nodes, job functions, and personnel. Through analyzing the likelihood and potential impact of these risks, enterprises can reclassify risk levels and reprioritize risk rankings.

In the area of compliance risk assessment, enterprises must pay particular attention to the ongoing oversight of third-party business partners and acquired entities. When engaging third parties, companies should conduct thorough due diligence, retain detailed documentation, communicate applicable compliance policies and procedures, provide training where necessary, and obtain explicit compliance commitments. To maintain continuous oversight, enterprises should implement a combination of mechanisms—such as periodic updates to due diligence, ongoing training, audits, and annual compliance certifications. In the context of mergers and acquisitions, companies must ensure that their compliance standards, policies, and procedures are promptly extended to newly acquired entities. For prospective acquisition targets, enterprises should conduct appropriate due diligence and adopt supplementary measures such as targeted compliance training and audits.

Second, enterprises should promptly maintain an up-to-date inventory of compliance requirements to ensure that changes in relevant laws and regulations are accurately incorporated into the company's internal compliance policies, standards, management procedures, operational workflows, and employee handbooks. Corporate compliance involves a process of internalizing external legal norms—that is, transforming "external laws" into "internal rules." The external norms most pertinent to business operations include administrative regulations, criminal law provisions, and international legal and regulatory frameworks. Once a compliance management system is in place, these external legal norms are likely to undergo continual revision. To maintain effective risk control, enterprises must promptly incorporate such updates into internal compliance instruments—by translating them into enforceable policies, updating employee handbooks accordingly, and embedding these requirements into compliance training and employee commitment mechanisms. Only through such transformation can a unified standard of conduct be achieved across all levels of personnel, thereby sustaining the effectiveness of compliance risk management in a constantly evolving regulatory environment.

Third, enterprises should implement periodic reviews and testing measures to evaluate the effectiveness of their compliance programs. In light of evolving legal requirements, regulatory expectations, and dynamic risk environments, companies must regularly assess and test their compliance management systems to determine how effectively they identify, mitigate, and prevent unlawful or non-compliant conduct. Based on the results of these evaluations, enterprises should promptly identify any weaknesses or deficiencies in their systems, take targeted measures to address identified gaps, and make necessary adjustments to their compliance policies and procedures.

Finally, the occurrence of unlawful or non-compliant conduct presents a critical opportunity for enterprises to enhance their compliance management systems. In such cases, companies should conduct internal investigations to ascertain the facts and assign responsibility. More importantly, they should identify the underlying structural and systemic deficiencies that contributed to the violation and implement targeted institutional corrections and remedial measures. Based on these findings, enterprises should refine and reinforce their compliance frameworks to address institutional vulnerabilities. Such post-incident improvements are essential to maintaining the effectiveness of the compliance system in preventing future violations and mitigating compliance risks.

3.8 Conclusion

Although corporate compliance management can take various institutional forms, achieving the goal of effectively preventing and controlling compliance risks requires the establishment of a set of generally applicable foundational principles that serve as the basis for all compliance management systems. Similar to legal principles in general, the core principles of effective compliance—while necessarily abstract—exert a sustained influence on the establishment, development, and refinement of compliance frameworks over time. The formulation of these principles should, on the one hand, reflect the essential requirements of effective compliance, thereby providing a primary basis for assessment and approval by regulatory and judicial authorities, and, on the other hand, abstract universally applicable concepts from more concrete management practices. In this way, these principles function as minimum governance standards for identifying and rectifying ineffective or merely symbolic ("paper-based") compliance.

The six core principles discussed in this chapter each play a distinct role in safeguarding the effectiveness of corporate compliance management. The risk-based principle provides enterprises with a strategic framework for designing their compliance systems, encouraging a shift away from impractical, management-based compliance models toward internal control structures founded on risk assessment, risk management, and risk mitigation. The principle of proportionality requires companies to establish risk control systems that are commensurate with their size, business scope, industry characteristics, and level of compliance risk, ensuring that the leadership structure, organizational framework, resource allocation, and management processes are adequately equipped to prevent unlawful conduct. The principle of top-level commitment underscores the responsibility of senior management for compliance governance, thereby preventing the marginalization of the compliance function and ensuring the effective operation of the compliance management system. Building on this foundation, the principle of authority requires enterprises to accord the compliance function a relatively independent status, with clear powers to carry out compliance reviews, veto unlawful or non-compliant business activities, and take disciplinary action against offending personnel. It further calls for the allocation of adequate resources to support the compliance function, thereby establishing the institutional safeguards necessary for its effective performance. The principle of business process integration emphasizes the deep embedding of compliance management within operational workflows, enabling the identification and control of compliance risk points throughout core business processes. This ensures that compliance remains an integral part of business management, rather than operating in isolation. Finally, the principle of sustainability underscores the importance of continuous improvement and dynamic adjustment. It requires enterprises to revise and upgrade their compliance frameworks in response to evolving risk landscapes, regulatory developments, and changes in the external environment—ensuring that the compliance system remains up to date and capable of preventing systemic compliance failures over time.

The six core principles of effective compliance discussed in this chapter are applicable to all scenarios in which enterprises establish compliance management systems. They constitute a set of general guidelines for the operation of effective compliance programs. In different compliance contexts, enterprises may need to adopt differentiated approaches. For example, the methods and procedures involved in building an autonomous compliance system may differ from those required in implementing a compliance remediation program for an implicated enterprise, and distinct guiding principles may also apply. Similarly, when developing targeted compliance systems—such as those for anti-commercial bribery, data protection, workplace safety, environmental and resource protection, or anti-money laundering—enterprises may adopt different compliance philosophies suited to the specific regulatory domain. Nevertheless, in carrying out these compliance activities, enterprises must avoid "paper compliance," "formalistic compliance," or "ineffective compliance." A minimum set of management standards must still be observed. The six principles discussed herein provide precisely such minimum behavioral norms for the design, implementation, and evaluation of effective compliance programs.

CHAPTER 4

Institutional Models for Corporate Compliance Systems

4.1 Introduction

Corporate compliance systems can generally be classified into two distinct models based on the timing and context of their establishment: routine compliance management systems (also referred to as ex ante compliance or autonomous compliance) and crisis-responsive compliance remediation (also known as ex post compliance).[1] The former denotes compliance systems proactively established by enterprises in the absence of external regulatory pressure. As a forward-looking mechanism, it is designed to identify and manage potential legal and regulatory risks in advance, and to ensure that corporate activities are conducted in accordance with applicable laws, administrative regulations, and internal governance standards. By contrast, the latter emerges in the aftermath of a legal or regulatory violation—typically in the context of administrative enforcement actions, criminal investigations, or international sanctions—and constitutes a remedial response aimed at mitigating adverse consequences, obtaining leniency, and restoring institutional legitimacy. In the context of routine compliance management systems, enterprises are generally not faced with immediate or clearly defined compliance risks. Accordingly, they tend to adopt a broad, management-oriented approach, constructing comprehensive systems that cover multiple regulatory areas and all stages of business operations. In contrast, crisis-responsive compliance remediation is usually initiated by enterprises implicated in misconduct. Driven by the imperative to avert legal sanctions and reputational damage, these enterprises often adopt a more targeted, risk-oriented strategy—focusing on remedying the specific type of violation

[1] Ruihua Chen, "Two Models of Effective Compliance Management," *Law and Social Development*, no. 1 (2022).

R. Chen, *An Introduction to Corporate Compliance*,
https://doi.org/10.1007/978-981-95-7257-1_4

involved and on building targeted compliance mechanisms to prevent recurrence.[2]

Within the dual-track framework of compliance system development outlined above, two markedly distinct models of compliance management can be identified. The approach adopted by enterprises in building a routine compliance management system is generally categorized as a management-based compliance model. In contrast, the approach taken during crisis-responsive compliance remediation is typically classified as a risk-based compliance model.

The management-based compliance model has been widely adopted in the development of compliance systems within China's state-owned enterprises (SOEs). At present, Chinese SOEs—drawing on compliance frameworks issued by international organizations and operating under the supervision of administrative regulatory authorities—have actively pursued the establishment of enterprise-wide compliance systems. This model embodies the philosophy of comprehensive compliance, premised on the principle that enterprises must conduct their operations in full conformity with applicable laws and regulations. It entails, as an initial step, a systematic review of domestic statutes, administrative regulations, policy directives, international legal instruments, internal corporate rules, industry standards, and professional ethical codes to determine the enterprise's complete set of compliance obligations. Building on this foundation, enterprises identify and evaluate priority compliance domains, and then establish an integrated compliance management framework that encompasses all business units, operational phases, and procedural workflows.

The risk-based compliance model is typically adopted by enterprises implicated in legal or regulatory violations in the context of crisis-driven compliance remediation. In such circumstances, Chinese regulatory authorities commonly require the enterprise to formulate a targeted compliance program. This model adheres to a risk-based logic, focusing on the specific type of unlawful conduct at issue, with the objective of preventing similar or related violations from recurring. Following an internal investigation into the underlying causes of the misconduct, the enterprise is expected to implement institutional corrections tailored to those findings and, on that basis, to introduce a targeted compliance program designed to address the identified risks.

Shen Nan, Chief Legal Officer of ZTE Corporation, has provided a vivid comparative analysis of these two compliance approaches. In his view, ZTE initially adopted a management-based model in the early stages of its compliance development, establishing a top-down compliance management system along four dimensions: the cultivation of compliance culture, the allocation of compliance resources, the construction of procedural and institutional mechanisms, and the enhancement of professional capacity. However, as the company's compliance governance entered deeper and more complex phases, this model—characterized by a rigid, one-size-fits-all approach to rule

[2] Ruihua Chen, "Two Models of Effective Compliance Management," *Law and Social Development*, no. 1 (2022).

application—began to reveal significant limitations. In response, ZTE gradually shifted its focus toward risk-oriented thinking and ultimately developed a risk-based compliance system. The fundamental difference between these two models lies in their respective conceptions of compliance risk. The management-based model emphasizes abstract compliance risk—that is, generalized, macro-level, and potential risks of legal or regulatory violations. By contrast, the risk-based model focuses on concrete compliance risk, referring to specific, micro-level, and immediate risks of unlawful or non-compliant conduct.[3] Based on this understanding, ZTE ultimately concentrated its compliance efforts on three high-risk areas: export control, anti-commercial bribery, and data protection. It accordingly established three targeted compliance programs: an export control compliance plan, an anti-commercial bribery compliance plan, and a data protection compliance plan.[4]

ZTE's experience in establishing a compliance management framework is not an isolated or exceptional instance, but one that carries broad applicability and generalizable value. Even before ZTE's compliance violations came to light, Siemens AG in Germany underwent a comparable process. In response to allegations of large-scale overseas bribery, Siemens became the subject of investigations by German prosecutors as well as U.S. enforcement and regulatory bodies. Under the supervision of the U.S. Department of Justice and the Securities and Exchange Commission, and with guidance from an independent compliance monitor, Siemens undertook a multi-year compliance remediation initiative. Through targeted institutional reforms, the company not only established a dedicated anti-commercial bribery compliance system, but also, following further risk identification and assessment, proactively launched additional programs in antitrust, data protection, and anti-money laundering.[5]

A review of compliance system development cases shows that both management-based and risk-based compliance models are widely adopted by various types of enterprises when establishing their compliance frameworks. While the risk-based compliance model has demonstrated particular success in post-violation compliance remediation settings, it should not be viewed as exclusive to enterprises facing enforcement actions. For companies undertaking proactive or voluntary compliance efforts, the management-based approach is not the sole—or necessarily optimal—option. From the standpoint of effective risk prevention and control, a risk- based compliance model may offer a more responsive and targeted framework for compliance governance. In this respect, whether in post-crisis compliance remediation or in ex ante compliance system development, the management-based compliance model tends to suffer from structural deficiencies that are difficult to overcome, whereas the risk-based compliance model exhibits unique institutional strengths that make

[3] Nan Shen, "A Cognitive and Managerial Roadmap to Compliance Risk Control," *Compliance Talker* (WeChat public account), July 19, 2022.

[4] Ruihua Chen, "ZTE's Targeted Compliance Program," *China Lawyer*, no. 2 (2020).

[5] Ruihua Chen, "Siemens' Compliance System," *China Lawyer*, no. 6 (2019).

it an indispensable alternative. It is therefore important to recognize that the risk-based compliance model—though originally developed as a remedial response to specific violations—can, with appropriate adaptation and contextualization, function as both a normative and operational blueprint for constructing robust, forward-looking compliance systems in non-crisis contexts.

In light of the foregoing, this chapter seeks to conduct a preliminary inquiry into the two principal models of corporate compliance management. It examines the management-oriented and risk-oriented models from multiple dimensions, including their respective compliance objectives, institutional foundations, approaches to risk identification, and methods of compliance implementation. The analysis further summarizes their underlying value orientations, core structural elements, and defining institutional characteristics. Building upon this comparison, the chapter offers a synthesized evaluation of the strengths and weaknesses of each model from the perspectives of normative coherence and practical efficacy. Rather than reaching a definitive conclusion as to which model is categorically superior, this chapter aims to underscore that enterprises engaged in the development or refinement of compliance systems should consider a broader range of institutional choices. With deliberate and rational evaluation, organizations may be better positioned to select a compliance model that best suits their particular circumstances.

4.2 Conceptual Models of Compliance Management

Contemporary corporate compliance management is shaped by two fundamentally distinct conceptual models. The first is the PDCA-based compliance management model—Plan, Do, Check, Act—rooted in the ISO standards framework. The second is the PDR risk control model—Prevention, Detection, Response—developed from practical experiences in corporate compliance governance. Because China's current national compliance standards essentially incorporate and mirror the ISO international standards, the PDCA model has come to represent the official managerial philosophy in Chinese compliance regulation. In particular, the architects of China's compliance standards have embraced this model as the theoretical foundation for constructing standardized compliance systems. Today, this management-driven philosophy serves as the normative blueprint for preventive compliance practices in Chinese state-owned enterprises.

Yet it should not be overlooked that an alternative, risk-based compliance philosophy has gained prominence in the compliance remediation processes adopted by certain Western jurisdictions. For instance, in the post-violation compliance remediation undertaken by Siemens AG and ZTE Corporation, the systems developed bore little resemblance to the ex ante frameworks commonly used by Chinese SOEs. Instead, these systems embodied a distinct risk-control orientation informed by empirical responses to compliance failures. Indeed, in any case where a company has committed legal or regulatory violations and come under the scrutiny of Western regulators or international financial institutions, the subsequent compliance reconstruction has consistently been grounded in this alternative management philosophy. Even after completing their formal compliance remediation obligations, such companies typically continue to build and operate compliance systems premised on this risk-centered approach.

The PDCA management model—first conceptualized by American statistician and management theorist Walter A. Shewhart, and later refined and widely promoted by W. Edwards Deming—provides a classic cyclical framework for organizational governance. The acronym "PDCA" encapsulates four iterative stages. P (Plan) refers to the planning phase, in which an organization, through investigation, evaluation, and analysis, sets its management objectives and identifies specific measures and methods to achieve them. D (Do) denotes the execution phase, in which the organization implements the planned measures in accordance with the established framework. C (Check) represents the review phase, in which implementation outcomes are assessed against the original plan, with successes and deficiencies identified. A (Act) signifies the improvement phase, in which the organization adopts corrective measures based on the review results, consolidates effective practices into standardized procedures, and institutes preventive measures to avert the recurrence of identified problems.[6]

Both the *ISO 37301:2021 Compliance Management Systems – Requirements with Guidance for Use* (hereinafter, the "ISO International Compliance Standard") and its equivalent Chinese national standard, *GB/T 35770-2022*, follow the PDCA (Plan–Do–Check–Act) management model described above. Under this framework, the Plan phase involves establishing a public statement of commitment to compliance, formulating the compliance policy, defining roles and responsibilities, and identifying compliance obligations and risks; the Do phase covers institutional support, competence and awareness building, communication and training, operational controls and procedures, and documentation; the Check phase entails internal audits, management reviews, monitoring and measurement of compliance performance, channels for raising compliance concerns, and investigation processes; and the Act phase focuses on taking corrective actions in response to non-compliance and ensuring the continual improvement of the compliance management system.

It is evident that a compliance management system built on the PDCA model encompasses virtually all key components of compliance governance, thereby framing compliance as a comprehensive internal control framework. Under this managerial philosophy, compliance is defined as the enterprise's systematic fulfillment of its legal and regulatory obligations, with the aim of reducing or eliminating both the likelihood and consequences of non-compliance. It also entails fostering a shared organizational culture shaped by

[6] Yiyi Wang et al., *Interpretation and Application of the Compliance Management Systems Standard: GB/T 35770–2022 / ISO 37301:2021* (Beijing: Enterprise Management Publishing House, 2022), 11.

values, ethical norms, belief systems, and behavioral practices committed to regulatory adherence. To achieve this objective, enterprises must first establish a robust compliance governance environment, define the scope of their compliance management system, identify applicable compliance obligations, and conduct corresponding compliance risk assessments. In accordance with the principle of top-level commitment, organizations are required to designate a compliance governance body, appoint senior management personnel to oversee compliance-related functions, and formulate a compliance policy aligned with fundamental standards. They must establish a dedicated compliance management department, define core compliance roles and responsibilities, and clarify lines of authority and accountability within the compliance governance framework. On this basis, enterprises should formulate compliance objectives across relevant departments and organizational levels, allocate sufficient resources, ensure that compliance personnel possess the requisite competencies, facilitate both internal and external compliance communication, and regularly maintain and update relevant documentation. In addition, enterprises must establish appropriate control mechanisms and procedures to manage their compliance obligations and associated risks. These measures should include the implementation of whistleblower reporting channels and the investigation of potential non-compliant behavior. Moreover, organizations are required to regularly monitor and assess the performance of their compliance management systems, conduct internal audits, and systematically evaluate the effectiveness of compliance measures. Most importantly, continuous improvements must be made to the compliance framework based on the findings derived from ongoing monitoring, auditing, and management review processes.

This model of compliance system construction is driven by two interrelated engines: the fulfillment of compliance obligations and the management of compliance risks, thereby reflecting a management-oriented approach to compliance control. Influenced by this paradigm, certain regulatory authorities in China define compliance as the lawful and rule-based operation of enterprises, taking the identification and observance of compliance obligations as the point of departure. This approach has resulted in the delineation of broad compliance management domains and the pursuit of "broad-scope compliance" or "comprehensive compliance" as institutional objectives. Within this framework, enterprises are expected to establish the "three lines of defense" for effective compliance governance and to embed compliance performance into core business management processes.

Beyond the PDCA model, an alternative approach to corporate compliance management has emerged: the PDR control model. The PDCA model may be viewed as grounded in a philosophy of rationalism—one that emphasizes the articulation of elevated management goals and the systematic deployment of organizational measures to achieve them. By contrast, the PDR model is informed by a philosophy of empiricism. Rather than advancing abstract or idealized objectives, it conceptualizes compliance as a practical exercise in risk mitigation, error avoidance, and misconduct prevention. Under this approach, compliance management is understood as the practical reduction or elimination of non-compliant conduct, which is regarded as the essential objective of compliance control.

The PDR control model refers to a compliance risk control framework that enterprises develop to reduce the likelihood of legal or regulatory violations and to minimize the risk of significant strategic loss. This risk-oriented approach to compliance defines compliance risk as the probability of major unlawful conduct and the resulting adverse consequences for the enterprise. To prevent or mitigate such strategic risks, enterprises are expected to construct compliance systems centered on risk control, structured around three core functions: prevention, detection, and response. The "P" in the PDR model stands for Prevent, referring to the proactive prevention or containment of compliance risks. In practice, this function is fulfilled through a range of institutional measures, including the establishment of compliance leadership structures and organizational systems, compliance risk assessments, due diligence procedures, compliance training, commitment statements, and the cultivation of a strong compliance culture. The "D" stands for Detect, denoting the mechanisms of monitoring, surveillance, and early warning embedded in business operations to uncover signs of potential violations. These tools enable the timely identification of unlawful or non-compliant conduct and allow for targeted interventions. The "R" refers to Respond, which encompasses the reactive and corrective measures taken in the aftermath of a compliance breach. These include investigations, internal audits, and remedial actions aimed at addressing the underlying causes of non-compliance and mitigating its consequences. This response function also entails the implementation of institutional improvements designed to close compliance loopholes and enhance the long-term resilience of the compliance management system.

In general, enterprises that have not experienced legal or regulatory violations tend to favor the PDCA management model when developing their compliance systems, using it as the foundation for building broad-based and comprehensive compliance management frameworks. In contrast, companies that have been subjected to investigations, penalties, or sanctions by regulatory or law enforcement authorities are more likely to adopt the PDR control model. These enterprises focus on addressing the specific compliance risks they have encountered and typically construct targeted control frameworks aimed at preventing the recurrence of similar violations. In the broader trajectory of corporate compliance development, companies such as Siemens AG in Germany and ZTE Corporation in China have adopted the PDR model in establishing their compliance systems. Likewise, the French anti-corruption compliance guidelines explicitly identify "prevention," "detection," and "response" as the three institutional pillars of effective compliance risk management—alongside the principles of top-level commitment and proportionality.

4.3 The Management-Based Model

The so-called *management-based compliance model* is a compliance governance approach that takes comprehensive adherence to rules as its core objective. To achieve this, enterprises must transform both the mandatory legal requirements imposed by the state and the voluntary compliance commitments made by the organization into concrete internal management standards. This process involves a systematic identification and classification of the enterprise's compliance obligations, followed by a risk assessment based on the nature and scope of its business operations. The overarching aim is to ensure effective prevention of high-priority compliance risks while also minimizing the likelihood of other forms of non-compliance across all operational domains. Building on this foundation, enterprises are expected to establish and implement a comprehensive compliance management system that spans all business functions, personnel, operational stages, and procedural flows. This management-based compliance model has been formalized in various international compliance frameworks and has been recognized by Chinese administrative regulators as an institutional guarantee for effective compliance governance. As such, it has been widely promoted across a broad range of state-owned enterprises in China. Notably, Chinese companies that have not been subject to regulatory sanctions or judicial enforcement actions by Western authorities or international organizations tend to prefer this model when responding to domestic administrative compliance requirements.

4.3.1 Compliance as Rule Adherence

The term *corporate compliance*—as rendered in English—literally refers to the adherence or conformity of enterprises to applicable rules. The management-based compliance model is rooted in this foundational understanding: it conceptualizes corporate compliance as the enterprise's systematic observance of legal and regulatory norms. Broadly speaking, the rules to be observed fall into two categories: (1) mandatory legal norms issued by the state; and (2) voluntary commitments made by the enterprise itself. To ensure that both externally imposed obligations and internally assumed commitments are effectively observed, enterprises must establish a dedicated compliance management system. This system rests on four foundational pillars: an organizational structure, a regulatory framework of internal rules and procedures, operational mechanisms, and a culture of compliance. Substantively, corporate compliance governance consists of two core components: first, the identification of the *rules* to be followed—namely, compliance obligations derived from laws, regulations, and related normative requirements; and second, the determination of how to *comply* with those rules—specifically, by translating them into internal managerial standards and operational practices.

The *Compliance Management Systems — Requirements with Guidance for Use* (*ISO 37301:2021*), issued by the International Organization for

Standardization (ISO) (hereinafter, the "ISO 37301 Compliance Guidelines"), defines compliance as "the fulfillment of the organization's compliance obligations." In the context of the ISO 37301 Guidelines, *compliance obligations* are defined as "requirements that an organization has to comply with and that it chooses to comply with." The identification of these obligations is regarded as the fundamental basis for establishing a compliance management system. *Non-compliance* is correspondingly defined as the "non-fulfillment of a compliance obligation." A *compliance management system* is described as an integrated framework that combines an organization's "fundamental structures, policies, processes, and procedures" with the aim of achieving "intended compliance outcomes," and is designed to enable the organization to take action to prevent, detect, and respond to non-compliance.

The *Administrative Measures for Compliance Management of Central State-Owned Enterprises* (2022), issued by the State-owned Assets Supervision and Administration Commission of the State Council (SASAC), represent the official regulatory position on compliance within China's administrative framework. The Measures largely adopt the definition provided in ISO standards, defining compliance as the enterprise's fulfillment of relevant compliance obligations. More specifically, compliance is understood as the requirement that "corporate management activities and employee conduct conform to national laws and administrative regulations, industry codes, international treaties and rules, as well as the company's articles of association and internal policies and procedures." According to the Measures, *compliance management* refers to an organized and systematic set of activities undertaken by enterprises with the aim of effectively controlling compliance risks, guided by the overarching goal of promoting lawful and rules-based business conduct. It applies to both organizational operations and individual employee behavior, and is operationalized through the establishment of compliance rules, the refinement of compliance mechanisms, the cultivation of a compliance culture, and the reinforcement of supervisory and accountability structures.

According to some scholars, corporate compliance should not be understood simply as conventional law-abiding behavior. Rather, it denotes a voluntary process through which enterprises internalize external regulatory requirements and convert them into structured internal management activities. This process involves the full participation of all employees and encompasses compliance controls across all procedures, stages, and operational functions. It is characterized by its routinized and sustainable nature. As a form of governance, compliance is substantively distinct from mere legality: what is legal is not necessarily compliant. Legality represents the minimum threshold for lawful business conduct, whereas compliance entails a higher standard—often encompassing ethical and moral expectations that exceed the letter of the law.[7] The initial objective of establishing a corporate compliance management system

[7] Zhile Wang, "Strengthening Compliance Management to Advance Sustainable Corporate Development," *Shenzhen Legal Review*, no. 3 (2020).

is to prevent and control compliance risks. However, its long-term goal is to foster a culture of lawful and rule-based business conduct. The broader goal is to transition from *reactive compliance* to *proactive compliance*—a shift from externally imposed mandates ("I am required to comply") to internally motivated commitment ("I choose to comply"). On the foundation of risk prevention and mitigation, enterprises are expected to develop comprehensive compliance frameworks, enhance their organizational soft power and competitiveness, and cultivate a deeply rooted compliance culture grounded in legality and integrity, ensuring the enterprise's ability to achieve sustainable development over time.[8]

4.3.2 Obligation-Oriented Compliance

Under the management-based compliance model, enterprises are expected to treat compliance obligations as the foundation for establishing, developing, implementing, evaluating, maintaining, and continually improving their compliance management systems. Based on their degree of binding force, compliance obligations may be divided into mandatory compliance obligations and voluntary compliance obligations. Mandatory compliance obligations are norms and requirements that an enterprise is legally bound to observe. Breach of such obligations will typically trigger legal sanctions and expose the enterprise to significant compliance risks. These obligations generally include: statutory laws and administrative regulations; licenses, permits, or other forms of official authorization; binding orders, rules, or guidelines issued by regulatory authorities; judicial decisions; and requirements set forth in international treaties, conventions, or protocols. Voluntary compliance obligations, by contrast, are commitments that an enterprise elects to assume at its own discretion. These may include: agreements with community organizations or non-governmental entities; internal corporate policies and procedures; self-adopted principles or codes of conduct; self-declared labels or voluntary environmental commitments; contractual commitments arising from business arrangements; and relevant industry or professional standards. Such obligations often reflect an enterprise's self-imposed governance norms, sectoral best practices, or contractual undertakings. Observing these obligations not only enhances the effectiveness of the enterprise's compliance management system but also serves to prevent and mitigate potential compliance risks to the greatest extent possible.

In delineating the scope of compliance obligations, some compliance scholars have followed the approach outlined above—and in certain cases, have extended it further by incorporating ethical and moral norms into the concept of compliance itself. Under this expanded framework, compliance obligations are understood to originate from two sources: external regulatory

[8] Zhile Wang, "Fundamentals of Corporate Compliance Programs," *Trends in Transformative Criminal Law* (WeChat public account), July 15, 2020.

requirements, which enterprises are legally bound to observe, and internal compliance commitments, which are voluntarily assumed. On this basis, the rules that enterprises are expected to follow—referred to collectively as compliance obligations—may be classified into three categories: external rules, which refer to the legal statutes and regulatory provisions of the jurisdictions in which enterprises operate; internal rules, which include an enterprise's internal policies, codes of conduct, and governance mechanisms; and ethical rules, which reflect standards of integrity and moral conduct to which the enterprise voluntarily commits.[9]

Where should enterprises obtain information on their legal and other compliance obligations? In general, enterprises should establish and maintain a dedicated set of compliance records that comprehensively enumerate all applicable obligations. They should also implement formal procedures for regularly reviewing and updating these records to ensure alignment with the latest legal and regulatory developments. To keep compliance obligations current and accurate, enterprises are advised to adopt a multi-channel information-gathering strategy. Common sources include: reviewing official announcements issued by regulatory authorities; maintaining membership in professional associations; attending industry forums, seminars, or compliance briefings; monitoring updates on official regulatory websites; taking part in regulatory consultations or interviews; seeking advice from legal counsel; and studying interpretive statements issued by regulators or relevant judicial decisions.

Under the guidance of regulatory authorities, many state-owned enterprises in China have identified the establishment of a *compliance obligations register* as the first step in building their compliance management systems. Within this framework, compliance obligations are regarded as the benchmark against which enterprises evaluate the lawfulness and appropriateness of their business activities. They also serve as a reference point for identifying potential compliance deviations throughout the course of operations. The development of a *compliance obligations register* entails the systematic identification, classification, and documentation of all applicable compliance obligations and is widely recognized as a foundational component of effective compliance governance. This process requires compliance personnel to possess comprehensive and structured knowledge of the domestic legal system, relevant foreign legal regimes, mandatory regulatory standards, corporate ethics, and the internal governance framework defined by the company's articles of association.

To ensure the effectiveness of a compliance obligations repository, enterprises should adopt a risk-based approach guided by the Pareto principle. This entails first identifying and prioritizing those obligations that are clearly defined and most relevant to the enterprise's core operations, before gradually expanding to other compliance areas. For example, manufacturing enterprises should

[9] Chenling Guo, Jihua Ding, and Zhile Wang, *Compliance: Evaluating the Effectiveness of Corporate Compliance Management Systems* (Beijing: Enterprise Management Publishing House, 2021), preface, ix.

focus on obligations concerning workplace safety, labor protection, and environmental compliance; sales and service enterprises should prioritize antitrust and anti-bribery regulations; while technology and research-driven enterprises should emphasize compliance in areas such as trade secret protection, trademarks, patents, and other aspects of intellectual property.[10]

4.3.3 *The Expanding Scope of Compliance Risk*

Compliance risk refers to the potential adverse consequences an enterprise may face during its business operations due to a failure to fulfill its compliance obligations. While the management-based compliance model underscores that identifying compliance obligations is foundational to establishing a compliance management system, it also places strong emphasis on risk—indeed, it actively promotes a risk-based compliance approach. But what, precisely, does "compliance risk" mean in this context?

According to the ISO 37301 Compliance Guidelines, compliance risk is defined as "the possibility of noncompliance with the organization's compliance obligations and the associated consequences." In ISO terminology, compliance risk is generally categorized into two types: inherent compliance risk and residual compliance risk. *Inherent compliance risk* refers to the level of risk that exists in the absence of any measures to modify the risk—essentially corresponding to the traditional concept of "the consequences of noncompliance." *Residual compliance risk* refers to the level of risk remaining after risk treatment measures have been applied, reflecting the consequences of ineffective or insufficient compliance controls. Regardless of type, compliance risks can result in a broad range of adverse outcomes, including civil, administrative, or criminal liability, as well as financial loss, reputational damage, and other forms of harm.

The management-based compliance model adopts an expansive understanding of "compliance risk," framing it in two distinct dimensions. The first dimension concerns the internal likelihood of unlawful or unethical conduct, including administrative violations, criminal offenses, civil wrongs, or breaches of industry norms and social ethics. Whether such misconduct is committed by the enterprise itself or by its employees, its occurrence is treated as the manifestation of internal compliance risk. The second dimension relates to the external consequences arising from such misconduct, including administrative penalties, criminal sanctions, civil liabilities, financial losses, reputational harm, and adverse public perception. In essence, external compliance risk refers broadly to the full range of punitive, financial, reputational, and societal repercussions that may result from noncompliance or other forms of corporate misconduct.

[10] Feng Liang and Jiubo Yue, "Five Key Points in Building and Maintaining a Corporate Compliance Obligation Database," *Business Compliance Watch* (WeChat public account), November 19, 2022.

A fundamental step in building an effective corporate compliance management system is the identification and assessment of compliance risks, which serve to delineate key areas of potential exposure and define the scope of targeted compliance programs. Compliance risk identification encompasses two essential components: the detection of risk sources and the classification of risk levels. Enterprises should conduct regular reviews to identify the sources of compliance risk and assign corresponding risk levels, thereby generating both a compliance risk inventory and a risk-level classification register. Based on this foundation, enterprises should carry out periodic compliance risk assessments. These assessments are particularly critical when launching new products, business lines, or services; undergoing changes in organizational structure or strategic direction; facing shifts in external regulatory conditions; experiencing modifications in compliance obligations; engaging in mergers or acquisitions; or following incidents of noncompliance.

Many enterprises also adopt a "risk-based" assessment approach, focusing their primary efforts and limited resources on business areas identified as high-risk, before gradually extending the scope to encompass a broader range of compliance risks. However, these enterprises often fail to differentiate between *abstract* and *concrete* compliance risks, or between *potential* and *imminent* risks. Consequently, they tend to designate numerous "priority compliance risk areas"—sometimes several, even more than a dozen—based solely on the perceived likelihood of noncompliance, without taking into account the organization's actual compliance capacity. This fragmented approach often results in the simultaneous development of multiple, sometimes over ten, targeted compliance programs.

In 2018, the State-owned Assets Supervision and Administration Commission of the State Council (SASAC) issued the *Compliance Management Guidelines for Central State-Owned Enterprises (Trial)*, which identified seven priority areas for compliance management: market transactions, safety and environmental protection, product quality, labor and employment, finance and taxation, intellectual property, and business partnerships. Within each of these domains, the Guidelines enumerated three to five categories of compliance risk. For instance, in the area of market transactions, prevalent risks include acts such as commercial bribery, antitrust violations, and unfair competition, as well as compliance issues arising in asset disposals and bidding and tendering processes. In the domain of safety and environmental protection, compliance risks primarily pertain to workplace safety and the conservation of environmental and natural resources.

Such enumerations of common priority compliance risk areas are essentially abstract regulatory guidelines intended to highlight potential domains that enterprises should focus on during compliance risk identification. However, this does not mean that every enterprise is required to treat all the listed categories as its own "priority compliance risks," nor does it justify the indiscriminate establishment of corresponding compliance programs across the board. In line with the principle of proportionality in compliance management, any corporate compliance framework must be tailored to the enterprise's specific characteristics—such as its size, industry sector, business model, product type, and risk profile. Both the identification of risk areas and the selection of targeted compliance programs should be based on a differentiated and well-focused approach. Such a tailored strategy constitutes a fundamental precondition for building an effective and sustainable compliance management system.

However, in response to regulatory pressures from administrative authorities, many state-owned enterprises (SOEs) have adopted a management-based compliance. Following a comprehensive review of their legal and regulatory obligations, and with due regard to their respective industry characteristics and operational scope, these enterprises undertake broad-based compliance risk assessments, identifying business areas with a higher propensity for legal or regulatory violations as their "priority compliance domains." Under this approach, it is not uncommon for enterprises to identify a dozen, or even several dozen, categories of compliance risk and to construct compliance management systems specifically tailored to mitigate these high-risk domains. Some enterprises have even explicitly adopted the concept of "de-emphasizing specialized compliance while reinforcing comprehensive compliance" as a guiding principle in the design of their compliance governance structures.[11]

For example, China Minmetals Corporation has identified eight priority areas for compliance management in light of its operational needs and strategic development. These areas include corporate governance, anti-bribery, economic sanctions and export controls, antitrust compliance, intellectual property and trade secret protection, data and privacy protection, business partner management, and workplace safety and environmental protection.[12]

Similarly, Sinopec has issued its *Code of Integrity and Compliance Conduct*, which outlines as many as sixteen priority areas for compliance management. These areas include corporate governance and business operations, safety management, environmental protection, employee health, public safety, anti-bribery and anti-corruption, consumer rights protection, antitrust and unfair competition, financial and tax compliance, asset management, corporate social responsibility, employee rights, intellectual property protection, data and information security, international trade and investment, and business partner management.[13]

Furthermore, as one of China's largest state-owned enterprises, China Merchants Group has issued a *Compliance Manual* that defines thirteen priority areas for compliance management, each linked to corresponding

[11] "Steps and Key Elements of Corporate Compliance Risk Identification and Assessment," *Senior Legal Management* (WeChat public account), April 10, 2022.

[12] Dingyuan Wang and Keyu Gong, "How Was the China Minmetals Compliance System Built?" *Senior Legal Management* (WeChat public account), March 16, 2023.

[13] Jiangbo Du, "Sinopec General Counsel Du Jiangbo: Eliminating Performative Compliance, Advancing Substantive Compliance," *Legal Community* (WeChat public account), December 27, 2022.

compliance obligations. These areas include labor and employment, taxation, antitrust, unfair competition, anti-bribery, anti-money laundering, export controls, business partner management, corporate information disclosure, workplace safety, environmental protection, product quality, and data protection and information security.[14]

4.3.4 *Comprehensive Compliance*

Building on a systematic review of compliance obligations and a comprehensive assessment of compliance risks, enterprises are expected to establish an extensive, integrated compliance management framework—this forms the core of the concept of *comprehensive compliance*. Within the management-oriented compliance model, comprehensive compliance entails the development of a multi-disciplinary, multi-sector, and multi-tier system designed both to prevent diverse categories of compliance risks and to respond effectively to compliance incidents. Many enterprises equate comprehensive compliance with *enterprise-wide risk management*, contending that compliance governance should encompass the entirety of corporate operations—covering every department, branch, subsidiary, and employee—and span the entire business cycle, from strategic decision-making and operational execution to oversight and remediation. It is further argued that comprehensive compliance systems are particularly essential for large-scale corporate groups. Such groups typically integrate manufacturing, research and development, trade, and finance, and operate simultaneously across multiple sectors, professional domains, and legal jurisdictions worldwide. This diversity of exposure necessitates the establishment of a full-spectrum, highly specialized compliance management system capable of addressing risks in a holistic and coordinated manner.[15]

In line with the concept of comprehensive compliance, enterprises should regard the establishment of fully law-abiding and rules-based operations as the primary objective of their compliance management efforts. All compliance risks arising within the organization should be treated as objects of systematic prevention and control. Taking into account factors such as the company's size, business scope, industry characteristics, and the results of compliance risk assessments, enterprises are expected to develop a compliance management system capable of effectively preventing all forms of unlawful or non-compliant conduct. In contrast to targeted compliance programs that address risks in specific areas, comprehensive compliance promotes a holistic approach to compliance risk management. According to some scholars, the shift from specialized compliance to comprehensive compliance represents an inevitable stage in

[14] "Compliance Manual of China Merchants Group," *Guangdong Enterprise Risk Management Research Association* (WeChat public account), August 16, 2022.

[15] Jiangbo Du, "Sinopec General Counsel Du Jiangbo Interprets the Classification of Compliance in the Chinese Context," *Corporate Legal Affairs Alliance* (WeChat public account), March 15, 2023.

the development and institutionalization of corporate compliance systems.[16]Compliance is a systemic process of managerial enhancement and organizational cultural transformation. Only by moving from fragmented, issue-specific practices to a unified, enterprise-wide compliance model can companies establish a truly effective and sustainable compliance management system.[17]

Under the concept of comprehensive compliance, enterprises are expected to implement the principle of full coverage. This principle requires that compliance obligations extend to all business functions, departments, subsidiaries at every level, branch offices, and employees and be integrated throughout all stages of corporate activity—including decision-making, execution, and oversight. Adherence to this principle serves a dual function: first, it facilitates the realization of fully law-abiding and rules-based operations by ensuring that compliance responsibilities are fulfilled across all business domains, operational phases, and procedural links; second, it helps prevent legal and regulatory violations by minimizing the occurrence of both major risk events and ordinary compliance breaches, thereby advancing the enterprise toward the ideal of zero compliance failures.

In contrast to comprehensive compliance, some enterprises have advanced the concept of "employee-wide compliance," which underscores that compliance management should not be regarded solely as the responsibility of legal or compliance departments. Instead, under the premise of strong top-level commitment, enterprises are encouraged to adopt a "three lines of defense" model for compliance risk control. The first line consists of all employees, who are expected to assume basic responsibility for compliance risk awareness and prevention; the second line comprises professional legal and compliance staff responsible for managing and implementing compliance programs; and the third line involves audit or supervisory departments that conduct investigations, remediation, and follow-up actions based on identified compliance risks. However, it is unrealistic to expect all employees to engage in professionalized compliance work. The essence of employee-wide compliance lies not in assigning expert-level duties to all personnel, but in reinforcing the expectation that every employee must comply with internal rules and regulations and adhere to established compliance procedures and standards.

Under the guiding framework of comprehensive compliance, enterprises are expected to establish a fully integrated compliance management system. Such a system consolidates the fundamental structures, policies, processes, and procedures related to compliance management, with the ultimate aim of preventing, detecting, and responding to non-compliant conduct. Over time, it incorporates a broad set of management elements and gradually develops into

[16]Pengcheng Xie, "From Targeted to Comprehensive Compliance: Four Points Enterprises Should Consider," *Compliance Forum* (WeChat public account), August 9, 2022.

[17]Zhile Wang, "From Targeted to Comprehensive Compliance," *Entrepreneur Magazine* (WeChat public account), January 16, 2023.

a governance framework that meets the baseline standards for effective compliance oversight. According to the ISO 37301 Compliance Guidelines, a comprehensive compliance system typically consists of the following core components: compliance governance structures and top-level management, compliance planning systems, compliance resource allocation mechanisms, compliance operations and implementation systems, and compliance performance evaluation mechanisms. Frequently emphasized elements—such as compliance culture, training programs, leadership commitment, whistleblowing channels, and compliance audits—are systematically embedded within the corresponding functional sub-systems.

Administrative regulatory authorities in China have provided multiple interpretations of what constitutes a comprehensive compliance management system. As regulatory practices—particularly within state-owned enterprises—have continued to evolve, an increasingly well-defined institutional framework has taken shape. This framework generally comprises four core elements. The first is compliance leadership and organizational structure, which includes the board of directors, executive management, compliance committee, chief compliance officer, dedicated compliance departments, and a three-tier risk prevention and control system. The second is fundamental compliance policies and systems, referring to the establishment of specialized compliance guidelines tailored to key areas of risk. The third is the compliance operational mechanism, which encompasses systems for compliance risk identification, assessment, and early-warning; compliance reviews; compliance reporting; mechanisms for rectifying non-compliance issues; whistleblowing and reporting channels; accountability and disciplinary measures for violations; evaluations of compliance effectiveness; and compliance performance appraisal mechanisms. The fourth is compliance culture development, which involves training programs, awareness campaigns, employee handbooks, and formal compliance commitments.[18]

4.4 The Risk-Driven Model

Beyond the management-driven model described above, another approach to compliance management has emerged in Chinese corporate practice: the risk-driven compliance model. This model was initially developed in the course of compliance reforms carried out by enterprises subject to legal or regulatory action. It has since been adopted by an increasing number of companies with a heightened awareness of risk, and has gradually become an established mode of compliance management in their day-to-day operations. Under this approach, compliance is regarded as a governance mechanism aimed at the prevention and control of specific, imminent, and escalating risks. The presence and potential eruption of such tangible compliance risks constitute the primary impetus

[18] State-owned Assets Supervision and Administration Commission (SASAC), *Compliance Management Measures for Central SOEs* (WeChat public account: Guozi Xiaoxin), September 17, 2022.

for establishing a compliance management system, while the effective mitigation of these real-world risks remains its fundamental objective. In defining compliance risks, the risk-based compliance model rejects the generalized notion of "potential illegality" as the basis for risk identification. Instead, it conceptualizes compliance risk primarily in terms of the actual penalties and associated consequences that may result from legal or regulatory violations. As these risks are typically concrete, clearly defined, and domain-focused, enterprises adopting this model tend to formulate targeted compliance programs tailored to specific areas of risk. Accordingly, the core focus of compliance management is placed on the prevention, monitoring, and response to these identifiable compliance threats.

In compliance management practice, enterprises that have been subjected to administrative penalties, criminal prosecution, or international financial sanctions are especially inclined to adopt the risk-based compliance model. During compliance remediation, these enterprises often implement targeted compliance programs aimed at addressing the specific compliance risks that gave rise to enforcement actions, frequently with the practical objective of obtaining leniency. After remediation is completed, they generally continue applying this risk-based logic by expanding the scope of such programs in a measured way, building on their existing baseline compliance structures. However, they rarely pursue the establishment of a comprehensive or fully integrated compliance management system.

4.4.1 *Risk-Control-Oriented Compliance*

The earliest iterations of the risk-based compliance model emerged in compliance remediation cases involving enterprises subject to enforcement proceedings. Following the occurrence of unlawful or noncompliant conduct, these enterprises no longer faced the *mere possibility* of sanctions; rather, they confronted the immediate and pressing challenge of minimizing penalties, liabilities, and other adverse consequences. Within this context, establishing a compliance management system through targeted remediation became an indispensable course of action for loss reduction and risk containment.[19]

For example, in the Siemens case, the company—accused of engaging in commercial bribery—entered into a settlement agreement with the U.S. Department of Justice and the Securities and Exchange Commission, and underwent a multi-year compliance remediation process. In response to its persistent exposure to bribery-related compliance risks, Siemens established a dedicated anti-commercial bribery compliance management system.[20] Similarly, in the case of ZTE Corporation, the company entered into separate settlement agreements with U.S. judicial and regulatory authorities and developed an export control compliance program to address the compliance risks it faced in

[19] Ruihua Chen, "ZTE's Export Control Compliance Program," *China Lawyer*, no. 3 (2020).
[20] Ruihua Chen, "ZTE's Export Control Compliance Program," *China Lawyer*, no. 3 (2020).

the area of export controls.[21] Another example is the case of Hunan Construction Engineering Group. After being sanctioned by the World Bank, the company reached a settlement agreement and conducted a compliance risk assessment related to its prior involvement in commercial fraud. It subsequently established a targeted integrity compliance management system.[22]

Is the risk-based compliance model merely applicable in the context of post-violation remediation? The answer is clearly no. In a number of cases, companies that had completed compliance remediation and passed official assessments—thereby receiving leniency from regulatory or judicial authorities—chose to institutionalize this risk-based approach as part of their long-term compliance strategy. Through ongoing efforts in compliance risk identification and assessment, these companies uncovered major risks that posed significant threats to their continued viability, prompting the development of additional targeted compliance programs. For instance, Siemens AG, after establishing its anti-commercial bribery compliance system, conducted multiple rounds of risk identification and designated antitrust, data protection, and anti-money laundering as new priority compliance areas. Corresponding compliance programs were subsequently created for each of these domains. Similarly, following the implementation of its export control compliance program, ZTE Corporation conducted in-depth risk assessments and identified commercial bribery and data protection as new priority areas of compliance risk. In response, it established dedicated anti-bribery and data protection compliance management systems. According to widely cited research, the risk-based compliance frameworks developed by Siemens and ZTE have proven both effective and successful. This suggests that even in the context of autonomous, internally driven compliance initiatives, the risk-based compliance model can serve as a necessary and effective approach for building a robust, adaptable, and high-performing compliance management system.

Unlike the management-based compliance model, the risk-based compliance model does not define corporate compliance merely as adherence to rules or lawful operations. Instead, it frames compliance as a core component of corporate governance aimed at the effective prevention and control of compliance risks. In the course of business operations, companies are exposed to a wide array of risks—defined broadly as the possibility of incurring losses or adverse outcomes. Among these, four types of risk are typically categorized as strategic risks, meaning they carry the potential to produce catastrophic consequences for the enterprise. The first is decision-making risk, which arises when errors in setting the company's strategic direction result in fundamental misjudgments. The second is operational risk, referring to failures in business execution or internal management that jeopardize sustainable profitability or lead

[21] Ruihua Chen, "The Compliance System of Hunan Construction Group," *China Lawyer*, no. 11 (2019).

[22] Ruihua Chen, *China's Experience in Effective Compliance* (Beijing: Peking University Press, 2023), 91.

to insolvency. The third is financial risk, which stems from weak financial oversight and may result in misconduct such as fraud or embezzlement, thereby causing significant financial damage. The fourth is compliance risk, which refers to the serious consequences—such as administrative penalties, criminal liability, or disqualification from key market activities—that may result from violations of applicable laws or regulations.

Under the risk-based compliance model, the compliance risks that enterprises aim to prevent and control are classified as strategic risks, standing alongside decision-making, operational, and financial risks. In global business practice, such strategic compliance risks typically take three main forms: administrative penalties, criminal prosecution, and international financial sanctions. These risks are unified by a common collateral consequence—disqualification from market participation. By contrast, general adverse outcomes such as monetary losses, reputational harm, or other less severe consequences resulting from legal or regulatory violations are not regarded as the primary focus of compliance management. The notion of "disqualification" refers to the suspension or revocation of an enterprise's qualifications to access or operate in particular markets. Examples include the suspension of business operations, revocation of licenses or permits, cancellation of franchise rights, exclusion from public procurement, ineligibility for loans or financing, delisting from stock exchanges, or the cancellation of business registration. It is precisely the imperative to avert these disqualification outcomes—arising from administrative, criminal, or international regulatory action—that elevates compliance risk to the level of a strategic concern and makes compliance management a critical component of modern corporate governance.

4.4.2 *Identification of Concrete Compliance Risks*

Under the management-based compliance model, enterprises are typically expected to identify risk areas based on the internal likelihood of legal or regulatory violations. The resulting compliance risks are often abstract, generalized, and latent in nature—evaluated primarily by reference to the company's industry characteristics and operational activities. Within this framework, "comprehensive compliance management" is essentially understood as the systematic prevention and control of all potential compliance risks an enterprise might face. By contrast, the risk-based compliance model does not require enterprises to maintain a comprehensive register of all compliance obligations, nor to give equal attention to every potential legal or regulatory violation. Instead, it employs empirical methods to identify and address compliance risks that are concrete, immediate, and already manifesting. Following the principles of specificity and effectiveness, this model prioritizes the resolution of high-impact, time-sensitive risks that—if left unaddressed—may expose the enterprise to catastrophic legal, financial, or reputational harm.

Under the risk-based compliance model, enterprises should avoid engaging in broad, unbounded reviews of all possible compliance obligations. Rather, the identification and assessment of compliance risks should constitute the foundational work upon which the entire compliance management system is built. This model discards abstract and overgeneralized notions of compliance risk, concentrating instead on three specific areas of legal exposure: administrative violations, criminal offenses, and breaches of international financial regulations. These correspond to three core categories of compliance risk—namely, administrative penalties, criminal prosecution, and international financial sanctions—each of which may result in disqualification from market access. In identifying compliance risks, enterprises are expected to adopt systematic, evidence-based methodologies—including investigation, verification, and targeted screening—to pinpoint operational domains where such risks are most likely to materialize. Once risks have been accurately identified, risk assessment should follow, focusing on two key dimensions: the likelihood of occurrence and the magnitude of potential consequences.

In identifying compliance risks, enterprises should focus on violations that have already occurred or are likely to emerge in the near future—what are commonly referred to as concrete or imminent compliance risks. The methods for identifying such risks differ depending on whether the enterprise is undergoing compliance remediation or conducting autonomous compliance initiatives. In the context of compliance remediation involving enterprises subject to investigation or sanctions, the relevant violations may include administrative infractions—such as monopolistic practices, unfair competition, data security breaches, money laundering, or commercial bribery—as well as criminal offenses like issuing fraudulent VAT invoices, selling counterfeit goods, polluting the environment, operating without a license, corporate bribery, collusive bidding, or smuggling. In some cases, enterprises may have breached the codes of conduct established by the World Bank or other international financial institutions. Under these circumstances, enterprises can identify specific compliance risks based directly on the unlawful conduct they have engaged in. For instance, if the violation pertains to national antitrust laws, monopolistic practices should be classified as a primary compliance risk. If the offense involves environmental crimes, then environmental harm should be designated as a core area of compliance concern. Similarly, if a company has engaged in fraud in the course of participating in World Bank-funded procurement projects, integrity-related risks should be prioritized accordingly.

In contrast, during routine autonomous compliance efforts—where no significant legal or regulatory violations have occurred—enterprises cannot rely on prior infractions to define their primary compliance risk areas. Under the risk-oriented compliance model, companies are instead expected to identify specific, high-priority compliance risks through systematic investigative and monitoring methods. Typically, this process begins by selecting a representative operational period during which the enterprise examines its own record of legal or regulatory incidents, analyzes the types of litigation it has faced, and reviews disciplinary or liability records involving employees and senior executives. In addition, the enterprise may assess patterns of misconduct observed in peer companies within the same industry sector. These investigative and monitoring efforts enable enterprises to identify specific operational areas that are especially prone to legal or regulatory violations. Based on this preliminary identification, companies should assess the relative urgency and severity of the various risks, and further narrow the scope of risk domains through a comparative analysis—taking into account factors such as organizational size, governance structure, industry characteristics, business scope, and management culture. The goal is to isolate a small number of compliance risks that are either critical to resolve or highly likely to escalate if left unaddressed. This approach to compliance risk identification is not derived from a comprehensive mapping of all compliance obligations, nor from theoretical assumptions based solely on business operations. Rather, it is grounded in the enterprise's past experience and is designed to identify those risks most likely to recur and result in future violations.

Once specific and concrete compliance risks have been identified, enterprises must conduct a scientifically grounded assessment of each. Such assessment generally unfolds along two key dimensions. First, the likelihood of the risk materializing must be evaluated—namely, the probability that the enterprise will engage in the relevant unlawful or non-compliant conduct in the absence of appropriate compliance controls. Second, enterprises should evaluate the impact of non-compliance by assessing both the direct and indirect consequences that may arise from potential violations, including the various forms of loss the enterprise may incur.

In practice, experienced compliance professionals often apply a 10-point scale to evaluate the likelihood of each compliance risk. The potential impact of non-compliance is then quantified, either as a monetary value or as an impact range. Multiplying the likelihood score by the impact value yields a risk rating for each identified compliance risk. Drawing on the findings of internal self-assessment reports, enterprises should identify operational areas with elevated compliance risk. These may include production, sales, finance, environmental management, procurement and bidding, import/export operations, and interactions with external stakeholders such as customers, suppliers, agents, and distributors. This process enables the detection of high-risk activities and the analysis of governance structures, business models, and management practices that contribute to such risks. After assigning risk ratings to specific positions, personnel, activities, and managerial arrangements, enterprises can determine their overall compliance risk profile. In general, any department, function, individual, or management model demonstrating a strong correlation with past or potential violations—particularly those of a criminal nature—should be classified as high-risk and designated as a priority for compliance remediation.[23]

[23] Ruihua Chen, *China's Experience in Effective Compliance* (Beijing: Peking University Press, 2023), 11–14.

4.4.3 Targeted Compliance Management Systems

In contrast to the management-based compliance model, which emphasizes the construction of a "comprehensive compliance management" system, the risk-based compliance model prioritizes the development of *targeted compliance management systems*, also referred to as *targeted compliance programs*. These programs are established based on the identification and assessment of specific compliance risks in targeted areas of corporate activity, and are designed to address such risks in a focused and effective manner. For instance, Siemens AG, following a period of compliance remediation and the establishment of a robust internal compliance framework, has implemented several targeted compliance programs, including anti-bribery, antitrust, anti-money laundering, and data protection compliance. Likewise, ZTE Corporation, through similar efforts, has developed specialized programs for export control, anti-bribery, and data protection. In another example, companies such as Alibaba, Meituan, and Yangtze River Pharmaceutical Group, after receiving administrative penalties from China's State Administration for Market Regulation, were required to complete compliance remediation within a three-year timeframe—an effort that involved the improvement and refinement of their respective *antitrust compliance programs*.

There exists a common misconception about targeted compliance programs—namely, that they constitute a form of "minor" or "piecemeal" compliance, limited to addressing narrow-scope or domain-specific risks, and thus incapable of fulfilling the overarching objective of ensuring lawful and rule-based corporate governance. In reality, from the perspective of effective risk prevention and control, the establishment of specialized compliance management systems—based on the identification and assessment of concrete risks in priority areas—is fully consistent with the internal logic of compliance system development. This approach reflects practical constraints inherent in corporate operations. Factors such as business scope, industry characteristics, organizational scale, resource limitations, and the urgency of particular compliance risks render the pursuit of fully comprehensive compliance impractical. Within this context, treating targeted compliance programs as the functional units of compliance governance is not only operationally feasible, but also essential for achieving substantive and effective compliance. Absent such programs, enterprises lack clearly defined and actionable compliance norms ("rules"), making it impossible to implement targeted and effective compliance measures ("actions"). In such cases, compliance management risks devolving into an abstract, fragmented, and purposeless exercise.

The establishment of targeted compliance programs does not suggest that compliance management should concentrate solely on specific compliance areas while disregarding broader domains. Rather, the rationale behind targeted compliance reflects a pragmatic and results-driven management philosophy: having addressed specific, high-priority areas of compliance risk, enterprises progressively expand the scope of targeted compliance management through ongoing risk identification and assessment. Siemens AG and ZTE Corporation offer illustrative examples. Each company developed its first targeted compliance program during the course of compliance remediation, and gradually expanded its compliance framework based on further risk assessments. In the future, additional targeted programs may be introduced, but such expansion will necessarily depend on the evolving outcomes of ongoing compliance risk assessment. Importantly, the design and implementation of targeted compliance programs must focus on structural compliance risks—that is, risks that endanger the enterprise's survival and long-term development. In this light, the common assertion that companies should "move from targeted compliance to comprehensive compliance" appears not only unsupported by empirical and normative evidence, but also premature and overly categorical.

A targeted compliance program should not be equated merely with a specialized compliance mechanism for preventing unlawful or non-compliant conduct. To be effectively implemented, such a program must be built upon two essential components: a foundational compliance management platform and targeted compliance elements. The foundational platform—analogous to a computer's operating system—serves as the structural backbone of the compliance system. It not only ensures the routine functioning of the compliance framework but also provides the necessary infrastructure for targeted compliance elements to operate effectively. It is on the basis of this foundational platform that targeted compliance elements can be developed and implemented in a practical and effective manner. A typical foundational compliance management platform may comprise a corporate compliance charter; designated compliance leadership bodies and governance structures; and systems for compliance risk prevention, such as risk assessments, third-party due diligence, employee training, compliance undertakings, and internal communication, and awareness programs. It may further incorporate mechanisms for compliance risk monitoring—including reporting channels, whistleblower systems, compliance investigation, and compliance audits—as well as frameworks for compliance risk response, such as internal investigation, disciplinary measures, sanction mechanisms, and the remediation of systemic deficiencies. The establishment and operation of this foundational platform should be guided by core principles recognized in effective compliance management practice—namely, the principle of proportionality, top-level commitment, effectiveness, the prioritization of compliance review, and sustainability.

Building upon the foundational compliance management platform, enterprises can construct targeted compliance elements tailored to specific areas of compliance. For example, in order to develop an anti-commercial bribery compliance program or an environmental compliance program, companies must incorporate targeted compliance elements into their overarching compliance management system. This entails translating relevant laws, administrative regulations, departmental rules, and internal policies pertaining to anti-bribery or environmental protection into clearly defined corporate compliance obligations. These obligations should then be codified into the organization's compliance policies and operating procedures in the form of concrete standards, protocols, and workflows. Likewise, when preparing employee handbooks, enterprises should incorporate relevant legal and regulatory requirements by formulating binding prohibitions and mandatory duties applicable to all employees, while also specifying the legal consequences of noncompliance.

Furthermore, in areas such as compliance training, compliance undertakings, and internal communication, enterprises should refrain from imposing vague or overly general compliance obligations on all employees. Instead, they should deliver targeted training modules—such as anti-commercial bribery compliance training or environmental compliance training—designed in accordance with the specific legal and regulatory requirements governing anti-bribery and environmental protection. Both employees and managerial personnel should be required to make explicit compliance commitments in these areas, thereby reinforcing a compliance culture that is thematically focused and legally grounded. Incorporating compliance into specific business processes and operational activities also requires tailored institutional arrangements under each specialized compliance program. For example, anti-commercial bribery compliance focuses on mitigating risks of prohibited conduct—such as offering, receiving, or facilitating bribes—particularly in areas such as business development, client acquisition, product sales, bidding and tendering, and cross-border transactions. By contrast, environmental compliance management places greater emphasis on controlling risks in production, waste disposal, and related operational processes, with a particular focus on preventing the discharge of hazardous substances prohibited by applicable environmental laws and regulations.

4.4.4 *Governance Based on Risk Control*

The management-based compliance model emphasizes the implementation of comprehensive compliance management, establishing a system that covers all aspects, stages, and processes of corporate operations. It advances lawful and rule-abiding business conduct by enhancing compliance leadership, organizational structures, operational mechanisms, performance evaluation, and the cultivation of a compliance culture. By contrast, the risk-based compliance model focuses more specifically on the effective control of compliance risks. It seeks to prevent, monitor, and respond to particular types of risk, aiming to avert their occurrence, detect them promptly, and implement timely institutional and systemic remedies when violations do occur. To that end, this model emphasizes both the proactive prevention of compliance risks and the effective management of risks that have already materialized.

Based on the experiences of enterprises engaged in compliance remediation, an effective compliance program typically consists of three essential components. First is the effectiveness of program design, which refers to whether the compliance plan is appropriately tailored, necessary, and feasible in light of the underlying causes of misconduct, and whether it can effectively prevent, monitor, and address the specific compliance risks facing the enterprise. Second is the effectiveness of program implementation, meaning whether the compliance remedial measures committed by the enterprise have been fully and faithfully executed. This includes establishing compliance leadership and organizational structures, conducting compliance reviews of business operations and product approvals, performing due diligence on third-party partners, providing targeted compliance training for employees and management, carrying out internal investigations, imposing disciplinary measures, and continuously improving the compliance system. Third is the effectiveness of program outcomes, namely, whether the implementation of the compliance program has demonstrably reduced the likelihood of repeated violations during the monitoring period, as verified through structured interviews, random checks, simulation testing, unannounced inspections, and in-depth audits.[24]

Based on the experiences of enterprises engaged in autonomous compliance management, once key areas of compliance concern have been identified through risk identification and assessment, companies must, in line with the objective of effective risk control, establish a general compliance management platform and construct targeted compliance mechanisms corresponding to each priority area.

First, even in the absence of any legal or regulatory violations, enterprises should proactively carry out compliance risk identification and assessment to uncover deficiencies in corporate governance structures, managerial controls, operational processes, and criminogenic elements embedded in their business models. In cases involving compliance remediation, such risk assessments are typically conducted during the enterprise's self-inspection or internal investigation phase. By contrast, within the framework of autonomous compliance management, these activities should be initiated during the preparatory stage, prior to the formal establishment of a compliance system. For enterprises not currently subject to regulatory investigations, administrative penalties, criminal liability, or international financial sanctions, conducting such risk assessments is no less important. It is through these assessments that companies can identify latent risks in their governance architecture, management practices, procedural operations, and commercial models. This constitutes the essential foundation for preventing formalistic, "paper compliance" and for achieving a truly effective and substantive compliance regime.

Second, once deficiencies in governance structures, managerial controls, operational processes, or business models have been identified, enterprises that are not subject to legal proceedings should nonetheless undertake necessary institutional corrections and systemic remediation. This involves adopting targeted measures to eliminate hidden risks, close structural loopholes, and address organizational shortcomings. Such corrective efforts represent not only the proven experience of enterprises undergoing compliance remediation,

[24] Ruihua Chen, *The Chinese Experience of Effective Compliance* (Beijing: Peking University Press, 2023), 11–14.

but also the necessary path for any organization seeking to establish a truly effective and integrated compliance management system. Without such institutional correction and systemic repair, the premature implementation of a broad, all-encompassing compliance framework is likely to result in paper compliance, formalistic compliance, or even outright ineffectiveness.

Third, in accordance with the principles of proportionality and top-level commitment, enterprises must allocate compliance resources—human, material, and financial—in a manner commensurate with their size, business operations, and risk exposure. Compliance structures and mechanisms should be proportionate to the nature and magnitude of the identified risks. Senior management must lead by example, demonstrating sustained and visible commitment to compliance. This entails ensuring the allocation of adequate resources necessary for effective compliance operations; cultivating a compliance culture through internal communication, training, and formal commitments; safeguarding the priority, independence, and authority of compliance review processes; and responding to violations with timely and effective disciplinary measures to reinforce accountability and ensure the rigorous implementation of the compliance management system.

Finally, in order to ensure effective control of compliance risks, the compliance management system may be structured as a comprehensive compliance risk management framework consisting of three interrelated components: prevention, monitoring, and response. To effectively prevent the occurrence of specific compliance risks, enterprises should formulate dedicated compliance policies, publish targeted employee handbooks, conduct continuous risk assessments, perform due diligence on clients, third-party partners, and acquisition targets, deliver tailored compliance training, obtain formal compliance commitments from managers and employees, and sustain internal communication initiatives to promote and embed a compliance culture. To effectively monitor potential compliance risks, enterprises should establish a real-time surveillance and early-warning system—akin to a 24-hour radar detection network. This entails introducing multiple monitoring mechanisms, including periodic compliance reports on risk exposures and incidents, anonymous whistleblower channels, internal investigations into suspected misconduct, and ongoing compliance performance monitoring and auditing. To effectively respond to compliance risks that have already materialized, enterprises should establish a structured response mechanism. This includes conducting independent internal investigations into violations, imposing disciplinary sanctions on responsible individuals, and addressing and correcting identified deficiencies within the compliance framework in a timely manner.

4.5 Comparing Compliance Management Models

Over the past two decades of experimentation and institutional development, two primary models of corporate compliance management have gradually taken shape in China. State-owned enterprises (SOEs), under the guidance of international compliance frameworks and domestic regulatory guidelines, have generally adopted a management-based compliance model in building autonomous, routine compliance systems. In contrast, a substantial number of enterprises that have been subjected to administrative investigations or sanctions imposed by international financial institutions due to legal or regulatory violations—commonly referred to as implicated enterprises—have adopted a risk-based compliance model in the course of their compliance remediation efforts. Importantly, however, many of these implicated enterprises, during the compliance remediation process, have also begun to experiment with autonomous compliance system building and have increasingly incorporated risk-based thinking into the design of their internal compliance frameworks. This development indicates that the risk-based model is not limited to post-violation remedial scenarios, but is equally applicable to enterprises engaged in proactive and self-initiated compliance management.

From the perspective of both the conceptual soundness of compliance governance and the practical effectiveness of compliance implementation, the two models outlined above possess distinct theoretical rationales and empirical foundations. Each carries its own set of advantages and limitations. This article does not aim to make a normative judgment as to which model is preferable; rather, it undertakes a preliminary comparative analysis from four analytical dimensions. As to which model will ultimately define the developmental trajectory of corporate compliance in China, a conclusive answer remains premature. The determination of this question will depend on the accumulation of empirical research evaluating the evolution of compliance governance and reform practices within Chinese enterprises, as well as on the reasoned, experience-based choices made by companies in response to the operational outcomes associated with each model.

First, in terms of compliance objectives, the management-based compliance model advances an appealing ideal—the notion that enterprises should fully and systematically adhere to rules across all aspects of their operations. In some cases, compliance is even framed as a cultural imperative that goes beyond mere legal conformity, reflecting an elevated expectation that aligns with the principles of corporate social responsibility. It underscores the enterprise's ethical obligations and its broader role as a socially responsible actor, embodying the highest normative aspiration within corporate governance. Yet an enterprise remains, fundamentally, a profit-driven commercial entity, constantly navigating pressures related to sustainable profitability, market competition, and long-term viability—and at times, existential survival. To impose overly expansive expectations of moral and social responsibility on such entities risks fostering a form of compliance utopianism, one that is disconnected from operational exigencies. While normatively appealing, such ideals often prove too lofty to gain broad internal resonance, making it difficult to secure consistent organizational support or sustained resource commitment.

In contrast, the risk-based compliance model adopts a more realist objective by conceptualizing compliance management as a process of compliance risk prevention and control. Within this framework, compliance risk is defined as a form of strategic risk, placed on equal footing with decision-making, operational, and financial risks. From this perspective, compliance is primarily understood as a collection of risk mitigation, crisis response, and liability segmentation measures aimed at preventing the enterprise from descending into catastrophic failure. Although this orientation does not reflect an elevated moral vision—and may, in fact, be perceived as a loss-avoidance strategy imposed by external pressures—it tends to generate stronger internal traction. Given its alignment with the enterprise's core interests, this model tends to garner stronger internal support and produce outcomes more closely aligned with corporate objectives.

Secondly, with respect to its foundational premise, the management-based compliance model places particular emphasis on the systematic identification and organization of compliance obligations. It treats both the binding legal norms enacted by the state and the voluntary commitments assumed by the enterprise as equally binding normative requirements to be observed in an integrated manner. In essence, this model defines compliance as ensuring adherence to the full spectrum of "rules"—both externally mandated and internally assumed—that regulate corporate conduct. Ideally, if a company could fully comply with every requirement set forth in its so-called compliance obligation inventory, this would constitute the most desirable and comprehensive compliance outcome. In practice, however, the legal and regulatory framework governing corporate conduct is both highly diverse and overwhelmingly voluminous. In addition to the multiplicity of national laws and administrative regulations, enterprises must navigate sector-specific regulatory rules, industry standards, ethical codes, and binding international treaties and customary practices—each differing in scope and applicability. Compounding these are the internal policies, contractual undertakings, and other self-imposed commitments that companies voluntarily adopt, the sheer volume of which defies quantification. A compliance model premised on the exhaustive enumeration of obligations risks becoming overwhelmed by the vast and ever-expanding sea of regulatory requirements. Even the process of identifying, classifying, and maintaining a comprehensive obligation register demands vast human, financial, and material resources—let alone the practical challenge of ensuring full and consistent compliance with each listed requirement.

The risk-based compliance model, by contrast, adopts a fundamentally different managerial logic. Rather than placing emphasis on the mapping of enterprise compliance obligations, it begins with the identification of compliance risks and treats the effective control of tangible, specific, and imminent risks as the foundation for building a compliance management system. At first glance, this approach may seem to diverge from the original intent of compliance, as it does not place "rule adherence" at the center. However, the philosophy it embodies arguably reflects a more advanced conception of compliance—namely, the identification of major compliance risks as a means to determine the specific regulatory areas where adherence is most urgently required. This approach is closely analogous to the logic of medical diagnosis and treatment.

Although it does not explicitly emphasize the ideal of holistic health, it relies on comprehensive assessment and applies targeted treatment to the most vulnerable areas, thereby achieving functional health outcomes in those domains.

Third, with respect to the definition of compliance risk, the management-based compliance model adopts an expansive approach by defining such risk as encompassing all adverse consequences that may result from rule violations. It emphasizes that compliance risk transcends legal risk, requiring enterprises to give due consideration not only to administrative or judicial penalties, but also to potential economic losses, reputational harm, and negative societal evaluations. In principle, if an enterprise were able to effectively prevent all such consequences, it could achieve an ideal state of internal governance. In reality, however, the most immediate and consequential risk confronting enterprises is the prospect of legal sanctions, which may result in the restriction or revocation of their license to operate, thereby triggering serious strategic losses or even existential threats. This is the core compliance concern for most companies. The urgency of this issue is particularly pronounced among Chinese enterprises that have undergone rapid, unregulated expansion under conditions of weak regulatory oversight. For these firms, the foremost challenge is how to develop a compliance management system capable of preventing administrative penalties, criminal prosecution, or financial sanctions imposed by either domestic or foreign authorities. Against this backdrop, abstract appeals to the prevention of "economic loss" or the avoidance of "ethical risk," though rhetorically elevated, often fail to resonate with companies facing immediate and tangible legal exposure. Such discourse, detached from the realities of corporate risk management, holds limited practical value.

In contrast, the risk-oriented compliance model rejects the moralized conception of compliance and defines compliance risk as the threat of administrative penalties, criminal liability, or state-imposed financial sanctions, as well as disqualification from market participation or other catastrophic consequences resulting from violations of law or regulation. Under this definitional framework, compliance risk is treated as a distinct subset of legal risk. It explicitly excludes relatively minor or non-critical infractions—such as civil breaches of contract, violations of labor and employment laws, failures to fulfill corporate social responsibilities, or disregard for public ethics. While these risks still require management and control, they fall within the remit of the enterprise's legal affairs department and lie outside the core objectives of compliance management.

What genuinely constitutes a strategic risk for enterprises is the potential exposure to administrative penalties, criminal prosecution, or international financial sanctions stemming from legal or regulatory violations. These sanctions may result in disqualification consequences—such as the revocation of business licenses, the termination of special operating permits, the suspension of production or commercial operations, the loss of critical clients or trading qualifications, and, in extreme cases, the cancellation of corporate registration. Only by defining compliance risk as a threat of this strategic magnitude can senior corporate leadership be effectively persuaded to place it on the same level as decision-making, operational, and financial risks. This is the only way compliance risk management can claim its rightful place within the broader framework of enterprise-wide strategic risk governance. After all, if minor economic losses, moral lapses, or negative public perceptions are also classified as compliance risks, how many companies would be willing to invest substantial resources into building a robust compliance management system? Under such an expansive and diluted definition, what foundation would the so-called principle of top-level commitment to compliance rest upon?

Finally, with respect to compliance management methodology, the management-based model promotes a vision of comprehensive compliance—extending across all business areas, operational stages, personnel categories, and managerial processes—with the ultimate aim of cultivating a compliance culture grounded in legality and regulatory adherence. If realized in full, this would indeed constitute an admirable and inspiring objective. Yet in a regulatory climate marked by escalating scrutiny and heightened risks of legal sanctions and disqualification, this model exhibits two critical structural flaws. First, given the severe limitations on compliance resources available to most enterprises, it is often challenging to construct and sustain a comprehensive compliance management system. Second, by requiring firms to disperse these limited resources across every dimension of operation, the model risks overextension and fragmentation. Compliance work, in this context, often becomes piecemeal, overly procedural, and detached from strategic risk priorities—ultimately weakening the enterprise's capacity to prevent and manage its most urgent and consequential compliance threats.

According to media reports and relevant empirical studies, several Chinese enterprises in the petroleum and petrochemical sectors have identified numerous key compliance areas and claimed to implement "comprehensive compliance management," yet continue to experience major liability incidents and growing safety risks in production and workplace management. Similarly, certain pharmaceutical and medical device manufacturers, though seemingly equipped with comprehensive compliance management systems, have exhibited entrenched patterns of commercial bribery and corruption, placing both corporate executives and entities at risk of administrative enforcement or even criminal prosecution. For such enterprises, strengthening anti-commercial bribery compliance mechanisms is a far more pressing and relevant task. Likewise, some state-owned enterprises that purport to have established comprehensive compliance management frameworks often encounter strict regulatory scrutiny when conducting overseas investment, operations, or listings. In jurisdictions with rigorous enforcement regimes—such as the United States and European Union member states—these enterprises have repeatedly committed legal violations, prompting settlements with foreign regulators or judicial authorities. Many have paid substantial fines and been compelled to carry out targeted compliance remediation, particularly through the reconstruction of their internal compliance systems.

In contrast, the risk-based compliance model embraces a philosophy of effective compliance risk control. It addresses major compliance risks through the implementation of targeted compliance programs and by organically integrating a foundational compliance management platform with targeted compliance elements. This allows enterprises to prevent, monitor, and respond to specific compliance risks, thereby achieving tangible and effective compliance outcomes. Although this model may seem at odds with the ideal of "comprehensive, rule-based corporate conduct," it in fact reflects a realist management approach—one that avoids utopian aspirations and instead seeks to resolve each identified compliance risk through pragmatic and incremental action. This model abandons superficial slogans such as "compliance in all areas," "compliance by all employees," or "compliance across all processes." Instead, it promotes a targeted, differentiated, and prioritized approach to risk control, based on the identification and assessment of specific risk areas, high-risk functions, and vulnerable personnel.

For example, enterprises should deliver compliance training and obtain formal compliance commitments from employees; conduct compliance due diligence on third-party business partners; and implement a compliance-prioritized management approach for personnel engaged in high-risk operations such as production, sales, import and export, bidding, and pollutant disposal. When a business activity or product is found to pose potential legal or regulatory risks, the enterprise must promptly assess the risk, take preventive or corrective action, and, where necessary, escalate the matter to senior management for a formal decision on suspension or rejection of the activity. Meanwhile, whether establishing compliance leadership and organizational structures, issuing compliance policies and employee handbooks, or constructing systems for risk prevention, monitoring, and response, all efforts should be centered on the effective control of compliance risk. The overarching objective is to ensure that the compliance management system is capable of substantively mitigating specific and identifiable compliance risks.

For this reason, enterprises need not devote their limited resources to overly formalistic or proceduralized management activities. Instead, they should implement targeted control measures to effectively prevent, monitor, and address real compliance risks, thereby making risk mitigation the central objective of compliance management. With respect to the notion of "compliance culture," there is no need for enterprises to engage in superficial or ceremonial promotional campaigns. A genuine culture of compliance can be gradually fostered through substantive management practices—such as compliance training, internal communication, hierarchical information flow, and mechanisms for incentives and sanctions. Compliance culture emerges organically from the effective functioning of a sound compliance risk control system; it arises naturally from effective compliance risk management. Enterprises should therefore avoid performative "cultural construction" initiatives, which often fail to produce substantive effects.

Given the respective strengths and limitations of the two compliance management models discussed above, how should enterprises determine which model to adopt? In general, according to conventional approaches to building a compliance system, enterprises that have not committed any unlawful or non-compliant acts typically opt for a management-based compliance system. As non-implicated enterprises, they are not under investigation, nor do they face imminent regulatory sanctions or criminal liability. As such, their compliance efforts are largely preventive in nature—often driven by the need to meet regulatory expectations or to respond to routine oversight and assessment by supervisory authorities. In contrast, enterprises suspected of administrative violations—implicated enterprises already subject to regulatory investigations—are exposed to an immediate risk of administrative penalties. For these enterprises, adopting a risk-based compliance system becomes a practical necessity. Their compliance efforts are generally shaped by the nature of the alleged violations and are aimed at preventing the recurrence of such misconduct through the development of targeted compliance programs.

Even so, the choice between compliance management models is not fixed or immutable, whether for implicated or non-implicated enterprises. In principle, once a non-implicated enterprise has established a comprehensive compliance management system under a management-based model, it should avoid becoming complacent or overly dependent on the initial structure. Instead, it should engage in regular risk identification and assessment to uncover systemic compliance risks—those with the potential to pose serious, even existential, threats to the company's operations or long-term viability. Upon identifying such critical risks, enterprises should treat them as priorities for enhanced compliance oversight, directing appropriate human and financial resources to strengthen targeted compliance structures. In line with the principle that it is more effective to address one critical risk thoroughly than to spread resources too thin, enterprises should adopt targeted and intensive compliance programs aimed at effectively preventing, monitoring, and responding to specific high-impact compliance risks.

At the same time, enterprises that have already been implicated in regulatory or legal violations—and have undergone successful compliance remediation under the supervision of regulatory authorities—should not regard the completion of a single targeted compliance initiative as the conclusion of their compliance efforts. Even where a specific compliance framework has been established or improved, regulatory assessments have been passed, and more lenient administrative outcomes have been granted, enterprises should continue to adopt a risk-based approach. This includes conducting specialized compliance risk identification and assessment to uncover additional risks that may have significant implications for the company's operations or long-term sustainability. The experiences of companies such as Siemens AG and ZTE Corporation demonstrate that effective compliance systems are built through a stepwise process—starting with targeted compliance remediation, followed by risk reassessment and the introduction of new specialized compliance programs. These phased efforts not only activated internal compliance control mechanisms but also gradually fostered a corporate culture of lawful and rule-based operation. Ultimately, the construction of a sound and sustainable compliance system depends on integrating the strengths of both management-based and risk-based models. Building a foundational compliance management platform and, on that basis, introducing targeted compliance programs to address high-priority risks constitute an essential pathway for enterprises to develop an institutionalized, dynamic, and effective compliance management framework.

CHAPTER 5

Corporate Compliance Risk Assessment

5.1 Introduction

At present, there are two prevailing theoretical models concerning the nature and function of corporate compliance: the management-based compliance model and the risk-based compliance model. The former is commonly applied in the context of autonomous compliance, where compliance is defined as the enterprise's adherence to legal and regulatory rules. This model emphasizes a comprehensive inventory of compliance obligations, with the aim of achieving full coverage across employees, business functions, and operational processes—thereby fulfilling the overarching objective of lawful and rule-based corporate governance. By contrast, the risk-based compliance model is typically adopted in the context of compliance remediation, particularly by enterprises that have been implicated in legal or regulatory violations. Under this model, compliance is conceptualized as a compliance risk control system, with emphasis placed on identifying the specific risks an enterprise faces and developing targeted compliance programs accordingly. The objective is to establish a system capable of effectively preventing, monitoring, and mitigating compliance risks.[1]

Under the management-based compliance model, compliance risk refers to the possibility that an enterprise may fail to fulfill its compliance obligations. It typically consists of two core components. The first is the likelihood of non-compliance—that is, the probability that the enterprise may internally engage in conduct that violates applicable norms, including external laws and regulations, internal policies and procedures, and ethical or moral standards. The second is the likelihood of loss, referring to the potential for the enterprise to incur external sanctions, administrative or criminal penalties, financial losses, reputational harm, or other adverse consequences resulting from such

[1] Ruihua Chen, *Two Models of Corporate Compliance Management System*, Legal Review, no. 1 (2024).

R. Chen, *An Introduction to Corporate Compliance*,
https://doi.org/10.1007/978-981-95-7257-1_5

violations. Based on this framework, compliance risk is understood as a category of corporate risk that surpasses conventional legal risk in scope and severity.

In contrast, under the risk-based compliance model, compliance risk—though rooted in legal risk—is not regarded as a conventional category of legal liability. Instead, it is conceptualized as a form of strategic risk that may subject the enterprise to significant adverse outcomes or even catastrophic losses. Within the broader framework of strategic risk management, compliance risk is typically considered alongside decision-making risk, operational risk, and financial risk, with particular attention paid to the likelihood of administrative sanctions, criminal prosecution, or international financial sanctions arising from serious legal or regulatory violations. First, with respect to the likelihood of noncompliance, compliance risk under this model refers primarily to the possibility that an enterprise may breach administrative regulations, criminal statutes, or international financial governance rules. By contrast, general civil liabilities or ethical and moral risks are not typically included within the scope of compliance risk management in this framework. Second, with respect to the likelihood of loss, compliance risk under the risk-based compliance model primarily refers to the possibility that an enterprise may be subjected to administrative penalties, criminal prosecution, sanctions imposed by international financial institutions, and associated disqualification from market access or participation. Corporate conduct that violates administrative regulations typically results in regulatory sanctions imposed by supervisory authorities; conduct that constitutes a criminal offense may lead to conviction and sentencing; and violations of the compliance requirements or integrity standards established by international financial institutions may trigger temporary or permanent sanctions. In all three cases, such sanctions may further result in collateral consequences—most notably, the revocation or restriction of licenses, permits, or other forms of operational qualification. By contrast, civil liability, general economic loss, or so-called reputational damage arising from ordinary legal violations typically falls outside the scope of compliance risk as defined under this model.

Regardless of how compliance risk is defined, enterprises generally regard compliance management as a risk-based governance activity and view compliance risk assessment as the foundational step in building an effective compliance management system. However, several foundational questions remain to be addressed: What, precisely, does "compliance risk assessment" entail? In what ways does it intersect with risk identification? And how is it connected to the delineation of compliance risk domains? On these issues, both domestic and international compliance guidelines—as well as major global compliance frameworks—tend to provide only vague, generalized, and non-operational definitions.

For example, under the UK anti-bribery regime, the principle of risk assessment is recognized as one of the six "adequate procedures" essential to effective compliance management. It emphasizes that enterprises must regularly assess the nature and severity of potential bribery risks and ensure that such assessments are both evidence-based and properly documented.[2] Similarly, the French anti-corruption framework identifies risk identification as one of the three foundational pillars of an effective compliance system. It requires enterprises to conduct structured risk identification processes in order to confirm, evaluate, and categorize existing corruption risks, and to adopt a tiered approach to compliance risk management accordingly. Based on the identification, evaluation, and prioritization of corruption risks, enterprises are expected to design, implement, and operationalize anti-corruption programs aimed at effectively preventing corruption, monitoring misconduct, and remedying institutional deficiencies.[3] In the United States, both criminal justice authorities and regulatory agencies regard ***compliance risk assessment*** as a critical factor in evaluating the effectiveness of corporate compliance programs under the *Foreign Corrupt Practices Act (FCPA)*. Enterprises are expected not to treat all compliance risks equally, but rather to allocate compliance resources in a risk-sensitive manner—prioritizing high-risk areas. Moreover, companies that sincerely implement a comprehensive and risk-based compliance program may receive tangible benefits in the form of mitigated penalties or leniency in enforcement outcomes.[4] Taken together, the anti-corruption frameworks of the United Kingdom, France, and the United States implicitly require enterprises to carry out ***targeted compliance risk assessments*** in the anti-bribery context, and treat such assessments as an essential element in the design and implementation of effective compliance programs. However, despite emphasizing the importance of risk assessment, these frameworks fail to provide clear and operational guidance regarding the specific requirements, methodologies, or procedures for conducting compliance risk identification and assessment in practice.

Another example is the *Compliance Management Systems—Requirements with Guidance for Use (ISO 37301:2021)*, issued by the International Organization for Standardization (ISO). The standard defines **compliance risk** as *"the likelihood of occurrence and the consequences of non-compliance with the organization's compliance obligations."* ISO 37301 mandates that organizations identify, analyze, and evaluate their compliance risks on the basis of a compliance risk assessment. This process requires linking their compliance obligations to the relevant activities, products, services, and operational processes, conducting compliance risk identification, performing periodic

[2] Yuanhuang Zhang et al., *Global Perspectives on Corporate Compliance*, Peking University Press, 2021, 112.

[3] Ruihua Chen, *The Chinese Experience of Effective Compliance*, Peking University Press, 2023, 280.

[4] Ruihua Chen, "Effective Compliance Standards in French Anti-Corruption Cases," *Qiaoqiao Legal Scholar* (WeChat public account), June 29, 2022.

compliance risk assessments, and reassessing compliance risks when significant changes occur in circumstances or the organizational environment.[5]

A further example can be found in the *Administrative Measures for Compliance Management of Central State-Owned Enterprises*, issued by the State-owned Assets Supervision and Administration Commission (SASAC) of the State Council of China. This document defines compliance management as a risk-based governance activity aimed at "effectively preventing and controlling compliance risks." It requires the business and functional departments of central SOEs to "carry out compliance risk identification and assessment, compile risk inventories and contingency plans," "regularly review compliance risks in key positions," and "promptly report compliance risks." Compliance management departments are further tasked with "organizing the identification, early warning, and response to compliance risks." In addition, the document mandates that central SOEs develop dedicated compliance policies or issue specialized compliance guidelines for high-risk areas such as anti-monopoly, anti-commercial bribery, environmental protection, workplace safety, labor and employment, tax administration, and data protection.[6] By emphasizing the importance of compliance risk identification and assessment, and by requiring enterprises to determine their *priority compliance risk areas*, the document reflects a noteworthy regulatory development. However, it falls short of offering concrete methodological guidance for conducting compliance risk identification and assessment. In particular, it does not clarify the relationship between the delineation of compliance risk areas and the process of compliance risk assessment.

It is evident that none of the aforementioned legal and regulatory documents provides a concrete definition or systematic account of critical issues such as the definition, scope, or methodology of compliance risk assessment, nor do they clarify its relationship to the broader notion of compliance risk. In many respects, these instruments exhibit ambiguity, inconsistency, and even conflicting interpretations. In light of these limitations, it is both necessary and timely to undertake theoretical reflection and conceptual clarification, grounded in effective corporate compliance practices and guided by recent institutional developments.

The central argument advanced in this chapter is that *compliance risk assessment* refers to the process through which an enterprise—by focusing on specific legal domains where violations are likely to occur—identifies, analyzes, and evaluates potential instances of noncompliance, taking into account the

[5] Research and Guidance Group on Corporate Compliance Cases, Supreme People's Procuratorate, *Manual on Corporate Compliance Cases*, China Procuratorate Press, 2022, 426.

[6] State-owned Assets Supervision and Administration Commission of the State Council, *Measures for the Compliance Management of Central Enterprises* (2022), Articles 13, 14, and 18.

significant adverse consequences such violations may trigger, including administrative penalties, criminal liability, and disqualification from relevant qualifications or market access. Prior to conducting a compliance risk assessment, enterprises must first undertake the ***delineation of compliance risk areas***—that is, the precise identification of legal domains in which compliance risks are likely to arise. This step serves as the foundation for developing targeted compliance programs and constitutes a necessary precondition for conducting meaningful risk assessments. Once compliance risk areas have been clearly delineated, the assessment process can be structured into three core stages: risk identification, risk analysis, and risk evaluation. This systematic approach enables enterprises to pinpoint specific compliance risk points, uncover the underlying structural causes of such risks, and categorize them according to their level of severity—thereby establishing a risk-based prioritization framework for compliance management. Based on the results of this assessment, enterprises can implement risk management and control measures aimed at the effective prevention, monitoring, and mitigation of compliance risks.

5.2 Defining Compliance Risk Areas

Empirical evidence indicates that corporate violations of laws and regulations typically occur within distinct compliance risk domains. When an enterprise engages in unlawful or noncompliant conduct, it often simultaneously breaches the legal norms specific to a particular regulatory field. For example, conduct that violates national anti-monopoly laws is typically classified as monopolistic behavior; violations of anti-money laundering legislation are commonly considered money laundering; breaches of environmental and natural resource protection laws are categorized as environmental violations; noncompliance with cybersecurity, data security, or personal information protection laws is referred to as cyber and data-related violations; and violations of tax administration laws are generally treated as tax-related violations. Accordingly, if an enterprise is reasonably likely to engage in such forms of conduct and thereby faces the risk of administrative penalties, legal sanctions, or disqualification from relevant qualifications, it is deemed to be exposed to compliance risks within the corresponding legal domain.

The term *compliance risk area* refers to the specific legal domain in which a compliance risk is likely to occur. In compliance management practice, the delineation of compliance risk areas is generally not treated as an integral part of the compliance risk assessment process. Nevertheless, it serves as a foundational prerequisite for conducting such assessments, a necessary basis for formulating targeted compliance programs, and a critical condition for ensuring the overall effectiveness of compliance management. First, the accurate delineation of compliance risk areas allows enterprises to move beyond a vague recognition of the mere possibility of noncompliance and instead identify the specific forms and types of legal and regulatory breaches that may occur. Only when these risk areas have been clearly defined can enterprises meaningfully engage in the identification, analysis, and evaluation of compliance risks. Second, delineating compliance risk areas provides the foundational basis for developing targeted compliance programs. As a general principle, an enterprise seeking to manage compliance risks within a particular legal domain must establish a corresponding compliance program. For example, where noncompliance may arise in areas such as tax administration, environmental protection, intellectual property rights, occupational safety, data and cybersecurity, or anti-bribery, the enterprise should establish targeted compliance programs—such as a tax compliance program, environmental compliance program, IP compliance program, occupational safety compliance program, data and cybersecurity compliance program, or anti-commercial bribery compliance program, respectively. Moreover, accurate delineation of compliance risk areas enables enterprises to allocate limited compliance resources to areas of highest concern. It supports the implementation of top-level commitment, facilitates the development of tailored compliance manuals and employee handbooks, and provides a foundation for targeted risk management activities, including risk assessments, due diligence, compliance training, commitment declarations, compliance reporting, and whistleblower procedures. Through this structured and domain-specific approach, enterprises can build effective systems for the prevention, monitoring, and mitigation of recurring or similar compliance violations.

How, then, should enterprises go about accurately delineating their compliance risk areas in practice? A useful analytical approach is to distinguish between two primary contexts in which compliance management typically takes place: compliance remediation and autonomous compliance.[7]

5.2.1 Compliance Remediation

When an enterprise has engaged in unlawful or noncompliant conduct and becomes subject to administrative enforcement proceedings, criminal prosecution, or regulatory actions initiated by international financial institutions, it may reach a settlement agreement with the relevant administrative authorities, judicial bodies, or global regulators. Under such agreements, the enterprise undertakes to implement compliance remediation measures and, upon meeting specified requirements and successfully passing a compliance assessment, may be granted more lenient treatment. In the context of compliance remediation involving legally implicated enterprises, a key question arises: how should the delineation of compliance risk areas be approached?

In principle, the occurrence of unlawful or noncompliant conduct indicates the materialization of a compliance risk—meaning that the enterprise has already committed a violation, thereby significantly increasing its exposure to

[7] Compliance remediation is also referred to as "post-crisis compliance," while autonomous compliance is often described as the "routine construction of a compliance management system." For a comparative analysis of these two compliance scenarios, see Ruihua Chen, "Two Models of Effective Compliance Management," *Law and Social Development*, no. 1 (2022).

administrative penalties, criminal liability, or international financial sanctions. Under the oversight of regulatory authorities, judicial institutions, or international financial organizations, enterprises typically identify relevant compliance risk areas based on the nature of the underlying misconduct and proceed to establish or enhance corresponding targeted compliance programs. For example, since 2021, companies such as Alibaba, Meituan, and Yangtze River Pharmaceutical Group have been investigated by China's State Administration for Market Regulation (SAMR) for violations of anti-monopoly laws. In response, these enterprises identified antitrust violations as a distinct compliance risk area and adopted anti-monopoly compliance programs as a core component of their compliance remediation efforts.[8] Similarly, Hunan Construction Engineering Group was subject to an enforcement action by the World Bank for engaging in fraudulent conduct during the bidding process for loan-funded projects. The company was sanctioned with a conditionally lifted debarment from future procurement opportunities. In the resulting settlement agreement, the enterprise designated integrity-related violations as a key compliance risk area and committed to developing an integrity compliance program as part of its targeted compliance remediation framework.[9]

From the perspective of effective compliance remediation, enterprises subject to regulatory or enforcement proceedings should adopt a narrowly tailored definition of compliance risk areas and prioritize the development and implementation of corresponding targeted compliance programs as the central task of their remediation efforts. Given the strictly prescribed compliance monitoring period, the limited compliance resources typically available, and the institutional pressure from regulatory agencies, judicial authorities, or international financial institutions, enterprises must delineate compliance risk areas in a pragmatic and focused manner. In practice, this delineation should proceed in two steps. First, the enterprise designates as a compliance risk area the specific legal domain corresponding to the misconduct already committed. Second, it includes within the same domain the potential for similar or recurring misconduct. Potential violations that fall outside the nature or scope of the original offense are, as a rule, excluded from the defined compliance risk areas for remediation purposes.

5.2.2 Autonomous Compliance

In contrast to enterprises engaged in compliance remediation, those undertaking autonomous compliance often face greater difficulties in delineating compliance risk areas. These enterprises have not committed any known legal or regulatory violations, are not subject to investigation by administrative

[8] Lei Wang, "Compliance Governance of Platform Monopolies," *Administrative Law Review*, no. 4 (2023).

[9] Ruihua Chen, "Compliance System of Hunan Construction Group," *China Lawyer*, no. 11 (2019).

agencies, judicial authorities, or international financial institutions, and do not currently face the prospect of penalties, sanctions, or disqualification. Rather, their compliance initiatives are typically undertaken voluntarily—either in response to regulatory expectations issued by administrative bodies or industry associations, or as a strategic decision aimed at strengthening their market competitiveness.

In most cases, enterprises do not establish compliance management systems at the time of their founding. Rather, such systems are typically introduced later—often when, in the course of business operations, the enterprise becomes aware of significant compliance risks. The impetus for building a compliance management system generally arises from the recognition that the enterprise's operations entail two types of potential exposure: first, the risk of engaging in specific types of unlawful or noncompliant conduct; and second, the risk of being subjected to administrative penalties, criminal liability, or international financial sanctions. Once an enterprise becomes aware of these potential exposures and conducts a rational, evidence-based assessment, it can begin to delineate the relevant compliance risk areas.

From the perspective of corporate compliance practice, enterprises may identify their compliance risk areas from three distinct angles: the internal perspective, the external perspective, and the comparative perspective.

The internal perspective refers to the enterprise's own efforts to detect potential compliance risks arising from its operational activities. Traditionally, companies have relied on factors such as business scope, industry characteristics, and operational scale to determine their risk areas. However, this approach often results in overly broad classifications that fail to capture the enterprise's specific vulnerabilities. To improve accuracy, many enterprises now undertake focused internal investigations to identify potential compliance risk areas. These investigations may involve: interviewing employees to uncover latent compliance risks, reviewing transaction records, contracts, and invoices to detect business segments prone to regulatory violations, examining past violations and enforcement actions to identify historically exposed areas, and analyzing litigation history to identify weaknesses in legal compliance. For example, through such internal investigations, Siemens AG identified three additional compliance risk areas beyond commercial bribery. Similarly, ZTE Corporation identified, in addition to compliance risks related to export control, two further major compliance risk areas—commercial bribery and data protection—through its risk investigation activities.

The external perspective refers to the identification of compliance risk areas based on the latest developments in legislation, regulatory policy, and the broader enforcement landscape. In many cases, the promulgation of new laws or the revision of existing regulations imposes more stringent compliance obligations on enterprises, thereby exposing them to elevated risks in previously unregulated or lightly regulated domains. For example, since 2023, China has launched a far-reaching anti-corruption campaign targeting the healthcare sector, alongside legislative amendments to the Criminal Law concerning penalties for bribery-related offenses. These legal and regulatory developments have markedly heightened the commercial bribery compliance risks faced by healthcare enterprises. As a result, establishing robust anti-commercial bribery compliance systems has become a top compliance priority across the industry. Similarly, when regulatory agencies introduce new supervisory priorities or intensify enforcement in particular areas, enterprises operating in those sectors may face newly emergent compliance risks. For instance, since 2022, China's public security authorities have launched a nationwide campaign against telecom and online fraud, intensifying enforcement efforts and adopting a preventive regulatory approach. In response, enterprises engaged in telecommunications and internet-based services have begun identifying anti-fraud compliance—particularly in relation to telecom and online fraud—as a key area of compliance concern.

The comparative perspective refers to the practice by which enterprises identify their own compliance risk areas through comparison with other entities operating in the same industry, engaging in similar business activities, or adopting comparable operational models. In China, administrative and judicial authorities often engage in selective enforcement, meaning that only certain enterprises are investigated and sanctioned despite widespread violations within an industry. For example, in sectors such as healthcare (where commercial bribery is prevalent), construction (where collusive bidding is common), or among small businesses (frequently involved in issuing fraudulent VAT invoices), it is often impractical for regulators or enforcement agencies to investigate all offenders. In such cases, selective enforcement is sometimes adopted as a matter of necessity. Given this reality, when enterprises in the same sector or with similar operational profiles become subject to administrative investigations, criminal prosecutions, or enforcement actions by international financial institutions, other enterprises facing similar risk conditions should take the opportunity to conduct compliance risk assessments. Drawing lessons from the enforcement experiences of their peers, they can more accurately identify and delineate their own compliance risk areas.

Naturally, through the above three investigative approaches, enterprises may uncover multiple compliance risk areas simultaneously. Given the limited resources typically available for compliance management, enterprises must take a comprehensive and balanced approach when confronted with multiple compliance risk areas, in order to achieve the goals of effective compliance governance. In practice, all enterprises are exposed to diverse types and degrees of compliance risk in the course of their operations. Some risks are potential, while others are actual; some arise at the macro level, while others are micro-level; some reflect the possibility of internal misconduct, while others involve the likelihood of external sanctions or penalties. Some compliance professionals distinguish between *abstract compliance risks*—which refer to generalized, potential, and often macro-level possibilities of legal or regulatory violations—and *concrete compliance risks*, which are specific, current, and directly associated with actual or imminent penalties, sanctions, or other adverse consequences.[10] The latter category is often referred to as systemic compliance risks—that is, risks that are current, pressing, and likely to result in substantial harm to the enterprise if not addressed. For example, during its compliance remediation process, Siemens AG ultimately classified money laundering and data violations as systemic risks on par with commercial bribery, and consequently extended its compliance framework to include anti-money laundering and data protection. Likewise, ZTE Corporation, upon completing its compliance remediation process, designated data privacy violations and commercial bribery as systemic risks with consequences equivalent to those associated with export control violations, and accordingly expanded its compliance program to address data protection and anti-bribery obligations.

5.3 Identifying Compliance Risks

Compliance risk identification refers to the process by which an enterprise—after defining the scope of compliance risk areas—investigates and confirms the specific risks it faces. Such risks may arise across a wide array of decision-making frameworks, managerial functions, business processes, and job positions. Even when two enterprises are exposed to compliance risks within the same legal domain—such as tax administration—the concrete mechanisms, operational steps, workflows, and personnel roles in which these risks manifest may differ substantially. An effective and scientifically grounded compliance risk assessment must begin with the precise and comprehensive identification of all relevant risk-bearing structures and functions. Only by locating where risks are most likely to occur can an enterprise proceed to develop meaningful risk control measures. This process is comparable to a medical diagnosis: identifying compliance risks plays a role similar to that of diagnosing a medical condition. Just as a physician must first identify the location and nature of a disorder before undertaking further diagnosis and treatment, so too must an enterprise first determine the loci of its compliance vulnerabilities before conducting more detailed assessments and implementing remediation measures.

From the perspective of practical compliance risk assessment, the identification of compliance risks involves the discovery and confirmation of specific risk exposures—that is, pinpointing the decision-making mechanisms, management processes, operational workflows, and organizational roles where such risks may reside. A useful example is the identification of commercial bribery risks. In many enterprises, instances of commercial bribery are often closely intertwined with internal control failures and organizational management practices. A seasoned compliance professional who had long served as a chief compliance officer described this risk identification process as follows:

[10] Nan Shen, "Advanced Insights on Compliance Risk Management," *Compliance Talker* (WeChat public account), July 19, 2022.

"Once the scope of compliance has been defined, we begin identifying the risks that fall within that scope, including the relevant business units, departments, and personnel. For example, if our focus is on conduct that violates the U.S. Foreign Corrupt Practices Act (FCPA), we start by listing associated risks—such as using third parties to pay bribes, maintaining off-the-books accounts, or engaging in excessive hospitality for public officials, like taking them on vacations under the pretext of attending conferences."[11]

According to the experience of this chief compliance officer, commercial bribery risks may emerge across multiple phases of corporate activity—including decision-making, management activities, and business operations. For instance, a company's legal representative or de facto controller may establish off-the-books accounts or maintain undisclosed "slush funds," thereby facilitating illicit payments. Where corporate and personal finances are not clearly separated, public funds may be misappropriated for private use, and senior executives may exploit personal accounts to engage in unlawful transactions. Financial personnel may approve reimbursement claims without due diligence, accepting suspicious invoices to disguise improper expenditures. Similarly, suppliers, agents, distributors, or intermediaries may bribe public officials while acting on behalf of the company. Sales personnel may also rely on bribery as a tactic to secure business or promote product sales.

This methodology for identifying commercial bribery risks can also be applied across other domains of compliance risk. Through the process of compliance risk identification, enterprises can pinpoint specific "compliance risk points" where non-compliant or illegal conduct is likely to occur. These points may be manifested as "risk mechanisms," "risk functions," "risk processes," "risk positions," or "risk personnel," all of which can be systematically compiled into a comprehensive compliance risk inventory. For instance, misconduct committed by the board of directors, the supervisory board, the executive team, or the ultimate controlling party during the decision-making process constitutes a "risk mechanism." Similarly, when violations are tolerated within key administrative procedures—such as invoice handling, contract management, expense reimbursement, hospitality, gift-giving, or charitable donations—these are categorized as "risk functions." Where illegal conduct emerges in operational processes—such as bidding and tendering, import and export activities, procurement, sales, or waste disposal—these are designated as "risk processes." In addition, individuals occupying specific roles—such as the legal representative, de facto controller, senior management, finance staff, production personnel, sales representatives, bidding officers, waste management staff, or branch managers—may present different degrees of compliance risk due to their functional responsibilities and operational exposure. These individuals are therefore classified as "risk personnel" operating in "risk positions."

[11] Qiong Pan, *Compliance Management: A Chief Compliance Officer's Work Notes*, China Machine Press, 2023, 55–56.

How, then, can enterprises comprehensively and accurately identify their compliance risk points? While many companies have developed relatively mature practices in this area, key conceptual disagreements persist. Two central questions remain at the heart of this debate. First, how does compliance risk identification differ between the contexts of compliance remediation and autonomous compliance? Second, what is the precise relationship between compliance risk identification and the mapping of compliance obligations? To resolve these issues, it is necessary to clearly differentiate between these two compliance contexts and, drawing on established compliance practices, to develop workable and context-sensitive approaches to risk identification that are both targeted and effective.

5.3.1 Compliance Remediation

Compliance remediation refers to post-violation compliance initiatives undertaken by enterprises under the supervision and assessment of relevant authorities. Compared with autonomous compliance, this remedial approach is marked by two defining features. First, the enterprise's compliance risks have already materialized, the affected legal and regulatory domains are clearly delineated, and the objectives of corresponding targeted compliance programs have been predetermined. Second, the enterprise conducts its compliance remediation under the supervision of compliance monitors, and the effectiveness of these efforts is subject to evaluation and acceptance by administrative authorities, judicial bodies, or international financial institutions. Under such circumstances, the identification of compliance risks should proceed in a sequential manner—starting with the mechanisms, business processes, positions, and personnel involved in past violations, and gradually expanding to include those risk points where future violations are reasonably foreseeable.

In the course of compliance remediation, enterprises subject to regulatory scrutiny are typically required to conduct internal investigations and submit a self-assessment report to the supervisory authorities. This report must thoroughly examine the unlawful conduct that occurred, identify the specific management functions and business processes involved, and determine both the directly responsible personnel and those bearing supervisory liability. For example, in cases involving the fraudulent issuance of value-added tax (VAT) invoices, the enterprise may exhibit multiple compliance risk points, such as autocratic decision-making by the de facto controller, the adoption of a business model marked by the separation of goods and invoices, the absence of inventory entry and exit records, arbitrary issuance of invoices, fabrication of contractual transactions, and the involvement of intermediaries offering excessive commissions to facilitate the fraud. In many instances, administrative authorities also conduct their own fact-finding investigations during enforcement proceedings to ascertain the basic facts of the violation. The case files generated in these proceedings—documenting the administrative enforcement process—often reveal pre-existing compliance vulnerabilities within the enterprise and serve as an important source for identifying risk points.

Naturally, the objective of compliance remediation extends beyond merely preventing the recurrence of the same violation; it must also aim to forestall the emergence of analogous forms of misconduct. Returning to the example of the fraudulent issuance of value-added tax (VAT) invoices, an enterprise must not only guard against the repetition of this specific offense, but also implement preventive measures against other related violations that jeopardize the integrity of tax administration. Accordingly, an enterprise should identify not only compliance risk points that have already materialized, but also those that are imminent, pressing, and likely to result in significant regulatory exposure or financial loss. To effectively identify such compliance risks, enterprises must adopt a scientifically grounded risk identification methodology. This process should proceed along two complementary dimensions. First, enterprises should compile a list of primary risk categories within the relevant legal domain, based on applicable laws and regulations. For example, in addition to the risk of issuing fraudulent invoices, an enterprise may also be exposed to risks such as tax evasion, refusal to pay taxes, obstruction of tax recovery, and fraudulent claims for export tax rebates. Second, for each of these risk categories, the enterprise should conduct a targeted compliance risk identification process to pinpoint decision-making procedures, management processes, business models, functional positions, and specific personnel that are realistically susceptible to noncompliance.

5.3.2 *Autonomous Compliance*

Drawing on the practical experience of compliance professionals, in the absence of any actual legal or regulatory violations, compliance risk identification may be initiated through the development of a compliance risk identification database. The foundational step in creating such a database is to establish a compliance obligations register, which systematically defines the normative sources of the enterprise's compliance obligations. This approach reflects the inherent relationship between compliance obligations and compliance risks—two sides of the same coin: any breach of a compliance obligation inherently gives rise to a compliance risk. Therefore, effective risk identification must begin with the comprehensive clarification of applicable obligations. In delineating its compliance obligations, an enterprise should not only identify all mandatory and voluntarily adopted laws, regulations, and other applicable standards currently in force, but also actively track legislative, regulatory, and policy developments. This ensures that the normative basis for compliance risk remains up to date, thereby enabling the enterprise to maintain continuous and dynamic compliance.[12]

[12] Zhi Mao, "Practical Construction of Corporate Compliance Risk Identification," *Zhuojian Compliance Research Institute* (WeChat public account), September 8, 2021.

Compared with the frequently asserted view that "compliance obligations constitute the prerequisite and foundation of compliance management," the approach outlined above more closely reflects the practical dynamics of enterprise compliance. Crucially, it acknowledges that risk identification must be grounded in the delineation of specific compliance risk areas. Once these areas are clearly defined, subsequent risk identification efforts become significantly more targeted and operationally feasible. Nevertheless, even within a relatively well-defined compliance risk domain, the task of mapping out relevant compliance obligations remains an extensive and complex undertaking. Take the anti-corruption compliance field as an example: applicable standards derive from a wide array of sources, including national laws, administrative regulations, ministerial rules, internal corporate policies, international conventions, industry norms, and ethical codes. These anti-corruption requirements may span dozens of operational areas and encompass hundreds of distinct provisions. Systematically consolidating these diverse and voluminous requirements into a comprehensive compliance obligations register can certainly help enterprises compare external regulatory demands with their internal business and management processes. This, in turn, supports the thorough identification of relevant compliance risk points. However, the obligation-based approach to risk identification also presents certain limitations—chief among them the tendency to generate large numbers of abstract risk points, i.e., risks characterized by generality, potentiality, or minimal severity. Such an approach may overlook concrete risk points—those involving real, imminent, and substantively significant risks of violation that demand prioritized attention.

To effectively identify concrete compliance risk points, enterprises should—after mapping out the relevant obligations within a specific compliance domain—conduct a structured classification of those obligations. Mandatory obligations whose breach may lead to significant legal, financial, or reputational consequences should be prioritized as the core focus of risk identification. Conversely, mandatory obligations whose violation would result only in minor repercussions may be treated as secondary. As for voluntary obligations—those whose noncompliance carries no regulatory or punitive consequences—they generally need not be regarded as a basis for compliance risk identification.

While mapping out compliance obligations, enterprises should also undertake concurrent assessments of their internal decision-making processes, management structures, business operations, and personnel functions that may give rise to legal or regulatory violations. Through practical and actionable methods, enterprises should aim to detect, at an early stage, those compliance risk points that are concrete, imminent, and materially significant. In the context of autonomous compliance initiatives, such risk identification may draw upon a range of diagnostic references, including the enterprise's own history of violations or litigation; past enforcement actions or sanctions imposed by administrative authorities, judicial bodies, or international financial institutions; enforcement actions against other enterprises with similar business models or operational structures, resulting in administrative, criminal, or international sanctions; and circumstances involving the development of new clients, engagement with third-party business partners, or corporate mergers and acquisitions.

Whether in mapping out compliance obligations or diagnosing potential violations, enterprises must adopt scientifically grounded methodologies for risk identification. Drawing on the practical experience of enterprises engaged in compliance management, the following basic methods are commonly employed: the interview method, which involves conducting structured interviews with department heads and personnel in key positions to identify potential compliance risks; the questionnaire method, whereby surveys are distributed to senior executives, employees, branch office personnel, customers, and third-party partners, and risk points are identified through systematic analysis of the responses; the case analysis method, which entails reviewing the enterprise's historical incidents of noncompliance—including litigation, administrative penalties, or other legal proceedings—to trace specific legal risk events to the underlying behaviors that caused them; and the surprise inspection method, typically used in highly regulated industries such as pharmaceuticals, food, and medical devices, where regulators or parent companies conduct random audits to detect potential violations in decision-making processes, business operations, critical functions, or key personnel.[13]

5.4 Analyzing Compliance Risks

Following the accurate identification of compliance risks, enterprises proceed to the next phase of compliance risk assessment—compliance risk analysis. This stage involves conducting causal analysis of the identified risks to determine their root causes and systematically evaluate the potential adverse consequences associated with each. In this respect, enterprises that have previously undergone compliance remediation often possess well-developed analytical practices. These accumulated experiences may serve as useful references for enterprises undertaking autonomous compliance initiatives.

5.4.1 *Compliance Remediation*

In principle, when enterprises become subject to administrative enforcement investigations or enforcement actions by international financial institutions due to unlawful or noncompliant conduct, they often seek to minimize potential losses by entering into settlement agreements that offer leniency in exchange for undertaking compliance remediation. Upon reaching such an agreement, enterprises are typically required to conduct internal compliance investigations and submit self-assessment reports disclosing the endogenous structural causes of the misconduct. Unlike external inducements for noncompliance, these

[13] Haixiao Gu and Shanshan Zhou, "Key Elements in Designing a Corporate Compliance Plan: Risk Identification," *King & Wood Mallesons Research Institute* (WeChat public account), July 5, 2022.

endogenous structural causes refer to systemic deficiencies within the enterprise's decision-making, operational, financial, and business management processes—deficiencies that directly or indirectly contribute to the emergence of compliance risks. Given that such remediation efforts are generally conducted under the oversight of administrative authorities, judicial agencies, or international financial institutions, enterprises must perform a comprehensive and accurate diagnosis of the structural drivers of compliance risk. Only through targeted corrective action and system-level compliance reform can they meet the evaluative standards required for passing institutional or regulatory compliance assessments.[14]

The internal compliance investigations conducted by enterprises in the course of compliance remediation represent a quintessential form of compliance risk analysis. Through such internal investigations, enterprises are often able to uncover multiple endogenous structural causes underlying unlawful or noncompliant conduct. These causes generally fall into four primary categories. First, significant deficiencies may exist in the corporate governance structure. Imbalances or dysfunctions in the allocation of authority among the shareholders' meeting, board of directors, board of supervisors, and executive management can lead to the breakdown of leadership, oversight, and internal checks and balances, thereby creating conditions conducive to unlawful or noncompliant conduct. Second, systemic weaknesses may be present in internal management systems. Deficiencies in human resources, compensation, finance, audit, or compliance oversight mechanisms can allow major business initiatives or product lines to circumvent necessary compliance review, thereby permitting unlawful or noncompliant conduct to go undetected and unaddressed and preventing timely accountability for responsible personnel. Third, structural vulnerabilities may be embedded in business processes. Significant procedural deficiencies in areas such as production, sales, import/export, bidding and procurement, environmental management, invoicing, contract execution, client development, and third-party onboarding can expose the enterprise to misconduct risks involving decision-makers, executives, subsidiaries, or operational staff, thereby increasing the likelihood of recurring violations. Fourth, the enterprise's business model or operational strategy may inherently embed illicit elements or even criminogenic structures, leading to systemic patterns of noncompliance. Such elements may include: reliance on a decoupled invoicing model, in which billing and goods delivery are artificially separated; sustained partnerships with entities engaged in bid rigging or bid padding; the use of unlicensed or extraterritorial mining operations; dependence on unauthorized data acquisition techniques, such as web scraping; or the engagement

[14] Ruihua Chen, "Basic Approaches on Effective Compliance Remediation," *Forum on Political Science and Law*, no. 1 (2022).

of agents who submit falsified customs declarations in cross-border transactions.[15]

During compliance remediation, implicated enterprises are often subjected to punitive obligations imposed by administrative authorities or international financial institutions. Such measures exert significant pressure on the enterprise to undertake substantive, system-wide reforms. Under this level of scrutiny, only those that implement genuine, far-reaching remediation efforts are likely to satisfy regulatory compliance assessments and secure more lenient resolutions. It is precisely this heightened regulatory pressure that often prompts enterprises to conduct comprehensive internal investigations, enabling them to uncover the structural drivers of their misconduct. Such investigations lay a critical foundation for effective and targeted compliance risk analysis.

5.4.2 *Autonomous Compliance*

In autonomous compliance contexts—where enterprises operate without external oversight from administrative authorities, judicial bodies, or international financial institutions—a central question arises: how should compliance risk analysis be effectively conducted in the absence of external scrutiny? According to mainstream theories of compliance management, it is essential to distinguish between compliance risk sources and compliance risk scenarios. The latter corresponds to what has previously been termed "compliance risk points," while the former refers to the individual or cumulative factors that may give rise to such risks. A rigorous compliance risk assessment requires not only the accurate identification of management functions and business workflows where compliance risks are likely to arise, but also a systematic analysis of the underlying sources and contributing conditions that may trigger such risks—culminating in the development of a compliance risk source inventory. Drawing on the empirical insights of compliance professionals and data from a wide range of corporate violations, a methodological framework known as the compliance risk source identification method has emerged. This approach centers on analyzing position-specific responsibilities within the enterprise and identifying the types and degrees of authority exercised across internal roles. These powers are then treated as potential sources of compliance risk. Specifically, any organizational function that entails the exercise of approval authority, customer management and sales authority, personnel decision-making, procurement, final release authority, measurement and valuation authority, financial control, or access to critical information constitutes a potential source of compliance risk. The mere exercise of such authority does not, in itself, create a compliance risk. However, when coupled with improper intent and facilitated by suitable business opportunities, the exercise of such power can enable the occurrence of

[15] Ruihua Chen, *The Chinese Experience of Effective Compliance*, Peking University Press, 2023, 43–49.

noncompliant conduct. This relationship may be conceptually expressed by the following formula:

Authority + Improper Motive + Opportunity = Noncompliant Conduct.[16]

The "compliance risk source identification theory" not only offers a methodological framework for identifying compliance risks but also holds considerable theoretical value in explaining their structural causes. Compared with compliance remediation, compliance risk analysis conducted in autonomous compliance settings faces an inherent limitation: in the absence of actual violations, it is difficult to trace the endogenous structural causes of noncompliant conduct. Without concrete instances of misconduct, the causal chain is effectively incomplete. In response to this challenge, recent theoretical advances have built upon the identification of specific compliance risk points to develop the "risk source identification" method, which seeks to uncover potential structural vulnerabilities by analyzing the allocation and exercise of internal corporate powers. This approach aims to demonstrate how particular configurations of authority may systematically predispose an enterprise to compliance risks. In this respect, the theory represents a significant contribution to the conceptual development of compliance risk analysis.

However, treating the exercise and distribution of key internal powers as the sole "source" of compliance risks may merely identify potential contributing conditions, without accurately uncovering the structural causes of noncompliant behavior. Drawing on practical experience in compliance remediation, it is clear that the likelihood of actual or imminent violations cannot be explained solely by flawed configurations of internal authority. Such risks may also arise—often to varying degrees—from deficiencies in corporate management systems, vulnerabilities embedded in business processes, or structural risks inherent in the company's commercial model, including elements that could be deemed unlawful or even criminogenic. For instance, exposure to anti-commercial bribery compliance risks may arise from critical gaps in the enterprise's procurement management framework—such as the absence of a robust supplier onboarding and due diligence system, the lack of continuous risk assessment procedures, the failure to maintain credit-based or compliance-qualified supplier lists, inadequate compliance training mechanisms for suppliers, and the absence of formalized exit protocols for disqualified vendors. Similarly, tax compliance risks may originate from the company's failure to implement an "invoice–goods integration" model in its operational controls. This may include the absence of unified inbound and outbound inventory documentation, inadequate supplier qualification systems, and the lack of compliance review mechanisms for critical control points such as transactions, invoicing, and contracting. These shortcomings are further exacerbated by the lack of essential compliance functions tied to invoice management, such as

[16]Guangzhong Fan, "How to Identify Corporate Compliance Risks (Part I)," *Ruisi Business School* (WeChat public account), March 10, 2024.

whistleblower channels, complaint procedures, veto mechanisms, internal compliance audits, and disciplinary measures.

Experience shows that enterprises engaged in autonomous compliance initiatives may, in order to establish an effective compliance management system, draw on the compliance remediation experience of sanctioned organizations. In the course of exploring so-called compliance risk source identification, they can conduct internal compliance investigations to determine the structural causes of risk across multiple dimensions, including governance structures, management systems, business processes, and business models. Only by identifying these structural vulnerabilities can enterprises implement targeted institutional corrections to remove the systemic factors that have led to noncompliance, thereby eliminating the possibility of repeated violations within the same risk domain. This constitutes an indispensable path toward achieving substantive and sustainable compliance.

5.5 Evaluating Compliance Risks

Following the identification and analysis of compliance risks within a specific domain, enterprises must conduct either qualitative or quantitative evaluations of the identified risks. As the final step in the compliance risk assessment process, compliance risk evaluation entails a comprehensive appraisal based on the results of prior identification and analysis, with particular focus on two key dimensions: the likelihood of the risk occurring and the probability and severity of its potential adverse consequences. In practice, even within a single risk domain, enterprises often face multiple and diverse compliance risks. For instance, in the area of anti-commercial bribery compliance, risks may emerge across numerous operational functions, such as strategic decision-making, personnel management, finance, procurement, sales, hospitality, gifts, travel, and charitable contributions. Some of these may be identified as critical risk points. The core function of compliance risk evaluation, therefore, is to establish a methodological framework for conducting qualitative or quantitative assessments of different types of compliance risks.

In practice, compliance risk evaluation is typically conducted through comparative approaches. Enterprises are expected to consolidate and assess multiple types of compliance risks in a structured manner. Qualitative analysis may be used to identify critical compliance risk points, which should be prioritized for control and mitigation. Alternatively, a quantitative scoring system may be applied to assign numerical values to each identified risk. Based on these scores, risks can be categorized into different risk levels, thereby establishing a clear prioritization framework for compliance risk management.

Let us begin with the application of qualitative methods. Identifying *critical compliance risk points* through effective risk identification is a best practice distilled from years of compliance management experience. For example, ZTE Corporation refers to such points as Key Control Points (KCPs). Drawing on its compliance framework, the enterprise recommends that once specific, tangible compliance risks have been identified and analyzed, organizations should determine which steps within their operational workflows constitute KCPs. A Key Control Point is defined as "a control measure capable of preventing, eliminating, or reducing a risk to an acceptable level." Such measures may include inspections, verifications, reviews, audits, reassessments, decision-making procedures, performance appraisals, budgeting processes, early-warning systems, data analytics, authorization protocols, inventory reconciliation, and the segregation of incompatible functions. In practice, enterprises may adopt a four-step analytical model to determine whether a particular control point qualifies as a KCP. First, does the step contain any risk control measures? Second, is there a dedicated mechanism for eliminating or reducing the relevant risk to an acceptable threshold? Third, does the potential impact of the risk exceed the organization's defined risk tolerance? Fourth, can subsequent steps in the process effectively mitigate or neutralize the risk? By establishing a structured model for evaluating the nature and function of control points, enterprises can categorize different types of risk controls, and—based on risk assessment outcomes and operational characteristics—identify the KCPs most critical to effective compliance. This enables more strategic resource allocation and enhances the enterprise's overall capacity for risk management and mitigation.[17]

Once each Key Control Point (KCP) has been identified, enterprises must design corresponding control measures aligned with the specific nature of the identified risks. For example, in export control compliance, concrete risks often center around four key elements: the transacting party, the destination country or region, the controlled item, and the end use. Accordingly, enterprises should formulate targeted KCP requirements for each risk point—such as restricted party screening, due diligence checks, sanctioned country/region filtering, and export license verification. At the same time, it is essential to ensure the effective operationalization of these control measures. Both control mechanisms and compliance tools must be tailored to the enterprise's business structure, resource capacity, and cost constraints. Enterprises should develop pragmatic and actionable implementation strategies that embed compliance controls into daily operations, thereby achieving seamless integration of compliance into core business workflows.[18]

In addition to qualitative methods, enterprises may also adopt quantitative approaches to compliance risk analysis. Typically, compliance risks can be quantitatively evaluated from two dimensions: first, the likelihood of compliance risk occurrence—that is, the probability that a violation or noncompliant act may occur if no compliance management measures are taken; second, the impact of noncompliance—that is, the types of direct or indirect consequences

[17] Ruihua Chen, "How Effective Compliance Management Is Forged: An Analysis Based on the ZTE Case," *Qiaoqiao Legal Scholar* (WeChat public account), November 4, 2023.

[18] ZTE Corporation, *Compliance Creates Value*, Law Press, 2023, 12.

the enterprise may face, and the potential losses it may incur, should such violations take place.[19]

By evaluating compliance risks along these two dimensions, enterprises can conduct a structured quantitative analysis: first, the likelihood of compliance risk occurrence can be categorized into probability levels of 100%, 75%, 50%, 25%, and 0%; second, based on the potential impact on the enterprise's business objectives, the severity of each compliance risk can be classified as "catastrophic," "very severe," "severe," "significant," or "minor."[20]

Some enterprises adopt a ten-point scale to assess the likelihood of compliance risk occurrence and convert the consequences of noncompliance into specific monetary values or defined economic intervals. Typically, the compliance risk level of each identified risk is calculated by multiplying the probability score by the corresponding impact value. After evaluating the risk profiles of relevant positions, personnel, activities, and management practices, enterprises can determine the final compliance risk level. In general, risks that have both a high probability of occurrence and severe consequences are categorized as high compliance risks. Those with a moderately high probability and less-than-severe consequences are classified as medium compliance risks. Risks with low likelihood and relatively minor consequences are considered low compliance risks.

Through the quantitative assessment of compliance risk levels, enterprises can, on the one hand, establish data-supported priorities for the management of different compliance risks, and on the other hand, allocate compliance resources in proportion to the level of risk identified. In principle, enterprises should adopt a zero-tolerance policy toward all forms of noncompliance and include even lower-level compliance risks within the scope of compliance control. Preventive, monitoring, and responsive measures should be applied accordingly. However, to effectively manage those compliance risks that are more likely to occur and have more serious consequences—and to avoid potentially catastrophic losses—enterprises should prioritize the allocation of efforts and resources to the management of high-level compliance risks, and subsequently expand their control strategies to address all identified risks.

5.6 Sustaining Risk Assessment Practices

After delineating compliance risk areas and completing the above assessment activities, can enterprises consider the task complete once and for all? The answer is no. Since compliance risks are continuously evolving, compliance risk assessments must also be maintained on an ongoing basis. Only in this way can enterprises identify changes in the nature of compliance risks, determine the

[19] "What is Proportionality in Corporate Compliance?" GAN Integrity, accessed July 21, 2022. https://www.ganintegrity.com

[20] Qiong Pan, *Compliance Management: A Chief Compliance Officer's Work Notes*, 56–57.

causes behind those changes, reclassify risk levels, and adjust the priority of compliance risk controls accordingly.

In corporate compliance practice, changes in compliance risk generally manifest in two key dimensions: first, changes in the external regulatory environment; and second, changes in internal business operations.

The external regulatory environment in which enterprises operate is constantly evolving and may result in significant shifts in compliance risk. Such changes typically fall into several categories: the enactment of new laws and regulations, which introduce additional compliance obligations for enterprises; amendments to existing legal frameworks, which may increase the severity of penalties for violations; changes in international trade, finance, or business conditions, which subject overseas operations to stricter regulatory requirements and elevate the risk of trade sanctions; and intensified regulatory enforcement by government agencies targeting specific industries, business activities, or operational models, thereby increasing both the frequency and intensity of enforcement actions and raising the likelihood of administrative penalties.

Second, changes in an enterprise's governance structure, business operations, product lines, client base, or commercial activities may also give rise to a range of new compliance risks. Such changes may be reflected in the following aspects: the enterprise initiates a new line of business, develops a new product, or establishes a branch office in a new domestic or overseas location, thereby creating new compliance risk points; significant adjustments in the company's governance structure, organizational setup, or strategic direction—such as going public, forming a board of directors, or appointing a new management team—may introduce new sources of risk in corporate decision-making; engaging new clients, signing contracts with new suppliers, agents, distributors, or intermediaries, or undertaking major mergers and acquisitions may also generate additional compliance risks; and finally, the occurrence of violations, administrative enforcement actions, criminal prosecutions, or investigations by international financial institutions may expose serious gaps or deficiencies in the enterprise's compliance risk control framework.

Precisely because enterprises may face new compliance risks stemming from changes in both the external regulatory environment and internal business operations, effective compliance management requires continuous and sustained risk assessment. In practice, such ongoing assessments typically take two forms: periodic risk assessments and ad hoc risk assessments.

Periodic risk assessments are routine compliance management activities carried out in the absence of major violations. To prevent noncompliant conduct, enterprises should establish a robust compliance risk prevention process, in which periodic risk assessments serve as a primary mechanism. Within this process, enterprises should adhere to the principle of top-level commitment, ensuring that senior management takes the lead in initiating, promoting, supervising, and implementing the assessment. They should also uphold the principle of proportionality, conducting targeted assessments based on compliance risks identified through regular compliance reports, whistleblower disclosures, audits, inspections, and disciplinary measures. In addition, enterprises should conduct due diligence on prospective clients, third-party partners, and acquisition targets to assess the potential compliance risks associated with these engagements. To prevent periodic assessments from becoming a mere formality, enterprises are encouraged to combine the efforts of internal compliance personnel with the expertise of external compliance professionals. This approach facilitates the accurate identification, analysis, and evaluation of specific compliance risk points that may have emerged over time due to deficiencies, gaps, or hidden vulnerabilities in the compliance management system. Furthermore, if the assessment process reveals a cross-sectoral shift in compliance risk—such as a transition from anti-bribery to anti-money laundering, cybersecurity, or other domains—enterprises should consider redefining their compliance risk areas and developing new specialized compliance programs. Once such changes in risk domains are identified, the scope, focus, and methodology of compliance risk assessments should be revised accordingly to address the evolving risk landscape.

Ad hoc risk assessments refer to responsive compliance evaluations initiated when an enterprise encounters significant, unplanned events or changes during the course of its operations. These assessments are designed to update and improve the compliance management system in response to new circumstances. According to relevant international compliance guidelines, enterprises should trigger such reassessment procedures under the following urgent conditions: updates or expansions in business activities; substantial changes in organizational structure or strategic direction; major external developments, including changes in the economic environment, market conditions, debt profile, or client relationships; modifications in applicable compliance obligations; the occurrence of mergers or acquisitions; and incidents of noncompliant behavior.

Certainly, although this categorization may not apply uniformly to all enterprises or to every operational context within the same enterprise, it nonetheless provides a practical framework for conducting ad hoc compliance risk assessments. Emergency events can generally be divided into two types: external compliance events and internal compliance events. As previously discussed, the former refers primarily to changes in the external regulatory environment, while the latter involves sudden disruptions in internal business activities. What distinguishes such events is their abrupt nature, which often prevents enterprises from responding in time through regular risk assessments. Among these events, the most consequential are crisis-level incidents—such as regulatory investigations initiated by administrative agencies, criminal proceedings brought by judicial authorities, or enforcement actions launched by international financial institutions. When such crises occur, enterprises must avoid both passivity and any form of unlawful response. Instead, they should establish and implement a comprehensive crisis response plan, in which ad hoc risk assessments serve as a core operational component. In accordance with the fundamental requirements of effective compliance management, enterprises should not only develop preventive and monitoring processes for compliance risks, but also establish a responsive mechanism for addressing actual violations. Within this mechanism, ad hoc risk assessments triggered by incidents of non-compliance form an essential element. In such situations, the ad hoc assessment process may incorporate internal compliance investigations and anti-fraud reviews as integral parts of the enterprise's broader crisis response strategy.

Experience has shown that no enterprise—regardless of how well-designed its compliance framework may be—can fully eliminate the risk of legal or regulatory violations. An effective compliance program requires both periodic and ad hoc compliance risk assessments, adapted to the enterprise's specific business conditions and external environment, to ensure the timely refinement and improvement of existing compliance policies and procedures. The core objective of compliance risk assessment lies in the ongoing identification, analysis, and evaluation of compliance risks, which enables enterprises to regularly update their specialized compliance policies, standards, and processes. This, in turn, enhances the relevance and effectiveness of risk control, ensuring that the compliance management system remains dynamic and up to date. Ultimately, it supports the sustained performance of the enterprise in preventing compliance risks, monitoring compliance operations, and responding effectively to violations.

5.7 Managing Compliance through Risk Assessment

Compliance risk assessment constitutes a foundational element of enterprise compliance management. In both theoretical discourse and practical application, compliance management is often referred to as "compliance risk management" or "compliance risk control." Under a risk-based approach, enterprises can define core compliance objectives, apply the principle of proportionality, establish or improve their compliance management systems, and scientifically evaluate their effectiveness—all on the basis of risks that have been identified, assessed, and classified. On this basis, the relationship between compliance risk assessment and compliance management may be briefly summarized as follows.

First, the delineation of compliance risk areas—as a necessary prerequisite to risk assessment—provides the foundation for developing targeted compliance programs. In principle, once an enterprise identifies a legal or regulatory domain in which compliance risks exist, it should establish a corresponding program tailored to that specific risk area. A targeted compliance program refers to a dedicated compliance management system designed to address risks in a defined area of concern. Following the delineation of risk areas, if an enterprise confirms the presence of significant compliance risks in fields such as anti-bribery, data protection, anti-money laundering, intellectual property protection, taxation, import-export operations, or occupational safety, it may consider establishing targeted compliance programs—such as an anti-bribery compliance program, data protection compliance program, anti-money laundering compliance program, IP compliance program, tax compliance program, import-export compliance program, or occupational safety compliance program. However, given the limited compliance resources available to most enterprises—and in the interest of effective risk control—the development of targeted compliance programs should generally follow a phased and prioritized approach. Enterprises should prioritize those areas where compliance risks are most likely to result in significant harm, and then progressively broaden the scope of targeted compliance management in accordance with the outcomes of ongoing compliance risk assessments.

Second, based on the results of compliance risk assessments, enterprises can set more reasonable and attainable objectives for their compliance management. To avoid adopting overly broad or impractical goals—such as the blanket pursuit of "full legal and regulatory compliance"—enterprises should formulate objectives grounded in the specific compliance risk points identified and the corresponding risk levels assessed. A more pragmatic and actionable goal is the effective control of compliance risks within a defined domain. To support this goal, enterprises should establish three interrelated sub-objectives. First, ex ante prevention, which refers to the proactive deterrence of unlawful or noncompliant conduct within the same risk area. Second, real-time monitoring, which involves the continuous oversight of decision-making, operational, and management processes, with the aim of providing an early warning or "compliance radar" function. Third, ex post response, which consists of targeted remedial measures designed to address institutional weaknesses exposed by incidents of noncompliance.

Third, based on the identified compliance risk points and the assessed levels of risk, enterprises may apply the principle of proportionality to determine the prioritization of risk control measures, the allocation of compliance management resources, the designation of compliance leadership and organizational structures, and the development of an appropriate institutional framework—all in response to the results of compliance risk assessments.[21] For example, if a risk assessment indicates that deficiencies in corporate governance and vulnerabilities in financial management rank among the enterprise's highest compliance risks, the enterprise should treat improvements in governance and financial oversight as top compliance priorities. Specific measures may include strengthening the supervisory role of the board of directors; limiting the financial approval authority of the legal representative, ultimate controller, or other senior executives; reinforcing the independence of the corporate legal person; eliminating off-the-books funds or "petty cash" accounts; enhancing both internal and external audits of corporate finances; and activating compliance review mechanisms specific to financial management.

Fourth, based on the results of the compliance risk assessment, enterprises should establish a two-step approach to compliance management: the targeted correction of institutional deficiencies and the systematic construction of a compliance framework. A key indicator of ineffective compliance is the

[21] Ruihua Chen, "The Principle of Proportionality in Corporate Compliance Remediation," *Comparative Law Studies*, no. 1 (2023).

tendency to disregard specific risk conditions while enthusiastically drafting broad compliance plans or issuing internal rules—resulting in paper-based or purely formalistic compliance structures. To avoid such outcomes, enterprises should align their compliance measures closely with the findings of the compliance risk assessment. First, in response to the results of the risk analysis, enterprises should implement targeted corrective measures to eliminate the structural causes of compliance risks—such as rectifying governance deficiencies, closing regulatory control gaps, addressing vulnerabilities in business processes, and reforming business operations or commercial models to remove unlawful or criminal risk elements. Second, based on the results of the risk evaluation, enterprises should establish targeted compliance systems that correspond to the nature and severity of the identified risks. This includes building a comprehensive compliance control system that integrates ex ante prevention, real-time monitoring, and ex post response mechanisms, and, on the basis of a foundational compliance platform, developing the necessary domain-specific compliance components tailored to the enterprise's risk profile.

Fifth, enterprises should evaluate the effectiveness of their compliance programs based on the results of compliance risk assessments. This evaluation should be conducted across three dimensions: the effectiveness of program design, the effectiveness of program implementation, and the effectiveness of program outcomes. The effectiveness of program design refers to whether, in response to identified, analyzed, and assessed compliance risks, the enterprise has developed targeted institutional corrective measures and committed to establishing a comprehensive compliance management framework. The effectiveness of program implementation concerns whether these corrective measures and compliance systems have been effectively executed and embedded into the enterprise's decision-making, operations, business activities, and internal management processes. This includes: the timely compliance review of high-risk business activities; the suspension or termination of business operations involving unlawful or noncompliant conduct; and the prompt imposition of disciplinary actions on responsible employees, managers, personnel in branches, or third-party business partners. The effectiveness of program outcomes evaluates whether the originally identified compliance risks have been properly managed and mitigated, thereby fulfilling the overall compliance objectives of ex ante prevention, real-time monitoring, and ex post remediation.

5.8 Conclusion

Compliance management is a risk-based managerial activity. To carry out effective compliance management, enterprises must establish a scientifically grounded compliance risk assessment mechanism. Such assessments should be based on a prior delineation of the legal domains in which compliance risks may arise, thereby defining the basic scope of the assessment. On this foundation, compliance risk assessment typically includes three fundamental components: risk identification, risk analysis, and risk evaluation. Through these processes, enterprises confirm specific compliance risk points, uncover the structural causes of those risks, and assign appropriate risk levels—thus enabling a rational determination of risk control priorities. By applying the results of compliance risk assessments, enterprises can effectively implement the principle of proportionality and develop a risk-based system for the prevention, monitoring, and mitigation of compliance risks. In doing so, they can achieve the essential objective of compliance management: to exercise effective control over compliance risks and prevent the occurrence of unlawful or noncompliant conduct.

Compliance risk assessment is a highly practice-driven management activity. In this regard, enterprises have developed a range of valuable experiences in risk control. Moving forward, scholars in corporate compliance theory may analyze these practical experiences and engage in a process of refining and validating them—distilling the essential from the incidental and identifying what is both reliable and replicable. Through such efforts, regularized patterns of practice may be abstracted into sound and dynamic theoretical models. Ultimately, compliance risks—like decision-making risks, operational risks, and financial risks—constitute strategic risks that demand sustained attention and adequate resource allocation. Compliance management, accordingly, should be recognized as one of the three core components of an enterprise's strategic risk control system. To strengthen compliance management in practice, enterprises should draw lessons from the risk assessment processes used during post-violation compliance remediation, and adapt these insights to their autonomous compliance programs. This will improve both the scientific rigor and practical effectiveness of compliance risk assessment.

CHAPTER 6

Evaluating the Effectiveness of Compliance Programs

6.1 Introduction

Corporate compliance efforts may be divided into two categories, based on the timing and impetus for establishing a compliance management system: *routine compliance management system* and *crisis-responsive compliance remediation mechanism*. The former—referred to as *ex ante compliance*—denotes a set of preventive measures initiated by an enterprise in the absence of any known legal or regulatory violations, and prior to being subjected to administrative investigations, criminal prosecution, or inquiries by international financial institutions. These efforts are typically driven either by regulatory expectations imposed by administrative agencies or industry associations, or by the enterprise's strategic objective of enhancing its market competitiveness. In contrast, *crisis-responsive compliance remediation*—commonly known as *ex post compliance*—refers to remedial measures undertaken in the wake of corporate misconduct and during the course of administrative enforcement, criminal proceedings, or investigations led by international financial institutions. These efforts are primarily aimed at addressing structural deficiencies and operational vulnerabilities within the existing compliance management system, with the goal of obtaining leniency or other compliance-based incentives.[1]

Whether in the context of *routine compliance management system* or *crisis-responsive compliance remediation mechanism*, the establishment of a corporate compliance framework is rarely the result of a purely voluntary effort to strengthen internal controls. Rather, such initiatives are typically undertaken under the impetus and supervision of regulatory authorities, industry associations, or judicial institutions. These external actors often prescribe an overarching objective for the compliance management system and articulate specific

[1] Ruihua Chen, "Two Models of Effective Compliance Management," *Law and Social Development*, no. 1 (2022).

R. Chen, *An Introduction to Corporate Compliance*,
https://doi.org/10.1007/978-981-95-7257-1_6

requirements aimed at achieving that objective. From a normative standpoint, such institutions tend to promote the goal of "lawful and compliant business operations" and use this as a baseline for assessing the effectiveness of a company's compliance program. However, driven by cost-efficiency concerns and a rational desire to avoid legal and financial exposure, enterprises are unlikely to commit unlimited resources to compliance initiatives. In practice, they often aim to meet only the minimum compliance standards set by external bodies, seeking to exchange compliance efforts for maximized regulatory leniency or minimized legal consequences. As a result of ongoing negotiation and implicit bargaining, enterprises and oversight institutions frequently arrive at a tacit understanding—one that, from a defensive perspective, centers on achieving the "minimum threshold for effective compliance." This threshold typically refers to preventing corporate misconduct and avoiding administrative penalties, criminal prosecution, or international financial sanctions. Consequently, the notion of an "effective compliance program" has emerged as a benchmark applied by regulatory authorities, industry associations, and judicial bodies in evaluating the adequacy of corporate compliance systems, and as a fundamental objective for enterprises seeking to establish an effective compliance management system.

But what, precisely, constitutes "effective compliance management"? And how should the effectiveness of a corporate compliance program be scientifically assessed? These fundamental questions have received scant attention in academic scholarship, and few comprehensive or systematic frameworks have been proposed to date. In practice, enterprises engaged in autonomous compliance system development often operate without meaningful external guidance and in the absence of strong compliance-related incentives. As a consequence, the systems they establish frequently fall short of meeting even the most basic standards of effectiveness. Administrative regulatory authorities, for their part, have also failed to develop or apply widely recognized benchmarks or methodologies for evaluating compliance effectiveness. Whether issuing administrative compliance guidance, imposing mandatory compliance obligations, or offering compliance-based incentives to enterprises under investigation, such authorities have generally lacked a coherent and accepted evaluative framework.

A review of international developments in compliance management reveals that even in jurisdictions such as the United States and Europe—where the concept of "effective compliance management" first emerged—there is still no mature or widely accepted standard or methodology for evaluating compliance effectiveness. As several Western scholars have observed, prevailing evaluation approaches fail to incorporate the actual outcomes of compliance programs and lack empirically robust methods for measuring effectiveness. Likewise, the compliance guidelines and evaluation frameworks issued by various international organizations for the promotion of corporate compliance largely adhere to a "oriented-oriented" assessment paradigm. Under this model, the focus rests primarily on whether a compliance system has been formally established and implemented, treating such procedural indicators as proxies for effectiveness. However, these approaches tend to overlook the two core objectives of compliance management: the effective mitigation of compliance risks and the substantive enhancement of organizational compliance culture.[2]

Both international and domestic efforts to evaluate the effectiveness of corporate compliance—whether theoretical inquiries or practical implementations—remain at an early and relatively superficial stage. These efforts predominantly concentrate on the formal establishment of compliance management systems, the promulgation of internal rules and policies, and the procedural assessment of their implementation. What is conspicuously lacking, however, is a sustained focus on the actual results of compliance remediation and the substantive impact of compliance management. There is an absence of practicable evaluation metrics and methodologies tailored to these concerns. In many cases, compliance assessments revolve around verifying whether enterprises have honored their compliance commitments, adopted necessary internal regulations, and operationalized the requisite compliance structures. Yet these assessments often fail to consider whether the implemented compliance framework functions as a genuine remedy for organizational deficiencies, whether it effectively corrects systemic faults, and whether it meaningfully contributes to preventing the recurrence of similar or related violations.

Establishing sound and rational standards for assessing the effectiveness of corporate compliance represents a global challenge in corporate governance and a critical research agenda within the field of compliance theory. This chapter aims to synthesize the comparative experiences of Western jurisdictions and China in implementing compliance effectiveness evaluations, with particular emphasis on the two prevailing paradigms: the process-oriented model and the outcome-oriented model. Building on this comparative analysis, the chapter advances a more integrated and pragmatic alternative framework—one that positions the effective control of compliance risks as the central objective of compliance management. Within this framework, the effectiveness of corporate compliance is to be evaluated across three interrelated dimensions: the formulation of compliance programs, the implementation of those programs, and the realization of intended compliance outcomes. To ensure that evaluations across these dimensions are conducted in a scientifically robust and practically reliable manner, the chapter further proposes tailored assessment methodologies corresponding to each evaluative dimension.

[2] Hui Chen, "The Application and Measurement of Compliance Mechanisms in Legal and Regulatory Contexts," in *Compliance Assessment and Measurement: Preventing Corporate Crime and Misconduct*, ed. Melissa Lawry and Benjamin van Rooij, trans. Zhu Qing and Fan Xiaoliang (Beijing: Contemporary China Publishing House, 2023), 46–49.

6.2 Process-Oriented Evaluation: Western Frameworks

In principle, the fundamental objective of compliance management is to ensure that enterprises are able to prevent and control unlawful or noncompliant behavior in the course of their business operations. An effective compliance management system, therefore, is not merely characterized by the establishment of a formalized set of written rules and structures, but also by the implementation of specific compliance measures aimed at realizing this core objective. This raises a critical question: how should the effectiveness of a corporate compliance program be evaluated? On this issue, two distinct evaluative paradigms have emerged—namely, the process-oriented model and the outcome-oriented model. These two approaches differ significantly in the elements they identify as constituting "effective compliance," in the standards they apply for evaluation, and in the methodologies they adopt for assessment. This section begins with a brief analysis and critique of the process-oriented model by examining its institutional development and practical implementation in Western jurisdictions.

The so-called process-oriented model of evaluation refers to an approach that assesses the effectiveness of compliance management based on the methods, procedures, and mechanisms adopted by a company in implementing its compliance program. Under this model, "effective compliance management" is measured against a set of relatively objective procedural benchmarks. As long as a company's efforts to establish or improve its compliance management system fulfill the fundamental elements associated with effective compliance, it is deemed to have met the standard of compliance effectiveness. For companies engaged in routine compliance system building, the establishment and operation of core compliance components—such as a dedicated compliance leadership and organizational structure, the issuance of compliance policies and employee handbooks, the provision of compliance training, the conduct of due diligence, and the implementation of whistleblowing mechanisms—are typically regarded as sufficient to constitute effective compliance. Likewise, for companies undergoing crisis-responsive compliance remediation, making formal commitments to corrective actions and fulfilling them point by point is generally viewed as achieving effective compliance remediation. In both cases, the completion of these procedural elements serves as the primary criterion for evaluating the effectiveness of the compliance system.

Since the 1990s, regulatory and judicial authorities in Western jurisdictions have not only actively promoted the establishment of corporate compliance systems but have also increasingly focused on the issue of compliance program effectiveness. In this context, countries such as the United States, the United Kingdom, and France have undertaken institutional efforts to articulate the objectives of effective compliance, define its core structural elements, and explore corresponding evaluation methodologies and criteria. These developments have contributed to a growing body of normative guidance on what constitutes an effective compliance program. However, such efforts remain predominantly situated within a process-oriented evaluation paradigm—emphasizing whether enterprises have implemented procedural components of compliance programs, while largely neglecting the assessment of actual compliance outcomes. To date, standards and methodologies for outcome-oriented evaluation have yet to be fully established or adopted in practice. For both implicated and non-implicated enterprises, a significant unresolved challenge persists: how to ensure that the construction and operation of compliance management systems serve not merely as formalistic structures, but as functionally effective mechanisms for preventing unlawful, unethical, or criminal conduct through meaningful risk control.

6.2.1 U.S. Standards for Effective Compliance

In 1991, the United States introduced two significant institutional innovations in the promotion of corporate compliance through amendments to the *Federal Sentencing Guidelines*. First, it established the seven core elements of an Effective Compliance Program. Second, it implemented a compliance-based incentive mechanism that enabled criminally implicated corporations to receive mitigated penalties if they had adopted such programs. Since then, the U.S. Department of Justice (DOJ) has consistently treated the existence of an effective compliance program as a critical factor in determining whether to bring charges against a corporation. Beginning in 2017, the DOJ further institutionalized this approach by issuing the *Evaluation of Corporate Compliance Programs*, a policy document that has since been revised multiple times. Drawing upon a range of prior DOJ-issued compliance manuals, guidance documents, and memoranda, this framework sets forth the evaluation standards to be applied by federal prosecutors in assessing the effectiveness of corporate compliance programs.

The 1991 revision of the U.S. Federal Sentencing Guidelines established seven core elements of an effective compliance program. Under the Guidelines, such a program should ensure that the organization "exercises due diligence to prevent and detect criminal conduct" and "fosters an organizational culture that encourages ethical conduct and a commitment to compliance with the law."[3] Through subsequent revisions, these core elements have remained largely consistent and have become a fundamental benchmark for assessing whether an organization can effectively prevent and detect criminal conduct.

According to the U.S. *Federal Sentencing Guidelines*, an "effective compliance and ethics program" must contain at least seven essential elements. First, the organization must establish standards and procedures reasonably designed to prevent and detect criminal conduct. Second, compliance management authority must be allocated across three levels: the governing body should be knowledgeable about the program and exercise reasonable oversight with

[3] Carole Basri, *Corporate Compliance* (Durham, NC: Carolina Academic Press, 2017), 72–73.

respect to its implementation and effectiveness; senior management should ensure that an effective program is in place and assume overall responsibility for it; and specific individuals should be assigned day-to-day operational responsibility, with adequate resources, appropriate authority, and direct access to the governing body or an appropriate subgroup thereof. Third, the organization must exercise due diligence to exclude from positions of substantial authority any individual known, or who should have been known through due diligence, to have engaged in illegal activities or other conduct inconsistent with an effective compliance and ethics program. Fourth, the organization should provide periodic and effective communication and training regarding its standards, procedures, and other aspects of the compliance and ethics program to the governing body, senior management, individuals with substantial authority, employees, and agents. Fifth, mechanisms for monitoring, auditing, and periodically evaluating the program's effectiveness must be implemented, including the establishment of a system for anonymous or confidential reporting without fear of retaliation. Sixth, the program should be promoted and enforced consistently throughout the organization through appropriate incentives for ethical conduct and disciplinary measures for engaging in misconduct or for failing to take reasonable steps to prevent or detect it. Finally, after detecting criminal conduct, the organization must take appropriate responsive action, including making any necessary modifications to the compliance and ethics program to prevent future misconduct.

From 1991 to 2018, the seven core elements of an effective compliance and ethics program remained largely unchanged. The 2018 revision of the *Federal Sentencing Guidelines*, however, added a further requirement that organizations periodically assess the risk of criminal conduct and incorporate such risk assessment into the operational implementation of their compliance and ethics programs.[4]

As the effectiveness of corporate compliance mechanisms became a statutorily recognized sentencing consideration, U.S. federal prosecutors began to treat the existence and adequacy of such mechanisms as a key factor in determining whether to bring charges against corporate defendants. Since 1999, the U.S. Department of Justice (DOJ) has issued a series of guidelines, manuals, and memoranda that underscore the importance and substantive components of effective compliance programs. Notably, the 1999 *Principles of Federal Prosecution of Business Organizations* identified "whether the corporation has a compliance program and whether it is well designed and implemented" as one of eight factors that prosecutors must consider in deciding whether to indict a company. Beginning in 2008, the DOJ formalized its corporate prosecution policy through issuance of the "*Principles of Federal Prosecution of Business*

[4] Hui Chen, "The Application and Measurement of Compliance Mechanisms in Legal and Regulatory Contexts," in *Compliance Assessment and Measurement: Preventing Corporate Crime and Misconduct*, ed. Melissa Lawry and Benjamin van Rooij, trans. Zhu Qing and Fan Xiaoliang (Beijing: Contemporary China Publishing House, 2023), 46–49.

Organizations." These principles, incorporated into the *Justice Manual*, direct prosecutors to consider ten discrete factors in evaluating corporate wrongdoing and appropriate resolutions—such as criminal charges, plea agreements, or deferred prosecution agreements. Notably, Factor 5—the adequacy and effectiveness of the compliance program at both the time of the offense and at the charging decision—and Factor 7—the corporation's remedial efforts, including whether it has sought to establish or improve an effective compliance mechanism—are particularly significant in assessing whether a company merits a more favorable outcome.[5] Taken together, these documents consistently emphasize the importance of establishing an effective compliance program and identify it as a key factor for prosecutors in deciding whether to initiate charges. Importantly, the DOJ's understanding of what constitutes an effective compliance program remains closely aligned with the standards originally set forth in the *Federal Sentencing Guidelines*.

In addition to treating the effectiveness of compliance programs as a key factor in prosecution decisions, the U.S. Department of Justice (DOJ) has also integrated the objectives and core components of effective compliance into the enforcement of the *Foreign Corrupt Practices Act (FCPA)*. In 2012, the DOJ and the Securities and Exchange Commission (SEC) jointly issued the *FCPA Resource Guide*, which provides practical information to corporations and the general public regarding the enforcement of the statute. Although the Guide itself does not carry the force of law, it reflects the official position of federal prosecutors and securities regulators on what constitutes an effective compliance program. The Guide reaffirms the foundational principles set forth in the *Principles of Federal Prosecution of Business Organizations*. It identifies several critical factors that prosecutors consider when deciding whether to initiate an investigation, bring charges, or enter into a resolution agreement. These include: whether the company had implemented a compliance program prior to the misconduct; whether that program was effectively designed and operationalized; and whether the company took appropriate remedial actions following the violation, such as adopting a new compliance program or improving an existing one.

At the same time, according to the views of the Department of Justice and the SEC, no compliance program can entirely prevent all criminal conduct by corporate employees, and the mere occurrence of misconduct does not necessarily mean that the company's compliance program is ineffective. The evaluation of compliance effectiveness should focus on ten key areas: first, the tone at the top and the demonstrated commitment of senior management, including top leadership's dedication to fostering a compliance culture, ensuring effective implementation of the compliance program throughout the organization, and

[5] Hui Chen, "The Application and Measurement of Compliance Mechanisms in Legal and Regulatory Contexts," in *Compliance Assessment and Measurement: Preventing Corporate Crime and Misconduct*, ed. Melissa Lawry and Benjamin van Rooij, trans. Zhu Qing and Fan Xiaoliang (Beijing: Contemporary China Publishing House, 2023), 50–51.

clearly communicating compliance expectations; second, the company's code of conduct, compliance policies, and procedures, meaning whether a code of conduct has been issued, reviewed, and updated on a regular basis, and whether appropriate policies, internal controls, auditing protocols, and disciplinary procedures have been developed; third, oversight, autonomy, and resources, referring to whether responsibility for implementing and overseeing the compliance program is assigned to sufficiently senior personnel with meaningful authority and adequate resources; fourth, compliance risk evaluation, that is, whether the company has implemented a genuinely risk-based compliance program and allocated proportionate resources and attention to higher-risk areas such as due diligence and internal auditing; fifth, training and continuous guidance, including whether the company regularly provides training and certification to ensure that compliance policies and procedures are effectively disseminated and understood across the organization; sixth, incentives and disciplinary measures, referring to whether the company has established a robust system to promptly sanction noncompliant behavior while appropriately rewarding employees who adhere to legal and compliance standards; seventh, third-party due diligence, assessing whether the company conducts risk-based background checks on third parties—including agents, consultants, and distributors—on a periodic and ongoing basis, communicates its compliance expectations to these parties, and secures their commitment through mechanisms such as certifications; eighth, confidential reporting and internal investigations, including whether the company has implemented anonymous and secure reporting channels for whistleblowing, conducts timely internal investigations of reported misconduct, and takes appropriate remedial measures; ninth, continuous improvement through regular testing and review, examining whether the company periodically revises its compliance program in response to changes in business operations, risk profiles, client base, and applicable laws, as well as in light of deficiencies identified in the existing program; and tenth, pre-acquisition due diligence and post-acquisition integration, evaluating whether the company performs adequate due diligence on target entities prior to mergers or acquisitions, disclose and cooperate in addressing any detected misconduct, and integrate the acquired entity into its compliance framework through measures such as training, risk evaluation, and operational audits.[6]

The ten factors outlined above represent the principal considerations adopted by the Department of Justice and the Securities and Exchange Commission in assessing the effectiveness of corporate anti-commercial bribery compliance programs. While they differ from the seven elements articulated in the *Federal Sentencing Guidelines* primarily in terms of scope and level of detail, they do not embody any substantive departure in content. Moreover, beyond the specific domain of anti-commercial bribery compliance, the DOJ has

[6] Ruihua Chen, *The Chinese Experience of Effective Compliance*, Peking University Press, 2023, 290–295.

formulated a broader evaluative framework applicable to corporate compliance programs across all sectors and legal domains.

In 2019, the U.S. Department of Justice issued the *Evaluation of Corporate Compliance Programs*, consolidating prior DOJ manuals, guidelines, and memoranda into a unified framework for prosecutors to assess the effectiveness of corporate compliance programs. Although revised multiple times since its release, the document has consistently retained three fundamental questions as the core criteria for evaluation: whether the program is well designed; whether it is being applied earnestly and in good faith; and whether it works in practice.

Some Chinese scholars have interpreted the three evaluative criteria set out by the U.S. Department of Justice as corresponding to three dimensions of compliance effectiveness: the effectiveness of program design, the effectiveness of program implementation, and the effectiveness of program outcomes. The Supreme People's Procuratorate of China, in a 2022 document on the review and assessment of compliance remediation for implicated enterprises, even adopted these three dimensions as the principal benchmarks for evaluations conducted by prosecutors and third-party organizations. A close reading of the DOJ's *Evaluation of Corporate Compliance Programs*, however, reveals a significant mismatch between the titles of these criteria and the substantive content they cover. Rather than articulating distinct, outcome-oriented standards for assessing effectiveness, the document largely reorganizes various structural components of a compliance program under three thematic headings and presents them as evaluation benchmarks.

For instance, the criterion "whether the corporation's compliance program is well designed" should, in principle, establish a comprehensive standard for determining whether the program's overall structure and framework are sound and effective. In practice, however, this section addresses only a subset of institutional elements primarily concerned with risk prevention and detection—such as risk evaluation mechanisms, internal policies and procedures, training and communication protocols, anonymous reporting and investigation systems, third-party due diligence mechanisms, and compliance controls in mergers and acquisitions. The second criterion— "whether the corporation's compliance program is being applied earnestly and in good faith"—is, in principle, meant to assess whether the commitments articulated in the written compliance plan have been substantively implemented and whether the corresponding risk control mechanisms have been effectively put into operation. However, in the DOJ's framework, this dimension is summarized as three institutional elements relating to compliance governance and disciplinary/reward structures: commitment by senior and middle management, autonomy and resources, and incentives and disciplinary measures. As for the third criterion — "whether the corporation's compliance program works in practice"—this should, in principle, be understood as evaluating whether the compliance program has effectively served its purpose of preventing unlawful, unethical, or criminal conduct, and whether it has fostered a corporate culture grounded in legal and regulatory compliance. However, within the DOJ's evaluative framework, this standard is largely narrowed to procedural considerations such as continuous improvement through regular updates, periodic testing, and review mechanisms; well-functioning mechanisms for investigating misconduct; and analysis and remediation of underlying misconduct. Conspicuously absent is any examination of whether the compliance program has played a demonstrable role in reducing or eliminating unlawful behavior, or whether there exists a direct causal link between the functioning of the program and the actual mitigation of corporate wrongdoing.[7]

6.2.2 UK Standards for Effective Compliance

Influenced by developments in the United States, the United Kingdom began incorporating corporate compliance mechanisms and focusing on the evaluation of compliance effectiveness after 2010. That year, the UK enacted the *Bribery Act*, which introduced the corporate offence of "failure of commercial organisations to prevent bribery." This provision imposes strict liability on companies involved in bribery but simultaneously provides a statutory defense if the company can demonstrate that it had implemented an effective compliance program. According to the Act and its associated guidance, an effective compliance program is defined through six principles of "adequate procedures." Where a company has adopted a compliance system consistent with these principles, the judiciary may recognize this as a valid defense and exempt the company from liability. This compliance-based defense mechanism was later extended to corporate criminal liability in tax-related offences. In 2020, the UK's Serious Fraud Office (SFO) released a revised *Operational Handbook on Evaluating Compliance Programs*, which outlines a systematic framework and evaluative criteria for prosecutors, investigators, auditors, legal counsel, and compliance professionals to assess the effectiveness of a company's compliance program during investigations.

The codification of a compliance-based defense mechanism represents a distinctive feature of the United Kingdom's corporate criminal liability regime. Under this framework, the law first imposes strict liability on corporate entities—meaning that if an employee engages in conduct such as bribery or tax evasion, the company is presumed to have committed the offence of failing to prevent such misconduct (e.g., failure to prevent bribery or failure to prevent the facilitation of tax evasion). Second, the law provides the company with a statutory defense: it may rebut the presumption of liability by demonstrating that it was not negligent, thereby severing the legal nexus between the corporation and the offending individual. Third, the primary method for mounting this defense is to show that, prior to the misconduct, the company had implemented an anti-bribery or anti-tax-evasion compliance program that was reasonably designed and effectively operated to prevent such offenses. Finally, if

[7] Ruihua Chen, *The Fundamentals of Corporate Compliance*, 3rd ed. (Beijing: Law Press, 2022), 102–109.

the company is able to prove the adequacy and effectiveness of its compliance measures, the judicial authorities are required to find the company not liable. If not, the company will be found to have committed the relevant failure-to-prevent offence.

In 2011, the UK Ministry of Justice issued guidance on the implementation of the Bribery Act, stating that a company may be deemed to have an effective anti-commercial bribery compliance program if it adheres to the six core principles of "adequate procedures." These principles were reaffirmed in the 2017 guidance accompanying the implementation of the Criminal Finances Act, which extended their applicability by recognizing them as a statutory defense for companies facing liability in tax-related offences. In general, "adequate procedures" refer to internal compliance systems designed to prevent risks of commercial bribery or tax evasion. Whether a corporate compliance framework satisfies the fundamental criteria of "adequate procedures" has become the central benchmark used by UK prosecutors to evaluate the effectiveness of corporate compliance programs.

In brief, the concept of "adequate procedures" consists of six fundamental principles used to evaluate the effectiveness of a corporate compliance program. The principle of proportionate procedures requires that the procedures designed to prevent misconduct be proportionate to the compliance risks the organization faces, taking into account its nature, size, and complexity; these procedures must also be clear, practical, accessible, and capable of effective implementation. The top-level commitment principle emphasizes that senior management should demonstrate a clear and active commitment to preventing bribery or tax evasion, and foster an internal culture of zero tolerance for such conduct. The risk assessment principle requires companies to conduct regular assessments of the nature and severity of internal and external compliance risks associated with persons performing services for or on behalf of the company, and to document both the process and findings of such assessments. The due diligence principle mandates the adoption of a risk-based and proportionate approach to conducting background checks on third parties and service providers, in order to mitigate identified compliance risks. The communication principle requires that compliance policies and procedures be clearly conveyed and effectively understood throughout the organization through both internal and external communication efforts. Finally, the monitoring and review principle requires companies to adopt procedures for monitoring and evaluating their compliance systems in order to prevent bribery or tax evasion by management personnel, and to implement timely improvements to these procedures based on periodic assessments.

In the practice of criminal justice in the United Kingdom, prosecuting authorities are required to evaluate the effectiveness of a corporate compliance program in four distinct scenarios: first, when determining whether prosecution is in the public interest; second, when deciding whether to enter into a deferred prosecution agreement (DPA) with the company; third, when assessing whether the company has satisfied the statutory "adequate procedures" defense in response to criminal charges; and fourth, when considering whether the compliance program may serve as a mitigating factor at the sentencing stage. To ensure the effectiveness of such evaluations, the Serious Fraud Office (SFO) published the *Operational Handbook on Evaluating Compliance Programmes* in 2020. This handbook extends the application of the six "adequate procedures" principles for crime prevention beyond anti-bribery and tax-related offenses to all forms of corporate criminal liability. These principles may be invoked both to prompt companies to make compliance-related commitments and to serve as benchmarks for assessing the effectiveness of corporate compliance remediation. Moreover, the handbook emphasizes that prosecutors should begin examining the effectiveness of a company's compliance framework at the earliest stages of a criminal investigation. They are encouraged to gather relevant information regarding the company's establishment or improvement of its compliance program from multiple sources. Common investigative tools include voluntary disclosures and interviews, compulsory production of documents and records, witness interviews, and suspect interrogations.

Given that prosecutors may be required to assess the effectiveness of a corporate compliance program in a variety of legal contexts, the SFO's *Operational Handbook on Evaluating Compliance Programmes* introduces a multidimensional evaluative framework. It calls for prosecutorial attention to three distinct temporal dimensions of compliance effectiveness. First is the retrospective evaluation of the company's pre-incident compliance program—namely, whether an effective compliance regime had been established prior to the commission of the offense. Second is the contemporaneous evaluation of the current compliance program—whether, in the period following the misconduct and preceding any prosecutorial decision, the company has taken steps to enhance its compliance infrastructure, adopt remedial measures, or implement a proactive and effective compliance initiative. Third is the prospective evaluation of the company's future compliance commitments—that is, the extent to which the company has pledged compliance remediation, and what positive developments can reasonably be anticipated. This future-oriented dimension often plays a decisive role in the prosecutor's determination of whether to enter into a deferred prosecution agreement (DPA).[8]

6.2.3 French Standards in Anti-Corruption Compliance

Much like the United Kingdom, France first established its compliance incentive mechanisms within the realm of anti-corruption enforcement. In 2016, France enacted the *Sapin II Law*, which established the French Anti-Corruption Agency, introduced mandatory compliance programs, created a deferred prosecution agreement (DPA) framework, and set out the core principles for

[8] Ruihua Chen, *The Chinese Experience of Effective Compliance* (Beijing: Peking University Press, 2023), 268–269.

effective compliance. In 2020, the French Anti-Corruption Agency released a comprehensive set of *Anti-Corruption Compliance Guidelines*, applicable to both public institutions and private enterprises. These guidelines articulate the core principles of anti-corruption compliance and delineate three institutional pillars that collectively serve as the principal evaluative standards for assessing the effectiveness of corporate compliance programs in France's anti-corruption legal framework.

The *Sapin II Law* of 2016 marked a pioneering step in France's anti-corruption enforcement by introducing a mandatory compliance program regime and a deferred prosecution agreement (DPA) framework. The law also established seven core elements that define the minimum requirements of an effective compliance program. First, the adoption of a code of conduct that clearly defines behaviors likely to constitute bribery or other illicit transactions. Second, the creation of an internal whistleblowing system to collect reports and alerts from employees regarding suspected misconduct. Third, the implementation of a risk assessment process to identify, analyze, and rank bribery risks according to the company's industry and geographical areas of operation, with regular updates. Fourth, the development of internal and external accounting control procedures designed to ensure that accounting records and books are not used to conceal corrupt practices. Fifth, the establishment of a training program for executives and employees most exposed to bribery risks, aimed at equipping them to prevent and detect corrupt conduct. Sixth, the creation of a disciplinary procedure to sanction violations of the code of conduct. Seventh, the introduction of an internal control and evaluation mechanism to monitor and assess the overall effectiveness of the compliance program.

To ensure the effective implementation of both the mandatory compliance framework and the deferred prosecution agreement (DPA) mechanism, the French Anti-Corruption Agency (AFA) issued a compliance guidance document in 2017 to assist companies in developing anti-corruption compliance programs. In 2020, the AFA significantly revised and expanded this document, releasing a more systematic and comprehensive Anti-Corruption Compliance Guidelines. While the Guidelines do not possess binding legal authority, they serve as a key reference for the AFA in evaluating the effectiveness of corporate anti-corruption compliance programs. Building on a set of foundational principles and three core institutional pillars, the Guidelines set out detailed requirements for anti-corruption compliance programs in both the private and public sectors.

The Guide designates the principle of proportionality as the core standard for anti-corruption compliance programs, requiring enterprises to establish programs tailored to the specific nature and severity of their corruption risks. On this basis, the Guide mandates that a corporate compliance framework be grounded in three interrelated institutional pillars. First, senior management's commitment to anti-corruption, which entails that leadership not only set an example in preventing and monitoring corrupt practices but also play an active role in promoting and supporting the program by ensuring adequate allocation of resources. Second, risk identification, which involves the concrete recognition, assessment, and categorization of corruption risks specific to the enterprise, along with the implementation of tiered risk management measures. Third, risk management, which entails designing, rolling out, and implementing the anti-corruption compliance program based on the results of risk identification and assessment, with the aim of effectively preventing and monitoring compliance risks and taking remedial measures to address any identified institutional deficiencies.[9]

To implement the core principles of anti-corruption compliance and ensure the effective operation of the three institutional pillars, the French Anti-Corruption Guide outlines detailed compliance requirements for both private-sector enterprises and public institutions. For instance, in support of the principle of top-level commitment, the Guide mandates that top executives actively lead the design, implementation, and oversight of the anti-corruption program. This includes ensuring that compliance personnel are equipped with adequate authority, resources, and access to relevant information; conducting regular evaluations of anti-corruption measures and protocols; personally leading or participating in the implementation of critical anti-corruption measures and procedures; clearly articulating the organization's anti-corruption strategy and commitments to internal stakeholders and external business partners; and imposing appropriate disciplinary sanctions on individuals found to have engaged in misconduct.

Similarly, to ensure the smooth and effective implementation of corruption risk identification, the Guidelines require companies to regularly update relevant documentation, refine their information analysis and management processes, accurately assess the severity of identified corruption risks, classify and rank such risks by level, and periodically update the risk identification process itself. Furthermore, to implement the risk management mechanism, the Guidelines require companies to operationalize preventive measures by formulating anti-corruption codes of conduct and policies, providing compliance training, and conducting third party due diligence. They also call for strengthening risk monitoring through the operation of internal whistleblowing mechanisms and the activation and maintenance of internal controls and audit procedures. Finally, to ensure timely remediation and continual enhancement of institutional arrangements, companies are required to impose disciplinary sanctions on violators and to systematically record and archive anti-corruption information for future reference.

[9] Ruihua Chen, *The Chinese Experience of Effective Compliance* (Beijing: Peking University Press, 2023), 279–281.

6.2.4 Preliminary Reflections

Once corporate compliance moves beyond its earlier stage as an internal control mechanism and becomes an external regulatory requirement imposed by supervisory authorities, judicial bodies, or industry associations, it can no longer be detached from its fundamental objective, and must be subject to certain minimum standards of effectiveness. To date, whether regulatory agencies are implementing mandatory compliance regimes, prosecutors are determining whether to initiate prosecution based on considerations of public interest, deciding whether to enter into deferred prosecution agreements with implicated companies, or courts are weighing compliance efforts in sentencing decisions, the evaluation of a company's compliance program has become an indispensable part of criminal and administrative proceedings. In order to ensure that such evaluations are conducted with rigor and fairness, several jurisdictions in the United States and Europe have developed institutional frameworks for assessing effective compliance programs. Through this process, a set of broadly accepted norms has emerged and been formalized in the practices of judicial and regulatory bodies in countries such as the United States, the United Kingdom, and France. These shared understandings reflect the following key propositions: that the fundamental purpose of a corporate compliance program is to effectively identify, prevent, and monitor compliance risks, particularly unlawful, unethical, or criminal conduct; that companies are expected to establish a risk-based compliance management system incorporating a defined set of institutional elements to ensure meaningful implementation; that it is insufficient for companies to merely demonstrate the formal existence of a compliance framework meeting minimum regulatory standards—they must also provide concrete, verifiable evidence that such a framework operates effectively in practice; and that both regulators and judicial authorities, when conducting such evaluations, should adhere to methodologically sound, evidence-based procedures using reliable assessment tools.

However, efforts in the United States and Europe to develop standards and methodologies for evaluating the effectiveness of corporate compliance programs have also encountered criticism and controversy. For instance, with respect to the effective compliance elements articulated in the U.S. Federal Sentencing Guidelines, some scholars have argued that while the Guidelines define the objective of compliance mechanisms as the prevention and detection of criminal conduct, they fail to provide measurable criteria for evaluating outcomes. The drafters of the Guidelines did not rely on empirical evidence to address fundamental questions such as whether the implementation of the Guidelines has, over the decades, actually reduced corporate criminal activity, or whether it has enabled earlier detection of such misconduct. Similarly, in the context of the settlement agreements entered into by U.S. prosecutors and corporate defendants—particularly the provisions requiring the establishment or enhancement of compliance programs—critics have pointed to the absence of any standards for determining whether the company has achieved the intended goal of preventing recidivism. Several core issues remain underexplored: How should the start date for measuring recidivism be determined? Should every instance of internal control failure be treated as a recurrence of misconduct? And must the subsequent offense be identical in nature, or merely similar, to the initial violation in order to qualify as recidivism? These questions have received limited academic or practical attention, and prosecutorial authorities have yet to offer definitive answers.[10]

These criticisms are undoubtedly well-founded. The objectives of effective compliance are generally clear: to prevent and monitor the occurrence of unlawful or noncompliant conduct, or to prevent the recurrence of the same or similar offenses. Yet significant uncertainties persist. How can enterprises actually achieve these goals through the establishment of compliance systems or through post-incident compliance remediation efforts? And how should regulatory or judicial authorities assess whether a given compliance program has genuinely fulfilled these objectives? In this respect, the institutional frameworks developed in Western jurisdictions appear to suffer from three key limitations.

First, there is a tendency to focus excessively on whether a company has formally established the *minimum elements* of a compliance management system, while insufficient attention is paid to the substantive relationship between each element and the overarching objective of achieving effective compliance. In practice, it is not particularly difficult for companies to quickly incorporate the structural components required by compliance guidelines into their internal governance frameworks. For example, adopting codes of conduct, formulating compliance policies and procedures, conducting risk assessments, and performing due diligence on third-party business partners can all be accomplished relatively swiftly and with minimal resistance. Yet the critical question remains: do the establishment, implementation, and operationalization of these components actually contribute to the prevention of internal misconduct? Empirical evidence suggests otherwise. Many enterprises issue well-drafted anti-bribery codes of conduct, regularly conduct compliance risk assessments, and carry out background checks on customers, suppliers, agents, and distributors. Nonetheless, instances of commercial bribery and similar violations continue to arise with considerable frequency. In many instances, the formulation and promulgation of compliance rules is one matter, whereas ensuring that they function effectively to prevent misconduct is quite another.

Second, there is an excessive reliance on a "oriented-oriented" approach, which tends to overlook the substantive effectiveness of compliance outcomes. In both the United States and Europe, the elements of effective compliance articulated by regulatory bodies—as well as the corresponding evaluations conducted by prosecutors and regulators—are predominantly procedural in

[10] Hui Chen, "The Application and Measurement of Compliance Mechanisms in Legal and Regulatory Contexts," in *Compliance Assessment and Measurement: Preventing Corporate Crime and Misconduct*, ed. Melissa Lawry and Benjamin van Rooij, trans. Zhu Qing and Fan Xiaoliang (Beijing: Contemporary China Publishing House, 2023), 49–59.

orientation, whether intentionally or not. According to this approach, a company is considered to have achieved "effective compliance" if it merely complies with the prescribed requirements, fulfills its declared compliance commitments, incorporates the minimum compliance elements into its management system, and translates its textbook compliance policies into operation or activates its internal control mechanisms. What remains largely ignored, however, is whether the company has, in practice, prevented the recurrence of similar or identical violations within a specific timeframe, or whether it has succeeded in fostering a genuine compliance culture. Regulatory and judicial authorities seldom undertake serious inquiry into such outcome-oriented indicators.

Third, there is a notable absence of scientifically grounded and practically viable methods for measuring whether a compliance program has achieved its intended outcomes. Consequently, there are no objective standards for determining whether a company has effectively prevented unlawful conduct or recidivism. Neither compliance guidelines issued by regulatory or prosecutorial authorities nor the settlement agreements reached with corporate defendants provide outcome-oriented benchmarks for evaluating compliance effectiveness. Instead, they tend to focus exclusively on enumerating the structural elements and procedural steps companies are expected to implement, without articulating any outcome-oriented criteria for assessing compliance effectiveness—let alone proposing empirically grounded, operational indicators for measuring whether the intended objectives have actually been achieved.

6.3 Process-Oriented Evaluation: Chinese Frameworks and Practices

As early as the 1990s, certain Chinese administrative authorities introduced compliance management systems within specific regulatory sectors. Since the turn of the twenty-first century, in response to growing international pressure for companies to establish sound compliance frameworks—and to tackle the increasingly acute problem of ensuring lawful and regulation-abiding corporate conduct—Chinese regulatory bodies have accelerated the institutionalization of corporate compliance mechanisms. By issuing compliance guidelines, regulators have provided official templates or baseline standards for enterprises to follow. In sectors such as finance and securities, mandatory compliance regimes have been established, turning the implementation of compliance systems into a legal obligation for designated enterprises. Firms that refuse to establish such systems or fail to meet regulatory requirements may face legal liability. Moreover, through the adoption of compliance incentive mechanisms, regulators have created space for "companies under investigation" to receive more lenient administrative treatment in exchange for undertaking post-violation compliance reforms, thus embedding a reward structure that encourages compliance remediation efforts.

The core purpose of establishing and implementing a corporate compliance management system is to effectively identify, manage, and mitigate specific compliance risks, thereby enabling the prevention, detection, and response to potential legal or regulatory violations. To this end, administrative regulatory authorities in China have increasingly recognized the importance of assessing the effectiveness of corporate compliance systems. As an international standard followed by Chinese regulatory authorities in promoting compliance management, the ISO compliance guidelines explicitly call for the establishment of effective compliance management systems. Several national-level compliance guidelines in China likewise stress the significance of building effective systems and promote the evaluation of their operational performance. Moreover, certain industry associations have begun formulating and publishing evaluation standards for compliance effectiveness, including defined assessment dimensions and measurable indicators. These developments provide a normative reference for regulators to accurately assess the effectiveness of enterprise compliance programs and offer practical guidance for companies seeking to improve and refine their compliance management systems in a targeted manner.

6.3.1 National Standards for Compliance Effectiveness

In 2022, China's State Administration for Market Regulation and the Standardization Administration jointly issued the national standard *Compliance Management Systems—Requirements with Guidance for Use* (GB/T 35770-2022, hereinafter the "National Standard"), which is an equivalent adoption of the ISO 37301:2021 *Compliance Management Systems—Requirements with Guidance for Use* (hereinafter the "ISO 37301:2021 International Standard") issued by the International Organization for Standardization (ISO). This standard sets out the fundamental requirements for establishing a compliance management system and provides guidance and recommended practices for its implementation. According to its drafters, the National Standard adopts the internationally recognized risk management cycle of Plan–Do–Check–Act, breaking risk control down into four interrelated stages aimed at achieving effective compliance outcomes. In line with this model, the standard outlines seven core components of compliance management: organizational context, leadership, planning, support, operation, performance evaluation, and continual improvement.[11]

The National Standard defines compliance effectiveness as "the extent to which planned activities are carried out and planned results are achieved." To achieve compliance effectiveness, enterprises must identify the sources of their compliance obligations in accordance with the legal and regulatory environment in which they operate. The governance structure and top management are required to demonstrate active commitment to compliance management

[11] Yiyi Wang et al., *Interpretation and Application of the Standard "Compliance Management System—Requirements and Guidance"* (Beijing: Enterprise Management Press, 2022), 10–15.

and integrate it into both strategic and operational planning. Enterprises should ensure adequate support for compliance by allocating necessary resources, developing personnel competencies, promoting compliance awareness, facilitating internal and external communication, and maintaining documented information. They are also expected to establish control measures across compliance policies, processes, and procedures; conduct appropriate evaluations of the effectiveness of the compliance management system; and implement improvement measures in response to changes in their internal or external environment and business operations.

Within this framework, performance evaluation is considered a critical management tool. It encompasses the processes of information gathering, internal auditing, and management review, all aimed at assessing both the effectiveness of the compliance management system and the organization's overall compliance performance. Enterprises are expected to develop, implement, and maintain a set of appropriate evaluation metrics to measure the achievement of compliance objectives and assess compliance outcomes. For example, in conducting performance evaluations, companies should monitor a range of indicators, including: the effectiveness of training programs; the effectiveness of internal controls; the proper allocation of responsibilities for compliance obligations; the timeliness of compliance actions; the effectiveness of corrective actions addressing previously identified deficiencies; instances of failure to conduct internal compliance audits; and the extent to which compliance risks are incorporated into business strategy reviews. To facilitate effective performance evaluation, enterprises may adopt a three-tiered indicator framework comprising basic, reactive, and predictive indicators. Basic indicators include the percentage of employees trained, the frequency of regulatory interventions, and the utilization rate of feedback mechanisms. Reactive indicators focus on the identification of compliance issues by type, location, and frequency; the consequences of non-compliance; and the time taken to report and implement corrective actions. Predictive indicators assess potential compliance risks based on projected losses or gains and monitor emerging trends in non-compliant behavior.

To ensure the timely identification of weaknesses in the compliance management system, enterprises should establish a compliance reporting mechanism and maintain records of non-compliance incidents along with the corrective measures undertaken. In parallel, they are expected to conduct regular internal audits of the compliance system and require governing bodies and top management to carry out periodic management reviews. These reviews serve to ensure that the system remains appropriate, adequate, and effective over time, and provide a direct basis for its continuous improvement and refinement.

6.3.2 Definitions by Central Regulatory Authorities

In promoting the establishment of corporate compliance management systems, China's administrative regulatory authorities have made proactive and notable efforts. By issuing administrative compliance guidelines and piloting mandatory administrative compliance mechanisms, they have articulated objectives and requirements for enterprises to develop and implement compliance frameworks. At the same time, in order to encourage enterprises under investigation to undertake compliance remediation and establish targeted compliance programs, some authorities have begun experimenting with administrative compliance incentive mechanisms—enabling enterprises to "exchange compliance for leniency" as a means of stimulating enthusiasm for building robust compliance systems. However, the mere establishment of compliance frameworks or the publication of compliance guidelines is far from sufficient to achieve the overarching goal of effectively preventing and controlling compliance risks. To avoid the emergence of superficial or purely formalistic compliance, certain regulatory authorities have shifted their focus toward evaluating the effectiveness of compliance management practices. Nevertheless, to date, administrative agencies have not yet developed a coherent and standardized framework of indicators or methodologies for assessing the effectiveness of corporate compliance systems.

For example, the *Administrative Measures for Compliance Management of Central State-Owned Enterprises*, issued by the State-owned Assets Supervision and Administration Commission (SASAC) in August 2022, explicitly designates the "effective prevention and control of compliance risks" as the core objective of enterprise compliance management. According to the Measures, compliance management is defined as a structured and planned set of corporate activities—including the establishment of compliance systems, the improvement of operational mechanisms, the cultivation of a compliance culture, and the strengthening of oversight and accountability. To prevent compliance management from becoming superficial or purely formalistic, the Measures set forth general requirements for assessing the effectiveness of compliance systems in central SOEs. Specifically, enterprises are required to "regularly evaluate the effectiveness of their compliance management systems, conduct focused evaluations of compliance practices in key business areas as needed, and enhance the application of evaluation results."[12]

Similarly, in 2024, the State Administration for Market Regulation (SAMR) issued the *Antitrust Compliance Guidelines for Business Operators.* Adopting a regulatory framework consistent with the aforementioned *Administrative Measures*, the Guidelines define antitrust compliance management as a structured, planned, and full-process management activity undertaken by enterprises with the aim of "preventing and mitigating antitrust compliance risks."

[12] State-owned Assets Supervision and Administration Commission of the State Council, *Measures for Compliance Management of Central Enterprises* (2022), arts. 13, 14, 18.

These activities encompass the formulation of compliance rules, risk identification and response, compliance review, compliance training, compliance commitments, compliance incentives and sanctions, and compliance oversight. The Guidelines enumerate 22 illustrative examples which, from the perspectives of antitrust compliance management principles, compliance governance structures, compliance risk management, operational safeguards, and compliance incentives, provide general guidance to business operators on establishing and implementing antitrust compliance programs. Moreover, the Guidelines explicitly underscore the importance of compliance evaluation and continuous improvement, encouraging business operators to regularly assess the effectiveness of their antitrust compliance systems, identify and rectify existing deficiencies, and continuously refine and enhance their compliance programs. In the event of significant antitrust risks or violations, operators are also required to conduct special evaluations of the effectiveness of their antitrust compliance management systems.

6.3.3 *Explorations by Industry Associations (I)*

To ensure that enterprises attain genuinely effective compliance management—and to prevent the emergence of "paper compliance" or ineffective formalism—several industry associations in China have taken the initiative to develop and issue advisory documents aimed at evaluating the effectiveness of corporate compliance systems. For instance, in 2021, the China Securities Association issued a revised version of the *Guidelines for the Effectiveness Evaluation of Compliance Management in Securities Companies*, marking the first time an industry-specific association introduced standards for assessing compliance effectiveness. In 2022, the China Enterprise Evaluation Association released a revised version of the *Guidelines for the Effectiveness Evaluation of Corporate Compliance Management Systems*, which provides baseline standards for a wide variety of enterprises conducting compliance assessments. That same year, the China Association of Small and Medium Enterprises issued the *Effectiveness Evaluation Guidelines for Compliance Management Systems in Small and Medium-Sized Enterprises*, establishing a structured framework specifically tailored to the compliance evaluation needs of SMEs.

Of course, the compliance effectiveness evaluation guidelines issued by relevant industry associations do not have the force of law and are not legally binding on administrative regulatory authorities or judicial bodies in their assessment of an enterprise's compliance program. To a large extent, these documents function as reference frameworks for enterprises conducting internal evaluations of compliance effectiveness, and they may also serve as assessment standards for third-party institutions engaged in evaluating corporate compliance systems. In practical compliance management, enterprises may either conduct self-assessments or commission independent third parties to carry out such evaluations. The aforementioned guidelines can serve as important references in both types of assessment. The analysis below takes the

Guidelines for the Effectiveness Evaluation of Corporate Compliance Management Systems (hereinafter referred to as the *Evaluation Guidelines*) as a representative example, in order to provide a brief overview of the evaluation standards for compliance effectiveness promoted by Chinese industry associations.

The *Evaluation Guidelines* establish an index system for assessing the effectiveness of corporate compliance management systems, structured around five core evaluation dimensions with corresponding indicators. These include: first, compliance environment evaluation, focusing on internal and external factors, stakeholder needs and expectations, the scope of the compliance system, and compliance obligations; second, leadership and resource allocation, assessing top-level participation, the functions and resources of compliance bodies, managerial responsibilities and performance, and the digitalization of compliance management; third, compliance systems and operational mechanisms, which examine the structure of the compliance framework and its operational implementation; fourth, compliance culture, covering compliance philosophy, compliance cultural promotion, and employee responsibilities and performance; and fifth, performance evaluation and continuous improvement, addressing monitoring and evaluation, internal audits, management reviews, continuous improvement, and the handling of nonconformities and corrective actions.

According to the *Evaluation Guidelines*, the effectiveness of a compliance management system is defined as "the extent to which the operation and outcomes of the established system achieve the intended objectives." This definition encompasses four key dimensions: (1) the system's alignment with relevant normative documents and the ISO 37301 International Standard issued by the International Organization for Standardization; (2) the consistency between the implementation process and internal compliance documentation; (3) the extent to which the implementation outcomes fulfill the enterprise's compliance objectives; and (4) the results of ongoing improvement efforts. Compliance effectiveness evaluations are based on a combination of enterprise self-assessments and expert assessments. A self-assessment involves the enterprise's internal review of its compliance operations and outcomes, while an expert assessment entails an independent, professional examination of the normative and evidentiary materials submitted by the enterprise. On the basis of the self-assessment, the designated assessment body conducts a comprehensive and systematic review, and where necessary, verifies the information on site through methods such as document review, questionnaires, interviews, and field visits. Whether performed internally or externally, the evaluation process may assign scores to each of the five evaluation dimensions, with the scores distributed across corresponding performance indicators. The total score then determines the enterprise's compliance effectiveness rating. For example, under a 1,000-point system, enterprises scoring below 600 are deemed to have failed to meet the evaluation threshold; those scoring between 601 and 900 are rated as "compliant," "good," or "excellent"; and those scoring above 901 are considered to have reached the "industry benchmark" level in compliance management. Both self-assessments and third-party assessments must culminate in a formal compliance effectiveness evaluation report, which sets out the enterprise's basic information, the evaluation basis and methodology, the key findings, recommended improvements, and an analysis of performance across the five core dimensions.

6.3.4 Explorations by Industry Associations (II)

The aforementioned *Evaluation Guidelines* establish general evaluation standards applicable to enterprises across sectors. Beyond this universal framework, however, some industry associations have developed evaluation standards specifically tailored to particular types of enterprises, which warrant closer examination. A particularly illustrative example is the *Guidelines for the Effectiveness Evaluation of Compliance Management in Securities Companies*, issued by the China Securities Association in 2021. These guidelines not only articulate sector-specific standards for assessing compliance effectiveness within securities firms, but also set out a range of concrete evaluation methodologies tailored to the securities industry.

According to these evaluation guidelines, the assessment of compliance effectiveness in securities companies is categorized into two types: comprehensive evaluations and special-purpose evaluations. Each company is required to conduct at least one comprehensive evaluation of its compliance management effectiveness annually. Such evaluations may be conducted internally at the company's discretion or commissioned to an external professional institution, with the latter required at least once every three years. The evaluation should primarily address four core areas: the compliance management environment; the fulfillment of compliance responsibilities; the support infrastructure for compliance management; and the establishment and operational effectiveness of management systems and mechanisms.

With respect to the evaluation of the compliance management environment, companies should focus on whether a robust compliance culture has been established, whether the compliance management system is comprehensive, and whether the basic requirements for compliant operations are being effectively observed.

In assessing the fulfillment of compliance responsibilities, particular attention should be given to whether compliance duties are being effectively performed at all organizational levels, including key functions such as compliance review, compliance consultation, compliance training, compliance monitoring, compliance performance evaluation, compliance accountability, and compliance reporting.

In evaluating the support infrastructure for compliance management, the assessment should examine whether mechanisms—such as the performance of the chief compliance officer's duties, the establishment of a compliance department, the allocation of compliance personnel, compliance oversight of subsidiaries, and institutional safeguards for compliance personnel—are well-structured and effectively implemented.

As for the evaluation of business management systems and operational mechanisms, the focus should be on whether internal systems and procedures are sound, aligned with applicable laws and regulations, and capable of being promptly revised in response to changes in the external regulatory environment.

In conducting evaluations of compliance management effectiveness, securities firms are expected to adopt a range of assessment methods, including but not limited to interviews, knowledge testing, sampling analysis, questionnaires, walkthrough testing, and system and data testing. Among these, sampling analysis and walkthrough testing are considered core methods and should be used regularly.

Evaluation teams may conduct sampling analysis based on key areas of concern by selecting business or management items for review. Samples should be drawn from a defined population according to factors such as transaction frequency, materiality, and levels of compliance risk, and evaluators should assess the selected samples accordingly. Concurrently, evaluators may carry out walkthrough testing on specific business processes. This involves reviewing original documentation and tracing the flow of transactions as recorded in the documents, with the aim of verifying how relevant internal policies and operational procedures are actually implemented in practice. Such testing serves to evaluate the firm's compliance with applicable laws and regulations throughout its operational and management activities.

6.3.5 Brief Commentary

The national standards for compliance management established by Chinese regulatory authorities—along with the administrative guidelines and regulatory measures issued on that basis—largely follow the international standards for compliance management promulgated by the International Organization for Standardization (ISO). Similar to the compliance management guidelines adopted in certain Western jurisdictions, these international standards essentially reflect a reproduction of the "oriented-oriented" model for evaluating compliance effectiveness. The strengths and limitations of this evaluative approach have already been addressed earlier and will not be reiterated here.

It is worth noting that in recent years, certain central-level regulatory authorities in China have placed increasing emphasis on the evaluation of compliance management effectiveness. These authorities now view the effective prevention and mitigation of compliance risks as the core objective of compliance management and have begun to assess compliance effectiveness based on the extent to which this objective is achieved. Moreover, the results of such evaluations are being used as an important basis for improving and optimizing enterprise compliance management systems. This trend is undoubtedly of positive significance.

Some industry associations in China have issued preliminary standards for evaluating compliance management effectiveness and have engaged in valuable exploratory efforts in this area. Although the main evaluation indicators currently in use remain largely process-oriented—emphasizing the assessment of how compliance management elements are implemented—these efforts have also incorporated a range of scientifically grounded assessment methods, such as interviews, knowledge testing, sampling analysis, questionnaires, and walkthrough testing. These methodologies have previously been employed to varying degrees in corporate risk assessment practices and are now being applied to the evaluation of compliance management effectiveness. Their integration into compliance assessment frameworks provides enterprises and regulatory authorities with a more objective and evidence-based foundation for evaluating compliance performance. This development is undoubtedly a positive and commendable step forward.

6.4 Emergence of Outcome-Oriented Evaluation Standards

In the evaluation of compliance management effectiveness, both European and American jurisdictions have, with remarkable consistency, adopted a oriented-oriented approach. Regulatory authorities and industry associations in China have largely followed suit. This process-oriented model has drawn criticism from some American scholars, who have undertaken theoretical reflection and made initial efforts to propose an outcome-oriented framework for assessing compliance effectiveness. Meanwhile, although U.S. prosecutors generally evaluate a company's compliance remediation based on its fulfillment of compliance commitments and the implementation of key compliance elements, in certain cases, they have placed additional emphasis on the actual outcomes of remediation efforts. In such cases, prosecutors have identified the prevention and detection of unlawful or criminal conduct, along with the establishment of a culture of lawful and compliant business operations, as the core objectives of effective compliance remediation. As a result, implicated companies have been required to restructure their corporate governance, modify flawed business practices, and address problematic corporate cultures—thereby undertaking substantive organizational reforms. These practices clearly go beyond formal assessments of compliance procedures and reflect a shift toward outcome-oriented evaluation of compliance effectiveness.

Indeed, it is not only the American academic and judicial communities that are calling for change. The International Organization for Standardization (ISO)—one of the primary institutions responsible for developing international standards on corporate compliance management—has in recent years initiated efforts to formulate a global standard for evaluating the effectiveness of compliance programs, and has released a draft for public consultation. Although this draft continues to focus largely on traditional process-based indicators of compliance effectiveness, it is noteworthy for the first-time inclusion of an "outcome dimension" as one of the three core evaluation categories. This outcome dimension is positioned as a key criterion for assessing the actual effectiveness of various compliance measures. Once this international standard is approved by ISO member states and formally adopted, it will mark the international community's official endorsement of an outcome-oriented approach to compliance evaluation—one that emphasizes tangible results and demonstrable improvements in compliance systems. Such a shift is likely to have a profound and lasting impact on the evolution of compliance evaluation models across jurisdictions.

6.4.1 *Scholarly Perspectives*

In the United States, an increasing number of corporations have adopted compliance programs, and regulatory agencies as well as prosecutors have broadly established compliance incentive mechanisms—granting leniency in administrative enforcement or criminal sentencing, and in some cases even opting for non-prosecution—when the implicated enterprise is deemed to have implemented an "effective compliance program." However, the actual effectiveness of such programs has not received sufficient scrutiny. Regulatory bodies, prosecutors, and the enterprises themselves have largely neglected the need to evaluate compliance outcomes, particularly through empirically grounded and scientifically rigorous methodologies. This phenomenon has been described as a "hope-based compliance," in which both internal and external stakeholders tend to assess compliance effectiveness by looking at levels of investment, the apparent good faith of the initiative, and the degree to which the program aligns with widely accepted industry practices. Consequently, such evaluative approaches fall well short of enabling corporations to engage in verifiable and sustained self-regulation.

Some American scholars argue that legal reform must advance the conditions necessary for establishing an evidence-based compliance—that is, a compliance management system rooted in empirical data and capable of scientifically verifying the effectiveness of compliance efforts in preventing and mitigating legal and regulatory risks. In the absence of rigorous outcome testing, compliance programs risk being reduced to little more than aspirational statements—subjective expressions of intent to protect employees, shareholders, and the public from corporate wrongdoing. From this perspective, any reform of the compliance regime must rest on empirical validation; otherwise, it should be regarded as a failed reform.[13]

Ms. Hui Chen, former Compliance Counsel at the U.S. Department of Justice, has extensive experience in promoting compliance remediation among corporations involved in legal violations. She has observed that an increasing number of governments around the world have begun implementing compliance incentive mechanisms, with stated goals such as the prevention, detection, and remediation of corporate misconduct. However, she notes that no judicial

[13] Brandon Garrett and Gregory Mitchell, "Measuring the Effectiveness of Corporate Compliance," trans. Xia Fei, *Criminal Studies* 6 (2022).

or regulatory authority in any jurisdiction has yet established a reliable framework for accurately measuring the effectiveness of compliance programs. Nearly all legal instruments and compliance guidelines continue to focus on evaluating corporate compliance efforts based on inputs—such as training programs, internal communications, and resource allocation—rather than outcomes. Chen offers a pointed critique of this prevailing approach, likening it to running a public health initiative that does not measure outcomes like life expectancy, infant mortality, or disease trends, but instead measures only the number of medical records, the hours worked and wages paid to healthcare personnel, or the number of educational campaigns and posters.[14]

Taking the United States as an example, the compliance industry as a whole has largely assessed the effectiveness of compliance programs by measuring the performance of specific compliance-related activities. For example, managerial commitment is evaluated based on the frequency with which senior leadership issues compliance-related communications; training is assessed by the number of sessions conducted and the number of participants involved; policies and procedures are measured by their quantity; reporting mechanisms are evaluated based on how information is disclosed; and third-party due diligence is gauged by the number of external partners subjected to background checks. However, none of these indicators provides meaningful evidence of whether any particular component—or the compliance program as a whole—is genuinely effective. At best, they merely demonstrate that the organization has "engaged in compliance-related activities," without verifying whether those efforts have produced the intended outcomes.

Hui Chen has also expressed criticism of the international certification standards for compliance systems issued by the International Organization for Standardization (ISO). Citing ISO 37001—the anti-commercial bribery compliance management standard—as a case in point, she argues that although ISO claims to assist organizations in implementing reasonable and appropriate measures to prevent, detect, and respond to bribery, it does not attempt to measure whether those prevention, detection, and response objectives are actually achieved. With respect to evaluating the effectiveness of anti-commercial bribery compliance mechanisms, ISO has neither developed scientifically robust measurement methodologies nor established operationally viable evaluation indicators.

Of course, in response to the above criticisms, some compliance professionals have offered counterarguments, asserting that the effectiveness of preventing unlawful or unethical conduct is inherently unmeasurable—"you cannot measure how bribery was prevented in the same way you measure the efficacy of a vaccine." In addition, some professionals have exhibited clear resistance to

[14]Hui Chen, "The Application and Measurement of Compliance Mechanisms in Legal and Regulatory Contexts," in *Compliance Assessment and Measurement: Preventing Corporate Crime and Misconduct*, ed. Melissa Lawry and Benjamin van Rooij, trans. Zhu Qing and Fan Xiaoliang (Beijing: Contemporary China Publishing House, 2023), 46–49.

the very notion of measuring compliance effectiveness. This resistance often arises from their limited access to accurate and comprehensive performance data within organizations, as well as a general lack of incentive or motivation to revise or improve existing evaluation methodologies.

Hui Chen argues that the prevailing oriented-oriented approach to compliance assessment should be replaced with an outcome-oriented measurement model, aimed at verifying whether current compliance mechanisms are effectively achieving their fundamental objectives. Based on her preliminary analysis, she maintains that it is indeed possible to introduce scientifically grounded methodologies to assess whether compliance programs are effective in preventing unlawful or unethical conduct. Regulatory authorities, she suggests, could draw on indicators such as perception, cost, risk mitigation, the number and proportion of high-risk transactions, audit anomalies, detection time, reporting rates, and investigative data to evaluate the preventive impact of compliance systems. Moreover, Chen contends that relying solely on internal corporate reform is inadequate. What is essential, she argues, is that legal and regulatory institutions recognize the importance of incorporating oriented-oriented metrics into compliance oversight. On that foundation, they should establish objective measurement standards and employ a range of scientific evaluation tools. "In order to align the stated objectives of corporate compliance mechanisms with their actual performance—and to serve the public interest in preventing and detecting misconduct—legal and regulatory regimes must begin to measure compliance effectiveness both quantitatively and qualitatively, at both the structural and programmatic levels." She further suggests that there is a pressing need to identify and refine empirically valid measurement methods to determine whether the compliance frameworks relied upon by the industry for decades are in fact capable of fulfilling their intended function: the prevention and detection of corporate misconduct.

Hui Chen emphasizes that the measurement of compliance effectiveness should proceed along two analytical dimensions: first, evaluating whether the compliance program as a whole is capable of effectively preventing and detecting misconduct; and second, assessing whether each individual component of the compliance framework performs its intended function. With respect to the latter, she argues that assessments—whether of management commitment, training, policies and procedures, reporting mechanisms, or third-party due diligence—must move beyond process-based questions such as whether specific compliance activities have been performed, whether training sessions have taken place, whether policies and procedures exist and are regularly updated, or whether a reporting mechanism is in place. Instead, objective, empirically grounded metrics must be employed to assess the actual preventive impact of each element. For example, rather than simply verifying that senior management has made public statements in support of compliance, the relevant question should be whether such commitment has helped foster a more compliant or ethically aware organizational culture. Similarly, compliance training should be assessed in terms of whether it leads to measurable improvements in employee behavior or organizational performance; policies and procedures should be evaluated based on what specific outcomes in prevention or detection they have produced; reporting mechanisms should be analyzed in terms of how frequently they are used, by whom, and for what types of incidents; and third-party due diligence efforts should be assessed based on the nature and severity of risks or red flags they help uncover.

6.4.2 *Compliance Incentive Practices*

According to the 1991 revision of the U.S. Federal Sentencing Guidelines, the core requirement for effective compliance is that a corporation must implement a risk-control system capable of preventing and detecting criminal conduct, and cultivate a corporate culture grounded in lawful and ethical business operations. This standard of compliance effectiveness is intended to apply uniformly to both companies engaging in proactive compliance efforts before any violations occur and those implementing compliance remediation measures after being implicated in misconduct.

The prosecutorial practices surrounding post-violation corporate compliance remediation in the United States have drawn sharp criticism from some scholars. They contend that prosecutors often reduce compliance remediation to little more than the provision of a formal checklist of written compliance policies, while seldom encouraging companies to pursue structural reform or undertake meaningful evaluations of their compliance remediation efforts. That said, in a limited number of cases involving non-prosecution agreements (NPAs) or deferred prosecution agreements (DPAs), prosecutors have indeed required implicated companies to adopt measures aimed at improving corporate governance structures.

For example, in certain cases, prosecutors have ordered companies to terminate specific business operations that were found to be in violation of the law or to shut down subsidiaries engaged in illegal activities. KPMG, for instance, discontinued all of its private client tax services, while Beazer Homes closed an entire subsidiary implicated in fraudulent mortgage lending practices.

In other cases, prosecutors required implicated companies to revise executive and employee compensation structures, including changes to both the method and basis of payment. Two banks involved in investigations clawed back bonuses previously awarded to senior executives held responsible for misconduct. GlaxoSmithKline (GSK), meanwhile, prohibited its sales representatives and managers from receiving commission-based compensation tied to sales volume. Restructuring sales compensation schemes—particularly within the pharmaceutical industry—has become a common provision in corporate compliance agreements and is widely regarded as a key measure for shifting industry practices and transforming corporate culture. Under its agreement, GSK was barred from using prescription volume as a basis for employee compensation and was instead required to evaluate performance based on criteria such as "business acumen, customer engagement, and scientific knowledge of the product." The agreement also prohibited promotional payments to physicians. Johnson & Johnson entered into a similar agreement that included provisions mandating changes to employee remuneration policies.

In certain cases, prosecutors have gone beyond general oversight and imposed specific personnel-related requirements on corporations under investigation. These measures have included not only mandates to recruit new employees but also, in some instances, conditions requiring prosecutorial pre-approval of key appointments. For example, under its settlement agreement, Bristol-Myers Squibb was required to formally separate the roles of Chief Executive Officer and Chairman of the Board, appoint new independent directors, and enhance its disclosures to the Securities and Exchange Commission. Similarly, Aibel Group was obligated to obtain the prosecutor's prior consent before appointing a new Executive Chairman of the Board, a majority of the Compliance Committee members, and the designated Compliance Consultant. Aurora Foods was required to consult with prosecutors before making any personnel decisions related to its compliance function. In an especially far-reaching case, Blackwater undertook a full-scale internal restructuring by replacing its entire senior management team, appointing a new Chief Compliance Officer, and expanding its board to include independent directors.

Compared with promoting structural reforms in corporate governance, U.S. prosecutors have increasingly prioritized the transformation of corporate culture within offending enterprises. Historically, American criminal justice policy placed primary emphasis on the punishment of offenders, often at the expense of offender rehabilitation and the prevention of recidivism. In recent years, particularly in cases involving corporate crime, prosecutorial objectives have evolved toward reengineering internal management practices and fostering a culture shift aimed at preventing future violations. Notably, this emphasis on cultural transformation does not imply a wholesale reconfiguration of the enterprise's entire organizational ethos. Rather, it focuses specifically on modifying those cultural norms and practices that are directly implicated in non-compliance with criminal law.

The 2003 prosecution of KPMG by federal authorities marked a significant shift in prosecutorial policy. At the time one of the Big Four accounting firms in the United States, KPMG had orchestrated a large-scale scheme to promote unlawful tax shelters to private clients, causing the federal government to incur tax losses totaling tens of billions of dollars—a violation constituting tax fraud under federal criminal law. Central to the case was the identification of a toxic corporate culture in which senior executives imposed sustained pressure on tax professionals to aggressively sell illegal tax avoidance products. As the prosecution revealed, "KPMG transformed its tax professionals into sales agents, compelling them to meet revenue targets, employing telemarketing tactics to recruit clients, misusing confidential client tax data to identify prospects, and marketing these schemes even to the firm's own audit clients." The firm went so far as to establish a telemarketing unit dedicated to promoting these abusive shelters, incentivizing personnel to target high-net-worth individuals and dramatically boost revenues. Profits from the untaxed income—typically around 1%—were then distributed among KPMG, participating banks, and other co-conspirators.

Criminological research on corporate wrongdoing suggests that one of the most effective means of transforming corporate culture is through the implementation of internal control mechanisms and procedures—particularly the development of compliance policies and programs that not only promote adherence to legal and regulatory obligations but also shape employees' attitudes and behaviors. Prosecutors may employ Deferred Prosecution Agreements (DPAs) and Non-Prosecution Agreements (NPAs) as tools of compliance incentivization, encouraging companies implicated in misconduct to undertake remedial actions—such as sanctioning responsible individuals and making voluntary disclosures—and to restructure their compliance systems. In doing so, these companies may secure more lenient criminal outcomes and avoid prosecution or conviction. In this capacity, prosecutors are increasingly cast as agents of positive change, advancing corporate integrity, improving organizational conduct, and supporting the prevention, detection, and punishment of white-collar crime.

Although most agreements do not contain specific provisions requiring the evaluation of compliance effectiveness, in certain cases, during the implementation of compliance remediation measures, prosecutors—often assisted by independent compliance monitors—have shown a greater interest in the actual efficacy of compliance programs and have taken empirical steps to assess their impact.

For instance, in the case of Bristol-Myers Squibb, former judge Frederick Lacey was appointed as the compliance monitor. Although he received a substantial compensation package from the company, the monitoring team under his leadership maintained operational independence and rigorously exercised its oversight responsibilities. The compliance monitor required the company to adopt concrete measures to ensure that the details of its compliance remediation plan were faithfully implemented. In addition to submitting quarterly reports on compliance progress to both the prosecutors and the Securities and Exchange Commission, Lacey also attended board meetings to directly supervise the execution of the compliance program. During the course of the monitoring period, the company engaged in further unlawful conduct. In response, the compliance monitor recommended the removal of the Chief Executive Officer and also oversaw the dismissal of the General Counsel.

Similarly, in the Siemens case, Dr. Theo Waigel, serving as the chief compliance monitor, established a supervisory team with the assistance of a U.S. attorney. The team comprised Siemens employees, American lawyers, and German legal professionals. They conducted an in-depth review of Siemens' global operations and organizational structure, examined documents related to compliance, financial controls, and internal audits, and gained a comprehensive understanding of the company's internal mechanisms—thus laying the groundwork for meaningful reforms. Over a four-year monitoring period, the team reviewed tens of thousands of documents, conducted site visits in more than 20 countries, and interviewed over 1,500 executives and employees. They also made multiple trips to the United States to report compliance progress to federal prosecutors. To drive compliance reforms, the monitors submitted several remediation reports and issued over 100 specific reform recommendations, all of which Siemens accepted and used to rebuild its compliance infrastructure. The monitors played an instrumental role in revitalizing Siemens' compliance program. They employed risk-based internal audits to identify high-risk areas, attended planning meetings, HR meetings, and other management sessions, and tested the company's whistleblower hotline using simulated complaints and employee response assessments. They also submitted reports to investors assessing the long-term impact of the compliance reforms. To evaluate program effectiveness, the monitors applied several technical methods. In each business unit, they randomly selected 10 to 12 transactions to examine for signs of improper payments. They were authorized to question the Chief Sales Officer, review reimbursement claims, and inspect relevant documentation. This risk-oriented sampling method was adaptable to various national contexts and industry sectors. Thanks to the sustained efforts of the compliance monitors, Siemens underwent a profound transformation and succeeded in building a robust and high-performing compliance management system.[15]

6.4.3 ISO's Initiative for Compliance Evaluation Standards

In April 2024, the International Organization for Standardization (ISO) released a draft document for public consultation titled *Compliance Management Systems—Guidelines for Effectiveness Evaluation* (hereinafter referred to as the "ISO 37302 Guidelines"). Although still in the stage of soliciting feedback from ISO member states, the ISO 37302 Guidelines represent the latest international initiative aimed at developing a standardized framework for evaluating the effectiveness of compliance management systems. According to the ISO 37302 Guidelines, enterprises, regulatory bodies, and judicial authorities in an increasing number of countries have expressed the need for reliable tools to evaluate compliance effectiveness. The ISO 37302 Guidelines underscore the importance of establishing more detailed assessment rules to support the effective implementation of ISO 37301 Guidelines and to provide ISO member states with a globally recognized benchmark for assessing the performance of compliance management systems.[16]

[15] Brandon Garrett and Gregory Mitchell, "Measuring the Effectiveness of Corporate Compliance," trans. Xia Fei, *Criminal Studies* 6 (2022).

[16] ANDA Risk Control Research Center, *ISO 37302: Compliance Management Systems—Guidelines for Evaluating Effectiveness*, "Integrated Compliance and Risk Control" WeChat Official Account, May 15, 2024.

According to the ISO 37302 Guidelines, the effectiveness of a compliance management system is defined as its "ability to consistently achieve its objectives and intended outcomes." The assessment of compliance effectiveness should be guided by several core principles, including objectivity, comprehensiveness and scalability, and traceability.

Under the ISO 37302 Guidelines, a compliance management system is structured around three core components: planning and establishment, implementation, and performance evaluation and improvement—each accompanied by detailed evaluation criteria. Under the "Planning and Establishment" section, the criteria include: analysis of the context of the organization and the requirements of interested parties; identification and update of compliance obligations; determination of the scope of the compliance management system and assessment of compliance risks; leadership and commitment of the governing body and top management; implementation of compliance governance principles; maintenance and promotion of a compliance culture; assignment of roles, responsibilities, and authorities for personnel at different levels; setting of compliance policies and objectives; and planning of actions to address risks and opportunities along with allocation of necessary resources. In the "Implementation" section, the criteria encompass: operational actions to address risks and opportunities; allocation of resources; competencies, capacity building, and awareness raising; employment processes, rewards, and disciplinary actions; training; internal and external communication; establishment of a mechanism for raising concerns; implementation of investigation processes; and management of documented information. Finally, the "Performance Evaluation and Improvement" section outlines the following five criteria: monitoring, measurement, analysis, and evaluation of performance; internal audits; management review; corrective actions in response to nonconformities and/or noncompliance; and planned continual improvement.

Judging from the content and categorization of its evaluation criteria, the ISO 37302 Guidelines—intended as an "international standard" for assessing the effectiveness of compliance management systems—do not significantly exceed the normative benchmarks already established in jurisdictions such as the United States, the United Kingdom, and France. In fact, the structure and substance of the Guidelines also appear to reflect considerable influence from China's national standards on compliance effectiveness evaluation, given its status as a principal ISO member. Notably, the Guidelines structure the assessment criteria into three distinct dimensions: the effectiveness of system planning and design, the effectiveness of implementation, and the effectiveness of outcomes. This reflects a broader trend among ISO member states toward emphasizing the assessment of implementation effectiveness as a critical dimension of compliance evaluation.

Particular attention should be given to the fact that the ISO 37302 Guidelines introduce an integrated evaluation methodology grounded in the three core components of a compliance management system. This methodology incorporates three mutually reinforcing dimensions: policies and procedures, conduct and culture, and results and impacts. According to the Guidelines, each evaluation criterion must be assessed across all three dimensions, and its level of effectiveness must be rated using a five-level scale. Under this framework, every indicator is evaluated from Level 1—the lowest degree of effectiveness—to Level 5, which represents the highest level of effectiveness attainable for that specific criterion.

For example, with respect to the evaluation criterion "Identification and Updating of Compliance Obligations," organizations are assessed across three dimensions: policies and procedures, conduct and culture, and results and impacts. Under the policies and procedures and conduct and culture dimensions, an organization that has not established any procedures for the identification and updating of compliance obligations shall be rated at Level 1. By contrast, an organization that has established comprehensive procedures, embedded them within operational processes, and systematically monitors, evaluates, and continuously improves them in response to both internal and external developments shall be rated at Level 5. Under the results and impacts dimension, an organization that has not yet determined its compliance obligations shall also be rated at Level 1. If an organization has only identified obligations in limited contexts—such as in relation to certain activities, products, or services, or in response to specific instances of non-compliance—it shall be rated at Level 3. An organization shall be assessed at Level 5 if it has comprehensively identified and documented both mandatory and voluntary compliance obligations related to its business activities, products, services, and relevant operational aspects; if this determination is based on independent data analysis; if sufficient resources have been allocated to ensure the timely and accurate identification of applicable obligations and their impact on the organization's operations.

For example, in relation to the evaluation criterion "Training," organizations are assessed across the dimensions of policies and procedures, conduct and culture, and results and impacts. Under the policies and procedures and conduct and culture dimensions, an organization that has not established any personnel training procedures, or has only developed incomplete procedures that have not been effectively implemented, shall be rated at Level 1 or Level 2, respectively. In contrast, an organization that conducts training in accordance with well-established procedures, applies quality control mechanisms to ensure the achievement of training outcomes, and maintains appropriate documented information evidencing training efforts shall be rated at Level 5. Under the results and impacts dimension, an organization that provides no training, or whose training is occasional and inconsistent, shall be rated at Level 1 or Level 2, respectively. An organization may qualify for Level 5 if its training programs are aligned with both organizational objectives and individual competency needs, the content is tailored to address the diverse requirements of the organization and its personnel, and targeted training is delivered in areas where incidents of non-compliance have occurred.

For instance, in relation to the evaluation indicator "performance monitoring, measurement, and analysis," evaluators assess organizations across the dimensions of policies and procedures, conduct and culture, and results and impacts. Under the dimensions of policies and procedures and conduct and culture, an organization that has not yet established relevant procedures for performance monitoring, measurement, and analysis, or has procedures that are incomplete or not consistently implemented, shall be rated at Level 1 or Level 2, respectively. By contrast, an organization that has fully integrated such procedures into its operational systems, implements performance monitoring, measurement, and analysis across all business functions, maintains appropriate documented information, and regularly reviews and analyzes performance data to drive continuous improvement, shall be rated at Level 5. Under the results and impacts dimension, organizations that either do not conduct any performance monitoring, measurement, or analysis, or whose practices are misaligned with organizational needs or operational realities, shall be rated at Level 1 or Level 2, respectively. Organizations that align these efforts with organizational needs, identify structural weaknesses and deficiencies in their compliance management system, and whose performance data supports root cause analysis and the identification of improvement opportunities, shall qualify for Level 5.

6.4.4 *Analytical Discussion*

Compared with process-oriented evaluation approaches, outcome-oriented evaluation shifts the focus of compliance effectiveness assessment toward measurable outcomes. It emphasizes the actual impact of the compliance management system in achieving its intended objectives—particularly in terms of preventing and detecting violations, and fostering a corporate culture of lawful and rule-based operations. Proponents of this approach have keenly identified a fundamental shortcoming of oriented-oriented evaluation: its disproportionate focus on the mere existence of compliance rules, structural elements, and management initiatives, without considering whether these elements generate tangible effects. This often leads to a state of "compliance for compliance's sake." Moreover, a wide range of compliance-related risk control measures—such as risk assessments, due diligence procedures, compliance training, top-level commitments, compliance reporting, whistleblower mechanisms, compliance audits, and internal investigations—may risk becoming abstract concepts or unverifiable assumptions ("compliance metaphysics") if their actual contribution to achieving compliance objectives cannot be substantiated by empirical evidence.

The proactive compliance incentives implemented by U.S. prosecutorial authorities in certain corporate enforcement cases illustrate that, from an outcome-oriented standpoint, post-violation compliance remediation can serve as a powerful driver of substantive corporate transformation. Such transformation may encompass reforms to corporate governance structures as well as shifts in corporate culture—both of which are often critical to achieving meaningful improvements in compliance outcomes. Concurrently, the compliance effectiveness evaluation standards issued by the International Organization for Standardization (ISO) have begun to emphasize oriented-oriented assessments of key compliance elements. This reflects the growing recognition of outcome-oriented assessment as a foundational principle in the emerging global standards for measuring compliance effectiveness.

Admittedly, the outcome-oriented approach to compliance evaluation remains at an early conceptual stage and is far from achieving methodological maturity. In particular, much of the existing scholarship reveals a pattern of "strong critique but weak construction"—namely, while offering extensive criticisms of oriented-oriented evaluation models, it fails to articulate robust and feasible alternatives. For a genuinely outcome-driven framework to take root and gain broader acceptance, it is necessary to define with precision what constitutes the "ideal outcomes" of compliance management and to establish appropriate evaluative benchmarks. This entails distinguishing between the primary objectives and subsidiary goals of compliance programs, and developing scientifically sound methods for tiered classification and quantitative assessment of a program's effectiveness in meeting those goals. However, current academic discourse and practical exploration suggest that this endeavor faces considerable obstacles, especially in terms of creating reliable theoretical foundations and practical methodologies for measuring actual compliance outcomes in a quantifiable manner.

6.5 Redefining the Objectives of Compliance Effectiveness

As discussed above, process-oriented evaluation models concentrate on whether compliance systems are properly implemented, but tend to overlook their actual performance in preventing and identifying compliance risks. Conversely, outcome-oriented approaches highlight the practical impact of compliance efforts in deterring violations and promoting a compliance culture, yet often fall short of offering empirically sound methods of assessment. Both models, in their current forms, appear to diverge from the fundamental objective of evaluating compliance effectiveness. In this landscape—where compliance evaluation remains suspended between procedural rigor and outcome validation—it may still be too early to propose a mature third model that surpasses both existing paradigms. Further theoretical inquiry and practical experimentation are needed. Nevertheless, it remains both possible and necessary to adopt a synthesized evaluation strategy that draws on the advantages of both models while avoiding their respective limitations.

Generally, the effectiveness of compliance management refers to the extent to which an enterprise's compliance management system achieves its intended objectives. A system that, through proper design and implementation, successfully meets its anticipated goals may be characterized as an effective compliance management system. Conversely, if the system fails to achieve these objectives, it should be regarded as ineffective. Effectiveness may also vary in degree: a system that significantly advances the attainment of the ideal objectives of compliance may be evaluated as relatively effective, whereas one that makes only limited progress may be assessed as having low compliance effectiveness.

So, what exactly constitutes the objective of compliance management? On this question, there is little consensus between scholars and practitioners in the field. Some normative frameworks define "effective compliance" as the capacity to prevent unlawful or noncompliant conduct, thereby emphasizing risk prevention as the central aim of compliance programs. Other guidelines underscore the importance of cultivating a "culture of legality and regulatory adherence," framing the promotion of compliance culture as a core objective. The U.S. Federal Sentencing Guidelines go even further by introducing the element of "detection" of unlawful or criminal behavior, recognizing the timely identification of compliance risks as a key goal of post-violation compliance remediation.

How, then, should the fundamental objectives of compliance management be defined? To address this question, it is useful to begin with a process of deconstruction before reconstruction. First, equating the effectiveness of compliance management solely with the *prevention* of unlawful or noncompliant behavior reflects an overly narrow and arguably flawed perspective. In reality, even the most sophisticated and well-designed compliance systems cannot entirely eliminate the possibility of violations, misconduct, or criminal activity. U.S. prosecutors and regulatory agencies have repeatedly emphasized that the occurrence of illegal conduct within a corporation does not, in and of itself, render its compliance program ineffective. This underscores the point that while preventing misconduct and mitigating compliance risks are undoubtedly important goals, they do not exhaust the full meaning or function of effective compliance management.

Second, the emphasis on cultivating a "compliance culture" is frequently reflected in both domestic and international compliance guidelines, and is often hailed as the most essential goal of compliance management. However, the notion of "compliance culture" is inherently subjective, typically referring to the development of an organizational atmosphere, value orientation, or behavioral norms aligned with lawful and rule-abiding conduct. This concept lacks clearly defined parameters and measurable indicators, making it difficult to assess in any objective or consistent manner. Furthermore, it is highly susceptible to shifts in corporate governance structures or changes in senior leadership. If such an amorphous and fluid concept were to serve as the foundational goal of compliance management, it would significantly undermine the definitional clarity of what constitutes "effective compliance management."

Third, while an effective compliance system must indeed be capable of *detecting* unlawful or noncompliant behavior when preventive mechanisms fail, detection alone is not sufficient. Once misconduct or major compliance risks have been identified, a robust compliance program must also be capable of implementing appropriate corrective and remedial measures to close governance gaps, rectify internal deficiencies, and mitigate future risks.

According to the author's earlier research, compliance management can be categorized into two basic models: a management-oriented model and a risk-oriented model.[17] Under the first approach, "effective compliance management" is defined as the enterprise's attainment of the ideal state of lawful and regulation-compliant operation. Under the second, the ideal objective of compliance management is framed as the effective control of compliance risks. While the aspiration for enterprises to operate in full accordance with laws and regulations is both important and commendable, it is inherently broad, lacks precise definitional boundaries, and provides limited guidance in addressing the concrete compliance risks that enterprises confront in reality. In contrast, the goal of effectively controlling compliance risks reflects a pressing and pragmatic managerial challenge faced by all businesses. Achieving this objective not only reduces the likelihood of illegal, noncompliant, or unethical behavior but also significantly lowers the risk of administrative sanctions, criminal liability, or international financial penalties. It further helps mitigate the threat of catastrophic consequences such as loss of market qualifications or exclusion from procurement systems. Accordingly, effective compliance management is herein defined as the capacity to effectively control compliance risks.

What, then, does it mean to "effectively control compliance risks"? To address this question, we may look to institutional practices in the United States and Europe concerning compliance remediation for corporate offenders, as well as the practical experiences of companies that have successfully implemented robust compliance programs. Based on these insights, this book proposes what may be termed the "PDR" control framework. Under this framework, the ideal objective of a compliance management system is to ensure the *accurate and timely control* of compliance risks. This requires first conducting precise identification, analysis, and assessment of such risks, and then managing them across three interrelated dimensions. First, prevention (Prevent) requires organizations to adopt proactive measures that avert misconduct before it occurs, thereby eliminating the possibility of compliance risks materializing. Second, detection (Detect) emphasizes real-time monitoring—akin to a 24/7 radar system—to promptly identify unlawful or noncompliant behavior and detect emerging risks. Third, response (Respond) involves taking timely and appropriate remedial actions, including investigation, disciplinary measures, and corrective efforts, to mitigate the impact of violations and prevent recurrence. Together, these three dimensions provide a structured and integrated approach to managing compliance risks within controllable boundaries.[18]

[17] Ruihua Chen, *Two Models of Corporate Compliance Management System*, Legal Review, no. 1 (2024).

[18] So far, the full application of the PDR compliance risk control model has been primarily demonstrated in the Siemens case. At the same time, the French National Anti-Corruption Agency has also relied on this model to establish the basic institutional framework for anti-corruption compliance risk management. See Ruihua Chen, *The Fundamentals of Corporate Compliance*, 3rd ed.

What, then, is the relationship among these three types of compliance management behavior—and how do they relate to the overarching goal of controlling compliance risks? From the perspective of compliance risk management, the act of controlling compliance risks should be regarded as the ultimate objective of corporate compliance management. To achieve this overarching objective, an enterprise should break it down into three stages—ex ante control, ongoing control, and ex post control—each of which constitutes a sub-objective of compliance risk management.

Ex-ante control, also known as prevention, refers to a management strategy that seeks to proactively avert unlawful or noncompliant conduct before it occurs. This is accomplished through the implementation of institutional measures aimed at mitigating compliance risks at an early stage. Typical preventive activities include conducting regular compliance risk assessments, performing due diligence on clients and third-party partners, and organizing compliance training programs. The ideal outcome of ex-ante control is effective deterrence—that is, preventing the occurrence of misconduct and reducing the likelihood of compliance risks materializing. However, experience shows that even the most well-designed compliance management systems cannot entirely prevent the occurrence of unlawful or non-compliant conduct. Compliance practices in nearly all jurisdictions demonstrate that the mere existence of legal, regulatory, or criminal violations does not necessarily mean a company's compliance system is ineffective. The essential question is whether the company has established and implemented a practical and effective set of controls for managing compliance risks both during and after such incidents.

So-called ongoing control, also known as monitoring, refers to a compliance management philosophy aimed at the accurate and timely detection of unlawful, non-compliant, or criminal conduct within an organization, as well as the ongoing surveillance of emerging compliance risks. In practice, a range of activities—such as compliance reporting systems, whistleblower mechanisms, and internal audits—serve as tools for implementing this monitoring function. From a pragmatic standpoint, when ex-ante controls fail to prevent the emergence of compliance risks, enterprises must deploy a real-time monitoring infrastructure—or, more vividly, a "24-hour radar warning system"—capable of continuously tracking operational, managerial, and decision-making processes. Once illegal conduct is detected or a significant risk of violation is identified, the enterprise must promptly strengthen its compliance response. Compared to the ex-ante control, this type of monitoring functions as a concurrent or real-time control mechanism and constitutes the second line of defense in an enterprise's overall compliance risk management system.

Ex post control, also known as response, refers to the set of remedial, corrective, and improvement measures adopted by an enterprise following the occurrence of unlawful, non-compliant, or criminal conduct, specifically aimed

(Beijing: Law Press, 2023), 130–136; and Chen, *Effective Compliance: The Chinese Experience* (Beijing: Peking University Press, 2023), 280–283.

at addressing weaknesses or deficiencies in the compliance management system. Since ante control cannot eliminate all compliance risks, and ongoing control primarily provides reactive responses to isolated incidents, it is essential for enterprises to establish a framework for the systemic remediation and enhancement of their compliance infrastructure. In practice, when a violation has occurred or a compliance risk has been identified, companies typically initiate targeted internal investigations to uncover the underlying structural causes of the misconduct. Based on the findings, they implement institutional reforms and corrective measures to address the identified gaps, prevent the recurrence of similar violations, and reduce the likelihood of future compliance failures.

In summary, compliance management effectiveness may be defined as the extent to which an enterprise successfully controls compliance risks. The overarching objective of compliance management is to achieve such effective control. To realize this goal, enterprises must meet three interrelated sub-objectives at distinct stages of risk management. First, the ex ante prevention of compliance risks—taking proactive measures to avert the occurrence of unlawful or non-compliant conduct. Second, real-time monitoring—the timely detection and identification of emerging compliance risks or violations as they arise. Third, post-incident response—the implementation of investigative, disciplinary, corrective, and remedial actions after a violation has occurred or a risk has materialized.

6.6 Establishing Three-Tiered Evaluation Standards

Redefining the objectives of compliance management merely sets an external ideal outcome for compliance efforts. To assess the actual effectiveness of a compliance management system, it is also essential to establish a set of internal evaluative standards. In principle, a compliance system may only be considered effective in controlling compliance risks—rather than merely symbolic, superficial, or ineffective—if it meets these standards. Such criteria not only allow evaluators to make binary judgments (i.e., whether the system is effective or not), but also facilitate more nuanced assessments of its relative strength or weakness, including graded classifications of effectiveness ranging from strong to weak. Enterprises and regulatory authorities can, based on such assessments, implement targeted corrective, remedial, or improvement measures, thereby achieving the dynamic objective of effectively controlling compliance risks.

How, then, can we establish a scientifically grounded set of criteria for evaluating the effectiveness of compliance management systems? The U.S. Department of Justice's *Evaluation of Corporate Compliance Programs* offers a normative framework that serves as a valuable point of reference. Under this framework, the effectiveness of a compliance program may be assessed from three interrelated dimensions: the effectiveness of its design, the effectiveness of its implementation, and the effectiveness of its outcomes.

Although the U.S. Department of Justice formally employs the aforementioned three-dimensional framework for evaluating corporate compliance programs, the specific criteria articulated under this model remain predominantly process-oriented. In practice, dozens of compliance-related policies, standards, procedures, and operational protocols are classified under the three dimensions, thereby giving rise to an evaluative approach that risks devolving into "compliance for the sake of compliance." This framework places insufficient emphasis on identifying structural weaknesses, systemic deficiencies, or functional gaps within an enterprise's compliance management system, and gives little consideration to the system's actual performance or real-world impact. Instead, its primary focus is on whether the enterprise has carried out its promised compliance remediation measures or has established and put into operation the required compliance structures.

To effectively resolve the problems of formalism, superficial documentation, and ineffectiveness in compliance management, it is necessary to build on the above three-dimensional evaluation framework by introducing scientifically grounded criteria for measuring compliance effectiveness within each dimension. This would infuse the evaluative dimensions with substantive, outcome-oriented elements, thereby transforming the framework into a more rigorous and meaningful instrument for assessing the effectiveness of corporate compliance systems.

6.6.1 Program Design Effectiveness

One of the fundamental criteria for evaluating the effectiveness of a compliance management system is the soundness of its program design. This standard emphasizes the extent to which the institutional structure of the compliance framework enables the enterprise to exert effective control over compliance risks. To meet this general requirement, several measurable and substantive indicators should be established. First, the compliance program must be purpose-driven—that is, it should be specifically formulated to address the organization's pre-existing structural deficiencies, systemic vulnerabilities, and latent risks through corresponding governance measures. Second, the compliance program should be risk-aligned, meaning it must directly correspond to the distinct areas of compliance risk that the enterprise faces and should take the form of a targeted or specialized compliance initiative. Third, the program's design must adhere to the principle of proportionality, ensuring that its scope and depth are commensurate with the enterprise's size, operational complexity, industry characteristics, and both internal and external risk environments. Fourth, the compliance plan must be functionally robust: it should be capable of supporting effective prevention, monitoring, and response mechanisms tailored to the specific risks identified, and must incorporate clear internal processes to operationalize these functions.

As a matter of principle, no enterprise can develop an effective compliance program without first conducting a precise and comprehensive diagnosis of its pre-existing structural deficiencies and systemic vulnerabilities. In the context of post-violation compliance remediation, evaluators must examine whether the company has submitted an internal investigation report or a self-assessment report that identifies the structural factors intrinsically linked to the occurrence of unlawful or criminal conduct. Likewise, in the process of routine compliance management system development, enterprises are expected to carry out compliance risk identification, analysis, and evaluation, with the aim of uncovering potential risk points and sources of compliance risk. Both types of efforts serve the overarching function of diagnosing the organization's structural weaknesses. Such deficiencies generally fall into four categories. First, deficiencies in corporate governance structures—for example, agent overreach, internal confusion regarding legal personhood, ineffective parent–subsidiary control mechanisms, or the absence of internal checks and balances. Second, institutional gaps in management rules and procedures, such as the separation of invoicing and goods delivery, fabrication of contracts, falsification of bidding documents, or failure to properly handle hazardous waste. Third, process-related vulnerabilities embedded in operational workflows—for instance, when business departments directly conduct customs clearance, when enterprises fail to perform due diligence on upstream suppliers, intermediary agents, or downstream distributors, or when they neglect to assess compliance risks in merger and acquisition targets. Fourth, latent illegality in commercial models, whereby certain business strategies or operational arrangements intersect with the constitutive elements of criminal offenses, rendering the model inherently unlawful or structurally criminogenic.[19]

Once the enterprise has accurately diagnosed its structural deficiencies and vulnerabilities, it must adopt targeted corrective and remedial measures to eliminate those weaknesses, close institutional loopholes, and resolve latent operational risks. The overarching aim of such efforts is to achieve the "decriminalization" or "de-illegalization" of the enterprise's business operations or commercial models. Only when the compliance program is expressly designed to address and rectify these underlying problems—by incorporating the logic of structural remediation and the mitigation of inherent illegality—can it be regarded as substantively effective at the design stage. Under such conditions, follow-up measures, such as the introduction of targeted compliance programs, are genuinely meaningful. Otherwise, any compliance framework introduced by the enterprise risks lacking specificity and contextual relevance, thereby becoming a formalistic, superficial, and ultimately ineffective management system.

In addition, the compliance program developed by an enterprise must be aligned with the specific categories of compliance risk identified through prior diagnosis, and should take the form of a specialized or domain-specific compliance framework. A targeted compliance program refers to a tailored compliance management system that corresponds to a particular type of compliance risk. For example, if the enterprise is exposed to anti-bribery risks, it should

[19] Ruihua Chen, "Basic Approaches to Effective Corporate Compliance Remediation," *Forum on Politics and Law*, no. 1 (2022).

establish an anti-commercial bribery compliance program; if it faces tax-related risks, a tax compliance program should be implemented; if the risks involve environmental and resource protection, an environmental compliance program should be developed; and if the risks pertain to intellectual property, a dedicated IP compliance program should be instituted. It is important to note that the creation of such targeted compliance programs requires both the establishment of a foundational compliance management platform and the incorporation of risk-specific compliance elements tailored to the regulatory and operational characteristics of each domain.[20]

In accordance with the principle of proportionality, a compliance program should be appropriately scaled and aligned with the enterprise's personnel size, industry sector, business operations, changes in its internal and external environment, and the scope and severity of its compliance risks. In building a foundational compliance management infrastructure, these variables must be carefully considered to ensure that the compliance leadership structure, organizational architecture, risk prevention mechanisms, compliance monitoring systems, and incident response systems are suitably calibrated to the enterprise's actual conditions. For instance, a medium- or large-sized company with a board of directors may establish a Compliance Management Committee under the board's supervision. By contrast, a small- or micro-sized enterprise without a board may opt to create a Compliance Leadership Team. Likewise, a large-scale enterprise or one exposed to substantial compliance risks may appoint a Chief Compliance Officer (CCO) and set up a dedicated compliance department, further subdivided into a compliance operations unit and a compliance audit unit. In comparison, a smaller enterprise with limited exposure to compliance risks may designate a single Compliance Officer to assume full-time responsibility for managing compliance affairs.

On the other hand, the design of targeted compliance elements must also reflect the enterprise's particular structural features and risk profile, with a view to establishing targeted systems for addressing identified categories of compliance risk. Once key risk areas have been identified, the enterprise should proceed to build corresponding specialized compliance mechanisms. For example, in the absence of an anti-commercial bribery compliance program, the enterprise should issue dedicated compliance policies and employee handbooks aimed at mitigating bribery-related risks, conduct risk assessments and due diligence, organize anti-bribery compliance training and require formal declarations of compliance from employees, and cultivate a culture compliance centered on anti-bribery values. Crucially, the enterprise must embed anti-commercial bribery management requirements into all operational procedures, business functions, critical roles, and high-risk personnel positions where violations are most likely to occur. This integrated approach seeks to eliminate or substantially reduce the space in which compliance risks may emerge, thereby

[20] Ruihua Chen, "Targeted Compliance Programs in Corporate Compliance Remediation," *Forum on Politics and Law*, no. 1 (2023).

neutralizing the potential for illegal conduct at each specific point in the enterprise's day-to-day operations.

6.6.2 *Implementation Effectiveness*

The second criterion for evaluating the effectiveness of a compliance management system concerns the effectiveness of its implementation. This standard underscores that a compliance system should not remain confined to written policies or formal documentation; it must ensure that all components of the compliance framework are fully activated, applied, and embedded within the organization's processes and practices. In other words, compliance must be fully embedded in the enterprise's day-to-day management to support the prevention, detection, and response to compliance risks. Implementation effectiveness refers not to the activation of isolated elements, but to the integrated and sustained functioning of the system as a whole—much like a machine that can only operate effectively when all its parts are running in coordination and fulfilling their intended functions. From a procedural standpoint, implementation effectiveness means that the compliance charters, policies, and employee handbooks promised by the enterprise have not only been issued but also put into practice. It means that compliance leadership structures and organizational mechanisms have been established and are effectively performing their governance and oversight roles. It further requires that all preventive compliance management components—such as risk assessments, due diligence, compliance training, compliance undertakings, and initiatives to foster a compliance culture—be duly established and effectively carried out. Monitoring elements, including internal reporting channels, whistleblowing mechanisms, compliance audits, and risk monitoring systems, must be not only established but actively enforced and demonstrably effective. Finally, responsive measures—such as internal investigations, anti-fraud inquiries, disciplinary procedures, the remediation of institutional vulnerabilities, and improvements to the compliance system—must be operational and functioning effectively.

In evaluating the effectiveness of compliance program implementation, particular attention should be given to the operation of four core elements within the compliance management system. First, the conduct of senior leadership should be examined to assess whether they have genuinely fulfilled their governance responsibilities—by demonstrating clear commitment to compliance, allocating sufficient managerial resources, taking disciplinary action against violators, and promoting a compliance culture throughout the organization. This ensures that the principle of top-level commitment is not merely symbolic, but operationalized in practice. Second, the compliance department must have effectively exercised its compliance review function by conducting thorough evaluations of managerial processes, business operations, and organizational practices identified as high-risk. This includes diagnosing potential violations, assessing legal exposure, and producing formal compliance assessment reports. Third, the compliance function should possess the authority to question, challenge, or even veto business activities, management practices, or operational models that present significant compliance risks or a heightened likelihood of serious violations. These objections should be taken seriously by senior leadership and meaningfully incorporated into the enterprise's decision-making processes. Fourth, where violations have already occurred—whether committed by employees, third-party partners, middle management, or senior executives—the compliance department must be empowered to launch internal investigations and recommend appropriate disciplinary measures. Senior management must give due consideration to these recommendations and respond with thoughtful and principled decisions.

6.6.3 Outcome Effectiveness

The third criterion for evaluating the effectiveness of a compliance management system concerns the effectiveness of its outcomes. This standard underscores that such a system must not only be duly established in written form and put into practical operation, but must also, moreover, produce tangible results in achieving the objective of effectively controlling compliance risks. Outcome effectiveness can be assessed from two principal dimensions. First, after a period of sustained implementation, the compliance management system should be demonstrably effective in performing its core functions—namely, preventing compliance risks, monitoring compliance operations, and responding promptly and effectively to violations. Second, through prolonged compliance management, the enterprise should have genuinely enhanced its corporate culture and underlying values of operating in accordance with laws and regulations, thereby fostering organizational norms and conduct consistent with lawful and ethical business practices.

The first evaluative dimension may be referred to as the degree to which the sub-objectives of compliance management outcomes are achieved. For instance, with respect to the goal of *preventing compliance risks*, if—after a certain period of compliance management—the enterprise has activated a comprehensive set of institutional elements, including risk assessments, due diligence procedures, compliance training, compliance undertakings, and initiatives to foster a compliance culture, and if these measures have demonstrably achieved positive results in preventing the occurrence of identical or similar compliance risks, it may be concluded that the compliance management has been effective in this regard. Likewise, regarding *compliance monitoring*, if reporting systems, whistleblowing mechanisms, and compliance audits have been effectively employed to identify risk exposures and detect violations, thereby realizing the goal of real-time oversight, the monitoring function of the program may be considered effective. Similarly, with respect to *responsive measures*, if—following incidents of non-compliance—the enterprise has conducted internal investigations and anti-fraud inquiries, imposed sanctions on responsible parties, closed governance gaps, and improved its compliance management practices to rectify and remedy systemic deficiencies, it may be concluded that the compliance management system has proven highly effective in achieving its compliance risk-control objectives.

By contrast, the second evaluative dimension may be described as the degree to which a compliance culture has been institutionalized and strengthened. While the assessment of compliance culture is inherently complex due to its subjective and qualitative nature, it is nonetheless possible to evaluate cultural development through a set of observable and objective indicators. For example, one may assess whether the enterprise has fostered a culture of preventing unlawful or non-compliant conduct by evaluating its implementation of due diligence procedures, compliance training programs, and compliance undertakings. The enterprise's adherence to the principle of top-level commitment can likewise be evaluated by reviewing the issuance of compliance bulletins, open letters, warning notices, internal and external communications, and the dissemination of compliance values. Moreover, an organization's commitment to a rule-based operational ethos may be evidenced by its willingness to conduct compliance reviews in high-risk areas, issue vetoes where appropriate, and promptly impose disciplinary measures on individuals responsible for misconduct—demonstrating a credible "zero-tolerance" policy toward violations. Finally, stakeholder perceptions—including those of employees, customers, third-party partners, and subsidiary personnel—regarding the legality and integrity of the company's business practices can also serve as meaningful indicators of whether a genuine compliance culture has taken root within the organization.

6.7 Methodologies for Evaluating Compliance Effectiveness

Following the redefinition of the core objectives of compliance management and the clarification of the standards for evaluating its effectiveness, it is essential to reflect on and systematize the methodologies by which such effectiveness may be assessed. This issue has long been overlooked in academic research, despite its practical significance. By contrast, compliance practitioners have persistently explored this area and developed a series of evaluative tools and techniques that have, over time, come to be widely recognized within the professional community. For instance, Chinese regulatory agencies and industry associations have referenced methods such as interviews, questionnaire-based surveys, sampling tests, and walkthrough testing in various guidelines for evaluating compliance effectiveness. Similarly, prosecutorial authorities in jurisdictions such as the United States and Europe have adopted techniques including simulated whistleblower reporting and random attendance at internal meetings. These approaches have garnered widespread attention and are frequently—though often uncritically—regarded as "scientific methods" for evaluating the functionality and credibility of compliance management systems.

Nonetheless, their application and methodological rigor remain subject to further critical examination and refinement.

Indeed, a closer analysis of the three criteria for evaluating compliance effectiveness reveals that empirically driven methods—such as sampling, surveys, and walkthroughs—may be operationally useful primarily for assessing the implementation of compliance programs. These methods can help determine whether the compliance systems an enterprise has established, or pledged to establish, have been genuinely activated and are functioning as intended. However, such empirical tools fall short when applied to the evaluation of compliance program design. The effectiveness of a program's design depends fundamentally on whether the enterprise has accurately diagnosed the structural causes behind compliance risks or violations, whether it has adopted targeted and remedial measures, and whether it has formulated targeted compliance programs that are appropriately tailored to its specific risk profile. Robust evaluation in this dimension requires substantive analysis of internal investigation or self-assessment reports and should be guided by principles analogous to "prescribing the right remedy," "treating the root cause," and "tailoring solutions to context." Only through such qualitative and context-sensitive review can one determine whether the program exhibits relevance, practicability, and substantive effectiveness. Similarly, the evaluation of compliance outcomes should not be limited to surface-level methods such as sample checks, surveys, or procedural walkthroughs. Instead, it demands the adoption of more rigorous and professional empirical methodologies. The fact that a compliance program is actively running does not automatically indicate that it has achieved its intended objectives. To assess whether the program has effectively controlled compliance risks and fostered a compliance culture, evaluators must employ a longitudinal perspective. This includes sustained measurement of how well the program prevents misconduct, monitors compliance practices, and addresses violations, as well as objective evaluation of whether it has meaningfully transformed the organization's ethical climate and enhanced its awareness of risk management and legal responsibility.

In light of the foregoing, it is essential to develop distinct evaluative approaches tailored to the three core dimensions of compliance program effectiveness. Generally, all methodologies for assessing compliance effectiveness can be categorized into three types: document-based assessments, operational assessments, and oriented-oriented assessments. Document-based assessments are best suited to evaluating the effectiveness of program design; operational assessments are appropriate for examining the effectiveness of program implementation; and oriented-oriented assessments are intended to measure the actual results achieved by the compliance program.

In evaluating the effectiveness of compliance program design, regulatory authorities, judicial bodies, third-party evaluators, and the enterprises themselves should perform a qualitative assessment based on three core documents. First, they should examine whether the enterprise's internal investigation report or self-assessment report accurately and comprehensively identifies the structural causes that led to the violation or triggered the compliance risk. Second, they should assess whether the submitted compliance program or remediation report includes targeted corrective and remedial measures—such as eliminating governance deficiencies, closing management loopholes, mitigating procedural vulnerabilities, and achieving the "de-criminalization" or "de-illegalization" of the company's business practices or commercial model. Third, they should determine whether the proposed compliance program qualifies as a risk-specific or domain-specific compliance framework that addresses significant risks in a particular area, and whether it incorporates control measures proportionate to the enterprise's size, industry sector, operational characteristics, internal and external environment, and overall risk exposure.

In evaluating the effectiveness of compliance program implementation, evaluators may flexibly employ a variety of empirical testing methods, selectively utilizing investigative techniques such as individual interviews, questionnaires, sample surveys, walkthrough tests, simulated complaints, and random observation of meetings. The goal is to produce assessment reports that meet the basic methodological requirements of social science and offer an accurate evaluation of the operational effectiveness of the enterprise's compliance management system. It is important to note that these methods must be applied under rigorous conditions: sampling should be conducted randomly rather than subject to human manipulation; the sample size and scope should be sufficiently large and comprehensive, rather than confined to specific domains, processes, or quantities; and the testing should be conducted independently, without interference or influence from the enterprise being evaluated.

In evaluating the effectiveness of compliance program outcomes, assessors should adopt a long-term perspective. On the premise that the compliance program has been effectively implemented and operationalized, they should evaluate both the program's actual impact in controlling specific compliance risks and its effectiveness in enhancing the organization's compliance culture. With respect to risk control, assessors should determine whether the enterprise has experienced recurring violations or risk events during the evaluation period, and whether previously identified structural deficiencies have been adequately corrected or mitigated. The evaluation should be guided by an outcome-oriented approach, with judgments based on measurable and verifiable results. As for evaluating the effectiveness of efforts to strengthen the culture of compliance, assessors should rely on a set of objective indicators, including the frequency of compliance risk assessments, the effectiveness of due diligence procedures, the outcomes of compliance training, the effectiveness of compliance undertakings, the application rate of compliance reviews, the effectiveness of the compliance department's veto power over non-compliant or high-risk activities, the effectiveness of sanctions imposed on responsible parties, and the frequency with which the compliance management system is tested and improved. These indicators should be integrated to form an evidence-based and holistic overall assessment of cultural development.

6.8 The Future of Compliance Evaluation

Within both academic and practical domains of corporate compliance, persistent concerns have been voiced regarding the legitimacy of compliance management systems. Critics argue that many widely accepted compliance frameworks may amount to little more than window-dressing—consuming significant corporate resources without demonstrable effectiveness in preventing or detecting violations. In response to such criticisms, regulatory and judicial authorities in Western jurisdictions have taken the lead in institutionalizing scientific, evidence-based evaluations of compliance effectiveness. Several international organizations have also issued global standards for assessing the effectiveness of compliance management systems. In China, regulators have shown a high degree of vigilance from the outset against superficial, formalistic, and ineffective compliance practices. Since the early stages of introducing compliance governance frameworks, Chinese authorities have gradually moved toward institutionalizing compliance effectiveness assessments.

However, to date, compliance management systems in Western jurisdictions—as well as the evaluation standards promoted by international standard-setting organizations—have largely adhered to a process-oriented model. Regulatory authorities and industry associations in China have similarly adopted many of these internationally endorsed methods for assessing compliance effectiveness. This approach, which emphasizes the implementation of compliance activities as the primary benchmark of effectiveness, has drawn pointed criticism from some scholars. In response, academic discourse has advanced an alternative, outcome-oriented evaluation paradigm—one that focuses on the actual results of compliance programs in achieving their intended objectives. This outcome-oriented approach advocates for the development of empirically grounded and scientifically valid measurement criteria. In parallel, judicial and regulatory authorities in several countries have begun experimenting with oriented-oriented assessments in the context of compliance remediation for offending enterprises. International organizations have also issued compliance evaluation guidelines with the aim of incorporating outcome-oriented indicators and outcome-oriented dimensions into existing evaluation models.

Against this backdrop, it is both necessary and timely to synthesize international and domestic experience in compliance effectiveness evaluation and to propose a comprehensive and integrated theory of effective compliance. Under this framework, the starting point for evaluating compliance effectiveness lies in redefining the overarching goal of compliance management as the effective control of compliance risks—a goal that can be further broken down into three sub-objectives: the prevention of compliance risks, the monitoring of compliance operations, and the response to violations. Based on this conceptual foundation, the assessment of compliance effectiveness can be structured around three analytical dimensions: the effectiveness of compliance program design, the effectiveness of compliance program implementation, and the effectiveness of compliance program outcomes. To conduct scientifically sound evaluations across these three dimensions, corresponding methodologies should be adopted: a document-based assessment method for evaluating the design of compliance programs; an operational assessment method for examining the activation and performance of compliance systems; and an oriented-oriented assessment method for measuring the actual impact of compliance efforts on risk control and the cultivation of a law-abiding corporate culture.

The evaluation of compliance management effectiveness remains a global challenge, prompting ongoing efforts by regulatory bodies, international organizations, and domestic authorities to explore and refine appropriate methodologies. Whether in issuing compliance guidelines, enforcing mandatory compliance frameworks, or reviewing corporate remediation efforts, regulators and judicial institutions require scientifically grounded standards and methods to assess the actual effectiveness of compliance systems. In this context, there is both a growing expectation that regulatory agencies, judicial bodies, and international institutions will continue to improve the rigor and precision of compliance evaluation tools, and a pressing need for academic engagement. Theoretical research—particularly that which proceeds along the path "from experience to theory"—can distill patterns and principles from practical exploration and institutional experimentation. Such scholarship is essential for building a durable theoretical foundation capable of guiding the long-term development of compliance effectiveness assessment.

CHAPTER 7

Administrative Settlements and Compliance Oversight

7.1 The Introduction of China's Administrative Settlement Regime

Corporate compliance was originally designed as an internal risk control mechanism aimed at addressing unlawful or improper conduct within enterprises. Over time, it has evolved into a core component of modern corporate governance. For an extended period, compliance either functioned as a means of self-regulation adopted voluntarily by enterprises to strengthen internal management or as a sector-specific tool of industry governance intended to promote self-monitoring and prevent destructive market competition. However, as enterprises have grown in scale, complexity, and specialization, traditional enforcement approaches—predicated on harsh punitive measures such as substantial fines, license revocations, and criminal penalties—have increasingly proven inadequate in addressing corporate misconduct. This is particularly evident in such areas as securities and futures, anti-unfair competition, anti-money laundering, and anti-commercial bribery. In these domains, administrative enforcement faces deeply entrenched and systemic challenges. Regulatory agencies often struggle to address the structural and cultural causes of widespread violations within large corporations. As a result, they frequently fail to detect or prevent structural illegality, and in some cases, even encounter regulatory failure. To enhance corporate supervision and compel enterprises to manage legal risks more effectively, governments across jurisdictions have gradually embraced the construction of compliance programs as a key strategy for regulatory oversight.[1] Within administrative enforcement, this has led to the emergence of a dual-track model that combines traditional "deterrence-based" approaches with an "incentive-based" logic. Under this emerging model,

[1] Feng Deng, "The Origins of Corporate Compliance and the Institutional Limitations in China," *Comparative Law Review*, no. 1 (2020).

R. Chen, *An Introduction to Corporate Compliance*,
https://doi.org/10.1007/978-981-95-7257-1_7

regulators may offer leniency in exchange for demonstrable compliance efforts. For enterprises that establish effective compliance programs, regulators may refrain from initiating enforcement actions, consider the existence of a compliance framework as a mitigating factor in administrative penalties, or treat compliance commitments as a precondition for concluding an administrative settlement agreement.[2] Through this process, compliance-based regulatory mechanisms have been progressively integrated into the administrative enforcement system in China.

Chinese regulatory authorities have placed considerable emphasis on the development of corporate compliance mechanisms. To promote the establishment of standardized compliance management systems, they have issued national compliance standards—particularly targeting central state-owned enterprises and companies engaged in overseas operations. Simultaneously, in key regulatory fields such as securities and futures, and anti-unfair competition, regulatory agencies have introduced a variety of institutional mechanisms designed to encourage or compel enterprises to implement compliance programs. These include mandatory compliance requirements, compliance-based defenses, penalty mitigation linked to compliance efforts, and administrative settlement mechanisms. Through these initiatives, China has begun to establish a preliminary institutional framework for administrative compliance regulation.

However, in comparison with the other three types of administrative compliance mechanisms, the establishment of an administrative settlement regime provides a significantly stronger incentive for enterprises to develop and maintain effective compliance management systems. As early as the late twentieth century, Chinese law had already recognized administrative settlements as a legal institution. However, these settlements were primarily applied in the context of administrative reconsideration and administrative litigation, where they served to resolve disputes between administrative agencies and private parties. In the investigative phase of administrative enforcement, by contrast, no such settlement mechanism previously existed. This landscape began to shift in 2015, when the China Securities Regulatory Commission (CSRC) issued the *Pilot Measures for Administrative Settlement*, thereby launching a pilot program for administrative settlements in the field of securities and futures regulation. Under this mechanism, when an administrative counterpart is suspected of violating securities laws, administrative regulations, or relevant regulatory provisions, the CSRC may, upon application by the counterpart, negotiate a settlement covering issues such as the rectification of alleged violations, the elimination of adverse consequences, the payment of a settlement amount, and the compensation of investor losses. Once a settlement agreement is reached, the CSRC may terminate its enforcement investigation accordingly. According to authoritative interpretations, adopting administrative settlements in such

[2] Yunxia Yin and Xiaoxia Li, "Motives and Implementation Paths of Corporate Compliance in China," *China Legal Review*, no. 3 (2020): 159.

cases facilitates the achievement of regulatory objectives, reduces legal and procedural disputes, stabilizes and clarifies market expectations, restores orderly market functioning, and safeguards the lawful rights and interests of investors.[3]

An analysis of administrative settlement agreements concluded between the China Securities Regulatory Commission (CSRC) and various enterprises reveals a consistent pattern: enterprises applying for administrative settlement typically agree to pay substantial settlement amounts while simultaneously committing to adopt necessary measures to "strengthen internal controls and corporate governance." Upon implementing these corrective actions, they are required to submit a written remediation report to the CSRC. In return, as specified in the settlement agreement, the CSRC undertakes to terminate its investigation and adjudicative proceedings concerning the applicant's alleged violations.[4]

In 2019, the revised Securities Law, enacted by the national legislature, formally incorporated the administrative settlement mechanism into China's statutory legal framework. Pursuant to Article 171 of the Securities Law, during an investigation by the China Securities Regulatory Commission (CSRC) into an entity or individual suspected of securities violations, the party under investigation may submit a written application committing to rectify the unlawful conduct, compensate affected investors, and eliminate any resulting harm or adverse impact within a timeframe approved by the CSRC. Upon receiving such a commitment, the CSRC may decide to suspend the investigation. If the party fulfills its commitments, the CSRC may terminate the investigation; otherwise, it may resume the enforcement process. Although the provision does not explicitly reference the term "administrative settlement" and remains relatively concise and abstract in its formulation, it is widely recognized that the mechanism established under this article constitutes a de facto administrative settlement regime.

In November 2021, the State Council promulgated the *Measures for the Implementation of the Commitment System by Parties in Securities and Futures Administrative Enforcement* (hereinafter the "*Implementation Measures*"), thereby formally establishing the "administrative enforcement commitment system" in the field of securities and futures regulation as an administrative regulation. Essentially, an administrative enforcement commitment is a variant of the administrative settlement mechanism. It refers to a process whereby, during an investigation by the securities regulatory authority under the State Council into a suspected violation of securities or futures laws, the investigated party undertakes to rectify the misconduct, compensate affected investors, and eliminate any resulting harm or adverse impact. Upon recognition of the

[3] Dongfang Li, "On the Administrative Settlement System in Securities Enforcement: A Commentary on the CSRC's Pilot Measures for Administrative Settlement," *Journal of China University of Political Science and Law*, no. 3 (2015).

[4] Tao Xi, "An Analysis of the Administrative Settlement System in Securities Law," *Journal of Comparative Law Studies*, no. 3 (2020).

commitment by the regulatory authority and full performance by the party, the investigation may be terminated. The *Implementation Measures* articulate key principles governing the commitment process—namely, fairness, voluntariness, and good faith—and establish a procedural framework encompassing application, acceptance, negotiation, determination of the commitment amount, execution of a formal commitment agreement, performance of obligations, suspension of the investigation, and eventual termination. The *Implementation Measures* further clarify the circumstances in which such commitments are not applicable, provide rules for the use and management of commitment payments, and establish mechanisms for supervision and accountability.[5]

Prior to the promulgation of the *Implementation Measures*, the Anti-Monopoly Commission of the State Council had already issued a compliance guideline on antitrust matters, along with the *Guidelines on Commitments by Undertakings in Monopoly Cases* (hereinafter the "*Commitment Guidelines*"). Although the *Commitment Guidelines* hold only the legal status of a ministerial regulation, they mark the first systematic recognition by Chinese regulatory authorities of an "administrative enforcement commitment" mechanism. This regime is directly grounded in the relevant provisions of China's *Anti-Monopoly Law*. As early as 2007, Article 45 of the *Anti-Monopoly Law*, as enacted by the legislature, had established the basic framework for administrative enforcement commitments in the antitrust context. According to this provision, where an undertaking under investigation for suspected monopolistic conduct offers to adopt remedial measures to eliminate the adverse effects of such conduct, the enforcement agency may decide to suspend the investigation. The agency is further authorized to monitor the undertaking's compliance with its commitments and may decide to terminate the investigation upon satisfactory fulfillment.[6]

Pursuant to the aforementioned provisions of the *Anti-Monopoly Law*, the *Commitment Guidelines* provide that an undertaking under investigation may propose a commitment to take concrete measures to eliminate the consequences of its conduct. The anti-monopoly enforcement agency under the State Council may accept such a commitment and decide to suspend or terminate the investigation accordingly. The *Commitment Guidelines* establish a comprehensive framework governing the application of the commitment regime, including the scope of its applicability, the procedures for submitting and withdrawing commitments, the nature of remedial measures, channels of communication between undertakings and enforcement authorities, the review of proposed commitments by the enforcement agency, as well as the procedures for suspending, terminating, and resuming investigations.

[5] "Breaking News! The Administrative Commitment System in Securities and Futures Enforcement Will Be Implemented Starting Next Year, Opening a New Channel for Investor Rights Remedies," *China Securities Journal*, November 29, 2021.

[6] Jiemin Sheng and Haitao Jiao, "The Enforcement Dilemmas and Incentives of the Commitment System under the Anti-Monopoly Law," *Tsinghua Law Journal*, no. 2 (2009).

To date, China's administrative enforcement commitment regime has been formally established in two key regulatory domains: anti-monopoly enforcement and securities and futures regulation. Substantively, this regime allows business operators suspected of regulatory violations to make formal commitments during the course of administrative investigations. These commitments typically involve measures to eliminate the adverse consequences of the alleged conduct, compensate affected parties, and rectify the unlawful behavior. Upon reaching a recognized commitment agreement with the enforcement authority and fulfilling the specified obligations, the investigation may be terminated. At present, this regime is implemented by regulatory bodies under the State Council and applies to both natural persons and legal entities suspected of misconduct. Regardless of whether the committing party is an individual or a corporate entity, they are generally required to pay a substantial settlement sum or commitment payment and to fully carry out the remedial measures they have pledged. In return, the administrative enforcement authority may grant leniency by refraining from pursuing administrative liability against the party.

In formal terms, the administrative enforcement commitment regime shares certain similarities with the compliance supervision and assessment mechanism promoted by procuratorial authorities. However, it is important to note that when prosecutors subject an enterprise suspected of criminal conduct to compliance assessment, this is not solely based on the enterprise's admission of guilt, cooperation with the investigation, or efforts to remediate harm. Crucially, these enterprises are also selected because they have submitted a compliance remediation plan and made a formal commitment to establishing or improving their internal compliance management systems.[7] By contrast, at least as reflected in existing written rules, administrative enforcement commitments do not explicitly incorporate compliance remediation requirements, nor do they impose any clear obligation on enterprises to adopt or enhance a compliance framework. Even in the limited number of cases handled by the China Securities Regulatory Commission (CSRC) during the pilot phase of the administrative settlement regime, although enterprises were required to "strengthen internal controls" and submit a "written rectification report," no substantive information was provided regarding compliance systems or remediation plans. Moreover, the CSRC did not undertake any acceptance review or evaluation of the compliance efforts undertaken. Evidently, in the design and pilot implementation of the administrative enforcement commitment regime, the compliance dimension—particularly the role of corporate remediation and institutional reform—was overlooked by regulatory policymakers. As a result, incentive-based mechanisms to promote compliance were not incorporated into the structure of the regime.

This chapter offers a preliminary inquiry into the relationship between administrative settlements and compliance incentives. It begins with an analysis

[7] Jiemin Sheng and Haitao Jiao, "The Enforcement Dilemmas and Incentives of the Commitment System under the Anti-Monopoly Law," *Tsinghua Law Journal*, no. 2 (2009).

of the compliance incentive mechanisms embedded in the U.S. administrative settlement system, aiming to develop a theoretical framework for understanding the interaction between settlement agreements and corporate compliance. The chapter then examines the implementation and effects of China's pilot administrative settlement regime, focusing on the institutional design of administrative enforcement commitments. Finally, from the perspective of strengthening compliance incentives, it puts forward initial proposals for reforming and improving China's administrative settlement framework.

7.2 A Comparative Perspective: The U.S. Regime

China's administrative settlement regime has been shaped in significant part by the U.S. model of administrative settlement agreements. This influence is particularly pronounced in the regulatory practices of the China Securities Regulatory Commission (CSRC), which has increasingly drawn on the enforcement strategies and regulatory experience of the U.S. Securities and Exchange Commission (SEC) in supervising securities and futures enterprises. The integration of corporate compliance mechanisms into administrative settlements serves as a key example of this transnational regulatory borrowing. To clarify the origins and institutional logic of China's administrative settlement framework, a brief analysis of the U.S. system is therefore warranted.

In the United States, when a regulatory agency uncovers a potential violation of administrative law by a corporate entity, it typically initiates a formal investigation led by the agency's enforcement division. If the investigation produces sufficient evidence of wrongdoing, the agency may choose between two principal enforcement mechanisms. The first is the administrative sanction process, through which the agency imposes penalties via internal adjudicatory procedures. The second is the civil enforcement route, whereby the agency files a lawsuit in court seeking judicial sanctions. In practice, agencies enjoy broad discretion in selecting between these two avenues and, in some instances, may pursue both simultaneously.

An administrative settlement agreement refers to an arrangement concluded between a regulatory agency and a corporate entity subject to administrative enforcement, typically in cases where the enterprise has cooperated with the investigation, voluntarily disclosed misconduct, or undertaken to implement a compliance program. Such agreements generally consist of two core components. First, the agency imposes a defined monitoring period during which the enterprise is required to fulfill a set of prescribed obligations. Second, upon satisfactory performance during the monitoring period, the agency agrees to impose a mitigated administrative sanction. In principle, an administrative settlement agreement may be reached at any stage of the administrative sanction process—from the initiation of the investigation to the issuance of the final sanction decision. Similarly, in civil enforcement proceedings, a settlement may be concluded after the agency files a complaint in federal district court but before the court renders a final judgment. In practice, the U.S. Securities and

Exchange Commission (SEC) frequently enters into Deferred Prosecution Agreements (DPAs) or Non-Prosecution Agreements (NPAs) with corporate defendants, while other federal regulatory agencies may enter into administrative settlement agreements of a similar structure and function.

7.2.1 SEC DPAs and NPAs

According to the U.S. Securities and Exchange Commission's *Enforcement Manual*, when conducting an enforcement investigation or initiating civil proceedings, the SEC takes into account a number of factors. These include: the statutory or regulatory provisions that may have been violated; the severity of the alleged misconduct; the potential consequences of the violation; whether the affected parties are especially vulnerable or at risk; whether the misconduct is ongoing; whether the conduct can be effectively investigated within the relevant statute of limitations; and whether other agencies—including federal or state authorities—are better positioned to undertake the investigation. The SEC also considers whether the case reflects widespread industry practices and whether the company has a record of prior violations.[8]

The U.S. Securities and Exchange Commission (SEC) has established a cooperation framework to guide enforcement decisions involving corporate entities. According to a 2001 investigative report issued by the SEC, authorities are instructed to consider whether a company has demonstrated cooperation in four key areas. First, whether the company engaged in self-policing prior to the discovery of misconduct, including the implementation of effective compliance procedures. Second, whether the company undertook self-reporting after the misconduct was identified—this includes conducting a comprehensive internal review of the nature, scope, source, and consequences of the misconduct and providing timely, complete, and effective disclosures to the public, regulatory bodies, and relevant self-regulatory organizations. Third, whether the company adopted remedial measures, such as terminating or appropriately disciplining responsible individuals, enhancing internal controls and procedures to prevent recurrence, and compensating those adversely affected by the misconduct. Fourth, whether the company cooperated with enforcement authorities by providing the SEC with relevant information concerning both the misconduct and the steps taken to remedy it.[9] While this framework provides structured criteria, the SEC retains discretion to apply these factors flexibly based on the specific circumstances of each case.

In May 2011, the U.S. Securities and Exchange Commission (SEC) entered into its first Deferred Prosecution Agreement (DPA) with a company for

[8] Securities and Exchange Commission, Division of Enforcement. *Enforcement Manual*. § 2.1.1, "Ranking Investigations and Allocating Resources."

[9] *Report of Investigation Pursuant to Section 21(a) of the Securities Exchange Act of 1934 and Commission Statement on the Relationship of Cooperation to Agency Enforcement Decisions (Seaboard Report)*, Securities Exchange Act Release No. 44969 and AAER-1470 (October 23, 2001).

violations of the Foreign Corrupt Practices Act (FCPA).[10] The case involved a manufacturer of steel pipe products that had bribed Uzbek government officials in connection with its bid to supply materials for oil and gas pipeline projects, thereby breaching the FCPA's anti-bribery provisions. As a result of the scheme, the company secured multiple contracts and earned approximately $5 million in profits. Following the discovery of the misconduct, the company voluntarily self-reported the violations, conducted a comprehensive internal investigation, and fully cooperated with both the SEC and the U.S. Department of Justice. It also undertook extensive remedial measures, including strengthening its anti-corruption procedures and expanding compliance training. Under the terms of the DPA, the company agreed to pay $5.4 million in disgorgement and a $3.5 million civil penalty.

Generally, a Deferred Prosecution Agreement (DPA) between the SEC and a company constitutes a form of settlement in which the SEC agrees to suspend enforcement actions for a specified monitoring period, typically not exceeding five years. If the company complies with all the terms of the agreement during this period, the SEC will refrain from initiating administrative sanctions. By contrast, a Non-Prosecution Agreement (NPA) reflects a commitment by the SEC not to initiate any enforcement action, and it does not involve any probationary period. Once an NPA is executed, the company is expected to adhere permanently to all the agreed-upon terms. However, should the company violate any provision of the NPA at any point, enforcement authorities may refer the case back to the SEC for potential follow-up action.

A Deferred Prosecution Agreement (DPA) typically contains the following provisions. First, the company must cooperate truthfully and fully with the SEC's investigation—this involves producing all relevant non-privileged documents, responding to inquiries, attending interviews, appearing in proceedings, and waiving territorial service limits. Second, it must enter into a tolling agreement, effectively extending any applicable statutes of limitation. Third, the company must commit to not violating securities laws during the deferred period. Fourth, it must make any agreed-upon payments—including disgorgement of ill-gotten gains and civil penalties. Fifth, if it fully complies with the DPA during the deferment (usually up to five years), the SEC will forego pursuing any further enforcement action related to the same conduct. Sixth, if the company breaches the agreement, the SEC may proceed with enforcement against it for both the original violation and any new misconduct. Seventh, the company consents to the SEC's use of any statements, materials, or information disclosed under the agreement in subsequent proceedings in the event of a breach. Eighth, the DPA typically includes additional undertakings designed

[10] Securities and Exchange Commission. "Tenaris to Pay $5.4 Million in SEC's First-Ever Deferred Prosecution Agreement." Press Release, 2011–112, May 17, 2011. https://www.sec.gov/news/press/2011/2011-112.htm

to protect investors, such as compliance-related policies or injunctive provisions.[11]

Non-Prosecution Agreements (NPAs) entered into by the SEC and corporate entities are, apart from the second and third elements noted above, substantively identical to Deferred Prosecution Agreements (DPAs).[12] In enforcement practice, however, it is the third element of a DPA—commonly referred to as the "compliance clause"—that typically imposes obligations on the company to improve or strengthen its internal compliance program. By contrast, NPAs generally do not contain analogous compliance-related requirements.

7.2.2 *Settlement Practices of the Department of Commerce and FTC*

The Bureau of Industry and Security (BIS) under the U.S. Department of Commerce may initiate a formal administrative enforcement proceeding by issuing a charging letter, after which it may negotiate a settlement agreement with the company under investigation. If the parties reach a settlement prior to the issuance of the charging letter, BIS may consider a reduction in the amount of civil penalties, and the case will not be referred to an Administrative Law Judge (ALJ). However, if a settlement is reached after the charging letter has been issued and the adjudicative process has already begun, BIS must request the ALJ to withdraw the case from the hearing docket. In situations where the matter has progressed to the review stage before the Under Secretary of Commerce, the effectiveness of the settlement agreement is subject to the Under Secretary's approval.[13]

The Federal Trade Commission (FTC) may enter into settlement agreements with corporate entities in both administrative and civil enforcement proceedings. In administrative investigations and actions involving alleged violations of consumer protection laws or antitrust statutes, the FTC is authorized to negotiate settlements with the companies under investigation. Similarly, in civil proceedings initiated by the FTC before a U.S. District Court, the Commission may reach a settlement with the defendant company. However, in such cases, the FTC is required to publicly disclose the basis for the settlement and must obtain judicial approval from the court before the agreement becomes effective.[14]

[11] Securities and Exchange Commission, Division of Enforcement. *Enforcement Manual.* § 6.2.2, "Deferred Prosecution Agreements."

[12] Securities and Exchange Commission, Division of Enforcement. *Enforcement Manual.* § 6.2.3, "Non-Prosecution Agreements."

[13] U.S. Department of Commerce, Bureau of Industry and Security. *Administrative Enforcement Proceedings.*

[14] Federal Trade Commission. *A Brief Overview of the Federal Trade Commission's Investigative, Law Enforcement, and Rulemaking Authority.* https://www.ftc.gov/about-ftc/what-we-do/enforcement-authority

For instance, in July 2019, the Federal Trade Commission (FTC) entered into an administrative settlement agreement with InfoTrax Systems, a Utah-based technology firm, following allegations that the company failed to implement reasonable data security measures, leading to the unauthorized access and theft of personal information belonging to nearly one million consumers.[15] According to the FTC, InfoTrax and its former CEO failed to adopt readily available, cost-effective, and reasonable safeguards for protecting and storing consumer data. These failures included: neglecting to inventory and delete unnecessary data; failing to conduct code reviews or perform network testing; failing to monitor for malicious file uploads; failing to adequately segment its network infrastructure; and failing to deploy appropriate cybersecurity tools to detect anomalous network activity. The FTC further alleged that the company stored sensitive personal information—including Social Security numbers, payment card details, bank account information, and login credentials—in plaintext, without encryption. As a result of these deficiencies, a hacker infiltrated InfoTrax's servers and affiliated websites on more than twenty occasions between May 2014 and March 2016, ultimately gaining access to the personal data of approximately one million paying customers. The breach was only discovered in March 2016, when the company received an alert that its servers had reached capacity—a condition caused by the large data files created by the intruder. The stolen information could be exploited for identity theft and financial fraud. The FTC alleged that the company failed to implement reasonable safeguards to protect the personal information under its custody, thereby engaging in unfair practices prohibited by the Commission.

Under the administrative settlement agreement between the FTC and InfoTrax Systems, the company is barred from engaging in any business activities involving the collection, sale, sharing, or storage of personal information unless and until it implements a comprehensive data protection program to remedy its prior security failures. This program must include: first, a systematic assessment of both internal and external risks to the security of personal data; second, the implementation of safeguards designed to protect such data against cybersecurity threats; and third, procedures for regularly testing and monitoring the effectiveness of those safeguards. The agreement further requires the company to undergo independent, biennial evaluations of its data protection program. These evaluations must involve practices such as sampling, employee interviews, and document reviews, and must be conducted independently from the company's management and influence. Notably, the agreement also grants the FTC the authority to designate the independent assessor responsible for these evaluations.

[15] Federal Trade Commission. "Utah Company Settles FTC Allegations It Failed to Safeguard Consumer Data." Press Release, November 2019. https://www.ftc.gov/news-events/press-releases/2019/11/utah-company-settles-ftc-allegations-it-failed-safeguard-consumer

7.2.3 *Compliance in Administrative Settlements*

In the United States, virtually all regulatory agencies vested with administrative enforcement authority are empowered to enter into settlement agreements with companies found to have violated legal or regulatory obligations. This practice is especially common in high-risk regulatory domains such as anti-bribery, anti-money laundering, data protection, unfair competition, and export control. Agencies including the Securities and Exchange Commission (SEC), the Department of Commerce, the Department of the Treasury, and the Federal Trade Commission (FTC) may also collaborate with the Department of Justice (DOJ) to initiate coordinated enforcement actions. Under such joint enforcement frameworks, companies may be subjected to both administrative enforcement proceedings and criminal prosecution. In these contexts, regulatory agencies and prosecutorial authorities are able to negotiate bundled settlement arrangements with implicated companies, which often combine administrative settlements with Deferred Prosecution Agreements (DPAs) or Non-Prosecution Agreements (NPAs). As a result, administrative settlement agreements may substantively and procedurally overlap with prosecutorial mechanisms.

In the majority of administrative settlement agreements, the establishment of an effective compliance program is not only a critical factor in enabling a company to reach a favorable settlement, but also a commonly included provision that serves to justify leniency in administrative sanctions. Regulatory authorities generally view the implementation of a compliance framework as a clear signal of the company's willingness to cooperate with enforcement efforts. In certain instances, regulators have characterized the post-violation adoption or enhancement of a compliance program as a "substantive remedial measure" that "reflects a cooperative attitude." When such measures are accompanied by voluntary self-disclosure and active cooperation during the investigation, they collectively form the basis for concluding an administrative settlement agreement.[16] This clearly illustrates that the development of a compliance program can play a pivotal role in facilitating both the negotiation and the successful execution of administrative settlements.

In cases where administrative settlement agreements have been concluded, regulatory authorities frequently impose a set of clearly articulated compliance obligations requiring the company to reconstruct or substantially enhance its internal compliance framework. These agreements often contain dedicated "compliance clauses" that mandate, for example, the implementation of training programs for both employees and senior management; the annual submission of compliance reports; the execution of written certifications by staff affirming their adherence to the company's code of conduct; and the reinforcement of internal controls and procedural safeguards, particularly with respect

[16] Securities and Exchange Commission, Division of Enforcement. *Enforcement Manual.* § 6.2, "Cooperation Tools."

to securities regulation and anti-bribery compliance.[17] Moreover, some settlement agreements go further by explicitly requiring the restructuring of the company's compliance governance architecture. Such provisions may include the establishment of a dedicated privacy oversight committee, the appointment of chief compliance officers, the periodic submission of independent compliance evaluation reports, and the retention of external experts to assess the operational effectiveness of specific compliance systems.[18]

Many regulatory authorities require companies entering into administrative settlement agreements to engage independent compliance monitors—neutral third parties tasked with evaluating and overseeing the company's fulfillment of the compliance-related obligations set forth in the agreement. The objective of such monitoring is to ensure that the company adopts corrective measures sufficient to mitigate the risk of future misconduct. For instance, the U.S. Securities and Exchange Commission (SEC) frequently requires the appointment of an independent compliance consultant to conduct a comprehensive review of the company's internal control systems.[19] These consultants are typically authorized to propose remedial measures designed to strengthen the company's compliance infrastructure and reduce the likelihood of recurrence. When a company implements the monitor's recommendations in good faith and successfully addresses the deficiencies identified during the monitoring period, it may emerge with a more robust and durable compliance program. In numerous enforcement actions, the Department of Justice (DOJ) and the SEC conduct coordinated investigations and jointly enter into Deferred Prosecution Agreements (DPAs) or Non-Prosecution Agreements (NPAs). In such cases, the two agencies may appoint a single compliance monitor to discharge dual oversight responsibilities on behalf of both institutions.[20]

By applying the administrative settlement framework to companies that have established compliance programs—and by embedding compliance provisions within such agreements that require firms to reconstruct their compliance systems as essential remedial measures—regulatory authorities have adopted a proactive, incentive-based approach to fostering corporate compliance. This approach has substantially increased corporate willingness to design and implement Effective Compliance Programs in response to identified legal and regulatory risks. It encourages companies to actively engage with regulators, pursue corrective reforms, and address structural deficiencies in their compliance architectures in order to prevent future violations. Crucially, it is through these

[17] Securities and Exchange Commission. *Deferred Prosecution Agreement with Tenaris.*

[18] Federal Trade Commission. "FTC's $5 Billion Facebook Settlement: Record-Breaking and History-Making." Business Blog, July 24, 2019. https://www.ftc.gov/news-events/blogs/business-blog/2019/07/ftcs-5-billion-facebook-settlement-record-breaking-history

[19] Veronica Root. "Modern-Day Monitorships." *Yale Journal on Regulation* 33 (2016): 109, 131.

[20] Michael S. Diamant, Christopher W. Sullivan, and Jason H. Smith. "FCPA Enforcement Against U.S. and Non-U.S. Companies." *Michigan Business & Entrepreneurial Law Review* 8 (2019): 353, 359.

collaboratively structured administrative settlements—characterized by mutual participation and embedded incentives—rather than through the imposition of punitive sanctions alone, that U.S. regulatory agencies have advanced the broader institutionalization of compliance mechanisms within the corporate sector.

7.3 Observations on China's Pilot Implementation

In 2015, the China Securities Regulatory Commission (CSRC) introduced the Measures for the *Pilot Measures for Administrative Settlement*, marking the first attempt to implement an administrative settlement mechanism within China's securities and futures regulatory system. Under this framework, an *administrative settlement* refers to a process in which, during the CSRC's investigation into alleged violations of securities and futures laws, administrative regulations, or related regulatory provisions, the investigated party may apply for a negotiated resolution. Upon CSRC's review and approval of the application, both parties may enter into a settlement agreement through negotiation. The core elements of such agreements typically include: remedial measures to address the alleged violations, actions to eliminate the adverse consequences of the misconduct, and the payment of an administrative settlement fund to compensate investors for losses. In exchange, the CSRC agrees to terminate the enforcement investigation and to refrain from imposing administrative penalties. More specifically, the settlement process must be initiated by the investigated party. Following a case-by-case review, the CSRC determines whether a negotiated outcome is appropriate. Where approved, the settlement agreement generally imposes two primary obligations on the investigated party: payment of the agreed settlement amount and implementation of corrective measures to address the alleged misconduct and its adverse effects. In return, the regulator agrees to discontinue its enforcement action and waive further administrative sanctions.

During the three years following the CSRC's pilot implementation of the administrative settlement regime, no settlement agreements were concluded with investigated parties. It was not until early 2019 that the first such agreement was concluded, providing an opportunity to observe how the mechanism operated in practice. In early 2020, the CSRC reached another administrative settlement in a distinct enforcement proceeding, offering further insights into the pilot program's application and effectiveness.

In April 2019, the China Securities Regulatory Commission (CSRC) entered into an administrative settlement with Goldman Sachs (Asia) L.L.C., Beijing Gao Hua Securities Company Limited, and seven other applicants. This was the first administrative settlement case concluded since the CSRC launched its pilot program in 2015. According to the CSRC's public announcement, from October 2013 to July 2015, a proprietary trader at Goldman Sachs (Asia) executed transactions through a Goldman Sachs brokerage account opened at Gao Hua Securities and provided trading instructions to a proprietary trader at

Gao Hua. On four trading days between May and July 2015, both parties engaged in additional transactions involving other related stocks and stock index futures contracts. The CSRC formally launched an investigation into the applicants' conduct in July 2016. Upon application by all nine parties, the CSRC agreed to enter into an administrative settlement, under which the applicants were required to pay RMB 150 million as a settlement amount. They were also ordered to take necessary measures to strengthen their internal control systems and, upon completion, to submit a written remediation report to the CSRC. In return, the CSRC agreed to terminate its investigation and enforcement proceedings relating to the alleged misconduct.[21]

In January 2020, the China Securities Regulatory Commission (CSRC) entered into an administrative settlement agreement with five companies, including Sidley (Shanghai) Trading Co., Ltd. According to Announcement No. 1 of 2020 issued by the CSRC, in 2015, Sidley (Shanghai), together with Fullgoal Fund Management Co., Ltd., CITIC Futures Co., Ltd., Guosen Futures Co., Ltd., and Qianshi Chuangfu Capital Management Co., Ltd., was subject to a regulatory investigation for suspected violations of account management rules and regulations governing asset management operations. Upon applications submitted by the five entities, the CSRC ultimately entered into administrative settlement agreements with each of them. Under the terms of the settlements, the five companies were ordered to pay settlement amounts of RMB 670 million, RMB 1.8 million, RMB 10 million, RMB 2.35 million, and RMB 1 million, respectively. They were also required to adopt necessary measures to strengthen their internal control systems and, upon completion, submit written remediation reports to the CSRC. In return, the CSRC agreed to terminate its investigations and enforcement proceedings concerning the alleged misconduct.

An examination of the two aforementioned administrative settlement cases suggests that the CSRC's pilot use of administrative settlements in the securities regulatory domain has, in practice, incorporated corporate compliance into the enforcement process. Specifically, the CSRC requires companies suspected of regulatory violations to propose remedial measures aimed at correcting the misconduct and mitigating its consequences as a precondition for reaching a settlement. The companies are not only expected to commit to strengthening internal governance, but are also required to implement concrete internal remediation measures. Only through such actions can they secure the regulator's agreement to terminate the investigation and thereby avoid more severe administrative penalties. This indicates that, at least within the sphere of administrative regulation, corporate compliance has begun to serve as an integral component of the incentive structure in regulatory enforcement.[22]

[21] Weiqiao Yang, "Behind the CSRC and Goldman Sachs Administrative Enforcement Settlement," *Board Magazine* WeChat Official Account, July 31, 2019;

[22] Xinyu Liu, "Settlement Exceeds 680 Million RMB! CSRC Reaches Administrative Settlement with Five Institutions Including Sidou," *Pengpai News* WeChat Official Account, January 20, 2020.

However, because the CSRC's pilot implementation plan for administrative settlements failed to incorporate a comprehensive incentive mechanism for corporate compliance, doubts remain as to how effective this approach can be in advancing substantive compliance practices. From the perspective of encouraging companies to develop compliance programs, the CSRC appears to lack the necessary institutional infrastructure.

To begin with, the CSRC has not issued any dedicated compliance management guidelines specifically tailored to enterprises operating in the securities and futures sector. Experience from Western jurisdictions indicates that administrative settlements can only serve as effective tools for preventing, detecting, and mitigating compliance risks when companies are required to implement customized compliance programs that address specific areas of concern. To support this, regulatory authorities must regularly issue industry-specific compliance guidelines to help companies establish or improve their compliance frameworks. Regrettably, during its pilot of the administrative settlement mechanism, the CSRC failed to provide any such compliance guidance tailored to the unique risks in the securities and futures market. As a result, companies involved in misconduct have lacked the basic compliance tools needed to "rectify unlawful conduct," "undertake meaningful remediation," or "build effective internal control systems." After paying the settlement fines, these companies typically do not adopt compliance charters, establish internal compliance structures, or formulate targeted compliance policies and codes of conduct addressing specific forms of misconduct—such as false disclosure, insider trading, market manipulation, or client fraud. In the absence of risk-specific prevention, monitoring, and response mechanisms, official mandates to "correct violations" or "actively implement remediation" risk becoming little more than rhetorical gestures.

Second, the CSRC has not made the establishment of a corporate compliance mechanism a prerequisite for entering into an administrative settlement. According to the CSRC's pilot measures for administrative settlements, aside from several vague and highly discretionary criteria, the only operable condition is that the case involves legal or factual complexity—i.e., it qualifies as a "difficult case"—and that the investigated party is willing to pay a substantial settlement amount. Nowhere do the measures require the prior establishment of a compliance system as a condition for settlement. Yet if a company has never had a compliance management framework in place, it makes little sense to speak of "improving" or "enhancing" such a system. If a compliance mechanism is created from scratch only after the conclusion of a settlement, how can it meaningfully serve to remedy past misconduct or demonstrate genuine remediation?

For compliance mechanisms to be widely adopted, regulators must design effective incentives—for example, by granting preferential access to administrative settlements for companies that have already implemented robust compliance programs. Only then can administrative settlements serve as a positive inducement for potentially noncompliant firms to proactively establish compliance systems in order to qualify for leniency. Conversely, if the existence of a compliance program is not treated as a threshold requirement, what incentive do companies in the securities and futures sector have to undertake such efforts proactively?

Third, the CSRC has not incorporated comprehensive compliance provisions into the administrative settlement agreements it concludes with companies applying for settlement. In the United States and the United Kingdom, regulatory authorities routinely publish the full text of administrative settlement agreements. This practice serves two principal functions: first, it enhances transparency and public accountability in administrative enforcement; second, it exerts a degree of punitive and deterrent pressure on the companies involved, compelling them to cooperate with regulatory authorities, improve their compliance programs, and prevent future violations. In addition, regulators in these jurisdictions frequently require companies to enter into dedicated compliance provisions or annexed compliance documents as an integral component of the settlement agreement. These provisions set forth specific and detailed obligations regarding the design, implementation, or enhancement of internal compliance systems. Such compliance commitments are either embedded within the main body of the agreement or appended as formal annexes, and they constitute the primary basis for assessing whether the company has fulfilled its post-settlement obligations.

To date, however, the CSRC has applied the administrative settlement mechanism in only two cases and has not made the full text of either agreement publicly available. As a result, it is impossible to determine what specific compliance obligations were imposed on the companies involved, or what commitments they may have undertaken. Based on the limited case summaries released by the CSRC, it appears that the companies were merely instructed to "take necessary measures to strengthen internal control" and to "submit a written remediation report" upon completion. Yet the CSRC did not clarify what such internal control improvements should involve, nor what substantive content the remediation reports should contain. Did the CSRC conclude dedicated compliance clauses or enter into formal compliance documents with these companies? On this point, no information has been disclosed. It is therefore reasonable to ask: to what extent has the CSRC, while collecting substantial administrative settlement payments, actually exercised substantive regulatory oversight in compelling companies to establish effective compliance management systems?

Finally, the CSRC has neither established a probationary period for companies to improve their compliance mechanisms, nor instituted a system of continuous oversight to monitor such improvements. In jurisdictions such as the United States and the United Kingdom, it is standard practice for regulatory authorities entering into administrative settlement agreements with noncompliant companies to impose a probationary period—typically lasting three years or more—during which companies are required to fulfill a range of obligations, most notably the establishment or enhancement of targeted compliance programs. Depending on the nature of the misconduct and the company's progress in implementing compliance measures, regulators may appoint compliance monitors or coordinators to conduct periodic reviews and oversee the company's remediation efforts. In cases where a company demonstrates a high degree of cooperation with the investigation, regulators may opt not to appoint external monitors, instead requiring the company to submit regular compliance progress reports. Ultimately, prior to concluding the settlement process, the regulatory authority conducts a final review to determine whether the company has fully met its obligations under the settlement agreement. Only upon such confirmation is the administrative enforcement process formally concluded.

However, under the CSRC's pilot measures for administrative settlements, no clear probationary period is imposed on companies involved in misconduct, nor is there any mechanism for the continuous supervision and evaluation of their internal management reforms or remediation efforts. The pilot framework does not establish a system for appointing compliance monitors, nor does it require companies to submit periodic compliance reports. Furthermore, it lacks any procedure for conducting a final assessment of a company's compliance progress before the conclusion of the probationary period. In the absence of such supervisory mechanisms, this laissez-faire regulatory approach raises serious concerns: how can it exert meaningful pressure on companies to improve their internal control systems or ensure that corrective measures are effectively implemented?

7.4 The Framework of Administrative Enforcement Commitments

China's administrative enforcement commitment regime has so far been implemented in two major regulatory domains: antitrust enforcement and securities and futures regulation. The *Anti-Monopoly Law*, enacted in 2007, was the first to establish this mechanism in the context of antitrust regulation. In 2019, the State Council Anti-Monopoly Commission issued the *Commitment Guidelines*, which formally promoted the operationalization of this regime within the antitrust sector. In 2015, the China Securities Regulatory Commission (CSRC) issued the *Pilot Measures for Administrative Settlement*, launching a trial application of administrative settlements in the regulation of the securities and futures markets. After four years of pilot implementation, the administrative settlement approach was formally absorbed into the revised *Securities Law* in 2019, which replaced the provisional mechanism with a codified administrative enforcement commitment regime. In 2021, the State Council promulgated the *Implementation Measures*, thereby establishing the institutional framework for administrative enforcement commitments in the securities and futures regulatory system.

On the surface, China's administrative enforcement commitment regime shares certain structural similarities with the administrative settlement mechanism employed in the United States. However, a key point of divergence lies in the treatment of corporate compliance obligations. In the United States, administrative settlement agreements almost invariably include compliance-related provisions, requiring implicated companies to establish or enhance internal compliance programs as a condition of the settlement. By contrast, China's administrative enforcement commitment regime, in its current design, does not incorporate compliance elements into its institutional framework. The commitment agreements concluded between enforcement authorities and the investigated parties generally do not contain explicit clauses mandating the development or improvement of corporate compliance systems. In the sections that follow, this chapter offers a brief examination of the normative rationale underpinning China's administrative enforcement commitment regime, and provides a focused analysis of its implementation in the antitrust and securities/futures regulatory sectors—specifically addressing key procedural stages such as application, commitment measures, agreement formation, suspension of investigation, and termination of enforcement proceedings.

7.4.1 Normative Foundations

Traditionally, China's administrative legislation and enforcement have adhered to the principles of legality of administrative authority and the non-disposability of public power. Within this doctrinal framework, the introduction of administrative settlement mechanisms—rooted in Anglo-American legal systems—has long been a subject of controversy. The recent adoption of the administrative enforcement commitment mechanism by central regulatory agencies, particularly in the fields of antitrust and securities/futures enforcement, marks a significant conceptual breakthrough in China's administrative enforcement philosophy. This institutional development signifies a broader transition in China's regulatory approach—from a coercive, command-and-control model to one that emphasizes initiative, negotiation, and regulatory cooperation.

As early as the initial phase of the administrative settlement pilot program, reform-oriented decision-makers in the securities regulatory sector articulated four primary objectives for introducing this mechanism. First, by requiring counterparties to pay substantial settlement amounts, the system aimed to provide prompt compensation for investors' economic losses. Second, by facilitating negotiated resolutions in complex and challenging enforcement cases, the mechanism was intended to expedite case closure and promptly clarify and stabilize market expectations. Third, by enabling dialogue, compromise, and agreement between regulators and administrative counterparts, the system sought to defuse disputes and reduce reliance on administrative reconsideration or litigation. Fourth, it was designed to address practical challenges arising from deficiencies in the existing legal framework, by providing a pragmatic mechanism to resolve conduct that is difficult to characterize legally—allowing such cases to be closed through settlement without issuing a definitive legal determination.[23]

As early as 2019, China's State Council antitrust authorities identified three key benefits of establishing an administrative enforcement commitment regime to strengthen antitrust enforcement and safeguard fair market competition. First, the regime facilitates the prompt restoration of a fair and competitive market order. By terminating investigations and waiving administrative penalties for undertakings that voluntarily cease illegal conduct and adopt remedial measures to eliminate its adverse effects, the system encourages the discontinuation of monopolistic practices and mitigates their consequences—thereby reinforcing fair competition. Second, it improves enforcement efficiency. Given the evidentiary difficulties and time-consuming nature of antitrust investigations, the regime incentivizes undertakings to proactively discontinue illegal practices and submit binding commitments, thus significantly reducing the time and effort required to resolve cases. Third, it helps conserve enforcement resources. By incorporating mechanisms of negotiation and settlement, the regime promotes early cessation of unlawful conduct and enables enforcement agencies to conclude cases with minimal resource expenditure and within a shorter timeframe.[24]

In 2021, the China Securities Regulatory Commission (CSRC) and the Ministry of Justice offered a renewed interpretation of the policy rationale for establishing an administrative enforcement commitment regime in the securities regulatory domain. The regime was deemed instrumental in improving enforcement efficiency, ensuring timely investor compensation, and restoring market order through the following four objectives. First, it enhances enforcement capacity by reconciling the inherent tension between the challenges of investigating capital market misconduct and the market's demand for swift regulatory responses. Second, it enables timely compensation for investor losses, thereby improving investor satisfaction and reinforcing perceptions of fairness. Third, it increases the cost of violations, strengthening deterrence by requiring alleged violators to bear significant economic consequences. Fourth, it promotes efficient dispute resolution and closure of cases, contributing to the mitigation of social tensions, the timely restoration of market order, and the stabilization of investor expectations.[25]

Indeed, as a major reform in administrative enforcement, the establishment of the administrative enforcement commitment regime represents the incorporation of a more consultative, compromise-based, and cooperative approach

[23] Gang Xiao. "Actively Exploring a New Model of Administrative Settlement in Regulatory Enforcement." *Administrative Management Reform*, no. 1 (2014).

[24] Jiang Wan and Cheng Guo. "Comments on the Anti-Monopoly Committee of the State Council's *Guidelines on Operators' Commitments in Monopoly Cases*." Published on the official WeChat account of *Grandall Law Firm*, August 19, 2020.

[25] "Breaking News! The Administrative Commitment System in Securities and Futures Enforcement Will Be Implemented Starting Next Year, Opening a New Channel for Investor Rights Remedies." *China Securities Journal*, November 29, 2021.

into regulatory practice. Viewed from the perspective of administrative enforcement reform, the regime serves three principal value objectives. First, from the standpoint of efficiency and resource optimization, the regime provides a pragmatic mechanism for resolving complex and technical enforcement cases—particularly in antitrust and securities regulation. Conventional investigations often require substantial time, manpower, and financial resources, and may stretch over several years without yielding definitive legal conclusions. By contrast, when business operators voluntarily cease unlawful conduct and adopt remedial measures to eliminate adverse effects, regulators may swiftly bring cases to a close—achieving resolution with far fewer costs. Second, the regime introduces a built-in system of institutional incentives. Business operators who take the initiative to eliminate harm, compensate victims, and fulfill remedial obligations may receive regulatory leniency in the form of suspended or terminated investigations—and, in some cases, exemption from administrative penalties. This incentivizes cooperation and encourages undertakings to proactively engage with enforcement authorities. Third, the regime reflects a paradigm shift in regulatory logic—from one rooted in investigation, punishment, and deterrence to a model emphasizing commitment, negotiation, reciprocity, and mutual gain. Rather than being passive recipients of regulatory sanctions, enterprises can participate in the negotiation process and help shape the outcome. By voluntarily halting illegal conduct and paying commitment sums in lieu of penalties, firms not only demonstrate legal awareness but also become more inclined to accept the regulatory outcome proposed by enforcement authorities. Finally, while the regime may forgo formal administrative penalties, the requirement to pay substantial commitment sums—often exceeding statutory fines—ensures that violators still bear meaningful economic consequences. In this way, the regime retains its punitive and deterrent functions while offering a more flexible and constructive enforcement pathway.

7.4.2 *Procedural Framework*

In contrast to traditional administrative enforcement procedures, the administrative enforcement commitment mechanism constitutes a special enforcement process initiated by a business operator's voluntary application and conducted through negotiation. The process begins when the operator formally submits a request for the application of a commitment. Upon accepting the application, the regulatory authority reviews the proposed undertakings and engages in consultations with the operator regarding the specific terms. If consensus is reached, a formal commitment agreement is executed, and the authority issues a decision to suspend the ongoing investigation. During the agreed performance period, if the regulator determines that the operator has fully complied with the terms of the commitment, a final decision is rendered to terminate the investigation.

7.4.2.1 Application for Administrative Enforcement Commitments

In principle, the application of an administrative enforcement commitment is premised on the business operator's voluntary request; regulatory authorities generally do not initiate the administrative enforcement commitment process ex officio. In the context of antitrust enforcement, business operators may submit a commitment application at any point prior to the issuance of a prior notice of administrative penalty. Enforcement agencies encourage operators to submit commitments at the earliest possible stage and may inform them of the basic conduct of the suspected monopolistic behavior and its potential effects, allowing necessary communication with the enforcement agencies. Based on such communication, the operator may voluntarily propose a commitment.

In the field of securities and futures enforcement, the securities regulatory authority under the State Council has established a dedicated unit to oversee administrative enforcement commitment matters, which operates independently from the investigative departments. When delivering legal documents related to an enforcement investigation, the authority is required to inform the concerned party of its right to apply for the administrative enforcement commitment mechanism. The party may submit such an application at any point from the date of receiving the investigation notice up until the issuance of an administrative penalty decision. Upon receipt of the application, the regulatory authority must decide whether to accept it as soon as possible within the legally prescribed time frame.

7.4.2.2 Obligations of the Business Operator

In the context of antitrust enforcement, a business operator's commitment application typically includes the following elements: a description of the suspected monopolistic conduct under investigation and its potential adverse effects; specific remedial measures the operator commits to implementing to eliminate such effects; a justification of how these measures are expected to effectively mitigate or eliminate the identified consequences; a proposed timeline and method for fulfilling the commitments; and any other relevant undertakings.

In practice, the proposed commitments generally fall into three categories: structural measures, behavioral measures, and comprehensive measures. Structural measures may include the divestiture of tangible assets, intangible assets such as intellectual property rights, or other relevant interests. Behavioral measures may involve adjustments to pricing strategies, the removal or modification of restrictive trade practices, the opening of access to networks, platforms, or other essential infrastructure, or the licensing of patents, trade secrets, or other intellectual property rights. Regardless of type, all proposed commitments must be clear, feasible, and independently actionable by the operator. Where implementation requires the consent of a third party, the operator must submit a written statement of consent from the relevant third party.

In the field of securities and futures enforcement, a commitment application submitted by a business operator must contain the following components: first, basic information about the applicant; second, the principal facts and legal or factual grounds supporting the request for application of the commitment mechanism; third, the specific measures the applicant has taken or undertakes to take, which fall into three categories—measures to rectify the suspected unlawful conduct, to compensate investors for incurred losses, and to eliminate the harm or adverse consequences caused by the conduct; and fourth, any other information or materials as required by the regulatory authority.

From a legal standpoint, the measures undertaken or proposed by the allegedly noncompliant operator are essentially remedial and loss-reparative in nature. Whether aimed at correcting the underlying violations, compensating affected investors, or mitigating the harmful consequences or negative social impact of the conduct, these measures are all ex post interventions designed to restore the disrupted legal and social order. While primarily remedial, such measures may also contribute to the prevention of future violations.

7.4.2.3 Conclusion of the Commitment Agreement

In antitrust enforcement, the enforcement authority and the business operator may engage in dialogue and negotiation regarding the content of the proposed commitments. The scope of negotiation may include the factual characterization of the case, the effectiveness of the proposed measures in eliminating the consequences of the suspected monopolistic conduct, and whether the commitments are confined to addressing the competition concerns identified by the enforcement authority. During the negotiation process, upon mutual agreement between the enforcement authority and the operator, third-party business operators, relevant industry regulators, trade associations, and academic experts may be jointly invited to participate in the discussion. If the operator's alleged monopolistic conduct has affected the rights and interests of a broader and indeterminate group of market participants, consumers, or the public interest, the proposed commitments may also be subject to public consultation. In light of the feedback received from various stakeholders, the enforcement authority may recommend that the operator revise the proposed measures or submit an entirely new set of commitments.

In the field of securities and futures enforcement, once the regulatory authority accepts an application for the administrative enforcement commitment procedure, it may initiate consultations with the applicant concerning the scope and substance of the proposed commitments, taking into consideration the losses, harms, or adverse effects caused by the alleged violations. The consultation period typically lasts for six months. These consultations must be conducted in person, with the participation of at least two regulatory officials, and written records of the discussions must be duly prepared. If, following the consultations, the regulatory authority agrees to the commitments proposed by the applicant, both parties shall execute a Commitment Acknowledgment Agreement. This agreement must include the following elements: first, the legal basis for the application of the commitment procedure; second, the key factual findings relating to the alleged misconduct; third, the specific remedial measures the applicant undertakes to adopt, including the rectification of the unlawful conduct, compensation for investor losses, and mitigation of any resulting harm or negative consequences; fourth, the amount of the commitment payment and the method of its remittance; fifth, the timeline for the fulfillment of the applicant's commitments.

7.4.2.4 Payment of Commitment Sums

In the realm of antitrust enforcement, current laws and regulations do not explicitly authorize enforcement authorities to collect commitment sums. By contrast, under the 2021 *Implementation Measures* governing securities regulation, when a business operator submits an application for the commitment procedure, the securities and futures regulatory authority under the State Council enters into consultations with the applicant regarding the amount and method of payment for the commitment sum. These terms are subsequently formalized in a Commitment Acknowledgment Agreement. To a considerable extent, the payment of a sufficiently substantial commitment sum functions as both a substantive obligation assumed by the operator and a necessary precondition for the regulatory authority to issue a decision to terminate the enforcement investigation.

The so-called commitment sum essentially refers to the payment made by a party seeking to enter the administrative enforcement commitment procedure in the context of securities and futures regulation. In principle, when determining the amount of such payment, regulatory authorities should comprehensively consider several factors: the potential gains the party may have realized or the losses it may have avoided as a result of the alleged misconduct; the fines or disgorgement of unlawful proceeds that would likely have been imposed absent the commitment; the actual losses suffered by investors; and the procedural stage of the enforcement case at the time the commitment agreement is executed. Empirical evidence from the pilot administrative settlement regime in the securities enforcement domain suggests that regulatory authorities have frequently imposed settlement payments amounting to tens of millions—and in some cases, exceeding RMB 100 million. Based on this experience, it is foreseeable that both securities regulators and antitrust enforcement agencies will continue to require commitment sums at similarly elevated levels, particularly amounts that substantially exceed the statutory ceilings for administrative fines prescribed by existing regulations.

7.4.2.5 Suspension of Investigative Proceedings

As an incentive mechanism, enforcement authorities are expected to issue a suspension decision for business operators who either propose credible remedial commitments or have begun implementing such measures. "Suspension of investigation" refers to a regulatory action whereby the authority temporarily halts its administrative enforcement proceedings following the conclusion of a commitment agreement with the operator suspected of regulatory violations. In evaluating the proposed commitments, the authority may take into account various factors, including the operator's intent in engaging in the suspected monopolistic conduct; the nature, duration, and severity of the conduct; its resulting harm or adverse impact; and the scope and anticipated effectiveness of the remedial measures undertaken. If, after such evaluation, the enforcement authority determines that the proposed commitments satisfy the statutory criteria for applying the administrative enforcement commitment mechanism, it may formally suspend the investigation. All such suspension decisions must be publicly disclosed without exception.

7.4.2.6 *Performance of the Commitment Agreement*

When issuing a decision to suspend the investigation, the regulatory authority shall specify a defined period within which the business operator must fulfill its commitments. This performance period also constitutes the effective duration of the suspension. During this time, the operator is required to submit written reports to the enforcement authority detailing the implementation status of its commitments, in accordance with the terms set forth in the suspension decision. The enforcement authority is responsible for overseeing the operator's compliance throughout this period. If, during the performance period, the operator wishes to modify the substance of its commitments, it may submit an application for amendment. Upon review, the enforcement authority shall determine whether to approve the proposed changes. Where the operator, for reasons attributable to itself, fails to perform or fails to fully perform its commitments, the regulatory authority shall terminate the application of the administrative enforcement commitment mechanism and resume formal administrative sanction proceedings.

7.4.2.7 *Termination of the Investigation*

Termination of the investigation refers to a formal decision by the enforcement authority to conclude the administrative enforcement process and to waive the imposition of administrative penalties, once the business operator has fully performed its commitments during the suspension period. If, within the prescribed performance period, the regulatory authority determines that the operator has duly fulfilled all obligations set forth in the Commitment Acknowledgment Agreement, it shall issue a written decision to terminate the investigation. Such decisions must be publicly disclosed. Upon issuance of the termination decision, the regulatory authority shall be precluded from reopening the investigation into the same alleged unlawful conduct by the operator.

7.4.3 *Commentary*

Compared with the administrative settlement mechanism piloted in 2015, the newly established administrative enforcement commitment regime introduces a number of significant institutional improvements. These include an extended window for submission of applications, revised criteria and expanded scope of applicability, streamlined procedures for initiating the process, clarified factors for determining the amount of the commitment sum, and the formalization of a collective decision-making mechanism. Taken together, these adjustments are undoubtedly beneficial in encouraging business operators to submit applications in a timely manner and in facilitating the expedited conclusion of commitment agreements with regulatory authorities. Furthermore, between 2019 and 2021, the State Council and its subordinate regulatory agencies progressively broadened the applicability of administrative enforcement commitments to include both antitrust enforcement and securities and futures regulation. This expansion marks a significant step toward enabling the administrative enforcement commitment regime to serve a more robust role across a wider spectrum of administrative enforcement domains.

Whether in the context of antitrust enforcement or securities and futures regulation, the application of China's administrative enforcement commitment regime remains marked by significant ambiguities that call for clarification through more detailed and operational implementation rules. The current framework also exhibits a degree of institutional indeterminacy. For example, the specific obligations that business operators are expected to undertake remain inadequately defined. In the antitrust domain, key terms such as "measures to eliminate the consequences of the conduct" and the so-called "structural" and "behavioral" remedies continue to lack concrete, enforceable content. Likewise, in the realm of securities regulation, obligations framed as "correcting suspected unlawful conduct," "compensating affected investors," and "eliminating harm or adverse impact" remain conceptually vague and require authoritative interpretation to ensure that operators fully understand the substantive content of their commitments. In addition, the current approach to determining commitment sums, while referencing certain criteria under existing rules, still grants enforcement agencies broad discretionary power. As evidenced by several cases arising during the pilot implementation of the administrative settlement regime, the imposition of commitment sums must strike an appropriate balance—ensuring sufficient punitive and deterrent force while also adhering to the principles of necessity, proportionality, and reasonableness. In practice, this means structuring commitment payments into modular components, such as punitive sums, disgorgement of unlawful gains, compensation for investors and other victims, back payments of tax liabilities, and financial contributions for the remediation of harm and restoration of legal interests. Furthermore, the timeframe for fulfilling such commitments should not be left entirely to the enforcement authority's discretion. Instead, a minimum and maximum duration—for example, no less than one year and no more than three years—should be clearly stipulated. Notably, although compliance remediation is not yet a standard requirement under current commitment measures, regulatory agencies have previously required companies to "establish internal control mechanisms" under the administrative settlement framework. Any such restructuring of internal governance or compliance systems will necessarily demand sufficient time and organizational capacity for meaningful implementation.

Admittedly, one of the most contentious features of China's newly established administrative enforcement commitment regime lies in its failure to incorporate compliance remediation as a core component of the required undertakings. In contrast to the administrative settlement mechanisms adopted by regulatory authorities in other jurisdictions, the Chinese framework does not mandate that companies under investigation establish or enhance internal compliance programs. The prescribed obligations to "correct unlawful conduct," "compensate for losses," and "eliminate damage or adverse effects" amount, in essence, to cooperative or remedial measures imposed by enforcement authorities. Even when fully implemented, these measures primarily serve to mitigate the consequences of past misconduct, without addressing the root causes that enabled such violations in the first place. As a result, even after fulfilling the agreed commitments, a company's governance structure may remain fundamentally unchanged. Structural weaknesses in key areas such as corporate decision-making, operational controls, personnel management, financial oversight, compensation practices, and legal compliance systems may persist. These systemic deficiencies may continue to support business models that are non-compliant with administrative regulations—or, in some cases, even criminal statutes—thereby leaving the company exposed to significant ongoing compliance risks. If enforcement agencies focus narrowly on securing high-value commitment payments without requiring institutional reforms to address internal governance failures or mandating corrective action to reshape defective corporate cultures, the regime risks becoming transactional rather than transformative. Once the investigation is formally concluded, a company may view the matter as resolved and lack any further incentive to pursue substantive compliance improvements. In the absence of such reforms, how can future violations be meaningfully prevented?

Since 2015, the China Securities Regulatory Commission (CSRC) has piloted an administrative settlement mechanism in the securities regulatory domain and, during this process, gradually incorporated elements of compliance remediation. Terms such as "internal control management" and "rectification reports" already embodied the introduction of compliance management systems into regulatory practice. Yet, with the formal codification of the administrative settlement mechanism into the Securities Law and its elevation into an administrative regulation under the title of "administrative enforcement commitment," it is regrettable that this hard-won institutional innovation—the compliance remediation framework developed through years of experimentation—was not formally embedded in the relevant legislation. Nor was it included among the required remedial measures to be undertaken by companies under investigation. Is it not a matter of concern that such a significant reform effort was left unrecognized in the very instruments meant to institutionalize regulatory innovation?

7.5 Integrating Compliance into Administrative Settlements

Drawing on the experience of jurisdictions in Europe and the United States that have implemented administrative settlement agreements, it is clear that the establishment of a corporate compliance management system prior to the discovery of a violation can facilitate the negotiation and conclusion of such agreements between enterprises and administrative authorities. Furthermore, a company's commitment—during the enforcement process—to establish or enhance its compliance program can constitute a central component of the settlement agreement and, in some cases, serve as the principal basis for lenient administrative treatment by regulators. In this context, compliance has emerged as both a critical strategy for enterprises seeking to benefit from regulatory incentives and an effective instrument for regulatory authorities to improve the quality and credibility of administrative enforcement. In enterprise-related cases, a settlement agreement that fails to include compliance-related provisions should be considered incomplete and structurally inadequate.

By drawing on administrative regulatory practices from Europe and the United States, China has undertaken pilot reforms of its administrative settlement system in the field of securities regulation and has formally introduced an administrative enforcement commitment regime in both antitrust enforcement and securities oversight. Since the launch of the pilot program in 2015, China's securities regulators have made initial efforts to incorporate corporate compliance mechanisms into administrative settlement agreements. However, due to the extremely limited number of cases included in the pilot and the broadly framed requirements related to "internal control management" and "rectification reports," it remains difficult to ascertain the concrete modalities of compliance implementation or to evaluate the effectiveness of such efforts. Following the formal institutionalization of the administrative enforcement commitment regime, Chinese regulatory authorities, in negotiating with companies under investigation, have largely retained only remedial measures—such as eliminating adverse consequences, compensating for losses, and rectifying unlawful conduct—while failing to impose specific requirements for compliance remediation or the rebuilding of internal compliance programs. At least from the perspective of codified legal norms, the administrative settlement framework currently in place in China represents a model that lacks an embedded compliance incentive mechanism.

Chinese administrative regulatory authorities have increasingly recognized the important role of corporate compliance in preventing administrative violations and are actively promoting the establishment of compliance management systems through multiple channels. In addition to issuing advisory compliance guidelines, regulators have also begun to employ methods such as administrative guidance and mandatory compliance, urging companies suspected of administrative violations to carry out compliance remediation or to establish formal compliance frameworks. In recent administrative enforcement cases in the fields of antitrust and unfair competition, regulators have imposed significant administrative fines on major internet platforms and, at the same time, required them to implement compliance remediation within a specified period and to make formal compliance commitments. These developments represent a significant step forward in integrating compliance into the administrative enforcement process.[26] However, to fully incorporate compliance-based incentive mechanisms into the broader processes of administrative regulation and enforcement, it is not sufficient to rely solely on the current institutional arrangements. If compliance mechanisms were systematically introduced into the more widely applicable and far-reaching administrative settlement framework—allowing companies under investigation to not only undertake remedial measures but also commit to substantive compliance remediation—regulatory agencies could condition the waiver of administrative penalties on the effectiveness of such remediation efforts. This approach could incentivize meaningful changes in corporate governance structures and organizational culture, thereby producing stronger preventative effects against future administrative violations.[27]

Drawing on the conceptual foundations of administrative settlement agreements in Europe and the United States, and building on the lessons learned from China's pilot programs—especially the experience of prosecutorial compliance supervision and evaluation—China may consider advancing a framework for integrating compliance mechanism into future administrative settlement regimes.

7.5.1 *Incentivizing Ex Ante Compliance*

To ensure that the administrative settlement mechanism functions as an effective compliance incentive, enforcement authorities should give priority to applying the administrative enforcement commitment regime to companies that had already established a compliance management system prior to the alleged violation and subsequently submitted a commitment application during the investigation. Under the current antitrust and securities enforcement frameworks, regulators may conclude commitment agreements with companies suspected of violations, provided they agree to pay a commitment sum and undertake the required remedial measures. In the author's view, to integrate compliance mechanisms into the administrative settlement regime, it is essential to incorporate compliance-related factors into the eligibility criteria for applying administrative enforcement commitments. While companies that lacked a pre-existing compliance program should still be permitted to apply for commitments, enforcement authorities should give preferential treatment to

[26] Ruihua Chen. "On the Status of Corporate Compliance in the Administrative Regulatory Mechanism." *Journal of Shanghai University of Political Science and Law*, no. 6 (2021).

[27] Youyong Zhou. "The Construction of the Corporate Compliance Agreement System under the Concept of Contractual Administration." *Law Forum*, no. 3 (2021).

those that had proactively implemented such systems before the incident. Furthermore, the amount and terms of the commitment sum could be tailored based on whether the company had an operational compliance program in place prior to the violation, thereby reinforcing incentives for early compliance adoption.

The primary objective of establishing a preferential commitment mechanism for companies with pre-existing compliance programs is to incentivize the widespread adoption of compliance frameworks by making such programs a strategic advantage in the application of administrative enforcement commitments. For companies with latent antitrust or securities compliance risks, the availability of more favorable regulatory treatment—such as eligibility for administrative enforcement commitments based on demonstrated compliance efforts—can serve as a strong inducement to adopt compliance measures proactively and to submit applications for commitments at an early stage of the enforcement process. At the same time, this differentiated approach may help foster a broader understanding within the business community that "compliance can yield leniency," thereby generating varying degrees of motivation for companies to establish or strengthen their antitrust and securities compliance systems.

7.5.2 *Incorporating Ex Post Measures*

Once a company under investigation applies for the administrative enforcement commitment procedure, the enforcement authority should initiate a process of consultation with the enterprise. During this process, in addition to requiring the payment of a commitment sum and the implementation of necessary remedial measures, the authority should also mandate the submission of a corporate self-assessment report and a compliance remediation plan. Any compliance-related obligations agreed upon through consultation should be incorporated into the commitment agreement and treated as a precondition for the authority's decision to suspend the investigation. In principle, for companies that had not established a compliance program prior to the alleged violation, the commitment agreement should require the establishment of an antitrust or securities compliance system. For those that already had a compliance program in place, the agreement should contain provisions mandating the enhancement of the existing compliance framework or the implementation of effective compliance remediation measures.

Experience indicates that companies are likely to take the establishment or improvement of compliance systems seriously, and to devote meaningful resources to substantive compliance remediation, only when requirements for compliance remediation are raised prior to the commencement of the compliance review process. Accordingly, enforcement authorities should engage in comprehensive consultations with the enterprise on its compliance remediation plan at the initial stage of the application. Where necessary, the authorities may conduct a preliminary inquiry into the enterprise's corporate profile, business operations, governance structure, management practices, and history of regulatory violations. This process is essential for identifying the institutional root causes of the misconduct, uncovering managerial weaknesses, systemic deficiencies, and structural flaws in corporate governance. Only on this basis can enforcement authorities propose tailored and enforceable compliance remediation measures, and compel the enterprise to establish a robust and effective compliance management system.

7.5.3 *Building Compliance Assessment Mechanisms*

Under the current administrative enforcement commitment framework, enforcement authorities are required to set an appropriate performance period following the decision to suspend an investigation. However, existing legal provisions do not specify a mandatory duration for this period, nor do they establish clear obligations for the regulators to supervise the company's implementation of remedial and corrective measures. Drawing on the prosecutorial compliance supervision model piloted in China, a comparable institutional structure may be developed for administrative enforcement. First, enforcement agencies should establish a performance period ranging from no less than one year to no more than three years, which would also function as the compliance remediation period. Second, throughout this period, regulatory authorities should strengthen oversight of the company's compliance remediation efforts. Depending on the company's prior compliance status, two supervisory models may be adopted. The first is the Periodic Reporting Model. For companies that had already implemented a compliance system prior to the incident, enforcement agencies may require the periodic submission of compliance remediation reports, detailing the progress of corrective actions and updates to the compliance management system. The second is the Compliance Monitor Model. For companies without a pre-existing compliance framework, regulators may—drawing on prosecutorial practice—appoint an independent third-party professional or institution to serve as a compliance monitor. This monitor would assist enforcement agencies in supervising, guiding, and reporting on the company's compliance remediation process and the development of its internal compliance infrastructure. Finally, during the performance period, the company should not only undertake compliance remediation but also fulfill other committed remedial obligations—such as eliminating the consequences of the unlawful conduct, compensating affected investors or other victims, and ceasing or correcting the underlying violations.

7.5.4 *Defining Effectiveness Standards*

In principle, effective compliance refers to a scenario in which the company under investigation successfully implements compliance remediation measures and establishes a compliance management system that enables it to detect and prevent violations, thereby fostering a corporate governance structure and organizational culture grounded in lawful and rule-based operations. To achieve this goal, enforcement authorities should supervise the company's implementation of necessary remedial actions, identify the institutional causes underlying the company's unlawful conduct, and require the adoption of targeted corrective and restorative measures aimed at addressing structural weaknesses, managerial deficiencies, and governance failures. On this basis, companies should, taking into account their own characteristics, governance structures, and management models, establish at least a minimum standard of tailored compliance programs.

Establishing such a baseline compliance framework should involve the adoption of specialized compliance policies, standards, and guidelines as its core, the creation of an organizational structure capable of effectively implementing and enforcing those policies, and the development of management procedures capable of performing preventive, monitoring, and responsive functions in a consistent and integrated manner.[28]

7.5.5 *Compliance Evaluation and Acceptance*

The establishment of any compliance system must be accompanied by a corresponding mechanism for compliance evaluation and acceptance. Before the expiration of the commitment performance period, enforcement authorities should, drawing on the experience of prosecutorial reform efforts, conduct a comprehensive evaluation and acceptance review of the company's progress in establishing or improving its compliance management system.

For enterprises whose compliance measures pass evaluation and acceptance, enforcement agencies may, based on a holistic assessment that also considers the amount of commitment payment made and the remedial actions taken, issue a decision to formally terminate the investigation. Conversely, if the evaluation concludes that the company has failed to implement effective compliance measures or that its remediation is unsatisfactory, enforcement authorities may terminate the administrative enforcement commitment procedure, resume their investigation, and proceed to impose administrative sanctions on the company.

[28] Ruihua Chen, "Basic Approaches to Effective Corporate Compliance Remediation," *Forum on Politics and Law*, no. 1 (2022).

CHAPTER 8

Regulatory Approaches to Promoting Corporate Compliance

8.1 Introduction

Corporate compliance refers to a system of risk prevention and control established by enterprises to avoid or mitigate violations of laws and regulations. Generally, companies may develop compliance management systems through two primary pathways. The first is a proactive approach, whereby the enterprise voluntarily initiates compliance efforts—motivated by the pursuit of competitive advantage, expanded business opportunities, or fulfillment of corporate social responsibility. The second is a reactive approach, in which the enterprise is prompted by the supervision, guidance, or pressure of administrative authorities, judicial institutions, or international financial organizations to establish a compliance framework, often through remedial measures in response to misconduct. These two modes of compliance development may be broadly categorized as autonomous compliance and externally driven compliance.[1]

Practical experience in corporate compliance management suggests that, in the absence of external pressure and oversight, enterprises often find it difficult to successfully implement autonomous compliance systems. This challenge arises primarily from a lack of strong supervisory mechanisms and expert guidance during the process of establishing such systems. Even when companies fail to develop effective compliance frameworks, they typically face no regulatory penalties. Likewise, enterprises that engage in compliance out of intrinsic motivation and manage to design relatively comprehensive compliance programs often receive little recognition or tangible reward. As a result, driven by rational choice considerations, the majority of enterprises undertaking autonomous compliance efforts tend to abandon them midway—ultimately producing only

[1] Ruihua Chen, "Two Models of Effective Compliance Management," *Law and Social Development*, no. 1 (2022).

R. Chen, *An Introduction to Corporate Compliance*,
https://doi.org/10.1007/978-981-95-7257-1_8

formalistic, paper-based compliance structures that are ineffective in mitigating compliance risks.

Compared to autonomous compliance, externally driven compliance enjoys notable institutional advantages. Administrative authorities, judicial bodies, and international financial institutions are able to provide companies with appropriate supervision and guidance, thereby offering the necessary incentives for enterprises to engage in meaningful compliance system development. However, the involvement of judicial authorities and international financial institutions in promoting corporate compliance typically occurs only after the enterprise is suspected of engaging in unlawful, irregular, or criminal conduct. In such cases, these institutions generally initiate compliance oversight or evaluation procedures, requiring the company under investigation to undertake compliance remediation measures. For instance, prosecutors may launch a compliance review procedure for an enterprise suspected of criminal wrongdoing, compelling it to design and implement a tailored compliance program. Similarly, international financial institutions—such as the World Bank—may require companies implicated in fraud or commercial bribery to establish integrity compliance mechanisms within a designated monitoring period. From the perspective of the enterprise, these interventions represent post-crisis compliance efforts, characterized by their remedial and retrospective nature. By contrast, in cases where no misconduct has occurred and the enterprise is not subject to criminal prosecution or international sanctions, judicial bodies and international financial institutions generally lack the institutional authority or procedural basis to directly supervise, guide, or promote the development of corporate compliance systems.

In contrast, administrative authorities can play a broader and more sustained role in promoting corporate compliance through regulatory oversight. Depending on the stage of compliance development, regulators may not only facilitate post-violation compliance reforms but also encourage or guide enterprises to undertake preemptive and ongoing compliance initiatives. Through such regulatory efforts, administrative bodies can advance the establishment or improvement of compliance management systems along three primary dimensions. The first is compliance guidance, wherein regulators issue compliance guidelines, model rules, or policy frameworks to provide enterprises with standardized references for designing and implementing their compliance systems. The second is mandatory compliance, which involves imposing legally binding obligations on enterprises—typically within specific regulated sectors—to establish compliance management structures. Where companies fail to fulfill these statutory duties, administrative authorities may impose legal liability for noncompliance. The third is incentivized compliance, whereby enterprises suspected of administrative violations are afforded the opportunity to obtain more lenient regulatory treatment in exchange for undertaking substantive compliance remediation. This typically involves a negotiated agreement, under which the enterprise makes binding compliance commitments, formulates and executes a tailored compliance program, and implements remedial measures.

Upon successful completion of compliance evaluation and acceptance, enforcement authorities may decide either to forgo administrative penalties altogether or to impose reduced sanctions.[2] By rewarding companies that complete compliance remediation, this framework not only strengthens regulatory incentives but also encourages other enterprises under investigation to actively pursue meaningful compliance reforms.

Following more than two decades of reform and institutional experimentation, the three principal modalities through which Chinese administrative authorities promote corporate compliance—namely, compliance guidance, mandatory compliance, and incentivized compliance—have largely matured and gained broad acceptance across all levels of government. Both central and local regulatory agencies have come to acknowledge the significant limitations and systemic flaws of traditional governance models characterized by punitive enforcement and campaign-style regulation. Against this backdrop, the incorporation of preventive and consultative regulatory approaches has increasingly been recognized as a necessary and inevitable evolution in administrative oversight. This transition is particularly salient in high-risk regulatory sectors such as antitrust enforcement, unfair competition, anti-commercial bribery, cybersecurity and data governance, environmental and natural resource protection, occupational safety, product quality assurance, and intellectual property rights enforcement. In these areas, conventional regulatory mechanisms have faced mounting challenges and diminishing efficacy. Consequently, a critical question now facing policymakers and scholars alike is how to further enhance the role of administrative authorities in fostering corporate compliance and to refine the institutional architecture of compliance-based regulatory governance.

This chapter undertakes a preliminary inquiry into the three primary modes of compliance-oriented regulation—namely, compliance guidance, mandatory compliance, and compliance incentives—building on a summary analysis and evaluative reflection of administrative regulatory practices in China. It aims to articulate the theoretical nature, categorical distinctions, and normative justifications of these regulatory approaches, while also identifying key implementation challenges. From the perspective of future institutional development, the chapter further proposes tentative directions for refining and advancing these mechanisms as part of a broader effort to modernize administrative compliance governance.

8.2 Administrative Compliance Guidance

Administrative compliance guidance constitutes the most regularized and institutionalized method by which regulatory authorities promote corporate compliance. It typically involves the issuance of compliance guidelines or regulatory advisories by administrative agencies, with the aim of assisting enterprises in

[2] Ruihua Chen, *The Chinese Experience of Effective Compliance*, Peking University Press, 2023, 213–218.

establishing or enhancing their internal compliance management systems. This form of guidance is grounded in the logic of preventive regulation—that is, the proactive mitigation of legal and regulatory risks by encouraging companies to adopt systems capable of preventing, monitoring, and responding to potential compliance failures. Such guidelines are generally recommendatory in nature rather than legally binding. Although they are designed to offer direction and serve as a reference point for enterprises seeking to establish or enhance their compliance management systems, they do not possess the force of law or impose enforceable obligations.

From the perspective of regulatory coverage, administrative compliance guidance can be classified into two categories: general compliance guidance and specialized compliance guidance. The former refers to broad-based regulatory instruments issued to assist enterprises in identifying and managing a wide array of compliance risks across all operational domains. The latter denotes targeted guidance designed to help enterprises address specific types of compliance risks within defined regulatory sectors. For instance, the compliance management measures issued by the State-owned Assets Supervision and Administration Commission (SASAC) for centrally administered state-owned enterprises, and the compliance guidelines jointly issued by the National Development and Reform Commission (NDRC) and other agencies for Chinese companies conducting overseas operations, are examples of general compliance guidance. By contrast, specialized compliance guidance includes industry- or issue-specific guidelines released by sectoral regulators such as financial supervisory authorities, the State Administration for Market Regulation (SAMR), and the Ministry of Commerce. These bodies have published tailored compliance instruments aimed at assisting financial institutions in mitigating financial compliance risks, securities firms in managing securities-related risks, general enterprises in addressing antitrust risks, and export-oriented companies in complying with export control regulations.[3]

From the perspective of regulatory hierarchy, administrative compliance guidance in China can be categorized into central-level and local-level initiatives. The former refers to nationwide guidance issued by central administrative authorities to address overarching regulatory needs, while the latter encompasses region-specific initiatives launched by local governments and their agencies to promote compliance management among enterprises within their respective jurisdictions. At the central level, ministries and commissions such as the State-owned Assets Supervision and Administration Commission (SASAC), the State Administration for Market Regulation (SAMR), the China Securities Regulatory Commission (CSRC), and the Ministry of Commerce have taken the lead in issuing comprehensive compliance guidelines to enterprises under their regulatory oversight. At the local level, administrative bodies—including local SASACs, market supervision authorities, and justice departments—have

[3] Ruihua Chen, *The Fundamentals of Corporate Compliance*, 3rd ed. (Beijing: Law Press, 2023), 181–184.

issued either general normative documents to guide enterprises in developing integrated compliance frameworks, or promulgated more targeted policy instruments. In particular, such localized measures often address risks in areas such as antitrust, data governance, unfair competition, intellectual property protection, and taxation, or focus on sector-specific compliance in industries such as pharmaceuticals, customs, fintech, e-commerce, chemical production, and food services.

Regardless of whether issued by central or local administrative authorities, compliance guidelines in China generally follow a similar structural template and encompass several core components: the normative value and guiding principles of compliance management, the organizational architecture for compliance oversight, sector-specific compliance programs, operational procedures, supporting enforcement mechanisms, and strategies for cultivating a culture of compliance. With respect to organizational architecture, these guidelines typically clarify the institutional roles and interrelationships among the board of directors, executive management, enterprise leadership, compliance committees, chief compliance officers (CCOs), and designated compliance departments in relation to compliance decision-making, monitoring, and implementation. Regarding targeted compliance management, the guidelines often delineate key compliance risk areas and establish baseline frameworks for the development of targeted compliance programs. In the operational domain, enterprises are generally expected to implement systems for risk identification and assessment, internal compliance review procedures, remedial protocols for addressing violations, whistleblower reporting mechanisms, and accountability frameworks for non-compliance. In terms of supporting mechanisms, the guidelines frequently require the establishment of institutional arrangements such as compliance commitments, compliance reporting structures, regular compliance evaluations, internal advisory procedures, incentive and disciplinary regimes, effectiveness assessments, and performance-linked compliance metrics. To promote a robust compliance culture, the guidelines emphasize exemplary leadership from top management, institutionalized compliance training programs, internal awareness campaigns, and formal compliance declarations by employees.[4] Some guidelines also enumerate typical risk scenarios through case studies tailored to specific industries or regulatory domains.[5] Others incorporate extensive references to statutory and regulatory provisions, providing enterprises with a detailed inventory of binding and prohibitory norms applicable to their operational activities—effectively functioning as sector-specific compliance obligation checklists.[6]

[4] State-owned Assets Supervision and Administration Commission of the State Council. *Measures for the Compliance Management of Central Enterprises*. Issued in 2022.

[5] State Administration for Market Regulation. *Anti-Monopoly Compliance Guidelines for Concentrations of Undertakings*. Issued in 2023.

[6] Beijing Municipal Administration for Market Regulation. *Compliance Guidelines for Advertising Release Behavior in Beijing*. Issued in 2023; Guangzhou People's Procuratorate, Guangzhou

At present, both central administrative authorities and local regulatory bodies in China increasingly view the issuance of compliance guidelines and regulatory advisories as a vital policy instrument for enhancing corporate supervision and promoting the institutionalization of enterprise compliance management systems. In practice, whenever a particular industry or sector experiences a surge in legal or regulatory violations—particularly in circumstances where conventional administrative oversight has proven inadequate—regulatory agencies tend to respond by issuing targeted compliance guidance. This approach has become a default strategy for reinforcing administrative governance and reasserting regulatory control. Why, then, have administrative authorities demonstrated such a strong institutional preference for expanding compliance-based regulatory guidance? This trend can be attributed primarily to three underlying factors.

First, the development and promulgation of compliance guidelines represent a cost-effective and administratively efficient form of regulatory intervention. In sectors where legal and regulatory violations persist despite repeated enforcement efforts, traditional governance approaches—such as deterrence-based punishment and campaign-style crackdowns—have largely lost their effectiveness. In such contexts, it has become practically unfeasible for regulatory authorities to eradicate or significantly reduce unlawful conduct within a short period of time. As a more pragmatic alternative, regulators have increasingly relied on industry-specific or issue-specific compliance guidance to steer enterprises toward the construction of internal compliance management systems and to promote the identification and control of key compliance risks. This regulatory strategy not only affirms the authorities' resolve to enhance corporate compliance governance, but also conveys a clear institutional signal that preventive and forward-looking regulatory supervision is becoming the dominant paradigm.

Second, the issuance of compliance guidelines by administrative authorities provides enterprises with an official model and a standardized procedural framework for developing and implementing compliance management systems. Compared with autonomous, self-initiated compliance efforts, state-issued guidance offers a uniform and authoritative policy framework that articulates the minimum institutional requirements for building a functional compliance infrastructure. These guidelines typically delineate the core components of a compliance system, including the adoption of formal compliance charters, the establishment of compliance leadership and governance structures, the identification of key compliance risk areas and sector-specific frameworks, the design of operational mechanisms for compliance implementation, and the development of institutional safeguards to support system effectiveness. In doing so, regulatory authorities provide enterprises with a foundational blueprint for structuring compliance management in line with public

Municipal Bureau of Commerce, and other regulatory authorities. *Compliance Guidelines for the Cross-Border E-Commerce Industry of Guangzhou (Trial)*. Issued in 2022.

regulatory expectations. Moreover, in some sectors, regulatory agencies further specify the substantive compliance obligations that enterprises must observe, thus ensuring that companies operate with a clear set of normative references. These detailed provisions also offer practical templates for drafting internal compliance policies and employee handbooks.

Third, the issuance of compliance guidelines enables administrative authorities to establish a foundational framework for the future implementation of mandatory compliance obligations and incentive-based compliance mechanisms. While such guidelines are generally non-binding and possess the characteristics of "soft law"—emphasizing advocacy, recommendation, and encouragement—they nonetheless serve as important normative references in regulatory practice. Whether conducting compliance performance assessments or determining administrative liability for regulated entities, authorities require evaluative benchmarks to assess whether a company has established an operational compliance management system and whether that system functions effectively. In this context, compliance guidelines function as preliminary evaluation standards, providing regulators with a framework for judgment. Should future legislation impose legally binding compliance duties on enterprises, administrative agencies would be able to invoke these guidelines as objective criteria for evaluating statutory compliance. Likewise, if the legal system strengthens compliance-based incentives, such as leniency or discretionary mitigation of administrative penalties, regulators could rely on these guidelines to assess the effectiveness of a company's compliance framework or remediation efforts, thereby using them as a direct basis for determining eligibility for favorable regulatory treatment.

However, due to persistent misconceptions regarding the normative function of compliance guidelines, as well as the lack of essential institutional support mechanisms, several structural issues have emerged in the current practice of administrative compliance guidance in China. Foremost among these is the prevailing tendency of regulatory authorities to adopt a philosophy of "comprehensive compliance" or "broad-scope compliance," which mandates the establishment of fully integrated, end-to-end compliance management systems encompassing all business units and operational processes. Notably, such guidance generally lacks adherence to a risk-based compliance approach.[7] Under this regulatory paradigm, compliance is often reduced to a formalistic exercise in rule adherence, with enterprises treating the compilation of regulatory obligations as the foundational task of compliance management. As a result, companies frequently identify numerous, and sometimes excessive, "priority compliance risk areas," and pursue the construction of compliance architectures that claim to cover "all dimensions," "all departments," and "every operational stage." In settings where enterprises operate with limited compliance resources and insufficient internal incentives, this model of compliance

[7] Zhile Wang. "Strengthening Compliance Management and Promoting Sustainable Development of Enterprises." *Shenzhen Rule of Law Review*, no. 3 (2020).

guidance inevitably hinders their capacity to identify and address systemic and imminent compliance risks. It impairs the development of targeted, proportionate risk control mechanisms, frustrates the core objective of effective risk mitigation, and often leads to patterns of "paper compliance" or structurally ineffective compliance frameworks.

Second, many of these compliance guidelines or regulatory advisories merely replicate generic compliance management structures, without establishing substantive criteria or scientifically grounded methodologies for evaluating the effectiveness of compliance programs. This gap inevitably produces a structural disconnect between compliance guidance, mandatory compliance obligations, and incentive-based compliance mechanisms. Consider, for instance, a scenario in which a mandatory compliance regime imposes legal obligations on enterprises to establish compliance systems. In the absence of defined effectiveness standards and operational evaluation methods, regulatory authorities would lack a credible basis for assessing whether a given compliance program is genuinely effective. Similarly, in a legal framework that incorporates compliance incentives, the absence of practicable and verifiable benchmarks for evaluating the outcomes of compliance remediation would seriously undermine the legitimacy and persuasiveness of any determination as to whether an enterprise qualifies for lenient administrative treatment.

Third, compliance guidelines or regulatory advisories issued by administrative authorities are generally non-binding and function merely as recommendatory standards. This lack of legal enforceability significantly diminishes their normative force and limits the ability of regulators to provide effective oversight or guidance to enterprises in establishing or improving their compliance management systems. Issuing such guidelines without the institutional means to ensure adherence is, in effect, akin to constructing the body of a carriage without attaching its wheels—the structure exists, but it cannot function. While these guidelines may offer enterprises useful policy frameworks, procedural standards, and operational models for compliance management, their widespread adoption in practice requires the support of corresponding institutional mechanisms. In addition to the mandatory compliance obligations and incentive-based mechanisms discussed in subsequent sections, regulatory authorities should also establish supporting tools such as compliance evaluation and acceptance procedures, third-party compliance certification systems, and licensing frameworks that treat adherence to compliance guidelines as a key criterion in regulatory decision-making. Unfortunately, both central and local administrative agencies in China have often adopted a "publish-and-forget" approach, whereby compliance guidelines are issued without any follow-up to monitor implementation or evaluate effectiveness. Rarely do regulators conduct compliance performance reviews or incorporate adherence to these guidelines into enterprise certification, regulatory assessments, or access-to-market qualifications. As a result, such guidance risks becoming purely symbolic, with compliance governance falling into a state of regulatory non-performance that fails to generate meaningful compliance outcomes.

8.3 Administrative Mandatory Compliance

Mandatory compliance constitutes another important mechanism through which administrative authorities promote the establishment of internal corporate compliance systems. Under a mandatory compliance regime, enterprises that meet certain statutory thresholds are legally required to implement and maintain compliance management frameworks. Failure to fulfill this obligation may subject enterprises to administrative liability. Once the obligation to establish a compliance system is codified in law, regulatory authorities are authorized to treat noncompliance—whether by omission or refusal—as an administrative violation. This, in turn, may trigger a range of enforcement actions, including the imposition of administrative sanctions, the revocation of market access qualifications, or, in severe cases, the suspension or cancellation of the enterprise's business license. Accordingly, mandatory compliance mechanisms are widely regarded as an effective form of administrative regulation that compels enterprises to institutionalize compliance structures.

As a form of administrative compliance regulation, mandatory compliance regimes exhibit three defining characteristics. First, relevant laws and administrative regulations impose a statutory obligation on enterprises to establish internal compliance management systems. These legal norms also provide for corresponding administrative liability in cases of noncompliance. On this basis, administrative authorities are authorized to supervise and verify whether enterprises have fulfilled their compliance obligations, and may impose administrative sanctions on noncompliant entities as well as on responsible individuals. Second, the mandatory compliance obligations imposed on enterprises typically fall into two distinct categories: a general obligation to develop a comprehensive compliance management system that addresses the full spectrum of major compliance risks to which the enterprise may be exposed; a specialized obligation to establish targeted compliance systems tailored to mitigating specific risks in defined regulatory domains. Third, based on these statutory mandates, administrative agencies are empowered not only to oversee the construction of compliance systems, but also to conduct acceptance reviews and effectiveness evaluations of such systems. Where enterprises fail to fulfill these obligations, or where their compliance frameworks are found to be inadequate, regulatory authorities may impose appropriate administrative penalties in accordance with law.

Of course, the application of mandatory compliance mechanisms is conditional. When designing such regimes, legislative bodies typically consider multiple factors, including the size of an enterprise's workforce, its annual revenue, the characteristics of the industry in which it operates, and the nature of its business activities. Particular emphasis is placed on whether enterprises operating in specific sectors or engaging in particular business types are exposed to major compliance risks that are structural, urgent, and widespread. As a general rule, in line with the principles of proportionality and necessity, statutory obligations to establish compliance management systems are imposed only on enterprises that simultaneously meet two criteria: they operate in industries or regulatory domains identified as high-risk or sensitive; and they exceed legally defined thresholds with respect to employment scale or business turnover. On this legal basis, administrative authorities are authorized to selectively implement mandatory compliance regimes targeting enterprises that meet these conditions.

France is among the earliest countries to establish a mandatory corporate compliance regime, which currently applies primarily to compliance programs aimed at preventing corporate corruption. Enacted in 2016, the *Sapin II Law* (Loi Sapin II) created the French Anti-Corruption Agency (Agence française anticorruption, AFA), the authority tasked with overseeing the prevention and monitoring of corruption within companies. The law introduced two distinct types of mandatory compliance mechanisms: criminal mandatory compliance, and administrative mandatory compliance. Under the criminal compliance framework, companies found to have committed acts of bribery may be ordered by a court to establish an anti-corruption compliance program within a legally prescribed timeframe. The AFA is responsible for supervising and assisting the implementation of such programs and must report regularly to the public prosecutor on the company's progress. If the company fails to meet the compliance requirements, the court may impose fines on both the legal entity and its senior executives, and may sentence individual offenders to up to two years of imprisonment. Under the administrative compliance framework, companies that are not subject to criminal proceedings but meet certain statutory thresholds are nonetheless legally obligated to establish and implement anti-corruption compliance programs. The AFA is similarly responsible for overseeing compliance efforts in these cases.

Pursuant to the *Sapin II Law*, a company is required to implement an anti-corruption compliance program if it meets both of the following conditions: it employs more than 500 individuals, either as an independent legal entity in France or as part of a group whose parent company is headquartered in France and employs more than 500 people globally; and it generates annual revenues exceeding €100 million. Companies that satisfy these thresholds but fail to comply with the legal obligation to implement a compliance program may be subject to administrative fines of up to €1 million, and their executives may incur personal financial penalties of up to €200,000. Furthermore, the AFA is authorized to require such companies or their executives to bring their compliance programs into conformity with legal requirements within a period not exceeding three years.[8]

To ensure the effective implementation of the administrative mandatory compliance regime, the *Sapin II Law* sets forth seven core components for corporate anti-corruption compliance programs. These include the adoption of a code of conduct to prohibit corrupt practices, the establishment of an

[8] Ruihua Chen, "The Sapin II Law and Corporate Compliance in France," *China Lawyer*, no. 5 (2019).

internal whistleblowing mechanism for reporting corruption-related concerns, the regular assessment of corruption risks, the implementation of internal and external accounting control procedures, the development of anti-corruption compliance training programs, the creation of a disciplinary system applicable to corruption-related violations, and the establishment of internal monitoring and evaluation mechanisms.[9] In 2020, building on the practical experience gained from the enforcement of mandatory compliance requirements, the French Anti-Corruption Agency (AFA) released a comprehensive *Anti-Corruption Compliance Guidelines*. This document identifies the principle of proportionality as the core normative foundation of corporate anti-corruption compliance and articulates three foundational pillars of an effective compliance framework: a demonstrable commitment to anti-corruption from senior management, the systematic identification of corruption risks specific to the organization, and the implementation of risk-based mitigation mechanisms tailored to those identified risks.[10]

Compared with administrative compliance guidance mechanisms, mandatory compliance measures imposed by administrative authorities can serve as a more forceful regulatory instrument in promoting the development of corporate compliance management systems, primarily in three respects. First, by employing mandatory compliance as a tool of enforcement, administrative authorities can exert substantial regulatory pressure on enterprises that are under a legal obligation to establish compliance systems. Pursuant to statutory requirements, authorities may compel such enterprises to fulfill their duties to implement compliance management frameworks, and may conduct legally grounded supervision, guidance, directives, and inspections. Facing such external regulatory pressure, enterprises—guided by rational incentives to avoid penalties and preserve reputational and economic interests—often respond by transforming compliance from a passive obligation into a proactive internal management initiative.

Second, when combined with substantive compliance guidance, the implementation of mandatory compliance regimes can more effectively compel enterprises to establish and maintain meaningful compliance management systems. For enterprises subject to statutory compliance obligations, administrative authorities may mandate the establishment of at least a baseline compliance management framework in accordance with officially issued compliance guidelines or regulatory provisions. Authorities may also conduct inspections, acceptance reviews, and performance evaluations to assess the actual effectiveness of such frameworks. This mechanism helps prevent enterprises from engaging in perfunctory or formalistic compliance efforts, and instead promotes the

[9] Yuanhuang Zhang et al., eds., *Global Survey on Corporate Compliance* (Beijing: Peking University Press, 2021), 95–96.

[10] Ruihua Chen, *The Chinese Experience of Effective Compliance* (Beijing: Peking University Press, 2023), 279–283.

adoption of substantive, risk-based compliances that are capable of addressing and mitigating specific regulatory risks in a targeted and effective manner.

Third, administrative liability may be imposed on enterprises that refuse to fulfill their compliance obligations or fail to pass assessments of compliance effectiveness. In such cases, both the enterprises and the responsible individuals may be subject to administrative sanctions. This form of enforcement serves not only as a credible deterrent but also as a preventive mechanism, incentivizing enterprises to draw lessons from regulatory failures and to expedite the establishment or improvement of their compliance management systems in order to satisfy regulatory expectations.

Taken together, these three dimensions demonstrate that, when properly implemented, mandatory compliance regimes can exert substantial institutional pressure on enterprises, thereby serving as a powerful catalyst for the development of effective and robust compliance infrastructures.

China has initiated preliminary efforts to implement an administrative mandatory compliance regime. This model was first applied in the field of securities regulation and has subsequently been extended to other regulatory domains, including cybersecurity, data and personal information protection, telecommunications, and financial services. In 2017, the China Securities Regulatory Commission (CSRC) promulgated the Administrative Measures for the Compliance Management of Securities Companies, requiring that all securities firms and securities investment fund management companies established within China implement comprehensive compliance management systems and establish dedicated compliance departments. For enterprises that fail to establish or maintain effective compliance frameworks, the CSRC is authorized to adopt a range of coercive administrative measures, such as issuing warning letters, requiring the submission of periodic compliance reports, ordering corrective actions, and conducting regulatory interviews. Where enterprises violate compliance obligations at various stages of internal governance—for example, by failing to appoint adequate compliance personnel, conducting improper compliance performance assessments, paying compliance officers below the company average, or making significant business decisions without prior compliance review—the CSRC may issue formal rectification orders, require the submission of remedial action reports within a prescribed timeframe, or issue official warnings. In some cases, administrative fines may be imposed, and individuals directly responsible may also be subject to administrative sanctions.[11]

Subsequently, in order to enhance regulatory governance over key domains such as cybersecurity, data security, personal information protection, telecommunications, and e-commerce, Chinese law has introduced a preventive regulatory framework that imposes statutory obligations on relevant enterprises to establish targeted compliance management systems. Enterprises that refuse to

[11] Zhiyong Xie. "Ideas for Constructing the System of Corporate Compliance Governance in Administrative Law." *Science of Law (Journal of Northwest University of Political Science and Law)*, no. 3 (2023).

fulfill these obligations may incur administrative liability, both corporate and individual. For example, under the *Data Security Law*, data processors are required to implement comprehensive data security governance systems, conduct security awareness training, and ensure the overall security of data processing activities. They must also strengthen risk monitoring mechanisms, promptly address vulnerabilities and systemic defects, take emergency response measures in the event of data security incidents, and conduct regular risk assessments throughout the data lifecycle.[12] Under the *Personal Information Protection Law*, personal information processors that provide internet platform services—particularly those with a large user base and complex business models—are required to establish a robust personal information protection compliance system. They must also establish independent supervisory bodies, primarily composed of external experts, to oversee compliance implementation. In addition, they are obligated to formulate platform governance rules, suspend services to providers that engage in serious legal violations, and publish periodic reports on their performance of personal information protection responsibilities.[13] Similarly, under the *Anti-Telecom and Online Fraud Law*, enterprises engaged in telecommunications, financial, or internet-based services are mandated to assume risk prevention responsibilities, establish internal control and accountability mechanisms, and conduct fraud risk assessments, particularly for emerging or high-risk business models. Financial institutions that fail to implement effective internal controls, perform due diligence, apply risk management protocols, or monitor and respond to abnormal accounts or suspicious transactions are subject to legal sanctions. Likewise, telecom operators and internet service providers that fail to establish internal controls, enforce real-name registration policies or verification protocols, or fulfill duties related to risk monitoring, identification, and mitigation may also be held legally liable.[14] These laws collectively establish a punitive legal framework targeting enterprises that fail to fulfill statutory obligations related to data security, personal information protection, and anti-fraud internal controls. Administrative authorities are empowered to issue orders for rectification, deliver formal warnings, and impose financial penalties. In cases of non-compliance or where significant harm has occurred, regulators may impose substantial fines, order suspension of business operations, mandate internal restructuring, or even revoke business licenses or operational permits. Individuals directly responsible may also be subjected to personal administrative fines.

It is fair to say that China's legal and regulatory framework has, in sectors such as securities, cybersecurity, data security, and personal information protection, begun to establish a system of mandatory compliance, or has introduced

[12] Standing Committee of the National People's Congress. *Data Security Law of the People's Republic of China*. Adopted in 2021, arts. 29, 30.

[13] Standing Committee of the National People's Congress. *Personal Information Protection Law of the People's Republic of China*. Adopted in 2021, art. 58.

[14] Standing Committee of the National People's Congress. *Anti-Telecom and Online Fraud Law of the People's Republic of China*. Adopted in 2022, arts. 40, 41.

preventive regulatory mechanisms with quasi-mandatory administrative features. These mechanisms impose statutory obligations on enterprises in the relevant sectors to develop compliance management systems or security governance frameworks, while also authorizing administrative authorities to supervise and guide their implementation. Enterprises that fail to fulfill such obligations or fall short of established compliance standards may be subject to administrative penalties. To a considerable extent, the emergence of this administrative mandatory compliance regime represents a shift from a purely external regulatory paradigm toward a model that also emphasizes internal and self-regulation by major platform enterprises in sectors such as telecommunications, internet services, and banking. This development enables legal and regulatory mandates to be more effectively transmitted, internalized, and operationalized within those enterprises responsible for critical security governance functions. In turn, this facilitates a more integrated and coordinated system of co-regulation, which bridges external oversight with internal compliance, helping to remedy the deficiencies and blind spots of traditional supervisory approaches.

Admittedly, the development of mandatory administrative compliance mechanisms under Chinese law remains in its early stages, and the scope of their application by administrative authorities is still quite limited. Currently, the legal provisions governing such mechanisms are fragmented and dispersed across multiple regulatory instruments, and a systematic and coherent framework for mandatory compliance has yet to be established. In most cases, the obligations imposed on enterprises—particularly those operating in cybersecurity, data security, and personal information protection—contain elements of compliance governance, but do not constitute well-defined or comprehensive compliance obligations in the institutional sense. Moreover, while incorporating the notion of mandatory compliance, the law has not yet introduced basic normative standards for what constitutes an effective compliance program, nor have administrative authorities been equipped with objective tools or methodologies for assessing the actual effectiveness of corporate compliance efforts. In essence, mandatory compliance holds great potential as a regulatory instrument—if applied properly, it can become a powerful institutional resource for promoting the structured and professionalized development of corporate compliance systems. This regulatory need is particularly acute in industries where legal violations are frequent, such as data services, financial markets, pharmaceuticals, and construction. In these high-risk sectors, the enforcement of mandatory compliance obligations is both necessary and urgent. Nevertheless, even within these sectors, it would be neither necessary nor advisable for administrative authorities to pursue a uniform, across-the-board approach. Instead, drawing on the French regulatory experience, Chinese authorities could establish differentiated thresholds for the applicability of mandatory compliance obligations—based on objective criteria such as workforce size and annual revenue. In this way, enterprises with substantial scale and market influence within a given sector would be legally required to build compliance management systems, thereby serving as benchmarks and exemplars of compliance governance.

8.4 Administrative Compliance Incentives

As an important tool for advancing corporate compliance, administrative compliance incentives refer to a regulatory mechanism under which administrative authorities—once an enforcement investigation has been initiated—may grant lenient administrative treatment to enterprises that have either established or committed to establishing an effective compliance management system. Traditional administrative enforcement has largely relied on a punitive model, emphasizing deterrence through severe penalties and strict sanctions. In contrast, the compliance incentive mechanism introduces a model of "compliance-for-leniency," whereby enterprises that undertake meaningful compliance remediation, implement effective compliance programs, and demonstrate an ability to prevent the recurrence of similar violations may receive reduced or waived administrative penalties. This incentive-based approach is intended to encourage enterprises to actively build internal compliance systems and to motivate more enterprises under investigation to commit to compliance transformation.

8.4.1 Typology of Compliance Incentives

In the context of administrative enforcement, compliance incentives can generally be classified into ex-ante, interim, and ex-post incentives, depending on both the timing of the enterprise's misconduct and the form of leniency granted by the administrative authority. Ex-ante compliance incentives refer to lenient administrative treatment granted to enterprises that had already implemented a compliance management system before the occurrence of any regulatory violation. In practice, enterprises may proactively establish such systems—motivated by goals such as enhancing market competitiveness, attracting high-value clients, or expanding business opportunities—and may operate under a genuinely effective compliance framework. When a violation later occurs, the administrative authority may, taking into account the effectiveness of the enterprise's pre-existing compliance program, decide to waive or reduce penalties, thereby enabling the enterprise to avoid serious losses or mitigate adverse consequences.

China's 2017 revision of the Anti-Unfair *Competition Law* preliminarily established an ex-ante compliance incentive mechanism. Under this law, when an employee of a company engages in commercial bribery, the misconduct is generally attributed to the employer, and the enterprise is presumed to bear administrative liability. However, if the enterprise can present evidence showing that the employee's conduct was unrelated to securing business opportunities or competitive advantages for the enterprise, it may be exempted from such liability. According to conventional legal doctrine, employers are subject to strict administrative liability for unlawful acts committed by employees in the course of performing their duties. Nevertheless, if the enterprise can demonstrate that it had established and implemented an effective compliance program, this may serve as compelling evidence that the employee's conduct was not aimed at benefiting the enterprise, but instead constituted a personal act, for which the employee alone should bear legal responsibility.[15] In substance, this provision creates a mechanism of compliance-based exemption from enterprise liability, which functions as an ex-ante incentive by encouraging companies to proactively adopt internal compliance systems prior to any regulatory infraction.

The concept of interim compliance incentives refers to cases where, following the occurrence of an administrative violation, an enterprise proactively implements institutional remediation measures—such as establishing or improving its compliance management system—in order to obtain lenient treatment from the enforcement authority. As the term suggests, interim compliance refers to self-initiated compliance remediation undertaken after the violation but before any formal regulatory intervention. Unlike ex-ante compliance, interim compliance does not involve the prior existence of a compliance program. Nor is it equivalent to ex-post compliance, which is typically carried out under the supervision or instruction of administrative authorities. Instead, interim compliance measures are independently initiated by the enterprise as an autonomous response to regulatory risk. In practice, enterprises pursuing interim compliance often conduct internal investigations to identify the underlying structural and systemic causes of the violation. They may impose disciplinary measures on directly responsible individuals, remedy deficiencies in internal management mechanisms, and introduce targeted compliance systems to address specific risks and prevent recurrence.

Interim compliance incentives typically arise when an enterprise independently undertakes compliance remediation measures in response to its own regulatory violation. Once an administrative enforcement procedure is initiated, enforcement authorities may consider the enterprise's proactive remedial efforts as a basis for granting lenient administrative treatment, including the possibility of waiving or reducing penalties. As of now, due to the absence of a widely institutionalized ex-post compliance incentive mechanism in China's administrative enforcement system—and in the absence of a systematic legal framework for administrative settlement agreements or compliance supervision programs—most compliance incentives extended to enterprises by administrative authorities continue to take the form of interim compliance incentives in practice.

Ex-post compliance incentives refer to a regulatory mechanism in which, after an administrative violation has occurred and enforcement proceedings have been initiated, an enterprise voluntarily acknowledges its misconduct,

[15] Jiangping Xiao, "Main Progress in the New Anti-Unfair Competition Law," *China Market Regulation Studies* 12 (2017).

cooperates with the investigation, and formally commits to undertaking compliance remediation. In such cases, the administrative authority may launch a compliance supervision and evaluation process, set a compliance monitoring period, and require the enterprise to establish or enhance a compliance program. Based on the outcome of the compliance assessment, the authority may subsequently decide to grant lenient administrative treatment. In practice, enterprises suspected of administrative violations—regardless of whether a prior compliance system was in place—may be eligible for mitigated penalties if they make a binding commitment to compliance reform, accept administrative oversight, and successfully pass the compliance evaluation process. Such compliance remediation, conducted under the supervision and direction of the administrative authority, is referred to as ex-post compliance, while the corresponding leniency offered upon its successful completion is termed an ex-post compliance incentive.

In 2015, the China Securities Regulatory Commission (CSRC) piloted an "administrative settlement" mechanism, under which securities firms found to have committed regulatory violations could avoid administrative penalties by promptly paying a settlement amount and implementing corrective measures, leading to the termination of the enforcement investigation.[16] With the 2017 amendment to the Securities Law, this administrative settlement mechanism was formally transformed into an "administrative enforcement commitment" regime, which was subsequently codified into statutory law. To date, Chinese legislation has established this commitment-based mechanism in areas such as antitrust enforcement and securities regulation.[17] However, its implementation has been largely confined to central regulatory authorities, and it has not yet been extended to the administrative enforcement practices of local-level agencies. In practice, when enforcement procedures are initiated by the CSRC or the State Administration for Market Regulation (SAMR), enterprises under investigation that acknowledge wrongdoing, pay a commitment sum, and undertake to rectify the violation may become eligible for suspension of the enforcement process. If the enterprise subsequently remedies the unlawful conduct within a prescribed time frame, compensates affected parties, and eliminates adverse consequences, the administrative authority may decide to terminate the investigation. Nonetheless, actual cases involving the use of commitment-based enforcement remain relatively rare. Furthermore, it remains unclear whether such procedures allow for the integration of compliance remediation mechanisms, and whether administrative authorities are authorized—or required—to supervise, evaluate, guide, or verify the compliance efforts undertaken by enterprises. No comprehensive experimentation or institutionalization of such supervisory functions has been initiated by

[16]Gang Xiao. "Actively Exploring a New Model of Administrative Settlement in Regulatory Enforcement." *Administrative Management Reform*, no. 1 (2014).

[17]Youyong Zhou. "The Construction of the Corporate Compliance Agreement System under the Concept of Contractual Administration." *Law Forum*, no. 3 (2021).

regulatory bodies to date. Accordingly, there remains both theoretical debate and practical uncertainty as to whether China's current administrative settlement and administrative enforcement commitment regimes can be considered to have formally introduced a model of ex-post compliance incentives.

8.4.2 *The Non-Penalty Regime for First-Time Violations*

Thus far, China's legal framework has only introduced compliance-incentive mechanisms in a limited number of sectors, notably in relation to major administrative violations in areas such as securities regulation and antitrust enforcement. These mechanisms have been primarily implemented by central administrative authorities. However, with the enactment of the revised *Administrative Penalty Law* in 2021, certain local administrative agencies have begun to explore the incorporation of compliance remediation into enforcement practices for minor violations, using the law's "no penalty for first-time violations" provision as a legal foundation. This trend marks a significant and innovative step toward embedding compliance-based incentives into local-level administrative enforcement.

The establishment of the Non-Penalty Regime for First-Time Compliance Violations in China's *Administrative Penalty Law* is widely regarded as a major reform aimed at implementing the principle of combining punishment with education, lowering the cost of administrative enforcement, promoting tolerant and prudent regulation, and further optimizing the business environment.[18] According to this regime, both enterprises and individuals may be exempted from administrative penalties if the violation is a first offense, the resulting harm is minor, and prompt corrective measures are taken. In cases involving corporate administrative violations, three cumulative conditions must be satisfied to qualify for such leniency: the enterprise must be a first-time violator; the violation must have caused only minimal harm; and the enterprise must have taken timely corrective action. Regarding the first condition, local administrative authorities across the country have adopted varying standards and formulated "exemption lists" that generally define a "first-time violation" as the initial infraction committed by an enterprise within a specific geographic jurisdiction and within a designated annual or multi-year period. As to the second condition, whether the harm is considered minor is typically assessed based on factors such as the frequency of violations, the amount of unlawful gain, the presence of subjective intent or malice, and the actual consequences caused. The third condition—timely correction—is commonly interpreted to require the enterprise to cease the unlawful conduct, mitigate or eliminate the harmful effects, or take restorative measures prior to the issuance of an administrative penalty decision. Nonetheless, many legal scholars have noted that the criteria for applying this exemption remain ambiguous under the current law, leaving

[18] Hong Zhang and Yang Yue. "The 'No Penalty for First Violation' Administrative Sanction System and Its Improvement." *Economic and Trade Law Review*, no. 3 (2021).

substantial room for administrative discretion in enforcement.[19] In particular, the requirement of "timely correction" has proven difficult to operationalize in practice.[20] In recent years, administrative authorities across different regions have pursued reforms in regulatory governance, experimenting with ex ante regulatory frameworks that place corporate compliance frameworks at their core. A key issue has thus arisen: if an enterprise, prior to the occurrence of the violation or before the penalty decision is issued, implements effective compliance remediation measures that demonstrably reduce the risk of repeat offenses, can such action be deemed "timely correction" within the meaning of the law? To date, neither the *Administrative Penalty Law* itself nor the explanations provided by its drafters has offered a clear interpretation of this issue.

Administrative authorities in Yinzhou District of Ningbo City, Zhejiang Province, became the first in China to pilot a Non-Penalty Regime for First-Time Compliance Violations under the framework of the *Administrative Penalty Law*. By integrating corporate compliance remediation with the "first violation exemption" mechanism, the district introduced a compliance incentive model into the handling of minor administrative infractions. Under this regime, the outcome of a compliance assessment may serve as a basis for waiving or mitigating administrative penalties against the offending enterprise. According to the policy, an enterprise that commits a minor violation for the first time, causes only limited harm, and promptly takes corrective measures may be eligible for compliance-based leniency—provided it satisfies several conditions: truthfully disclosing the facts of the violation; voluntarily submitting relevant evidence; maintaining normal business operations; committing to establishing or improving its internal compliance system; and consenting to regulatory inspections and oversight. If these conditions are met, the administrative authority may initiate compliance proceedings for the enterprise. Drawing on the institutional experience of prosecutorial compliance reform, the Yinzhou market regulation authority introduced a pre-assessment mechanism to determine whether the enterprise qualifies for compliance-based supervision. Once deemed eligible, the enterprise is required to submit a compliance improvement plan and is then subject to a 60- to 90-day compliance remediation period under regulatory supervision. At the end of the remediation period, authorities conduct a formal assessment of the effectiveness of the compliance measures undertaken. If the enterprise passes the compliance evaluation, the market regulation authority may issue a decision to exempt it from administrative penalties or to impose a reduced sanction.[21]

[19] Cheng Chen. "Existing Problems and Regulatory Approaches of the Ecological Environment 'No Penalty for First Violation' System." *Journal of Nanjing University of Technology (Social Sciences Edition)*, no. 2 (2023).

[20] Guohua Jiang et al. "'No Penalty for First Violation': Legal Principles and Application." *Hubei Social Sciences*, no. 3 (2021).

[21] *Guidelines for Corporate Compliance Work in the Market Regulation Field of Yinzhou District, Ningbo City (Trial)*. Published on the official WeChat account of the Binjiang District Corporate Compliance Promotion Association, August 7, 2023.

This pilot reform of the Non-Penalty Regime for First-Time Compliance Violations represents a locally developed administrative incentive mechanism grounded in national legislation and constitutes a significant step toward advancing corporate compliance management in China. Although the *Administrative Penalty Law* establishes the general framework for exempting first-time offenders from administrative sanctions, it fails to provide a clear definition of the prerequisite condition of "timely correction." According to the interpretation adopted by administrative authorities in Yinzhou District, Ningbo City, the notion of "timely correction" encompasses not only conventional remedial actions—such as truthfully disclosing the facts of the violation, actively cooperating with the investigation, voluntarily compensating for any harm caused, and ceasing the unlawful business conduct—but also a range of compliance remediation measures. These include a voluntary commitment to implement compliance measures, the articulation of preliminary compliance remediation strategies, and the submission of a formal compliance plan. In essence, when enterprises undertake corrective actions related to codes of conduct, organizational structures, compliance mechanisms, and compliance culture—particularly those aimed at identifying, preventing, and addressing compliance risks—such efforts substantively fulfill the requirement of timely correction. Interpreting compliance remediation in this way not only aligns with the legislative purpose of the *Administrative Penalty Law* but also marks a meaningful development in integrating compliance incentives into the Non-Penalty Regime for First-Time Compliance Violations.

8.4.3 *Institutional Advantages of Compliance Incentives*

At present, Chinese law has yet to establish a comprehensive and systematic framework for administrative compliance incentives. As a result, the institutional space available for administrative authorities to promote the development of corporate compliance systems through incentive-based mechanisms remains limited. However, regulatory trends in several Western jurisdictions suggest that introducing compliance incentives—such as granting lenient treatment to enterprises that have implemented or pledged to implement effective compliance programs—can serve as a highly effective tool for encouraging the institutionalization of compliance frameworks within enterprises. In essence, as a regulatory policy instrument, administrative compliance incentives offer two key institutional advantages.

First, by offering leniency to enterprises that have adopted or committed to adopting compliance programs, administrative authorities can generate strong internal motivation for enterprises to establish robust compliance systems. In situations where no administrative violation has yet occurred or no enforcement action has been initiated, enterprises often lack sufficient incentive to engage in voluntary compliance efforts, which in turn diminishes the effectiveness of such efforts. The introduction of compliance incentives, however, reframes compliance as a rational strategy rooted in a cost-benefit analysis—allowing enterprises to exchange meaningful compliance remediation for lenient treatment and thereby avoid the most serious administrative sanctions. This incentive structure creates significant motivation for enterprises to pursue compliance as a means of maximizing both legal protection and reputational value. Once an enterprise's compliance program is recognized as effective by the administrative authority, it may be shielded from severe penalties or substantial economic losses—thereby receiving a concrete "compliance reward." This, in turn, may foster a broader cultural shift, encouraging potential violators and enterprises under investigation to actively pursue compliance as both a viable strategy and a worthwhile objective.

Second, the implementation of administrative compliance incentives enables enterprises to develop truly effective compliance management systems—avoiding the pitfalls of superficial, formalistic, or ineffective compliance. While enterprises may pursue "autonomous compliance" in the absence of crisis or enforcement pressure, such efforts frequently result in overly broad, generalized frameworks that fail to address the enterprise's specific and systemic compliance risks. A prominent example is the "comprehensive compliance systems" adopted by certain state-owned enterprises in China, which often focus on cataloguing legal obligations rather than constructing responsive, risk-based compliances. By contrast, an incentive-based compliance regime encourages enterprises to undertake targeted remediation measures that enhance their ability to prevent compliance risks, monitor business operations, and respond effectively to unlawful conduct. Whether compliance efforts are initiated before, during, or after regulatory intervention, administrative authorities typically conduct structured assessments to evaluate the design, implementation, and outcomes of the compliance program. Only those enterprises whose programs meet established effectiveness criteria are eligible for lenient administrative treatment; those failing to meet such standards may face more severe regulatory sanctions. As a result, enterprises operating under an incentive regime are more likely to submit to regulatory supervision, external review, and ongoing evaluation, and to implement targeted compliance programs that conform to standards set by administrative authorities. This helps ensure that compliance systems function substantively—as mechanisms for identifying, preventing, and correcting legal and regulatory violations. To a large extent, the three pillars of an effective compliance program—the effectiveness of its design, the effectiveness of its implementation, and the effectiveness of its outcomes—are shaped and reinforced by the administrative compliance incentive framework itself.

8.5 Reform Prospects

Compared with purely autonomous compliance efforts initiated by enterprises themselves, the establishment of compliance management systems under the proactive guidance and impetus of administrative authorities offers distinct institutional advantages and is more likely to achieve meaningful and effective compliance outcomes. In recent years, Chinese legislative bodies have gradually embraced the concepts of preventive regulation and collaborative regulation, incorporating elements of administrative compliance guidance, mandatory compliance measures, and compliance incentives into a range of laws and regulations. These developments have not only conferred a degree of authority on administrative agencies to strengthen compliance oversight, but have also expanded the institutional space for promoting corporate compliance practices. Nevertheless, it must be acknowledged that Chinese legislation in this area remains relatively conservative and underdeveloped. The legal framework has yet to deliver a robust normative response to the increasing societal demand for effective corporate compliance governance. Moreover, the role of administrative agencies in advancing enterprise compliance has received limited legislative attention and has not been endowed with sufficient legal authorization. Both central and local administrative authorities have, as a result, approached administrative compliance reform with considerable caution, demonstrating a stronger inclination to preserve the status quo rather than to engage in genuine innovation. This reticence can be attributed, on one hand, to the absence of a clear statutory foundation for more assertive or experimental compliance regulation. On the other hand, it also reflects a lack of institutional incentives and reform momentum, as well as apprehension about the potential risks associated with regulatory experimentation. In light of these challenges, it is necessary to undertake a comprehensive reassessment of existing administrative approaches to compliance promotion, to articulate a broader vision for legislative development in this domain, and to redesign the pathways through which administrative agencies can strengthen compliance regulation. In the discussion that follows, the author sets out several preliminary reform proposals regarding how administrative authorities might enhance their approaches to compliance guidance, mandatory compliance enforcement, and compliance incentives.

8.5.1 Reforming Administrative Guidance

In response to the growing tendency of administrative compliance guidance to become vague and overly generalized, it is essential to reform the way administrative authorities design and issue such guidance, with a view to enhancing its regulatory effectiveness and strengthening the supervisory and instructive functions of compliance guidelines and protocols.

First, through the issuance of compliance guidelines or formal compliance protocols, administrative authorities should direct enterprises to adopt a risk-based compliance, thereby avoiding the inherent limitations of a management-based compliance approach. Experience has shown that both central and local administrative authorities, in implementing what is often referred to as a "general compliance guidance" system, tend to promote the construction of comprehensive compliance management frameworks. These frameworks typically seek to ensure that enterprises operate in accordance with the law and relevant regulations, are premised on the exhaustive cataloguing of legal obligations, apply indiscriminately to all categories of compliance risks, and emphasize full-process, organization-wide compliance management—a model frequently described as broad-scope compliance. However, this compliance model is often overly ambitious in scope, fails to target key areas of compliance risk, and cannot be adequately supported due to limited organizational resources and capacity. Consequently, it tends to devolve into mere "paper compliance" or a formalistic exercise, falling short of producing substantive regulatory effects. To overcome the shortcomings of the management-based compliance model, administrative authorities should recalibrate their approach and progressively promote to enterprises a risk-based compliance framework. This specialized compliance model is oriented toward the prevention of specific compliance risks, grounded in systematic risk identification and assessment, organized around targeted compliance domains, and directed toward effective risk control and mitigation. Compared to broad and formalized compliance systems, this model—often developed organically through compliance remediation efforts arising from administrative enforcement cases—is significantly more targeted, pragmatic, and operationalizable. It has proven more effective in enabling enterprises to prevent, monitor, and respond to core compliance risks.

Second, administrative authorities should strengthen industry-specific compliance guidance by leveraging the institutional capacity and expertise of industry associations to promote the collective development of targeted compliance programs across groups of enterprises. Given the administrative costs associated with regulatory oversight, it is often unrealistic for authorities to require all enterprises within their jurisdiction to establish fully integrated, comprehensive compliance management systems. A more practical and effective approach, consistent with the principles of risk-based compliance, is for regulators to issue sector-specific guidance tailored to the systemic compliance risks prevalent in particular industries. In this regard, administrative authorities can collaborate with relevant industry associations to improve the quality and impact of compliance guidance in key sectors. For example, in the financial, securities, futures, and insurance sectors, regulators may issue anti-money laundering (AML) compliance guidelines; for pharmaceutical and healthcare companies facing elevated risks of commercial bribery, authorities may publish specialized guidance on anti-bribery compliance; and for large enterprises exposed to antitrust risks—such as those involving mergers, acquisitions, or the abuse of market dominance—authorities may support or mandate the adoption of industry-specific antitrust compliance protocols.

Third, in the course of providing compliance guidance, administrative authorities should not only urge enterprises to establish baseline compliance risk control systems but also issue clear and practicable standards for evaluating the effectiveness of compliance programs, thereby promoting more rigorous and scientific methods for assessing compliance performance. To achieve the core objectives of administrative compliance guidance, regulators—through the issuance of compliance guidelines—should articulate concrete and actionable compliance requirements, encompassing both a foundational compliance management platform and targeted compliance elements. Furthermore, authorities should progressively formulate and institutionalize standards for effective compliance, particularly by incorporating the three core benchmarks that have emerged from compliance remediation practices in regulated enterprises: the effectiveness of program design, the effectiveness of program implementation, and the effectiveness of program outcomes. These criteria should be clearly defined, refined, and standardized to serve as operational benchmarks guiding enterprises in the development and operation of robust compliance systems. In addition, administrative authorities should draw on proven practices from enterprises with mature compliance programs and actively promote streamlined and practical methods for evaluating compliance effectiveness. Such techniques may include random interviews, spot checks of transaction records, unannounced (fly-in) inspections, and simulated complaint testing. These tools are indispensable for preventing enterprises from adopting superficial or paper-based compliance and for ensuring that compliance programs are structured and implemented in a way that effectively identifies, prevents, and addresses legal and regulatory risks.

8.5.2 *Strengthening Mandatory Compliance*

To strengthen the mandatory compliance regime, it is essential to consider gradually introducing comprehensive compliance obligations for enterprises that either exceed a certain operational scale or are engaged in sectors characterized by significant compliance risks. For example, large-scale enterprises—such as those with more than 1000 employees, annual revenues exceeding RMB 100 million, those seeking public listing, or those involved in cross-border business activities—should be legally required under national legislation to establish internal compliance management systems. Furthermore, sector-specific mandatory compliance frameworks should be progressively implemented in industries where regulatory violations are more frequent. For instance, enterprises engaged in medical and pharmaceutical activities should be required to develop and maintain anti-commercial bribery compliance programs; companies operating in the construction and infrastructure sectors should be mandated to establish bidding and procurement compliance mechanisms; enterprises involved in mineral resource extraction and petrochemical operations should be required to adopt environmental and resource protection compliance programs; firms engaged in international trade or overseas business should be compelled to implement export control compliance frameworks; companies operating in the financial, securities, futures, and insurance sectors should be mandated to establish anti-money laundering (AML) compliance systems.

Second, enterprises that fail to fulfill their statutory obligation to establish a compliance management system should be subject to proportionate legal liability. Drawing on the implementation experience of France's mandatory compliance regime, enterprises that do not establish the required compliance systems within the prescribed legal timeframe should be subject to appropriate administrative penalties imposed both on the enterprise itself and on its responsible personnel. For enterprises that are unable to complete the establishment of a compliance system on time due to objective constraints, or whose compliance programs fail to pass evaluation and acceptance, regulators may order them to complete or improve their compliance systems within a specified period. Furthermore, enterprises that are repeatedly sanctioned over consecutive years for failing to meet their compliance obligations, or that fail to complete, enhance, or remediate their compliance systems within the timeframe set by the administrative authority, may be subject to more stringent administrative measures. Such measures may include restrictions on, or revocation of, the enterprise's operating licenses, franchise rights, or qualifications for public listing.

Third, strengthening the mandatory compliance regime also requires the introduction of a more scientific, rigorous, and evidence-based mechanism for compliance evaluation and acceptance. Building on improvements to the administrative compliance guidance framework, regulators should adopt the compliance management requirements, effectiveness standards, and evaluation methodologies issued by administrative authorities as the primary criteria for assessing enterprise compliance performance. Specifically, for enterprises that are legally obligated to establish compliance management systems, administrative authorities should implement a systematic and authoritative assessment mechanism to evaluate the fulfillment of such obligations. This may include establishing specialized compliance evaluation bodies, promoting standardized benchmarks for effective compliance, applying robust methodologies for assessing compliance effectiveness, and enhancing transparency and procedural fairness throughout the evaluation process. Furthermore, enterprises whose compliance programs fail to meet the prescribed standards should be afforded the opportunity to seek administrative remedies and to implement corrective measures, thereby ensuring that the evaluation process remains both fair and constructive.

8.5.3 *Enhancing Compliance Incentive Mechanisms*

Given the absence of a systematic administrative compliance incentive mechanism in China, it is imperative to develop a comprehensive framework for embedding compliance incentives into the country's regulatory architecture. On the one hand, it is necessary to establish a structured regime of ex-ante, interim, and ex-post compliance incentives that correspond to the specific stage at which an enterprise becomes suspected of administrative misconduct. On the other hand, the institutional design of ex-post compliance incentives should address both central and local enforcement practices, with tailored improvements introduced at each level. From the perspective of central administrative authorities, reforms should build upon the lessons learned from previous administrative settlement mechanisms and draw on the beneficial experiences of the existing administrative enforcement commitment system, with a view to gradually establishing a comprehensive framework for administrative settlement agreements. At the local administrative level, efforts should focus on expanding pilot programs for the "first violation compliance exemption" mechanism and progressively institutionalizing its application across the broader landscape of administrative enforcement. This would help strengthen incentive structures for enterprises involved in minor regulatory violations and encourage them to adopt meaningful compliance reforms in exchange for lenient treatment.

8.5.3.1 Establishing the Three-Tiered Compliance Incentive Mechanism

In designing ex-ante compliance incentives, it is essential to distinguish between systemic organizational violations and non-systemic violations, and to develop differentiated incentive mechanisms accordingly. The term systemic organizational violation refers to an administrative offense committed under the direction, instruction, acquiescence, or tacit authorization of the enterprise's decision-making body or senior management. In such cases, the enterprise is deemed to possess a unified institutional intent to commit the violation and, in principle, should bear administrative liability. However, enterprises may assert a compliance-based defense of non-liability, arguing that by having established and effectively implemented a relevant specialized compliance management system, they can demonstrate the absence of any such unified intent to commit wrongdoing. If this defense is successful, the administrative authority should exempt the enterprise from administrative liability.

By contrast, non-systemic violations refer to administrative offenses committed by ordinary employees, clients, agents, branch offices, or acquired entities operating within the corporate structure. Although these actors may have a legal agency relationship with the enterprise, their conduct does not necessarily reflect the unified institutional intent of the organization, nor is it always undertaken to advance the enterprise's interests. In such cases, the burden of proof rests with the administrative authority, which must demonstrate that the enterprise exhibited significant deficiencies or gaps in its compliance management system—such as managerial negligence, failure of oversight, or latent structural risks. Conversely, the enterprise may seek to achieve effective risk segregation by submitting evidence that it duly fulfilled its duties of care, prevention, and monitoring with respect to the relevant compliance risks, thereby demonstrating the absence of managerial fault or omission in its compliance governance. If such a defense is successfully established, the administrative authority should exempt the enterprise from administrative liability.

In the context of interim compliance incentive mechanisms, it is necessary to strengthen the degree of leniency afforded to enterprises that autonomously implement compliance remediation measures following the occurrence of a violation. Enterprises that proactively initiate such compliance measures in the aftermath of an unlawful incident effectively demonstrate the existence of a responsive risk management system capable of remedying and mitigating the consequences of regulatory breaches. This, in itself, constitutes compelling evidence of the enterprise's practical capacity to establish and maintain an effective compliance management system. At the same time, when enterprises independently undertake targeted compliance remediation efforts—without direct regulatory oversight—and develop internal control mechanisms addressing the relevant compliance risks, such actions can significantly reduce the costs of compliance supervision for administrative authorities and help achieve more optimal preventive outcomes. For these reasons, once the effectiveness of interim compliance remediation has been verified, administrative authorities should, wherever possible, grant exemption from administrative penalties as an incentive to encourage mid-process compliance efforts.

Compared to the previous two forms of compliance incentives, ex-post compliance incentives offer a significantly broader scope of application. In recent years, China's procuratorial authorities have implemented a series of criminal compliance reforms targeting enterprises suspected of criminal misconduct, gradually developing a relatively mature and effective set of institutional practices. Administrative authorities may draw on these experiences when designing and implementing ex-post compliance incentive mechanisms. For example, regulators could leverage the emerging institutional framework of the Third-Party Mechanism Management Committee to oversee the initiation of compliance supervision and assessment procedures by administrative agencies. Through this framework, qualified third-party organizations may be engaged to appoint compliance monitors responsible for supervising and guiding the compliance rectification process of enterprises under investigation. These monitors would subsequently issue compliance supervision reports that serve as the basis for regulatory evaluation and administrative decision-making. Furthermore, administrative authorities could establish monitoring periods to ensure that enterprises have sufficient time to address institutional deficiencies and build effective compliance management systems. Additionally, it would be beneficial to develop a public and transparent compliance assessment mechanism under which, in major cases, the Management Committee may convene public hearings to evaluate the effectiveness of an enterprise's compliance remediation efforts. With respect to substantive standards for assessing effective compliance, administrative authorities should also consider incorporating the evaluative criteria developed through the procuratorate's compliance reform experience, thereby establishing clear, specific, and operational benchmarks for determining compliance effectiveness.

8.5.3.2 Reconstructing the Compliance Incentive Mechanism of Central Administrative Authorities

To date, the "administrative settlement mechanism" piloted by the China Securities Regulatory Commission (CSRC) in 2015 has not evolved into a formalized system of administrative compliance incentives. Similarly, the "commitment-based administrative enforcement mechanism" subsequently promoted by both the CSRC and the State Administration for Market

Regulation (SAMR) has neither explicitly incorporated compliance remediation as a central component nor established corresponding mechanisms for supervision, assessment, and outcome evaluation. Furthermore, the relatively limited number of cases in which this mechanism has been applied makes it difficult to extract meaningful institutional lessons or best practices from its implementation. Accordingly, it can be concluded that, at the national level, central administrative authorities have not yet developed mature experience in systematically exploring, piloting, or institutionalizing administrative compliance incentive mechanisms.

In the future, drawing on the regulatory philosophies of preventive and negotiated supervision, it will be necessary to comprehensively introduce an administrative settlement agreement mechanism at the level of central administrative authorities. Under this framework, administrative regulatory bodies vested with the authority to impose administrative penalties may, in cases involving significant administrative violations, enter into an administrative settlement agreement with the enterprise under investigation—provided that the enterprise admits to the unlawful conduct, ceases the violation, actively undertakes remedial and loss-mitigation measures, and has made substantial contributions to society. Through dialogue and negotiation, the parties may agree that the enterprise, in addition to submitting a self-assessment compliance report, will develop a targeted compliance remediation plan. Upon review and approval of this plan, the regulatory authority may request the central-level Third-Party Mechanism Management Committee to initiate a compliance supervision and evaluation process. If the enterprise successfully completes the compliance remediation and passes the assessment conducted by the third-party organization, the administrative authority may decide to waive or reduce the applicable administrative penalties as a form of lenient treatment.

8.5.3.3 Comprehensive Promotion of Compliance Incentive Mechanisms by Local Administrative Authorities

At present, administrative authorities in certain economically developed regions have begun to experiment with the Non-Penalty Regime for First-Time Compliance Violations. From the perspective of local governance, it is necessary for administrative authorities to systematically evaluate the experiences accumulated through these pilot reforms and to gradually extend this mechanism to other jurisdictions. One potential approach would be to recognize enterprise compliance remediation as a key form of "timely correction" within the statutory framework of the *Administrative Penalty Law*, thereby providing a clear legal basis at the national level for piloting compliance supervision and assessment mechanisms targeting enterprises under investigation. It should be noted, however, that the "non-penalty lists" issued by various local administrative bodies indicate that this mechanism is, at present, primarily applied to minor administrative violations committed by enterprises. Looking ahead, as pilot reforms continue to deepen, local administrative authorities at all levels may consider extending the application of the Non-Penalty Regime for

First-Time Compliance Violations to cover more serious administrative violations committed by large-scale enterprises.

From a long-term perspective, the fundamental solution to the issue of fully legalizing the Non-Penalty Regime for First-Time Compliance Violations lies in further amending the *Administrative Penalty Law* to explicitly incorporate compliance remediation as one of the statutory conditions for applying such exemptions to enterprises under investigation. At the same time, the law should clearly specify the requirements for initiating a compliance supervision and assessment process, including the conditions for applicability, the procedures for initiation, the duration of the monitoring period, the methods of oversight by third-party organizations, and the procedures for evaluating and accepting compliance outcomes. Moreover, it should unambiguously establish that successful completion of compliance remediation—verified through an appropriate assessment process—constitutes a legal basis for exempting or mitigating administrative penalties. In this way, the ex-post compliance incentive mechanism would be formally enshrined in national legislation.

CHAPTER 9

Criminal Compliance Incentives I: Models of Compliance-Based Exculpation

9.1 Introduction

Against the backdrop of policies aimed at strengthening judicial protections for private enterprises, China's procuratorial authorities have begun to explore the implementation of a system of non-prosecution based on corporate compliance. Unlike the traditional model of discretionary non-prosecution—where the primary justification lies in the minor nature of the offender's conduct and the possibility of exemption from punishment under the Criminal Law—the core rationale for compliance-based non-prosecution is different. In this model, non-prosecution is contingent upon the enterprise's active cooperation and effective remediation: the company has established a corporate compliance program, carried out comprehensive reforms of its management systems, addressed institutional weaknesses and regulatory blind spots that facilitated the offense, and taken effective measures to prevent the recurrence of similar misconduct. Through compliance oversight and evaluation procedures, procuratorial authorities may ultimately decide not to prosecute enterprises that have established and operated an effective compliance program. The application of this compliance-based non-prosecution framework thus makes corporate compliance itself the direct legal basis for a decision not to pursue criminal liability, thereby conferring on compliance an important function of exculpation.[1]

However, in the process of exploring the system of corporate compliance-based non-prosecution, there remain divergent views within both the legal academy and the judicial community regarding whether, and to what extent, compliance should serve as a basis for exempting enterprises from criminal liability. Some scholars argue that, drawing on the experience of legal systems in Western countries and in view of the crime-preventive functions inherent in

[1] Ruihua Chen. "The Compliance Incentive Model in Criminal Procedure." *China Legal Science*, no. 6 (2020): 233.

R. Chen, *An Introduction to Corporate Compliance*,
https://doi.org/10.1007/978-981-95-7257-1_9

compliance management frameworks, corporate compliance should possess both substantive and procedural exculpatory functions. Substantively, they contend that compliance ought to constitute a statutory ground on which an accused enterprise can assert a defense of non-culpability. Procedurally, a decision by the procuratorial authority to grant non-prosecution on account of an enterprise's effective compliance measures, in itself, produces an "exculpatory effect." By contrast, other criminal law scholars maintain that once an enterprise has been found to have committed an offense, the subsequent establishment of a compliance system should, at most, serve as a basis for mitigating punishment, but not as a sufficient justification for declaring the enterprise not guilty. They draw an analogy to cases in which a natural person who has committed a criminal act cannot be absolved of liability merely because of post-offense repentance or efforts at reform. Some scholars even go further, contending that even in the context of compliance-based non-prosecution, compliance should not independently constitute the legal basis for exempting an enterprise from criminal responsibility. Rather, it should be considered only in conjunction with other factors—such as the minor nature of the offense, the enterprise's active cooperation in the investigation, and the implementation of effective remedial measures—which together may warrant a procuratorial decision not to prosecute.

In judicial practice, procuratorial authorities across different regions have articulated divergent interpretations regarding the function of corporate compliance. Some local procuratorates maintain that corporate compliance constitutes a procedurally complex and financially burdensome system of corporate governance, which should primarily be applied to large enterprises suspected of committing serious crimes, rather than to small and medium-sized enterprises involved in relatively minor offenses. Certain procurators have expressly argued that compliance-based non-prosecution should be distinguished from discretionary non-prosecution. In their view, for corporate offenses in which the directly responsible individuals are likely to receive sentences of up to three years' imprisonment, the procuratorial authority may directly apply discretionary non-prosecution without the necessity of imposing a compliance assessment process. By contrast, a considerable number of procuratorial authorities have adopted a relatively cautious stance toward piloting compliance-based non-prosecution. These authorities tend to regard compliance-based non-prosecution as merely a variant of discretionary non-prosecution and conceptualize corporate criminal liability as inseparable from the liability of responsible individuals. According to this perspective, compliance-based non-prosecution is appropriate only in cases where the directly responsible persons face potential sentences of no more than three years' imprisonment. For cases involving offenses where the responsible persons could be sentenced to more than three years, procuratorial authorities generally exclude such enterprises from compliance assessment procedures and, at most, consider compliance efforts as grounds for recommending leniency in sentencing.

In exploring the system of compliance-based non-prosecution, China's procuratorial authorities must indeed take into account the country's distinctive legal and institutional context, rather than simply transplanting the frameworks developed in the United States or Europe. For example, in cases involving suspected corporate crime, it is common practice in Western jurisdictions for prosecutors first to impose substantial fines on the enterprise and then to conclude deferred prosecution agreements (DPAs) or non-prosecution agreements (NPAs). However, such compliance assessment mechanisms—routinely employed in Europe and the United States—may not be readily applicable to China's circumstances.[2] Similarly, in the United States and many European countries, enterprises are treated as institutionally separate from their senior managers. Prosecutors may decide to forgo prosecution of the enterprise after compliance monitoring has verified that an effective compliance program has been implemented, while simultaneously pursuing criminal charges against the individuals directly responsible. This model of "exempting the enterprise but strictly punishing the responsible individuals" would be difficult to adopt in China. Under China's doctrine of corporate crime, the prosecution of directly responsible individuals is predicated on a finding that the enterprise itself has committed a criminal offense. If the enterprise is not determined to be criminally liable, there is no legal foundation for convicting and sentencing the responsible individuals.[3] Furthermore, in the United States and Europe, even enterprises suspected of serious offenses—such as large-scale commercial bribery, money laundering, or violations of personal data privacy—can enter into deferred prosecution agreements requiring them to establish or improve compliance management systems within a defined monitoring period. The prosecutor may then decide whether to forgo prosecution based on the effectiveness of the compliance measures undertaken. However, constrained by the fundamental principles of legality of punishment and proportionality between crime and punishment, Chinese procuratorial authorities cannot be vested with such broad discretionary power when applying compliance-based non-prosecution.[4] For enterprises suspected of especially serious criminal conduct, prosecutors cannot apply compliance-based non-prosecution at all and can, at most, treat compliance efforts as grounds for recommending leniency in sentencing.

Nevertheless, the experience in Europe and the United States—where compliance has been integrated into the criminal law framework and has been used to fully harness its incentivizing function—constitutes a legal development worthy of serious consideration. In reality, no enterprise is inclined to voluntarily adopt a costly and resource-intensive compliance management system, nor does any industry association possess the authority to compel companies to

[2] Yanan Shi. "Conditional Non-Prosecution in Corporate Criminal Cases and the Theory of Corporate Governance." *China Criminal Law Journal*, no. 3 (2020): 58.

[3] Jun Zhang, Wei Jiang, Sheng Lang, and Xingliang Chen. *A Comprehensive Discussion on Criminal Law*. Beijing: Law Press, 2003, 306.

[4] Ruihua Chen, "Deferred Prosecution Agreements in the Context of Corporate Compliance," *Journal of Comparative Law*, no. 1 (2020).

establish sophisticated compliance programs. Effective compliance initiatives are almost invariably built on the foundation of robust and credible incentive mechanisms. Among the currently recognized models, none are more impactful than the combination of administrative incentives provided by regulatory authorities and criminal incentives administered by prosecutorial agencies. For enterprises suspected of criminal conduct, the most powerful incentive lies precisely in the prospect that the procuratorial authorities will decide on lenient criminal treatment based on the effectiveness of the compliance measures undertaken. In practice, procurators have two principal mechanisms for activating this criminal incentive: first, by issuing a decision not to prosecute, thereby effectively exempting the enterprise from criminal liability; and second, by recommending a lenient sentence. By comparison, for an enterprise facing criminal charges, the possibility of achieving exculpation through compliance ("compliance-based exculpation") is considerably more compelling than the prospect of merely receiving a mitigated sentence. After all, once an enterprise is convicted, even if lenient punishment is imposed, the consequence is, at most, merely a reduction in the fine. In contrast, if an enterprise is declared not guilty, it not only avoids being stigmatized as a "criminal entity" and escaping criminal punishment altogether, but also avoids a series of severe collateral consequences, such as disqualification from licenses and qualifications, exclusion from government procurement and bidding processes, and the reputational damage inevitably associated with a criminal conviction.[5]

Precisely for this reason, as we explore the establishment of a compliance-based non-prosecution regime, it is essential to introduce a framework for compliance-based exculpation, thereby ensuring that a company's proactive efforts to implement compliance measures can serve as a legitimate ground for exempting it from criminal liability. Achieving such an institutional transformation requires a systematic theoretical analysis and justification of the concept and function of compliance-based exculpation. This chapter begins by distinguishing between two principal forms of corporate crime: systemic corporate crime and non-systemic corporate crime. Building on this distinction, I propose that compliance-based exculpation can itself be conceptualized in three discrete models: the "subjective fault exculpation model," the "statutory management duty exculpation model," and the "compliance assessment exculpation model." This chapter examines the constitutive elements and normative foundations of these three models and offers both predictions and critical commentary regarding the future evolution of China's criminal compliance regime. The core argument advanced here is that different forms of corporate crime should be matched with the corresponding model of compliance-based exculpation. In this way, corporate compliance can be fully established as a legal basis on which judicial authorities may exempt enterprises from criminal liability, thereby advancing the objectives of integrated social governance.

[5] Ruihua Chen, "Fundamental Issues of Corporate Compliance," *China Law Review*, no. 1 (2020).

9.2 Forms of Corporate Crime

To analyze the issue of compliance-based exculpation, it is first essential to distinguish between different forms of corporate criminality. As a legal entity endowed with a form of fictitious personality, a corporation is capable of independently incurring criminal liability. This institutional concept originated within the Anglo-American legal tradition. To date, Anglo-American law has primarily recognized two principles of corporate criminal liability: the doctrine of vicarious liability and the doctrine of identification. Under the former, a corporation is held criminally liable for offenses committed by its employees or agents acting within the scope of their employment and in furtherance of corporate interests. Under the latter, liability attaches through the acts and mental state of the corporation's senior representatives—namely, directors, managers, and other high-level agents—who commit offenses to benefit the corporation. Both attribution doctrines effectively impute the unlawful conduct of internal agents to the corporation itself. In practice, however, cases of this nature typically do not involve crimes that arise from collective decision-making processes within the corporation as an organized body.[6]

It was not until the late twentieth century that the framework of corporate criminal liability was formally established in several civil law jurisdictions. In both Italy and France, the design of corporate liability was influenced by the attribution principles developed in Anglo-American law, ultimately leading to the recognition of corporate criminal responsibility within continental legal systems. In France, under the doctrine of representation liability, a corporation may be held criminally responsible only for offenses committed by its governing bodies or representatives acting in pursuit of the corporation's interests. In Italy, Legislative Decree No. 231 of 8 June 2001 (hereinafter "Law 231") provides that individuals who exercise management powers and act on behalf of, or for the benefit of, the company will result in the company incurring legal liability for intentional criminal acts committed either domestically or abroad. Such individuals primarily include directors and managers who represent, effectively manage, or control the company, as well as persons acting under their direction and supervision. Law 231 explicitly stipulates that the adoption and effective implementation of a compliance program may exempt a corporation from criminal liability. However, this exculpation mechanism does not extend to situations involving systemic corporate crime. Accordingly, in Italy and comparable civil law jurisdictions, compliance-based exculpation primarily applies to offenses committed by persons who represent, manage, or control

[6] VP Nanda. "Corporate Criminal Liability in the United States: Is a New Approach Warranted?" Accessed September 21, 2019. https://link.springer.com/chapter/10.1007/978-94-007-0674-3_2; Crystal Jezierski. "Corporate Liability in U.S." Accessed September 21, 2019. https://globalcompliancenews.com/white-collar-crime/corporate-liability-united-states/

the enterprise, and does not encompass criminal conduct arising from systemic decisions or wrongdoing by the organization as a whole.[7]

In China, the Criminal Law has consistently rejected both the vicarious liability doctrine and the identification doctrine, and instead adheres to the principle of the unity of subjective and objective elements. Under this principle, the imposition of criminal liability on a unit (i.e., a legal person or other organization) requires demonstrating that the criminal conduct was committed in the name of the unit, for the purpose of advancing the unit's interests, and expressed the collective will of the organization itself. Typically, corporate crimes in China are understood to refer to offenses carried out either through collective decision-making by the organization or by resolution of its principal responsible persons. Regarding criminal acts perpetrated by individuals who represent, manage, or control an enterprise, there has been longstanding debate in both legal scholarship and judicial practice as to whether such conduct should automatically trigger criminal liability for the unit. As a matter of principle, the conduct of these individuals can be attributed to the organization only insofar as it reflects the collective will of the unit itself.[8]

Accordingly, whether under Anglo-American law, continental European law, or Chinese law, corporate crimes may generally be classified into two fundamental categories, depending on whether the conduct was carried out through collective decision-making or by authorization from within the enterprise itself: systemic corporate crime and *non-systemic corporate crime.*

Systemic corporate crime refers to socially harmful acts committed by an enterprise—as a legal-person commercial organization—based on either collective resolutions or determinations made by its principal responsible persons. This form of crime encompasses two specific subtypes. The first subtype involves offenses committed pursuant to collective decisions adopted within the enterprise. Typically, such crimes arise when a board of directors or senior management team deliberates and votes to engage in unlawful conduct. For example, if a company's board resolves to carry out smuggling, issue fraudulent VAT invoices, infringe trade secrets, pollute the environment, or manufacture and sell counterfeit pharmaceuticals, or if the management team decides to adopt illegal business models—such as unlicensed operations, the large-scale infringement of citizens' personal information, or the unlawful absorption of public deposits—these would all constitute systemic crimes based on collective organizational decision-making. The second subtype consists of systemic corporate crimes carried out on the basis of authorization or instructions issued by principal responsible persons. In these cases, the board or management team may not have formally adopted a collective resolution to engage in criminal

[7] Aurelio Giovannelli and Roberto Cursano. "Corporate Liability in Italy." Accessed September 6, 2019. https://globalcompliancenews.com/white-collar-crime/corporate-liability-in-italy/

[8] Liangfang Ye. "On the Morphological Structure of Corporate Crime: With Comments on the Separation of Corporate and Member Liability." *China Legal Science*, no. 6 (2008): 103; Hong Li. "Defining Corporate Intent in Corporate Crime." *Law Science*, no. 12 (2013): 158.

conduct, but the chairman, general manager, or other senior leaders nonetheless direct or authorize departments, subsidiaries, senior managers, employees, or third parties to commit illegal acts. For example, an enterprise may not have issued a collective decision to discharge pollutants, yet the chairman or general manager may instruct or permit subordinates to engage in such environmental violations. This too would fall within the scope of systemic corporate crime.[9]

Non-systemic corporate crime, by contrast, refers to circumstances in which, absent any collective decision of the enterprise or any authorization or instructions issued by its principal responsible persons, an internal actor—such as a senior executive, director, employee, subsidiary, or affiliated third party—commits a criminal act in the name of the enterprise and for the purpose of advancing its interests. Because the enterprise either tolerated, acquiesced in, or failed to take measures to prevent or correct such conduct, the act is attributed to the enterprise and treated as constituting corporate criminal liability.

Compared with systemic corporate crimes, the determination of non-systemic corporate crimes is more contested. Generally speaking, whether the perpetrator is a senior executive, an employee, a subsidiary, or a third party, it is seldom difficult to establish that the conduct was undertaken in the name of the enterprise or for the purpose of advancing its interests. So long as there is evidence demonstrating that such individuals exploited their involvement in the enterprise's operations with the intent to enhance its competitive advantage, expand its business opportunities, or improve its commercial performance, these two elements can typically be established without significant controversy. The greater challenge lies in assessing whether the individual's intent can be deemed to reflect the enterprise's overall subjective will. In this respect, Anglo-American law has developed a principle of strict liability: where an agent or senior representative commits a criminal act, the enterprise is presumed to bear criminal liability. While certain continental European jurisdictions have not formally adopted such a strict liability doctrine, they nonetheless accept that an enterprise may be held criminally accountable for offenses committed by those who represent, manage, or control it. Chinese criminal law does not recognize the principle of strict liability. Nevertheless, in practice, when adjudicating whether a criminal act committed by internal management personnel gives rise to corporate criminal liability, courts and prosecutors often apply a presumption of subjective intent. Under this approach, if the enterprise fails to take measures to prohibit, rectify, or prevent the misconduct of its senior managers, employees, subsidiaries, or third parties, it is presumed to bear criminal liability for such conduct.[10]

[9] Lei Shi. "Research on Corporate Criminal Intent." *Journal of Law and Business Studies*, no. 2 (2009): 70.

[10] Guanyu Li. "A New Theory on the Principles of Corporate Crime Sanctions: Focusing on the Connection between Presumed Subjectivity and Objective Attribution." *Politics and Law*, no. 5 (2015): 37.

On the basis of the foregoing distinction between different forms of corporate crime, it becomes possible to articulate a clearer evaluation of compliance-based exculpation. In principle, for systemic corporate crimes—where the enterprise has engaged in conduct that is not only socially harmful but also clearly characterized by subjective culpability—criminal liability ought to be imposed. In such cases, there is generally little scope within criminal law to establish compliance-based exculpation mechanisms. As some criminal law scholars have rightly observed, for this category of cases, even where an enterprise establishes or undertakes to establish a compliance management system, such efforts should, at most, serve as a basis for sentencing mitigation, rather than constituting a statutory ground for a declaration of non-liability. Moreover, when applying compliance-based non-prosecution mechanisms, systemic corporate crime cases—unless the offense is relatively minor in nature and the enterprise demonstrates active cooperation with the investigation, genuine remedial measures, and effective rectification—should in principle not be included within the scope of compliance assessment. As a general rule, in systemic corporate crime cases, compliance assessment measures should be reserved for situations in which the directly responsible persons are likely to face sentences of no more than three years' imprisonment. If, during the observation period, the enterprise successfully implements an effective compliance program, the procuratorial authority may then issue a non-prosecution decision. In this context, compliance-based non-prosecution can be understood as a special form of discretionary non-prosecution.

By contrast, in cases involving non-systemic corporate crimes, criminal law should—on the premise of adopting a strict liability framework—establish a dedicated compliance-based exculpation mechanism. In principle, where an enterprise has not established a compliance management system, it should be presumed to possess subjective culpability for criminal acts committed by its employees, senior managers, subsidiaries, or affiliated third parties, and therefore bear corresponding criminal liability. However, where the enterprise has implemented a compliance system and has fulfilled its duties of due care, supervision, and management—by taking measures to prohibit, prevent, and discipline such conduct—this should be sufficient to demonstrate that the enterprise did not possess subjective intent to cause social harm. In effect, the enterprise achieves a clear separation of liability from the culpable individuals and should no longer be held criminally responsible. At the same time, in areas where unlawful conduct occurs frequently and enterprises are particularly prone to management failures, criminal law could further establish specific categories of "negligence-based corporate crime." Under this approach, an enterprise's failure to actively fulfill its supervisory obligations, resulting in criminal acts by associated persons, would constitute a distinct form of negligent offense. In such cases, where no effective compliance program has been implemented, the negligent crime would be deemed established. Conversely, where an enterprise has instituted an effective compliance framework and has actively discharged its supervisory and managerial duties, it should not be held criminally liable for the offenses committed by relevant personnel.

In the process of exploring the application of compliance-based non-prosecution, it is generally appropriate that, for non-systemic corporate crime cases, procuratorial authorities may include any enterprise within the scope of compliance assessment so long as the enterprise has either already established a compliance management system or has demonstrated a genuine commitment to developing one. Under this approach, conditional non-prosecution measures may be applied. During the observation period, provided that the enterprise establishes a compliance management system, fulfills its compliance commitments, and effectively implements the compliance program, the procuratorial authority may issue a decision not to prosecute. For such cases, it is unnecessary for prosecutors to confine the applicability of compliance-based non-prosecution exclusively to minor criminal offenses. Rather, this compliance assessment regime could appropriately be extended to encompass corporate crimes in which the directly responsible individuals face potential sentences of up to ten years' imprisonment.

Accordingly, it is possible to classify compliance-based exculpation into three distinct models, depending on the nature of the corporate offense: the subjective fault exculpation model, the statutory management duty exculpation model, and the compliance assessment exculpation model. The first two models are primarily applicable to non-systemic corporate crime cases, while the third model may be applied both to non-systemic corporate crimes and to minor instances of systemic corporate crime. In contrast, for more serious forms of systemic corporate crime, there is no institutional basis for recognizing compliance-based exculpation.

9.3 The Subjective Fault Model

The subjective fault exculpation model refers to a form of compliance-based exculpation whereby an enterprise demonstrates, through the establishment and effective implementation of a compliance program, that it lacked subjective culpability for criminal acts committed by relevant personnel, thereby exempting itself from criminal liability. China's Criminal Law does not formally recognize a criminal compliance regime, nor does it explicitly stipulate that compliance may serve as a statutory basis for exculpating an enterprise from criminal liability. Nevertheless, in judicial practice, where corporate managers or employees engage in criminal conduct, an enterprise that can demonstrate the adoption of compliance measures—such as issuing compliance policies and employee handbooks, providing compliance training, imposing disciplinary sanctions, or offering incentives—may thereby establish that it lacked subjective fault in relation to the offense, enabling judicial authorities to exempt it from criminal liability. A typical example is the 2017 decision of the Lanzhou Intermediate People's Court, in which several Nestlé employees were convicted of infringing citizens' personal information. However, Nestlé itself was not held criminally liable because it had established and maintained a robust compliance system.[11]

Generally speaking, the subjective fault exculpation model comprises three essential elements. First, an associated person of the enterprise—such as an employee, senior manager, subsidiary, third party, or acquired entity—commits a criminal act with the purpose of advancing the enterprise's interests. Second, the enterprise would, in principle, be presumed liable for the acts of such associated persons. Third, the enterprise adduces evidence that it had established or implemented an effective compliance program to demonstrate that it exercised adequate compliance management over those associated persons. Specifically, it must show that it adopted compliance policies explicitly prohibiting such unlawful conduct and established compliance management procedures designed to prevent violations. Accordingly, the enterprise neither acted with intent by pursuing or tolerating the harmful outcome, nor engaged in recklessness or gross negligence that resulted in the occurrence of the harm.

9.3.1 Comparative Perspectives

The subjective fault exculpation model is widely reflected in the corporate compliance frameworks of common law jurisdictions. Within these frameworks, the doctrines of vicarious liability and identification establish that a corporation's criminal liability may arise either from criminal acts committed by its agents within the scope of their duties for the corporation's benefit, or from offenses carried out by directors, managers, or other senior executives in the exercise of their managerial functions to further the corporation's interests. In either scenario, the corporation is held legally responsible—meaning it assumes unified criminal liability for the misconduct of its agents or senior representatives.[12] If a corporation seeks to absolve itself of such liability and achieve a clear separation between its own responsibility and that of its agents or executives, it must adduce evidence demonstrating that it established and effectively implemented a robust compliance management system and thereby fulfilled its compliance obligations. It must further show that it neither authorized nor negligently failed to prevent the unlawful conduct. Only by satisfying these conditions can the corporation persuade the judicial authorities to issue an acquittal or a decision declining to prosecute.

According to the doctrine of vicarious liability (or respondeat superior), when employees commit criminal offenses in the course of performing their duties for the benefit of the corporation, the enterprise itself is deemed criminally liable for their conduct. Under the doctrine of identification, criminal acts

[11] Ruihua Chen, "Corporate Criminal Liability from the Perspective of Compliance," *Global Law Review*, no. 1 (2020); Ruihua Chen. "The First Case of the Compliance-Based Defense of No Guilt." *China Lawyer*, no. 5 (2020): 83–85.

[12] Yanan Shi. "Implementation of Compliance Programs and Corporate Criminal Attribution." *Law Journal*, no. 9 (2019): 21.

perpetrated by senior managers—whose decisions and intentions are treated as the directing mind and will of the company—are likewise attributed to the corporation, thereby establishing corporate criminal liability. However, if the corporation can demonstrate that it has established and effectively implemented a robust compliance management system—such as by issuing corporate compliance policies and employee codes of conduct, creating an internal compliance governance structure, explicitly prohibiting and sanctioning unlawful conduct by employees and managers, and conducting ongoing compliance training—it can show that it lacked subjective culpability. In this way, the company may establish that the criminal acts of its employees or senior managers were purely personal in nature and thereby rebut the presumption of strict liability. U.S. law also recognizes the doctrine of parent-subsidiary vicarious liability, whereby a parent company may be held criminally responsible for offenses committed by subsidiaries over which it exercises agency or control. Nonetheless, if the parent can demonstrate that it had implemented an effective compliance framework governing the subsidiary—including documented compliance protocols, training and awareness programs, risk assessments, continuous oversight and monitoring, disciplinary measures, and corrective action processes—it may effectively sever liability and avoid criminal responsibility for the subsidiary's misconduct. Furthermore, with respect to third-party business partners—including upstream suppliers and vendors, midstream agents and service providers, and downstream contractors and distributors—U.S. law similarly applies vicarious liability, requiring companies to answer for the criminal conduct of these parties. To achieve exculpation in such cases, the enterprise bears the burden of demonstrating that it had established a comprehensive compliance system addressing third-party risks, encompassing due diligence, training, tiered risk management, and disengagement mechanisms, thereby enabling it to legally distance itself from third-party liability. Additionally, U.S. law recognizes the doctrine of successor liability, under which an acquiring company may be held strictly liable for criminal offenses committed by the target entity prior to the merger or acquisition. To rebut this form of inherited liability, the acquiring company must demonstrate that it conducted thorough pre-acquisition due diligence and, following the transaction, strengthened compliance management and internal controls over the acquired business.[13]

In recent years, several continental European jurisdictions have incorporated compliance-based exculpation mechanisms into their criminal law frameworks. Although these countries have not embraced the doctrines of vicarious liability and identification derived from Anglo-American law, they nevertheless hold corporations criminally liable for offenses committed by senior managers acting in the interests of the enterprise and exercising managerial authority. However, if a company has established and effectively implemented a compliance program, it may be eligible for exemption from criminal liability. For example, under Italian law, when a corporation is subject to criminal

[13] Ruihua Chen. *The Fundamentals of Corporate Compliance*. Beijing: Law Press, 2020, 211 ff.

prosecution, it can advance an affirmative defense by demonstrating that it had adopted an effective compliance program. Specifically, in cases involving criminal acts committed by ordinary employees, a company can avoid liability by proving that it had instituted and enforced a compliance program sufficient to effectively prevent such misconduct. By contrast, for offenses committed by senior managers, the company bears a heightened burden of proof: it must not only show that it maintained an effective compliance framework but also demonstrate that its supervisory body exercised adequate oversight, and that the senior manager circumvented internal controls through deceptive means in order to perpetrate the offense.[14]

Italian law has also established six specific criteria that an effective compliance program must meet in order to serve as a basis for exculpation: first, it must identify activities or operational areas within the company that are exposed to criminal risk; second, it must set out procedures for managing financial resources in ways that are suitable to prevent the commission of offenses; third, it must provide for detailed protocols designed to guide the formulation and implementation of corporate decisions so as to reduce the likelihood of criminal conduct; fourth, it must establish an independent supervisory body endowed with autonomous powers to monitor the development and implementation of compliance measures; fifth, it must include continuous training for relevant employees and representatives of the company; and sixth, it must establish appropriate disciplinary procedures for employees and representatives who fail to comply with the standards set out under Legislative Decree No. 231.[15]

Article 31 bis, paragraph 2 of the Spanish Criminal Code similarly stipulates that when a company has implemented an effective compliance system specifically designed to prevent criminal offenses, it shall not be held criminally liable for offenses committed by individuals within the organization. To secure this exculpatory effect, the company bears the burden of demonstrating the following: first, that it has effectively adopted and enforced the compliance system; second, that the compliance body and personnel have been adequately empowered and possess both independence and professional competence; third, that this body has fully exercised its supervisory and control functions; and fourth, that no systemic criminal conduct has occurred.

The Spanish Criminal Code also enumerates detailed criteria that an effective compliance program must meet: first, conducting risk assessments to identify activities and behaviors likely to entail criminal liability; second, establishing policies and procedures governing corporate decision-making and its implementation; third, implementing appropriate measures for financial and

[14] Roberto Pisano. "Corporate Criminal Liability under Italian Law." Accessed September 6, 2019. https://globalinvestigationsreview.com/review/the-european-middle-eastern-and-african-investigations-review/2020/article/corporate-criminal-liability-under-italian-law

[15] Aurelio Giovannelli and Roberto Cursano. "Corporate Liability in Italy." Accessed September 6, 2019. https://globalcompliancenews.com/white-collar-crime/corporate-liability-in-italy/

accounting management; fourth, ensuring timely reporting of potential risks and violations; fifth, creating a disciplinary framework to appropriately sanction breaches; and sixth, periodically reviewing and updating the compliance system—requiring regular verification, especially if the system's provisions have been seriously breached or if the company's organizational structure or activities undergo significant changes.[16]

It is clear that both Italy and Spain, in formally incorporating compliance-based exculpation mechanisms into their legal frameworks, regard the implementation of an effective compliance program as a critical basis for severing the liability of the enterprise from that of individuals within the organization. The success of this separation of liability fundamentally rests on the premise that establishing and operating a compliance system demonstrates that the enterprise has duly fulfilled its management responsibilities and duty of care. Under these circumstances, the criminal conduct of internal personnel is considered to have exceeded the scope of the enterprise's authorization or instruction, and their subjective intent cannot be equated with the subjective intent of the enterprise itself.

9.3.2 *Compliance-Based Defense in Chinese Judicial Practice*

In China's criminal justice practice, when adjudicating cases involving criminal acts committed by company employees or senior management personnel, judicial authorities are required to ascertain three essential facts: first, whether the unlawful conduct was carried out in the name of the corporate entity; second, whether the conduct was undertaken for the purpose of advancing the entity's interests; and third, whether the conduct reflected the collective will of the entity itself. With respect to the first two inquiries, judicial authorities typically encounter little difficulty in establishing the relevant facts. In numerous cases involving employees or senior managers who exploit their professional positions to engage in acts of commercial bribery, fraud, or infringement of others' rights, the perpetrators often act under the banner of being "company employees" or "company executives." While their motives may partially involve personal gain, their actions frequently have the objective effect of increasing the company's commercial profits or enhancing its competitive position in the market. By contrast, the more contentious issue is whether such conduct can be deemed to embody the organization's collective intent. If the enterprise has serious deficiencies in its compliance management—such as failing to issue codes of business conduct, compliance policies, or employee behavioral guidelines, and neglecting to establish compliance mechanisms including risk assessments, compliance training programs, and internal reporting channels—it is likely to be regarded as bearing significant managerial culpability for the occurrence of unlawful acts by its personnel. In such circumstances, judicial

[16] *Overview of Anti-Bribery Laws and Regulations in Spain*. Published on the WeChat account "Compliance Xiaodaoke," June 3, 2020.

authorities may conclude that the enterprise has committed a grave omission in fulfilling its management responsibilities and thus bears criminal liability on the basis of this substantial subjective fault.

In 2017, the Lanzhou Intermediate People's Court of Gansu rendered a final judgment in a case involving employees of Nestlé who had committed the crime of infringing upon citizens' personal information. In this decision, the court sought to address the above-mentioned dilemma. The court held: "Corporate crime refers to conduct undertaken for the purpose of securing illegal benefits for the enterprise itself, which is objectively implemented either through a collective decision by the enterprise or a decision made by its responsible persons. The evidence—including the Nestlé employee handbook and codes of conduct—demonstrates that Nestlé expressly prohibited employees from engaging in illegal acts infringing upon citizens' personal information. The criminal conduct committed by the appellants, who violated the company's internal management regulations in order to enhance their personal performance, constituted individual acts."[17]

It can thus be seen that even in the absence of an established doctrine of strict liability, there remains institutional space within Chinese criminal law for compliance-based exculpation. If, after an employee or managerial staff member has committed a criminal offense, the enterprise can demonstrate to the judicial authorities that it had established a compliance management system, fulfilled its compliance obligations toward the employee or manager, exercised due diligence in identifying and preventing compliance risks, and maintained mechanisms for timely detection, monitoring, active cooperation, effective remediation, and conscientious rectification following any violations, the judicial authorities may conclude that the misconduct did not conform to the enterprise's compliance policies, breached internal regulations, fell outside established compliance procedures, and was inconsistent with the enterprise's organizational will—thus constituting conduct of a purely personal nature. In this way, the establishment and implementation of an effective compliance management system can demonstrate that the enterprise possessed neither subjective intent nor negligence, and thus should not bear criminal liability for the acts of its employees.

9.3.3 *Normative Justifications*

Why is it that, when affiliated personnel of an enterprise commit criminal offenses, the establishment of an effective compliance program can serve to demonstrate that the enterprise lacks subjective culpability and therefore should not bear criminal liability? To answer this question, two theoretical foundations may be invoked: the "theory of corporate independent will" and the "theory of effective regulation."

[17] Lanzhou Intermediate People's Court. (2017) Gan 01 Xing Zhong No. 89, Criminal Ruling.

First, according to the "theory of corporate independent will," an enterprise—though lacking the physiological consciousness and volition characteristic of a natural person—can nonetheless possess a form of consciousness and intent that is legally cognizable. Traditional theories of corporate criminal liability have generally grounded liability exclusively in the criminal acts of internal personnel, thereby overlooking the independent will of the enterprise itself. In reality, whether the criminal conduct is committed by corporate managers, internal employees, subsidiaries, or third-party partners, such conduct does not necessarily reflect the enterprise's collective will. When it is not possible to ascertain whether the actions of these individuals embody the will of the organization as a whole, determining whether the enterprise should bear criminal liability becomes a crucial question. Generally speaking, the company's articles of association, compliance policies, and employee codes of conduct—adopted through collective decision-making—constitute "abstract corporate acts" that express the enterprise's collective will. Meanwhile, the adoption of measures such as compliance risk assessments, due diligence, compliance training, the promotion of a compliance culture, disciplinary incentives, and remediation efforts represent "concrete corporate acts" that likewise embody the enterprise's collective will in practice.

Through these abstract and concrete corporate acts, the enterprise demonstrates a form of consciousness and intent entirely distinct from that of its affiliated personnel. On the one hand, the enterprise has clearly recognized the possibility that affiliated individuals may engage in unlawful or even criminal conduct, and by promulgating compliance charters, policies, and employee handbooks, it has fulfilled its duty of care and its duty to warn. This not only reflects a clear awareness of the risk that internal violations could occur but also shows a deliberate judgment that such risks should be actively mitigated through the implementation of compliance management measures. On the other hand, with respect to the socially harmful consequences that such conduct may produce, the enterprise has adopted compliance mechanisms to impose disciplinary measures on responsible parties and has established dynamic processes for preventing, detecting, and responding to violations. This demonstrates that the enterprise neither possessed the subjective intent to pursue or tolerate the occurrence of harmful outcomes nor exhibited negligence in the form of carelessness or overconfidence. Accordingly, where an enterprise has implemented a compliance management system, it has, through these measures, manifested a subjective will to discourage and even prohibit unlawful or criminal behavior. Any criminal conduct committed by affiliated personnel in this context no longer reflects the enterprise's own consciousness and intent but rather constitutes purely individual acts. It is precisely the establishment of such a compliance system that plays the decisive role in severing the liability of the enterprise from that of the individuals involved.

Secondly, according to the "theory of effective regulation," once an enterprise grows to a considerable scale, it frequently encounters the problem of regulatory failure on the part of external authorities. How to strengthen internal oversight within the enterprise—so that the numerous affiliated personnel can conduct business activities in accordance with laws and regulations and thereby prevent a broad array of legal risks—has become a practical challenge for corporate governance. Generally speaking, even if the enterprise's decision-making body possessed a figurative "clairvoyance" capable of scrutinizing every operational activity within the organization, it would still be difficult to prevent unlawful or non-compliant conduct committed by senior executives, employees, subsidiaries, or third parties. For example, despite repeated prohibitions issued by the board of directors, executives responsible for business operations may, in pursuit of performance targets, encourage or acquiesce in departmental personnel engaging in violations such as infringing personal information, conducting illegal business activities, or issuing fraudulent invoices. Likewise, although management repeatedly emphasizes environmental protection, executives or employees in charge of environmental affairs may still, in order to reduce operational costs, engage in the unlawful discharge of pollutants. Even when the enterprise promulgates policies requiring lawful conduct, a subsidiary, in the interest of pursuing commercial opportunities, may nonetheless resort to misappropriating trade secrets. Furthermore, while the company requires suppliers, agents, and distributors to adhere to legal business practices, these third parties, seeking to reinforce their own competitive advantages, may still engage in illegal conduct, including commercial bribery. In the face of such violations, administrative regulatory authorities attempting to prevent, detect, and respond effectively from the outside are confronted not only with a low probability of success but also with outcomes that are frequently unsatisfactory.

In circumstances where the effectiveness of external regulation is limited, strengthening internal self-regulation within enterprises has become an essential pathway for preventing illegal and criminal conduct. However, establishing a compliance framework and implementing a compliance management system is a governance strategy that entails substantial costs. Without robust external incentives, few enterprises would be willing to proactively adopt such an approach to corporate governance. Among the available incentives, the establishment of a compliance-based exculpation mechanism—under which a company would no longer bear criminal liability for offenses committed by its affiliated personnel if it has established an effective compliance management system—constitutes one of the most important inducements.[18] To achieve this compliance incentive effect, criminal law must adopt a logic of subjective intention inference: namely, that when an enterprise has implemented a compliance management system, it is presumed to possess the awareness and intent to prevent and deter its affiliated personnel from engaging in unlawful or criminal conduct, and therefore should not bear criminal liability arising from such

[18] Ruihua Chen, "Three Dimensions of the Corporate Compliance System: A Comparative Law Perspective," *Journal of Comparative Law*, no. 3 (2019); Feng Deng, "The Origins of Corporate Compliance and the Institutional Limitations in China," *Comparative Law Review*, no. 1 (2020).

conduct. Accordingly, the implementation of a compliance management system not only serves as the basis for demonstrating the absence of corporate culpability but may also constitute grounds for exempting the enterprise from criminal liability.

The foregoing arguments are applicable to cases involving non-systemic corporate crime. After all, in circumstances where the offense is neither the result of a collective decision by the enterprise nor the decision of its principal responsible persons, the critical issue in distinguishing corporate liability from the liability of affiliated personnel lies in determining whether the enterprise itself bore subjective culpability for the criminal conduct of those individuals. The establishment and implementation of a compliance mechanism precisely serves to sever the liability of the corporation from that of its affiliated personnel and helps enable the enterprise to exercise effective internal oversight. However, once an enterprise engages in systemic criminal conduct, its subjective awareness and intent can generally be substantiated to a considerable degree, and both the criminal acts of the enterprise and its culpable mental state can be clearly established. Under such circumstances, even if the enterprise has formally instituted a compliance management system, that system is effectively rendered a mere formality and fails to exert any meaningful preventive or deterrent effect against unlawful conduct. The existence of such a compliance framework, at most, may provide a basis for imposing a more lenient criminal penalty but cannot serve as grounds for exempting the enterprise from criminal liability.

9.4 The Statutory Management Duty Model

The so-called statutory management duty exculpation model refers to a framework whereby, in cases where the law establishes criminal liability for dereliction of duty, an enterprise can demonstrate that it has fulfilled its legally mandated obligations of supervision and management by establishing or implementing a compliance management system. By doing so, the enterprise may be exculpated from criminal liability, thereby effecting compliance-based exculpation. The application of this model presupposes that, when affiliated personnel of the enterprise engage in specified criminal conduct, the law presumes the enterprise has failed in its duty to prevent and control such misconduct. The operation of an effective compliance management system then serves as evidence that the enterprise did not neglect its duties and provides a foundation for exemption from criminal responsibility.

Where an enterprise commits an offense without having made a collective decision or a decision by its principal responsible persons, a *dereliction offense* essentially refers to criminal conduct arising from the enterprise's failure to fulfill its statutory management obligations.[19] The term *dereliction offense* denotes circumstances in which an enterprise, due to significant deficiencies in

[19] Libin Wang. "A Study on the Criminalization of Serious Regulatory Failures by Internet Service Providers." *Hunan Social Sciences*, no. 4 (2018): 100.

supervising and managing its affiliated personnel—including internal employees, senior executives, subsidiaries, and third parties—fails to prevent such individuals from committing criminal acts that cause serious harm to society. Under the statutory elements constituting these offenses, the enterprise's failure or refusal to discharge the management obligations prescribed by laws or administrative regulations constitutes a key precondition for the imposition of criminal liability. These statutory management obligations substantially encompass, or at least overlap with, compliance management obligations. Where an enterprise faces allegations of such a dereliction offense, it may rebut the presumption of dereliction and achieve compliance-based exculpation by demonstrating that it has fulfilled its statutory management duties and established an effective compliance management system.

Specifically, the statutory management duty exculpation model comprises the following three constituent elements. First, the law imposes specific mandatory compliance obligations on enterprises, requiring them to establish a compliance management system. Second, where affiliated personnel within the enterprise—including employees, senior executives, subsidiaries, or third parties—engage in certain unlawful or criminal conduct, the enterprise's failure to discharge its supervisory and managerial duties toward these individuals constitutes dereliction of duty. Third, if the enterprise has established or implemented a compliance management system, it may invoke this as a defense, demonstrating that it adopted compliance policies and employee codes of conduct, provided compliance training to affiliated personnel, and imposed disciplinary measures on violators. By doing so, the enterprise can establish that it fulfilled its compliance management obligations and should therefore be exempted from criminal liability.

9.4.1 *The U.K. Experience*

In the area of corporate criminal attribution, the United Kingdom has long maintained the concurrent application of the doctrines of vicarious liability and identification, although in practice the identification principle has been applied more broadly. In recent years, as large corporate groups have increasingly engaged in unlawful and criminal conduct such as commercial bribery and violations of tax administration regulations, the traditional attribution principles have revealed increasingly pronounced limitations in effectively pursuing corporate criminal liability. For example, under the doctrine of vicarious liability, a company may be held liable for unlawful acts committed by its employees or third parties, which can readily result in an overextension of criminal prosecution against corporations. Conversely, under the identification doctrine, only the acts and intentions of senior managers or directors are regarded as constituting the acts and intentions of the corporation itself. While this approach does not typically pose significant challenges in establishing the criminal liability of small companies, in the case of large corporate groups with numerous employees and highly complex governance structures, determining which senior managers or directors' intentions can be equated with the corporation's own will frequently proves challenging on multiple fronts. Consequently, efforts to impose criminal liability on such enterprises often become exceedingly difficult.[20] This is also one of the reasons why, in recent years, the United Kingdom has initiated so few criminal proceedings against large corporations.[21]

In 2010, the United Kingdom enacted the *Bribery Act*, introducing a new corporate offense: the failure of a commercial organization to prevent bribery. In 2017, the United Kingdom further introduced two additional corporate offenses under the Criminal Finances Act: first, the failure of a commercial organization to prevent the facilitation of UK tax evasion; and second, the failure of a commercial organization to prevent the facilitation of foreign tax evasion. These new offenses embody a model of corporate criminal liability predicated on a failure to prevent specified criminal conduct. When employees or third parties engage in the underlying offenses, the enterprise itself is subject to strict liability and is deemed to have committed a dereliction-type offense. However, English criminal law does not establish corporate criminal liability on the basis that the enterprise and the individual offenders share liability for the same offense; rather, it provides that the enterprise incurs independent liability for a failure-to-prevent offense arising from the conduct of its employees or associated persons. Consequently, the sanctions imposed for these dereliction-type offenses are generally much less severe than the criminal penalties applicable to the predicate offenses of bribery, tax evasion, and related crimes committed by individuals.

The implementation of the dereliction-based criminal liability regime has, in effect, significantly lowered the threshold for imposing criminal liability on enterprises. To prevent this expansive approach to corporate liability from producing unreasonable negative consequences, it has been necessary to establish a corresponding system of exculpatory defenses. On this basis, English law has introduced a compliance-based defense mechanism applicable to each of the three dereliction offenses described above. If an enterprise can adduce evidence demonstrating that it had implemented "adequate procedures" to prevent bribery or the facilitation of tax evasion, it will not be held criminally liable. The notion of "adequate procedures" refers to a compliance management system designed to effectively prevent criminal conduct, encompassing six core elements: the principle of proportionality, the principle of top-level commitment, the principle of risk assessment, the principle of due diligence, the

[20] Benqi Ouyang. "On the Establishment of Conditional Non-Prosecution for Corporate Crime in China." *China Criminal Law Journal*, no. 3 (2020): 69.

[21] "Corporate Criminal Enforcement: A Continuing Trend?" Accessed September 4, 2019. https://www.ashfords.co.uk/news-and-media/general/corporate-criminal-enforcement-a-continuing-trend; Mark Dunn. "Compliance Risk in the UK: What Companies Need to Know." Accessed September 21, 2019. https://bis.lexisnexis.co.uk/blog/categories/governance-risk-and-compliance/compliance-risk-uk

principle of effective communication, and the principle of monitoring and review.[22] Accordingly, where an "associated person" of a commercial organization commits bribery for the purpose of obtaining or retaining business or securing a commercial advantage for the organization, the organization bears the burden of demonstrating that it had established a compliance management system sufficient to discharge its duty to prevent such criminal conduct and thereby avoid liability for dereliction. This compliance-based exculpation framework may be described as the "statutory management duty exculpation model."

9.4.2 The Chinese Framework

In order to compel enterprises to effectively discharge their management responsibilities toward employees, subsidiaries, third parties, and other related actors, and to hold them accountable for dereliction in preventing criminal conduct by such persons, Chinese criminal law has likewise established dereliction offenses in which enterprises themselves constitute special subjects of crime. At present, the most representative of these offenses is the crime of refusing to perform information network security management obligations. Under the Criminal Law, the establishment of this offense requires the concurrent satisfaction of four elements: first, that laws or administrative regulations impose information network security management obligations on network service providers; second, that the enterprise has failed to fulfill these statutory management obligations; third, that regulatory authorities have ordered the enterprise to adopt corrective measures, which the enterprise has refused to implement; and fourth, that the enterprise's refusal to discharge its information network security management obligations has resulted in the widespread dissemination of illegal information, the disclosure of user data, or other serious consequences.

According to the legislative intent, where an enterprise refuses to fulfill the "information network security management obligations" established by law, fails to comply with corrective measures ordered by regulatory authorities, and thereby causes the statutorily defined serious consequences, it shall bear corresponding criminal liability. Such liability arises from the enterprise's dual omissions: first, its failure or dereliction in requiring employees, subsidiaries, third parties, and other relevant actors to comply with their statutory information network security management obligations; and second, its resistance to or passive response toward the corrective measures prescribed by the regulatory authorities.[23] Under these circumstances, if the enterprise does not actively raise an exculpatory defense, the judicial authorities may initiate criminal proceedings against it and pursue criminal liability accordingly.

[22] Ruihua Chen, "The UK Bribery Act and Corporate Compliance," *China Lawyer*, no. 3 (2019).

[23] Wangyuan Xie. "On the Crime of Failing to Perform Information Network Security Management Obligations." *China Legal Science*, no. 2 (2017): 243.

How, then, can an enterprise facing such charges raise an exculpatory defense? On this question, Chinese criminal law does not provide any statutory grounds for exculpation, nor does it, as English law does, expressly recognize the enterprise's adherence to "adequate procedures" in compliance management as a legally defined defense. In particular, whether the "information network security management obligations" required under Chinese criminal law are equivalent to the "compliance management obligations" applicable in the domains of network data and personal information protection remains a matter of debate. Nevertheless, the "information network security management obligations" referred to in the Criminal Law primarily denote the management duties imposed on network operators by Chinese laws and administrative regulations.[24] These obligations, at least in part, are intended to close gaps in network governance, eliminate potential vulnerabilities in data protection frameworks, and prevent the unlawful infringement of personal information. Accordingly, they can, to a certain extent, perform functions of preventing and identifying network compliance risks. For this reason, at least some of these obligations may be regarded as constituting a form of "network compliance management obligations."

For example, under the current *Cybersecurity Law of China*, network operators are subject to both "network operations security obligations" and "network information security obligations." These obligations incorporate elements akin to codes of conduct governing corporate commercial activities. Accordingly, both a company's network compliance policies and its employee codes of conduct should integrate these requirements so that they become compliance obligations embedded within the enterprise's operational processes. Among these, the obligations relating to network operations security primarily include fulfilling statutory protection duties in accordance with the graded cybersecurity protection system; ensuring that network products and services comply with mandatory national standards; requiring users to provide authentic identity information when entering into agreements or confirming the provision of services; and formulating emergency response plans for cybersecurity incidents to promptly address system vulnerabilities and other security risks. The network information security obligations mainly comprise the duty to maintain strict confidentiality of collected user information; to collect and use personal information in accordance with the principles of legality, propriety, and necessity; to publicly disclose the rules governing such collection and use; to clearly inform users of the purposes, methods, and scope of information processing, and to obtain their consent; to refrain from disclosing, altering, or damaging collected personal information or providing it to third parties without the user's consent; and to adopt technical and other necessary measures to safeguard personal information security and prevent its disclosure, damage, or loss,

[24] Wenhua Wang. "Application Analysis of the Crime of Failing to Perform Information Network Security Management Obligations." *People's Procuratorial Review*, no. 6 (2016): 25.

while promptly implementing remedial measures in the event of any such incident.

As China continues to strengthen the regulation of network security management and personal information protection, a series of forthcoming laws and administrative regulations are expected to impose additional network security management obligations on network operators. These legal instruments, while emphasizing the incorporation of such obligations into corporate codes of commercial conduct and compliance policies, also provide clearer definitions of the organizational structures and procedural requirements essential for effective network compliance. For example, the *Data Security Law* and the *Personal Information Protection Law*, both currently under consultation, require enterprises engaged in data and personal information processing to establish comprehensive data security management systems covering the entire data lifecycle; to appoint data security officers and dedicated management bodies; and to designate personal information protection officers responsible for supervising relevant processing activities and associated protective measures. These requirements clearly pertain to the establishment of a compliance organizational framework. Both draft laws further mandate that enterprises conduct data security education and training programs, enhance monitoring of data risks, and carry out periodic risk assessments of data activities and statutorily designated important information processing activities, with the results to be submitted to the competent authorities. These provisions plainly constitute procedural mechanisms aimed at preventing compliance risks. In addition, the two laws stipulate that enterprises providing data brokerage services must require data providers to disclose the sources of data, verify the identities of both parties to the transaction, maintain verification and transaction records, and adopt necessary measures to prevent unauthorized access as well as the disclosure, theft, alteration, or deletion of personal information. Enterprises are also required to conduct regular audits of the legality of personal information processing activities and the protective measures in place. These requirements are manifestly directed toward the identification and mitigation of compliance risks. Moreover, the two laws obligate enterprises, upon discovering data security risks or experiencing information breaches, to take prompt remedial action and to notify the relevant information protection authorities. These provisions clearly pertain to compliance response measures in the event of violations.

Precisely because the network security management obligations established by laws and administrative regulations serve the function of compliance management obligations, enterprises may invoke the fulfillment of such obligations as a ground for exculpation. Specifically, if an enterprise produces evidence demonstrating that it has established a network compliance management system, this is effectively tantamount to fulfilling its information network security management obligations. In doing so, the enterprise can establish that it has not engaged in any dereliction or omission, thereby enabling the judicial authorities to terminate criminal proceedings and to determine that the enterprise does not constitute the offense of refusing to perform information network security management obligations.

9.4.3 *Theoretical Underpinnings*

The core feature of this model is that, by imposing criminal liability on enterprises for dereliction in preventing criminal conduct by affiliated personnel, the law compels enterprises to establish compliance management systems while also affording them an opportunity for compliance-based exculpation. In both the United Kingdom and China, this type of criminal legislation remains at a nascent stage of development. It should be noted that this model is not applicable to cases involving systemic corporate crime. In such cases, the criminal conduct is carried out by the enterprise as a whole, and the enterprise possesses the subjective intent to commit the offense. Even if the enterprise were to establish a compliance system, it could not negate its own subjective culpability. At the same time, this model is also inapplicable to ordinary cases of non-systemic corporate crime. In such cases, the liability imposed on the enterprise is predicated on managerial dereliction. The establishment of a compliance system is not intended to sever the enterprise's liability from that of the affiliated individuals but rather to demonstrate that the enterprise did not fail in its duty to prevent or deter criminal conduct by such persons and therefore should not bear criminal liability for dereliction.

How, then, can the establishment of this exculpation model based on the fulfillment of management obligations in dereliction offenses be theoretically justified? This question can be briefly examined from three perspectives.

First, the statutory management duty exculpation model establishes mandatory compliance obligations for enterprises by creating a liability framework under which non-compliance entails guilt. In this way, it effectively incentivizes enterprises to establish compliance management systems. In general, for cases involving non-systemic corporate crime, criminal law adopts an approach characterized by compliance may lead to exculpation. However, this approach has a clear limitation: when an enterprise establishes a compliance system, it merely creates the possibility of achieving exculpation. Whether the establishment or implementation of such a system can actually demonstrate the absence of corporate intent or negligence, or sever the liability of the enterprise from that of its affiliated personnel, remains uncertain and is subject to the discretion of judicial authorities. This uncertainty can substantially diminish the deterrent and incentive effect of compliance measures under criminal law. By contrast, for certain types of non-systemic corporate crime, when criminal law adopts the statutory management duty exculpation model, it effectively imposes a mandatory duty of compliance upon enterprises. Under this liability framework—characterized by non-compliance entails guilt—enterprises, in order to mitigate potential criminal liability, are compelled to establish compliance programs and implement effective compliance management systems. If the model of compliance may lead to exculpation merely provides enterprises with a compliance-based incentive mechanism, then this model—grounded in non-compliance entails guilt—establishes a system of compliance-based sanctions. By comparison, the statutory management duty exculpation model can exert a significantly stronger incentive effect in promoting the implementation and enhancement of corporate compliance systems.

For enterprises in which affiliated personnel have committed such offenses, criminal law establishes a special form of strict liability that presumes the enterprise to have been derelict in its duty to prevent and deter criminal conduct by those individuals—that is, to have acted with subjective negligence. This presumption shifts the burden of raising an exculpatory defense onto the enterprise itself.[25] To assert an effective defense, the enterprise must produce evidence demonstrating that it has established or implemented a compliance management system and has thereby discharged its duty of care to prevent or deter criminal conduct by affiliated personnel. For enterprises that have not established such a system, this defense will inevitably fail to persuade judicial authorities, leaving them to bear the consequences of conviction. This dynamic compels enterprises to promptly implement compliance management systems in order to mitigate the risk of future criminal liability for dereliction. For those enterprises that have not yet faced prosecution, the experiences of others serve as a cautionary example, prompting them to adopt compliance programs or implement effective compliance management systems to avoid similar outcomes. Accordingly, the implementation of the statutory management duty exculpation model can, to the greatest extent possible, incentivize both enterprises subject to enforcement and those not yet implicated to establish robust compliance management frameworks.

Secondly, this compliance-based exculpation model integrates enterprises' management obligations with their compliance obligations, thereby elevating compliance management duties to the level of criminal law obligations and significantly enhancing the legal status of corporate compliance. The UK *Bribery Act* establishes six "adequate procedures" for corporate compliance, while Chinese criminal law requires enterprises to discharge the "information network security management obligations" prescribed by administrative regulations. Because these management obligations are primarily directed at employees, senior executives, subsidiaries, third parties, and other affiliated actors, they inherently encompass duties to prevent, identify, and address unlawful or non-compliant conduct by such persons. By incorporating compliance management obligations into the framework of criminal law, corporate compliance becomes a legally enforceable duty rather than merely an internal governance measure. Enterprises that fail to fulfill such obligations are directly subject to liability for dereliction offenses. Accordingly, this compliance-based exculpation model markedly elevates the legal standing of corporate compliance.

Thirdly, an enterprise's fulfillment of its statutory management obligations is sufficient to demonstrate the absence of subjective negligence with respect to

[25] Ruihua Chen, "On the Sinicization of Corporate Compliance," *Legal Science* 3 (2020).

the criminal conduct of affiliated personnel, thereby exempting the enterprise from liability for dereliction in preventing or deterring such offenses. So-called corporate dereliction offenses are, in essence, criminal acts arising from the enterprise's subjective negligence. Such negligence is primarily reflected in the enterprise's failure to discharge adequate management obligations, thereby allowing employees, managers, subsidiaries, or third parties to engage in unlawful or non-compliant conduct and, in some cases, cause harm to society. By establishing a compliance management system, an enterprise can demonstrate that it has exercised due care toward its affiliated personnel, fulfilled its supervisory and managerial responsibilities, and neither acted carelessly nor with overconfidence regarding the potential harmful consequences of their conduct. Rather, the enterprise has made adequate preparations and efforts to prevent unlawful acts, identify violations, and respond effectively to criminal incidents. However, when affiliated personnel willfully disregard the rules and management protocols established by the enterprise, this may result in the failure of the compliance management system. For an enterprise that has implemented such a system, the criminal conduct of these affiliated actors effectively constitutes an "accidental event" or a circumstance of "force majeure" that exceeds the scope of what the compliance framework could reasonably anticipate, address, or control.[26] Accordingly, it is precisely the existence of a compliance system that severs the causal link between the enterprise's management and the criminal conduct of affiliated personnel, thereby providing a direct basis for exempting the enterprise from negligence liability.

9.5 The Compliance Assessment Model

The first two compliance-based exculpation models are mechanisms under criminal law that provide enterprises with statutory grounds for raising an exculpatory defense when they have already implemented compliance management systems. Just as natural persons may invoke self-defense or necessity as a basis for exculpation, enterprises may invoke the establishment of compliance management systems as a legally recognized ground for exemption from liability. By contrast, in circumstances where the procuratorial authorities apply a compliance assessment mechanism, enterprises that have already committed criminal offenses may, upon being ordered to cooperate actively and undertake effective remedial measures, be designated as subjects of compliance assessment. Such enterprises are required to formulate effective compliance programs, and the procuratorial authorities determine whether to decline prosecution based on the enterprise's progress in implementing compliance management and carrying out institutional reforms. This mechanism—in which enterprises seek to persuade judicial authorities to exempt them from

[26] Jianing Geng. "The Advocacy of Inherent Corporate Criminal Liability and Its Doctrinal Shaping." *Chinese Journal of Comparative Law*, no. 6 (2020): 1501.

criminal liability by undergoing compliance assessment—may be referred to as the "compliance assessment exculpation model."

The United States was the first jurisdiction to establish the compliance assessment exemption model. Since the 1990s, U.S. federal prosecutors have applied the system of pre-trial diversion agreements to corporate criminal cases, thereby creating the frameworks of deferred prosecution agreements (DPAs) and non-prosecution agreements (NPAs). Under this framework, enterprises suspected of criminal offenses may, following negotiations with prosecutors, enter into agreements requiring them to pay substantial fines, cooperate actively, and undertake effective remedial measures. During a designated compliance assessment period, they are obligated to implement robust compliance programs. The prosecutorial authorities then determine whether to initiate formal prosecution based on the enterprise's performance in advancing compliance management and implementing institutional reforms. Because enterprises subject to compliance assessment can secure non-prosecution and avoid potentially catastrophic consequences if they successfully implement effective compliance programs, most enterprises undergoing such assessments actively fulfill their compliance obligations. In practice, this dynamic has contributed to the widespread adoption of compliance management systems.[27] Twenty years later, the compliance assessment exculpation model gradually came to be accepted in the United Kingdom, France, and other jurisdictions. In 2014, the United Kingdom introduced the deferred prosecution agreement system, under which prosecutorial authorities—subject to judicial oversight—apply compliance assessment mechanisms to enterprises under investigation. Subsequently, France, Australia, Canada, Singapore, and other countries adopted deferred prosecution agreement regimes, using the UK approach as a model.[28]

Since 2020, as corporate compliance systems have been increasingly integrated into enterprise regulatory frameworks, Chinese procuratorial authorities have begun exploring reforms to the non-prosecution mechanism for corporate compliance. Under the guidance of the Supreme People's Procuratorate, certain local procuratorial offices have launched pilot programs for a "corporate compliance assessment system." For enterprises suspected of committing minor offenses, provided that they admit guilt, accept punishment, and demonstrate a willingness to adopt compliance measures, the procuratorial authorities designate them as subjects of compliance assessment. During the prescribed assessment period, such enterprises are required to engage external independent monitors and implement compliance management mechanisms. If, upon review and verification, the enterprise is found to have successfully established a compliance management system, the procuratorial authorities issue a decision

[27] Ruihua Chen, "Deferred Prosecution Agreements in the Context of Corporate Compliance," *Journal of Comparative Law*, no. 1 (2020); Ruihua Chen. "The Deferred Prosecution Agreement System in the U.S. and Corporate Compliance." *China Lawyer*, no. 4 (2019): 78–80.

[28] Ruihua Chen. "Judicial Review Models of Deferred Prosecution Agreements." *China Lawyer*, no. 10 (2019): 76–79; Ruihua Chen, "The Sapin II Law and Corporate Compliance in France," *China Lawyer*, no. 5 (2019).

not to prosecute. Because this compliance-based non-prosecution mechanism applies to enterprises that have already satisfied the elements of a criminal offense, and because the decision not to prosecute is rendered following a period of compliance assessment, this system effectively constitutes a model of "compliance assessment-based exculpation."

The compliance assessment exemption model is characterized by four fundamental elements. First, the enterprise has already committed a specified criminal offense under the Criminal Law. Second, the enterprise voluntarily admits guilt and accepts punishment, actively cooperates with the investigation, undertakes remedial measures to mitigate harm and losses, and demonstrates a willingness to pursue institutional reforms. Third, the procuratorial authorities designate the enterprise as a subject of compliance assessment, requiring it to engage external independent monitors and, during the assessment period, to establish and implement a compliance management system. Fourth, upon completion of the compliance assessment, the procuratorial authorities issue a decision not to prosecute enterprises that have successfully implemented effective compliance programs, thereby exempting them from criminal liability.

9.5.1 *Assessment as a Basis for Exculpation*

Although China's compliance-based non-prosecution system differs substantially from the deferred prosecution agreement regimes in Western jurisdictions, it has, in general, evolved into a compliance assessment exculpation model. In this context, some observers have raised objections, arguing that within the operation of the compliance-based non-prosecution framework, compliance is not the sole basis for exempting enterprises from liability but merely one important factor among several considerations. If an enterprise fails to admit guilt and accept punishment, refuses to cooperate with the investigative authorities in evidence collection, or does not undertake remedial measures such as compensation, restitution, tax repayment, or environmental restoration, then even if it establishes a compliance management system, the procuratorial authorities will not issue a decision not to prosecute. On this basis, some commentators contend that compliance is not the exclusive ground on which procuratorial authorities base their non-prosecution decisions, and they even go so far as to deny that the compliance assessment mechanism serves any genuine exculpatory function.

In fact, even a brief comparative examination reveals that both deferred prosecution agreements and non-prosecution agreements are, in essence, conditional non-prosecution contracts concluded between enterprises suspected of criminal conduct and the prosecutorial authorities. In jurisdictions such as the United States, the United Kingdom, and France, prosecutorial authorities typically impose an assessment period of approximately three years, thereby postponing the decision whether to prosecute and entering into a written agreement with the enterprise under investigation. The obligations assumed by the enterprise generally include: admitting the criminal facts; paying substantial fines; restoring the status quo ante; disgorging unlawful gains; compensating victims; cooperating with ongoing investigations conducted by law enforcement authorities; removing or restructuring the board of directors or senior management team; disciplining individuals who bear direct responsibility for the corporate offense; implementing an effective compliance program; accepting the appointment of a compliance monitor designated by the prosecution; and submitting to compliance supervision and assessment.

A review of the provisions governing deferred prosecution agreements and non-prosecution agreements in Europe and the United States reveals that enterprises are required to undertake a series of contractual obligations, the core of which remains the obligation to implement an effective compliance program. Generally speaking, the existence of an established compliance management system is one of the preconditions for prosecutorial authorities to enter into such agreements. For an enterprise that has never implemented a compliance program, the likelihood of reaching such an agreement with the prosecution is exceedingly low. Before entering into such an agreement, the enterprise must submit a compliance improvement plan that satisfies the prosecutorial authorities. Once approved, this plan is incorporated into the deferred prosecution agreement or non-prosecution agreement and serves as the benchmark for evaluating whether the enterprise has implemented an effective compliance program. Among the various provisions contained in these agreements, the assessment period itself is designed to compel the enterprise to carry out the compliance program. Clauses requiring the payment of fines, active cooperation, and diligent remediation are likewise necessary measures to ensure effective compliance implementation, and can even be regarded as preconditions for the prosecution to initiate the compliance assessment process. Once the agreement is signed and the compliance assessment process is underway, the primary factor determining whether the prosecutorial authorities will issue a decision not to prosecute is the enterprise's performance in fulfilling its obligations. As a practical matter, enterprises that fail to undertake protective measures—such as admitting guilt, paying fines, actively cooperating, and implementing effective remedial measures—will not even be considered for compliance assessment. Accordingly, at the conclusion of the assessment period, the principal determinant of whether the prosecutorial authorities will decide not to prosecute is the progress made in compliance implementation. Therefore, in the criminal procedures of Western jurisdictions, compliance clearly serves an exculpatory function.

In China's recent reform initiatives concerning compliance-based non-prosecution, the procuratorial authorities have implemented a "compliance assessment system," and non-prosecution decisions issued following such assessments are referred to as "corporate compliance non-prosecution." These developments underscore the central role of corporate compliance within this institutional framework. From the perspective of basic institutional logic, the procuratorial authorities typically conduct two separate reviews of an enterprise under investigation: the first review examines whether the enterprise meets the conditions for initiating compliance assessment, and the second assesses whether the enterprise satisfies the requirements for applying non-prosecution.

In the first review, the procuratorial authorities consider a range of factors, including whether the criminal facts have been established; whether the enterprise admits guilt and accepts punishment; whether the enterprise has the capacity to implement compliance measures; and whether it has undertaken remedial actions such as refunding illegal gains, returning illicit property, repaying taxes, or restoring the environment. It can be said that the enterprise's admission of guilt, active cooperation, and effective remediation are all critical considerations for the procuratorial authorities in determining whether to place the enterprise within the compliance assessment process.[29]

Once the procuratorial authorities issue a decision to place an enterprise under compliance assessment or to grant conditional non-prosecution, the enterprise is required to assume new compliance obligations. These obligations include engaging a compliance monitor and entering into a compliance monitoring agreement; submitting a criminal compliance plan and establishing an effective corporate compliance system; submitting to oversight by the procuratorial authorities and the compliance monitor; disclosing relevant factual information; regularly reporting on the progress of compliance implementation; and promptly identifying, disclosing, and preventing any potential unlawful or criminal conduct. Accordingly, before the conclusion of the compliance assessment period, the procuratorial authorities must conduct a second review of the enterprise. The central focus of this review is the enterprise's fulfillment of its criminal compliance obligations, in particular the actual effectiveness of implementing the compliance program. In deciding whether to issue a non-prosecution decision, the procuratorial authorities primarily consider whether the enterprise has established and implemented an effective compliance program; whether pre-existing institutional risks have been eliminated; whether structural deficiencies have been remedied; whether the proposed remediation measures have been carried out; and whether the likelihood of reoffending has been significantly reduced.[30]

Accordingly, among the many factors considered by the procuratorial authorities, whether the enterprise has implemented an effective compliance program is clearly the decisive factor in determining whether to issue a non-prosecution decision. Other factors—including the enterprise's admission of guilt and acceptance of punishment, active cooperation, and effective remediation—are indeed primary considerations when the procuratorial authorities

[29] Yong Li. "Constructing Corporate Compliance in China from the Perspective of the Procuratorate." *Journal of the National Prosecutors College*, no. 4 (2020): 102–107; Yuhua Li. "Corporate Plea Bargaining System Centered on Compliance." *Journal of Zhejiang Gongshang University*, no. 1 (2021): 69.

[30] Ruihua Chen, "Research on Deferred Prosecution Agreements for Corporate Compliance," *Chinese Journal of Criminal Law*, no. 1 (2021): 92.

decide whether to initiate compliance assessment. However, once the compliance assessment process has been commenced, these considerations give way to the question of whether a compliance management system has been effectively established. If the enterprise under investigation implements the compliance management system in accordance with its committed compliance plan during the assessment period, the procuratorial authorities may rely on this as the basis for a decision not to prosecute. This fully demonstrates that, once an enterprise is placed under compliance assessment, the implementation of compliance measures has a clear exculpatory function.

9.5.2 *Application in Non-Systemic Offenses*

In the course of exploring reforms to the compliance-based non-prosecution system, procuratorial authorities have applied compliance assessment mechanisms to enterprises under investigation that have admitted guilt and accepted punishment, demonstrated a willingness to implement compliance measures, and undertaken active remedial efforts. On this basis, they have rendered decisions to exempt such enterprises from criminal liability through compliance. However, as discussed earlier, corporate crime can be categorized into systemic and non-systemic offenses. For enterprises that have engaged in systemic criminal conduct, the scope for applying the compliance assessment exemption mechanism is relatively limited. By contrast, for enterprises involved in non-systemic offenses, there is significantly greater scope for the application of compliance assessment. This raises an important question: why should the compliance assessment exculpation mechanism be applied to enterprises that have committed non-systemic crimes?

In essence, non-systemic corporate crime is characterized by the fact that the criminal conduct of the enterprise is not the result of collective decision-making or the deliberate actions of its principal responsible persons. Rather, it involves criminal acts committed by an affiliated individual in the name of the enterprise and for the purpose of advancing corporate interests, for which the enterprise bears a form of presumptive criminal liability due to its failure to establish a robust compliance management system or to adopt adequate preventive and deterrent measures. Once the procuratorial authorities designate such enterprises as subjects of compliance assessment and impose compliance monitoring measures requiring them to establish an effective compliance program, three positive outcomes can be achieved. First, through the implementation of a compliance framework, the enterprise can successfully repair and remediate the legal interests harmed by the criminal conduct. Second, through institutional reforms, adjustments to its business model, and the establishment of internal self-regulation mechanisms, the enterprise can effectively prevent similar criminal conduct from occurring in the future. Third, by exempting the enterprise from liability, the authorities can prevent it from suffering catastrophic losses and thereby safeguard the public interest. The following sections will briefly analyze these three aspects in turn.

First, according to the theory of "legal interest restoration," the very act of an enterprise establishing an effective compliance program constitutes the remediation and repair of the legal interests that have already been harmed, and this serves as the principal basis for applying compliance-based exculpation measures to the enterprise. Under traditional criminal law theory, crime is regarded as socially harmful conduct that infringes upon legal interests, which may include the interests of the state, the public, or individual victims. The rationale for imposing criminal liability on offenders is to fulfill the retributive and deterrent functions of criminal law by depriving those who have committed offenses of the benefits gained through their conduct and subjecting them to corresponding loss and suffering. In this respect, traditional theory adopts a retrospective perspective that focuses on punishing those who have infringed upon protected legal interests. By contrast, under the compliance assessment framework, when an enterprise accepts compliance assessment and establishes an effective compliance program, it takes measures to remediate and restore the legal interests harmed by the offense, thereby eroding the foundation for imposing criminal liability.[31] This reflects a forward-looking perspective that emphasizes leniency toward enterprises that have undertaken to repair the harm caused by their conduct.

In cases of non-systemic corporate crime, the offenses are directly committed by affiliated individuals such as managers, employees, subsidiaries, or third parties, while the enterprise itself becomes entangled in criminal proceedings due to deficiencies in its compliance management. By participating in the compliance assessment process administered by the procuratorial authorities, enterprises undertake a series of proactive measures, including admitting guilt and accepting punishment; cooperating with law enforcement investigations; actively disclosing and reporting criminal conduct; imposing strict sanctions on the affiliated individuals directly responsible; and adopting remedial measures such as compensating victims, repaying taxes, disgorging illicit gains, and restoring the status quo ante. Beyond these steps, enterprises also implement targeted corrective measures to address management deficiencies and systemic vulnerabilities, thereby establishing a governance framework designed to prevent, detect, and respond to compliance risks. In this respect, through the establishment of a compliance system and related measures, enterprises engage in a comprehensive process of legal interest restoration, repairing the legal interests damaged by the criminal conduct. Among these measures, cooperation with law enforcement facilitates the full clarification of the facts of the case; remedial actions help to compensate the state, society, and victims for their losses; sanctions against those directly responsible mitigate the risk of future offenses at the personnel level; and the establishment of a compliance system addresses the prevention of criminal conduct at the institutional level. Taken together, these acts of legal interest restoration demonstrate that, for

[31] Weidong Chen. "From Substance to Procedure: Corporate Compliance and Corporate 'Decriminalization' Governance." *China Criminal Law Journal*, no. 2 (2021): 121.

enterprises that have established effective compliance programs, the social harmfulness of the corporate offense has been reduced to the minimum. Under such circumstances, pursuing criminal convictions is neither necessary nor equitable. Accordingly, in view of the demonstrated effect of effectively restoring legal interests, it is both reasonable and justified to adopt compliance-based exculpation measures for enterprises undergoing compliance assessment.

Secondly, according to the theory of effective crime prevention, by establishing an effective compliance program, enterprises strengthen internal compliance management and effectively eliminate the likelihood of affiliated personnel reoffending. This constitutes another basis for granting compliance-based exculpation. Traditional criminal law theory is founded on the principle that all crimes must be punished, adhering to the doctrine of proportionality between culpability and punishment. Under this approach, any actor who commits a criminal offense must be convicted in accordance with the statutory elements of the crime. Even if the actor subsequently adopts proactive and effective measures to prevent further offenses, thereby significantly reducing the risk of recidivism, such efforts are not regarded as sufficient to negate the criminal liability that would otherwise be imposed. As an exception, only where statutory grounds for exculpation—such as self-defense or necessity—are present may the judicial authorities decide not to convict the offender. However, these statutory defenses have traditionally been designed primarily for natural persons, and for enterprises that have engaged in socially harmful conduct, no comparable exculpatory grounds have been established.[32]

However, unlike natural persons, enterprises are commercial organizations endowed with a legally fictitious personality and characterized by highly complex governance structures. Establishing a compliance-based exculpation mechanism for enterprises suspected of criminal conduct can create a powerful incentive for them to develop internal control systems and prevent criminal activity. In cases involving non-systemic corporate crime, the offenses are committed by affiliated personnel, while the enterprise's primary deficiency lies in the absence of an effective management system and internal controls, resulting in structural shortcomings in preventing and deterring such conduct. Once an enterprise accepts compliance assessment by the procuratorial authorities and establishes a relatively robust compliance management system, it can achieve effective crime prevention in three key respects. First, the enterprise can undertake substantial reforms of previously flawed business models and operational practices, thereby eliminating pre-existing unlawful, non-compliant, or criminal elements. Second, the enterprise can enhance its ability to prevent and detect internal misconduct arising from its specific compliance risks. This can be achieved by issuing targeted compliance policies and employee codes of conduct, and establishing compliance training programs to ensure that employees and subsidiaries operate in accordance with applicable laws and regulations.

[32] Mingliang Ma. "Corporate Compliance as a Method of Crime Governance." *Political Science & Law Forum*, no. 3 (2020): 172.

By conducting compliance risk assessments and due diligence, and implementing periodic compliance risk reporting, the enterprise can integrate third-party activities into its compliance monitoring framework; simultaneously, by establishing internal whistleblowing channels and compliance audit procedures, it can promptly identify potential violations or instances of non-compliant conduct. Third, the enterprise can implement mechanisms for internal compliance investigations, compliance remediation, and compliance incentives and sanctions, thereby closing pre-existing management gaps, eliminating institutional vulnerabilities, and enhancing the overall compliance management system.

By implementing a compliance governance system, enterprises establish an internal supervision framework targeting affiliated personnel, thereby providing a necessary supplement to the inherent limitations of external regulatory oversight by administrative authorities. This internal monitoring system employs compliance management as its principal instrument and designates as its subjects of supervision the enterprise's managers, employees, subsidiaries, third parties, and even acquired entities. Its primary objective is to ensure that these affiliated actors conduct business lawfully and in compliance with regulations, thereby forming an effective management framework for preventing criminal conduct.[33] To encourage enterprises to adopt such self-regulation and crime prevention measures, procuratorial authorities must provide a robust system of incentives. Accordingly, by establishing a compliance-based exculpation mechanism, the authorities can create powerful incentives for enterprises under investigation that have successfully developed self-monitoring mechanisms aimed at preventing criminal offenses.[34] Indeed, it is not difficult to see that in the absence of such a compliance assessment exemption mechanism, few enterprises would be willing to engage voluntarily in time-consuming and resource-intensive compliance management activities that offer little immediate economic return.

Thirdly, according to the public interest consideration theory, issuing a non-prosecution decision for an enterprise that has undergone a compliance assessment and successfully implemented a compliance management system aligns more closely with the broader interests of society. Traditional criminal procedure theory maintains that mandatory prosecution and discretionary prosecution should be applied in combination. Under this approach, where the conduct of an individual satisfies the statutory elements of a criminal offense and meets the evidentiary threshold, prosecution is generally required as a matter of uniform policy. Only in cases where the offense is minor and criminal punishment is not necessary under the Criminal Law may the procuratorial authorities exercise discretion to issue a non-prosecution decision. In cases involving more

33 Ruihua Chen, "On the Nature of Corporate Compliance," *Journal of Zhejiang Gongshang University*, no. 1 (2021).

34 Yuhua Li. "Criminal Procedure Incentives for Corporate Compliance in China." *Journal of Comparative Law Studies*, no. 1 (2020): 26–29; Shaojun Liu. "Possibilities and Limits of Localizing the Non-Prosecution System for Corporate Compliance." *Law Journal*, no. 1 (2021): 54–57.

serious criminal conduct, there is typically no institutional space for non-prosecution. In corporate crime cases, the prevailing principle is that procuratorial authorities should, in general, issue non-prosecution decisions only where the directly responsible individuals would likely be sentenced to no more than three years' imprisonment.

In cases where an enterprise has undergone compliance assessment and, in accordance with prosecutorial supervision requirements, established an effective compliance program and strengthened its internal monitoring systems, thereby effectively preventing the recurrence of criminal conduct by affiliated personnel, there is no need—based on considerations of public interest—for the procuratorial authorities to initiate prosecution. Instead, adopting a compliance-based exculpation approach is more appropriate. Specifically, the compliance-based exculpation mechanism serves to protect the public interest in several respects. First, it avoids potentially bankrupting consequences for the enterprise, thereby preventing social tensions and conflicts arising from employee layoffs, investor losses, and failed third-party investments. Second, it prevents the conviction of the enterprise or its directly responsible personnel, thus avoiding outcomes such as disqualification from public listing, the loss of franchise qualifications, or the revocation of business licenses. Third, it averts catastrophic consequences that could result from the enterprise's conviction, including the loss of tax revenue, economic decline, and setbacks to emerging industries. Fourth, it provides incentives for technologically advanced enterprises to reform their business practices and operating models through the establishment of effective compliance programs, thereby achieving sustainable development and, over time, potentially evolving into dynamic, long-lasting enterprises.

By implementing the compliance assessment system, the procuratorial authorities do not merely conduct an evidentiary review and an examination of whether the statutory elements of the offense have been satisfied. Rather, they engage in a broader public interest consideration, determining whether to initiate prosecution based on the imperative of safeguarding the public interest.[35] This represents a significant innovation in prosecutorial philosophy and in the exercise of public prosecution. Under this approach, the procuratorial authorities no longer adhere solely to the objectives of "arrest whenever there is guilt," "prosecute whenever there is guilt," or "punish all crimes." Instead, they adopt the maximization of the public interest as their primary guiding principle. For enterprises under investigation that have established internal monitoring systems and undertaken measures to prevent criminal conduct by affiliated personnel, the authorities may opt for compliance-based exculpation. This

[35] Fenfei Li. "On Prosecutorial Recommendations for Corporate Compliance." *China Criminal Law Journal*, no. 1 (2021): 112–113; Yueping Wei. "From 'State Presence' to 'Social Presence': A Study on the Structure of Protected Interests in Non-Prosecution Practice for Compliance." *Law Journal*, no. 1 (2021): 45–46.

measured relinquishment of the state's punitive authority is, in fact, better aligned with the broader interests of both the state and society.

9.5.3 *Application in Minor Systemic Offenses*

The theoretical foundations for compliance-based exculpation discussed above are fully applicable to enterprises involved in non-systemic offenses. However, in cases where criminal conduct results from collective decisions of the enterprise or from decisions made by its principal responsible persons, these grounds for exculpation may not be entirely applicable. After all, such enterprises possess a *subjective intent* to engage in criminal conduct, with their decision-making bodies effectively functioning as criminal collectives. The policies and decisions adopted by these enterprises are themselves characterized by a criminal orientation. For such enterprises, compliance assessment aimed at reforming their business and operational models and establishing internal monitoring mechanisms over affiliated personnel is unlikely to produce meaningful results in practice. Accordingly, in cases where criminal conduct is perpetrated through collective decision-making or by principal responsible persons, there is generally limited scope for the application of compliance-based exculpation.

Nevertheless, in cases involving minor systemic corporate offenses, the procuratorial authorities may still, pursuant to the principle of prosecutorial discretion, apply discretionary non-prosecution. In the course of applying discretionary non-prosecution, the procuratorial authorities may also designate enterprises that have committed minor systemic offenses as subjects of compliance assessment and, upon verifying that they have indeed established effective compliance programs, issue non-prosecution decisions. In light of this possibility, it becomes necessary to address the following question: why is it appropriate to adopt compliance assessment-based exculpation for enterprises that have engaged in minor systemic offenses?

To address this question, the author proposes a *procedural exculpation theory* as a preliminary explanation. Under the current framework of Chinese criminal legislation, there exists a substantial body of excessively severe substantive criminal provisions that have subjected enterprises to an ever-expanding spectrum of criminal liability risks. Chinese criminal law has established an increasing number of offenses applicable to corporate actors, the vast majority of which are statutory crimes, meaning offenses that originated as administrative violations but were subsequently criminalized by law. The threshold for corporate criminal liability is relatively low and often exhibits a form of *homogenization* with administrative misconduct. Apart from factors such as "serious circumstances," "large amounts," "grave consequences," or "failure to rectify following administrative penalties," there are few substantive distinctions between criminal and administrative liability. The scope of corporate criminal offenses has become extremely broad, with a continuing trend of expansion. From food and drug safety, tax administration, financial regulation, intellectual property protection, and environmental protection to corporate governance, cybersecurity, and data protection, enterprises may now potentially face charges under more than 150 distinct offenses spanning dozens of sectors of production and commercial activity.

Against the backdrop of increasingly pervasive and severe substantive criminalization, it is necessary for the procuratorial authorities to establish a mechanism of procedural exculpation to serve a moderating and remedial function. After all, although this category of systemic corporate offenses arises from collective decisions made by the enterprise or its principal responsible persons, the resulting harm is not particularly severe. If, through the compliance monitoring process, the enterprise establishes an effective compliance program sufficient to prevent the recurrence of criminal conduct, there is no compelling need for the procuratorial authorities to pursue prosecution. Instead, they may adopt a more lenient approach to criminal disposition. Such compliance-based exculpation decisions for enterprises that have committed systemic offenses not only advance the public interest but also embody the criminal justice policy of combining punishment with leniency. They represent a procedural remedy designed to counterbalance the expansion of substantive criminalization.

Of course, in cases involving such systemic corporate offenses, the procuratorial authorities may impose more stringent compliance requirements during the compliance assessment process. In addition to requiring the enterprise to engage a compliance monitor and establishing a longer assessment period, the authorities should also impose more severe sanctions on those directly responsible. For example, the procuratorial authorities may order the dissolution of the board of directors, mandate the replacement of the management team, and impose stringent penalties on the individuals directly accountable. Furthermore, the authorities may prescribe more rigorous compliance remediation measures, such as extending the duration of the assessment period, requiring the enterprise to engage a more specialized compliance monitoring team, and formulating broader and more detailed compliance obligations. Additionally, the procuratorial authorities may issue more specific compliance guidelines and establish clearer standards for compliance verification.

9.6 Future Directions

On the basis of distinguishing among different categories of corporate crime, this study has analyzed three compliance-based exculpation models and set out the normative justifications for each. At this point in the analysis, we may offer some concluding observations and address certain questions that have emerged in the course of China's reform of the compliance-based non-prosecution system.

First, it is clear that when enterprises establish effective compliance programs, such programs can serve distinct exculpatory functions in different types of cases. In ordinary cases of non-systemic corporate crime, the existence of a compliance mechanism can constitute direct evidence that the enterprise lacked criminal intent or negligence and can serve to sever the enterprise's liability from the criminal liability of affiliated individuals. In cases involving dereliction offenses, the establishment of a compliance management system can provide grounds for demonstrating that the enterprise fulfilled its statutory management obligations and did not act with dereliction, thereby supporting exemption from such liability. In cases where the enterprise has already satisfied the elements of a criminal offense, the procuratorial authorities may, by placing the enterprise under compliance assessment and issuing a decision to exempt it from criminal liability, achieve objectives such as restoring legal interests, preventing recidivism, and establishing effective internal supervision mechanisms. For enterprises that have committed systemic offenses, there is generally little scope for compliance-based exculpation, as these cases typically involve clear subjective culpability on the part of the enterprise itself. Only in minor cases may the procuratorial authorities regard the establishment of a compliance management system as an indicator of the minor nature of the offense and, on this basis, issue a non-prosecution decision. In this respect, compliance-based exculpation serves as a procedural remedy to counterbalance the excessively severe substantive criminalization of corporate conduct.

Secondly, *compliance-based non-prosecution* and *discretionary non-prosecution* cannot be regarded as entirely equivalent. In principle, discretionary non-prosecution is a form of lenient criminal disposition by which the procuratorial authorities exercise discretion to exempt enterprises involved in minor criminal offenses from prosecution, reflecting a model of *discretionary exculpation*. By contrast, compliance-based non-prosecution is a form of lenient criminal disposition grounded in the enterprise's participation in compliance assessment and the establishment of an effective compliance program, with the objectives of restoring legal interests, preventing recidivism, and establishing internal self-regulation mechanisms. This reflects a model of compliance-based exculpation. For cases of non-systemic corporate crime, the compliance-based exculpation mechanism may be applied regardless of whether the offense is minor or serious. In cases involving systemic corporate crime, however, there is generally little scope for compliance-based exculpation. Only in minor cases may the procuratorial authorities afford enterprises the opportunity to undergo compliance assessment and regard the establishment of an effective compliance program as an indication of the minor nature of the offense, thereby issuing a non-prosecution decision. In such circumstances, compliance-based non-prosecution and discretionary non-prosecution may overlap. Accordingly, the assertion frequently made by prosecutors—that "compliance-based non-prosecution applies only to minor criminal cases"—is defensible in the context of systemic corporate crime but does not apply to cases of non-systemic corporate crime.

Thirdly, the question arises whether compliance-based non-prosecution is applicable solely to the enterprise itself or also to the directly responsible individuals. In cases of non-systemic corporate crime, the criminal conduct of affiliated personnel occurs first, and the enterprise is subsequently held liable on the basis of its subjective culpability or dereliction. If the enterprise successfully raises a defense grounded in the implementation of compliance measures demonstrating the absence of fault or dereliction, the corporate offense can be recharacterized as an individual offense, meaning that the affiliated individuals alone bear criminal liability. In this way, the liability of the entity and that of the directly responsible individuals can be appropriately separated. This fully accords with a core principle of compliance theory: "Be lenient with the enterprise, but punish the responsible individuals severely." However, in cases of systemic corporate crime, traditional principles of attribution continue to apply—namely, that the criminal liability of the enterprise constitutes the premise and foundation for the liability of the directly responsible individuals. In such cases, applying compliance-based non-prosecution cannot achieve a separation between corporate and individual liability. Where the procuratorial authorities decide to apply the compliance assessment exemption mechanism in these cases, they must issue non-prosecution decisions for both the enterprise and the directly responsible individuals. Nonetheless, since these cases involve minor corporate offenses, there are no legal obstacles to applying discretionary non-prosecution to both the enterprise and the individuals involved.

Finally, the question arises whether compliance-based non-prosecution is more appropriate for small and medium-sized enterprises or for large corporate groups. Experience shows that non-systemic corporate crimes typically occur in the course of business operations by large corporate groups. These enterprises have complex internal governance structures, numerous commercial partners, and frequently engage in investment and acquisition activities, all of which increase the likelihood that affiliated individuals will engage in criminal conduct and necessitate substantial investments in internal governance. For such large enterprises, applying compliance-based non-prosecution can enhance internal supervision, help overcome the limitations of external regulatory oversight, and effectively prevent criminal conduct. By contrast, systemic corporate crimes often arise in the business activities of small and medium-sized enterprises. For these enterprises, the scope for applying compliance-based non-prosecution is relatively limited and is generally confined to cases involving minor corporate offenses. The position adopted by many procuratorial authorities—namely, that compliance-based non-prosecution should primarily be applied in cases where the directly responsible individuals would likely be sentenced to no more than three years' imprisonment—is broadly defensible. However, in such cases, the procuratorial authorities should, in addition to requiring the replacement of the board of directors and management team and the imposition of severe sanctions on those responsible, mandate that the enterprise actively cooperate with investigations, undertake effective remedial measures to mitigate harm and losses, and comply with more stringent compliance monitoring procedures.

CHAPTER 10

Criminal Compliance Incentives II: Compliance and Deferred Prosecution Agreements

10.1 Emergence of the Deferred Prosecution System

Traditionally, whether in cases involving individual defendants or corporate entities, prosecutorial authorities in the United States have had three principal options for handling criminal cases: first, initiating a public prosecution; second, issuing a non-prosecution decision; and third, entering into a plea agreement or sentencing agreement with the defendant, whereby, on the basis of the defendant's voluntary admission of guilt, the prosecutor recommends that the court impose a more lenient sentence.

However, in addition to these established practices—prosecution, non-prosecution, and plea or sentencing agreements—the United States also developed the *pre-trial diversion agreement* system. Under this framework, prosecutors and defendants may conclude an agreement by which the prosecution commits to suspending the initiation of formal criminal proceedings for a specified monitoring period, during which the defendant must fulfill a series of obligations. These obligations typically include voluntarily admitting the factual basis of the alleged offense, compensating victims, and pledging full cooperation with investigative authorities. If, upon review at the conclusion of the monitoring period, the prosecutor determines that the defendant has satisfactorily complied with all obligations under the agreement, the prosecution is formally withdrawn, and the case is closed without any conviction being recorded against the defendant. Originally, the pre-trial diversion agreement system emerged within the juvenile justice context in the United States, where it was used to dispose of cases involving minors suspected of minor criminal conduct. Over time, its application was gradually extended to drug-related cases requiring mandatory treatment measures. In 1974, the U.S. Congress enacted the Speedy Trial Act, which formally recognized the legal basis for the pre-trial diversion system. In 1990, the U.S. Department of Justice issued the United States Attorneys' Manual, setting out detailed guidance on the

R. Chen, *An Introduction to Corporate Compliance*,
https://doi.org/10.1007/978-981-95-7257-1_10

objectives, conditions, and procedures governing prosecutors' use of pre-trial diversion agreements. To this day, the pre-trial diversion agreement system remains an important mechanism for U.S. prosecutors to resolve minor criminal cases.

Since the 1990s, U.S. federal prosecutors have gradually extended the application of the pre-trial diversion agreement system to cases involving alleged corporate criminal conduct. In particular, in cases where corporations are suspected of offenses such as commercial bribery, money laundering, violations of export control regulations, breaches of personal data protection laws, financial fraud, environmental pollution, and violations of healthcare regulations, federal prosecutors have increasingly opted to enter into either Deferred Prosecution Agreements (DPAs) or Non-Prosecution Agreements (NPAs) with the corporations involved, as alternatives to initiating formal prosecutions or issuing outright non-prosecution decisions. Unlike plea bargaining, under which a defendant enters a guilty plea and is ultimately subject to a formal conviction by the court, these two forms of pre-trial diversion agreements operate on a different premise. Specifically, if, at the conclusion of the agreed monitoring period, the prosecutor determines that the corporation has fully complied with all terms and obligations set out in the agreement, the prosecutor may formally decline to pursue charges, thereby concluding the case without any criminal conviction. In other words, corporations that enter into plea agreements remain subject to an official finding of guilt by the court, whereas corporations that enter into a deferred prosecution agreement or a non-prosecution agreement may, upon successful completion of the monitoring period, be formally discharged from criminal liability without any record of conviction.[1]

Unlike the traditional pre-trial diversion agreements applied to individual defendants, deferred prosecution agreements and non-prosecution agreements involving corporations impose a series of additional obligations on the corporate defendant. On the one hand, the corporation is required to pay substantial fines, disgorge all illicit gains, and provide compensation to any victims who suffered losses as a result of the criminal conduct. On the other hand, as a condition of its continued cooperation with prosecutorial authorities, the enterprise must commit to rebuilding its compliance program or enhancing its existing compliance management system, accept the appointment of an independent compliance monitor designated by the prosecution, and submit periodic reports to the prosecutorial authorities detailing the progress of its compliance remediation efforts. Throughout the monitoring period, the prosecution maintains ongoing compliance oversight, and, at the conclusion of this period, determines whether to proceed with formal prosecution based on the enterprise's performance in establishing or improving its compliance framework.

[1] Cindy R. Alexander and Mark A. Cohen, "The Evolution of Corporate Criminal Settlements: An Empirical Perspective on Non-Prosecution, Deferred Prosecution, and Plea Agreement," *American Criminal Law Review* 52 (2015): 537.

From the perspective of institutional design, deferred prosecution agreements (DPAs) and non-prosecution agreements (NPAs) exhibit certain nuanced differences. Generally, where prosecutors have already initiated criminal proceedings, they may enter into a DPA with the corporate defendant. A DPA explicitly sets out the relevant facts underlying the alleged offense and must be submitted for judicial approval. In contrast, when charges have not yet been filed, prosecutors may instead conclude an NPA with the enterprise. Such agreements do not require court approval and typically do not contain detailed factual admissions regarding the alleged conduct; rather, they are negotiated exclusively between the prosecutor and the corporation. Nonetheless, in practice, once a DPA or NPA has been concluded by U.S. prosecutorial authorities, there is little substantive distinction between the obligations imposed under either framework. In 1992, the U.S. Attorney's Office for the Southern District of New York utilized the NPA mechanism for the first time in a securities fraud case involving Salomon Brothers. Two years later, that same office applied the DPA mechanism for the first time in a case against Prudential Securities concerning the misrepresentation of investment returns.[2]

The pre-trial diversion agreement system implemented by U.S. prosecutors in corporate cases has had a significant impact on the development of criminal procedure in other jurisdictions. This influence stems largely from its demonstrable benefits in reducing litigation costs, preventing recidivism among corporate offenders, and mitigating collateral harm to innocent stakeholders. However, because the non-prosecution agreement model confers excessively broad discretionary powers on prosecutors while effectively circumventing judicial oversight, many jurisdictions have shown a stronger preference for adopting the deferred prosecution agreement model refined in the United States. Following the American example, the United Kingdom formally established a deferred prosecution agreement regime through the enactment of the *Crime and Courts Act* in 2014.[3] In June 2018, Canada amended its Criminal Code to create a comparable system, thereby authorizing prosecutors to enter into deferred prosecution agreements with corporations suspected of committing serious economic crimes such as fraud, bribery, and money laundering. Also in 2018, Australia, drawing on the U.K. legislation as a legislative template, enacted the *Criminal Code Amendment* (Bribery of Foreign Public Officials) Act. This reform both revised provisions on transnational bribery and formally introduced a deferred prosecution agreement framework.[4] In March 2018, Singapore likewise established a deferred prosecution agreement regime

[2] Liangfang Ye, "The Development of the U.S. Corporate Deferred Prosecution Agreement System," *China Criminal Law Journal*, no. 3 (2014).

[3] "Deferred Prosecution Agreements: Key Differences Between the US and UK," August 24, 2019, https://www.marsh.com/content/dam/marsh/Documents/PDF/USen/Marsh%20Insights_Deferred%20Prosecution%20Agreements.pdf

[4] "Australia's New DPA System and What It Means for General Practitioners," August 24, 2019, https://learn.asialawnetwork.com/2019/03/05/deferred-prosecution-agreements-singapore/

modeled on the U.K. approach. The Singapore Parliament passed the *Criminal Justice Reform Act*, which empowers prosecutors to conclude conditional deferred prosecution agreements with corporations suspected of offenses including bribery and money laundering.[5]

On December 8, 2016, the French Parliament adopted the *Sapin II Law*, which was designed to strengthen sanctions against corporate bribery. Alongside the implementation of a mandatory corporate compliance framework, the legislation introduced a U.S.-style deferred prosecution agreement mechanism. This development represented France's second major embrace of an adversarial, negotiation-based justice model derived from the common law tradition, following its earlier adoption of the Anglo-American approach to plea bargaining and sentencing agreements. Under this framework, prosecutorial authorities may, in cases involving corporations suspected of commercial bribery, enter into conditional settlement agreements based on a pre-trial guilty plea procedure (*Comparution sur Reconnaissance Préalable de Culpabilité*, CRPC). This procedure—known as the Judicial Public Interest Agreement (Convention Judiciaire d'Intérêt Public, CJIP)—has come to be regarded as the French analogue of the deferred prosecution agreement. It signifies the formal integration of the American model of negotiated prosecution and settlement into a continental European civil law jurisdiction.[6]

It is noteworthy that whether in the United States—where deferred prosecution agreements and non-prosecution agreements have been extensively utilized—or in jurisdictions such as the United Kingdom, Canada, Australia, Singapore, and France, the requirement that enterprises reconstruct or enhance their compliance frameworks has consistently been incorporated as a core component of these agreements and regarded as a critical precondition for prosecutors' suspension of criminal proceedings. In practice, a corporation's commitment to establishing or strengthening an effective compliance program has become a fundamental prerequisite for prosecutors to consider concluding a deferred prosecution agreement. The degree to which an enterprise succeeds in implementing and improving its compliance measures has likewise emerged as a principal determinant of whether prosecutorial authorities ultimately elect to terminate prosecution. To a significant extent, the opportunity to negotiate a deferred prosecution agreement—and thereby persuade prosecutors to withdraw criminal charges—has become one of the most powerful incentives motivating corporations to rebuild or refine their compliance systems.

At present, government regulatory authorities in China are vigorously advancing the establishment of corporate compliance management systems through administrative initiatives, and an increasing number of state-owned and private enterprises have begun to attach greater importance to the

[5] "Commentary: Deferred Prosecution Agreements in Singapore," August 24, 2019, https://learn.asialawnetwork.com

[6] "French Announces Its First Deferred Prosecution Agreement," August 24, 2019, https://www.skadden.com>2017/12.

development of compliance programs. In stark contrast, however, China's Criminal Law remains notably rigid in its approach to the conviction and sentencing of corporate offenders. Similarly, the Criminal Procedure Law has yet to establish any dedicated procedural framework for handling cases involving corporate crime. In particular, neither of these laws has incorporated compliance mechanisms, nor have they created criminal law incentives for enterprises to adopt compliance systems or procedural pathways through which enterprises might obtain leniency in exchange for implementing compliance measures. Consequently, enterprises currently lack sufficiently strong incentives to proactively develop robust compliance frameworks.

In light of this gap, the author proposes to undertake a preliminary study, from a comparative law perspective, of the deferred prosecution agreement regimes in jurisdictions such as the United States, the United Kingdom, France, Australia, Canada, and Singapore. This chapter will classify these regimes into two primary models—prosecutorial discretion and judicial review—analyze the relationship between deferred prosecution agreements and corporate compliance systems, and set forth the normative justifications for these regimes. On this basis, it will offer preliminary commentary on the necessity and feasibility of introducing such mechanisms into China's legal system.

10.2 Models of Deferred Prosecution Agreements

When U.S. prosecutors began applying pre-trial diversion agreements to corporate defendants, they developed two distinct mechanisms: the deferred prosecution agreement (DPA) and the non-prosecution agreement (NPA). The latter confers on prosecutors an almost unilateral authority, allowing them to enter into agreements with corporate defendants entirely at their own discretion, without any form of judicial oversight. Although DPAs in the United States formally require review and approval by a judge, in practice every aspect of these agreements—including their substantive content, the duration of the monitoring period, monitoring arrangements, and the ultimate determination of outcomes—remains almost entirely under prosecutorial control, rendering judicial review and supervision largely nominal. By contrast, jurisdictions such as the United Kingdom and France, as well as Canada, Australia, and Singapore, which have followed the British model, have not only rejected the U.S.-style NPA system characterized by prosecutorial dominance but also undertaken substantial reforms of the DPA framework to subject it to more rigorous judicial scrutiny. Under these systems, once the prosecutor and the corporate defendant have reached a deferred prosecution agreement, the prosecutor must submit the agreement to the court. The agreement only acquires legal effect upon judicial confirmation following a hearing. During the monitoring period, the court is responsible for overseeing the implementation of the agreement, in particular the enterprise's efforts to rebuild or enhance its compliance program. Upon the conclusion of the monitoring period, the prosecutor must submit a recommendation to the court, which then decides whether to dismiss the case or to reinstate judicial proceedings. As a result, in jurisdictions such as the United Kingdom and France, a model of judicially supervised deferred prosecution has emerged that stands in clear contrast to the U.S. approach.[7] In the following discussion, the author will draw on the deferred prosecution agreement regimes of the United States, the United Kingdom, France, Canada, Australia, and Singapore to compare these two models and offer a brief commentary.

10.2.1 *The Prosecutorial Discretion Model*

In the United States, the decision whether to apply a deferred prosecution agreement or a non-prosecution agreement to a corporate defendant lies entirely within the discretion of federal or state prosecutors. Judicial review or approval of a deferred prosecution agreement frequently amounts to a purely formal procedure that lacks substantive oversight. Deferred prosecution agreements may be used in a broad array of corporate criminal cases, including—but not limited to—monopolistic conduct, fraud, bribery, tax evasion, environmental pollution, violations of export control laws, and infringements of personal data protection regulations. Such cases typically implicate a complex matrix of legal regimes, including securities law, trade law, unfair competition law, environmental protection statutes, the Foreign Corrupt Practices Act, food and drug safety legislation, tax and currency transaction law, anti-fraud provisions, and anti-money laundering regulations.

U.S. law grants prosecutors broad enforcement authority, including significant discretion to negotiate and enter into deferred prosecution agreements or non-prosecution agreements with corporate defendants. In practice, because nearly all forms of corporate misconduct simultaneously constitute both criminal offenses and administrative violations, prosecutors frequently collaborate with other government regulatory agencies to conclude so-called "global settlement agreements" with the enterprises involved. Government agencies that commonly participate alongside the Department of Justice in negotiating deferred prosecution agreements include the Securities and Exchange Commission (SEC), the Food and Drug Administration (FDA), the Department of Commerce, the Department of the Treasury, and the Federal Trade Commission (FTC). In many cases, state prosecutors likewise coordinate with state-level regulatory authorities to enter into deferred prosecution agreements. For example, in the well-known Siemens foreign bribery case, the Department of Justice and the SEC jointly entered into a deferred prosecution agreement with Siemens AG. Similarly, in the case involving ZTE Corporation's violations of export control laws, the Department of Justice, acting in

[7] Jennifer Arlen, "The Potential Promise and Perils of Introducing Deferred Prosecution Agreements Outside the U.S.," NYU School of Law, Public Law Research Paper No. 19–30, July 29, 2019. SSRN: https://ssrn.com/abstract=3428657. Accessed August 24, 2019.

coordination with the Department of Commerce and the Department of the Treasury, entered into a deferred prosecution agreement with ZTE.[8]

Within the pre-trial diversion agreement frameworks employed by U.S. prosecutors, non-prosecution agreements are invoked with markedly greater frequency than deferred prosecution agreements. To some extent, this pattern reflects prosecutors' preference for the exercise of discretionary authority, as non-prosecution agreements entirely circumvent even the most minimal forms of judicial scrutiny. In cases involving deferred prosecution agreements, prosecutors typically engage in extensive settlement negotiations with corporate defendants lasting several months or even over a year. Only after reaching a consensus do they submit the draft agreement to the court. In practice, judges generally conduct a purely formal review and almost never reject or revise the agreements presented by the prosecution. Once a DPA has been approved, judicial monitoring of its implementation tends to be extremely limited. For example, in *USA v. Fokker Services B.V.* (2016), a federal district court judge refused to approve a deferred prosecution agreement on the grounds that prosecutors had declined to indict individual corporate executives and that the agreement's terms were excessively lenient toward the company. However, on appeal, the D.C. Circuit Court of Appeals reversed the district court's decision, holding that determinations as to whether to enter into a DPA and how to define its specific terms fall wholly within the prerogative of federal prosecutors.[9] In another case in 2017, the U.S. Court of Appeals for the Second Circuit explicitly limited the authority of judges to oversee the performance of DPAs. Available evidence suggests that, to date, whether in reviewing and approving deferred prosecution agreements or in monitoring their execution, U.S. courts have generally adopted a hands-off approach and have rarely exercised substantive oversight.[10] Furthermore, at the conclusion of the monitoring period, the evaluation of a company's compliance with the agreement and the decision whether to bring charges remain almost exclusively within the discretion of the prosecution, with judges virtually never overturning prosecutorial decisions. The increasingly perfunctory nature of judicial review has prompted growing criticism. Many commentators contend that prosecutors have, in effect, circumvented the formal legal system when entering into DPAs, thereby giving rise to significant constitutional and public policy concerns. Others have expressed apprehension that prosecutors wield an undue advantage in negotiating such agreements and may abuse prosecutorial authority during discussions with corporate defendants.[11]

In the application of deferred prosecution agreements, judicial review imposes only minimal constraints on prosecutorial discretion. To mitigate the

[8] Peter Spivack and Sujit Raman, "Regulating the 'New Regulations': Current Trends in Deferred Prosecution Agreements," *American Criminal Law Review* 45 (2008): 159.

[9] United States v. Fokker Services B.V., 818 F.3d 733, 742–745 (D.C. Cir. 2016).

[10] United States v. HSBC Bank USA, N.A., 863 F.3d 125 (2d Cir. 2017).

[11] Wilson Ang et al., *Deferred Prosecution Agreement—Justice Delayed or Justice Denied?* Norton Rose Fulbright, March 2018.

risk of abuse inherent in such discretion, the U.S. Department of Justice has, over time, issued a series of guidelines and memoranda setting forth standards of conduct for federal prosecutors when determining whether to bring criminal charges against corporations. Among these instruments, the 1999 Holder Memorandum, titled Bringing Criminal Charges Against Corporations, enumerated eight factors that prosecutors should weigh when deciding whether to pursue corporate indictments. The 2003 Thompson Memorandum, Principles of Federal Prosecution of Business Organizations, instructed prosecutors to regard corporate cooperation with governmental investigations and the voluntary disclosure of misconduct as grounds for leniency. It further emphasized that, wherever feasible, prosecutors should resolve matters through DPAs and NPAs rather than formal indictments. The 2006 McNulty Memorandum imposed certain restrictions on the measures prosecutors could adopt to secure corporate cooperation. In 2008, the Filip Memorandum revised the Thompson Memorandum and was incorporated into the United States Attorneys' Manual. That same year, the Morford Memorandum established detailed guidance for the appointment of compliance monitors by prosecutors and delineated the scope of monitors' authority. Finally, the 2010 Grindler Memorandum provided additional clarification regarding the role of compliance monitors in deferred prosecution agreements, particularly concerning the resolution of disputes between the corporation and the monitor arising during the implementation of such agreements.[12]

What, then, are the principal components of a typical deferred prosecution agreement? A review of numerous DPAs concluded between U.S. prosecutors and corporate defendants makes it possible to summarize the core obligations typically imposed on enterprises. First, the corporate defendant must formally admit the factual basis underlying its criminal conduct. Second, the company is required to accept the sanctions imposed by law enforcement authorities, including monetary fines, restitution, disgorgement of illicit profits, compensation to victims, and other remedial measures. Third, the enterprise has a continuing obligation to cooperate fully with any ongoing investigations conducted by enforcement agencies. Fourth, the company must implement a robust compliance program designed to prevent and deter the recurrence of similar unlawful or improper practices in the future. Fifth, it must replace or even restructure its board of directors or senior management team and impose stringent disciplinary measures on employees or executives directly responsible for the misconduct. Sixth, the enterprise is required to accept the appointment of an independent compliance monitor designated by the prosecution and to submit to continuous compliance oversight, typically for a period of no less than three years. Seventh, throughout the monitoring period, the company must refrain from committing the same offense again or otherwise violating any provisions of the agreement. Eighth, the corporate defendant must waive its right to a

[12] Matt Senko, "Prosecutorial Overreaching in Deferred Prosecution Agreements," *Southern California Interdisciplinary Law Journal* 19 (2009–2010): 163.

speedy trial and any defenses relating to statutes of limitation. Ninth, the enterprise is prohibited from making any statements that contradict the content or purpose of the agreement. Finally, the agreement may include other related obligations as specified in the negotiated terms.

By implementing deferred prosecution agreements, U.S. federal prosecutors have routinely required corporate defendants to pay fines that often reach hundreds of millions of dollars. Each year, the Department of Justice enters into DPAs and NPAs with companies worldwide, generating billions of dollars in aggregate financial penalties. In recent years, the revenue derived from such settlements has demonstrated a consistent upward trajectory. This practice has become particularly controversial in relation to foreign corporations that either conduct business within the United States or are listed on U.S. securities exchanges. A growing number of commentators have accused the Department of Justice of acting with questionable motives and have even characterized these settlement fines as a form of "extortion" directed at foreign enterprises. Nonetheless, from an objective standpoint, the use of deferred prosecution and non-prosecution agreements has undeniably subjected companies engaged in bribery, money laundering, and other serious misconduct to powerful sanctions. Perhaps most significant is that, in addition to imposing substantial monetary penalties, prosecutors routinely set monitoring periods during which corporate defendants are required to establish or strengthen compliance frameworks. In this way, compliance regimes and compliance cultures have been propagated on a global scale. In a very real sense, the U.S. system of deferred prosecution agreements has compelled multinational corporations worldwide to prioritize the development and enhancement of compliance mechanisms, making this regime one of the most influential drivers of corporate compliance internationally.

10.2.2 The Judicial Review Model (I)

In the United Kingdom, a deferred prosecution agreement (DPA) refers to a conditional suspension of prosecution concluded between the prosecuting authority and a corporate defendant, under judicial supervision, after the initiation of criminal proceedings. The principal agencies empowered to negotiate such agreements are the Serious Fraud Office (SFO) and the Crown Prosecution Service (CPS). These bodies hold the statutory authority to prosecute criminal cases and may apply for a DPA in cases involving eligible offenses such as fraud, bribery, and other forms of corporate misconduct.

Unlike the U.S. deferred prosecution system, the UK's DPA regime is applicable solely to legal entities suspected of criminal activity and does not extend to individual defendants. While the agreement is voluntarily negotiated between the prosecution and the company, it acquires legal force only following judicial examination and formal approval. Once approved, the DPA suspends the underlying criminal proceedings. Throughout the monitoring period prescribed by the agreement, the corporate defendant is obligated to fulfill all specified requirements, in particular the payment of financial penalties and the implementation of an effective compliance program. At the conclusion of the monitoring period, if the prosecuting authority, upon review, determines that the company has satisfactorily performed its obligations under the DPA and that discontinuing the prosecution would better serve the public interest, it may formally withdraw the charges. In such circumstances, the matter is concluded without a conviction, allowing the enterprise to avoid criminal liability.

To prevent prosecutors from abusing their discretion, UK law establishes two principal standards that must be satisfied before a deferred prosecution agreement may be pursued: the evidential test and the public interest test.

Under the evidential test, the prosecutor must be satisfied either that there is sufficient evidence to establish that the alleged offense has been committed or that there is a reasonable suspicion, based on some admissible evidence, that the company has engaged in criminal conduct, together with reasonable grounds to believe that further investigation will produce additional admissible evidence such that the existing evidence would be capable of proving the offense.

With respect to the public interest test, the prosecutor must assess whether refraining from prosecution and instead entering into a deferred prosecution agreement would better serve the public interest. In conducting this assessment, prosecutors are required to take into account a range of factors, including whether the enterprise has a history of similar misconduct; whether it has previously been subject to criminal, civil, or regulatory sanctions, in which case a deferred prosecution agreement is less likely to be appropriate; whether the company has established an effective compliance program; and, in cases involving suspected violations of the *Bribery Act* 2010, whether it has adhered to the guidance on adequate procedures. Prosecutors must also consider whether, upon discovery of the misconduct, the company has cooperated fully with the prosecuting authorities, among other relevant considerations.

Ordinarily, a comprehensive deferred prosecution agreement in the United Kingdom contains provisions requiring the company to pay an agreed financial penalty; compensate victims for their losses; cover the costs incurred by the prosecuting authority; cooperate fully with law enforcement agencies; comply with prohibitions against engaging in specified activities; submit financial reports; establish a robust compliance or monitoring program; and maintain cooperation with the prosecution in any future proceedings against individual employees, among other obligations.

Compared with the U.S. model, the UK deferred prosecution agreement regime is marked by a distinctive feature: any such agreement must undergo judicial review, receive formal approval, and be subject to ongoing judicial oversight. During negotiations with the corporate defendant, the prosecutor may submit a unilaterally prepared statement of facts, together with details of each alleged offense. The parties may agree to maintain the confidentiality of the factual materials during the negotiation process, and a DPA may be concluded only if consensus is reached regarding the statement of facts. Before the agreement is signed, the prosecutor must satisfy the judge that entering into the DPA is likely to serve the interests of justice and that all of its provisions are fair, reasonable, and proportionate. After the DPA is submitted, the judge conducts a private (in camera) hearing to review its terms in detail. Once the judge has accepted the agreement, a public hearing is convened at which the court formally approves the DPA. Only thereafter may the prosecutor make the contents of the agreement publicly available.[13]

Specifically, UK law establishes a four-stage procedure for the application of a deferred prosecution agreement (DPA). First, the initiation stage. A DPA may be initiated when a company suspected of economic crime engages in self-reporting, a whistleblower submits a report, or the prosecuting authority undertakes a preliminary investigation. During this stage, the prosecutor and the company engage in preliminary discussions to ascertain whether there is a mutual intention to explore the possibility of entering into a DPA. Second, the negotiation stage. The prosecutor issues a formal invitation to the company to commence DPA negotiations. The parties must then identify the factual basis for the suspected misconduct and determine the applicable legal provisions. Third, the drafting stage. The prosecutor and the company prepare a draft DPA in accordance with the relevant provisions of the Prosecution of Offences Act and the applicable prosecutorial guidance. Fourth, judicial scrutiny and approval. Once an agreement is reached, the draft DPA must be submitted to the court for a two-stage review: (1) the preliminary hearing, conducted in private, during which the prosecutor submits supporting materials, including a statement of facts, and demonstrates to the court that the proposed DPA is likely to serve the interests of justice and that its terms are fair, reasonable, and proportionate. At this stage, the judge may propose modifications to the terms of the DPA or decline to approve the proposed agreement; (2) the final hearing, during which the prosecutor applies to the Crown Court for a declaration that the DPA is indeed in the interests of justice and that its terms are fair, reasonable, and proportionate. Once the DPA has been approved, the court is required to publish the full text of the agreement in a public hearing.[14]

Since the *Crime and Courts Act* entered into force in 2014, and up to December 2018, UK prosecuting authorities had successfully concluded deferred prosecution agreements (DPAs) with four companies: Standard Bank (2015), an anonymized company (2016), Rolls-Royce (2017), and Tesco (2017). As a principal component of these agreements, the four companies collectively paid financial penalties amounting to £670 million to the UK government. On 30 November 2018, the Serious Fraud Office announced that the UK's first DPA had formally expired. The company involved—Standard

[13] E. Chua and B. Chan, "Deferred Prosecution Agreements in Singapore: What Is the Appropriate Standard for Judicial Approval?" *International Commentary on Evidence*, published online August 1, 2019. https://doi.org/10.1515/ice-2019-0002

[14] "The Mechanics of Deferred Prosecution Agreements in the UK," August 7, 2019, https://www.gov.uk/speeches

Bank PLC (now known as ICBC Standard Bank)—had fully complied with the terms of the agreement, and the prosecution was accordingly withdrawn.

On 30 November 2015, the UK Serious Fraud Office (SFO) entered into a deferred prosecution agreement (DPA) with Standard Bank. Prior to this, prosecutors had filed charges alleging that Standard Bank had violated Section 7 of the *Bribery Act* 2010 by failing to prevent commercial bribery carried out by the bank's employees in Tanzania. Under the terms of the agreement, Standard Bank undertook the following obligations. First, it was required to cooperate fully and transparently with the investigating authorities, including disclosing information and materials related to the conduct of relevant individuals. Second, it agreed to pay $6 million in compensation to the Tanzanian government, together with accrued interest. Third, profits of $8.4 million were to be confiscated by the SFO and transferred to the UK Treasury. Fourth, the bank was fined $16.8 million, also to be paid to the UK Treasury. Fifth, it committed to rebuilding its corporate compliance program. Sixth, Standard Bank agreed to pay £330,000 in costs to the SFO. By August 2017, Standard Bank had fully discharged all obligations stipulated in the agreement. The SFO confirmed the bank's complete compliance with the DPA. With the court's approval, the SFO formally withdrew the prosecution.[15]

10.2.3 The Judicial Review Model (II)

Under the influence of the UK approach, Canada, Australia, and Singapore have likewise adopted a model of deferred prosecution agreements characterized by judicial supervision. In France, the Judicial Public Interest Agreement (CJIP) regime similarly incorporates the key feature of a negotiated settlement between the prosecuting authorities and the corporate defendant, but places the resulting agreement firmly within a framework of judicial scrutiny. Accordingly, this mechanism may be regarded as the French equivalent of a deferred prosecution agreement and is classified here as part of the "judicial review model."

For example, Canadian prosecutors may enter into a deferred prosecution agreement with a corporate defendant. Under such an agreement, if the enterprise fulfills its obligations during the designated monitoring period—including paying fines and compensation and establishing or improving a compliance program—the prosecution will withdraw the criminal charges at the conclusion of that period. Consistent with the approach in the United Kingdom, Canada's DPA regime applies exclusively to legal entities and does not extend to natural persons. After negotiations have been concluded and an agreement reached, the prosecutor must submit the DPA to the court for judicial review. In assessing the legality of the agreement, the judge is required to ensure that its terms are fair, reasonable, and proportionate. Once judicial approval has been

[15] "SFO Agrees First UK DPA with Standard Bank," August 7, 2019, https://www.sfo.gov.uk/News-Release/SFO-Agrees-first-UK-DPA-with-Standard-Bank

granted, the agreement must be publicly disclosed to ensure transparency and accountability in the DPA process.

Similar to their counterparts in the United Kingdom, Canadian prosecutors, when deciding whether to enter into a deferred prosecution agreement and determining the specific terms to be included, must consider a range of factors. These include: first, whether the enterprise has voluntarily reported and acknowledged its misconduct; second, whether the company has cooperated fully with governmental authorities; third, whether the enterprise has demonstrated a genuine commitment to reforming its business practices and corporate culture; fourth, the nature and seriousness of the alleged offense; fifth, the degree of culpability involved (for example, whether senior management tolerated or facilitated the misconduct); sixth, whether the company has strengthened or established an effective compliance program; and seventh, whether a criminal conviction would result in significant adverse consequences for innocent third parties.[16]

In Australia, for example, a deferred prosecution agreement (DPA) is a voluntary arrangement entered into between prosecutors and a corporate defendant, under which the company may avoid prosecution by fulfilling certain obligations—such as compensating victims, paying financial penalties, and establishing or enhancing a compliance program. Closely resembling the UK model, Australia's DPA framework applies exclusively to corporate entities and does not extend to natural persons. DPAs are reserved for relatively serious forms of corporate crime, including bribery, fraud, insider trading, and other misconduct involving market transactions. The terms of a DPA are negotiated between the prosecutor and the company and typically encompass requirements to pay fines, compensate victims, and implement compliance measures. Judges bear responsibility for reviewing the content of the agreement, ensuring that its terms serve the interests of justice and are fair, reasonable, and proportionate. Once judicial approval is granted, the DPA must be made public. Following such approval, prosecutors undertake not to initiate criminal proceedings against the company provided that it fulfills its obligations during the monitoring period.

Under Australian law, a comprehensive deferred prosecution agreement (DPA) typically includes the following elements. First, a statement of facts describing all unlawful conduct attributed to the corporate defendant, although the agreement does not require the company to formally admit guilt regarding the offenses alleged by the prosecution. Second, obligations imposed on the company to comply fully with the terms of the agreement. Where appropriate, the prosecutor may appoint an independent monitor to oversee compliance. Third, provisions specifying the financial penalties to be imposed. In determining the amount, the prosecutor considers factors such as the company's degree of cooperation, the gravity of the criminal penalties that would result from

[16] "Features of Canada's New DPA Scheme," August 24, 2019, https://www.mondaq.com/canada/crime

conviction, and the profits obtained through the misconduct. Fourth, detailed provisions enumerating the circumstances that constitute a breach of the agreement and the legal consequences arising from such breaches. Fifth, an obligation requiring the company to cooperate with and support any investigations or prosecutions brought against individual employees implicated in the conduct. Sixth, requirements for the company to strengthen its compliance program or implement other remedial measures aimed at preventing future violations. Seventh, provisions obliging the company to reimburse the prosecution for costs incurred in negotiating and concluding the agreement, to compensate victims, and to bear any additional financial or legal consequences resulting from non-compliance with the DPA's terms.[17]

Similarly, in Singapore, the deferred prosecution agreement (DPA) framework closely resembles the model adopted in the United Kingdom. Under this system, a DPA constitutes a conditional suspension of prosecution negotiated between the prosecutor and a corporation suspected of economic offenses such as bribery and money laundering. Pursuant to the agreement, the corporate defendant undertakes to fulfill a range of specified obligations, including implementing a comprehensive compliance program, strengthening internal policies and controls, appointing an independent compliance monitor, cooperating with investigations and prosecutions of individual employees, compensating victims, and paying financial penalties, among other measures. Should the company fail to discharge its obligations under the DPA, the prosecutor retains the authority to reinstitute criminal proceedings against the enterprise. For the corporate defendant, opting for a DPA offers the prospect of avoiding a formal conviction by the court, thereby mitigating the significant commercial and reputational harm typically associated with a criminal judgment and subjecting the company to sanctions that are generally less severe than those imposed through conventional criminal prosecution.

After concluding a deferred prosecution agreement (DPA) with the corporate defendant, the prosecutor must submit the agreement to the High Court of Singapore for judicial review. The Court must be satisfied that the agreement serves the interests of justice and that its terms are "fair, reasonable, and proportionate" before granting approval. Once the DPA has been approved, the prosecution is required to make its content publicly available. During the period in which the DPA remains in effect, the prosecutor retains the authority to propose amendments to its terms; however, any such modifications must be reviewed and approved by the High Court. If the prosecutor determines that the corporate defendant has failed to comply with the agreement during the monitoring period, the prosecutor must petition the Court for relief. The Court may authorize the reinstatement of criminal proceedings against the

[17]"How Might a Deferred Prosecution Agreement Scheme Work in Australia?" August 24, 2019, https://www.lexology.com/detail

company only if it is satisfied, on the balance of probabilities, that the defendant has breached the agreement.[18]

Whether in Canada, Australia, or Singapore, all of these jurisdictions are Commonwealth countries that were subject to prolonged British colonial rule and that have adopted the common law system. As a result, the acceptance of a deferred prosecution agreement (DPA) regime has not encountered significant institutional or cultural obstacles. By contrast, France is a civil law country, which raises the question: in what respects does the French Judicial Public Interest Agreement (CJIP) differ from the UK's DPA system?

Unlike the frameworks in the United Kingdom and the United States, French law imposes stringent restrictions on the content of agreements negotiated between prosecutors and corporate defendants and grants judges the authority, ex officio, to conduct a substantive review of such settlement agreements. Under the *Sapin II Law*, a prosecutor may enter into a CJIP with a corporation only if the company agrees to pay a financial penalty not exceeding 30% of its average annual turnover over the preceding three years. In addition, the company must undertake, under the supervision of the French Anti-Corruption Agency (AFA) and with the assistance of an independent third-party expert, to establish or enhance its compliance program within a period of three years. In cases involving identifiable victims, the company is further required to compensate the victims for their losses in the agreed manner within one year. Once the agreement has been concluded, the prosecutor must submit it to the court, which may confirm the CJIP only after conducting a hearing. The settlement becomes legally effective upon judicial approval. At the conclusion of the monitoring period—which may not exceed three years—the prosecutor reviews whether the company has fulfilled all obligations under the agreement. If so, the prosecutor applies to the court to terminate the criminal proceedings. Conversely, if the company has failed to comply, the prosecutor reports the breach to the court, which then determines whether prosecution should be resumed.

Compared with the deferred prosecution agreements employed in the United States and the United Kingdom, the French Judicial Public Interest Agreement (CJIP) exhibits several distinctive features. First, the corporate defendant is not required to enter a guilty plea. However, it must acknowledge the "statement of facts" prepared by the prosecution and accept its legal qualification—namely, that these facts constitute the offenses alleged against the company. This acknowledgment does not, however, amount to an admission of guilt and does not result in a criminal conviction or the creation of a criminal record. Second, the agreement is concluded exclusively between the prosecutor and the legal entity; it cannot be concluded with any natural persons. Third, the CJIP is limited to specific categories of offenses, notably corruption, money laundering, and related forms of misconduct. Fourth, the agreement typically

[18] Wilson Ang et al., "Deferred Prosecution Agreements in Singapore—Five Things You Should Know," August 24, 2019, https://www.regulationtomorrow.com

imposes a range of obligations on the company, including payment of financial penalties, compensation of victims, and implementation or enhancement of a compliance program under the supervision of the Anti-Corruption Agency.[19]

In terms of judicial review, the French CJIP is more comparable to the UK's deferred prosecution agreement (DPA) model, in that it grants judges broad authority to conduct comprehensive scrutiny of the agreement submitted by the prosecution. Once the prosecutor has filed the agreement with the court, the judge examines it and, if satisfied, issues formal approval. After approval, the full text of the agreement must be published on an official website. Judicial scrutiny primarily focuses on several questions: whether there is a justified need for applying a deferred prosecution agreement; whether the procedural requirements have been properly observed; whether the sanctions proposed fall within the limits permitted by law; and whether the penalties are proportionate to the profits derived from the unlawful conduct. Beyond these aspects, the court is only empowered to accept or reject the proposed agreement in its entirety; it is not authorized to modify any of its terms. Furthermore, after the agreement has been approved, the judge does not assume any supervisory role over its subsequent implementation and has no power to assess whether the company has fulfilled its obligations under the agreement.

On 27 November 2017, the French National Financial Prosecutor's Office (Parquet National Financier, PNF), responsible for prosecuting serious financial crimes, concluded the country's first Judicial Public Interest Agreement (CJIP) with the Swiss branch of HSBC Bank, which had been under investigation for money laundering offenses. The agreement was subsequently approved by the Paris High Court. According to the statement of facts acknowledged by the bank, the prosecution alleged that a former employee of HSBC's Swiss branch had stolen client records and transmitted them to the French authorities. These records revealed that numerous French clients had concealed their actual income and assets from the tax authorities, thereby engaging in tax evasion. The bank itself was suspected of facilitating money laundering and engaging in activities beyond the scope of legitimate banking operations. During the ensuing investigation, HSBC implemented comprehensive reforms of its internal governance structures and business procedures, undertaking significant efforts to mitigate legal risks.

Following six months of negotiations, the National Financial Prosecutor's Office announced the agreement, which was formally endorsed by the Paris High Court. Under its terms, HSBC's Swiss branch agreed to pay a total of €300 million in financial penalties and compensation, including €142 million in reparations to the French state, €86 million in disgorgement of profits, and €72 million in fines. The latter two amounts did not exceed 30% of the branch's

[19] "The French Prosecutor Office Has Entered Into the First French DPA in History With HSBC Private Bank Suisse," August 24, 2019, https://www.kramerlevin.com

average annual revenue over the preceding three years; however, the compensation payment was not subject to this cap.[20]

It is noteworthy that the agreement concluded between the prosecution and HSBC did not include any provisions obliging the bank to establish or further enhance a compliance program. This omission was primarily attributable to the fact that, in the years prior to the conclusion of the agreement, HSBC—as a UK-headquartered multinational banking group—had already implemented substantial reforms aimed at addressing compliance deficiencies in the credit management practices of its Swiss operations. In particular, the bank had taken proactive measures to strengthen its anti-money laundering and tax compliance frameworks, which were regarded by the authorities as demonstrating a significant and genuine commitment to mitigating legal and compliance risks.

In summary, whether in Canada, Australia, Singapore, or France, these jurisdictions have essentially followed the United Kingdom's example, establishing a framework of judicially supervised deferred prosecution agreements (DPAs). Once a prosecutor has reached a preliminary settlement with a corporate defendant suspected of economic crime, the agreement must be submitted to the court for review. If, following a hearing, the court determines that the agreement serves the interests of justice and satisfies the requirements of fairness, reasonableness, and proportionality, it may approve the agreement. The prosecutor is then obligated to disclose the full text and substance of the agreement to the public. During the implementation phase, if the company fails to comply with any of the agreed terms, the prosecutor must apply to the court for a determination. The court has the authority to revoke the agreement and authorize the resumption of criminal proceedings, at which point the case proceeds to trial. Upon the expiration of the monitoring period, the court retains the authority to conduct a comprehensive review of the company's performance under the agreement and to decide whether to terminate the proceedings definitively or to permit the prosecutor to pursue formal charges. In short, although prosecutors maintain considerable discretion in negotiating, executing, and monitoring such agreements, this discretion is subject to meaningful judicial constraints and oversight.

10.3 Compliance and Deferred Prosecution

The system of deferred prosecution agreements (DPAs) originated in the United States, where it has been applied both to individuals accused of minor offenses and to corporations implicated in economic crimes. For individual defendants, a DPA is essentially a conditional non-prosecution arrangement concluded by a prosecutor in consideration of the defendant's demonstrated willingness to reform, and it bears no inherent connection to corporate compliance mechanisms. In contrast, when applied to corporations suspected of

[20] "The French Prosecutor Office Has Entered Into the First French DPA in History With HSBC Private Bank Suisse," August 24, 2019, https://www.kramerlevin.com

commercial offenses, DPAs have become inextricably linked with the establishment and enhancement of compliance programs. In the United States, the use of DPAs in corporate cases remained relatively rare throughout the 1990s. It was only in the early 2000s—following the high-profile collapses of Enron, WorldCom, and Arthur Andersen—that the Department of Justice began to deploy DPAs on a broader scale. Although federal prosecutors obtained convictions in these cases, the prosecutions also triggered severe collateral consequences, including corporate bankruptcies, widespread job losses, and profound disruptions to economic and financial stability. These experiences prompted the Department of Justice to adopt DPAs more systematically, embedding compliance obligations in nearly every agreement as a means of encouraging corporate reform while avoiding the devastating repercussions of formal convictions. Beginning in 2014, the United Kingdom and France, in establishing their own deferred prosecution frameworks, also incorporated corporate compliance requirements as a core component of these agreements, making the development or improvement of compliance programs both a central condition of settlement and a prerequisite for the ultimate decision not to proceed with prosecution. Since 2018, Canada, Australia, and Singapore, in adopting deferred prosecution regimes modeled in part on the UK approach, have likewise without exception required corporate compliance commitments as an integral element of their agreements.

Although the manner and extent to which different jurisdictions have incorporated corporate compliance mechanisms into deferred prosecution agreements differ to some degree, it can be stated in general terms that the development and implementation of compliance programs have become an integral component of such agreements. More specifically, in these jurisdictions, the relationship between corporate compliance and deferred prosecution agreements manifests itself in three principal ways. First, the existence of at least a preliminary compliance program is typically regarded as one of the preconditions for a prosecutor to consider entering into a deferred prosecution agreement with a corporate defendant. Second, within the agreement itself, the company is ordinarily required to undertake a commitment to improve its compliance framework, including presenting a detailed plan for comprehensively rebuilding its compliance management system. Third, during the monitoring period, the prosecution engages in continuous oversight of the company's progress in implementing the compliance program. This may include appointing an independent compliance monitor to conduct sustained supervision or requiring the company to submit periodic reports documenting the status and effectiveness of its compliance reforms. The following sections will briefly analyze each of these aspects in turn.

10.3.1 Compliance as a Precondition for DPAs

In both the United States and the United Kingdom, when dealing with corporations suspected of economic crime, prosecutorial authorities consider the existence of a compliance program not only as a factor in deciding whether to initiate a prosecution but also as an important criterion in assessing whether to enter into a deferred prosecution agreement with the enterprise. Compared to companies that have never established any form of compliance program, those that have already taken preliminary steps to implement compliance measures are substantially more likely to be considered eligible for negotiating a deferred prosecution agreement. In such cases, the agreement will typically include a series of provisions aimed at further strengthening compliance management and ensuring that the compliance program achieves real and demonstrable effectiveness. By contrast, where a company has never adopted any compliance framework, prosecutors are generally reluctant to believe that the mere conclusion of a deferred prosecution agreement will be sufficient to prompt the company to develop an "effective compliance program" entirely from scratch.

According to the *United States Attorneys' Manual*, when determining whether to initiate a prosecution and whether to pursue a deferred prosecution agreement or a non-prosecution agreement, prosecutors are required to consider at least the following ten significant factors: first, the nature and seriousness of the offense, including the risk of harm to the public and any applicable policies and priorities governing the prosecution of corporations for particular categories of crime; second, the pervasiveness of wrongdoing within the corporation, including the complicity in, or the condoning of, the misconduct by corporate management; third, the corporation's history of similar misconduct, including prior criminal, civil, and regulatory enforcement actions; fourth, the corporation's willingness to cooperate in the investigation of its agents; fifth, the existence and effectiveness of the corporation's pre-existing compliance program; sixth, the corporation's timely and voluntary disclosure of wrongdoing; seventh, the corporation's remedial actions, including efforts to implement an effective compliance program or improve an existing one, to replace responsible management, to discipline or terminate wrongdoers, to pay restitution, and to cooperate with relevant government authorities; eighth, collateral consequences, such as whether prosecution would cause disproportionate harm to shareholders, pension holders, employees, and others not personally culpable; ninth, the adequacy of remedies such as civil or regulatory enforcement actions; and tenth, the adequacy of the prosecution of individuals responsible for the corporation's malfeasance.

Prosecutors exercise broad discretion in weighing the factors outlined above. In practice, the process from the initiation of a prosecutorial investigation to the conclusion of a deferred prosecution agreement typically entails a negotiation period of variable duration. During this period, companies under investigation often undertake proactive measures to facilitate the conclusion of a settlement agreement, such as disclosing information about unlawful conduct, cooperating with investigative authorities, and improving their compliance programs. The progress made in these areas constitutes a critical consideration for prosecutors when deciding whether to enter into a deferred prosecution agreement. A substantial body of case experience demonstrates that prosecutors are particularly inclined to conclude such agreements with companies that have already established a compliance framework and demonstrated significant cooperation with enforcement agencies, but whose compliance mechanisms nonetheless require further enhancement. In these instances, the deferred prosecution agreement is regarded as an effective instrument for incentivizing improvements in corporate compliance systems, while simultaneously serving the punitive, deterrent, and rehabilitative functions traditionally associated with criminal sanctions.[21]

For example, on November 18, 2018, the U.S. Department of Justice and the U.S. Attorney's Office for the Southern District of New York entered into a deferred prosecution agreement with Société Générale (SG). Under the agreement, SG agreed to pay a criminal penalty of $880 million to the U.S. federal and New York State governments in exchange for a commitment by the federal and state prosecuting authorities not to pursue criminal conspiracy charges during a specified three-year monitoring period. According to the Statement of Facts annexed to the deferred prosecution agreement, the resolution of the matter fully considered SG's substantial cooperation with investigators and its efforts to enhance its compliance program. After the inquiry commenced, SG not only disclosed information concerning its unlawful conduct but also conducted a comprehensive review of the relevant transactions, entered into settlement and deferred penalty agreements with the government, produced extensive written materials and investigative reports, responded to inquiries from enforcement authorities, and arranged interviews with relevant employees. Importantly, SG had ceased the underlying misconduct before the investigation began and had already implemented significant improvements to its sanctions compliance framework. Between 2009 and 2017, the bank established a centralized sanctions compliance function, increasing its staff in this unit to 31 employees, and expanded the headcount of its global compliance department from 169 to 785 employees. In addition, it upgraded its compliance-related information technology systems and increased its overall compliance budget from €53.8 million in 2010 to €186 million in 2016. To further strengthen adherence to sanctions regulations, SG issued comprehensive compliance policies, instituted a policy requiring the termination of employees involved in sanctions violations, and conducted training for employees on sanctions compliance obligations.[22]

In the United Kingdom, under the Deferred Prosecution Agreement Code of Practice issued by the Serious Fraud Office and the Crown Prosecution Service, prosecutors are required to apply both an evidential test and a public interest test when assessing whether to enter into a DPA with a corporate defendant. The existence of a corporate compliance program is regarded as a

[21] Guo Linjiang, "The Use of Deferred Prosecution in U.S. Corporate Crime," *China Criminal Law Journal*, no. 7 (2010).

[22] "USA v. S.G.S.A.," August 24, 2019, https://www.justice.gov/usao-sdny/press-release/file/1112461/download

significant factor in the public interest assessment. To determine whether concluding a deferred prosecution agreement would better serve the public interest, prosecutors must take into account the seriousness of the alleged offense, together with four additional considerations: first, the company's record of similar misconduct; second, the existence and effectiveness of the company's compliance arrangements before, during, and after the offending; third, the timing of the company's disclosure of its misconduct and the accuracy and completeness of the information provided; and fourth, the extent of the company's cooperation with the criminal investigation. At the same time, in reviewing a DPA submitted by the prosecution, the judge is likewise required to consider whether the company has established an effective compliance program, among other factors, in order to determine whether approving the agreement is consistent with the interests of justice.

10.3.2 Compliance as a Core Component

Whether in the United States—the birthplace of the deferred prosecution agreement regime—or in jurisdictions that later adopted similar frameworks, such as the United Kingdom and France, it has become almost universally recognized that enhancing a corporate compliance program constitutes a central element of these agreements. On the one hand, to conclude such conditional deferred prosecution agreements, prosecutors typically require corporate defendants not only to pay substantial fines but also to commit to strengthening their compliance programs, to accept ongoing oversight of the improvements, and to pledge comprehensive cooperation with investigative and enforcement authorities. On the other hand, in order to avoid harsher sanctions and to mitigate the risk of more severe losses, corporate defendants commonly undertake, beyond disclosing misconduct and cooperating with regulatory investigations, to make further efforts to reinforce their compliance management systems. Such measures are intended to close gaps in the compliance infrastructure, prevent, detect, and effectively monitor potential compliance risks, ensure the accountability of individuals responsible for violations, and minimize the likelihood of recurrence. To a significant extent, what is referred to as a deferred prosecution agreement is, in essence, a negotiated arrangement between prosecutors and the corporation, centered primarily on the development and improvement of the company's compliance management system.

With respect to the provisions requiring the reconstruction of compliance programs under deferred prosecution agreements, no jurisdiction imposes uniform or formulaic requirements. Rather, the specific compliance enhancement measures are calibrated to the particular facts and circumstances of the alleged misconduct and to the identified high-risk areas within the company's operations. In this regard, jurisdictions such as the United States, the United Kingdom, and France have each issued baseline standards defining the minimum elements of an effective compliance program. For example, the

U.S. Department of Justice regularly publishes detailed guidance for prosecutors outlining the essential criteria for evaluating whether a compliance program satisfies these benchmarks. Accordingly, in supervising the reconstruction of compliance frameworks, prosecuting authorities are expected both to adhere to these minimum standards and to exercise discretion in tailoring obligations to the unique context of each case. This approach reflects a deliberate balance between principled consistency and necessary flexibility.

For example, in 2019, the U.S. Department of Justice entered into a deferred prosecution agreement with Lumber Liquidators. Under the terms of this agreement, the company was required to improve or reconstruct its compliance program by strengthening its internal controls, policies, and procedures, so as to establish an effective internal accounting control system and a robust anti-fraud compliance framework. In addition, the agreement included a dedicated annex specifically detailing the requirements for rebuilding the corporate compliance structure. This annex comprehensively enumerated obligations across a broad spectrum of areas, including top-level commitment, policies and procedures, periodic risk assessments, appropriate oversight mechanisms, employee training and guidance, internal reporting and investigations, disciplinary measures, management of third-party relationships, compliance in mergers and acquisitions, and continuous monitoring and testing.[23]

Similarly, following a four-year anti-bribery investigation, the UK Serious Fraud Office entered into a deferred prosecution agreement with Rolls-Royce in 2017, which was approved by the Queen's Bench Division of the High Court. Under the terms of this agreement—which imposed penalties approaching £500 million—the company was required to continue retaining the team led by Sir Gold to conduct an independent review of its anti-bribery and corruption compliance practices. Building on the two interim reports that had already been completed, Rolls-Royce was obligated to produce a third independent report addressing the reconstruction of its compliance program. Following the completion of the third report, the company was required to develop a written implementation plan to give effect to the recommendations set forth in the first two reports for improving its compliance framework. Additionally, it was recommended that the third report should conduct a focused risk assessment in four specific areas: first, the company's provision of "privileges" or improper benefits to customers in the form of cash, credit, or other benefits; second, the geographic distribution, staffing levels, and professional qualifications of the company's compliance personnel; third, the effectiveness of compliance training initiatives aimed at mitigating bribery and corruption risks; and fourth, the adequacy of Rolls-Royce Power Systems' anti-bribery policies, procedures, and internal controls.[24]

[23] "USA v. Lumber Liquidators Holdings, Inc.," August 10, 2019, https://www.justice.gov/opa/press-release/file/1143011/download

[24] "Deferred Prosecution Agreement—SFO v. Rolls Royce PLC," August 10, 2019, https://www.sfo.gov.uk/case/rolls-royce-plc

10.3.3 Ongoing Monitoring of Compliance Enhancements

In the deferred prosecution agreement regimes of the United States, the United Kingdom, and France, prosecutors not only require corporate defendants to commit to improving their compliance programs during the specified monitoring period but also obligate them to engage independent compliance monitors. These monitors are responsible for continuously overseeing and evaluating the company's adherence to the agreement, the transformation of its business practices, and the development or enhancement of its compliance systems. They are required to submit regular reports on their findings to law enforcement or regulatory authorities. This mechanism of appointing an independent compliance monitor functions as a critical means of sustained oversight over the company's efforts to reconstruct its compliance framework in response to identified risks and represents an essential institutional safeguard against the recurrence of unlawful or improper conduct. Indeed, in practice, the effective and continuous supervision by an independent monitor is indispensable; without it, corporate commitments to rebuild compliance programs under deferred prosecution agreements would remain largely aspirational and difficult to enforce.

In the United States, compliance monitors are typically drawn from individuals with prior experience as prosecutors, judges, or securities regulators. The initial shortlist of candidates is proposed by the corporate defendant, but the final selection is made by the prosecuting authority, with the company responsible for covering the monitor's compensation. In practice, a significant proportion of compliance monitors are former prosecutors who previously served in the Department of Justice. In jurisdictions such as the United Kingdom and France, compliance monitors may likewise be distinguished professionals from the legal, financial, or other relevant sectors.

Once appointed, the compliance monitor is tasked with conducting a comprehensive assessment of the company's prior misconduct, the principal areas of compliance risk, deficiencies in the compliance program, and the adequacy of third-party oversight mechanisms. The monitor subsequently formulates recommendations to improve the compliance management framework. Upon receiving the monitor's findings and recommendations, the company is expected to implement targeted corrective actions. These may include revising the composition of the board of directors, replacing senior management, expanding the compliance function, and, more broadly, rebuilding the compliance system in accordance with recognized standards of effective compliance programs. This process involves drafting employee handbooks, developing systems for the prevention, detection, and response to compliance risks, and establishing robust monitoring mechanisms. The compliance monitor is required to submit periodic reports to the prosecuting authority on the company's remediation measures and progress in enhancing its compliance program. Typically, these reports are filed quarterly, or at a minimum, semiannually. Furthermore, throughout the entire monitoring period, the compliance monitor is authorized to provide advice on the company's day-to-day operations, major corporate decisions, and personnel arrangements, all from the perspective of mitigating compliance risks.

For example, under the deferred prosecution agreement concluded in 2015 between the U.S. Department of Justice and Louis Berger International, the company was required to submit to oversight by a compliance monitor, approved by both parties, for a period of three years. Within thirty days of the agreement's entry into force, the company was obliged to provide a list of three proposed candidates, from which the Department of Justice would independently select one to serve as the designated compliance monitor. The monitor was required to meet several qualifications: possessing expertise and competence in the Foreign Corrupt Practices Act (FCPA) and other relevant anti-corruption laws; demonstrating experience in designing or assessing corporate compliance policies, procedures, and internal controls—particularly those addressing FCPA and anti-corruption obligations; having the capacity to access and deploy resources necessary to perform monitoring duties; and maintaining sufficient independence to carry out these responsibilities effectively and impartially. The monitor's primary duty was to assess and oversee the company's adherence to the terms of the agreement, including its obligation to implement the compliance program reforms specified therein, so as to mitigate the risk of future misconduct. To fulfill these responsibilities, the monitor was authorized to conduct an initial review of the company's compliance with anti-corruption requirements and to submit an initial report. Subsequently, the monitor was required to conduct follow-up reviews and provide follow-up reports to the Department of Justice. In addition, the monitor was entitled to communicate relevant findings concerning corrupt practices and any false statements or records to the company's senior management and was under an obligation to report any such violations to the Department of Justice. Following the submission of each report, the monitor was required to meet with Department officials to discuss the findings and recommendations in detail.[25]

For example, in 2014, the UK Serious Fraud Office (SFO) entered into the first deferred prosecution agreement in British legal history with Standard Bank PLC. Under the terms of this agreement, the bank was required, throughout the monitoring period, to cooperate fully and transparently with the SFO and other investigative authorities. Additionally, the bank was obliged to engage PricewaterhouseCoopers (PwC) to conduct an independent assessment of its internal anti-bribery and anti-corruption compliance procedures, in accordance with the scope and depth of review prescribed by the SFO. Upon completion of this assessment, Standard Bank was required to accept the recommendations for compliance reforms and to implement the proposed

[25] "USA v. Louis Berger International, Inc.," August 12, 2019, https://www.justice.gov/criminal-fraud/file/642061/download

measures within twelve months. PwC was also mandated to submit periodic reports to the SFO verifying the bank's progress in enhancing its compliance program.[26]

Naturally, prosecutors do not appoint a compliance monitor in every case. Since 2016, the U.S. Department of Justice has implemented a compliance incentive framework designed to reward companies that voluntarily disclose misconduct.[27] Under this framework, if, in the course of an investigation by prosecutors or other regulatory authorities, a corporate defendant proactively engages in self-disclosure—including reporting violations and identifying responsible individuals previously unknown to investigators—the prosecution may elect not to require the mandatory appointment of an independent compliance monitor in any deferred prosecution or non-prosecution agreement concluded with the company. Instead, the enterprise assumes the obligation to submit periodic compliance reports. In recent years, U.S. prosecutors have increasingly employed this corporate compliance reporting mechanism in DPAs, requiring companies, for the duration of the monitoring period, to submit annual reports to the Department of Justice or other supervisory agencies detailing the development and implementation of their compliance programs. Some DPA texts not only specify obligations to strengthen compliance measures and submit periodic reports but also append detailed plans setting out the improvements to be undertaken and outlining the specific content and schedule of the annual reporting requirements.

For example, in the deferred prosecution agreement concluded in 2018 between the U.S. Department of Justice and Transport Logistics International, the corporate defendant undertook a comprehensive commitment to enhance its compliance program and assumed an obligation to submit at least one periodic report per year detailing its progress in strengthening its anti-foreign corruption compliance framework. Pursuant to the agreement, within one year of execution, the company was required to complete an initial review and submit an initial report. Over the remaining two years of the monitoring period, the company was further obligated to conduct two additional reviews and to submit two follow-up reports. All reviews and reports were to focus specifically on measures to strengthen the anti-corruption compliance program and to improve the company's internal controls, policies, and procedures designed to ensure adherence to the Foreign Corrupt Practices Act (FCPA) and other applicable legal requirements.[28]

[26] "Serious Fraud Office v. Standard Bank PLC," August 10, 2019, https://www.sfo.gov.uk/download

[27] Ruihua Chen, "Three Dimensions of the Corporate Compliance System: A Comparative Law Perspective," *Journal of Comparative Law*, no. 3 (2019).

[28] "Transport Logistics International Inc. Agrees to Pay $2 Million Penalty to Resolve Foreign Bribery Case," August 12, 2019, https://www.justice.gov/opa/press-release/file/1043241/download

10.4 Theoretical Foundations

Some scholars, drawing on research and observations of the U.S. pre-trial diversion agreement system, have argued that the primary rationale for applying such agreements to corporations lies in the objective of avoiding the so-called "ripple effects of punishment." In other words, prosecutors seek to prevent the adverse consequences that criminal sanctions imposed on a corporate offender may inflict on other parties—third persons who were not involved in the wrongdoing but maintain economic or social ties with the corporation. It was precisely the severe lessons of the early 2000s—most notably the bankruptcies of Enron, WorldCom, and Arthur Andersen—following prosecutions by U.S. authorities, which triggered widespread layoffs and substantial collateral damage to the economy, that prompted the Department of Justice to recalibrate its enforcement policies. Within this context, the Department sought to harness the deterrent effect of the threat of prosecution as leverage to compel internal reforms in corporate governance. By employing pre-trial diversion agreement mechanisms—including deferred prosecution agreements—the Department has aimed to avoid harming innocent stakeholders such as investors, employees, pensioners, and customers, thereby mitigating the broader ripple effects that criminal punishment could otherwise produce.[29]

Indeed, a substantial body of literature examining the U.S. pre-trial diversion system frequently references the Enron and Arthur Andersen cases, observing that these events were closely connected to the subsequent widespread adoption of deferred prosecution agreements in corporate criminal enforcement. The present author broadly concurs with the assessment that one of the principal motivations for applying DPAs to corporate defendants lies in the desire to avoid the ripple effects of punishment. However, even in the United States, interpreting the legitimacy of pre-trial diversion agreements solely through this lens appears unduly reductive. If prosecutors concluded such agreements merely to avoid bringing criminal charges against corporate entities, how can one account for the requirement that companies pay fines reaching near-astronomical amounts? Why insist that corporations commit to comprehensive cooperation with investigations, including proactively disclosing unlawful conduct and identifying culpable individuals? Why impose obligations to rebuild compliance programs and, in many cases, to submit to the oversight of independent compliance monitors? These features cannot be adequately explained by reference to the objective of avoiding collateral harm alone. Moreover, in jurisdictions such as the United Kingdom, France, Canada, Australia, and Singapore, legislators have not simply replicated the U.S. model. Instead, they have established deferred prosecution frameworks characterized by narrowly defined scopes of application, stringent procedural safeguards, and judicial review models distinct from those in the United States. From a

[29] Liangfang Ye, "The Development of the U.S. Corporate Pre-Trial Deferred Prosecution Agreement System," *China Criminal Law Journal*, no. 3 (2014).

comparative law perspective, the fact that so many jurisdictions have adopted deferred prosecution agreements and designated them as alternative sanctions for corporate criminal conduct must be understood as reflecting a combination of internal and external rationales that extend well beyond the mere aspiration to mitigate the collateral consequences of criminal prosecution.

In essence, a deferred prosecution agreement constitutes a contract or agreement entered into by the prosecution and the corporate defendant through a process of equal negotiation and voluntary decision-making. As with any contractual arrangement, the parties engage in rational assessments of their respective interests, seeking to maximize their gains and minimize their losses, and ultimately agree upon terms acceptable to both sides. For this reason, much like plea bargaining, deferred prosecution agreements are premised on the fundamental principle of mutual advantage. However, considerations of self-interest alone are insufficient to fully account for the legitimacy of any institutional reform. In most cases, deeper motivations are also operative, introducing factors such as the protection of the public interest and the promotion of justice into the calculus. This is precisely why the United Kingdom and several other Commonwealth jurisdictions have emphasized that deferred prosecution agreements must be subject to judicial scrutiny—to ensure that they "serve the interests of justice" and satisfy requirements of fairness, reasonableness, and proportionality. In light of these considerations, the present discussion will offer a theoretical account of the legitimacy of deferred prosecution agreements along three principal dimensions.

10.4.1 The Principle of Mutual Advantage

One of the principal criticisms directed at the system of deferred prosecution agreements is that it vests prosecutors with an expansive degree of discretion, effectively allowing them to supplant the courts as the ultimate arbiters in cases involving alleged corporate criminal conduct. Critics contend that this framework deprives corporate defendants of fundamental procedural safeguards, including the attorney–client privilege against compelled testimony, the right to a fair trial before an impartial tribunal, and the opportunity to seek the exclusion of unlawfully obtained evidence. In particular, once a corporate defendant consents to a deferred prosecution agreement, it is typically required to acknowledge the factual allegations set out by the prosecution. These admissions may subsequently be introduced as evidence if prosecutors elect to reinstitute criminal proceedings at a later stage. Consequently, once a company has chosen to enter into such an agreement, it is, in practical terms, almost impossible for it to secure an acquittal should the matter proceed to trial.

Indeed, the criticisms directed against deferred prosecution agreements bear a striking resemblance to those historically leveled at plea bargaining. However, the plea bargaining system is founded on the principle of mutual advantage, which enables it to accommodate and reconcile the interests of all stakeholders involved. This utilitarian rationale has allowed plea bargaining to endure as the principal procedural mechanism through which the vast majority of criminal cases in the United States are resolved over the long term. In much the same way, notwithstanding the numerous criticisms to which it is subject, the system of deferred prosecution agreements is likewise capable of serving the interests of society at large, prosecuting authorities, and corporate defendants alike. By achieving this balance, it mitigates many of the adverse social consequences that can result from corporate prosecutions and, consequently, has secured a broad foundation of practical legitimacy and acceptance.

By entering into deferred prosecution agreements with corporate defendants, prosecutors ensure that the vast majority of companies suspected of criminal conduct ultimately avoid the initiation of formal proceedings and are spared the prospect of criminal conviction by a court. In consequence, these enterprises are relieved of a range of collateral consequences, such as the risk of bankruptcy, mass employee layoffs, investors or shareholders losing their capital, pensioners being deprived of their means of subsistence, and customers or other innocent third parties bearing substantial losses. Moreover, this approach helps prevent broader economic disruption or financial crises that could threaten the stability of governmental regulatory systems. The avoidance of these "ripple effects of punishment" is quite evidently a form of political benefit actively pursued by prosecutorial authorities across jurisdictions. After all, whether in the United States, the United Kingdom, or other countries, decisions regarding whether to indict a corporate defendant invariably involve public interest considerations and cannot be dissociated from political factors. To a significant extent, the decision to conclude a deferred prosecution agreement is motivated by the imperative to avert corporate insolvency, forestall large-scale unemployment, and preempt wider economic decline.

Beyond these considerations, prosecuting authorities also pursue deferred prosecution agreements as a means of enhancing procedural efficiency. By employing this mechanism, prosecutors can avoid protracted and cumbersome judicial proceedings, mitigate the inherent uncertainties of trial outcomes, and relieve themselves of the extraordinarily onerous investigative and evidentiary burdens associated with corporate criminal prosecutions. This approach, in turn, maximizes enforcement efficiency and bolsters the state's capacity to ensure corporate accountability. Experience has shown that indicting corporations and subjecting them to trial often entails prolonged and resource-intensive litigation, with cases frequently remaining unresolved for many years. Moreover, the prospect of securing a conviction is by no means assured. On the one hand, corporate crime typically involves highly specialized economic misconduct embedded within complex operational structures and largely shielded from external scrutiny. As a result, prosecutors routinely face formidable obstacles in collecting evidence sufficient to establish guilt beyond a reasonable doubt. On the other hand, corporate defendants generally possess considerable financial resources and are able to engage exceptionally experienced legal counsel. In such circumstances, prosecutors must contend with vigorous defense strategies, which may involve challenging the admissibility and probative value of prosecutorial evidence or disputing whether the case satisfies the applicable standards for conviction. This dynamic substantially increases the difficulty of obtaining a successful judgment against corporate defendants.

With the rapid proliferation of corporate crime, prosecuting authorities in many jurisdictions have significantly intensified their enforcement efforts against offenses such as commercial bribery, unfair competition, violations of export controls, money laundering, infringement of personal data, and business fraud. This escalation in enforcement activity has, in turn, placed tremendous strain on judicial systems, which have increasingly suffered from severe case backlogs and protracted litigation delays. In such overburdened environments, it has become almost inevitable that prosecutors must endure extended periods before they can bring corporate offenders to justice. Empirical research conducted by U.S. scholars has demonstrated that in numerous corporate crime cases, the interval between the occurrence of the misconduct and the issuance of a final judgment routinely extends to seven years or more. This reality forces prosecuting authorities to allocate substantial time, financial resources, and personnel to the litigation of a relatively limited number of cases. Consequently, they are frequently left without the capacity to investigate and indict other corporations engaged in economic wrongdoing, thereby contributing to various degrees of enforcement deficiency.

The widespread adoption of deferred prosecution agreements (DPAs) has effectively extricated prosecutorial authorities from the difficulties described above, substantially improving both the efficiency and the rigor of enforcement in corporate crime cases. First, the conclusion of a DPA is predicated on the corporation's acknowledgment of the factual basis underlying the alleged misconduct and its commitment to provide extensive cooperation and support in the investigation and any related proceedings. Corporate defendants not only cooperate fully with prosecutorial and regulatory inquiries—by proactively producing evidence, consenting to document disclosures, facilitating interviews of relevant employees, and engaging in self-disclosure regarding both the unlawful conduct and those responsible—but also, much like individual defendants who plead guilty, agree to waive important procedural safeguards. These waivers typically include the right to challenge the admissibility of evidence and the right to assert attorney–client privilege. As a result, DPAs significantly reduce the time and resources required of prosecutors and remove many procedural barriers that would otherwise complicate evidence collection and case preparation. Second, DPAs enable prosecutors to secure a relatively predictable and advantageous outcome. During the monitoring period—when the corporate defendant is obliged to comply with commitments to cooperate, remediate compliance failures, and submit to ongoing oversight—and at the conclusion of that period—when prosecutors conduct a final assessment of performance—prosecuting authorities retain considerable leverage to supervise, evaluate, and enforce compliance with the agreement's terms. Finally, empirical research shows that in most cases resolved through DPAs, the process from the commission of the offense to the expiration of the monitoring period typically lasts about four years. Of course, this timeframe alone does not fully capture the comparative efficiency gains relative to formal criminal trials. Throughout this period, prosecutors are able to rely on corporate self-disclosure and the oversight conducted by independent compliance monitors, which frees them from the burdens of protracted investigation and litigation. This dynamic enables prosecutors to pursue additional cases against other corporations suspected of economic crime, thereby significantly enhancing both the effectiveness and the scope of enforcement efforts.[30]

So what, in practical terms, are the benefits for corporations that elect to enter into a settlement with prosecuting authorities by signing a deferred prosecution agreement (DPA)?

Substantively, when a company is convicted, the immediate consequence is typically the imposition of a court-ordered financial penalty. However, in the United States, the United Kingdom, France, Canada, Australia, and other jurisdictions, a criminal conviction almost invariably triggers additional collateral sanctions beyond fines—such as disqualification from bidding on government contracts or, in some instances, the revocation of critical business licenses. These collateral consequences frequently attach automatically to a conviction and can be tantamount to a corporate "death sentence." For example, in the 2002 Arthur Andersen case, the day after prosecutors filed charges, the U.S. Securities and Exchange Commission ordered Andersen to cease auditing public companies effective August 31, 2002—a sanction that effectively forced the firm to shut down and has often been described as a "death sentence."[31]

Consider the example of financial institutions: they often opt to conclude DPAs precisely to avoid incurring much greater losses and suffering more severe repercussions. These potential consequences generally include the following. First, the loss of business licenses. If U.S. regulatory authorities suspend or revoke a bank's license, the institution loses access to the U.S. market—its most important market—and is effectively unable to continue operations, resulting in potentially devastating losses. Second, the erosion of market share, customer base, and employee retention. In many cases, even if proceedings eventually proceed to trial, the protracted and burdensome nature of litigation entangles the company in prolonged uncertainty, prompting the departure of clients, the flight of talented personnel, and significant damage to the business franchise. Third, a sharp decline in share price. Once regulators publicly disclose adverse findings, the company's stock price often falls precipitously, inflicting substantial financial harm. Fourth, the risk of sustained and aggressive regulatory scrutiny. If the company declines to enter into a settlement agreement with enforcement authorities, it faces a significantly heightened

[30] W. A. Kaal and Timothy A. Lacine, "The Effect of Deferred and Non-Prosecution Agreements on Corporate Governance: Evidence from 1993–2013," *Business Law* 70 (2014–2015): 61.

[31] Liangfang Ye, "The Development of the U.S. Corporate Pre-Trial Deferred Prosecution Agreement System," *China Criminal Law Journal*, no. 3 (2014).

likelihood of being subjected to ongoing, and potentially retaliatory, investigations and further prosecutions.

Against this backdrop, when regulatory authorities bring charges—particularly when prosecutors initiate criminal proceedings—corporate defendants almost invariably engage in closed-door negotiations with enforcement agencies. Their objective is to secure the most advantageous settlement terms possible, typically by negotiating for the lowest feasible financial penalties and the least burdensome compliance obligations in exchange for the authorities' commitment not to pursue the matter through formal indictment and trial. In practice, nearly all cases resolved via such settlement agreements conclude with prosecutors formally withdrawing the charges upon the expiration of the monitoring period. By avoiding a criminal conviction, the company not only evades the stigma of a formal finding of guilt but also circumvents collateral consequences such as disqualification from government contracting or the revocation of regulatory licenses essential to the continuation of core business operations. In a system where bringing a criminal prosecution against a company can be tantamount to imposing an organizational "death sentence," the decision to enter into a deferred prosecution agreement is, for many enterprises, a question of existential survival. The benefits derived from securing such agreement are incalculable.

10.4.2 Substitution for Penal Functions

A prominent criticism frequently leveled against the system of deferred prosecution agreements (DPAs) is that prosecutors, in effect, decline to pursue criminal indictments against corporations whose conduct plainly satisfies the elements of serious offenses, opting instead to replace conventional criminal sanctions with the imposition of substantial monetary penalties. This approach is often alleged to dilute the retributive and deterrent purposes traditionally associated with criminal punishment and to risk fostering a climate of impunity. Indeed, once a DPA has been concluded, it is almost always the case that, following the expiration of a multi-year monitoring period, no formal prosecution is subsequently initiated. Nonetheless, the combination of significant financial penalties imposed on the corporate defendant and mandatory obligations to cooperate fully with enforcement authorities and to implement or strengthen compliance frameworks—although formally classified as civil or administrative measures—can generate punitive and deterrent effects that are functionally comparable to those of a criminal conviction and sentence. This capacity to operate as an effective substitute for criminal punishment constitutes a central pillar underpinning the normative legitimacy of the deferred prosecution agreement regime.

According to the principle of structural functionalism articulated in contemporary sociology, the continued existence of any institutional arrangement or structural framework depends on the functions it performs and the contributions it makes to sustain the broader social system. Structure and function are mutually interdependent, maintaining an equilibrium that preserves the coherence of the system as a whole. Where an established structural arrangement manifests inherent deficiencies, any newly created institutional mechanism intended to replace it must ensure that it is capable of discharging the functions formerly performed by its predecessor. In this respect, although prosecuting corporations and securing convictions and sentences undeniably presents serious drawbacks, any substitution of this approach with the deferred prosecution agreement regime must nonetheless guarantee that this alternative framework is capable of fulfilling the core purposes traditionally ascribed to criminal punishment. Otherwise, if the only rationale were the avoidance of corporate convictions, the likely consequence would be that corporate misconduct not only escapes meaningful sanction but is effectively legitimized, prompting other enterprises to adopt similar practices and ultimately eroding the foundational integrity of the legal order.

The operation of the deferred prosecution agreement regime typically results in prosecutors refraining from filing formal charges against the implicated corporation, thereby objectively shielding the enterprise from the consequences of criminal conviction and sentencing. However, the vitality of this regime lies precisely in the fact that, while it spares the company from being formally punished under the label of a "convicted offender," it nonetheless imposes an alternative form of sanction. Through a constellation of institutional mechanisms, the regime obliges the enterprise to disclose the relevant criminal conduct and identify the individuals responsible, to reconstruct and strengthen its compliance program, and to submit to sustained monitoring and oversight. These remedial measures not only help prevent the recurrence of corporate wrongdoing but also exert a meaningful deterrent effect on other market actors. Accordingly, the deferred prosecution agreement framework enables corporations suspected of criminal misconduct to avoid the formal stigma associated with criminal punishment, while still achieving the core punitive and deterrent functions traditionally ascribed to criminal sanctions—and, in certain respects, accomplishing these objectives even more effectively than conventional prosecution and sentencing.

10.4.2.1 Deferred Prosecution Agreements as a Substitute for Punitive Functions

Punishment can only fulfill its inherent retributive function if it generates a sufficiently concrete punitive impact. To achieve this, offenders must be subjected to penalties that are proportionate to the nature and gravity of their criminal conduct. In the sphere of corporate crime, the most widely applied criminal sanction across jurisdictions is the imposition of monetary fines. However, the amount of such fines is generally subject to strict statutory ceilings. In cases resolved through plea bargains or guilty plea agreements, the fines imposed are, on the one hand, constrained by the limits established under criminal law and, on the other hand, are often moderated to reflect the company's voluntary admission of wrongdoing and its cooperation with enforcement authorities. Accordingly, whether in the United States, the United Kingdom, or France, when a corporate defendant voluntarily pleads guilty and concludes an agreement with prosecutors, the fines imposed by the court upon conviction typically range from several hundred thousand dollars or euros to, at most, a few million.

However, in cases resolved through deferred prosecution agreements, prosecutors exercise a considerable degree of discretion and negotiate the amount of the financial payment with the corporate defendant, without being constrained by statutory caps applicable to criminal fines. Such payments do not constitute criminal fines in the strict legal sense but rather take the form of a *settlement sum*—that is, a compensatory payment undertaken by the defendant enterprise in exchange for entering into the agreement. These sums typically encompass several components: purely punitive amounts, disgorgement of unlawfully obtained profits, compensation to victims, and reimbursement of investigative and enforcement costs incurred by regulators and prosecuting authorities. In recent U.S. practice, settlement payments under deferred prosecution agreements frequently reach tens of millions of dollars or euros, with cases involving penalties exceeding USD or EUR 100 million becoming increasingly common. For example, a study of cases from 1987 to 2011 found that the median financial penalty imposed under deferred prosecution agreements was USD 189 million, while the median penalty in non-prosecution agreements was even higher, at USD 219 million. By contrast, during the same period, plea agreements resulted in a median fine of only USD 75.7 million.[32] Similar trends are observable in the United Kingdom. Of the four deferred prosecution agreements concluded by the Serious Fraud Office to date, two involved financial penalties exceeding EUR 100 million. Notably, in the Rolls-Royce case, the company agreed to pay nearly GBP 300 million to the UK authorities, in addition to USD 170 million to the United States and USD 25.5 million to Brazil.[33] France offers further illustration: in 2016, a French court approved a guilty plea agreement (*Comparution sur Reconnaissance Préalable de Culpabilité*, CRPC) between the National Financial Prosecutor's Office and a Swiss bank accused of money laundering, convicting the bank and imposing a fine of EUR 2.8 million. Yet, in 2017, the same court approved a deferred prosecution agreement in another matter involving a Swiss bank, under which the defendant agreed to pay a record EUR 300 million in fines and compensation.[34]

Indeed, when a court convicts and sentences a corporation, the judgment not only formally designates the enterprise as a *criminal offender* and imposes

[32] Cindy R. Alexander and Mark A. Cohen, "The Evolution of Corporate Criminal Settlements: An Empirical Perspective on Non-Prosecution, Deferred Prosecution, and Plea Agreement," *American Criminal Law Review* 52 (2015): 537.

[33] "Approval of UK's Fifth DPA Concludes SFO Investigation into Serco Companies," August 24, 2019, https://hsfnotes.com/2019/07/10

[34] "First French DPA Ever Approved in France," August 24, 2019, https://www.allenovery.com/en-gb/pages

a financial penalty, but also triggers a range of collateral consequences that can disqualify the company from entering into contracts with public entities or engaging in certain regulated lines of business. This combination of direct sanctions and ancillary penalties often results in devastating economic losses for the corporation. By contrast, the use of a deferred prosecution agreement spares the company the formal stigma and legal consequences of a criminal conviction. Nevertheless, it obliges the enterprise to absorb financial penalties of extraordinary magnitude—frequently reaching tens or even hundreds of millions of dollars or euros. For any corporation, such obligations constitute an exceptionally severe burden. Moreover, given that corporate crimes are typically profit-driven, reflecting the pursuit of improper economic advantage, these substantial financial sanctions often serve a critical function: ***depriving the offender of the benefits unlawfully obtained***. In many cases, the financial losses imposed under deferred prosecution agreements substantially exceed the company's illicit gains, thereby achieving an effect that is, in economic terms, even more punitive than traditional fines.

10.4.2.2 Specific Deterrent Effects of Deferred Prosecution Agreements

The specific deterrent effect of criminal sanctions typically arises from the fact that offenders, once subjected to severe and timely punishment, incur substantial costs and losses, thereby forfeiting both the incentive and the capacity to reoffend. The use of deferred prosecution agreements (DPAs) incorporates several mechanisms that reinforce this specific deterrent effect. First, the corporate defendant is required to formally acknowledge having engaged in the criminal conduct alleged by the prosecution. This acknowledgment is functionally equivalent to an individual confession of guilt and conveys contrition and acceptance of responsibility. Second, for companies that have pursued illicit profits in the course of their operations, the imposition of large-scale financial penalties in itself constitutes a formidable deterrent, compelling them to refrain from similar conduct in the future. Third, the obligations imposed by the agreement—including cooperation with investigative authorities, proactive disclosure of misconduct and culpable individuals, the rebuilding of compliance programs, and submission to comprehensive compliance monitoring—force the company to eliminate structural factors that might otherwise facilitate recidivism. These measures close compliance gaps and enable more effective prevention, detection, and management of potential violations, substantially reducing the likelihood of repeated offenses. Finally, if the corporate defendant fails to fulfill the terms of the agreement, the prosecution retains the right to reinstate criminal proceedings and may rely on all evidence collected during the monitoring period as well as the company's own admissions. This dynamic effectively means that ***"a conviction in court becomes virtually inevitable."*** As a result, there are virtually no cases in which a company that has entered into a DPA engages in new criminal conduct during the monitoring period, and even after prosecutors formally decline to bring charges, the probability of recidivism remains exceedingly low.[35]

10.4.2.3 General Deterrent Effect of Deferred Prosecution Agreements

The general deterrent function of criminal sanctions primarily lies in demonstrating to potential offenders the certainty and severity of punishment, thereby removing any incentive to engage in unlawful conduct. The use of deferred prosecution agreements (DPAs) subjects corporate defendants to financial penalties that are often of staggering magnitude. This, in itself, exerts a powerful psychological deterrent on other companies contemplating the pursuit of illicit gains. Moreover, once a DPA has been concluded—and particularly after it has been approved by a court—the agreement text, including the indictment, the statement of facts, and the provisions acknowledging the corporation's culpability, is typically made public through statutory disclosure mechanisms. Such publication effectively amounts to an official declaration and condemnation of the company's wrongdoing. The resulting reputational damage diminishes the corporation's credibility and standing in the marketplace, impairing its ability to conduct business, secure contracts, and maintain a competitive edge. Additionally, the fact that a corporate defendant may ultimately secure the dismissal of charges—provided it establishes a robust compliance program and submits to sustained compliance oversight—creates a strong incentive for other enterprises to accelerate the development of effective internal compliance frameworks in hopes of benefiting from similar leniency. The capacity of deferred prosecution agreements to drive the adoption of compliance management systems ensures that companies are motivated to implement measures for preventing, detecting, and responding to misconduct. In this respect, DPAs make a meaningful contribution to the broader objective of reducing corporate crime.[36]

10.4.3 Prosecutorial Engagement in Corporate Governance

Another frequently voiced criticism of the deferred prosecution agreement (DPA) regime is that it enables prosecutors to subject corporations to measures that resemble those imposed on convicted offenders, despite the absence of any judicial determination of guilt. Critics contend that this practice undermines the presumption of innocence and allows prosecuting authorities—institutions whose mandate is limited to criminal investigation and prosecution—to exercise a form of "behavioral correction" that properly belongs within the exclusive domain of the judiciary. In this respect, the criticism is not without merit.

[35] E. Illovsky, "Corporate Deferred Prosecution Agreements," *Criminal Justice* 21 (2006–2007): 36.

[36] F. Mazzacuva, "Justification and Purposes of Negotiated Justice for Corporate Offenders: Deferred and Non-Prosecution Agreements in the UK and US Systems of Criminal Justice," *The Journal of Criminal Law*, June 1, 2014.

Nevertheless, when contrasted with the traditional model of public prosecution, the DPA regime represents a significant evolution. It empowers prosecutors to engage proactively in shaping corporate governance structures without requiring a formal conviction as a prerequisite. In doing so, it shifts the focus of enforcement away from purely punitive and deterrent aims and toward the supervisory facilitation of organizational reform, thereby creating a corrective function specifically designed to prevent corporate misconduct.

First, by entering into a deferred prosecution agreement with the prosecution, the corporate defendant undertakes comprehensive cooperation and, based on the voluntary acknowledgment of the factual basis of its misconduct, effectively "opens the door" to investigations conducted by prosecutors and other regulatory authorities. Such cooperation typically involves a thorough overhaul of the company's decision-making structures, management teams, and auditing functions, including the removal of senior executives responsible for the violations. Moreover, through either proactive or reactive acceptance of self-disclosure obligations, the company not only provides prosecutors with new evidence of unlawful conduct but also identifies the wrongdoing of employees and members of senior management. This extensive collaboration with criminal and regulatory inquiries both signifies the company's recognition and remorse for its past violations and enables the timely and effective prosecution of all individuals responsible, thereby achieving a clear separation between culpable employees and the corporate entity itself. Evidently, these measures lay a solid foundation for prosecutors and regulatory bodies to compel companies to undertake sweeping reforms and fundamentally transform their governance practices.

Second, as a core requirement of a deferred prosecution agreement, the prosecution mandates that the corporate defendant undertake a comprehensive reconstruction of its compliance program. This process entails a thorough assessment of the company's compliance risks, the reorganization of its compliance infrastructure, and the enhancement of its compliance management system across multiple dimensions, including preventive measures, continuous monitoring, and post-incident response mechanisms, so as to effectively forestall future violations. At the same time, throughout the monitoring period prescribed by the agreement, prosecutors exercise continuous oversight by appointing independent compliance monitors or instituting corporate compliance reporting obligations. Under these arrangements, the company's progress in implementing its compliance reforms is subject to real-time monitoring, periodic assessments, and mandatory reporting, with prosecutors retaining the authority to issue additional recommendations for corrective action when necessary. In this capacity, prosecutors effectively assume the role of supervisors, reviewers, and, to some extent, adjudicators in overseeing the transformation of the corporate governance framework. The deferred prosecution agreement thereby functions as an instrument for correcting the company's prior unlawful business practices through structural reforms, with the objective of gradually fostering mechanisms for lawful and compliant operations over the course of the multi-year monitoring period. This comprehensive reshaping of the company's compliance management practices and organizational culture represents the most salient and distinctive contribution of the deferred prosecution agreement regime.

Finally, the implementation of the deferred prosecution agreement regime has prompted companies not only to strengthen compliance management with respect to their own employees and senior management, but also to enhance oversight of compliance practices among counterparties in mergers and acquisitions and third-party business partners. This development has significantly reduced the likelihood that external actors will engage in unlawful or improper conduct. A substantial body of case evidence demonstrates that major compliance risks frequently arise in the context of corporate investments and acquisitions. Companies are particularly vulnerable to violations when developing relationships with third-party partners such as suppliers, distributors, and agents. Where a counterparty in an investment or acquisition engages in unlawful activities, the acquiring or investing company is often exposed to "successor liability," thereby assuming joint responsibility for the prior misconduct. Likewise, if third-party partners commit criminal or regulatory violations, the company may incur derivative legal liability as a result. Accordingly, in deferred prosecution agreements, prosecutors routinely require corporate defendants to improve compliance frameworks specifically targeting the risks associated with mergers and acquisitions and third-party engagements. These obligations typically include conducting thorough compliance risk assessments and due diligence inquiries into third parties, as well as formulating corrective measures addressing the business models and transactional practices of such partners to compel them to establish mechanisms and a culture of lawful, compliant operations. As a result, under prosecutorial supervision, the corporate defendant—through the reconstruction of its compliance program—becomes capable of exercising effective monitoring, oversight, and even corrective influence over a broad network of third-party partners. This, in turn, generates a pronounced "radiating effect," extending the reach and impact of the company's compliance management system well beyond its organizational boundaries.[37]

[37] M. Kochler, "Measuring the Impact of Non-Prosecution and Deferred Prosecution Agreements on Foreign Corrupt Practices Act Enforcement," *UC Davis Law Review* 49 (2015–2016): 497.

CHAPTER 11

Criminal Compliance Incentives III: The Chinese Experience in Enterprise Compliance Reform

11.1 Introduction

Since the beginning of the twenty-first century, the evolution of China's legal system has gradually shifted away from an approach primarily driven by ***institutional transplantation***, moving instead toward a development trajectory characterized by ***practical experimentation, theoretical consolidation, and legislative refinement***. In the field of criminal law in particular, local judicial authorities—either under the guidance of higher judicial organs or through their own initiatives in institutional innovation—have often taken the lead in piloting reforms. After a period of exploration and experimentation, the academic community has distilled and synthesized the successful practices that emerged, progressively building consensus on their legitimacy and structural design and articulating more mature theoretical frameworks to underpin reform. Subsequently, through the combined efforts of practitioners and scholars, the legislature has extracted those institutional arrangements considered relatively mature and less controversial, incorporating them into national legislation as foundational legal norms. This process has served, on the one hand, to confer legal legitimacy on the reforms and to defuse criticisms such as the claim that "the reforms lack a statutory basis." On the other hand, it has formally integrated the institutional breakthroughs achieved in practice, endowing them with binding legal authority. Taken together, this approach has come to represent one of the most important models shaping the development of China's legal system over the past two decades.

The compliance reform for enterprises involved in criminal cases is a major judicial initiative driven by the procuratorial authorities, and it has now undergone nearly four years of exploratory development. Beginning in March 2020, when the Supreme People's Procuratorate launched pilot programs in selected grassroots procuratorates, the reform was extended in March 2021 to ten provincial-level procuratorial offices nationwide, and by April 2022, it had

R. Chen, *An Introduction to Corporate Compliance*,
https://doi.org/10.1007/978-981-95-7257-1_11

entered a phase of comprehensive pilot implementation across the country. China's enterprise compliance reform has thus advanced along a path of sustained experimentation, iterative trial and error, and gradual institutional refinement. From its initial emergence as a *"spark of innovation"* to its later expansion into a *"raging prairie fire,"* the reform has evolved into a prominent undertaking that has drawn significant attention from all sectors of society. As the legislature has now placed amendments to the Criminal Procedure Law on its agenda, a pressing question has emerged: how to incorporate the outcomes of this reform into the Criminal Procedure Law itself and thereby establish, at the level of fundamental legislation, the legitimacy and authority of a compliance supervision and assessment system for enterprises involved in criminal cases.

According to data released by the Supreme People's Procuratorate, from the launch of enterprise compliance reform in March 2020 through September 2023, procuratorial authorities across the country handled a total of 7815 compliance cases involving enterprises suspected of criminal conduct. Among these, non-prosecution decisions were issued for 2898 enterprises and 6102 responsible individuals who participated in compliance remediation. In contrast, 136 enterprises failed to pass the compliance acceptance assessment, and the enterprises and responsible individuals concerned were prosecuted and held criminally accountable in accordance with the law. Over the same period, of the 7815 compliance cases handled nationwide, 5527—accounting for 70.72%—involved the application of the third-party oversight and assessment mechanism.[1] It is fair to say that this reform initiative, led by the procuratorial authorities, has played a positive role in safeguarding enterprises' survival and development, facilitating their transformation away from criminal conduct, and strengthening the procuratorate's role in social governance. The large number of enterprises and individuals who, through compliance remediation, received lenient treatment—particularly those who were issued non-prosecution decisions and thereby obtained certificates of "no criminal record," avoiding the collateral consequences of criminal sanctions—has contributed to protecting the interests of the state, the public, enterprises themselves, and their stakeholders. This outcome reflects the active and constructive role of the procuratorial authorities in social governance. Moreover, the operation of the compliance supervision and assessment system has never been a matter of simply "letting enterprises off" or "closing cases without prosecution." Nor has compliance remediation been treated as a mere formality. The procuratorial authorities have applied rigorous standards when evaluating and accepting compliance outcomes and have consistently retained the authority to initiate prosecution against enterprises failing to achieve effective compliance. Additionally, the vast majority of these compliance cases have involved the

[1] Jingfeng Gao, "Actively Promoting the Legislative Implementation of a Modern Chinese Corporate Compliance System," *Jimen Integrated Criminal Law Forum* (WeChat Official Account), November 27, 2023.

participation of third-party organizations. Compliance monitors serving within these bodies have played a critical role by conducting substantive compliance remediation and ensuring that enterprises fulfill effective compliance objectives.

At present, the theoretical foundations, institutional arrangements, and social outcomes of enterprise compliance reform for criminally implicated companies have been positively evaluated across society, and there is a growing consensus within both academic and practical circles. However, it must be acknowledged that, constrained by various factors, the reform still faces numerous challenges, and some scholars and practitioners have voiced criticisms and reservations about certain aspects of its design. Indeed, in the context of any reform initiative, it is unrealistic to expect unanimous acceptance of every institutional arrangement. Once a reform has undergone a period of experimentation and iterative adjustment, and has produced demonstrably positive social effects, if its theoretical foundations and structural framework have won broad recognition and have shown themselves capable of effectively addressing major practical problems, it can reasonably be incorporated into fundamental legislation. As for those institutional components that remain contested, it is appropriate to adhere to the principle of *"seeking common ground while preserving differences,"* temporarily refraining from codifying them into law and instead leaving room for continued reform and exploration.

In view of the foregoing, this article aims to offer a preliminary discussion on how the achievements of enterprise compliance reform might be incorporated into legislation. The author will begin by providing a concise overview of the theoretical foundations of the reform, in order to establish a rationale for formally enshrining a compliance supervision and assessment mechanism for enterprises involved in criminal cases within the legal framework. On this basis, the article will analyze and evaluate the relatively mature institutional designs that have developed through the reform process and will present preliminary proposals for addressing the supporting measures and safeguards that urgently require attention. As for certain institutional arrangements that remain the focus of substantial controversy, the author will briefly consider the arguments on both sides and outline basic approaches to resolving the related disagreements.

11.2 The Theoretical Foundations

While the compliance reform for enterprises involved in criminal cases has achieved positive outcomes, it has consistently faced questions about its *legitimacy* and whether it possesses a sufficient legal basis. Some critics have argued that this reform "rests solely on utilitarian considerations and lacks legal grounding," and that it risks undermining the uniform application of criminal law.

In reality, any reform that rigidly adheres to the provisions of existing legislation without introducing appropriate institutional innovation is unlikely to have substantial significance. To resolve these controversies, it would be sufficient for the legislature to amend the Criminal Procedure Law and formally establish the mechanism of compliance supervision and assessment for enterprises involved in criminal cases. Doing so would effectively put an end to debates over its "legitimacy." Nevertheless, even if this were accomplished, a further and more challenging question would remain: What is the justification for procuratorial authorities to issue non-prosecution decisions or other lenient dispositions to enterprises by applying the compliance assessment mechanism? In this regard, several theories advanced by scholars and practitioners—such as the public interest consideration theory, the alternative criminal sanctions theory, the legal interest restoration theory, and the effective prevention of corporate crime theory—are persuasive, widely accepted by researchers, and can provide important theoretical foundations for guiding compliance reforms in enterprises involved in criminal cases.

11.2.1 Public Interest Consideration Theory

The so-called *public interest consideration* holds that when deciding whether to initiate a public prosecution, the procuratorial authorities should conduct a comprehensive assessment and balancing of the various impacts that prosecution may have on the public interest, and should make their decision in accordance with the principle of minimizing harm to public welfare.[2] Specifically, guided by the concept of rational choice, the procuratorial authorities must weigh the potential public interest benefits arising from prosecuting the enterprise against the public interest losses that prosecution would entail, in order to reach the optimal litigation decision. If, after this balancing, it is determined that prosecution would generate substantial benefits while the associated losses would be negligible, a decision to proceed with prosecution may be justified. Conversely, if a careful assessment shows that prosecuting the enterprise would cause significant social, economic, or even political harm, and that the public interest served by prosecution is clearly disproportionate, a decision of non-prosecution or deferred prosecution should be adopted.

To regulate the exercise of prosecutorial authority and to limit prosecutorial discretion, some Western countries have explicitly incorporated a *public interest test* into their legal frameworks. For example, in the United Kingdom, when reviewing whether to prosecute, prosecutors must apply two tests: first, the *evidential test*, and second, the *public interest test*. The latter requires prosecutors to consider whether, rather than initiating proceedings against the enterprise, it would better serve the public interest to enter into a deferred prosecution agreement.[3] In the United States, prosecutorial authorities apply the system of *pretrial diversion agreements* to corporations primarily to avoid

[2] Xiaoqing Zhu, "Public Interest Considerations in Prosecutorial Discretion," *Journal of the National Prosecutors College*, no. 3 (2023).

[3] Ruihua Chen, *The Fundamentals of Corporate Compliance*, 3rd ed. Beijing: Law Press, 2023, 339.

the so-called *ripple effects of punishment*. This concept refers to the various adverse consequences that criminal penalties imposed on an enterprise may have for other parties—particularly the potential harm to innocent third parties such as the company's investors, employees, pensioners, and customers. In this way, authorities seek to prevent criminal sanctions from generating such "ripple effects."[4]

In China, before deciding whether to initiate the compliance assessment procedure, procuratorial authorities are required to conduct a thorough evaluation of the potential benefits and drawbacks of prosecuting the enterprise involved and to give priority to applying this procedure to enterprises that make significant contributions to society. This approach reflects the core principles of the *public interest consideration theory*. Specifically, public interest considerations can be divided into *positive public interest considerations* and *negative public interest considerations*. The former refers to the procuratorial authorities' comprehensive examination and assessment of factors such as the enterprise's employment scale, tax contributions, the technological sophistication of its products, its performance in generating foreign exchange through exports, its growth prospects, whether it is a listed or pre-IPO company, whether it constitutes a local pillar enterprise, and whether it occupies a key position within an industrial chain. For enterprises making major contributions to society, prosecutorial authorities should exercise particular caution in deciding whether to bring criminal charges.

By contrast, *negative public interest considerations* refer to the weighing of the adverse consequences that prosecuting an enterprise may produce. Typically, once an enterprise is prosecuted, convicted, and sentenced, it faces a range of collateral consequences associated with criminal penalties. These include restrictions on, or the revocation of, various market access qualifications imposed by state agencies or relevant organizations, resulting in varying degrees of limitations on procurement, business operations, import and export activities, participation in bidding processes, listing on stock exchanges, obtaining loans, and securing franchise rights. In the most severe cases, an enterprise may be forced to suspend operations, declare bankruptcy, or permanently shut down. Accordingly, when reviewing whether to prosecute, procuratorial authorities should comprehensively consider whether prosecution would damage the interests of stakeholders such as shareholders, investors, employees, creditors, banks, local governments, and communities. They must assess whether prosecution might trigger adverse consequences, including employee layoffs or widespread unemployment, significant losses to investors, reductions in tax revenue, disruptions to industrial supply chains, increases in crime rates, outbreaks of collective incidents, or the emergence of new sources of social instability. Where doubts or disputes arise over whether to apply the compliance assessment procedure to a particular enterprise, procuratorial authorities

[4] Liangfang Ye, "The Development of the U.S. Corporate Pre-Trial Deferred Prosecution Agreement System," *China Criminal Law Journal*, no. 3 (2014).

should conduct a thorough evaluation and balancing of the relevant social, public, and national interests, and make a rational and prudent decision that satisfies the fundamental requirement of maximizing the public interest.

11.2.2 Alternative Sanctions Theory

During the process of compliance reform for enterprises involved in criminal cases, some have expressed concerns that procuratorial authorities' decisions not to prosecute—based on enterprises' compliance remediation efforts—could result in the toleration of criminal conduct and undermine the uniform application of criminal law. In reality, a careful examination of the conditions governing the application of the compliance assessment mechanism, along with an analysis of the compliance remediation process itself, reveals that such concerns lack any factual basis. In implementing the compliance assessment mechanism, procuratorial authorities have not abandoned the imposition of sanctions on enterprises; on the contrary, they have often adopted measures that, in certain respects, are more stringent and demanding than traditional criminal penalties. These measures serve to realize a compliance penalty function that criminal punishment alone is unable to achieve. This is precisely the rationale underlying the theory of alternative criminal sanctions in the context of compliance reform for enterprises involved in criminal cases.[5]

First, the application of the compliance assessment mechanism for enterprises involved in criminal cases is marked by clear punitive characteristics.[6] As a precondition for applying the compliance assessment procedure, the enterprise must admit guilt and accept punishment, cease all criminal activities, and actively cooperate with criminal investigation, prosecution, and compliance assessment. This, in itself, means that the enterprise relinquishes the right to mount a defense of innocence and voluntarily expresses its willingness to accept sanctions. At the same time, in order to persuade the procuratorial authorities to initiate the compliance assessment procedure, enterprises typically adopt various remedial measures to mitigate the social harm caused by their offenses. Such measures may include paying fines, surrendering illicit gains, paying outstanding taxes and late fees, restoring environmental resources damaged by the crime or covering restoration costs, compensating victims or victim entities, obtaining their forgiveness, or concluding settlement agreements with them.

[5] Ruihua Chen, *The Fundamentals of Corporate Compliance*, 3rd ed. Beijing: Law Press, 2022, 359.

[6] Liuchang Yue, ed., *U.S. Anti-Money Laundering Compliance Supervision—Case Collection of U.S. Regulatory Agency Sanctions*, Beijing: China Financial Publishing House, 2019, 76. This book comments on the Deferred Prosecution Agreement (DPA) reached between U.S. regulatory authorities and HSBC Bank, noting that "the DPA required HSBC Bank to pay a fine of USD 1.256 billion and to admit the illegal acts listed in the statement of facts. Overall, the DPA compelled HSBC Bank to take a series of significant measures, and considering that HSBC Bank, as a corporation, cannot be imprisoned, the effect of the DPA is almost equivalent to a criminal conviction."

For enterprises involved, implementing these remedial measures amounts to accepting a special form of penalty and exposes them to a range of adverse social, economic, and reputational consequences.

Second, the sanctions resulting from the compliance assessment procedure for enterprises involved in criminal cases are often more severe than conventional criminal penalties. On the one hand, once the judicial authorities convict an enterprise, the typical penalty imposed is a criminal fine. By comparison, the fines, back taxes, surrendered illicit gains, environmental restoration costs, and victim compensation payments that procuratorial authorities require enterprises to pay can result in economic losses far exceeding those of the criminal fine alone, amounting to a substantially harsher sanction. On the other hand, once the procuratorial authorities initiate the compliance assessment procedure, they do so with the objective of effectively preventing future violations. They order the enterprise to undertake targeted compliance remediation. This process requires the enterprise not only to submit a self-assessment report disclosing the endogenous structural causes of its criminal conduct, but also to accept strict oversight by third-party organizations. Under such supervision, the enterprise must carry out targeted institutional corrections to its governance structures, management systems, and business processes, and must establish or improve a specialized compliance management framework. In terms of the costs incurred and the losses sustained by the enterprise, this compliance remediation process, in itself, constitutes a sanction that is often significantly more severe than conventional criminal punishment.

Third, once compliance assessment for an enterprise involved in criminal cases is successfully completed, it can achieve distinctive functions that traditional criminal punishment cannot substitute. Traditional criminal penalties pursue the dual aims of retribution and prevention. Although compliance assessment enables the enterprise to avoid the direct consequences of criminal conviction, it can, in a new way, realize more effective retributive and preventive functions. This is because the unique punitive consequences arising from compliance assessment can fulfill a compliance-based retribution function, subjecting the enterprise to significant social, reputational, and economic losses. At the same time, compliance assessment directly addresses the endogenous structural causes of the enterprise's criminal conduct through targeted institutional corrections and the establishment of a specialized compliance management system as part of the compliance remediation process. This approach helps prevent the recurrence of the same or similar violations. In terms of effective crime prevention, such compliance assessment often delivers a superior special prevention effect compared to traditional criminal penalties and can also generate a stronger general deterrent impact across society.

11.2.3 *Legal Interest Restoration Theory*

Crime is an unlawful act that seriously infringes upon legally protected interests and entails varying degrees of social harm. This is one of the principal grounds for holding offenders criminally accountable. The reason why enterprises involved in criminal cases may be subjected to the compliance assessment procedure—and, depending on the effectiveness of their compliance remediation, ultimately receive a procedural non-conviction disposition—is primarily that these enterprises have undertaken a range of remedial measures. Such measures include admitting guilt and expressing remorse, ceasing criminal activities, cooperating with criminal investigations, compensating victims, and repairing harm. Through these efforts, the enterprises have implemented effective compliance remediation, helped prevent the recurrence of similar offenses, and contributed to reducing the negative consequences to society.[7]

The legal interest restoration theory provides an important theoretical foundation for enterprises' post-offense compliance remediation. First, as a precondition for the procuratorial authorities to apply the compliance assessment mechanism, the enterprise must admit guilt and accept punishment, cease its criminal conduct, and cooperate fully with all prosecutorial and compliance oversight efforts. This signifies that the enterprise has renounced adversarial litigation and expressed a willingness to accept criminal accountability and undergo compliance assessment. This stance is not only the basis for restoring legally protected interests but also a key justification for the procuratorial authorities to exercise leniency. Second, the remedial measures undertaken by the enterprise—such as paying fines, surrendering illicit gains, paying back taxes and late fees, repairing environmental damage, and compensating victims—have significantly reduced the harmful consequences inflicted on protected legal interests. These measures have also helped restore, at least partially, the interests and social relationships disrupted by the offense, thereby fulfilling a function that can serve as a substitute for criminal punishment. Third, under the supervision of the procuratorial authorities and the Third-Party Mechanism Committee, the enterprise, by accepting compliance assessment and evaluation conducted by an independent organization, has implemented effective institutional corrections and established or improved specialized compliance management systems. These efforts have closed management loopholes prone to harming protected interests and, at the cultural level, have instilled values oriented toward safeguarding legal interests. Given that the enterprise, through compliance remediation, has effectively prevented the recurrence of conduct that infringes upon protected interests, the necessity for the procuratorial authorities to bring a public prosecution is correspondingly greatly diminished.

[7] The theoretical summary that corporate compliance has a "public interest restoration" function was first observed in the reform experience of the Longhua District Procuratorate in Shenzhen, Guangdong. See Lei Wei et al., "Helping Enterprises Identify Risks and Fill Gaps—Shenzhen Longhua: Establishing a Public Interest Restoration Observation Period System to Promote Corporate Compliance Rectification," *Procuratorial Daily*, June 21, 2021.

11.2.4 Effective Control of Corporate Crime Theory

The traditional theory of criminal law has long maintained that imposing criminal penalties on offenders serves the purpose of crime prevention. However, in the context of corporate crime, relying solely on harsh punishment rarely achieves effective deterrence. This is because, in practice, judicial sanctions imposed on offending enterprises generally amount to nothing more than the imposition of a fine. Combined with the widespread phenomenon of selective enforcement, criminal enterprises often have ample opportunities to evade accountability. As a result, criminal penalties exert limited deterrent force on enterprises already engaged in misconduct and provide little dissuasion to other enterprises that might contemplate similar violations. Moreover, when an enterprise suffers from structural defects in corporate governance, loopholes in internal management systems, hidden risks in business processes, or even a business model containing a "criminal gene," purely punitive measures leave these entrenched pathologies unaddressed. The likelihood that the enterprise will reoffend therefore remains substantial. The implementation of the compliance assessment mechanism for enterprises involved in criminal cases abandons the traditional approach of preventing crime solely through punishment. Instead, it adopts a governance strategy aimed at identifying and eliminating the underlying causes of corporate criminality. The theoretical logic embodied in this system is a theory of effective control of corporate crime, grounded in a philosophy of realism.[8]

According to this theory, procuratorial authorities can require enterprises involved in criminal cases to adopt compliance remediation measures and implement Effective Compliance Programs, thereby achieving meaningful crime prevention. Corporate compliance is a form of corporate governance oriented toward risk control. If an enterprise, through compliance remediation under the supervision of the procuratorial authorities and compliance monitors, ultimately succeeds in establishing and implementing an effective compliance program, the endogenous structural causes underlying its criminal conduct can potentially be eliminated, and the likelihood of reoffending is greatly reduced.[9] In terms of effective crime prevention, post-offense compliance remediation can play a positive role in several respects. First, by carrying out internal investigations and submitting self-assessment reports, the enterprise can accurately identify and assess compliance risks, pinpoint governance structures, management systems, business processes, and business models prone to criminal conduct, and then carry out targeted institutional corrections and robust remedial measures. Second, by transforming its corporate governance structure and elevating compliance management to a strategic priority equal to decision-making management, operational management, and financial man-

[8] Ruihua Chen, *The Chinese Experience of Effective Corporate Compliance*, Beijing: Peking University Press, 2023, 154.

[9] Philip Weller, *Effective Compliance Programs and Corporate Criminal Litigation*, translated by Wanfang, *Finance and Law Review*, no. 3 (2018).

agement, the enterprise can establish a compliance management committee or leadership group under the board of directors or other top decision-making body. It can create an independent and authoritative compliance department with adequate resources, set up a compliance review mechanism covering all business lines and products, and adopt a "one-vote veto" system for activities and products that pose compliance risks. This compliance framework, which embodies the principle of top-level commitment, can effectively deter and monitor unlawful conduct. Third, the enterprise can develop targeted compliance programs addressing the specific types of offenses that have occurred, embedding applicable legal and regulatory requirements into the company's special compliance policies and employee handbooks. These, in turn, become behavioral guidelines binding all levels of the organization and the foundation for compliance training, compliance risk assessments, and compliance due diligence. Fourth, based on compliance risk identification and assessment, the enterprise can establish a set of compliance risk management processes—especially mechanisms for activating due diligence, compliance training, compliance reporting, internal whistleblowing, regular compliance audits and monitoring, internal investigations, incentives and disciplinary measures, and continuous improvement. Such a system enables the compliance framework to play an active role in preventing misconduct in advance, monitoring it during execution, and responding to it afterward.

11.3 Institutional Experience of Enterprise Compliance Reform

To date, in order to advance enterprise compliance reform, the Supreme People's Procuratorate has participated in issuing a number of normative documents and has released dozens of guiding cases concerning the compliance supervision and assessment of enterprises involved in criminal cases.[10] An analysis of these normative documents and guiding cases shows that several groundbreaking institutional arrangements have already been established and have been implemented with considerable success. As a kind of "living organism," once the compliance supervision and assessment system is set in motion and cultivated through careful experimentation within an appropriate social, economic, political, and cultural environment, it gradually grows and develops into an institutional element capable of integration into the existing system and legal framework. To preempt continued challenges regarding its legitimacy, it

[10] As of August 2022, the Supreme People's Procuratorate, in coordination with eight other departments, issued two significant normative documents to advance corporate compliance reforms: first, the *Guiding Opinions on Establishing a Third-Party Supervision and Evaluation Mechanism for Corporate Compliance in Criminal Cases (Trial)* on June 3, 2021; and second, the *Measures for the Construction, Evaluation, and Review of Corporate Compliance in Criminal Cases (Trial)* on April 19, 2022. Moreover, as of November 2023, the Supreme People's Procuratorate has published four batches of "Pilot Cases of Corporate Compliance Reform," including a total of 20 representative cases covering more than 12 types of criminal offenses.

is necessary to systematically sort through and summarize these relatively mature institutional arrangements so that they can be smoothly incorporated as an organic component of the criminal procedure law system.

11.3.1 *Third-Party Mechanism Committees*

To ensure the smooth progress of compliance supervision and assessment reform, procuratorial authorities at all levels have promoted the establishment of Third-Party Supervision and Evaluation Mechanism Management Committee (hereinafter referred to as the "Third-Party Mechanism Committee"). These committees, with the All-China Federation of Industry and Commerce and its local branches serving as their permanent offices, have become the leading bodies and supervisory authorities overseeing enterprise compliance reform. As of the end of September 2023, procuratorial authorities across the country had facilitated the establishment of one national-level Third-Party Mechanism Committee, 32 provincial-level committees, 329 municipal-level committees, and 1805 county and district-level committees. At present, a third-party supervision and evaluation mechanism characterized by "procuratorial leadership, multi-party participation, objectivity and neutrality, and enhanced supervision" has been largely established nationwide.[11]

In the practice of enterprise compliance reform for companies involved in criminal cases, the Third-Party Mechanism Committees play a critically important leadership and supervisory role. First, the Third-Party Mechanism Committee has the authority to decide whether to initiate the third-party oversight and assessment mechanism. For enterprises that meet the applicable conditions, the procuratorial authorities may, either upon the enterprise's application or ex officio, decide to launch the compliance supervision and assessment procedure. However, to activate the third-party oversight and assessment mechanism, the procuratorial authorities must consult with the Third-Party Mechanism Committee for review and approval. Second, the Third-Party Mechanism Committee selects personnel from the roster of qualified professionals to form a Third-Party Oversight and Assessment Organization (hereinafter referred to as the "Third-Party Organization"), which is responsible for investigating, supervising, assessing, and evaluating the enterprise's compliance remediation efforts. Each level of committee has formulated and published a directory of qualified professionals—referred to as compliance monitors—from which candidates are drawn to constitute Third-Party Organizations for cases where the compliance supervision procedure has been initiated. These organizations then undertake the supervision and assessment work. Third, the committees have established joint conference mechanisms responsible for the routine selection, training, and evaluation of compliance

[11] Jingfeng Gao, "Actively Promoting the Legislative Implementation of a Modern Chinese Corporate Compliance System," *Jimen Integrated Criminal Law Forum* (WeChat Official Account), November 27, 2023.

monitors serving as members of Third-Party Organizations. Where compliance monitors engage in illegal or improper conduct, the committees may conduct investigations and impose disciplinary measures. Fourth, the committees have formed inspection teams to carry out on-site spot checks and ongoing supervision of the compliance oversight activities performed by Third-Party Organizations. Finally, once a Third-Party Organization has completed its compliance supervision and assessment work, the committee may review the organization's assessment report and participate in the compliance acceptance hearing convened under the leadership of the procuratorial authorities, expressing its opinion on whether the enterprise's compliance remediation satisfies the required standards.

After several years of reform, experimentation, and institutional development, the Third-Party Mechanism Committee have become a key institutional platform for leading and supervising compliance assessment work. In ensuring the effectiveness of compliance reform, these committees play roles in four principal respects. First, they exercise effective oversight and checks over the procuratorial authorities' initiation of compliance supervision procedures, the evaluation and acceptance of compliance remediation, and decisions to grant lenient treatment to implicated enterprises. This promotes adherence to the fundamental rule-of-law principles of power restraint and balance. Second, they provide robust supervision over the Third-Party Organizations composed of compliance monitors, requiring them to uphold essential professional ethics, avoid conflicts of interest or other misconduct, and maintain integrity and self-discipline. Third, they oversee, track, and inspect the compliance assessment activities conducted by Third-Party Organizations, ensuring that compliance monitors discharge their duties in accordance with the law and driving enterprises' compliance remediation toward the goal of effectively preventing future violations. Fourth, through the mechanism of joint conferences, the committees involve relevant administrative regulatory authorities in the assessment, acceptance, and evaluation of enterprise compliance remediation. This approach not only leverages the active engagement of these regulators but also ensures smooth coordination between administrative enforcement and criminal justice, as well as the implementation of sector-specific compliance initiatives. In doing so, the committees help tax, customs, environmental protection, market regulation, workplace safety, and other administrative authorities carry out "root-cause governance" of unlawful conduct by enterprises and ensure that compliance remediation produces lasting effects.

11.3.2 Third-Party Organizations

Since 2021, with the progressive establishment of the third-party oversight and assessment mechanism for enterprise compliance, the Third-Party Mechanism Committees have begun piloting a system under which designated professionals serve as third-party experts to conduct compliance supervision and assessment. The term "third-party mechanism professionals" refers to individuals selected and appointed by the committees to serve as members of Third-Party Organizations, participating in the supervision and evaluation of enterprises involved in criminal cases. These professionals include lawyers, certified public accountants, tax advisors, corporate compliance officers, subject-matter experts and scholars, as well as professionals affiliated with relevant organizations. Qualified personnel with specialized expertise from government departments—such as those responsible for ecological and environmental protection, taxation, market regulation, and workplace safety—may also be appointed as third-party mechanism professionals. In principle, the national, provincial, and municipal Third-Party Committees each establish a directory (roster) of approved professionals. County-level committees may also establish such directories, subject to review and approval. The Third-Party Mechanism Committees are responsible for the comprehensive coordination of the selection, training, evaluation, reward and disciplinary measures, and oversight of these professionals within their respective jurisdictions.

After the procuratorial authorities decide to initiate the compliance supervision and assessment procedure for an enterprise involved in a criminal case, they may, with the approval of the Third-Party Mechanism Committee, activate the third-party oversight and assessment mechanism. A group of qualified professionals is then selected from the roster to constitute a Third-Party Organization, which is tasked with understanding, evaluating, supervising, and assessing the effectiveness of the enterprise's dedicated compliance remediation plan and issuing a determination as to whether the compliance efforts satisfy the prescribed standards. Generally, a Third-Party Organization is composed of three to seven professionals. For small and micro-sized enterprises, it may be composed of two professionals. The assessment process and the conclusions reached by the Third-Party Organization are subject to review by both the Third-Party Mechanism Committee and the procuratorial authorities. Where the compliance remediation is determined to meet effectiveness standards, a conclusion of qualified compliance may be issued. On this basis, the procuratorial authorities may decide not to prosecute or may recommend lenient penalties.

The evaluation and assessment conducted by the Third-Party Organization constitute a critical stage in determining whether an enterprise's compliance remediation will be genuinely effective. The Third-Party Organization may develop a tailored compliance assessment work plan based on the enterprise's specific circumstances. The assessment should focus on the remediation and mitigation of compliance risks associated with the offense. Drawing on sector-specific compliance evaluation benchmarks, the Third-Party Organization should develop an assessment index system adapted to the enterprise's operational realities. The assessment process should primarily address key areas, including risk identification, the handling of violations, organizational staffing and structure, resource allocation, the functioning of compliance management mechanisms, and the cultivation of a robust compliance culture. Upon completion of the compliance assessment, the Third-Party Organization carries out a comprehensive inspection and evaluation of the enterprise's implementation of its compliance plan and prepares a detailed compliance assessment report. These institutional arrangements, after more than two years of practical application, have been shown to be both feasible and indispensable for enabling enterprises to achieve effective compliance remediation.

Of course, there remain a number of issues to be addressed regarding the participation of Third-Party Organizations in evaluating the compliance remediation of enterprises involved in criminal cases. For example, in some localities, the funding for third-party oversight and assessment comes from government budgets, and the remuneration provided to professionals in Third-Party Organizations is relatively modest given the complexity and significance of their work. This disparity has dampened professionals' motivation and made it difficult to ensure that assessments are conducted to a high standard.[12] In addition, in certain regions, the Third-Party Mechanism Committees have not carried out rigorous vetting when selecting professionals to include in the rosters of eligible experts. As a result, individuals unfamiliar with compliance management have been enrolled, and further due diligence has often been lacking when assembling Third-Party Organizations. Consequently, some members lack meaningful experience in specialized compliance remediation, causing the supervision and assessment work to become largely perfunctory and formalistic and failing to ensure the reliability and quality of compliance remediation outcomes. Moreover, neither the procuratorial authorities nor the Third-Party Mechanism Committees have yet established robust mechanisms to supervise the work of Third-Party Organizations. There has been little substantive review of the quality of their compliance assessments and a lack of adequate oversight to identify conflicts of interest or breaches of professional ethics among compliance monitors. In many cases, their assessment conclusions are accepted uncritically, without independent scrutiny. These shortcomings have significantly undermined the effectiveness of compliance remediation efforts.[13]

11.3.3 Conditional Non-prosecution for Enterprises

After nearly four years of reform and experimentation, China's procuratorial authorities have preliminarily established a conditional non-prosecution system for enterprises involved in criminal cases. Under this system, where an enterprise meets certain prescribed conditions, the procuratorial authorities may entrust the Third-Party Mechanism Committee to appoint a Third-Party Organization to investigate, evaluate, supervise, and assess the enterprise's compliance commitments. The results of this assessment serve as an important

[12] Yanhong Liu, "Key Issues in the Third-Party Supervision and Assessment Mechanism for Corporate Compliance Involved in Criminal Cases," *Chinese Applied Jurisprudence*, no. 6 (2022).

[13] Yan Kong and Jia Han, "Improving the Third-Party Supervision and Assessment Mechanism for Corporate Compliance Involved in Criminal Cases," *People's Procuratorial Journal*, no. 7 (2023).

reference point for the procuratorial authorities when deciding how to dispose of the case. In judicial practice, once the procuratorial authorities obtain the consent of the Third-Party Mechanism Committee and decide to initiate the third-party oversight and assessment procedure, they establish a compliance monitoring period, typically lasting several months. During this period, the Third-Party Mechanism Committee designates a Third-Party Organization to conduct supervision, monitoring, and evaluation of the enterprise's compliance remediation efforts. This compliance supervision and assessment mechanism essentially functions as a deferred prosecution decision made by the procuratorial authorities with respect to the enterprise. Only if the enterprise fulfills the compliance remediation requirements it has committed to within the monitoring period will it become eligible for a non-prosecution decision. Accordingly, this system is often referred to as the *conditional non-prosecution system for enterprises involved in criminal cases.*

At present, the conditional non-prosecution system for criminally implicated enterprises has developed a relatively mature institutional framework. First, for an enterprise to be eligible for this system, it must meet specific conditions before the procuratorial authorities may initiate the procedure. These conditions mainly include: the enterprise or responsible individuals must admit guilt and accept punishment; the enterprise must be capable of maintaining normal business operations; the enterprise must commit to establishing or improving its internal compliance system; the enterprise must voluntarily agree to the application of the third-party oversight mechanism; the enterprise must fully cease all unlawful and criminal activities; the enterprise must return any unlawful gains, pay back taxes and late fees, and pay applicable fines; and the enterprise must fully cooperate with investigations, prosecutions, and the work of the Third-Party Organization. Second, to initiate the compliance supervision and assessment procedure, the procuratorial authorities must submit the case level by level for review and approval by the provincial procuratorial office. For cases involving the third-party mechanism, the consent of the corresponding Third-Party Mechanism Committee at the same level is also required. Third, once the procuratorial authorities and the Third-Party Mechanism Committee decide to commence the compliance supervision procedure, they must set a compliance monitoring period and assemble and appoint a Third-Party Organization to conduct supervision, monitoring, and evaluation of the enterprise's compliance remediation. Under the time limits prescribed by the current Criminal Procedure Law regarding the review and prosecution stage, this monitoring period is typically between three and six months. In a small number of particularly significant cases or those requiring an extension, the period can last between 6 and 12 months. Fourth, before the monitoring period concludes, the procuratorial authorities and the Third-Party Mechanism Committee must conduct an acceptance review of the enterprise's compliance remediation. Acceptance can take the form of either a written review or a hearing. The procuratorial authorities and the Third-Party Mechanism Committee comprehensively examine and evaluate the effectiveness of the compliance remediation and the establishment of the special compliance system based on the assessment report submitted by the Third-Party Organization, and then issue a conclusion on whether the compliance remediation has passed. Finally, for enterprises that pass the compliance assessment, the procuratorial authorities may decide not to prosecute or may recommend lenient sentencing to the court. For enterprises that fail the compliance assessment, the procuratorial authorities retain the authority to file charges and recommend appropriate criminal penalties to the court.

Of course, this conditional non-prosecution system still has ample room for further improvement. In particular, regarding eligibility criteria, current normative documents have yet to establish sufficiently clear and operational standards, resulting in considerable discretion for some local procuratorial authorities in deciding whether to initiate the procedure. In the future, building on the achievements of compliance reform and drawing on successful case experiences, four main categories of eligibility criteria could be developed. First, the foundational conditions require that the enterprise or responsible individuals must admit guilt and accept punishment, cease the relevant unlawful or criminal conduct, fully cooperate with investigations conducted by law enforcement agencies, the procuratorial authorities, regulatory bodies, and the Third-Party Organization, and demonstrate the capacity to maintain normal business operations. Second, the legal interest restoration conditions emphasize that the enterprise must have undertaken proactive remedial measures that significantly reduce the social harm caused by the offense; depending on the specific circumstances, these measures could include paying fines, surrendering illicit gains, paying back taxes, repairing environmental damage or covering environmental restoration costs, compensating victims, and obtaining their forgiveness. Third, the public interest conditions require that applying the compliance assessment procedure to the enterprise should serve important social and public interests, which may be evaluated by reference to factors such as the enterprise's employment scale, tax contributions, the technological sophistication of its products, export performance, its position within critical industry chains, and whether it is listed or preparing for listing. Finally, the compliance remediation foundations stipulate that the enterprise must demonstrate a strong willingness to engage in compliance remediation by submitting a self-assessment report identifying the endogenous structural causes of the offense, presenting a targeted compliance remediation plan, or having already established a pre-existing compliance program.

Regarding the duration of the compliance monitoring period, it could be considered to amend the Criminal Procedure Law in order to formally establish the conditional non-prosecution system for enterprises involved in criminal cases, create a mechanism to suspend the prosecution review process, and set a dedicated compliance monitoring period that aligns with the requirements of compliance supervision and remediation. The monitoring period could range from one to three years, with the procuratorial authorities determining the specific duration based on factors such as the enterprise's size, type of business operations, industry characteristics, and the level of compliance risk. This determination should be guided by the overarching objective of ensuring that compliance remediation is both effective and comprehensive.

Regarding the compliance acceptance mechanism, the conditions and procedures for applying the two acceptance methods could be clearly stipulated based on the type of case. In principle, for cases in which the third-party mechanism has not been activated, the procuratorial authorities may independently determine whether to conduct acceptance through written procedures or by convening a hearing. However, for cases in which the third-party mechanism has been applied with the consent of the Third-Party Mechanism Committee, the procuratorial authorities should generally organize a hearing-based acceptance process. Under this procedure, a panel of hearing officers is selected, and the hearing is chaired by at least three prosecutors. The enterprise's legal representatives, along with their defense counsel or compliance advisors, participate in the hearing, while members of the Third-Party Organization attend to present the findings of the compliance assessment and respond to questions raised by all parties. The procuratorial authorities should also invite representatives of the Third-Party Mechanism Committee, people's supervisors, investigators, and any victims or victim entities to attend. Upon conclusion of the hearing, the procuratorial authorities, taking into account the hearing officers' votes, the effectiveness of the enterprise's compliance remediation, and the Third-Party Organization's assessment conclusions—and after soliciting the views of the relevant units within the Third-Party Mechanism Committee — issue a final determination on whether the compliance assessment has been successfully passed.

To prevent judicial personnel from abusing the compliance assessment procedure, consideration could be given to establishing a judicial remedy mechanism for compliance assessment applications. Specifically, when an enterprise or a responsible individual applies to initiate the compliance assessment procedure and the procuratorial authorities or the court refuse the application, they should be required to issue a written decision stating the reasons for the refusal. If the procuratorial authorities decide not to initiate compliance assessment, the applicant should have the right either to file an objection with the higher-level procuratorial authority or to apply to the court for the initiation of compliance assessment. In cases where a first-instance court denies an application to initiate compliance assessment, the applicant should be entitled to appeal that decision, and the second-instance court should be required to issue a ruling on whether to uphold the appeal. The appellate decision should be in writing and should clearly state the factual grounds and legal reasoning underlying the determination.

11.3.4 Standards for Effective Compliance Remediation

In the operation of the compliance supervision and assessment system, the standards for effective compliance remediation serve both as the criteria applied by Third-Party Organizations in assessing and evaluating enterprises and as the basis on which the procuratorial authorities and the Third-Party Mechanism Committees accept and approve compliance remediation outcomes. Through several years of reform and practice, China's procuratorial authorities have preliminarily established such standards.[14] First, effective compliance must meet the requirements of a targeted compliance program, namely, it must be capable of effectively preventing the recurrence of the same or similar illegal or criminal conduct. Second, effective compliance must embody the principle of top-level commitment,[15] requiring the actual controllers and principal responsible persons of the enterprise to make explicit compliance commitments and demonstrate that compliance is a core corporate value, adopting a zero-tolerance attitude toward unlawful conduct and ensuring that compliance is integrated into the enterprise's development objectives, strategies, and management systems. Third, effective compliance must reflect the principle of proportionality,[16] meaning that the enterprise should establish compliance management institutions or designate compliance personnel in a manner commensurate with its type, size, business scope, and industry characteristics. Finally, effective compliance must address risk prevention and control requirements by establishing and improving compliance mechanisms in accordance with risk management needs and the responsibilities of its compliance management structures. These mechanisms should include the provision of adequate resources and safeguards, procedures for addressing violations, compliance performance appraisal systems, and continuous improvement measures.

The establishment of these standards for effective compliance remediation is undoubtedly of great significance for strengthening and refining China's conditional non-prosecution system for enterprises involved in criminal cases. Looking ahead, as research on criminal procedure legislation continues to advance, it will be possible to further distill practical and operable standards for effective compliance by systematically analyzing successful cases and reform experience. For example, in view of the distinctive characteristics of post-offense compliance remediation, it is necessary to adopt approaches different from those applied in pre-existing compliance management and to develop a method for assessing the effectiveness of compliance remediation. Such a method should define three core elements as essential criteria for effective remediation: diagnosing the endogenous structural causes underlying the enterprise's criminal conduct, implementing targeted corrections to address

[14] Yanhong Liu, "Standards for Effectiveness of Corporate Compliance Construction: From the Perspective of Crime Prevention in Criminally Involved Enterprises," *Eastern Jurisprudence*, no. 4 (2022).

[15] Ruihua Chen, "The Proportionality Principle in Corporate Compliance Rectification," *Comparative Law Research*, no. 1 (2023).

[16] Ruihua Chen, "The Senior Management Commitment Principle in Compliance Rectification," *Legal Science*, no. 3 (2023).

deficiencies in the compliance system, and building a systematic and specialized compliance framework.[17]

For example, to meet the practical needs of compliance assessment, evaluation, and acceptance, a multidimensional methodology for effective compliance evaluation could be established for Third-Party Organizations, procuratorial authorities, and Third-Party Mechanism Committees. This approach would introduce three core evaluation components: the effectiveness of compliance plan formulation, the effectiveness of compliance plan implementation, and the effectiveness of compliance outcomes. Specifically, in evaluating the effectiveness of compliance plan formulation, assessors could analyze the compliance remediation plan submitted by the enterprise. If the written materials substantively incorporate the three essential elements of effective compliance—namely, the diagnosis of the endogenous structural causes of the offense, the adoption of targeted corrective measures, and the establishment of a systematic and specialized compliance framework—a positive determination can be rendered. In evaluating the effectiveness of compliance plan implementation, the assessment should focus on whether the measures promised by the enterprise have been effectively put into practice. This includes determining whether the pledged rules and policies have been promulgated and enforced, whether the promised compliance leadership and management structures have been established, whether compliance review procedures have been integrated into relevant business processes, whether non-compliant decisions, activities, or products have been vetoed, and whether individuals responsible for violations have been held accountable. Finally, in assessing the effectiveness of compliance outcomes, evaluators should scientifically determine whether the enterprise has transformed its previous pathological operating practices, whether it has ceased reliance on unlawful or improper business models, and whether it has developed a corporate culture firmly committed to compliance with laws and regulations.

11.3.5 Forms of Leniency Based on Compliance

For enterprises that successfully pass compliance acceptance, the procuratorial authorities generally have two forms of lenient disposition available. First, they may issue a compliance-based non-prosecution decision, which means that, relying on the enterprise's effective compliance remediation, the procuratorial authorities choose not to prosecute the case. Second, they may make a compliance-based lenient sentencing recommendation, under which they propose that the court impose a mitigated sentence in recognition of the enterprise's verified compliance efforts. In practice, beyond granting lenient treatment to the enterprise itself, the procuratorial authorities may also extend such leniency to relevant responsible individuals within the enterprise, either by

[17] Ruihua Chen, "Basic Ideas for Effective Corporate Compliance Rectification," *Political and Legal Forum*, no. 1 (2023).

issuing non-prosecution decisions for them or by recommending that the court apply lighter penalties.

At present, there remain differences of opinion in both practice and scholarship regarding whether lenient treatment should also be extended to the responsible individuals of an enterprise that has passed compliance acceptance. However, with respect to granting a non-prosecution decision to the enterprise itself after it has successfully completed compliance remediation, there is broad consensus in practice and little controversy in theory. In principle, the decision by procuratorial authorities not to prosecute an enterprise that has passed compliance acceptance has become an effective incentive measure. This is because, once a non-prosecution decision is issued, the enterprise not only avoids the imposition of criminal penalties but also obtains a certificate confirming the absence of a criminal record. Consequently, it is exempt from the collateral consequences of criminal punishment: it is not barred from holding special operating qualifications, participating in public bidding processes, pursuing a stock exchange listing, or other activities, nor does it risk revocation of its business license. Precisely for these reasons, issuing a compliance-based non-prosecution decision can maximize an enterprise's motivation to undertake compliance remediation and establish robust compliance management systems. This is the fundamental institutional safeguard upon which the effectiveness of compliance programs depends.

At present, the main area of controversy concerns the scope and extent of applying compliance-based lenient sentencing. To date, both the normative documents issued in the course of compliance reform and the relevant compliance remediation cases indicate that successfully passing compliance acceptance is treated merely as a discretionary mitigating circumstance. Whether applied to the enterprise itself or to its responsible individuals, the procuratorial authorities, when relying on successful compliance remediation, can only recommend mitigated penalties within the statutory sentencing range. For the enterprise itself, if the procuratorial authorities proceed with prosecution, they are limited to recommending that the court impose a moderately reduced fine. However, even if the procuratorial authorities propose such a reduction, how much incentive does this actually create for the enterprise? From the perspective of these companies, once prosecution has been initiated and the court issues a conviction, they are legally designated as offenders and are subject to the collateral consequences associated with criminal punishment. In this context, even a lowered fine carries little substantive significance for the enterprise's operations, development, or survival—and fails to generate the compliance incentives that the system is intended to achieve.

Experience from compliance reform demonstrates that in order to create genuine incentives for enterprises involved in criminal cases to pursue compliance, it is not sufficient merely to establish a system of compliance-based non-prosecution in law. For enterprises suspected of committing serious corporate crimes, it is also worth considering the introduction of broader sentencing incentives. Specifically, successful completion of compliance remediation could be formally recognized as a statutory ground for reducing or exempting criminal penalties. In general, for enterprises that meet the conditions for non-prosecution, the procuratorial authorities could issue a non-prosecution decision based on successful compliance acceptance. For enterprises that are prosecuted due to suspicions of major corporate crimes, the procuratorial authorities could recommend to the court that the penalties be substantially mitigated. Based on such recommendations, the court could significantly reduce the amount of fines imposed, and, where appropriate, even depart from the statutory fine ranges. Moreover, for enterprises that have both passed compliance acceptance and presented other mitigating or exempting circumstances, the procuratorial authorities could recommend that the court consider a complete exemption from criminal penalties. The court could then issue a judgment waiving the punishment altogether.

11.4 Controversial Issues

At the initial stage of enterprise compliance reform, the procuratorial authorities primarily piloted the approach in cases involving minor corporate crimes committed by small and micro enterprises. In such cases, they applied a "dual non-prosecution" policy, issuing non-prosecution decisions both for the enterprise itself and for the responsible individuals. This institutional experimentation did not generate significant controversy among scholars or practitioners. However, as compliance reform has gradually deepened, some large enterprises suspected of committing serious crimes have come within the scope of compliance assessment. Cases involving offenses perpetrated by actual controllers, senior management personnel, or key technical staff have also been included in the compliance framework. In these matters, the procuratorial authorities have not only adopted a "case separation" approach but also treated successful compliance remediation as a basis for granting lenient treatment to the individuals responsible. These reform measures have attracted criticism from some commentators, who argue that they undermine the fundamental principles of corporate criminal accountability, risk condoning serious wrongdoing by enterprises and their executives, and violate the principle of equality before the law. At the same time, these criticisms have also prompted responses and targeted rebuttals from other scholars and practitioners supportive of the reforms. In addressing these contested issues, it is essential to adopt a calm and objective perspective, to conduct systematic analysis and balanced evaluation, and to make every effort to identify constructive solutions to these areas of disagreement.

11.4.1 Full-Process Compliance Supervision and Assessment

Since 2023, building on the positive outcomes of prosecutorial compliance reform, relevant authorities and legal scholars have proposed the concept of full-process compliance. This approach envisions establishing an institutional framework in which public security, procuratorial, judicial, and correctional authorities collaboratively advance enterprise compliance across the entire criminal procedure, ensuring that compliance remediation becomes a legally recognized basis for leniency at every stage.[18] According to normative documents issued in various regions, full-process compliance means that investigative, prosecutorial, judicial, and enforcement agencies apply procedural or substantive leniency to cases meeting the criteria for compliance assessment and place such cases within dedicated procedural tracks. For example, at the investigation stage, once a case is formally filed, investigative authorities may adopt procedural leniency measures for eligible cases, such as applying non-custodial coercive measures, refraining from seizure, impoundment, or freezing of assets, and conducting a preliminary review of whether the case is appropriate for compliance assessment. These decisions must be documented, and the case should be promptly transferred to the procuratorial authorities. At the prosecution stage, procuratorial authorities are expected to initiate the compliance supervision and assessment procedure without delay, organizing compliance oversight, evaluation, and acceptance, and granting lenient treatment to enterprises that successfully complete remediation. During the trial phase, courts may, in cases meeting compliance assessment conditions, independently commence compliance supervision and assessment, request that procuratorial authorities initiate the procedure, or evaluate the effectiveness of compliance efforts undertaken independently by the enterprise. For enterprises determined to have satisfied compliance requirements, the court may impose mitigated criminal penalties.[19] Finally, in the enforcement phase, judicial administrative authorities may, in cases involving probation or community correction, implement compliance assessment, activate the third-party mechanism, and grant leniency to enterprises that complete effective compliance remediation.

It must be acknowledged that if the concept of full-process compliance were to be implemented, it could indeed yield certain positive effects. However, to date, neither investigative authorities, the courts, nor judicial administrative agencies have attached sufficient importance to this reform, nor have they engaged in systematic exploration or pilot experimentation. Relevant pilot cases have remained exceedingly scarce. Consequently, both the academic community and practitioners have found it difficult to draw lessons from practice or to distill consistent and replicable institutional designs. Furthermore, regarding the institutional arrangements for full-process compliance, there remain a number of unresolved and contentious issues that will require careful examination and resolution.

[18] Fenfei Li, "Full-Process Leniency for Corporate Compliance Involved in Criminal Cases," *China Legal Science*, no. 4 (2023).

[19] Ruihua Chen, "Institutional Models for Courts Promoting Corporate Compliance Rectification," *Chinese Applied Jurisprudence*, no. 1 (2023).

First, how to coordinate the relationship between the compliance supervision and assessment procedure and the leniency procedure based on admission of guilt and acceptance of punishment is an issue that warrants thorough exploration in future criminal procedure legislation. Some commentators argue that, since one of the prerequisites for applying the compliance assessment procedure is that the enterprise or individual admits guilt and accepts punishment, this procedure should be subsumed within the broader leniency framework applicable to such cases.[20] However, others maintain that the compliance assessment procedure and the leniency procedure based on admission of guilt and acceptance of punishment are fundamentally different in nature. Specifically, the compliance assessment procedure constitutes an educational and corrective mechanism directed primarily at enterprises, with the principal purpose of promoting the "de-criminalization" and rehabilitation of corporate operations and governance structures. In contrast, the leniency procedure is applicable to all criminal cases and is designed chiefly to incentivize guilty pleas, conserve judicial resources, and enhance procedural efficiency. I concur with the latter view.

Second, with respect to whether investigative authorities should directly initiate the compliance assessment procedure, this is an issue that requires careful study before any institutional decision is made. One view holds that if the "full-process compliance" reform approach is to be adopted, then—similar to how plea-based leniency cases are handled—investigative authorities should be able to accept applications from enterprises to commence compliance assessment during the investigation stage. Consistent with the principle of "the earlier, the better," investigative authorities could themselves initiate the compliance procedure and invite the procuratorial authorities to engage the third-party oversight mechanism. However, another perspective maintains that allowing investigative authorities to directly launch compliance assessment does not necessarily result in more effective compliance remediation. During the investigative stage, it may be sufficient for the investigative authorities, when dealing with enterprises that meet the criteria for compliance assessment, to adopt non-custodial measures wherever possible, refrain from coercive actions that would unduly interfere with normal business operations, and transfer the case to the procuratorial authorities without delay. In this view, substantive compliance assessment should still be initiated and conducted in a unified manner by the procuratorial authorities. I concur with the latter view.

Third, regarding the models for court participation in compliance reform, no comprehensive normative framework has yet been established, and the number of publicly disclosed pilot cases remains extremely limited in both authority and scope. As a result, the available examples are too few to allow researchers to draw objective conclusions or to distill consistent insights. One perspective contends that courts should assume a certain leading role in

[20] Yong Li, "Direction and Path for Legalization of Corporate Compliance in China," *Guizhou University Journal (Social Science Edition)*, no. 3 (2023).

compliance reform. Under this approach, in cases that satisfy the criteria for compliance assessment, courts could independently initiate the compliance supervision and assessment procedure or invite the procuratorial authorities to launch it jointly. Regardless of how the process is triggered, courts would rely on the third-party mechanism as an institutional platform to evaluate and verify the enterprise's compliance remediation efforts, and, on that basis, to decide whether to grant lenient treatment.[21] However, others are concerned that overly proactive involvement by the courts in the compliance assessment process could compromise their neutrality and impartiality as adjudicators. According to this view, courts should adopt a more passive posture: accepting cases referred by the procuratorial authorities after compliance remediation has been completed and reviewed, and then conducting their own examination of the results. Alternatively, if the procuratorial authorities decline to initiate compliance assessment, enterprises may, with assistance from counsel, independently carry out compliance remediation, after which the courts could assess the process and outcomes and, where appropriate, impose more lenient criminal penalties.[22] In my view, whether courts should actively initiate compliance assessment or instead confine themselves to passively reviewing completed compliance efforts is a question best resolved by observing the practice of pilot reforms and undertaking a comprehensive evaluation. Nevertheless, two difficult issues warrant close attention when defining the courts' role in compliance reform. First, if courts restrict themselves to reviewing cases in which compliance remediation has already been completed and then grant leniency solely in sentencing, such leniency is likely to be confined to reduced penalties for individual responsible persons. Courts will seldom issue decisions that fully exempt enterprises from criminal liability on the basis of compliance, which severely limits the incentive for enterprises to undertake meaningful reforms. Second, for cases meeting the criteria for compliance assessment, courts could consider suspending or adjourning proceedings and recommending or consenting to the withdrawal of prosecution by the procuratorial authorities, thereby allowing them to carry out compliance assessment independently. If the enterprise successfully completes the compliance process, the procuratorial authorities could then issue a non-prosecution decision. While this approach may create powerful incentives for enterprises, it would also require significant reforms to the legal framework governing withdrawal of indictments.

Finally, at the stage of criminal penalty enforcement, although some local jurisdictions have begun experimenting with pilot programs to conduct compliance assessment during this phase, such practices are likely to generate even greater controversy. While certain scholars have proposed introducing mechanisms akin to "corporate probation" in China, this concept is unlikely to be

[21] Fenfei Li, "Three Models of Incorporating Corporate Compliance into Criminal Trials," *China Criminal Law Journal*, no. 4 (2023).

[22] Pengcheng Xie, "Scope of Cases for Application of Leniency Policy by Courts in Corporate Compliance," *Chinese Applied Jurisprudence*, no. 5 (2023).

realized in the short term. Within the existing enforcement framework, absent any substantial institutional reforms, the judicial administrative authorities may only initiate compliance assessment procedures in cases where probation has been granted to individual responsible persons. This approach may indeed produce some incentive effects for those individuals. However, for the enterprise itself, even where comprehensive compliance remediation has been successfully undertaken, it is improbable that any significant benefits or rewards will be conferred. Given the lack of meaningful incentives for enterprises, their willingness to actively engage in compliance remediation will inevitably be constrained.

11.4.2 Compliance in Cases Involving Natural Persons

Unlike the compliance assessment mechanisms in many Western jurisdictions, which are limited to corporate crime cases, China's procuratorial authorities have defined the scope of compliance assessment to encompass two categories of cases. First, unit crime cases, in which the company or enterprise itself is deemed the perpetrator of the offense. Second, cases involving natural persons, where actual controllers, senior managers, or key technical personnel of the company or enterprise commit offenses that are closely related to the enterprise's production and business activities. In the second category, even if the enterprise does not satisfy the criteria for unit crime, the procuratorial authorities may nevertheless initiate a compliance assessment procedure directed at the enterprise itself. Upon successful completion and acceptance of the compliance remediation, the outcome can serve as a basis for granting lenient criminal dispositions to the enterprise's senior management, controlling persons, or technical staff.

Why, then, do procuratorial authorities initiate a compliance assessment procedure for an enterprise even when the enterprise itself has not committed a crime? To date, scholars have primarily advanced two lines of reasoning. First, the argument of effectively protecting small and micro enterprises. According to this perspective, in China, most criminal conduct involving enterprises arises within small and micro businesses. These enterprises typically lack sound corporate governance structures, making it difficult to maintain a clear separation between the legal personality of the company and that of its senior management. A small number of actual controllers or executives often exercise de facto control over the enterprise's operations and fate. To protect such enterprises from collapse as a consequence of individual wrongdoing, procuratorial authorities have expanded the scope of compliance assessment beyond corporation crime cases to include cases in which the offenses are committed by corporate managers. Second, the argument of effectively preventing crime. Under this reasoning, the fact that senior managers engage in criminal conduct during business operations is attributable not only to their personal culpability or external inducements, but also to structural factors within the enterprise itself: deficiencies in governance arrangements, weaknesses in management systems, vulnerabilities in business processes, or even problematic aspects of the business model. To prevent the recurrence of similar offenses, procuratorial authorities, with the enterprise's consent, may initiate a compliance assessment procedure directed at enterprises that do not formally constitute unit crime.

Even so, this reform experiment—namely, initiating compliance assessment procedures in cases involving offenses committed by corporate management personnel—remains subject to considerable controversy, both in theory and in practice. Critics of this approach typically advance three principal objections. First, for enterprises that are not themselves suspected of criminal conduct, there is neither an imminent external pressure nor a compelling internal incentive to engage meaningfully in compliance assessment. Consequently, it is exceedingly difficult for such enterprises to implement compliance remediation measures capable of effectively preventing future offenses. Second, although this approach may retain some practical justification in the context of small and micro enterprises lacking modern corporate governance structures, it is far less persuasive when applied to large enterprises that have established such frameworks. In these companies, the legal personality of the enterprise is genuinely separate from that of its senior managers or controlling shareholders, and the company's operations are no longer substantially dependent on any single individual. Accordingly, pursuing compliance remediation primarily to shield entrepreneurs in these circumstances lacks broader normative legitimacy. Third, extending compliance assessment to non-offending enterprises has given rise to serious concerns about "using enterprise compliance as a vehicle to enable natural persons to evade criminal liability." The original purpose of the compliance assessment mechanism was to provide incentives for enterprises implicated in criminal conduct to adopt remedial measures that would prevent the recurrence of similar offenses. By contrast, broadening the scope to encompass enterprises that have not committed offenses reorients the mechanism's objective toward facilitating leniency or exoneration for individual managers, a shift that is manifestly at odds with the rationale underpinning the creation of compliance assessment.

In my view, given the existence of these controversies, it is necessary to impose clear and well-defined limitations on the practice of initiating compliance assessment procedures for enterprises that are not themselves implicated as criminal suspects. In principle, when addressing offenses committed by actual controllers, senior managers, or key technical personnel in the course of business operations, the initiation of compliance assessment procedures directed at the enterprise should be contingent upon satisfying three basic prerequisites. First, the offense was perpetrated by internal personnel in the name of the enterprise and for the enterprise's benefit, even though the Criminal Law does not classify such conduct as a unit crime. Second, the enterprise demonstrably suffers from clear and substantial deficiencies in its governance arrangements, management systems, business processes, or business model. Third, there is a causal relationship between those structural deficiencies and the criminal conduct committed by the individual.

11.4.3 Leniency for Responsible Individuals

In implementing the compliance-based non-prosecution system, China's procuratorial authorities have, upon determining that an enterprise has successfully completed compliance remediation, generally granted lenient treatment not only to the enterprise itself but also to the directly responsible individuals within it. Specifically, they may issue non-prosecution decisions regarding such individuals or submit recommendations to the court for the imposition of mitigated sentences. This approach contrasts with the prevailing philosophy in many Western jurisdictions, which typically emphasizes "forgiving the enterprise while punishing the responsible individuals." By comparison, China's procuratorial authorities have embraced a reform model characterized by "leniency toward both the enterprise and the individuals." As a result, in many criminal cases, effective compliance remediation has become the direct basis for affording lenient treatment to corporate managers and other responsible personnel.

This practice—using an enterprise's successful compliance remediation as the basis for granting leniency to responsible individuals—has generated significant controversy, giving rise to two opposing schools of thought: the opposing view and the supporting view. According to the opposing view, once an enterprise has admitted guilt, undertaken remedial measures, and established or improved its compliance management system, it acquires the capacity to prevent the recurrence of criminal conduct and fosters a culture of lawful and compliant business operations. This is regarded as the principal justification for permitting the enterprise itself to "exchange compliance for leniency."[23] However, critics question why compliance remediation at the enterprise level should entitle individuals who are criminal suspects to benefit from lenient treatment. What is the causal relationship between collective compliance measures and the exoneration or mitigation of liability for the individual offenders? In practice, if enterprise compliance is used as the basis for granting non-prosecution or lenient dispositions to natural persons, there is a substantial risk that procuratorial authorities may contravene the foundational principles of compliance reform by effectively conflating "enterprise compliance" with "entrepreneur compliance." This conflation could result in a scenario in which large numbers of corporate managers who would otherwise be subject to criminal liability exploit the enterprise's participation in compliance assessment to evade punishment, thereby undermining the legitimacy and normative integrity of criminal sanctions.[24]

However, proponents of this approach contend that granting lenient treatment to responsible individuals following the successful completion of compliance remediation is justified for several principal reasons. First, many of these

[23] Ruihua Chen, "Deferred Prosecution Agreement System from the Perspective of Corporate Compliance," *Comparative Law Research*, no. 1 (2020).

[24] Hong Li, "Corporate Compliance Non-Prosecution: Misunderstandings and Corrections," *China Legal Review*, no. 3 (2021).

individuals serve as the enterprise's legal representatives, actual controllers, or senior technical personnel. If they were convicted and sentenced, such outcomes could sever the enterprise's cash flow, disrupt production and operational continuity, and ultimately push the business into a catastrophic crisis—thereby defeating the underlying objective of preserving and rehabilitating the enterprise through compliance measures. Second, the successful implementation of compliance remediation not only contributes to preventing the enterprise itself from engaging in future criminal conduct but also has a deterrent effect on recidivism by the responsible individuals. From this perspective, if compliance can be shown to diminish the risk of recidivism among responsible individuals, granting lenient treatment to them emerges as a logical and well-founded conclusion.[25]

In my view, while the practice of granting lenient treatment to responsible individuals on the basis of enterprise compliance does have a practical foundation, it remains the subject of considerable theoretical and practical controversy. To address this issue and to break through the current impasse in institutional reform, I propose an approach that may be described as the compliance relevance theory. This theory underscores that leniency for individuals predicated on enterprise compliance must not be unconditional or automatic. Rather, it should be premised on the principle that responsible individuals have made a meaningful contribution to, and played an active role in, the enterprise's compliance remediation efforts.[26] For the successful completion of compliance remediation to serve as a direct basis for granting lenient treatment to responsible individuals, those individuals must have demonstrably contributed to the compliance process—either by actively participating in compliance remediation work and driving the establishment, implementation, and effective functioning of the enterprise's compliance management system; or facilitating the enterprise's admission of guilt and acceptance of punishment, the cessation of unlawful business operations, cooperation with criminal enforcement authorities, or the adoption of remedial measures to mitigate the social harm resulting from the offense.

11.4.4 Case Separation in Major Corporate Crimes

In the early stages of compliance reform, procuratorial authorities adopted a "dual non-prosecution" approach as a form of lenient treatment in cases where enterprises had successfully completed compliance remediation. Specifically, in minor corporation crime cases—where the anticipated sentence did not exceed three years of imprisonment—the authorities would issue non-prosecution decisions simultaneously for both the enterprise itself and the directly

[25] Pengcheng Xie, "The Intrinsic Logic of Prosecutorial Reform on Leniency for Corporate Compliance," *Democracy and Legal System Weekly*, no. 42 (2021).

[26] Ruihua Chen, *The Chinese Experience of Effective Corporate Compliance*, Beijing: Peking University Press, 2023, 189.

responsible individuals. This practice generally did not encounter substantial legal obstacles. However, as the scope of pilot reforms has gradually expanded, some large enterprises suspected of committing more serious offenses have increasingly come under scrutiny. Certain enterprises in this category are influential state-owned companies, and in some instances, the offenses in question constitute major corporation crimes carrying potential sentences exceeding three years of imprisonment. In such more serious cases, if procuratorial authorities persist in applying dual non-prosecution, they will inevitably face significantly greater legal controversy.[27]

On the one hand, under China's current corporation crime regime, once an enterprise is determined to have committed a criminal offense, the law mandates a "dual penalty system," whereby both the corporation itself and the responsible individuals must be subjected to sanctions. The criminal liability of the corporation and that of its responsible persons are legally inseparable. Accordingly, if the authorities exempt the enterprise from criminal liability but continue to prosecute its managers and other responsible personnel—or conversely—this approach of splitting cases lacks a clear basis in law and does not possess normative legitimacy. On the other hand, the principal policy rationale underpinning the procuratorial promotion of compliance-based non-prosecution reforms has been to protect not only enterprises suspected of criminal conduct but also the entrepreneurs whose decisions exert a decisive influence over the enterprise's viability. If the authorities were simply to "exonerate the enterprise" while simultaneously punishing the responsible individuals, this would contradict the original objectives of the reform and could result in catastrophic consequences for the enterprise if its legal representative or controlling shareholder were to be imprisoned. Furthermore, if case separation were to be adopted in practice, there is a substantial risk that enterprises suspected of committing serious crimes could be shielded from criminal liability merely by undertaking compliance remediation measures. Such an outcome would effectively condone serious corporate criminality and undermine the uniform application of criminal law.

In response to the theoretical objections and controversies outlined above, the case separation mechanism in major corporate crime cases can be defended from three perspectives.

First, case separation is premised on the conceptual distinction between corporate liability and individual liability. The liability borne by responsible individuals is essentially analogous to that in ordinary natural-person criminal cases, as they are personally accountable for their conduct. By contrast, the liability attributed to the enterprise primarily arises from failures in governance, deficiencies in internal management systems, and neglect of institutional

[27] For issues concerning the controversy arising from the procuratorial authorities applying "dual non-prosecution" to both the involved enterprises and responsible personnel, see Yuhua Li, "'Dual Non-Prosecution' in the Localization of Corporate Compliance," *Rule of Law and Social Development*, no. 1 (2022).

responsibilities. Because the factual and normative foundations of corporate liability and individual liability are substantively different, it is appropriate to separate the treatment of the enterprise and its managers.

Second, it is necessary to distinguish between compliance-based non-prosecution and discretionary non-prosecution. When the procuratorial authorities, following compliance assessment, decide not to prosecute an enterprise that has successfully completed compliance remediation, such a decision does not equate to ordinary discretionary non-prosecution, which is typically grounded in the minor nature of the offense. Rather, it constitutes a form of *conditional non-prosecution*. The decision to refrain from prosecution in these circumstances is informed by three important considerations: the collateral consequences of convicting the enterprise are disproportionately severe and may cause significant harm to stakeholders, local government interests, and national economic objectives; the enterprise has undertaken active and effective measures to remedy the harm caused by the offense, including admitting guilt, ceasing unlawful operations, and adopting remedial actions; the enterprise has successfully established a robust compliance program, thereby substantially reducing the risk of recidivism. Viewed in this light, applying a case separation mechanism to major corporate crime cases reflects the understanding that conditional non-prosecution of the enterprise is procedurally and substantively distinct from the prosecution of individual offenders.

Third, the case separation mechanism serves as an important safeguard for ensuring that corporate crime is effectively addressed. From the perspective of public interest, where the procuratorial authorities are compelled to prosecute responsible individuals, they should nevertheless, in the interest of protecting broader social and economic interests, afford the enterprise an opportunity to undertake systemic reforms aimed at addressing the underlying causes of criminal conduct. By doing so, the enterprise may secure exoneration, provided that it can demonstrate both the substantive restoration of the infringed legal interests and the effective measures taken to prevent future misconduct.

11.5 Conclusion

Compliance reform for enterprises involved in criminal cases, after nearly four years of exploration, has produced significant positive outcomes across political, social, and economic dimensions, thereby laying a solid practical foundation for its eventual incorporation into the Criminal Procedure Law. At present, scholars and practitioners have articulated several mature theoretical frameworks to substantiate the legitimacy of the compliance supervision and assessment system, including the Public Interest Theory, the Theory of Alternative Criminal Sanctions, the Legal Interest Restoration Theory, and the Theory of Effective Prevention of Corporate Crime. Taken together, these frameworks have provided a robust theoretical underpinning for the reform's continued development. In parallel, through the issuance of normative documents, the publication of guiding cases, and iterative experimentation, the procuratorial authorities have gradually established a series of groundbreaking institutional arrangements, such as the Third-Party Mechanism Committee system, the Third-Party Organization system, the Enterprise Compliance Supervision and Assessment system, the Effective Compliance Remediation Standards system, and the Lenient Treatment system for enterprises that have successfully completed compliance remediation. These institutional innovations warrant systematic consolidation, rigorous evaluation, and further refinement, so that they can ultimately be incorporated into the Criminal Procedure Law as integral components of China's evolving criminal justice framework.

Of course, as corporate compliance reform continues to deepen, scholars and practitioners have expressed divergent—even opposing—views regarding certain exploratory institutional designs. The most contested issues include full-process compliance assessment encompassing all stages of criminal procedure; the application of compliance assessment to cases not involving corporate crime; the use of compliance remediation as the basis for granting lenient treatment to responsible individuals; and the case separation mechanism in major corporate crime cases. On these questions, researchers frequently hold divergent positions, and debates are often sharp and polarized, making it difficult to reach a unified perspective. For these contentious arrangements, the legislature should adopt an approach of "seeking common ground while reserving differences," striving to build as much consensus as possible and, where necessary, setting aside unresolved controversies. In circumstances where consensus cannot realistically be achieved in the near term, or where certain institutional designs may produce unintended negative consequences in practice, it would be prudent for lawmakers to allow judicial authorities across different regions to continue experimenting with reform initiatives, deferring final resolution of these issues until conditions are more conducive to agreement and implementation.

CHAPTER 12

Compliance Incentives in International Financial Organizations

12.1 The World Bank's Sanctions System

In international economic law, certain international organizations frequently impose conditional economic sanctions on enterprises. In order to have such sanctions lifted, enterprises are generally required to establish effective compliance programs and to put in place managerial mechanisms aimed at preventing the recurrence of unlawful or irregular conduct. Accordingly, corporate compliance has become not only an essential basis for the removal of sanctions imposed by international organizations, but also an important incentive mechanism for enterprises themselves. This form of compliance may be referred to as "anti-sanctions compliance."

A paradigmatic example in this respect is provided by international financial institutions, with the World Bank being the most representative case. As an international financial organization, the World Bank is empowered to impose a variety of sanctions on enterprises that engage in misconduct during bidding or procurement processes. In 2006, the Bank issued its first *Sanctioning Guidelines* (WBG Sanctioning Guidelines). After several rounds of revision, the most recent version of the Guidelines was promulgated in 2024. Under these Guidelines, misconduct by enterprises or individuals is generally classified into five categories:

1. Corrupt practice. In general terms, a corrupt practice refers to *"the offering, giving, receiving, or soliciting, directly or indirectly, of anything of value for the purpose of improperly influencing the actions of another party."* In determining whether corrupt conduct has occurred, the World Bank applies the evidentiary standard of "more likely than not."
2. Fraudulent practice. A fraudulent practice is defined as *"any act or omission, including misrepresentation, that knowingly or recklessly misleads, or*

R. Chen, *An Introduction to Corporate Compliance*,
https://doi.org/10.1007/978-981-95-7257-1_12

attempts to mislead, a party in order to obtain a financial or other benefit, or to avoid an obligation."

3. Collusive practice. Also referred to as collusion, this denotes *"an arrangement between two or more parties designed to achieve an improper purpose, including the improper influencing of the actions of another party."*
4. Coercive practice. A coercive practice is defined as *"impairing or harming, or threatening to impair or harm, directly or indirectly, any party or the property of a party for the purpose of improperly influencing that party's actions."*
5. Obstructive practice. This category encompasses conduct such as *"deliberately destroying, falsifying, altering, or concealing evidence material to an investigation; making false statements to investigators with the intent to materially impede a World Bank investigation; threatening, harassing, or intimidating any party in order to prevent the disclosure of information relevant to an investigation or to obstruct the investigation; or otherwise acting to materially impede the Bank's contractual rights of audit or access to information."*

With respect to the aforementioned forms of misconduct, the sanctions imposed by the World Bank are characterized by both *cross-debarment* and *joint sanctions.* Cross-debarment signifies that the World Bank not only sanctions the enterprise directly responsible for the misconduct, but also extends the sanction to all other enterprises maintaining an "affiliated relationship" with the sanctioned entity. More concretely, the scope of sanctions encompasses all recipients of loan proceeds—not merely the borrower, but also all ultimate users of loan funds, including project contractors, suppliers, service providers, subcontractors, agents, and other related parties. Joint sanctions, by contrast, refer to the practice whereby the World Bank cooperates with other multilateral development banks (MDBs)—notably the Inter-American Development Bank, the European Bank for Reconstruction and Development, the Asian Development Bank, and the African Development Bank. Pursuant to this arrangement, if any one of these institutions imposes a debarment exceeding one year, the other participating institutions may automatically give effect to and impose the same sanction.

According to the 2024 revised version of the *World Bank Sanctioning Guidelines*, six types of sanctions may be imposed on non-compliant enterprises or individuals: (1) Letter of Reprimand; (2) Restitution; (3) Debarment for a Fixed Period; (4) Conditional Non-Debarment; (5) Debarment with Conditional Release; and (6) Indefinite Debarment.

Among these sanctions, Conditional Non-Debarment and Debarment with Conditional Release are the measures most frequently applied by the World Bank. To date, several dozen Chinese enterprises have been sanctioned by the World Bank, the majority of which are state-owned enterprises. Their misconduct has primarily involved fraudulent practices in the bidding and tendering process, with a smaller number of cases concerning corrupt practices. For

Chinese enterprises, the sanctions most commonly imposed have been Conditional Non-Debarment and Debarment with Conditional Release.[1]

So, what incentives can enterprises obtain by establishing integrity compliance programs in order to lift World Bank sanctions? First, during the sanctioning process, the World Bank may consider the establishment of a compliance program as a primary basis for mitigating sanctions. According to relevant World Bank rules, if sanctioned enterprises meet the following conditions, the World Bank may reduce the sanctions to varying degrees: (1) If the sanctioned entity played only a minor role in the misconduct, sanctions may be reduced by up to 25%; (2) If the sanctioned entity has undertaken voluntary remedial measures, such as promptly reporting the misconduct, disciplining responsible employees, establishing an effective compliance system, or providing restitution for economic losses, the World Bank may reduce sanctions by up to 50%, and in exceptional circumstances this percentage may be exceeded; (3) If the sanctioned entity has actively cooperated with the World Bank's investigation, such as by conducting an internal investigation and sharing the results with the Integrity Vice Presidency (INT), admitting misconduct at an early stage, accepting sanctions, or voluntarily refraining from bidding on World Bank projects during the investigation, the World Bank may reduce sanctions by up to 33%, and in exceptional circumstances this percentage may also be exceeded.

Second, in cases where the World Bank imposes Debarment with Conditional Release or Conditional Non-Debarment, enterprises subject to sanctions are required to enter into a settlement agreement with the World Bank, under which they must implement a comprehensive integrity compliance program before they may have the sanctions lifted and regain eligibility for World Bank financing or bidding. In 2010, the World Bank appointed an Integrity Compliance Officer (ICO), responsible not only for supervising the progress of sanctioned enterprises in establishing or improving their compliance programs, but also for reviewing whether the compliance and other conditions imposed by the Sanctions Board or the Evaluation and Suspension Officers have been fulfilled. In 2017, Hunan Construction Engineering Group of China was released from several years of sanction by the World Bank after successfully implementing its integrity compliance program.[2]

12.2 The Sanctioning Procedure

In order to safeguard the integrity of its projects, the World Bank has established three specialized bodies responsible for addressing misconduct: (1) the Integrity Vice Presidency (INT), which includes the Integrity Compliance

[1] Zhen Liu and Xianfeng Zhou, "Fourteen Years of Refinement: A Brief Analysis of the Significant Impact of the Major Revision of the World Bank Sanctions Guidelines," *Junhe Law Review* (WeChat official account), December 13, 2024.

[2] Ruihua Chen, "The Compliance System of Hunan Construction Group," *China Lawyer*, no. 11 (2019).

Office (ICO); (2) the Office of Suspension and Debarment (SDO); and (3) the World Bank Sanctions Board and its Secretariat.

When the World Bank receives a report of alleged misconduct, the matter generally proceeds through three stages of review. First, the investigative phase is conducted by INT, which seeks to determine whether there is credible evidence supporting the allegations. Second, the decision-making phase follows, during which either an SDO officer or the Sanctions Board adjudicates whether the evidence is sufficient to establish misconduct and, if so, determines the appropriate sanctioning measure. Third, the ICO engages with the sanctioned enterprise or individual to assess whether the conditions for release from sanctions have been fulfilled.[3]

Once INT completes its administrative investigation and concludes that the evidence establishes misconduct on a more-likely-than-not basis, it prepares a Final Investigation Report. On this basis, INT drafts two subsequent documents: a Referral Report, submitted to relevant national authorities, and a Redacted Report, submitted to the World Bank's Executive Directors. Following completion of the investigation, INT may submit a Statement of Accusations and Evidence (SAE) to the SDO, thereby initiating the first level of review, or it may negotiate a settlement agreement with the respondent. In practice, many enterprises or individuals under investigation prefer to pursue settlement discussions with INT as a means of mitigating sanctions or reducing their practical impact.

The World Bank has established a two-tier administrative sanctioning system, which operates primarily during the second stage of the sanctioning procedure described above. Upon receiving INT's investigative report, the Office of Suspension and Debarment (SDO) conducts the first-tier administrative review to determine whether the evidence submitted by INT is sufficient to initiate sanctioning proceedings. The SDO officer examines whether the alleged misconduct occurred, determines the appropriate sanction, issues a *Notice of Sanctions Proceedings* to the respondent, imposes a temporary suspension of the respondent's eligibility for World Bank-financed contracts, reviews the respondent's written explanations, and evaluates any proposed settlement agreement to ensure that it was entered into voluntarily and that its terms do not manifestly conflict with the *World Bank Sanctioning Guidelines.* Once the SDO officer concludes that there is sufficient evidence to establish the misconduct, the sanctioning process may be formally initiated and appropriate sanctions imposed. At that point, the respondent is suspended from eligibility for World Bank-financed contracts. The respondent, however, retains the right to appeal to the Sanctions Board, which is responsible for the second-tier administrative review. If no appeal is filed, the SDO's decision takes immediate effect.

[3] "Research Series on Multilateral Development Bank Sanctions Compliance (I): Overview of the World Bank Group Sanctions System," *Panda Legal* (WeChat official account), November 18, 2024.

Upon receiving an appeal, the Sanctions Board conducts the second-tier review. This body is composed of seven external jurists, with the Chair and other members appointed by the President of the World Bank. Functioning as an independent administrative tribunal, the Sanctions Board issues final decisions in sanction cases arising from projects financed or guaranteed by any member institution of the World Bank Group. It is empowered to conduct a comprehensive, fair, and independent review of each contested case, unconstrained by the determinations made at the first-tier review by the SDO officer. The Board may request additional submissions, hold hearings, and render determinations not only on sanctions but also on related evidentiary and procedural issues. Once the Board determines that it is *more likely than not* that the respondent engaged in sanctionable conduct, it may issue a final decision upholding the sanction. Conversely, if it finds insufficient evidence, or deems the SDO's sanction inappropriate, the Board may issue a decision departing from that of the SDO.

After a sanction decision rendered by the Office of Suspension and Debarment (SDO) has taken effect, or following a final ruling by the Sanctions Board, the Integrity Compliance Office (ICO)—an office operating under the World Bank's Integrity Vice Presidency (INT)—becomes involved in the subsequent stage of the sanctioning process. The ICO is primarily responsible for monitoring the compliance status of sanctioned firms and overseeing the adherence of sanctioned individuals to prescribed codes of conduct.

Given that the vast majority of sanctions imposed by the World Bank take the form of Debarment with Conditional Release or Conditional Non-Debarment, the central task of the ICO, once a sanction decision has entered into effect, is to evaluate whether the compliance conditions attached to the sanction have been satisfied. Where enterprises are found to have met the compliance requirements specified in the sanction decision, and where individuals have demonstrated conformity with the applicable codes of conduct, the ICO issues a *release notice*, thereby restoring their eligibility to participate in World Bank–financed projects.

12.3 The Dual Incentive Function of Integrity Compliance Programs

According to the World Bank Sanctioning Guidelines and the *Integrity Compliance Guidelines*, the establishment of an integrity compliance management system by enterprises that have engaged in misconduct functions both as an important condition for the application of more lenient sanctions and as the principal basis for the removal of sanctions. Accordingly, when enterprises involved in violations establish or implement integrity compliance programs, such programs may operate as compliance incentives in two respects. First, prior to the occurrence of violations, if the enterprise has already established or implemented an integrity compliance program, the World Bank may take this into account as a mitigating factor when determining the applicable sanction. Second, following the occurrence of violations, if the enterprise voluntarily undertakes compliance remediation, or establishes and implements an integrity compliance program under the supervision of the World Bank, such measures may serve as the primary basis for lifting sanctions.

12.3.1 Compliance as a Condition for Sanctions

Since the World Bank Sanctioning Guidelines were first issued in 2016, the Bank has consistently regarded the existence or implementation of an integrity compliance program as a major factor in determining sanctions for noncompliant enterprises. In principle, where enterprises have established or implemented compliance management systems, the World Bank may adopt relatively lenient sanctioning measures or treat such compliance efforts as a primary basis for mitigating penalties imposed on the enterprise. Following the 2024 revision of the Sanctioning Guidelines, this provision—recognizing integrity compliance as a condition for the application of specific sanctions—has been significantly reinforced.

In the 2024 revision of the *World Bank Sanctioning Guidelines*, the conditions for applying the sanction of fixed-term debarment were explicitly clarified for the first time. The fact that a sanctioned enterprise has already established and implemented an integrity compliance program is now regarded as an important consideration in determining whether this sanction should be imposed. In the past, the World Bank most frequently applied debarment with conditional release to noncompliant enterprises. Only where grounds for mitigation existed would the Bank consider lighter sanctions such as fixed-term debarment, conditional non-debarment, or a letter of reprimand. For sanctioned enterprises, fixed-term debarment entails disqualification from participation in World Bank–financed projects for a specified period of time, but generally without any obligation to undertake actions to satisfy release conditions during that period. To activate this sanction, the revised Guidelines for the first time enumerated key factors to be considered, including: (1) whether the respondent has established and is actively implementing an integrity compliance management system; (2) whether the misconduct is attributable solely to an isolated and incidental act of an employee who is no longer employed by the respondent; and (3) whether the proposed sanction period is so short as to make it impracticable for the respondent to satisfy release conditions within the prescribed timeframe.[4]

The 2024 revision of the Sanctioning Guidelines also clarified the conditions for the application of a letter of reprimand, expressly incorporating the implementation of an integrity compliance program as a factor for

[4] Zhen Liu and Xianfeng Zhou, "Fourteen Years of Refinement: A Brief Analysis of the Significant Impact of the Major Revision of the World Bank Sanctions Guidelines," *Junhe Law Review* (WeChat official account), December 13, 2024.

consideration. In general, a letter of reprimand constitutes the least severe sanction: the sanctioned enterprise is neither disqualified from World Bank–financed projects nor required to meet specific release conditions. Its principal consequence lies in the fact that, in the event of a subsequent violation, the World Bank may take the prior reprimand into account when determining whether to impose a more severe sanction. According to the revised Guidelines, in issuing a letter of reprimand the Bank must consider the following factors: (1) whether the actor was a lower-level employee who played only a minor role in the misconduct; (2) whether the actor was a supervisor who neither participated in nor conspired in the misconduct but permitted it to occur through negligent oversight; and (3) whether the actor was a controlling shareholder who failed to exercise oversight over the direct perpetrator of the misconduct.

The 2024 revision of the Sanctioning Guidelines also introduced, for the first time, the concept of composite sanctions. This allows the World Bank, in cases of certain types of misconduct, to impose two or more sanctioning measures simultaneously, or to convert one sanction into another that is either lighter or more severe. For example, depending on the circumstances of the misconduct, the Bank may impose restitution in combination with another sanctioning measure. Likewise, a sanctioned enterprise may be subject to fixed-term debarment while simultaneously being placed under conditional non-debarment for a specified period. Furthermore, the Bank may decide to apply conversion sanctions: if the sanctioned enterprise fails to satisfy the compliance requirements for release within the prescribed period, a sanction of conditional non-debarment may automatically be converted into debarment with conditional release. This mechanism is intended to underscore both the significance and the urgency of completing effective compliance remediation.

In addition, the 2024 revision of the Guidelines introduced a number of new aggravating and mitigating factors, including: whether the sanctioned party complied with confidentiality obligations; whether public officials were involved in the misconduct; the extent of harm caused by the misconduct; whether false statements were made, perjury committed, or witnesses threatened; whether the party was subject to improper external pressure; and whether the misconduct occurred a significant time ago. Particularly noteworthy is that the Guidelines explicitly designate the effectiveness of the sanctioned party's internal investigation and its cooperation with the World Bank's investigation as primary factors in determining the sanction to be imposed. This effectively strengthens the role of autonomous compliance remediation in the Bank's sanctioning decisions. In practice, both sanctioned enterprises and individuals may obtain a reduction in sanctions if they submit an effective internal investigation report. The effectiveness of such reports is evaluated by the World Bank from three perspectives: (1) the sufficiency of the internal investigation; (2) the truthfulness, completeness, and credibility of the information disclosed to the Integrity Vice Presidency (INT); and (3) any restrictions on the use of such information. At the same time, where the sanctioned enterprise or individual demonstrates cooperation with the investigation—such as by conducting an internal investigation, admitting misconduct, or adopting self-restrictive measures—the World Bank may reduce the penalty, with the extent of mitigation reaching up to 50%.

12.3.2 Compliance as a Condition for Lifting Sanctions

From the perspective of most sanctioning decisions issued by the World Bank, since such decisions typically establish additional conditions for the lifting of sanctions, sanctioned enterprises are generally required—under the supervision of the World Bank—to establish or implement an Integrity Compliance Program (ICP). The Integrity Compliance Office (ICO) first undertakes an assessment of the sanctioned enterprise, examining its size, governance structure, operational model, geographical scope of business, industry sector, risk profile, and existing compliance management systems. The ICO then appoints independent integrity compliance monitors or compliance advisors to oversee the sanctioned enterprise, generally for a monitoring period not exceeding three years. During this period, the monitors conduct periodic assessments of the enterprise's compliance management processes and outcomes, while providing corresponding recommendations for improvement. At the conclusion of the monitoring period, the ICO conducts a final evaluation to determine whether the enterprise's compliance management has achieved the intended objectives. The primary factors considered include: whether compliance measures are tailored to the enterprise's risk profile; whether the control measures conform to the principles established in the World Bank *Integrity Compliance Guidelines*; and whether such measures have been effectively implemented. If, following this evaluation, the enterprise is deemed to have implemented effective compliance management and satisfied the release conditions specified in the sanctioning decision, the World Bank may issue a Notice of Release, thereby lifting the sanction.

The 2024 revision of the Sanctioning Guidelines also, for the first time, established explicit conditions for the lifting of sanctions imposed on natural persons. Prior to this revision, the Guidelines enumerated only the general conditions applicable to enterprises—such as implementing or enhancing compliance management measures and undertaking remedial steps in response to misconduct—without specifying how natural persons could obtain release. The revised Guidelines now stipulate that natural persons may achieve release by participating in and completing designated integrity compliance training programs. In this way, the Guidelines expressly require sanctioned individuals to take part in their enterprise's compliance programs, thereby encouraging them to play an active role in the implementation of corporate compliance management.

12.4 The World Bank's Integrity Compliance Program

The *World Bank Group Integrity Compliance Guidelines* (hereinafter *Integrity Compliance Guidelines*) constitute the operative compliance standards issued by the World Bank. Only when a sanctioned enterprise establishes or enhances its compliance system in accordance with the requirements of these Guidelines can it obtain the opportunity for release from sanctions. To date, dozens of Chinese enterprises have been sanctioned by the World Bank, the majority of which are state-owned enterprises penalized primarily for engaging in fraudulent practices. For instance, the Hunan Construction Engineering Group was sanctioned with Debarment with Conditional Release for misrepresenting its past performance in a World Bank–financed bidding project. During a three-year probationary period, the company, under the World Bank's guidance and supervision, restructured its corporate compliance system in line with the *Integrity Compliance Guidelines.* Having satisfied the Bank's compliance management requirements, the company was eventually removed from the "sanctioned entities list" in 2017.[5]

What, then, are the principal components of the World Bank's *Integrity Compliance Guidelines*? Broadly speaking, the Guidelines set forth ten fundamental requirements. Among them, "Prohibition of Misconduct" constitutes the overarching principle of corporate compliance; "Responsibility" concerns the organizational structure of compliance; "Internal Policies" and "Internal Controls" form part of the entity's compliance policies; while the remaining requirements delineate the procedural dimensions of compliance. Specifically, "Program Initiation, Risk Assessment, and Review," "Policies on Business Partners," and "Training and Communication" establish mechanisms for the prevention of compliance risks; the "Reporting Mechanism" creates a system for identifying and monitoring risks; while the "Incentive Mechanism" and "Remedial Measures for Misconduct" constitute responsive mechanisms for addressing violations.

To satisfy the World Bank's compliance requirements, sanctioned enterprises must formulate a Code of Business Conduct or an equivalent document explicitly prohibiting misconduct such as fraud, corruption, collusion, and coercion. This requirement represents the general principle of corporate compliance.

To build a genuinely effective compliance program, enterprises must foster and sustain a compliance culture rooted in trust—cultivating an environment that encourages integrity while imposing stringent consequences for misconduct. To this end, corporate executives and boards of directors should fully promote the implementation of the compliance program; employees at all levels must treat adherence to the program as a binding obligation; and senior compliance officers charged with supervising program implementation must be

[5] Ruihua Chen, "The Compliance System of Hunan Construction Group," *China Lawyer*, no. 11 (2019).

vested with full autonomy, adequate resources, and effective enforcement authority.

To establish an effective compliance program, a company must formulate a Code of Business Conduct from two dimensions. First, through the adoption of internal policies, the company should articulate values, policies, and procedures designed to prevent, detect, investigate, and remedy misconduct. The enterprise should conduct due diligence on employees vested with decision-making authority or capable of influencing operational outcomes, in order to determine whether they have engaged in improper conduct. Employment contracts or other agreements with former government officials or related entities or individuals should be restricted. The company should establish controls and procedures regarding gifts, hospitality, entertainment, travel, and other expenditures; make political contributions strictly in accordance with the law and ensure disclosure; adopt measures to prevent charitable donations from being used as a cover for misconduct and require disclosure; prohibit facilitation payments of any kind; maintain comprehensive documentation of all aspects of the compliance program; and adopt appropriate measures to detect and prevent corruption, fraud, collusion, and coercion.

Second, the enterprise should establish specialized internal control mechanisms governing its financial systems, contractual obligations, and decision-making processes. This entails three principal components: (1) implementing checks and balances within the financial and organizational structure to regulate corporate finance, accounting, recordkeeping, and other business activities, thereby ensuring that accounting and recordkeeping systems are subject to periodic review through both internal and external independent audits; (2) incorporating into employment contracts and partnership agreements explicit contractual obligations concerning misconduct, together with remedial or punitive measures; and (3) designing decision-making procedures to ensure that both the process and the decision-makers reflect proportionality to the significance of the obligations involved and to the risks associated with potential misconduct.

An effective compliance program must also provide timely and effective prevention and monitoring of compliance risks, while ensuring the adoption of appropriate response mechanisms once violations occur. These matters pertain to the procedural implementation of compliance. In this respect, the World Bank's *Integrity Compliance Guidelines* establish corresponding requirements to guide enterprises in the design and operation of their compliance systems.

To effectively prevent potential compliance risks, enterprises should establish targeted policies and procedures in areas such as risk assessment, business partner policies, and training and communication. To develop an effective compliance risk prevention system, companies need to conduct a comprehensive risk assessment of potential misconduct—such as fraud and corruption—that may arise in the course of their business operations, taking into full account factors such as enterprise size, business sector, geographical location, and other relevant circumstances. Risk assessments should be subject to periodic review and updating in light of changing circumstances, and adjustments or modifications to the compliance program should be made where necessary.

With respect to business partners, enterprises should encourage them to make reciprocal commitments to prevent, detect, investigate, and remedy misconduct. Business partners primarily include agents, advisors, consultants, representatives, distributors, contractors, subcontractors, suppliers, joint venture partners, and other third parties. Enterprises should conduct risk-based due diligence on their partners to avoid associations with third parties engaged in misconduct; inform partners of the compliance program and monitor their adherence to it; require partners to make reciprocal commitments to compliance and encourage them to establish Effective Compliance Programs; maintain comprehensive records of relationships with business partners; ensure that all payments to partners constitute legitimate and lawful remuneration; and supervise the performance of all contracts with business partners.

Training and communication are also integral components of the compliance risk prevention system. Enterprises should adopt practical and reasonable measures to publicize the compliance program on a regular basis, provide effective training to employees at all levels as well as to business partners, and maintain training records. Senior management should also report on the compliance program in the company's annual report, or otherwise publicly disclose and promote the content of the compliance program.

To effectively identify and monitor potential compliance risks, enterprises should establish a robust reporting system. This system should include four basic procedures:First, all employees must have a duty to report issues related to the compliance program.Second, effective measures should be adopted to provide management, employees, and business partners with guidance and advice on compliance with the program.Third, enterprises should establish whistleblowing mechanisms and reporting hotlines, offering secure communication channels and protective measures for employees who, despite instructions or pressure, refuse to violate the compliance program, as well as for individuals willing to report internal misconduct.Fourth, employees with decision-making authority or the ability to influence business outcomes should be required to submit periodic written statements confirming that they understand the code of conduct, strictly comply with the compliance program, and have reported to the internal compliance department any misconduct by other employees or business partners.

When misconduct occurs, enterprises should adopt compliance responses in two respects. First, timely reward and sanction measures should be implemented. To encourage and support compliance with the program across all levels of the organization, enterprises should adopt positive incentive mechanisms to promote the effective implementation of the compliance program. At the same time, appropriate disciplinary measures should be imposed on individuals involved in misconduct—including senior management and board members—and, where necessary, such measures may extend to termination of employment contracts. Second, enterprises should implement procedures to conduct internal investigations into detected misconduct. Once misconduct is confirmed, the enterprise should, through reasonable measures, take appropriate corrective steps to prevent the recurrence of similar or more serious violations.

12.5 The Hunan Construction Engineering Case: A Model for Compliance Remediation

Hunan Construction Engineering Group Co., Ltd. is a large state-owned enterprise ranked among China's top 500 companies. The company once participated in a World Bank–financed road renovation project and submitted a full set of documents intended to demonstrate its construction experience and competitive capacity. Upon review, however, the World Bank's Integrity Vice Presidency (INT) determined that the business experience documents submitted during the bidding process were not authentic, thereby constituting fraudulent conduct as defined under the *Integrity Compliance Guidelines*. Hunan Construction acknowledged this violation and cooperated with the World Bank's investigation. In October 2013, the World Bank imposed a two-year sanction of debarment with conditional release on the company. Under this sanction decision, Hunan Construction Engineering Group (including its affiliated entities) was prohibited, for a period of two years, from participating in World Bank–financed projects or benefiting from World Bank loans. After the expiration of the two-year term, the company could apply for reinstatement provided that it satisfied two conditions: (1) it had taken appropriate remedial measures with respect to the sanctioned misconduct; and (2) it had established and implemented an effective integrity compliance program consistent with the requirements of the World Bank.

The sanction imposed by the World Bank resulted in both financing difficulties and significant reputational damage for Hunan Construction Engineering Group. In order to restore its reputation, avoid further losses, and secure release from the sanction, the company, under the World Bank's supervision and guidance, undertook the establishment of an effective compliance program. On June 29, 2017, the World Bank formally recognized the company's efforts in implementing its integrity compliance system and issued a Notice of Release, thereby lifting the sanction. This marked the official termination of the World Bank's sanction against Hunan Construction Engineering Group.

So, what kind of integrity compliance system did Hunan Construction Engineering Group establish over the course of three years to gain the World Bank's recognition? We may first examine the company's principal practices in building its compliance system and then analyze the basic components of its integrity compliance framework.

First, promulgating compliance policies and procedures.

Following the World Bank's recommendations and in line with the standards set forth in the World Bank *Integrity Compliance Guidelines*, Hunan

Construction Engineering Group formulated and implemented its Integrity Compliance Policies and Procedures, which became the foundational norms for the company's compliance system. At the same time, the Group issued supplementary Integrity Compliance Management Measures, which established a comprehensive compliance framework covering top-level institutional design, organizational structure, staffing, and work procedures.

Second, establishing a compliance organizational system.

The Group created an Integrity Compliance Committee directly under the authority of the Board of Directors, chaired by the Secretary of the Discipline Inspection Commission, with the Group's senior management serving as members. A Chief Compliance Officer was appointed, concurrently held by the Group's General Counsel. In parallel, the Group established a dedicated compliance department by incorporating compliance functions into the existing Legal Affairs Department, renaming it the Legal and compliance department. Within this department, a Compliance Division was created, tasked with establishing and implementing the Group's integrity compliance system, staffed by several compliance officers. Moreover, all subsidiaries' legal departments were uniformly renamed Legal and compliance departments, expanding their functions to include integrity compliance management, each with its own compliance officers.

Third, organizing compliance training. All employees were required to read aloud and adhere to a Compliance Declaration, participate in annual compliance training, and sign a Compliance Certificate.

Fourth, strengthening compliance management of business partners. Before entering into cooperation with business partners (third parties), the Group required them—after undergoing compliance due diligence—to sign an Anti-Bribery Statement, a Warranty and Undertaking, and a Compliance Certificate, thereby committing themselves to observe the Group's Integrity Compliance Policies and Procedures as well as relevant anti-bribery laws throughout the contract period.

Fifth, conducting compliance risk assessments. The Group's Compliance Committee regularly carried out compliance risk assessments, classifying each department, branch, and subsidiary into high, medium, or low risk levels.

Sixth, organizing compliance audits. The Group's Audit Department conducted annual compliance audits on adherence to anti-bribery and anti-fraud laws and on the implementation of the Integrity Compliance Policies and Procedures, with particular attention devoted to high-risk departments, branches, and subsidiaries.

Seventh, establishing a whistleblowing system. The Group and its subsidiaries set up consultation and reporting hotlines to encourage employees and third parties to report acts of fraud, bribery, corruption, collusion, coercion, or any other conduct inconsistent with compliance policies.

Eighth, fully cooperating with the World Bank's compliance review and ongoing supervision. Under the World Bank's compliance requirements, sanctioned companies are obligated to submit periodic compliance progress reports and to undergo integrity compliance inspections by the World Bank's Chief Compliance Officer and Strategic Committee advisors. The World Bank also appointed an independent compliance monitor to oversee and review the company's compliance-building progress. In implementing its compliance system, Hunan Construction not only submitted regular compliance progress reports but also hosted multiple on-site inspections by the chief compliance officer and independent compliance monitor, accepting their recommendations and requirements for improvement. The Group underwent several on-site reviews by the World Bank's compliance department, carried out rectifications as required, and complied with the oversight and guidance of the independent compliance monitor. Ultimately, the World Bank approved the company's compliance system.

As a state-owned enterprise, Hunan Construction Engineering Group overcame significant resistance and difficulties and, with the support of top management, established a comprehensive set of integrity compliance policies and procedures modeled on the World Bank Integrity *Compliance Guidelines.* Broadly speaking, this compliance framework consists of 13 components: (1) Prohibited conduct; (2) Due diligence on business partners; (3) Anti-bribery and anti-fraud prevention in business activities; (4) Post-contractual supervision; (5) Special expenditures; (6) Personnel; (7) Accurate recordkeeping; (8) Compliance committee and chief compliance officer; (9) Evaluation and audit; (10) Training; (11) Compliance certificates; (12) Communication and reporting; (13) Rewards and sanctions. Among these, the first seven constitute compliance policies specifically designed to prevent corruption and fraud, while the latter six provide the organizational framework and procedural mechanisms necessary for implementing those policies.

To ensure consistency with the World Bank's compliance guidelines, Hunan Construction Engineering Group's compliance policies provide precise definitions of terms such as "kickbacks, bribery and remuneration," "fraud, collusion and coercion," and "payments involving government officials," thereby drawing clear distinctions between lawful and unlawful conduct. With respect to potential misconduct by business partners, the policies establish general requirements and procedures for due diligence, while also specifying exemptions from due diligence obligations. In order to effectively prevent bribery and fraud in business activities, the policies set out detailed compliance requirements concerning conflict of interest, contract execution, contract review, bidding and tendering, submission of documents, retention of external legal counsel, and contract archiving. With regard to post-contractual supervision, the policies prescribe specific measures, including timely notification, re-certification of business partners, payment review, result handling, and archiving. Furthermore, the policies establish specific behavioral standards for special expenditures, including gifts, hospitality, travel expenses, donations and sponsorships, and facilitation payments. They also set forth targeted rules for personnel selection, accurate bookkeeping, and the systematic maintenance of compliance archives.

In terms of compliance organization and compliance implementation procedures, Hunan Construction Engineering Group's Integrity Compliance Policies and Procedures established a compliance organizational framework consisting of the Integrity Compliance Committee, the Chief Compliance Officer, the Group's Legal and Compliance Department, and the Legal and Compliance Departments of its subsidiaries. It further specified the responsibilities of the Group's Integrity Compliance Committee, the Chief Compliance Officer, and the compliance officers of its subsidiaries, while also instituting a joint meeting mechanism for compliance work and a system of compliance review. With respect to implementation procedures, the document established an evaluation and audit system requiring periodic assessments of compliance risks, enhanced compliance audits, timely revisions of compliance policies, and the preparation of annual reports on compliance risks and compliance audit activities. To encourage employees and third parties to report misconduct, the document further provided procedures on open communication, compliance consultation, reporting and whistleblowing hotlines, handling of reports, and the protection of whistleblowers. In addition, it created a reward mechanism for employees and third parties who help uncover misconduct, as well as a disciplinary mechanism for employees who bear responsibility for violations of laws and regulations.

Chinese enterprises, in the course of overseas investment, mergers and acquisitions, listings, and participation in public bidding, are facing increasing compliance risks. These risks differ substantially from traditional operational and financial risks, and are also distinct from the general notion of "legal risk." Rather, they refer to the possibility of regulatory penalties and criminal sanctions resulting from violations, and the consequent economic, reputational, qualification-related, and opportunity costs. For Chinese enterprises, compliance risks may arise not only from potential investigations and penalties by foreign regulators in fields such as anti-bribery, anti-money laundering, export control, personal data protection, and anti-unfair competition, or from investigations by foreign criminal enforcement authorities, but also from sanctions imposed by international organizations such as the World Bank. In responding to such regulatory investigations, penalties, and sanctions, the establishment and implementation of an effective compliance program is often an indispensable avenue for reaching settlements with regulators, persuading international organizations to lift sanctions, and securing other forms of leniency. Hunan Construction Engineering Group's experience of undergoing World Bank compliance inspections and ultimately obtaining the lifting of sanctions illustrates the efforts of a large Chinese state-owned enterprise to establish a compliance system aligned with international standards. It constitutes a successful attempt to persuade an international organization to terminate sanctions. Its experiences and lessons merit close attention for Chinese enterprises, including state-owned enterprises.

Appendix: Typical Corporate Compliance Cases

ZTE Corporation's Targeted Compliance Program

ZTE Corporation regards integrity and adherence to ethical standards as the cornerstone of its global business operations. The company's *Code of Business Conduct* articulates the fundamental principles of integrity and ethical behavior, mandating that the company, its employees, customers, business partners, and investors comply with all applicable laws and regulations. It further establishes the obligation of every employee to "conduct business on behalf of the company in an ethical manner." In accordance with the *Code of Business Conduct*, ZTE is dedicated to developing an efficient and well-structured compliance system. By embedding compliance mechanisms throughout all business processes, the company aims to achieve an organic integration between compliance and business operations. This integration enables ZTE to establish a best-in-class compliance management framework within the industry and to transform compliance into a distinctive source of competitive advantage.

ZTE Corporation has established a Compliance Management Committee (CMC), which operates under the direct leadership of the President. The CMC oversees a coordinated structure comprising business units, specialized compliance departments, and the Compliance Audit Department, collectively forming a three-lines-of-defense framework for compliance risk management. The specialized compliance departments consist of four distinct units: the Export Control Compliance Department, the Anti-Commercial Bribery Compliance Department, the Data Protection Compliance Department, and the Compliance Organization Management Department. These units are primarily responsible for managing compliance in their respective specialized areas, including export controls, anti-bribery measures, and data protection. In organizational terms, ZTE has implemented a "penetrative compliance management system" under the guidance of the CMC. Within this system, each specialized compliance

R. Chen, *An Introduction to Corporate Compliance*,
https://doi.org/10.1007/978-981-95-7257-1

department establishes a Center of Excellence (COE) staffed with legal and regulatory experts and forms dedicated teams to address key risk domains. Dedicated compliance teams are also deployed within each Business Unit (BU), serving as a bridge between the COEs and operational units. Furthermore, Points of Contact (POCs) are appointed within each business unit to facilitate subsidiary-level penetrative compliance management, ensuring that compliance policies are effectively communicated and operationalized at the front lines of business activities.

Following its substitute settlement agreement with the U.S. Bureau of Industry and Security (BIS) in 2018, ZTE Corporation undertook a series of systematic efforts to reconstruct its compliance framework and restore institutional integrity. First, regarding compliance culture, the chairman and president of ZTE issued company-wide statements reaffirming the organization's commitment to compliance and ethical business conduct. Senior executives, designated as the primary compliance officers within their respective domains, signed letters of compliance responsibility to formalize their personal accountability and demonstrate the company's determination to institutionalize compliance governance. In addition, ZTE has continuously promoted compliance awareness through comprehensive training programs, encouraged internal reporting and supervision mechanisms, and fostered a culture of integrity characterized by both internal vigilance and external cooperation. Second, in relation to compliance resources, the company significantly increased its investment in compliance management, strengthened support for the internal compliance and inspection teams, and expanded collaboration with external law firms and consulting organizations. Moreover, ZTE enhanced its IT-based compliance infrastructure by optimizing key systems such as the Global Trade System (GTS), Business Partner Scanning System (BPS), and Legal and Compliance Management System (LCM). These developments have bolstered risk assessment mechanisms and advanced the company's overall compliance governance capacity. Third, with respect to institutional and procedural design, ZTE reinforced the authority and coordination functions of its Compliance Management Committee, which now oversees the formulation of compliance policies, deliberation of compliance matters, and final decision-making on critical issues. The company has embedded compliance checkpoints throughout specific business processes and integrated them into its IT systems to ensure real-time monitoring and automated verification, thereby reducing reliance on manual inspection. Finally, in terms of professional capacity building, ZTE has collaborated with leading law firms and accounting firms to jointly address complex compliance-related issues, thereby enhancing the company's professional competence and ensuring the sustainable operation of its compliance governance system.

ZTE Corporation has developed a comprehensive and industry-leading export control compliance framework. The company has established a dedicated Export Control Compliance Department composed of a Chief Export Compliance Officer, several Regional Directors of Export

Compliance—located respectively in China, Europe, the Americas, and the Middle East—and additional directors, managers, supervisors, and supporting personnel based in China and other jurisdictions. ZTE has issued and regularly updated its *Export Compliance Policy* and *Export Compliance Manual*, both of which are applicable to the corporate headquarters and all subsidiaries worldwide. To ensure full compliance throughout its supply chain and distribution network, ZTE and its subsidiaries have also published the Export Control Classification Numbers (ECCNs) applicable to ZTE products subject to U.S. export control regulations. Moreover, ZTE and its affiliates have implemented comprehensive compliance training programs covering all employees. These include company-wide awareness sessions on export compliance as well as specialized training tailored to the responsibilities of specific functional departments. The company has also maintained close and proactive cooperation with the Special Compliance Coordinator (SCC) and compliance monitors appointed by the U.S. government.

ZTE Corporation's export control compliance program was established pursuant to the "substitute settlement agreement" reached with the U.S. Department of Commerce. Under this agreement, the U.S. government assigned a Special Compliance Coordinator (SCC) and compliance monitors to oversee the reconstruction and operation of ZTE's export compliance program over a ten-year period. The export control compliance program has since become the central pillar of ZTE's overall compliance management system. According to the official announcement of the U.S. Department of Commerce, the SCC team stationed at ZTE is responsible for real-time monitoring of the company's adherence to U.S. export control regulations. Their duties encompass continuous oversight of compliance processes, investigation of specific cases, and the conduct of periodic compliance assessments. The SCC team reports directly to the U.S. Department of Commerce and operates with complete institutional independence. Internally, ZTE has established a Special Audit and Compliance Committee under its Board of Directors, consisting of no fewer than three non-executive directors. The chairman of the board serves as a member of this committee but is not permitted to act as its chair. In addition, ZTE has appointed an independent internal Special Compliance Coordinator who performs coordination, monitoring, evaluation, and reporting functions. Through these institutional arrangements, ZTE has constructed a three-tiered compliance defense system within its export control framework: the internal Compliance Committee, the independent internal Special Compliance Coordinator, and the externally appointed SCC team deployed by the U.S. government.

In parallel with the establishment of its export control compliance program, ZTE Corporation initiated the development of an anti-bribery and anti-corruption compliance framework. This framework is designed to ensure conformity not only with China's domestic anti-corruption and anti-bribery laws and regulations but also with major international legal regimes, including the U.S. *Foreign Corrupt Practices Act* (FCPA), the U.K. *Bribery Act*, and corresponding anti-corruption legislation in other jurisdictions where ZTE conducts business. The management and implementation of ZTE's anti-bribery and anti-corruption compliance framework are overseen by the Anti-Commercial Bribery Compliance Department under the leadership of the company's Compliance Management Committee.

ZTE Corporation has issued the *Anti-Commercial Bribery Compliance Policy* and the *Anti-Commercial Bribery Compliance Manual*, thereby establishing eight fundamental elements of its anti-bribery management system. First is top-level commitment to compliance management. Senior executives actively participate in the planning, decision-making, and consultation of anti-bribery compliance; assume direct responsibility for the compliance of their respective business areas; and personally engage in compliance training and communication to ensure the smooth operation of internal reporting and communication channels. Second is a sound compliance organization. Each business unit constitutes the first line of defense against bribery risks; the dedicated Anti-Commercial Compliance Department serves as the second line of defense; and the Compliance Audit Department functions as an independent third line of defense. In practice, ZTE has transformed the "Plan–Do–Check–Act" (PDCA) cycle into a closed-loop mechanism of "reasonable rules—effective implementation—rigorous enforcement—robust inspection," establishing a dual cycle of compliance operations and management. Third is adequate resource allocation. ZTE has reinforced its compliance structure across three levels—the Expert Center, BU compliance teams, and compliance liaisons within business units—while introducing and optimizing IT systems and tools to enhance compliance management efficiency and effectiveness. Fourth is systematic risk assessment. The Anti-Bribery Compliance Department and BU compliance teams conduct annual risk assessments, prepare corresponding risk reports, and adjust compliance measures in response to business and risk changes. Fifth is a comprehensive anti-bribery compliance policy framework. The company regularly maintains and updates its *Anti-Bribery Compliance Policy*, *Anti-Bribery Compliance Manual*, and related management rules and guidelines. These anti-bribery standards cover gifts and hospitality, external travel, business partners, procurement transactions, sponsorships, charitable donations, customer training, mergers and joint ventures, and employment. Sixth is effective process control. Utilizing the Legal and Compliance Management (LCM) and Team Collaboration Management (TS) systems, ZTE has embedded compliance approval procedures into sales, procurement, finance, employment, and investment workflows. Business activities cannot proceed without completion of the mandatory compliance approval process. Seventh is comprehensive training and communication. ZTE provides regular anti-bribery compliance training to all employees and specialized training for new employees, management, compliance personnel, key functional staff (marketing, finance, procurement), and external business partners. All employees are required to sign the *Anti-Bribery Compliance Commitment Letter*. Eighth is continuous monitoring and improvement. The Anti-Bribery Compliance

Department and BU compliance teams continuously supervise program implementation and address identified deficiencies. The Compliance Audit Department conducts periodic compliance audits to detect weaknesses and ensure corrective actions. Potential violations identified through whistleblowing or audits are investigated in accordance with established procedures, with recommendations for disciplinary measures where appropriate.

The Data Protection Compliance Program is a recently established targeted compliance program at ZTE Corporation. The company complies with globally applicable data protection laws and regulations, with particular emphasis on the European Union's General Data Protection Regulation (GDPR), integrating data protection requirements throughout its business processes. The Compliance Management Committee functions as the highest governing authority for data protection compliance. Consistent with the company's other targeted compliance programs, the Data Protection Compliance Program implements a three-tiered control structure: first, compliance liaisons within business units; second, the Data Protection Compliance Department; and third, the Compliance Audit Department. In line with GDPR requirements, ZTE has progressively appointed Data Protection Officers in key EU countries to oversee data protection management and compliance.

ZTE Corporation has established its core compliance policies on data protection. Under these policies, in business operations subject to the jurisdiction of the GDPR, the company has preliminarily developed a *Personal Data Dictionary*, embedded data protection compliance requirements into supplier management, and progressively advanced the integration and optimization of these requirements within its IT systems and business processes. ZTE has also instituted an emergency response mechanism for personal data breaches. In the event of a data breach, an emergency response team is promptly convened to mitigate potential losses and ensure that affected data subjects are duly notified in a timely manner. Furthermore, the company provides regular data protection compliance training to its employees to ensure that all personnel and business partners operating within the scope of the GDPR fully understand the obligations of data protection compliance and strictly implement the corresponding policies and procedures.

ZTE Corporation's Export Control Compliance Program

On June 8, 2018, China's ZTE Corporation entered into a *Substitute Settlement Agreement* (SSA) with the U.S. Bureau of Industry and Security (BIS). Earlier, in March 2017, ZTE had concluded a *Plea Agreement* with the U.S. Department of Justice, a *Settlement Agreement* with BIS, and a separate *Settlement Agreement* with the Office of Foreign Assets Control (OFAC). Pursuant to the SSA, ZTE was obliged to cooperate fully with the Monitor appointed by the U.S. Court and the Special Compliance Coordinator designated by BIS, and to accept their supervision and guidance in rebuilding its export control compliance program. Under the terms of the agreement, ZTE made several key compliance commitments: first, to establish a world-class export control compliance program grounded in industry best practices; second, to implement multiple improvements to its export compliance operations; third, to strengthen both internal and external compliance training programs; fourth, to publish the Export Control Classification Numbers (ECCNs) of its products; and fifth, to enhance its export compliance guidelines and procedures.

First, ZTE Corporation restructured and rebuilt its organizational system for export control compliance. Under the authority of the Board of Directors, the company established a Compliance Management Committee, which serves as the highest internal body responsible for formulating and implementing export control policies and procedures. Any transaction, export, or other business activity involving controlled products or technologies must be reviewed by the Compliance Management Committee, which holds *veto power* over whether such business activities may proceed. Under this committee, ZTE appointed a Chief Export Compliance Officer (CECO), who assumes overall responsibility for the execution and implementation of export control compliance policies and procedures. Reporting to the CECO, the Legal and Compliance Management Department functions as the secretariat of the Compliance Management Committee and exercises compliance oversight across all business functions, including research and development, sales, logistics, engineering, and services. By 2019, this department had more than forty compliance professionals and received support and guidance from external legal advisors and consulting experts. The company also significantly increased its compliance budget and allocated additional resources to strengthen its compliance capacity.

Second, ZTE Corporation established the core principles of its export control compliance program and actively fostered the development of a company-wide compliance culture. The company emphasized that building a robust export compliance system is of vital importance to its sustainable operations, stressing that export compliance is *"everyone's responsibility."* According to ZTE, compliance *"not only creates value but also protects value."* To enhance compliance awareness and ensure the effective dissemination of compliance policies and values across the organization, ZTE has undertaken a series of initiatives since 2018. The company issued an open *Export Compliance Letter* to all business partners, underscoring its export compliance policies and procedures. It also circulated multiple *Management Commitment Statements on Export Control Compliance* to all directors, managers, employees, and contractors, reaffirming the value-generating role of compliance and informing them about the ongoing updates and progress of the export compliance program. Furthermore, ZTE released several *Open Letters and Notices to Directors, Managers, Employees, Contractors, Suppliers, and Business Partners Regarding the Prohibition on Transfers of Items Controlled under the Export Administration Regulations (EAR) to Restricted Regions*, reiterating that strict adherence to

U.S. export control laws is a fundamental requirement for the company's global operations. In addition, the company's Chief Export Compliance Officer (CECO) regularly issued *Quarterly Newsletters* to business partners, providing updates on the progress and key developments of ZTE's compliance initiatives.

Finally, a critical step in ZTE Corporation's reconstruction of its export control compliance program was the issuance of the *Export Control Compliance Policy*. Initially published in 2018, this policy serves as a comprehensive document codifying the company's export compliance management framework. In 2019, a revised version was released to incorporate several enhancements and refinements. Pursuant to this policy, ZTE undertakes to *"comply with all applicable laws and regulations in the countries where it conducts business, including restrictions under economic sanctions and export control laws and regulations,"* and further commits to *"take measures based on export compliance risk assessments to ensure that all transactions conducted on behalf of ZTE, including those by agents, distributors, and resellers, comply with applicable export control and sanctions laws and regulations."* Recognizing that violations of these laws and regulations may result in severe criminal and civil penalties—including fines, imprisonment, denial of export licenses, revocation of export privileges, and other sanctions that could materially impact ZTE's global operations—the company stipulates that employees who breach the policy may be subject to disciplinary action or termination. This prompts the question: what are the specific provisions and operational contents set forth in ZTE's Export Control Compliance Policy? Broadly speaking, ZTE Corporation's Export Control Compliance Policy can be divided into five sections.

First, obligations of all employees: All personnel are required to adhere to compliance commitments, applicable laws and regulations, and participate in compliance training. This includes signing attestations confirming adherence to the Export Control Compliance Policy and complying with all applicable export control and economic sanctions laws and regulations, as well as internal policies and procedures established by ZTE to ensure compliance. Employees must provide accurate, complete, and timely information to the Export Control Compliance Department and internal or external compliance monitors, maintain a thorough understanding of the applicability of export control and economic sanctions laws to their work, and fully participate in all compliance training programs. Furthermore, employees are required to report any potential compliance risks or violations, ensure the accuracy and completeness of all records, data, and information, and properly preserve such documentation.

Second, restrictions on dealings with restricted regions and parties: The company must not engage in any business with restricted regions or restricted parties. Before exporting, re-exporting, procuring, or otherwise transferring goods, software, or technology, or providing related services, ZTE must verify the correct Export Control Classification Number (ECCN) and confirm whether prior authorization or licenses from the U.S. government or other relevant authorities are required. If such authorization is required, no export, re-export, provision of services, or other transfer may occur prior to obtaining it. The company must not conduct business with any party located in, registered in, or operating within countries or regions subject to U.S. sanctions, including companies originating from these restricted regions. The company also must not engage in business with any restricted parties sanctioned by the U.S. government or other authorities, including individuals or entities listed on the OFAC *Specially Designated Nationals (SDN) List* or on BIS' *Denied Persons List* or *Entity List*.

Third, due diligence and compliance procedures: ZTE employees must perform appropriate due diligence and comply with established procedures aimed at mitigating export compliance risks. Key elements of these procedures include recording comprehensive information on business partners in ZTE's internal systems; accurately classifying ZTE products; understanding all counterparties involved in a transaction; screening third parties against sanctions lists; obtaining relevant information or representations from third parties regarding business in restricted regions in accordance with export compliance risk requirements; conducting special reviews for transactions in high-risk regions; securing end-user or end-use statements when necessary; and identifying any red flags that suggest potential violations, dealings with restricted regions, or involvement of sanctioned parties.

Fourth, restrictions on public commentary: Employees are strictly prohibited from making any public statements regarding relevant settlement agreements or matters related to export control compliance on any communications platform without prior approval from the Export Control Compliance Department.

Fifth, reporting obligations: Employees are obligated to report any potential export compliance issues or violations. Reports may be submitted directly to the compliance department or anonymously. Retaliation against employees for making reports is strictly forbidden. Employees who knowingly fail to report violations may face disciplinary action, up to and including termination.

Concurrently with the issuance of the *Export Control Compliance Policy*, ZTE Corporation established comprehensive mechanisms for the prevention and monitoring of export control compliance risks, primarily encompassing compliance risk assessments, due diligence, compliance training, and end-to-end process monitoring. First, regarding compliance training, ZTE has implemented a multi-tiered framework combining all-employee training, business-process training, and specialized training for key positions. All-employee training addresses the fundamental requirements of export control compliance; business-process training focuses on the core compliance obligations embedded in specific operational workflows; and key-position training delivers targeted instruction for personnel in critical roles. This multi-level approach spans general awareness courses for all employees and specialized programs for mid-to-senior management and personnel in specific functions, continuously enhancing compliance awareness and communicating business-specific requirements. Export control compliance training covers an expanding range of operational areas, including the responsibilities of mid-level management, after-sales services, audits, export classification, finance, human resources, legal, logistics, procurement, research and development, restricted-party screening, sales and marketing, and the application of the *Export Control Compliance Manual.*

Second, implementation of the Subsidiary Compliance Enhancement Program (SCEP): ZTE strengthened the export control compliance management systems of its subsidiaries and provided targeted compliance training to their management personnel.

Third, leveraging technological tools to prevent and identify compliance risks: In accordance with U.S. government requirements, ZTE actively implements automated screening procedures. Using restricted-party list screening tools, the company conducts regular automated scans of business partners across multiple operational, financial, and communication platforms, enabling timely and effective identification of companies, entities, or individuals located in restricted regions. Additionally, ZTE has established effective communication mechanisms with its business partners to collect Export Control Classification Numbers (ECCNs) and related classification information, ensuring that its supply chain and distribution channels comply with export requirements. ZTE's Export Control Compliance Manual further requires all units to conduct commercial activities in accordance with the company's Code of Business Conduct, export control compliance program, import and export management measures, and material inventory operation guidelines. Export control laws, regulations, and manual requirements are embedded into business processes, while IT systems are employed to screen partners and review the compliance of products involved in business activities, enabling information-based and automated compliance control over core operational segments.

Fourth, establishment of compliance reporting channels: ZTE has publicized its compliance reporting options, reminding employees and stakeholders that suspected violations may be reported either directly to the Export Control Compliance leadership team or through other company communication channels, including anonymous reporting methods. The company's website provides information on reporting hotlines, domestic and overseas reporting portals, and reporting addresses.

Moreover, during the reconstruction of its export control compliance program, ZTE Corporation engaged in comprehensive cooperation with the U.S. government–appointed Special Compliance Coordinator team and Monitor team. This collaboration primarily involved the following: the company's Chief Export Compliance Officer (CECO) held regular meetings with the teams to implement recommendations for enhancing the compliance program; ZTE provided periodic updates on the progress of the revised compliance implementation plan; the company hosted visits from the Special Compliance Coordinator and Monitor teams, ensuring that employees were available to respond to inquiries and that the teams participated in ZTE's global training sessions and meetings; and ZTE supported the teams' work and implemented their recommendations regarding improvements to the export control compliance program.

So far, under the supervision of the U.S. government—primarily the Bureau of Industry and Security (BIS)—and with guidance from the Special Compliance Coordinator and Monitor teams appointed by the U.S. government, ZTE Corporation's export control compliance program has achieved significant milestones. Whether ZTE will ultimately have U.S. trade sanctions lifted at the end of the multi-year monitoring period depends on the continued implementation of a thorough and effective export control compliance program.

Based on the current progress of its compliance initiatives, ZTE—once under severe trade sanction pressure—has indeed rebuilt its export control compliance program in accordance with internationally recognized standards. The company's efforts and results provide a concrete example of an effective export control compliance program. For Chinese companies that have already faced similar trade sanctions, ZTE's program may serve as a reference model for lifting restrictions. For companies potentially at risk of comparable trade sanctions, emulating ZTE's approach to establishing a robust export control compliance program may offer an effective preventive measure.

Developing Effective Compliance Managers: ZTE Corporation's Management Experience

Shortly after the National Day holiday, I received a WeChat message from Mr. Huang Zhiyu of ZTE Corporation, informing me that the company's Legal and Compliance team had completed a manuscript presenting ZTE's compliance experience and inviting me to write a preface. Having been previously invited by Mr. Huang to visit ZTE on several occasions, and having collaborated with him on a compliance research project, coupled with my long-standing admiration for ZTE's compliance management, I was delighted to accept the invitation.

Upon receiving the manuscript, titled *Creating Value Through Compliance*, I carefully read several chapters, gaining an initial understanding of the book's structure and content, and developing a more direct appreciation of ZTE's compliance management practices. It should be noted that the growing interest in, and in-depth understanding of, corporate compliance in China—spanning academia, practice, and broader society—is closely linked to the "ZTE incident" that occurred between 2016 and 2018. Following that event, Chinese enterprises, regulatory authorities, and judicial institutions began paying extraordinary attention to corporate compliance management, gradually exploring mechanisms for autonomous corporate compliance, regulatory compliance, and compliance remediation. In July 2020, during a brief lull in the COVID-19 pandemic, I was invited to attend a compliance forum at ZTE and visited the company's Communications Museum, where I held a dedicated discussion with the Legal and Compliance team, gaining a preliminary understanding of ZTE's compliance management system. In May 2021, I led my students on a second research visit to ZTE. Subsequently, through collaborative research on the compliance officer system, my team conducted a third visit for further exchange and discussion. Based on the literature concerning ZTE's compliance management system, I authored two articles—*ZTE's Specialized Compliance Programs* and *ZTE's Export Control Compliance Program*—published in *China Lawyer*, aiming to showcase ZTE's compliance management experience.

Since 2018, ZTE Corporation has undergone a profound transformation in compliance management, effectively experiencing a "rebirth from the ashes." The company has developed distinctive, self-contained practices across multiple dimensions, including cultivating a compliance-oriented mindset, establishing a compliance organizational structure, developing risk management systems, and improving compliance operations and assurance mechanisms.

ZTE's senior executives have shared their experiences on various aspects, such as the company's compliance culture, organizational structure, the three major compliance focus areas, and risk-based compliance management, frequently emphasizing the unique mechanism of *"integrating compliance into business processes."* However, due to space constraints and interpretive gaps in written materials, current knowledge of ZTE's compliance practices remains preliminary and superficial, and many questions persist regarding the design and operational implementation of these practices.

To some extent, in the broader context of domestic initiatives—such as state-owned enterprises pursuing "comprehensive compliance," administrative regulators advancing corporate compliance in practice, and judicial authorities piloting compliance reforms in involved enterprises—ZTE's compliance practices retain a certain "mystique," making it difficult for outsiders to fully discern their essence and extract core insights. This is especially true given ZTE's location in Shenzhen, at the forefront of China's reform and opening-up, where the city has initiated a comprehensive *"urban compliance construction"* process. Shenzhen's administrative and judicial authorities are leading nationwide efforts to promote corporate compliance management. Under these circumstances, accurately interpreting ZTE's compliance experience and providing practical guidance for other enterprises seeking to build effective compliance systems has become a widely discussed topic within the professional community.

Creating Value Through Compliance provides a systematic account of ZTE Corporation's compliance system from an internal perspective, offering a comprehensive view of the company's journey—from compliance philosophy to methods, and from institutional frameworks to practical implementation. Remarkably, the authors, with vision, generosity, and selflessness, have fully disclosed what might otherwise have remained a corporate "trade secret," presenting society with a complete picture of ZTE's compliance architecture and offering highly valuable insights for other enterprises seeking to establish or enhance their own compliance programs. Organized into six chapters, the book systematically introduces ZTE's compliance governance philosophy, summarizes the company's compliance-building methods, reveals its overall operational system, and analyzes practical experiences in export control compliance, anti-bribery compliance, and data protection compliance. It also provides a detailed exposition of the company's specialized compliance audit practices. Reading the book gave me a far deeper understanding of ZTE's compliance management, resolving many previous uncertainties and offering clearer insight into the essence of its approach. To help readers better appreciate ZTE's compliance experience, I will provide a professional interpretation of *Creating Value Through Compliance* from several key perspectives.

ZTE's Compliance Philosophy

ZTE Corporation regards adherence to business ethics and compliance with the laws and regulations of the countries in which it operates as the cornerstone of corporate compliance. The company is committed to building an efficient compliance management system, embedding compliance across all business processes, and achieving deep integration between operations and compliance. Its objective is to establish a best-in-class compliance framework within the industry, ensuring that compliance becomes a competitive advantage and truly embodies the principle of "creating value through compliance."

Within ZTE's operations, compliance functions as a "strategic foundation for corporate development" rather than merely a functional department. The company places the highest priority on "business sustainability," enhancing management efficiency under secure operational conditions, maintaining zero tolerance for violations, and protecting the long-term interests of customers, partners, shareholders, employees, and other stakeholders. Over time, ZTE has evolved its compliance management from an initial system-oriented approach—focused on structural elements—to a more flexible, risk-oriented model. The company emphasizes the progression from "effective" to "efficient" compliance, continuously optimizing the integration of compliance into business controls and the productization of compliance tools.

ZTE Corporation's compliance culture is reflected not only in its written policies but also through a comprehensive set of institutional practices. The Chairman and President regularly issue open letters to all employees, shareholders, and business partners, reaffirming the company's commitment to effective compliance management. Senior executives, as first-line responsible persons in their respective domains, sign compliance accountability statements and reinforce their commitment through internal meetings, video messages, written communications, and internal lecture series. The company further embeds its compliance culture by conducting organization-wide training, actively promoting employee oversight, establishing a robust internal reporting system, and engaging in broad external collaborations. Collectively, these measures cultivate a corporate culture rooted in lawful and regulated business practices, shaping shared values and habitual behaviors.

ZTE's compliance management has evolved through three distinct stages, reflecting its understanding of "compliance value." The first, the "Protecting Value" stage, followed crisis events and involved establishing corporate red lines, embedding compliance into business processes, and implementing subsidiary-level oversight to prevent systemic compliance failures. The second, the "Collaborative Development" stage, focused on continuously enhancing the efficiency and precision of compliance controls, strengthening compliance audits, and achieving closed-loop management. The third, the "Creating Value" stage, seeks to establish compliance benchmarks, enhance the company's compliance brand, and build a best-in-class compliance management system fully aligned with business operations. The book's title, *Creating Value Through Compliance*, thus reflects not only ZTE's core compliance philosophy but also captures the essence of its compliance management practices.

Risk-Based Compliance Model

Under the pressure and guidance of regulatory authorities and judicial bodies, many domestic enterprises have begun exploring the establishment of compliance management systems. Yet, whether viewed from the perspective of regulators, judicial authorities, or the enterprises themselves, the dominant concept remains "broad-scope compliance" or "enterprise-wide compliance." This approach emphasizes constructing a compliance management system focused on rule adherence, mapping out compliance obligations, identifying multiple key risk areas, and covering all personnel, operations, and business processes throughout the organization. ZTE Corporation's Chief Legal Officer, Shen Nan, describes this as a "management-based approach to compliance system construction." Following the 2018 crisis, ZTE initially built its compliance system along these lines, focusing on four dimensions: developing a compliance culture, allocating resources for compliance, establishing processes and institutional frameworks, and enhancing professional capabilities. By investing significant resources, the company quickly established a "top-down" export control compliance system. This framework was structured around eight key elements of compliance system construction and incorporated the PDCA (Plan–Do–Check–Act) cycle into compliance management, creating a dual-loop model that integrates business operations with compliance. The core pillars of compliance management were defined as rule formulation, comprehensive training, strict execution, and effective auditing. However, as compliance management entered more complex operational contexts, ZTE gradually recognized the limitations of a rigid, one-size-fits-all approach. Blind adherence to rules led to inefficiencies and failed to accommodate the flexible, scenario-specific demands of real-world business operations. To address these challenges, enterprises must monitor and mitigate compliance risks in real time, advance risk governance proactively, and implement a risk-based compliance management system.

Based on its risk-based compliance philosophy, ZTE Corporation has established a "Risk–Control–Process–Tool" framework for managing compliance risks. The company differentiates between abstract compliance risks and concrete compliance risks: the former are macro-level, generalized, and potential, whereas the latter are micro-level, specific, and tangible. Building on the identification of concrete compliance risks, ZTE defines the sources of compliance rules and establishes adherence baselines, providing both the foundation and practical means for compliance control. To ensure effective implementation, the company embeds compliance rules into Key Control Points (KCPs) within business processes, thereby preventing a disconnect between compliance and operations. Additionally, through the deployment of automated compliance control systems, ZTE "productizes" compliance tools, ensuring that rules are applied consistently and effectively. By combining compliance-oriented thinking, concrete risk identification, and management tools, ZTE achieves deep integration of compliance rules with business operations, resulting in a compliance management system fully aligned with practical business realities.

ZTE's Compliance Organizational Structure

To achieve effective compliance management and control compliance risks, ZTE Corporation has established and progressively refined its compliance leadership and organizational framework. In accordance with the principle of top-level commitment, the company has established a Compliance Management Committee at the board level, serving as the primary leadership and decision-making body for compliance. The committee is chaired by the company's President and includes all Senior Vice Presidents and higher-level executives. In addition, ZTE appoints a Chief Legal Officer at the Senior Vice President level, functioning as the enterprise's Chief Compliance Officer (CCO).

Adopting a risk-based compliance management approach, ZTE has identified export control, anti-bribery, and data protection as its key systemic risk areas. Accordingly, the company has established three specialized compliance departments at headquarters: the Export Control Compliance Department, the Anti-Commercial Bribery Compliance Department, and the Data Protection Compliance Department. Each department operates a Center of Excellence (COE), together forming an expert team of approximately 100 professionals. These experts lead the development of risk control systems in their respective domains and ensure that compliance requirements are effectively localized and embedded throughout the organization.

To ensure seamless integration of compliance with business operations and avoid a disconnect between the two, ZTE Corporation established the Compliance Organizational Management Department, recruiting personnel from frontline business units who possess in-depth knowledge of operational processes. The company also innovatively created dedicated Business Unit (BU) compliance functions, forming 11 BU teams corresponding to its business divisions, each responsible for liaising with business personnel and addressing management needs within its respective area. Within the overall compliance framework, the Compliance Organizational Management Department acts as both an intermediary and a bridge: upward, it channels policies and directives from the COE departments; downward, it receives inquiries and reports from business units. According to the book, members of the BU compliance teams "are experienced employees who have worked extensively within business units and have an in-depth understanding of operational workflows. Their familiarity with processes across production, logistics, finance, commercial operations, sales, engineering services, and delivery enables them to pinpoint the precise 'critical points' where compliance controls should be applied, while balancing control requirements with management costs." They "quickly grasp the principles and requirements of compliance controls and, leveraging their knowledge of business processes and personnel, ensure that compliance measures are implemented efficiently." Furthermore, these teams "help to address the common criticism of COE departments being 'ivory tower' units by enabling frontline issues to be reported promptly, facilitating bottom-up feedback, and ensuring that compliance insights are grounded in operational realities rather than abstract policy considerations."

To ensure the rapid establishment of effective compliance channels within a large organization, ZTE Corporation has implemented a "Compliance Liaison Officer" mechanism. Each management unit and subsidiary appoints a liaison officer responsible for conveying compliance rules, standards, and guidelines, as well as executing related compliance tasks in accordance with the requirements of the professional compliance teams and the unit itself. In business units or subsidiaries without a designated liaison officer, the General Manager assumes this role by default.

Building on this organizational framework, ZTE has established a three-lines-of-defense model for compliance risk control. Business units serve as the first line of responsibility, ensuring that all employees actively participate in risk prevention and control. The COE compliance departments constitute the second line of defense, identifying and managing compliance risks through rule formulation and ongoing monitoring. The Compliance Audit Department forms the third line of defense, tasked with handling reports of violations, investigating incidents, disciplining personnel, and conducting continuous compliance audits. These three lines are interconnected and operate collectively to manage compliance risks effectively.

For the compliance management organization to achieve its objectives, it must be integrated with the operational mechanisms of compliance risk management. After more than five years of institutional development, ZTE has preliminarily established a comprehensive compliance operation system that encompasses compliance risk assessment, rule development, process monitoring, and crisis response.

Three Major Risk Areas

Unlike many large domestic enterprises that pursue "broad-scope compliance" or enterprise-wide compliance systems, ZTE Corporation has developed a specialized compliance management system focused on controlling systemic risks. Systemic risks are not ordinary compliance risks; they are major compliance risks that could materially threaten the sustainable operation of the enterprise. Based on its industry characteristics and following careful risk identification and assessment, ZTE has concentrated its specialized compliance governance on three key risk areas: trade compliance risk, corruption risk, and data compliance risk.

Trade compliance risk primarily concerns the import and export of goods and technologies. Operating in the telecommunications industry with a complex international supply chain, ZTE must ensure that all transactions comply with the export control laws of the countries involved to maintain supply chain security and sustainable operations. Moreover, following the severe crises in 2016 and 2018 due to violations of U.S. export control regulations, ZTE engaged in extensive negotiations with U.S. judicial and regulatory authorities, reaching settlement agreements. The company committed to implementing compliance remediation during the monitoring period, establishing and executing an export control compliance program, and subjecting itself to compliance assessments by both judicial and regulatory bodies. Accordingly, ZTE designates trade compliance as its primary systemic compliance risk and has developed a comprehensive export control compliance management system to address it.

Corruption risk, also known as commercial bribery risk, is a systemic compliance risk commonly faced by outward-oriented enterprises. As a capital-intensive company engaged in major infrastructure projects, ZTE is particularly exposed to potential corruption incidents. Furthermore, its overseas investments and operations create compliance challenges with anti-corruption laws and regulations in the countries or regions where its subsidiaries, branches, offices, and agents operate. To mitigate this risk, ZTE has established a dedicated anti-commercial bribery compliance management system.

Data compliance risk constitutes another major risk that outward-oriented enterprises must address amid increasingly stringent domestic and international data regulations, and it is a characteristic compliance challenge for the telecommunications industry. As a sector foundational to the data economy—responsible for the generation, processing, and transfer of data—telecommunications companies like ZTE must manage risks related to personal data protection and cross-border data transfers. Accordingly, ZTE has implemented a data protection compliance management system.

According to ZTE Vice President Li Wen, these three risk areas "constitute the three systemic compliance risks that could materially affect the sustainable operation of a telecommunications company." To address them, ZTE has "built a closed-loop business process encompassing rule formulation, operational execution, and audit supervision, thereby establishing an effective specialized compliance governance system." Other non-systemic compliance risks are typically managed through first-line business process controls and generally do not require dedicated compliance governance programs.

Integrating Compliance into Business Processes

How can enterprises prevent compliance from becoming disconnected from business operations, creating a "two-layer" phenomenon? How can compliance management be genuinely integrated into business processes? These questions are central to establishing an effective compliance system. Over the years, ZTE Corporation has explored these challenges and developed a robust approach to embedding compliance into business operations.

First, after identifying the compliance control areas, it is essential to define and clarify compliance obligations precisely. The company translates applicable laws, regulations, and related rules into concrete compliance obligations, incorporating them into compliance policies and employee handbooks, ensuring that they serve as behavioral standards consistently followed throughout the organization. ZTE has also established a multidimensional, real-time "external law monitoring channel" and a dedicated policy tracking team tasked with monitoring relevant compliance policies, analyzing their impact on business operations, and updating compliance obligation lists across all compliance areas.

Second, based on the defined compliance obligations, abstract compliance risks are systematically translated into concrete risks. Through continuous risk assessment, ZTE gains a comprehensive understanding of its operational environment and identifies compliance risks—first recognizing macro-level, potential, and generalized abstract compliance risks and then narrowing the focus to micro-level, immediate, and specific concrete compliance risks. In practice, this involves mapping potential violations of compliance obligations onto specific business activities, establishing key compliance risk points within those activities, and setting corresponding compliance management requirements to ensure effective risk control.

Next, after identifying and analyzing concrete compliance risks, enterprises must determine the Key Control Points (KCPs) within their business processes. A KCP is defined as "a control measure capable of preventing and eliminating the impact of a risk or reducing it to an acceptable level," encompassing activities such as inspections, verifications, reviews, audits, rechecks, decision-making, evaluations, budgeting, early warning, analysis, authorizations, inventories, and segregation of duties.

Determining whether a risk control point qualifies as a KCP typically involves four steps: (1) assessing whether the process step includes any risk control measures; (2) evaluating whether it incorporates specific measures to eliminate risk factors or reduce them to acceptable levels; (3) judging whether the impact of the risk factors would exceed acceptable thresholds if left uncontrolled; and (4) considering whether subsequent steps could eliminate or mitigate the risk's impact. By establishing a model to evaluate control point attributes, enterprises can classify risk control points and, based on risk assessment results and business characteristics, designate the KCPs, thereby allocating compliance management resources efficiently and enhancing risk control capabilities.

Once KCPs are identified, enterprises develop corresponding control methods tailored to the specific risks. For instance, in export control compliance, concrete risks typically involve four elements: the entity, the country, the item, and the end use. Targeted KCP measures for each risk point may include restricted party screenings, due diligence procedures, sanctioned country or region screenings, and confirmation of export authorizations.

Equally important is the effective implementation of KCP control measures. Control methods and compliance tools should be adapted to the operational context, available resources, and management costs, forming practical and actionable compliance plans. By embedding these requirements into business processes, enterprises achieve true integration of compliance into operational workflows, ensuring that compliance becomes a seamless and routine part of daily business activities.

Finally, for emerging compliance risks, ZTE optimizes its compliance management system from both management and business perspectives. From the management side, in response to changes in external regulations, the company adopts a top-down rule optimization approach. By systematically reviewing the compliance "rule pyramid"—covering compliance policies, principle-based standards, process-based standards, and Key Control Points (KCPs)—ZTE identifies gaps and blind spots in compliance principles, process norms, and KCP controls. From the business side, following a business-driven principle, the company collects compliance improvement suggestions from operational personnel to quickly pinpoint areas for optimization. This process refines KCPs within workflows, ensuring that compliance procedures remain aligned with evolving business needs. In practice, this bottom-up, business-initiated optimization is implemented through four key strategies: elimination, simplification, integration, and automation, enhancing both the efficiency and effectiveness of the compliance management system.

Siemens' Compliance Remediation Journey

Enacted in 1977, the Foreign Corrupt Practices Act (FCPA) introduced two fundamental legal provisions. The Anti-Bribery Provision prohibits U.S. companies from offering or providing "anything of value" to foreign government officials to secure or retain business. The Books and Records Provision, also called the Accounting Provision, obliges U.S.-listed companies to maintain books, records, and accounts in reasonable detail, accurately reflecting transactions and the disposition of assets, and to establish and maintain a suitable system of internal accounting controls. This provision is further divided into the Accounting Clause, which requires the preparation and maintenance of accurate, detailed, and fair books and records of transactions and asset handling, and the Internal Control Clause, which mandates the establishment and upkeep of appropriate internal accounting control systems.

The U.S. Department of Justice (DOJ) and the Securities and Exchange Commission (SEC) are responsible for enforcing the FCPA. From 1977 to 2017, over a span of 40 years, the DOJ initiated more than 300 enforcement actions against companies, while the SEC brought over 170 cases, including some in coordination with foreign authorities. Collectively, these agencies imposed over $10 billion in fines. Such enforcement actions are commonly referred to as FCPA enforcement.

Notably, the 2008 enforcement action against Germany's Siemens AG set a record at the time for the largest FCPA settlement. Siemens agreed to pay $800 million to the U.S. government and €800 million to the German government. In addition, the company incurred approximately $850 million in internal expenses for accounting, legal services, and related costs in response to the enforcement proceedings.

The Siemens Case

In November 2006, Siemens AG was investigated by the Munich Public Prosecutor's Office for suspected commercial bribery. During the investigation, authorities discovered that over 20 recipients and entities worldwide had received "suspicious payments" from Siemens, with millions of euros transferred to accounts in the United Arab Emirates, Indonesia, Sudan, and other countries. These recipients and entities had previously received multiple payments from Siemens, which were used to facilitate commercial bribery, secure business contracts, and build extensive international business networks.

Subsequently, Siemens proactively self-reported its bribery activities across multiple countries to the U.S. Department of Justice (DOJ) and the Securities and Exchange Commission (SEC). The company retained the U.S. law firm Debevoise & Plimpton to conduct a two-year independent internal investigation. Following this investigation, the DOJ filed criminal charges against Siemens AG and its subsidiaries in Argentina, Bangladesh, and Venezuela. The indictment alleged that the defendants had paid substantial bribes to government officials in several countries via consulting firms and recorded these payments in their books and records as "consulting fees" and "legal fees."

The U.S. Securities and Exchange Commission (SEC) filed a civil lawsuit against Siemens AG, alleging that from March 2001 to September 2007, the company engaged in extensive and systematic bribery of foreign government officials to secure business. During this period, Siemens made at least 4283 payments, totaling approximately $1.4 billion, through third parties to bribe officials across multiple countries. These corrupt practices resulted in 332 projects and generated profits exceeding $1.1 billion. Notably, between 1998 and 2008, Siemens allegedly paid over $70 million in bribes to Chinese officials and related personnel, securing contracts worth $2.3 billion, covering medical equipment, high-voltage transmission lines, metro trains, and signaling systems.

To mitigate further losses, Siemens reached a criminal settlement with the DOJ. Under this agreement, the DOJ declined to pursue criminal charges against Siemens AG on the condition that fines be paid for violations of the FCPA's Books and Records and Internal Controls provisions. The settlement required Siemens AG to pay $448.5 million, Siemens Argentina to pay $500,000, and both Siemens Venezuela and Siemens Bangladesh to pay $500,000 each for violations of anti-bribery and accounting provisions.

In response to the SEC's civil action, Siemens chose a civil settlement, under which it neither admitted nor denied the allegations of violating anti-bribery provisions, but agreed to return $350 million in ill-gotten gains to the Commission. At the same time, Siemens reached a settlement with the Munich Public Prosecutor's Office in Germany. The prosecutors concluded that Siemens had gained at least €394.75 million through bribery and, citing inadequate board-level supervision, imposed a fine of €395 million, while declining to pursue criminal charges. These agreements allowed Siemens to limit its losses in two key ways: it was not formally deemed to have committed bribery, keeping Germany's public export credit insurance valid, and as a responsible contracting party, it could continue engaging in relevant transactions with the U.S. government.

Following the bribery scandal, Siemens implemented comprehensive management restructuring. The Chairman of the Supervisory Board and the CEO resigned, around 200 managers were terminated, and more than 100 senior executives were required to cooperate with investigations. The company also revamped its compliance function, appointing Dr. Ulrich Wegner, former German Finance Minister, as an Independent Compliance Monitor, who began overseeing Siemens' compliance improvements from 2009 onward. Siemens engaged independent accounting and law firms, launching Germany's first-ever independent corporate investigation. This exhaustive review covered over 5000 consulting agreements, 40 million bank statements, 100 million documents, and 127 million transactions, along with numerous internal interviews. The investigation alone cost Siemens hundreds of millions of euros, underscoring the magnitude and seriousness of the compliance reform.

Siemens' Compliance Organization

Siemens has established an independent and authoritative compliance framework. The compliance function is led by a Chief Compliance Officer (CCO), who reports to the General Counsel and has the authority to submit reports directly to both the Management Board and the Supervisory Board. The General Counsel, in turn, reports directly to the President and CEO of Siemens. Under the CCO's leadership, each business group and regional company appoints a Group Compliance Officer or Regional Compliance Officer, responsible for implementing the compliance program in their area and reporting back to the CCO. Across all business groups and over 80 regional companies, these officers, supported by additional compliance staff, oversee the execution of compliance policies, provide continuous employee training, and ensure that management submits written confirmation of adherence to the Code of Conduct every two years. They are also responsible for investigating alleged violations, safeguarding whistleblowers from retaliation, and enforcing disciplinary actions when misconduct is confirmed. In addition to these officers, Siemens has appointed or assigned hundreds of compliance personnel across functional departments, business groups, divisions, foreign subsidiaries, and the healthcare sector. Assignments are determined not only by business size but also by the specific compliance risks relevant to each area. To maintain independence, all compliance officers and personnel are prohibited from holding external positions that could create conflicts of interest while performing their compliance duties.

Building upon its anti-corruption foundation, Siemens has broadened its compliance scope to cover four key areas: (1) anti-corruption, aimed at preventing bribery and undue influence; (2) antitrust, ensuring compliance with fair competition principles; (3) data protection, safeguarding personal and sensitive information; and (4) anti-money laundering (AML), preventing the company from being used for money laundering or terrorist financing activities. Moreover, Siemens undertakes internal investigations and enforces disciplinary measures when employees are suspected of breaching criminal laws, administrative regulations, or internal policies, or in connection with criminal or administrative proceedings involving the company or its personnel. These measures are integral to the overall compliance program.

The Siemens compliance framework comprises two core components: the Code of Conduct and three institutional pillars. The Code of Conduct represents the core of the compliance system, setting fundamental behavioral standards for all employees and reflecting the principle that "only ethical business is Siemens' business." The three institutional pillars—prevention, monitoring, and response—constitute the structural foundation of the compliance program and will be discussed in detail below.

Code of Conduct

Siemens' Code of Conduct is organized into eight sections, covering fundamental behavioral requirements, dealings with business partners and third parties, conflict-of-interest avoidance, use of company assets, information handling, environment, safety and health, mechanisms for complaints and suggestions, and compliance implementation and oversight. Together, these sections form the cornerstone of Siemens' compliance framework.

The fundamental behavioral requirements articulate four core principles for all employees: adherence to applicable laws and regulations and avoidance of unlawful activities; treating colleagues and partners with respect and conducting oneself honestly and ethically; accountability for protecting Siemens' reputation; and ensuring that managers actively fulfill their responsibilities in compliance management and supervising employees' lawful conduct.

In terms of dealings with business partners and third parties, the Code specifies standards across multiple areas, including fair competition and antitrust compliance, anti-corruption measures, prohibition of unlawful political contributions, charitable donations, and sponsorships, compliance with government procurement rules, adherence to anti-money laundering regulations and procedures, compliance with export control and customs laws in relevant jurisdictions, and requiring suppliers to observe applicable laws, among other obligations.

Siemens' Code of Conduct underscores the importance of avoiding conflicts of interest. Employees are required to act in the best interests of Siemens when making business decisions and to avoid any situation that could give rise to an actual or potential conflict of interest. Specifically, employees must not engage in or assist any business that competes with Siemens, nor may they hold secondary employment with a competing company. Employees who hold or acquire a financial interest in Siemens' business partners or affiliated companies must disclose this to the human resources department if their duties involve dealings with such entities or if they hold any position within them.

The Code also strictly prohibits using company assets for personal purposes or for any activities that are illegal, create conflicts of interest, increase costs, interfere with company operations, or otherwise harm Siemens.

Regarding information handling, employees must (1) maintain complete and accurate books and records that truthfully reflect all transactions and expenditures in accordance with applicable accounting standards; (2) protect internal confidential or proprietary Siemens information; (3) comply with laws and regulations on data privacy and security, refraining from unauthorized disclosure; and (4) avoid disclosing insider information obtained in the course of their duties, whether intentionally or inadvertently.

In the environment, safety, and health domain, the Code of Conduct requires employees to operate in an environmentally responsible manner while safeguarding the health and safety of all personnel.

The Code also sets out protocols for employee complaints, allowing staff to report concerns to supervisors, compliance officers, HR managers, or designated internal labor organizations. There are four primary reporting channels: (1) the Chief Compliance Officer; (2) Compliance Officers in business groups, regions, or functional departments; (3) the "Tell Us" platform (compliance help portal); and (4) Siemens' global special investigators. Complaints can be submitted confidentially or anonymously, are thoroughly investigated, and are kept strictly confidential, with a zero-tolerance policy for retaliation.

For compliance implementation and oversight, the Code requires Siemens' management to actively enforce adherence and regularly monitor compliance across all global operations.

Prevention System

The prevention system consists of proactive measures aimed at mitigating potential compliance risks before they materialize. Siemens' system includes six key components: compliance risk management, policy and process development, training and other communication channels, advice and support, integration with HR processes, and joint initiatives such as integrity programs. Among these, compliance risk management and training serve as the core pillars.

A fundamental prerequisite for effective prevention is ensuring that all employees adhere to the Code of Conduct. Building on this foundation, Siemens applies a range of compliance tools to manage risks comprehensively.

An effective compliance system relies on the timely and accurate identification of compliance risks within business processes, along with mechanisms to mitigate or eliminate them. Practically, this requires that each business process complies with applicable laws, regulations, and Siemens' internal standards. For certain projects, decision-makers conduct compliance risk assessments before pursuing actions such as bidding for contracts or acquiring equity. Similarly, potential business partners are evaluated for integrity, with senior management making risk-based decisions or implementing measures to reduce exposure. Beyond individual assessments, Siemens' compliance risk management system identifies risks at both the departmental and corporate levels. This is achieved through integrated bottom-up and top-down identification approaches, ensuring a comprehensive understanding of compliance risks across the organization.

The bottom-up risk assessment at Siemens engages business unit CEOs and managers together with their compliance officers to identify and evaluate the compliance risks specific to their departments. In odd-numbered years, assessments cover business groups, key operational countries, and Siemens' healthcare sector; in even-numbered years, the focus shifts to high-risk countries. These assessments address major compliance domains, including anti-corruption, antitrust, data protection, and anti-money laundering (AML).

The top-down risk assessment, by contrast, focuses on evaluating the effectiveness of Siemens' compliance controls. This involves continuous monitoring to ensure that compliance processes are properly implemented and achieve their intended results. The Chief Compliance Officer (CCO), in collaboration with the Management Board and the Supervisory Board Compliance Committee, reviews company-wide compliance risks, reports to Siemens' Enterprise Risk Management department, and implements measures to reduce these risks.

Complementing these approaches, Siemens conducts a cross-departmental risk audit each quarter. Led by the CCO, the "Compliance Risk Radar" initiative brings together the compliance organization, relevant functional departments, internal control units, and the audit department to systematically identify and track emerging compliance risks throughout the enterprise.

Even the most well-designed compliance system cannot function effectively if employees are unaware of its rules or unsure how to apply them. Accordingly, a key component of Siemens' prevention system is ensuring that all employees are fully informed about relevant laws, internal compliance policies, and procedures. This is complemented by ongoing training, guidance, and clear communication from senior leadership, reinforcing the company's commitment to compliance at every organizational level.

Training is structured into two main categories. First, employees in "sensitive" roles—including frontline sales staff, personnel interacting directly with government officials or clients, and those involved in government procurement—participate in mandatory, in-person, instructor-led sessions. These sessions cover Siemens' fundamental compliance concepts, data protection, and annual integrity dialogues and may include targeted antitrust and competition law training based on periodic risk assessments. Second, all employees participate in company-wide online training, which addresses the Code of Conduct, collaboration with business partners, sponsorships, donations, memberships, and the use of compliance tools. Online training is generally voluntary, providing a flexible complement to the in-person programs.

Beyond training, Siemens places strong emphasis on continuous communication with employees, ensuring they remain up to date on the latest laws, internal regulations, compliance procedures, and tools. The compliance organization facilitates this primarily through regular updates to the internal compliance intranet. Moreover, internal communication reinforces senior management's commitment to compliance across all organizational levels. Compliance teams within each business unit further support this effort through diverse media channels and activities, consistently amplifying the compliance message.

In addition to training and communication, Siemens' prevention system features a "guidance and support system," enabling management and employees to consult directly with their assigned compliance officers on interpreting and applying compliance rules in business decisions. Ultimately, Siemens seeks to embed integrity and compliance into employees' mindsets, cultivating a distinctive and pervasive compliance culture throughout the organization.

Monitoring System

Siemens' monitoring system is built around four main processes: control management, auditing, complaint handling, and reporting responsibilities. To complement existing violation-reporting channels, the company also established a Global Special Investigator mechanism to address complaints from employees and third parties.

Control management requires managers to conduct continuous oversight within their areas of responsibility during business operations, including random project checks to ensure compliance with antitrust and anti-corruption regulations.

Auditing entails periodic assessments by company auditors to confirm that the compliance program is effectively implemented across all business groups and subsidiaries and to identify any instances of non-compliance.

Complaint handling provides a formal process for uncovering potential misconduct. Employees can report complaints or violations of the Code of

Conduct to their supervisors, HR managers, or other designated personnel or departments. Upon receiving a complaint, the Chief Compliance Officer (CCO) launches a special investigation led by internal auditors and reports findings to the Audit Committee. All complaints are thoroughly investigated, securely documented, and treated confidentially, with a strict zero-tolerance policy for retaliation against complainants.

Simultaneously, complaints can also be directed to Siemens' Global Special Investigators, who are typically practicing attorneys retained by the company. When these investigators uncover suspected violations of the Code of Conduct or criminal law, the findings are referred to the Corporate Compliance Office, which subsequently launches a special investigation. All company departments are required to fully cooperate and support these investigations.

To reinforce the effectiveness of the complaint system, Siemens has established a 24/7 compliance help platform, "Tell Us." Serving as an extension of the Global Special Investigator program, this platform allows employees, customers, and business partners to report potential legal, regulatory, or criminal issues online or by phone in multiple languages. The service is managed by professional external providers to ensure strict confidentiality. Additionally, every Siemens employee email automatically includes a notice directing recipients to report any suspected violations of business ethics or law—particularly anti-corruption or antitrust breaches—via the Siemens "Tell Us" platform, with the relevant web link provided.

The reporting responsibility within Siemens refers to its comprehensive internal reporting framework, which consists of several core elements. First, the Chief Compliance Officer (CCO) delivers regular or ad hoc reports on compliance issues to the Board of Directors and the Audit Committee, covering the company's adherence to legal and regulatory requirements, progress in implementing compliance programs, and other key internal compliance activities. Second, Siemens has set up a Disclosure Committee accountable to the CEO and CFO, with the CCO and relevant department heads as members. This committee's main role is to review all documents submitted to the U.S. Securities and Exchange Commission (SEC) to ensure their accuracy and completeness. The CCO is responsible for linking compliance procedures with financial reporting, while department heads must ensure that the financial data submitted to the CEO and CFO is complete and reliable. Finally, the Disclosure Committee provides quarterly reports to the CEO and CFO regarding any criminal activity affecting company assets. Siemens' enterprise-wide reporting system, Treulufo, operates effectively, enabling internal audits to investigate relevant cases and allowing compliance personnel to offer legal guidance when necessary.

Response System

Siemens' response system covers the timely detection and investigation of violations, the disciplinary management of employees involved in misconduct, and the global tracking of individual cases.

Employees, third parties, or other stakeholders can report suspected violations through the reporting system or via independent Global Special Investigators. Once a report is received, the compliance organization within the relevant business unit initiates a review and evaluation process. Compliance officers assess the credibility of the allegations and, if sufficiently substantiated, examine the substantive aspects of the case to determine whether an internal investigation is warranted. The Chief Compliance Officer (CCO) may then authorize a centralized investigation. Upon conclusion of the investigation, compliance personnel prepare a comprehensive report detailing all factual findings, providing a legal assessment, and making disciplinary recommendations. The report also identifies any systemic weaknesses discovered during the investigation and proposes corrective measures to further strengthen Siemens' compliance framework.

For employees who violate laws and regulations, including the Siemens Code of Conduct, the company has established two disciplinary mechanisms. First, the Central Disciplinary Committee (CDC) administers global disciplinary actions at the group level, with the Chief Compliance Officer serving as a standing member. Second, for cases outside the CDC's jurisdiction, business unit leaders and the human resources department carry out disciplinary actions according to standard procedures, ensuring compliance with relevant rules. Prior to imposing any disciplinary measures, outcomes are evaluated at the group or local level, with responsible departments taking all aspects of the case into account and respecting the collective decision-making rights of employee representatives.

Siemens' global case tracking system requires the compliance organization to maintain centralized records of all violations and track the handling of each case, ensuring that all actions comply with applicable laws, regulations, and company policies. Each case is assessed based on its impact and included in compliance reports submitted by the Chief Compliance Officer to the Management Board and the Supervisory Board.

Following disciplinary actions, the relevant departments are responsible for implementing the recommendations in the investigation reports, addressing any systemic weaknesses or operational deficiencies to prevent recurrence of similar violations.

Anti-Money Laundering Compliance Case: Agricultural Bank of China

In November 2016, the Agricultural Bank of China (ABC) and its New York branch reached an administrative settlement with the New York State Department of Financial Services (NYDFS) for violations of U.S. anti-money laundering (AML) regulations. The settlement concluded that ABC's New York branch had deliberately concealed U.S. dollar settlement transactions, including falsifying documents related to transactions between China and Russia and omitting information on sanctioned counterparties in U.S. dollar settlements. Bank management also sought to silence whistleblowers who were conducting internal investigations into suspicious transactions. Within ten days of signing the settlement, the New York branch was required to pay a fine of $215 million. In addition, regulators mandated the establishment of an effective internal control system and ongoing independent testing of the branch's U.S. dollar settlement activities over an 18-month period.

Under the settlement agreement, ABC was required to appoint an independent monitor within 60 days to conduct a comprehensive review and assessment of the AML compliance program at its New York branch. Based on the monitor's assessment, ABC and its New York branch were to submit a detailed remediation plan to the regulators, designed to strengthen the AML compliance program comprehensively. The plan encompasses the AML compliance framework, suspicious transaction reporting, customer due diligence, internal auditing, and senior management oversight. The monitor is responsible for overseeing the implementation of these remediation measures over a two-year period and reporting to the regulators on both the progress and effectiveness of the measures.

Over the two years preceding the 2016 NYDFS settlement, ABC's New York branch faced multiple regulatory investigations for violations of U.S. anti-money laundering (AML) laws. Notably, the NYDFS investigation in 2016 culminated in the administrative settlement described above. Additionally, in September 2016, the U.S. Federal Reserve conducted its own AML enforcement review of the branch, resulting in a separate settlement under which the New York branch committed to enhancing its AML compliance program. The Federal Reserve identified deficiencies largely similar to those found by the NYDFS. Aside from the absence of a financial penalty and the appointment of an independent monitor, the terms of the Federal Reserve settlement were generally consistent with those agreed upon with the NYDFS.

According to the Consent Order issued by the New York State Department of Financial Services (NYDFS), the Agricultural Bank of China (ABC) and its New York branch demonstrated deficiencies in four major areas.

First is disregard for regulatory warnings. Since 2014, the NYDFS had repeatedly warned the branch during inspections that its monitoring systems were inadequate in transaction controls, risk assessments, and ongoing compliance procedures. U.S. dollar settlements, widely used in international trade, are considered high-risk due to their potential for money laundering or terrorist financing. The NYDFS highlighted shortcomings in the branch's AML and economic sanctions controls and recommended that the volume of U.S. dollar settlements remain at current levels until remediation was completed. Despite commitments to remediate, ABC's New York branch continued to expand high-risk U.S. dollar settlement activities. From January to July 2014, the branch processed an average of 148 daily U.S. dollar settlement transactions, totaling $2.6 billion; in the first half of 2015, the daily average increased to 330 transactions, totaling $7.2 billion.

Second is lack of transparency in transaction processing. Under U.S. AML regulations, transactions above certain thresholds require that both sender and receiver information be automatically screened by the bank's monitoring system. However, many U.S. dollar transactions at ABC's New York branch omitted required counterparty information, using unidentifiable codes instead. This practice prevented the bank's monitoring and screening systems from automatically identifying the true participants, creating a risk of AML non-compliance.

Third is failure to report suspicious transactions and improper undermining of the Chief Compliance Officer's independence. In September 2014, the then Chief Compliance Officer (CCO) of ABC's New York branch identified significant issues with the lack of transparency in U.S. dollar transactions and uncovered several suspicious transactions. These included a series of "abnormal transactions"—some high-risk transactions went undetected and unaddressed, the branch was suspected of falsifying potential investigative documents involving China and Russia, and suspicious transactions were not investigated promptly. The CCO reported these findings and the associated compliance risks to the branch's senior management. However, the branch's management disagreed with the CCO's assessments and only allowed the CCO to communicate with regulators in a highly restricted manner, framed as "seeking guidance." In February 2015, regulators responded, highlighting that the branch processed substantial volumes of U.S. dollar trade financing, operated with non-transparent transaction practices, and faced risks of violating AML regulations as well as sanctions and embargo laws. Regulators further advised management to enhance transparency regarding transaction counterparties. Despite these warnings, ABC's New York branch failed to implement the regulators' recommendations. Instead, management began constraining the CCO's independent authority, including limiting direct communications with regulators. Requests by the CCO to investigate relevant transaction information at the head office and other branches were subjected to managerial review. In April 2015, the CCO was placed on forced leave and departed two months later. By August of that year, nearly all compliance personnel at the New York branch had resigned. Although external consultants were subsequently engaged to manage compliance functions, management's restrictions on the compliance department remained in place.

Fourth is failure of the AML compliance mechanism at ABC's New York branch. Regulatory reviews revealed that the branch could not retain a qualified Chief Compliance Officer (CCO) for a sustained period. Temporary compliance consultants had only limited interaction with ABC's headquarters, and the shortage of compliance personnel impeded effective remediation of previously identified deficiencies. Amid the expansion of cross-border trade financing and related affiliated transactions, the branch's compliance capabilities were clearly inadequate. Oversight of high-risk transactions was seriously deficient: more than half of all transactions lacked effective monitoring, high-risk jurisdictions were not updated promptly, and numerous financial transactions went unsupervised. The branch failed to prioritize monitoring of high-risk areas, such as U.S. dollar settlements and trade finance, resulting in over 700 suspicious transactions remaining uninvestigated.

Under the settlement agreement with regulators, ABC's New York branch paid substantial fines and undertook comprehensive remediation, issuing the following anti-money laundering (AML) statement:

"As a bank licensed in the State of New York, the Agricultural Bank of China, New York Branch, and its management are fully committed to strict compliance with all requirements set forth by the New York State Department of Financial Services (NYDFS) and the U.S. Federal Reserve (FRB), as well as with applicable regulations issued by the U.S. Department of the Treasury's Financial Crimes Enforcement Network (FinCEN) and the Office of Foreign Assets Control (OFAC), including the Bank Secrecy Act and the USA PATRIOT Act. The New York Branch has implemented a comprehensive AML compliance program to promptly identify and prevent any individual or organization from using the branch to launder money or to fund terrorism and other criminal activities. In its daily operations, the branch will take all necessary measures, including reporting transactions involving currency, specified financial instruments, and suspicious activities, as well as conducting appropriate due diligence, to prevent the branch from being misused by money launderers or terrorists."

The headquarters of the Agricultural Bank of China (ABC) places great emphasis on building a robust anti-money laundering (AML) compliance management system, especially in areas concerning money laundering, terrorist financing, and breaches of international sanctions. The bank has undertaken comprehensive measures to strengthen its global compliance and risk control framework. ABC views compliant operations as the lifeline for its overseas institutions and the foundation and prerequisite for its international development. To this end, the bank has established an Anti-Money Laundering Center.

The AML Center is considered "the hub and core of ABC's internal AML control management system, serving as the unified management center for AML strategies, plans, and policies across domestic and overseas institutions; the organizational and coordination center for AML work across business lines; and the monitoring and risk prevention center for money laundering and terrorist financing." The bank aims to strengthen the Center across three dimensions: system, team, and technology. ABC has committed to, within three years, building a professional and comprehensive AML team, developing an intelligent and efficient AML system, and establishing a sound internal control framework for AML. In operational terms, the headquarters AML Center focuses on policy formulation and the handling of significant risks; branch-level centers concentrate on daily monitoring and risk reporting; and sub-branches and outlets prioritize customer identification and due diligence. Horizontal collaboration between internal control and business departments is emphasized: business units are responsible for balancing risk prevention with business development, performing AML functions such as customer due diligence, risk assessment, and risk control to maintain the first line of defense; internal control and compliance departments enhance policy management and guidance, strengthen monitoring and analysis, and conduct supervision to uphold the second line of defense; the audit department performs continuous independent audits of AML compliance management to fortify the third line of defense under a "zero tolerance" principle. Regarding key AML initiatives, ABC highlights accelerating the development of an AML compliance culture, implementing priority regulatory requirements, and improving AML management systems and mechanisms. Specific measures include: executives at all levels must personally oversee internal controls, compliance, and AML work, taking the lead in studying AML laws, regulations, and supervisory requirements; strengthening compliance training and assessments, with institutions unable to meet AML audit standards barred from operation, personnel failing AML assessments barred from positions, and business lines or products failing AML risk assessments prohibited from launch; raising customer due diligence standards, enhancing monitoring and reporting of suspicious transactions, and ensuring adherence to international sanctions to avoid crossing regulatory red lines. Within the comprehensive risk management framework, money laundering risk management must comply with the most stringent global standards and international best practices. Furthermore, ABC integrates AML performance into its overall evaluation and incentive systems, linking AML compliance directly to the comprehensive performance assessment of all levels of the bank, with serious violations or compliance failures resulting in automatic disqualification.

The Enron and Arthur Andersen Cases

In the history of corporate compliance in the United States, two corporate bankruptcies represent landmark events. The bankruptcy of Enron prompted U.S. administrative regulators to implement substantive corporate oversight mechanisms, thereby strengthening internal controls and compliance management systems within companies. The bankruptcy of Arthur Andersen subsequently led to significant changes in the U.S. Department of Justice's approach to corporate criminal prosecutions. Prosecutors began to make extensive use of deferred prosecution agreements (DPAs) and non-prosecution agreements (NPAs), while administrative agencies increasingly relied on administrative settlement agreements, replacing the previously dominant "strict punishment" approach. These developments created strong incentives for companies to establish effective compliance programs. Corporations could obtain more lenient administrative and criminal outcomes by engaging in robust self-regulation, self-reporting, voluntary disclosure, and full cooperation. Over time, corporate compliance mechanisms became standard tools for both incentivizing and enforcing lawful corporate behavior in the U.S. regulatory and prosecutorial framework.

Enron was once a leading U.S. energy company and one of the world's largest providers of electricity, natural gas, and telecommunications services, ranking seventh on the Fortune 500 list at its peak. In 2000, the company reported revenues of $101 billion and employed 21,000 people. On October 16, 2001, Enron released its second-quarter financial report, announcing a loss of $618 million and revealing that shareholders' equity had declined by $1.2 billion due to mismanagement. On October 22, the U.S. Securities and Exchange Commission (SEC) requested detailed transaction records and launched a formal investigation into Enron and its affiliated entities. On November 1, Enron pledged some of its assets to secure a $1 billion credit line from two financial institutions. Nevertheless, Merrill Lynch and Standard & Poor's subsequently downgraded the company's credit rating. On November 8, Enron was compelled to admit to accounting fraud, having overstated profits by $600 million since 1997. On November 28, Standard & Poor's further downgraded Enron's debt to junk bond status. By November 30, Enron's stock had fallen to $0.20 per share, reducing its market capitalization from a peak of $80 billion to $200 million. On the same day, Enron's European subsidiaries filed for bankruptcy, followed two days later by bankruptcy protection filings in the U.S. Northern District. Remaining personnel were tasked with liquidating assets, managing the bankruptcy process, and handling legal claims. On December 2, 2001, Enron formally filed for bankruptcy protection with assets totaling $49.8 billion, marking the largest bankruptcy in U.S. history at that time.

Following Enron's bankruptcy, numerous former executives faced criminal investigations and prosecutions for insider trading and related offenses. On December 28, 2005, Enron's former Chief Accounting Officer pled guilty to securities fraud and was sentenced to seven years in prison, along with a $1.25 million fine. In January 2006, prosecutors charged the former Chairman, CEO, and CFO of Enron with multiple crimes, including loan fraud, financial statement fraud, securities fraud, email fraud, money laundering, and insider trading. On May 25 of the same year, the U.S. Federal District Court in Houston rendered guilty verdicts against several of these former executives.

Enron's bankruptcy triggered a wide-ranging cascade of consequences. The company was exposed for financial fraud, corruption, and various other regulatory violations. Since 1990, Enron had contributed over $6 million in political donations to officials in the United States and United Kingdom. Arthur Andersen LLP, Enron's auditing firm, was convicted of obstructing justice and subsequently collapsed. Other affected companies, including WorldCom, also went bankrupt, marking some of the largest corporate failures in U.S. history. Financial institutions such as Citibank, JPMorgan Chase, and Bank of America paid $2 billion, $2.2 billion, and $69 million, respectively, to compensate victims of the Enron bankruptcy. The Enron scandal directly led to the enactment of the Sarbanes–Oxley Act, widely regarded as the most significant revision of U.S. securities law since 1930.

The full title of this legislation is the "Sarbanes–Oxley Act of 2002" (SOX), formally known as the *Public Company Accounting Reform and Investor*

Protection Act of 2002. It substantially amended the Securities Act of 1933 and the Securities Exchange Act of 1934, introducing numerous new provisions regarding corporate governance, oversight of the accounting profession, and regulation of the securities markets. The bankruptcies of companies such as Enron and WorldCom, caused by financial fraud and corruption, "shattered investor confidence in the capital markets." Accordingly, the primary purpose of SOX is to ensure that public companies comply with securities laws to enhance the accuracy and reliability of corporate disclosures, thereby protecting investors and serving other related objectives.

The Act reinforced the regulation of both accounting professionals and corporate conduct in several key areas: (1) establishment of an independent Public Company Accounting Oversight Board (PCAOB) to oversee audits of public companies; (2) enhancing auditor independence through measures such as mandatory rotation of lead audit partners and prohibiting auditors from providing certain non-audit consulting services; (3) restrictions on corporate executives' conduct and improvements to corporate governance structures to strengthen accountability for corporate reporting; (4) strengthening financial reporting and disclosure requirements to ensure that statements are accurate and comprehensive; and (5) increasing the enforcement capacity of the U.S. Securities and Exchange Commission (SEC) through additional funding and personnel. Simultaneously, SOX imposed stricter criminal liability on corporate executives and white-collar offenders. To enhance the reliability of financial reporting, it further required the establishment of an independent body to oversee the audits of publicly listed companies, the regular rotation of auditors, comprehensive revisions to accounting standards, clear criteria for the composition of audit committees, and immediate management assessments of internal controls as well as timely financial disclosures.

The enactment of this legislation represented a fundamental transformation in U.S. corporate governance, shifting the focus from simple information disclosure to substantive regulatory oversight. Central to the Act is the requirement for companies to establish comprehensive internal control systems, with corporate management bearing full responsibility for their design, operation, evaluation, and disclosure. Under the Act's guidance, the U.S. Public Company Accounting Oversight Board (PCAOB) set foundational standards for corporate internal control systems. These standards mandate that management evaluate the effectiveness of internal controls and document and report their findings. Specifically, management must: record the design of controls for all financial statement accounts and disclosures; test internal controls across all elements; perform procedures to obtain sufficient evidence and maintain supporting documentation; ensure that evaluations are conducted by management itself, possibly with support from internal auditors, other company personnel, or third parties—but never directly delegated to external auditors or other third parties; and, if any material weaknesses are identified, refrain from asserting that the internal control system is effective. All material deficiencies must be fully disclosed in management reports.

If the Enron scandal directly triggered a major transformation in U.S. corporate governance, the associated Arthur Andersen case directly led to significant changes in U.S. prosecutorial policy toward corporations implicated in wrongdoing.

Arthur Andersen, once one of the Big Five accounting firms, had provided internal audit and consulting services to Enron since its inception. In October 2001, following the exposure of Enron's financial scandal, the U.S. Securities and Exchange Commission (SEC) initiated a regulatory investigation. Upon learning of the investigation, Arthur Andersen's Houston office began destroying a substantial volume of Enron's accounting records, a practice that continued until November 8, when the firm received a subpoena from the SEC. On March 7, 2002, after a preliminary investigation, the U.S. Attorney's Office for the Southern District of Texas concluded that Arthur Andersen had potentially committed obstruction of justice and, with grand jury approval, drafted an indictment against the firm. The indictment was not disclosed to Arthur Andersen at the time. Prosecutors proposed a plea agreement, which Arthur Andersen's executives and defense counsel refused. On March 14, the indictment was formally filed in court, and the case entered the judicial process.

After its indictment, Arthur Andersen faced a mounting credibility crisis, as numerous clients severed ties with the firm. In an effort to contain the fallout, Andersen attempted to negotiate a deferred prosecution agreement (DPA) with federal prosecutors. However, the firm found the prosecutors' conditions—including payment of substantial fines, full cooperation with ongoing investigations, and reconstruction of compliance programs—unacceptable, and ultimately no agreement was reached. On June 15, 2002, following a trial in the U.S. District Court, Arthur Andersen was convicted of obstruction of justice, fined $500,000, and prohibited from providing accounting services for five years. Andersen appealed the verdict. On June 16, 2004, the U.S. Court of Appeals for the Fifth Circuit upheld the conviction, and the firm subsequently petitioned the U.S. Supreme Court. On May 31, 2005, the Supreme Court identified a procedural error in the jury instructions at trial, overturned the conviction, and remanded the case for a new trial.

Despite the Supreme Court's ruling, Andersen's fate was effectively sealed. Following the 2002 indictment, the SEC had already revoked Andersen's authorization to audit public companies, effective August 31, 2002, precipitating massive client losses. Clients terminated their relationships, and employees sought alternative employment, leaving 28,000 U.S. staff unemployed. In 2001, Andersen had maintained 390 offices across 85 countries, employed 85,000 people worldwide, and generated $9.34 billion in revenue. By the end of 2002, over 2300 public company clients had departed, global offices were either closed or sold, and the workforce had dwindled to just 3000 employees.

Following the Arthur Andersen case, against the backdrop of an economic downturn in the United States, the U.S. Department of Justice (DOJ) came under intense criticism. The frequent prosecution of corporations provoked significant controversy. One viewpoint argued that prosecuting Andersen brought minimal benefit to the government: no individuals responsible were held personally accountable, and the $500,000 fine was insignificant. Yet the prosecution and conviction had devastating consequences for Andersen and broader negative effects on the U.S. economy. Another perspective held that merely indicting a corporation could destroy it, likening such prosecution to a "death sentence" for the entity. Observers also noted that Andersen's conviction for destroying Enron's financial records ultimately forced the firm to close, resulting in tens of thousands of job losses—an emblematic case of the severe repercussions of corporate criminal liability.

A U.S. federal prosecutor famously testified before Congress, stating, "The Andersen case profoundly shocked every federal prosecutor, prompting them to actively seek a 'third path' for handling corporate crime." Scholars in China have noted that prosecuting and convicting a corporation produces a "ripple effect," harming innocent third parties such as investors, employees, pensioners, and clients. This understanding gained broad recognition in U.S. society after the Andersen case and became a major impetus for the rise of criminal pre-trial diversion agreements. Since then, when federal prosecutors encounter corporate economic crimes and a plea agreement cannot be reached, they typically employ deferred prosecution agreements (DPAs) or non-prosecution agreements (NPAs) to avoid formal indictment and conviction. Under these agreements, corporations may pay substantial fines while committing, during the monitoring period, to cooperate with investigations, implement compliance programs, submit to ongoing supervision by compliance monitors, and voluntarily disclose relevant information. This system created a genuine incentive for corporations to establish and maintain robust compliance frameworks, elevating the role of compliance in corporate governance to an unprecedented level.

The Nestlé Compliance Defense Case

Since the establishment of China's corporate criminal liability system, courts have generally assessed a company's criminal responsibility based on the actions of its directly responsible personnel. If these individuals—or other accountable staff—commit criminal acts in the name of the company, aimed at advancing corporate interests and reflecting the organization's collective will, such acts are typically treated as corporate crimes. Traditionally, when a criminal act is deliberated and approved by the company's decision-making body (e.g., the board of directors or party/government office) or carried out by the legal representative on behalf of the company, classifying it as a corporate offense has rarely been disputed. However, with the increasing complexity and specialization of corporate governance, large and multinational companies face greater challenges in managing, controlling, and supervising branch offices, third parties, and ordinary employees. When an employee at a branch commits an illegal act in the name of the company to further corporate objectives, a key question arises: under what circumstances should the company itself be held criminally liable? In other words, when employees claim their misconduct represents "corporate behavior," how can a company effectively distinguish corporate liability from individual employee responsibility?

In 2017, the Lanzhou Intermediate People's Court issued its final judgment in a case involving Nestlé employees' infringement of citizens' personal information, marking an important development in differentiating corporate liability from individual employee responsibility. According to the 2016 criminal judgment by the Chengguan District People's Court of Lanzhou, between 2011 and September 2013, defendants Zheng and Yang—serving as the Marketing Manager of Nestlé (China) Northwest Infant Nutrition Department and Gansu Regional Manager of the Lanzhou Branch Infant Nutrition Department, respectively—directed employees (defendants Yang, Li, Du, and Sun) to illegally obtain personal information from medical personnel at several hospitals, including the First Affiliated Hospital of Lanzhou University, the General Hospital of Lanzhou Military Region, and Lanzhou Lanshi Hospital. This was done to expand market share and promote Nestlé infant formula, using methods such as leveraging personal relationships and offering bribes. During this period, defendant Wang, an obstetrics nurse at the First Affiliated Hospital of Lanzhou University, illegally provided 2074 pieces of personal information collected during her work to defendants Yang and Sun in exchange for 13,610 RMB. Defendant Ding, an obstetrics nurse at the General Hospital of Lanzhou Military Region, provided 996 pieces of personal information to defendant Li for 4250 RMB. Defendant Yang, an obstetrics nurse at Lanzhou Lanshi Hospital, provided 724 pieces of personal information to defendant Du in exchange for 6995 RMB.

During the first-instance trial, defendants Zheng, Yang, Yang, Li, and Du claimed that the collection of citizens' personal information was conducted solely to fulfill company tasks and argued that the indictment misrepresented the amount of information obtained illegally. Evidence submitted in court—including instructions issued by Nestlé (recorded in employee training materials) and a company statement from Nestlé (China) Ltd.—demonstrated that Nestlé strictly prohibited employees from directly or indirectly contacting pregnant women, nursing mothers, or the general public for the purpose of promoting infant formula, and forbade any proactive collection of personal information without proper procedures or company authorization. The company's statement on DR (Data Research) objectives, target tasks, and methods for gathering related information made clear that DR tasks were not designed to collect consumers' personal information. The actual execution of DR tasks was monitored and evaluated by the Nutrition Consultation Center (NCC), operated by the Chinese Association for Health Promotion and Education, through telephone surveys. While some voluntarily provided consumer information was required for the surveys, Nestlé explicitly prohibited providing any money or other benefits to medical staff and never offered bonuses to employees or medical personnel in connection with this work.

Nestlé clearly stipulated in the "Nestlé Instructions" and the "Illustrated Guidelines on Interactions with the Healthcare System" that employees were strictly forbidden from offering any monetary or material incentives to healthcare professionals. All nutrition specialists were required to complete training on these policies and sign formal commitment letters to ensure compliance. Court-admitted evidence—including WHO online test results, completed test papers, instructions for engaging with healthcare professionals in high-risk countries, and employee bonus records—demonstrated that defendants Zheng, Yang, Li, Du, Yang, and Sun had participated in Nestlé's training and testing, which explicitly prohibited paying healthcare personnel for personal information.

Nestlé's internal policies, corporate instructions, the Nestlé Charter, and the illustrated guidelines confirmed that the company adhered to the World Health Organization's International Code of Marketing of Breast-milk Substitutes as well as Chinese health regulations. These rules prohibited employees from distributing free infant formula samples to mothers or offering monetary or material rewards to healthcare professionals to encourage formula promotion.

On October 31, 2016, the first-instance court ruled that Nestlé employees Zheng, Yang, and Sun, among six others, had obtained citizens' personal information through illegal means, constituting serious offenses. Additionally, hospital staff Wang, Ding, and another individual violated national regulations by selling or unlawfully providing citizens' personal information obtained during their official duties or services, also constituting serious offenses. The court determined that the actions of these nine individuals constituted the crime of infringing upon citizens' personal information.

Following the first-instance verdict, all defendants filed appeals. Defendant Zheng argued that his actions were corporate acts; Yang's defense counsel contended that the case involved corporate criminal liability; Li appealed on the grounds that all his actions were tasks assigned by the company; and Du claimed that his actions were carried out in accordance with company directives and that the information obtained was provided to the company.

On May 31, 2017, the Lanzhou Intermediate People's Court, after reviewing the case without holding a new hearing, held that: "Corporate crime occurs when an entity, with the purpose of obtaining illegal benefits for itself, objectively carries out acts collectively decided by the entity or decided by its responsible personnel. Evidence from Nestlé's handbooks and employee codes of conduct demonstrates that the company prohibited employees from engaging in illegal acts infringing upon citizens' personal information. The appellants violated company regulations and committed crimes to enhance personal performance; therefore, their actions constitute individual conduct." Accordingly, the Lanzhou Intermediate People's Court dismissed the appeals and upheld the original verdict.

This case has been described in legal circles as the "first corporate criminal compliance defense case." While this characterization is not without merit, China's criminal law has not yet established a strict liability system that automatically attributes employee misconduct to the corporation; thus, there is currently no legal basis for a corporate innocence defense. Furthermore, corporate compliance programs are primarily promoted by administrative regulators, and Chinese criminal law does not provide explicit incentives for companies to implement compliance systems. The idea that a company could avoid criminal liability or receive reduced penalties for having a compliance program has not yet been codified in law.

Nonetheless, this ruling remains a milestone in corporate criminal compliance jurisprudence. In this case, the defendants' actions of infringing upon citizens' personal information were carried out in the name of Nestlé employees and for the benefit of Nestlé, which are indisputable facts. The critical issue, however, was whether their conduct reflected Nestlé's subjective intent. Under widely accepted theories of criminal liability, the mental element (mens rea) consists of both cognitive and volitional components. Regarding the cognitive component, Nestlé could clearly demonstrate that neither its top decision-making bodies nor senior management authorized these actions nor were aware of them, meaning they had no knowledge of the employees' conduct. For a multinational enterprise of Nestlé's size, often employing thousands or even tens of thousands of staff, it is simply unrealistic for senior management to be aware of every individual employee's actions. In light of this, any discussion of whether Nestlé as a company "intended" to bring about a harmful outcome becomes irrelevant.

A potentially contentious issue lies in whether Nestlé could be held negligently liable for the criminal acts committed by its employees. Negligence, as a form of culpability, arises when an actor should have foreseen the harmful consequences of their actions but, due to carelessness or overconfidence, mistakenly assumes that such outcomes can be avoided—results that the actor did not intend to occur. In certain circumstances, Nestlé's toleration of employees' unlawful conduct could also indicate indirect intent. In these cases, the actor anticipates the possible occurrence of harmful outcomes but allows them to happen, adopting a stance that neither prevents nor seeks such results. For large enterprises, a lack of adequate employee oversight, insufficient training, or absence of enforceable internal regulations could expose the company to liability for negligence or even indirect intent, stemming from its failure to act or omissions.

In this case, Nestlé relied squarely on its internal governance structure as the foundation for its defense. The company demonstrated that it explicitly prohibited employees from distributing free infant formula samples to mothers, offering monetary or material incentives to healthcare professionals to promote formula, and collecting personal information without proper authorization. These policies and rules were not only codified in normative documents such as the Nestlé Charter, corporate instructions, and employee manuals, but also incorporated into employee training programs, which several of the defendants had completed and been tested on. Consequently, the employees' actions were carried out to achieve personal performance objectives rather than reflecting corporate intent. Nestlé had fulfilled its duty of care and exercised appropriate management, supervision, education, and training responsibilities. Because the employees' conduct violated Nestlé's internal regulations, it inherently contradicted the company's subjective intent. Given that Nestlé was unaware of these actions and had implemented proper oversight and training, the company cannot be held legally liable for the criminal acts committed in violation of its internal policies.

It is clear that the decisive factor in distinguishing corporate liability from individual employee responsibility lies in whether the company possessed the "subjective intent" to commit a criminal act. In the Nestlé case, the company's established compliance management system both eliminated the possibility that the corporation recklessly permitted harmful outcomes and ruled out any negligence or overconfidence, thereby providing a concrete basis for the company not to bear criminal liability.

The landmark aspect of this ruling is the court's reliance on the corporate compliance management system to determine that the entity lacked the necessary mens rea for criminal liability, effectively separating corporate responsibility from individual employee liability. Nonetheless, the underlying logic still follows the traditional theoretical approach of inferring corporate liability from employee conduct. In the context of China's administrative authorities actively promoting corporate compliance programs, state-owned enterprises have initiated comprehensive pilot programs, while private enterprises are gradually developing compliance systems. Experience from Western legal systems indicates that the strongest driver for full corporate compliance programs is often the creation of a compliance incentive mechanism. A compliance incentive mechanism allows a corporation to receive leniency in administrative penalties or criminal liability in recognition of its compliance efforts. In criminal law, such a mechanism is particularly valuable for enterprises already under investigation: it can provide a direct basis for corporate exoneration, justify mitigation of criminal penalties, or serve as a prerequisite for negotiating a deferred prosecution agreement with prosecutors. Currently, China's criminal and procedural law does not formally establish such a compliance incentive mechanism, potentially weakening enterprises' motivation to implement compliance programs and limiting their ability to leverage compliance efforts to obtain lenient treatment in criminal proceedings.

References

Epstein, M. J., and K. O. Hanson, eds. *Corporate Governance.* Translated by Nian Dianzong and Zhang Yue. Beijing: Peking University Press, 2014.

Chen, Ruihua. *Theoretical Foundations of Corporate Compliance*, 3rd ed. Beijing: Law Press, 2022a.

Chen, Ruihua. *China's Experience in Effective Compliance.* Beijing: Peking University Press, 2022b.

Friedrichs, David O. *Trusted Criminals: White Collar Crime in Contemporary Society.* Translated by Liu Rong. Beijing: Law Press, 2017.

Guo, Lingchen, Ding Jihua, and Wang Zhile. *Compliance: Effectiveness Evaluation of Corporate Compliance Management Systems.* Beijing: Enterprise Management Press, 2021.

Garrett, Brandon L. *Lessons from U.S. Prosecutors Handling Corporate Cases.* Translated by Liu Junjie et al. Beijing: Law Press, 2021.

Kaye, Andrew. *The Company's Objective.* Translated by Sun Hongyou et al. Beijing: Renmin University of China Press, 2014.

Li, Bencan, ed. and trans. *Compliance and Criminal Law: A Global Perspective.* Beijing: China University of Political Science and Laew Press, 2018.

Monks, Robert A. G., and Nell Minow. *Corporate Governance.* Translated by Li Weian et al. Beijing: Renmin University of China Press, 2017.

Micklethwait, John, and Adrian Wooldridge. *The Company: A Short History of a Revolutionary Idea.* Beijing: Peking University Press, 2021.

Ye, Haibo, ed. *Guidelines for Anti–Overseas Corruption Compliance Practice.* Beijing: Law Press, 2021.

Zhang, Yuanhuang, et al. *Global Studies on Corporate Compliance.* Beijing: Peking University Press, 2021.

Research and Guidance Group on Corporate Compliance Cases, Supreme People's Procuratorate. *Case Handling Manual for Corporate Compliance Involved in Criminal Cases.* Beijing: China Procuratorial Press, 2022.

Basri, Carole. *Corporate Compliance.* Durham, NC: Carolina Academic Press, 2017.

R. Chen, *An Introduction to Corporate Compliance*,
https://doi.org/10.1007/978-981-95-7257-1

Index[1]

A

B

C

[1] Note: Page numbers followed by 'n' refer to notes.

R. Chen, *An Introduction to Corporate Compliance*,
https://doi.org/10.1007/978-981-95-7257-1

D

E

F

G

H

I

J

L

M

FSC
www.fsc.org
MIX
Papier | Fördert
gute Waldnutzung
FSC® C083411

Kolibri 360 GmbH
Ferdinand-Jühlke-Straße 7
99095 Erfurt, Deutschland
produktsicherheit@kolibri360.de